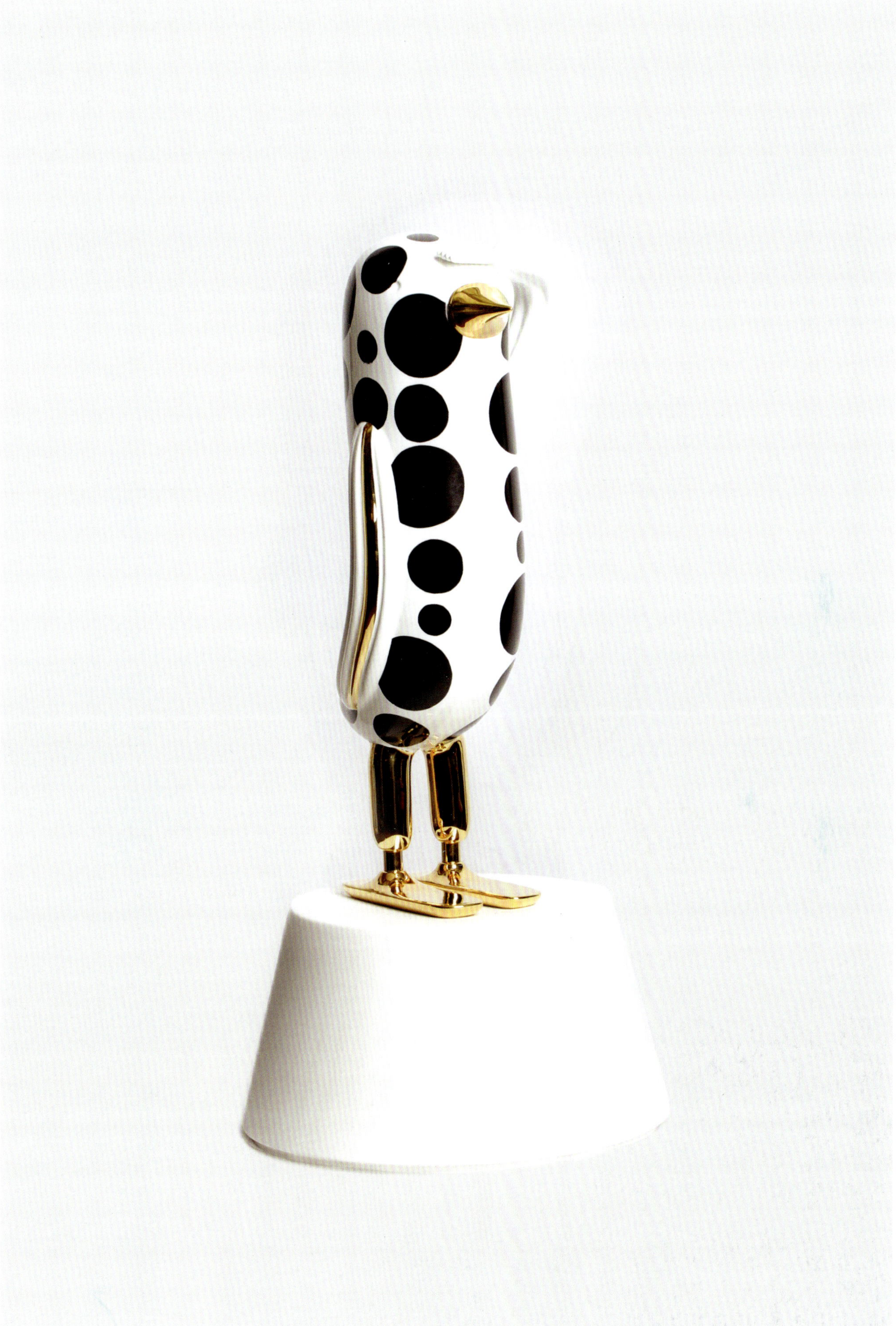

↓ Hope Bird—Limited-edition ceramic sculpture for Bosa, 2017

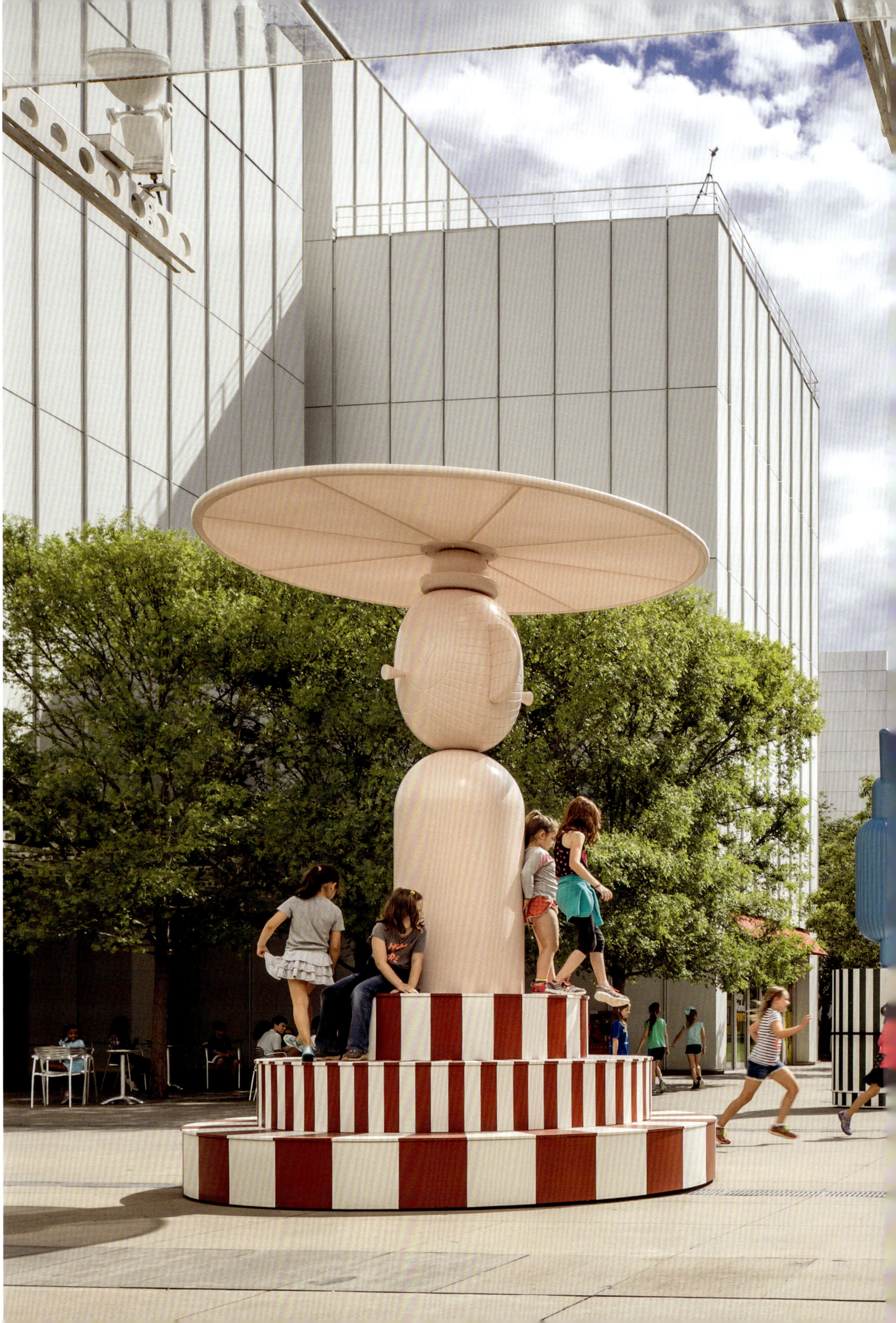

↓ Merry Go Zoo—Installation at the High Museum of Art, Atlanta, USA, 2017

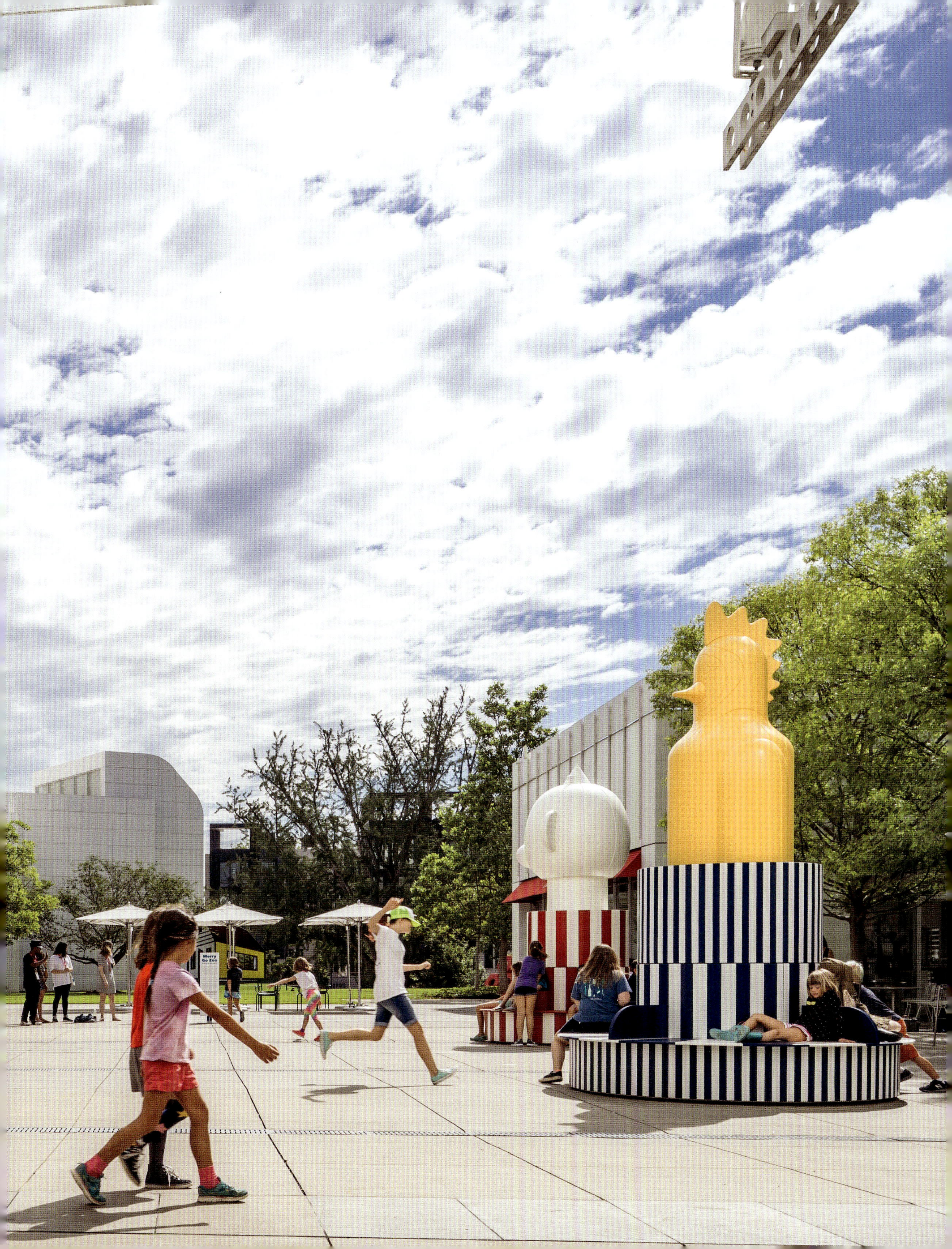

Merry
Go Zoo

→ Mixing ingredients, allowing myself to be influenced, feeling the amazement and innocence of the child in me are all traits of a creative philosophy based on the idea of constant rebirth.

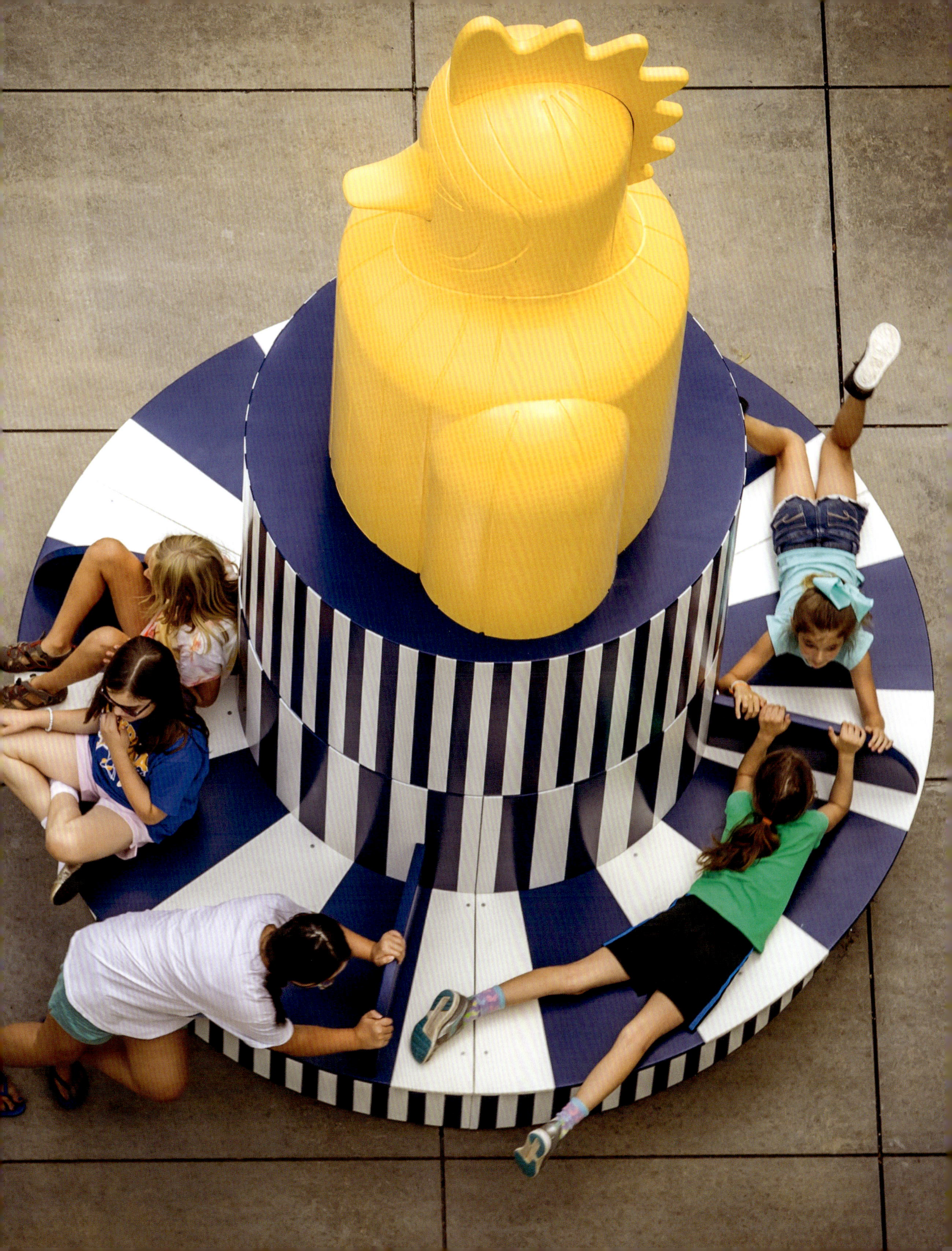

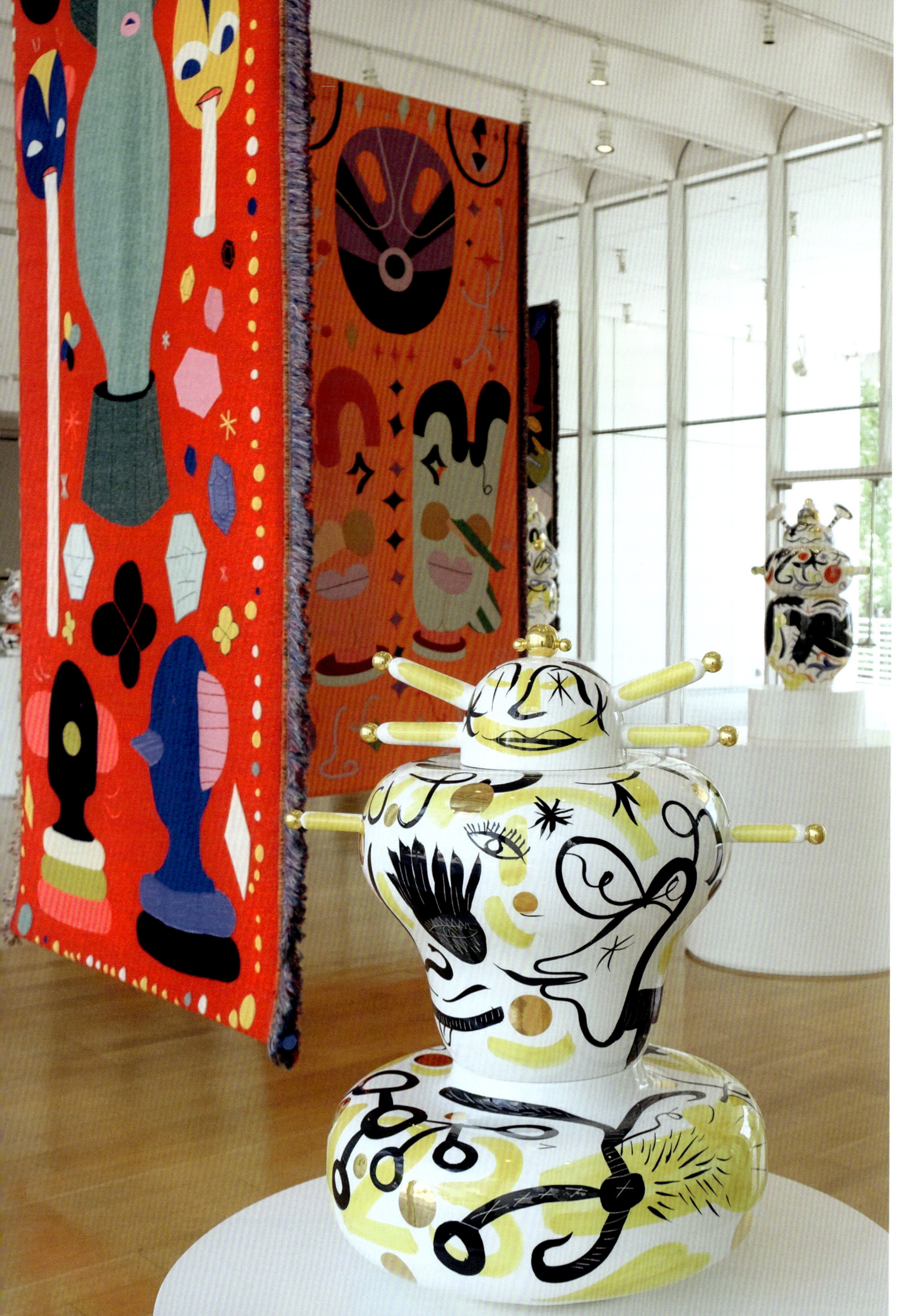

↑ Technicolor—Hand-painted ceramic vases and tapestries, High Museum of Art, Atlanta, USA, 2017
↓ Technicolor—Hand-painted ceramic vase and view of Merry Go Zoo exterior installation, High Museum of Art, Atlanta, USA, 2017

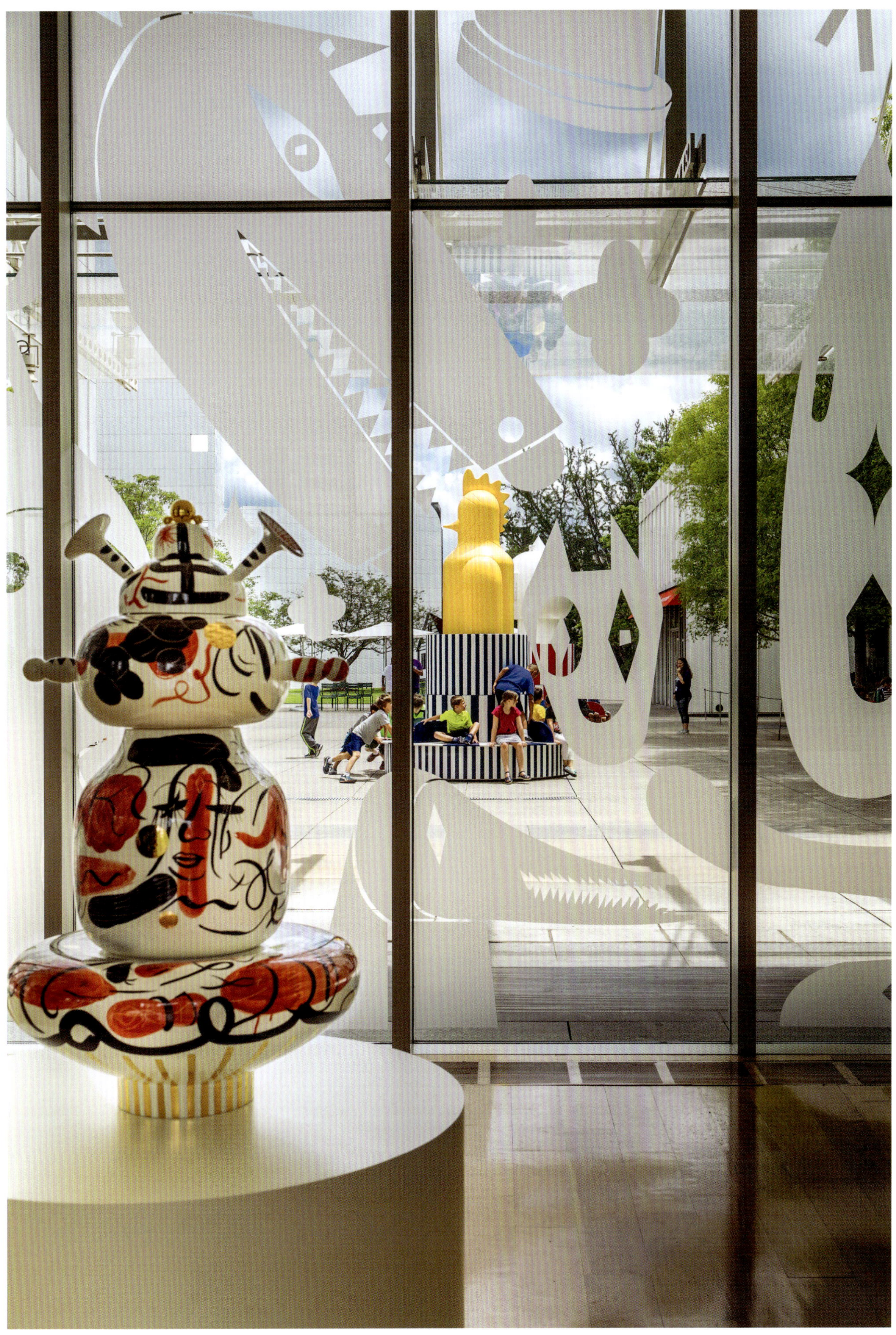

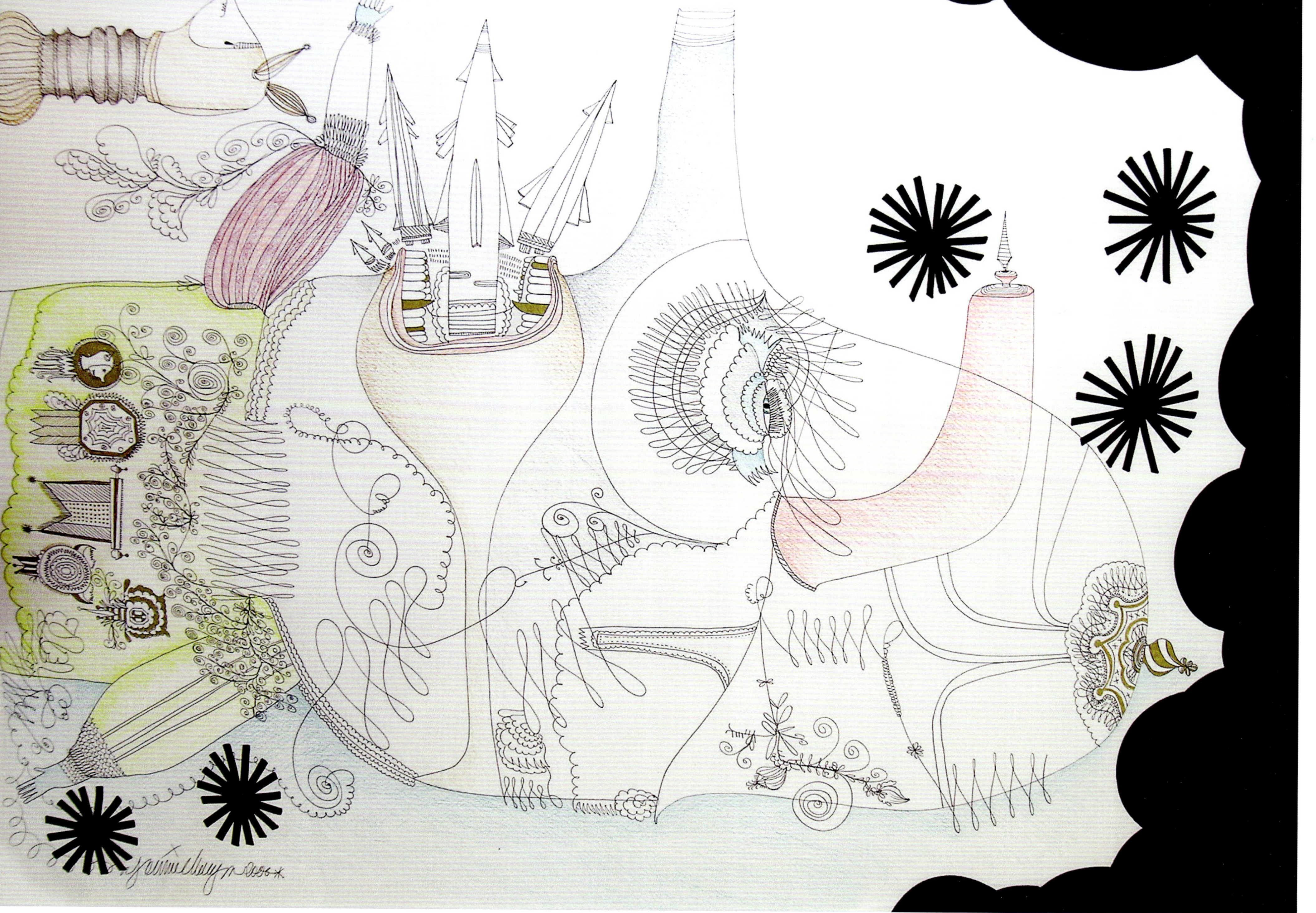

↑ Mon Cirque—Pencil drawing, 2005
↓ The Tournament—Interactive chess installation, Trafalgar Square, London Design Festival, U.K., 2009
Chess pieces made of hand-painted ceramic and turned wood

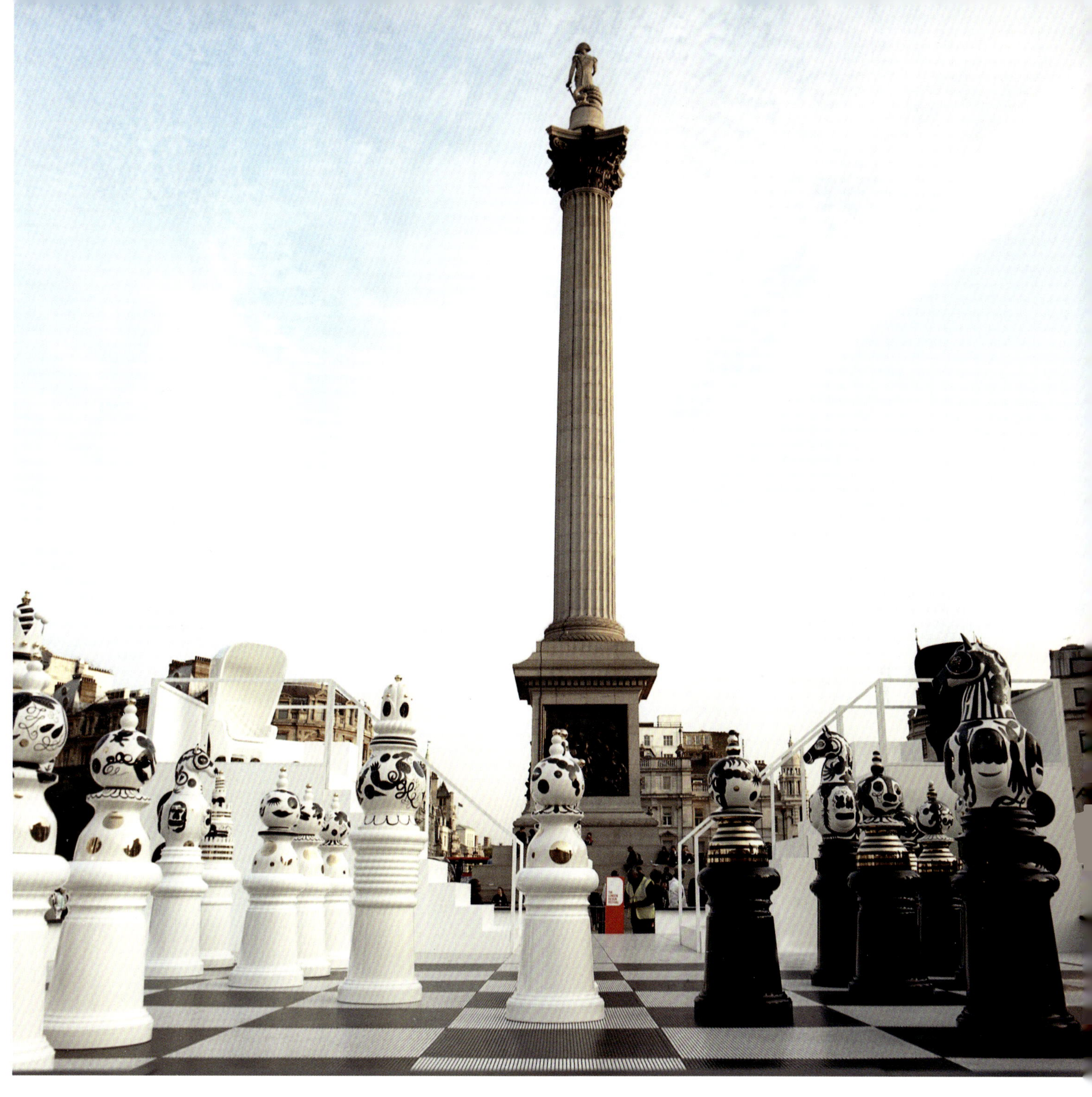

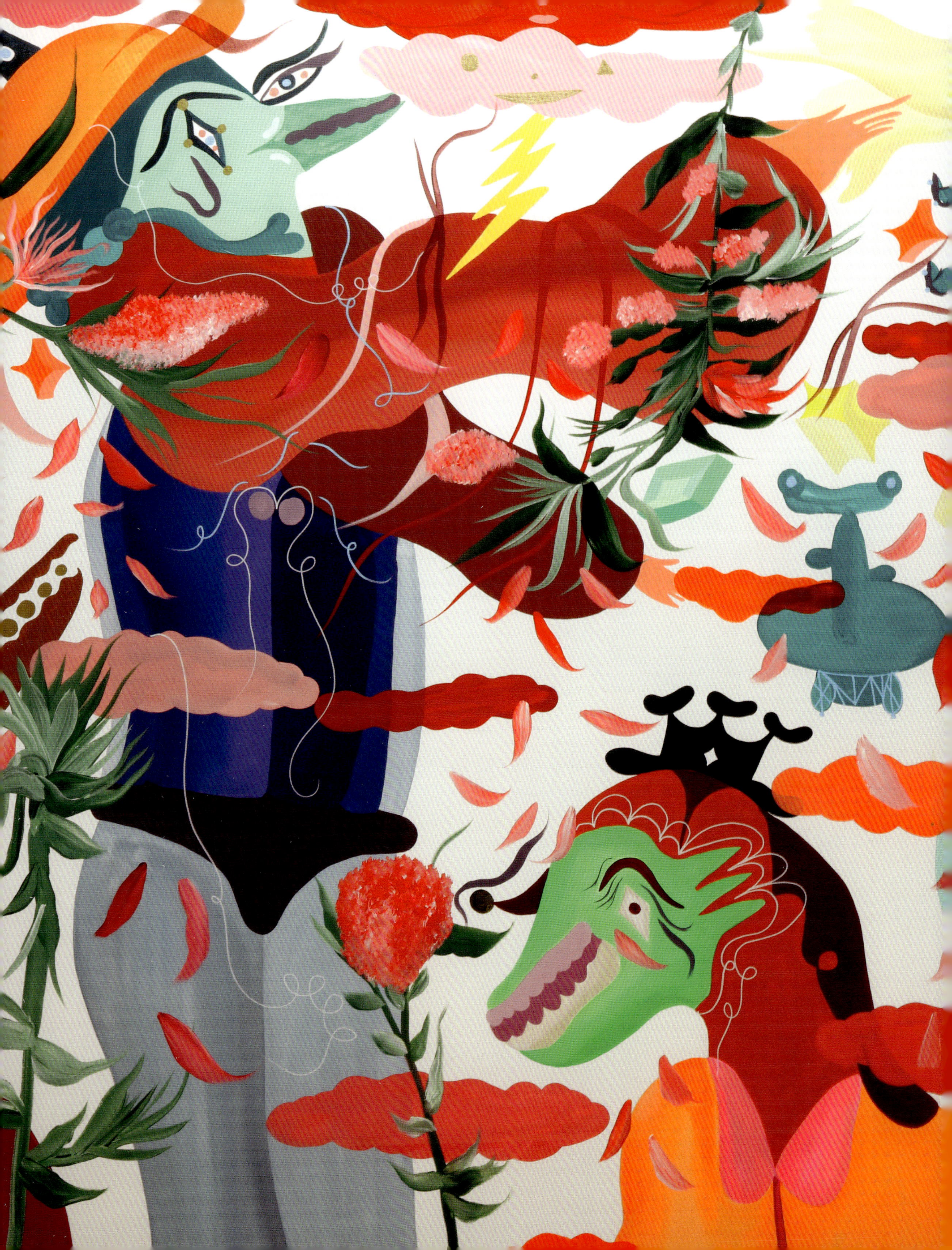

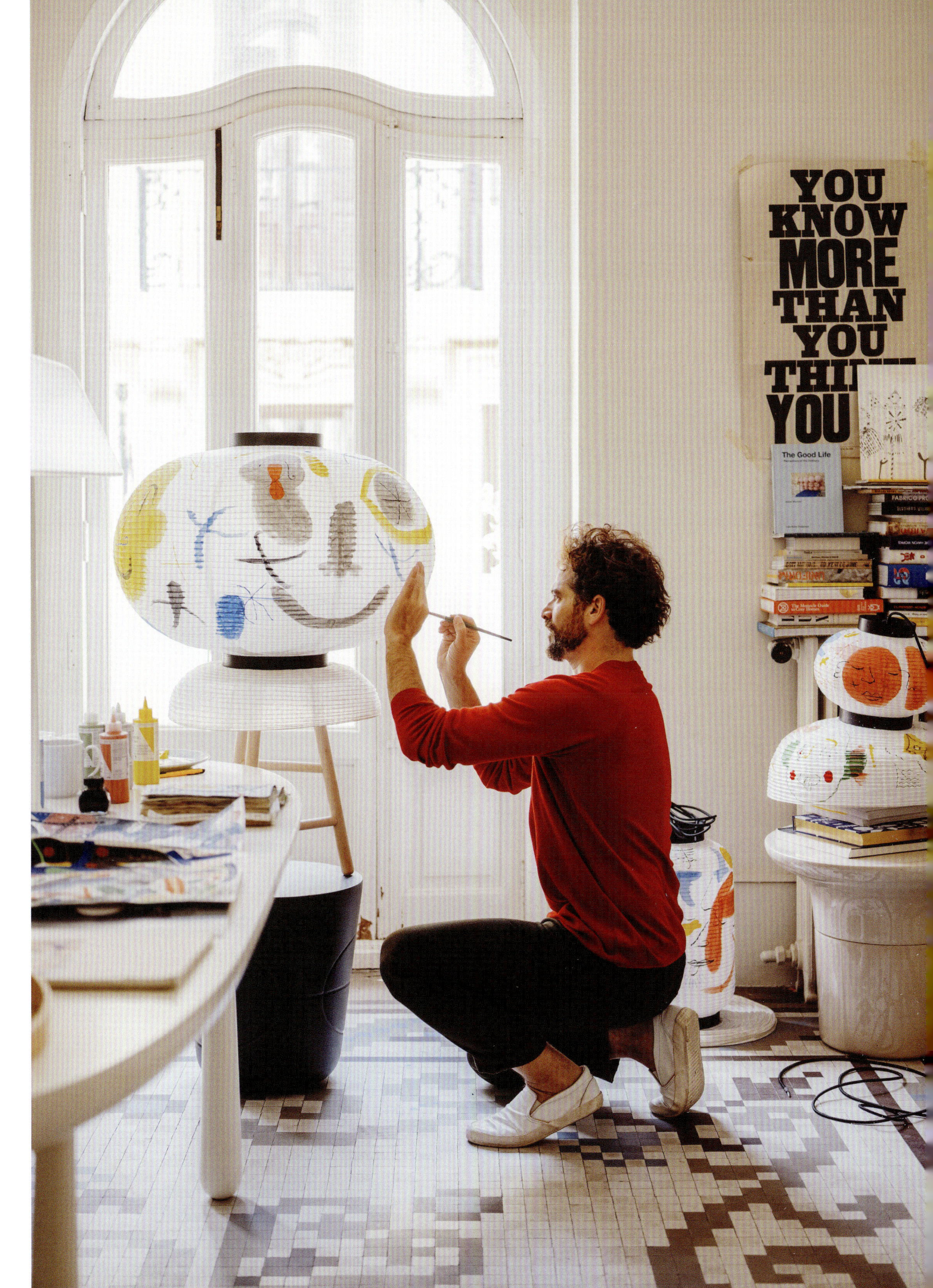

↑ The Answers in the Clouds—Acrylic on canvas, detail, 2022
↓ Hand-painting a Formakami lamp on top of Game On ceramic table, Valencia, Spain, 2019

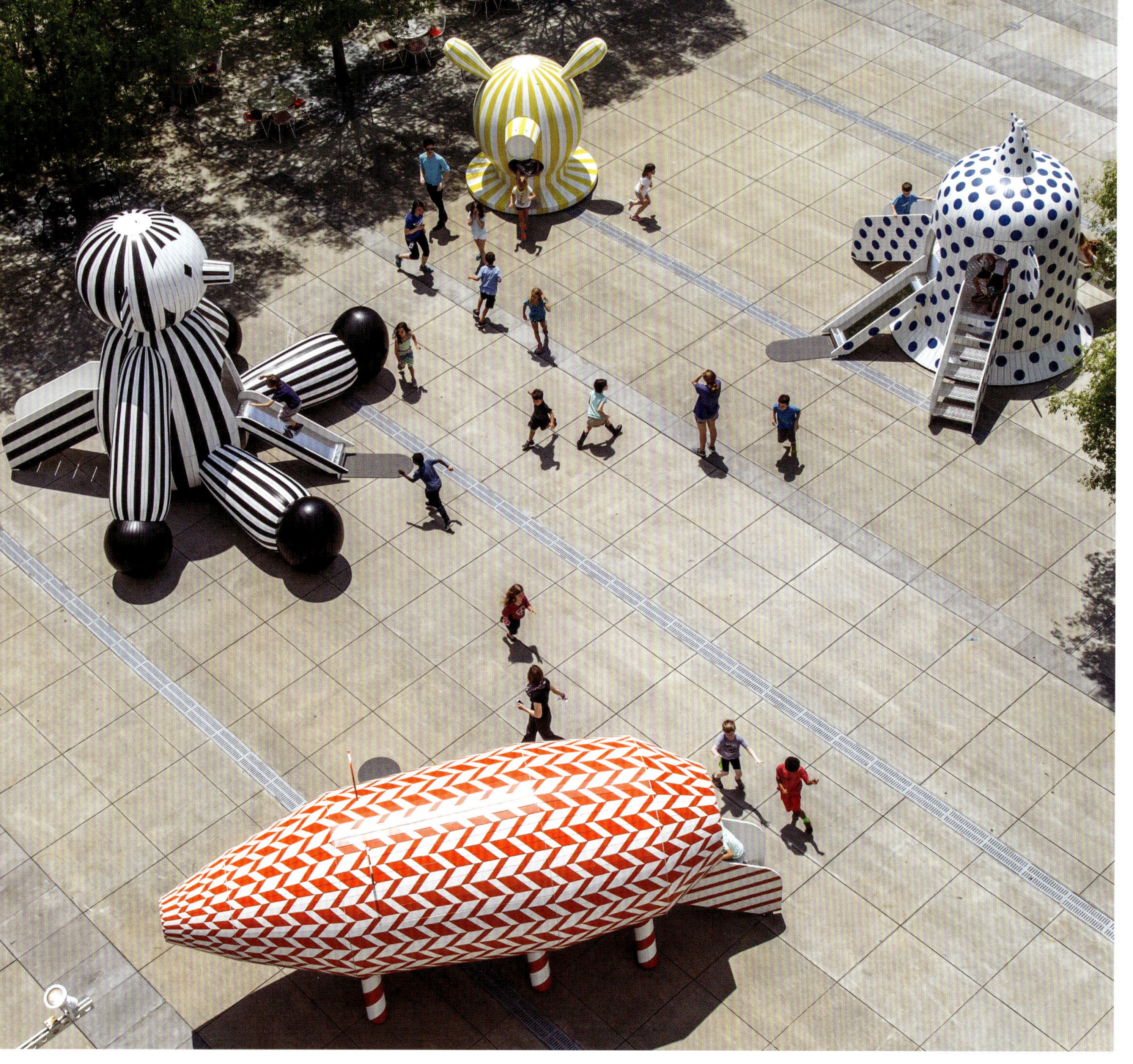

↑↓ Tiovivo—Installation at the High Museum of Art, Atlanta, USA, 2016

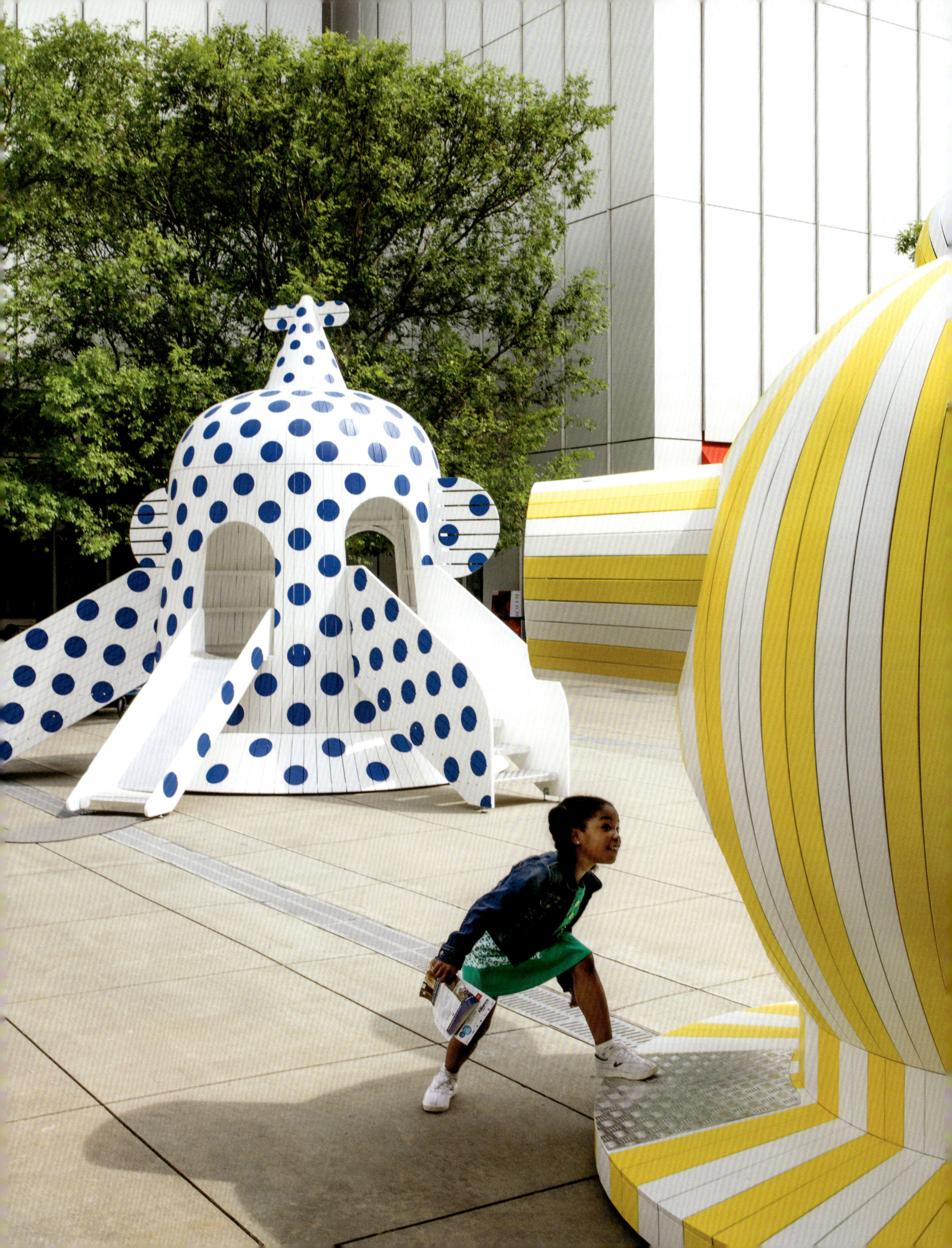

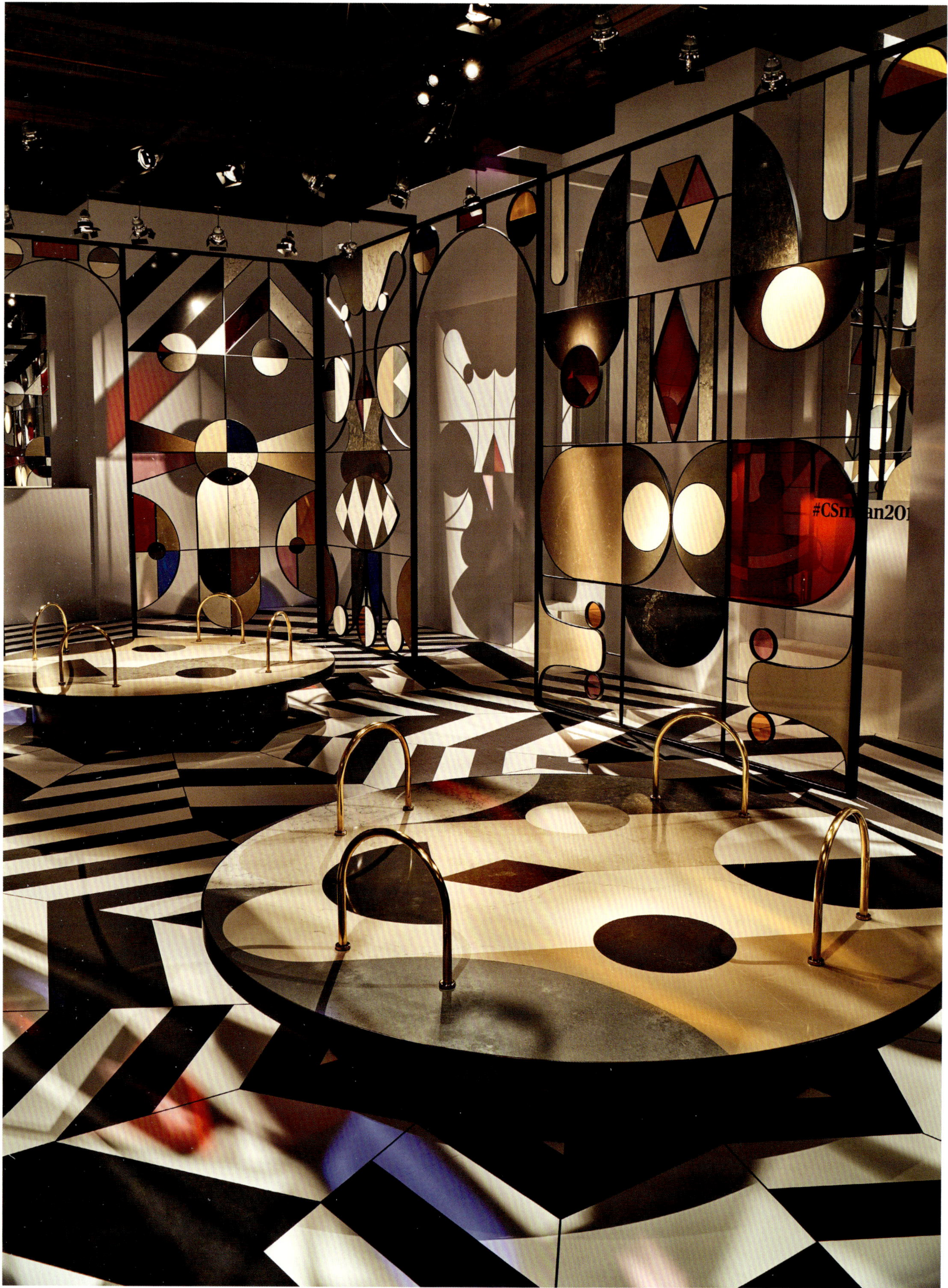

↓↑ Stone Age Folk—Installation at Palazzo Serbelloni for Caesarstone, Milan, Italy, 2017

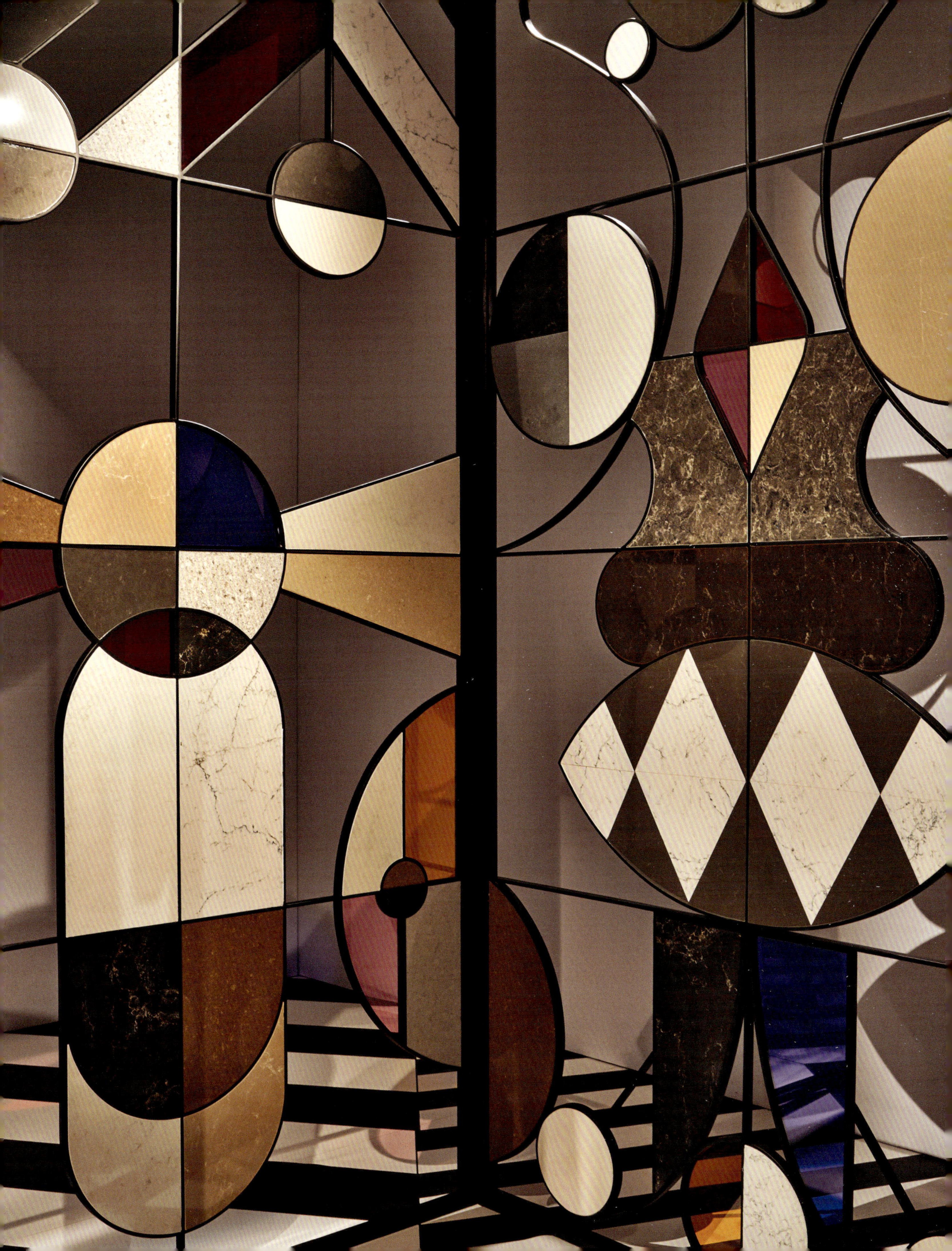

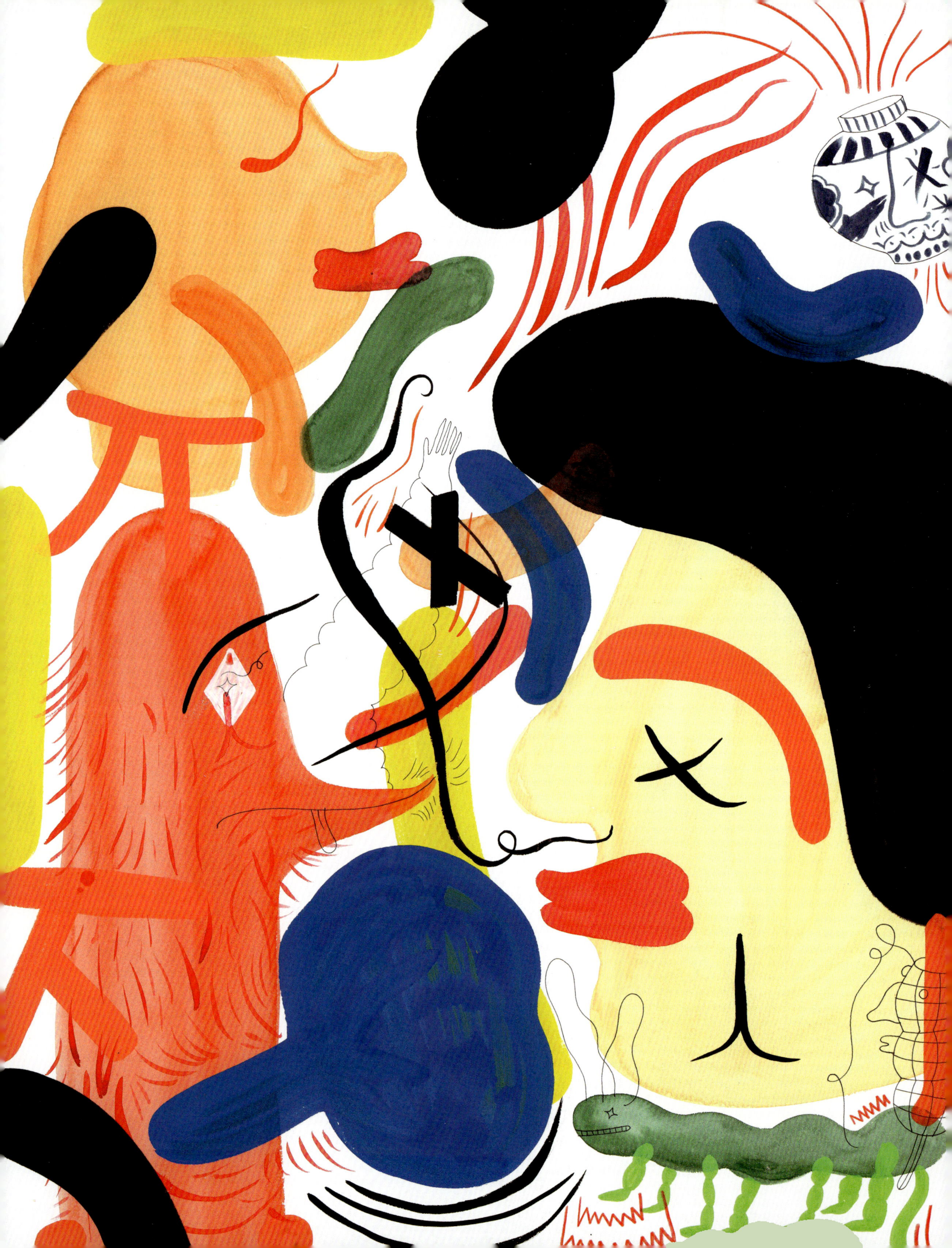

↑ Hall of Heads—Limited-edition print for Wrong Shop, 2021
↓ Lightolight—Metal wall appliqué for Parachilna, 2018

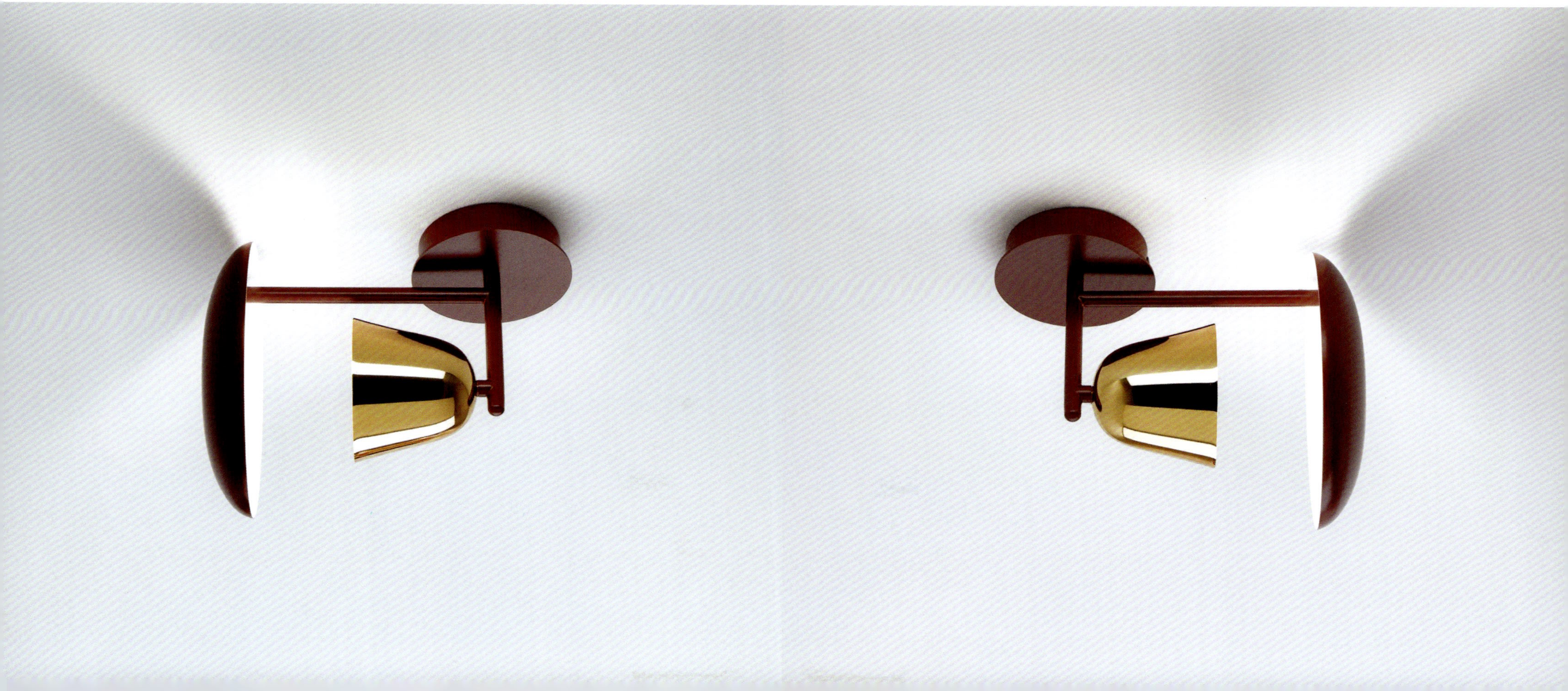

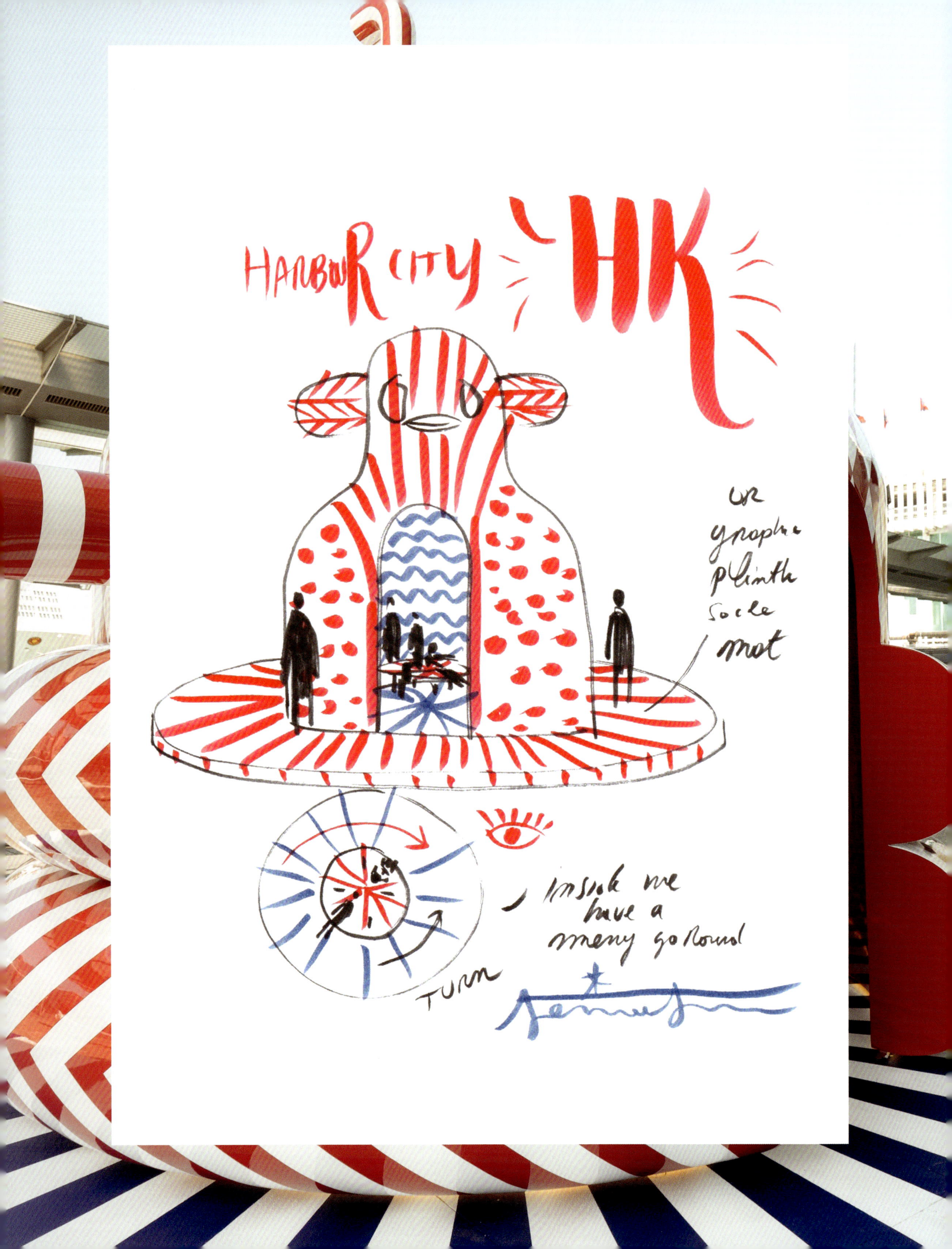

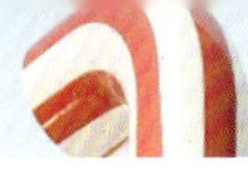

HARBOUR CITY
HK
or
graphic
plinth
socle
mot
inside we
have a
merry go Round
TURN

↑ Sketch for Archisculptures installation

↓ Archisculptures—Rabbitdoubledome and Duckodome, elements of the installation at Ocean Terminal Forecourt, Harbour City, Hong Kong, 2018

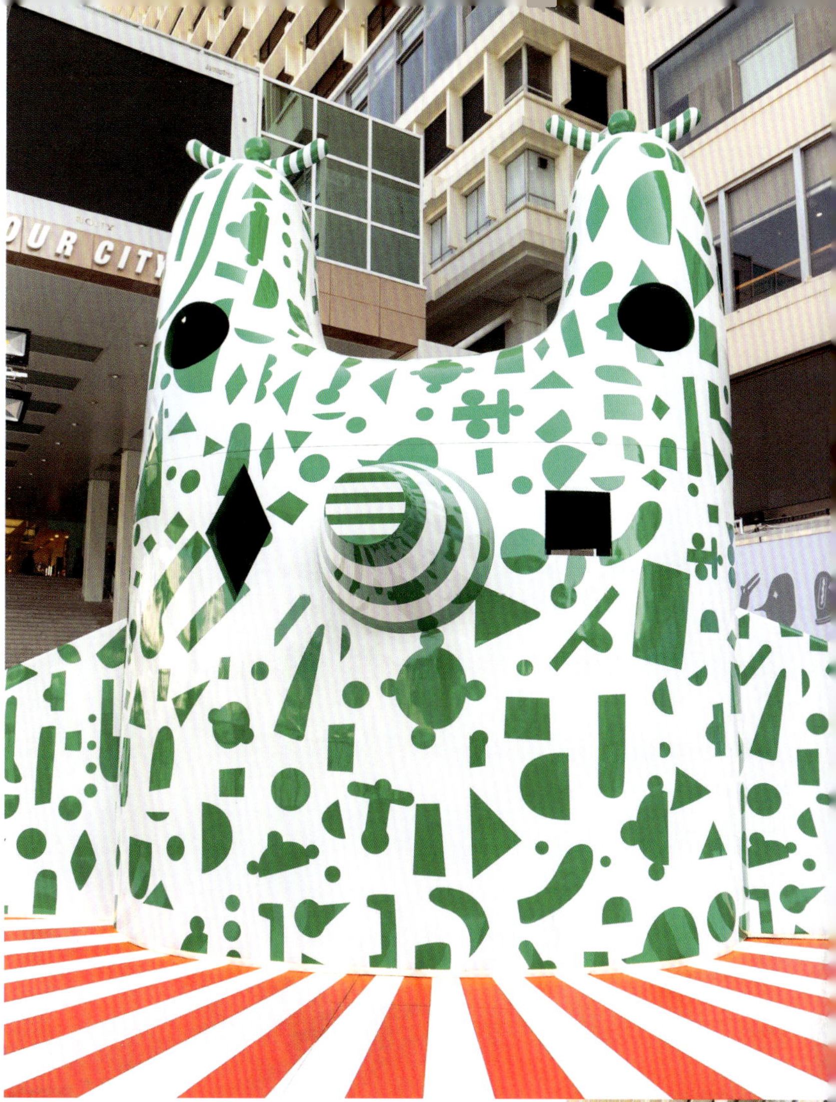

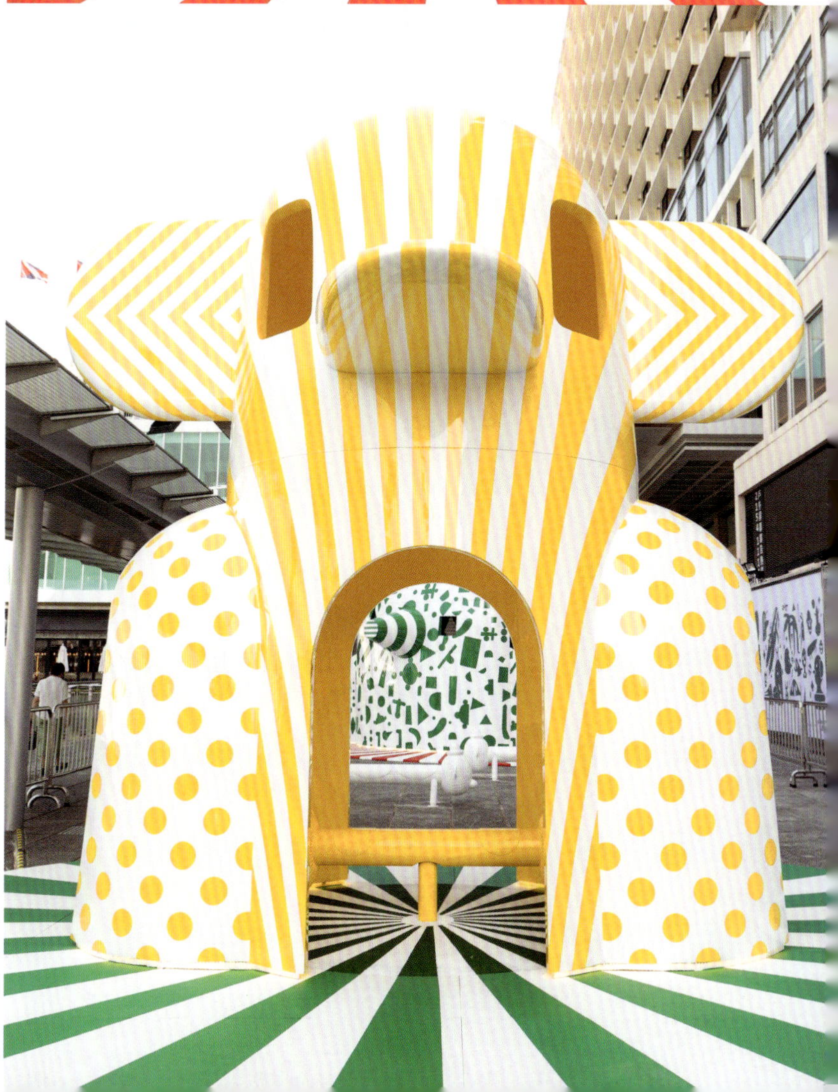

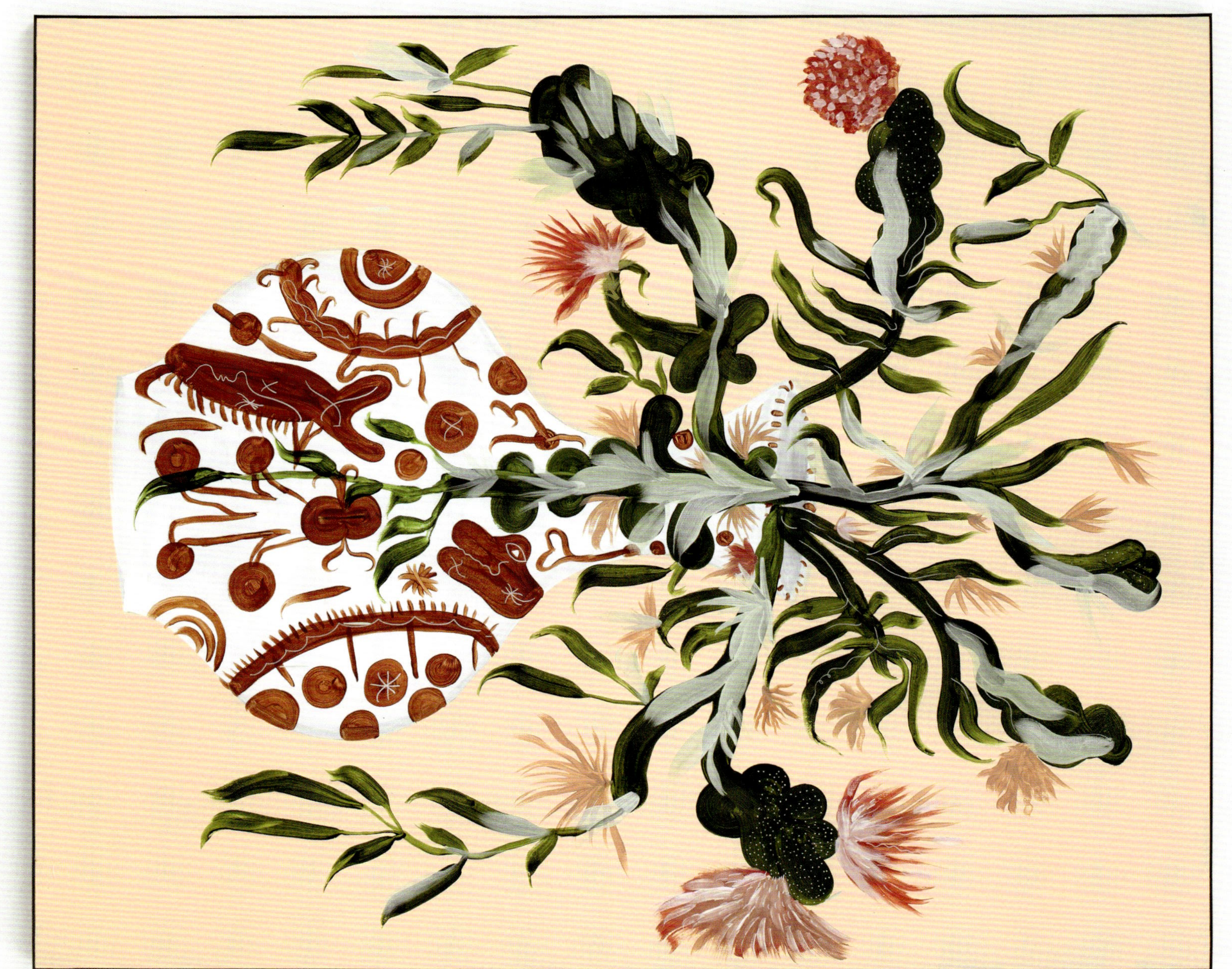

↓ Ming Med Terracotta—Acrylic on canvas, 200 ×160 cm, 2021
↓ Okobo-Kabuki Dog—Fiberglass sculpture, part of the Cosmotik Jungle exhibition at L21 Gallery, Mallorca, Spain, 2021

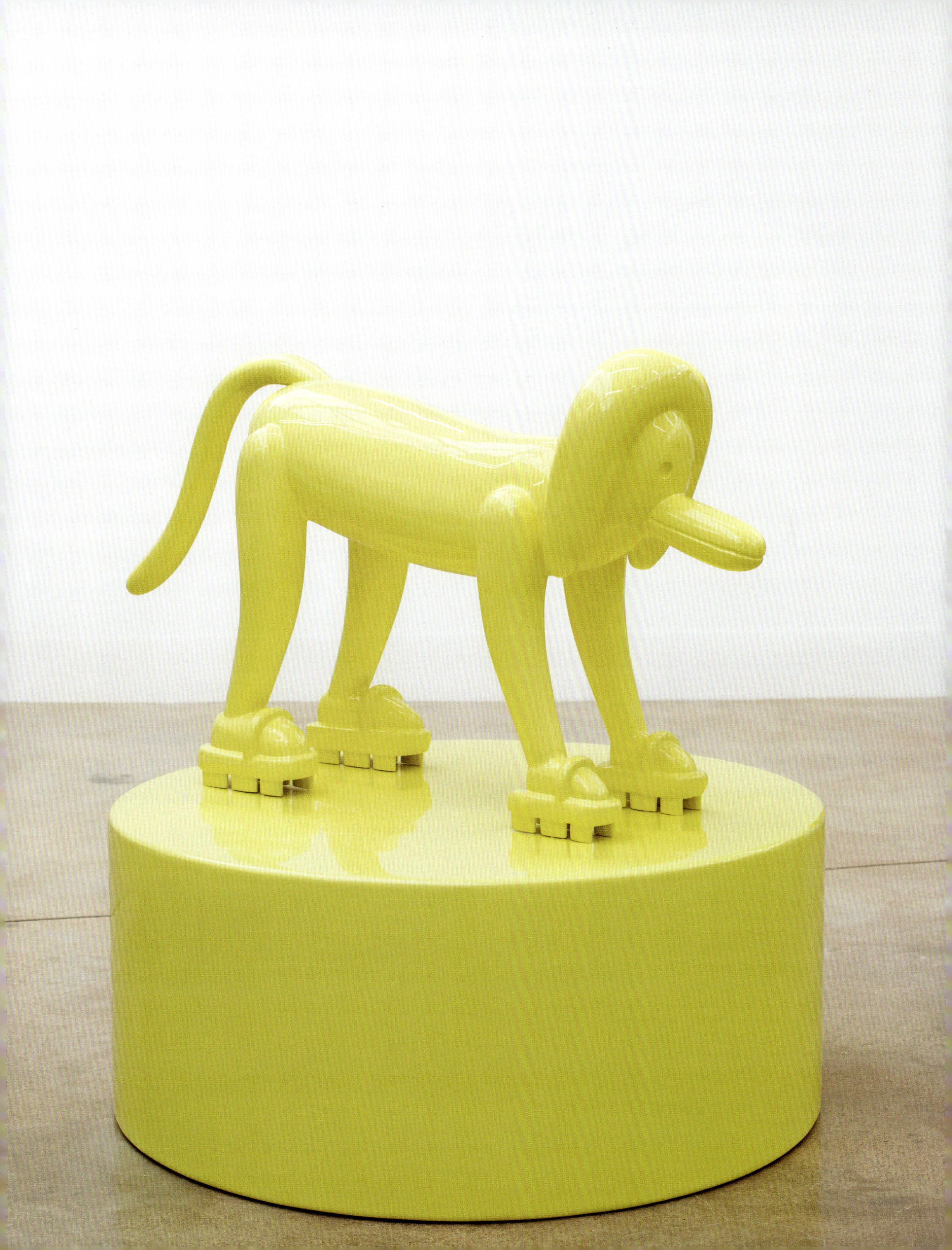

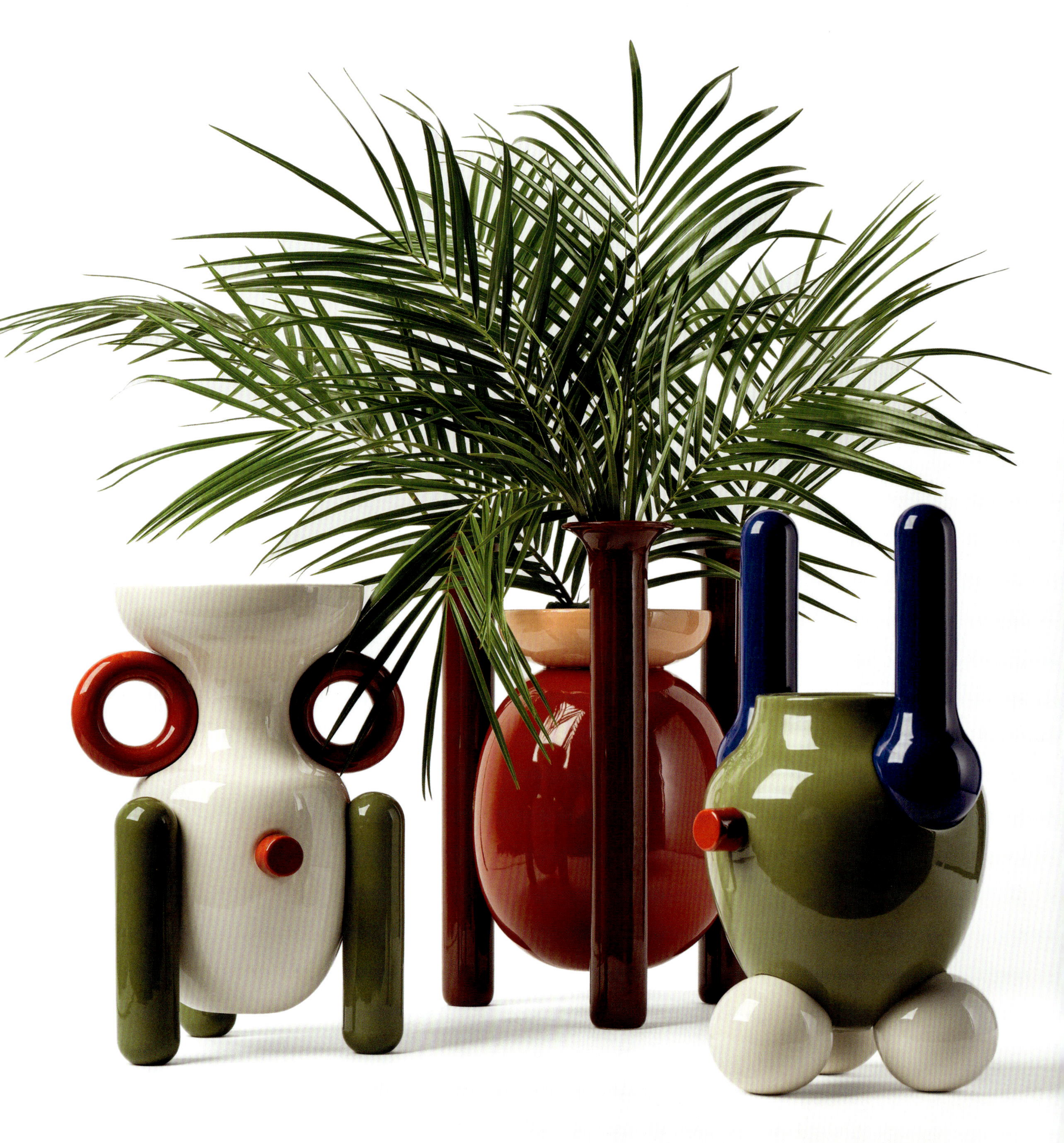

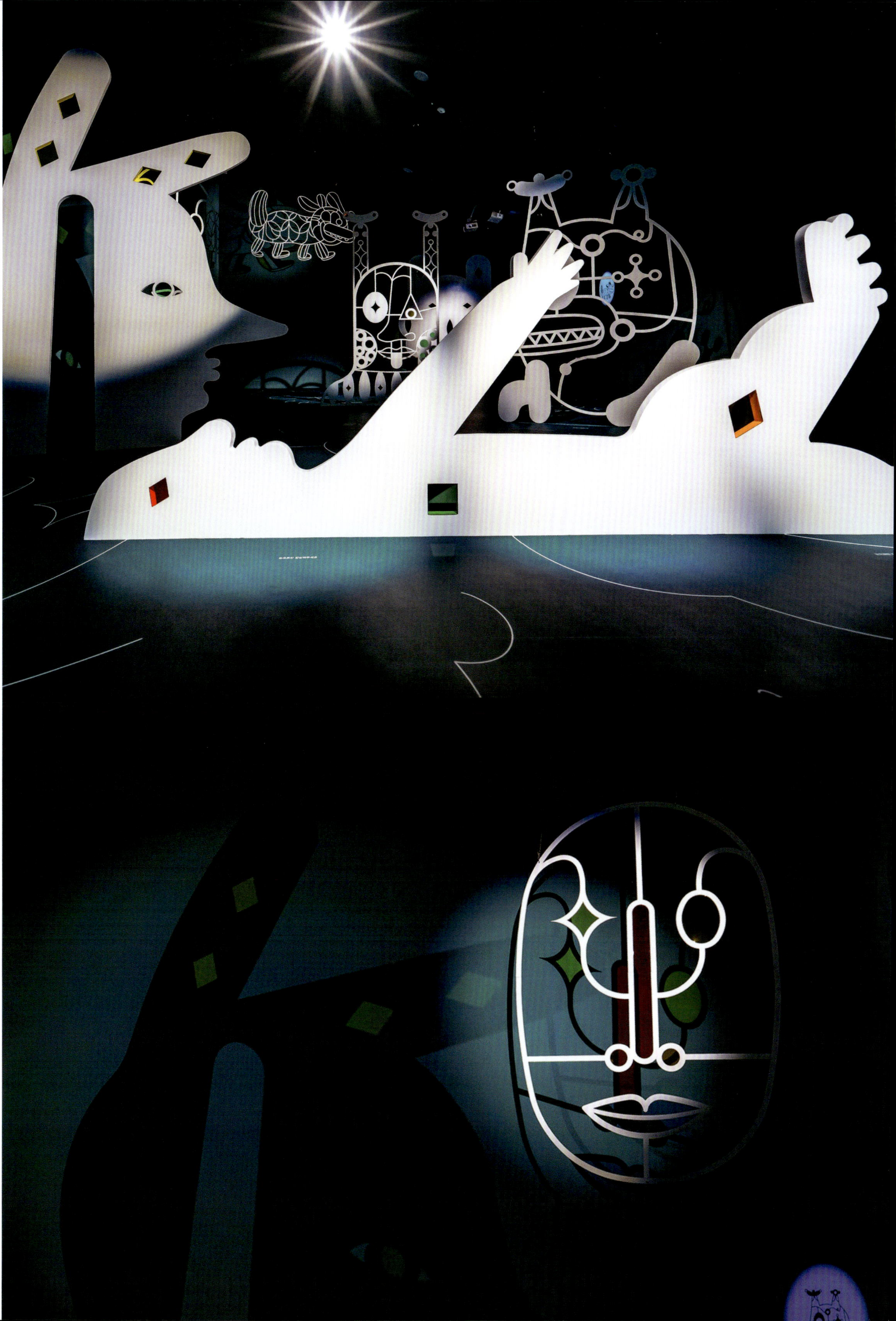

↑ Explorer—Vases for BD Barcelona Design, 2022

↓ Shadow Theatre—Installation from Serious Fun exhibition at the Daelim Museum, Seoul, South Korea, 2019

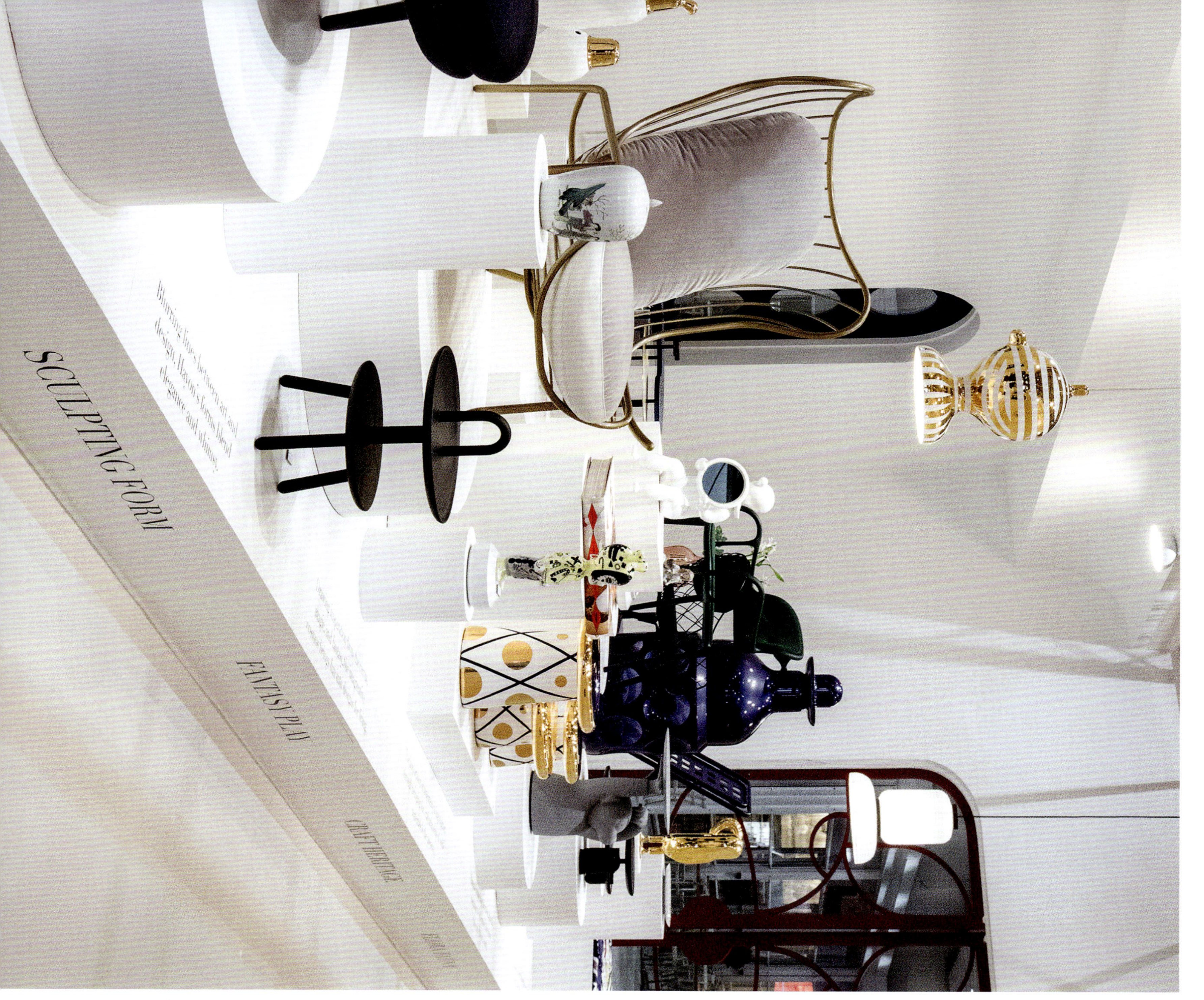

↑ Hayon DNA Gallery at the Stockholm Furniture & Light Fair, Guest of Honour, 2016

Pavillion showcasing: Réaction Poétique side table, Arpa armchair, Clown Mirror, T-Tables, The Guest, Mon Cirque sculpture, Monkey Table, Formakami lamp, etc.

↓ Entrance door detail

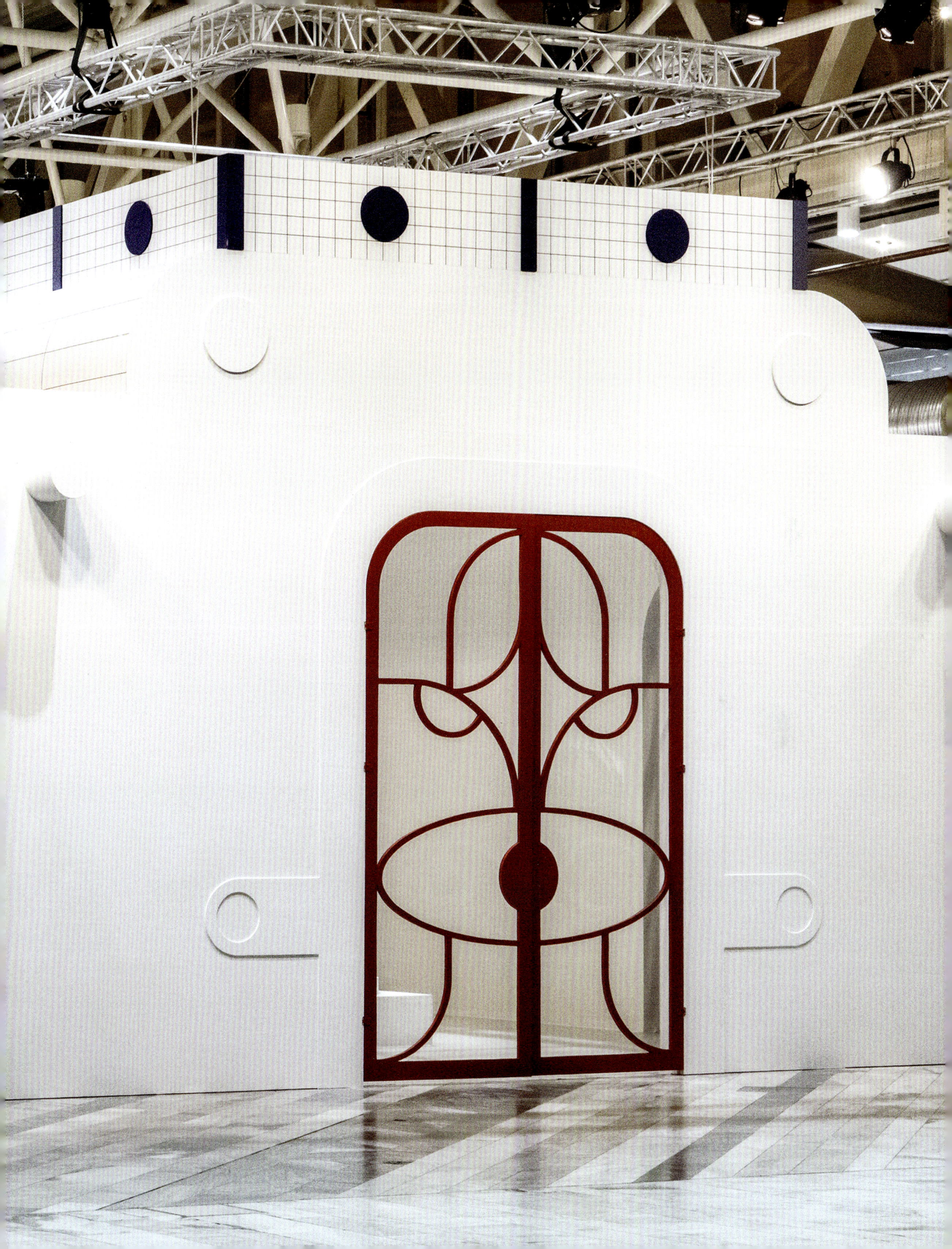

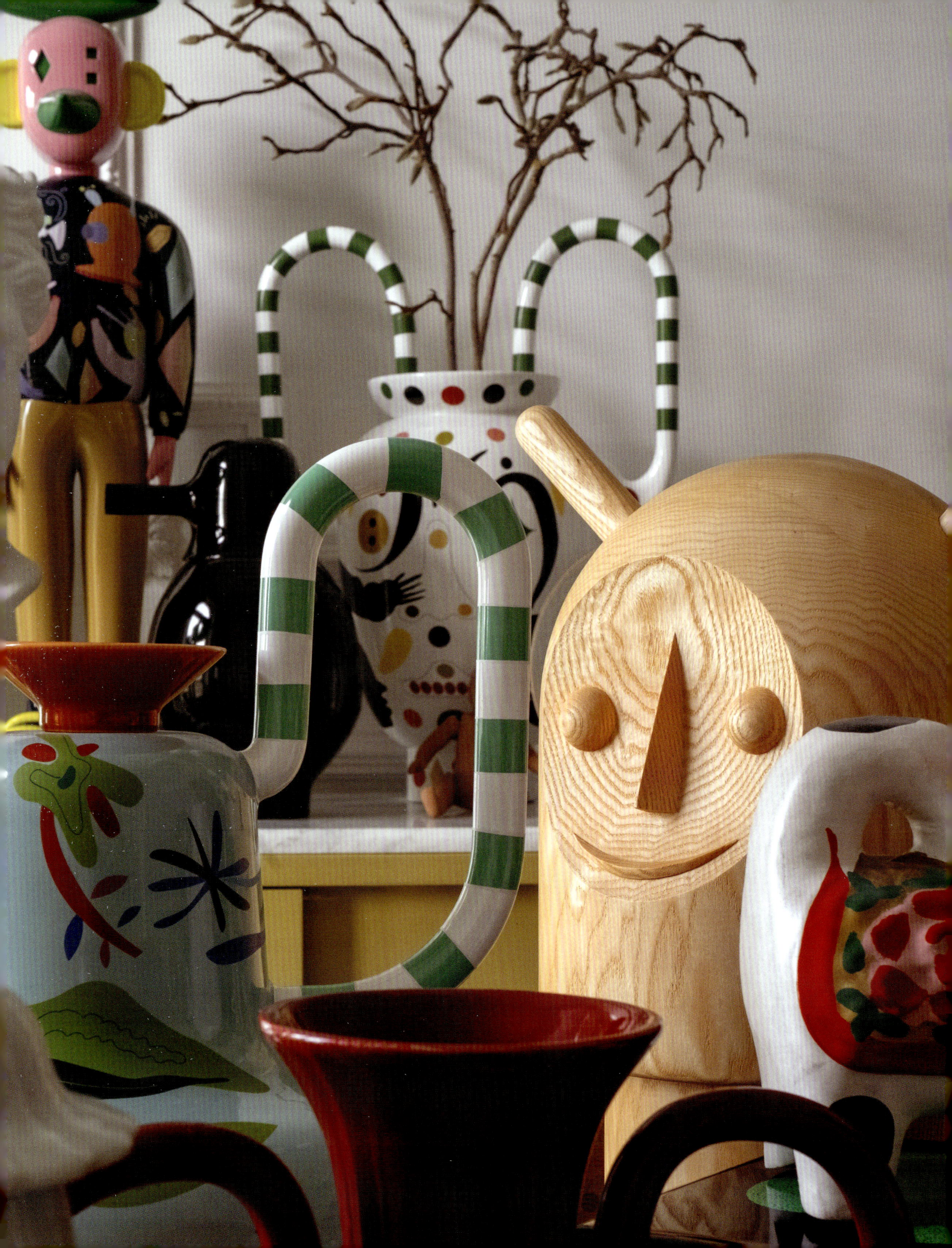

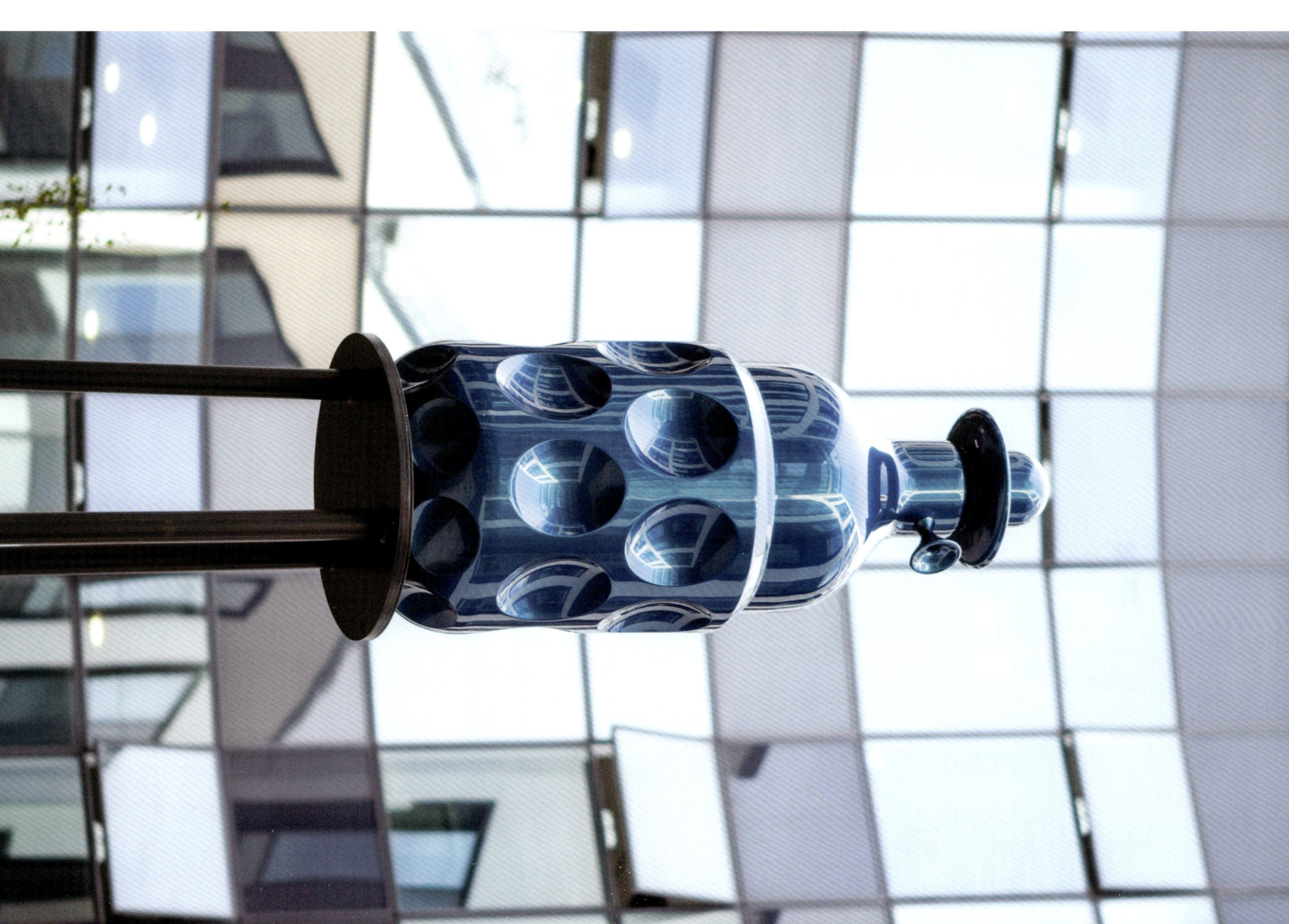

↑ Miscellaneous: Folkboy—Aeromaticolor Vase for Maison Matisse—Showtime Vase, black—Smilo wood sculpture
↓ Mon Cirque—Sculptures installed at the Southmead Hospital courtyards in Bristol, U.K., 2014

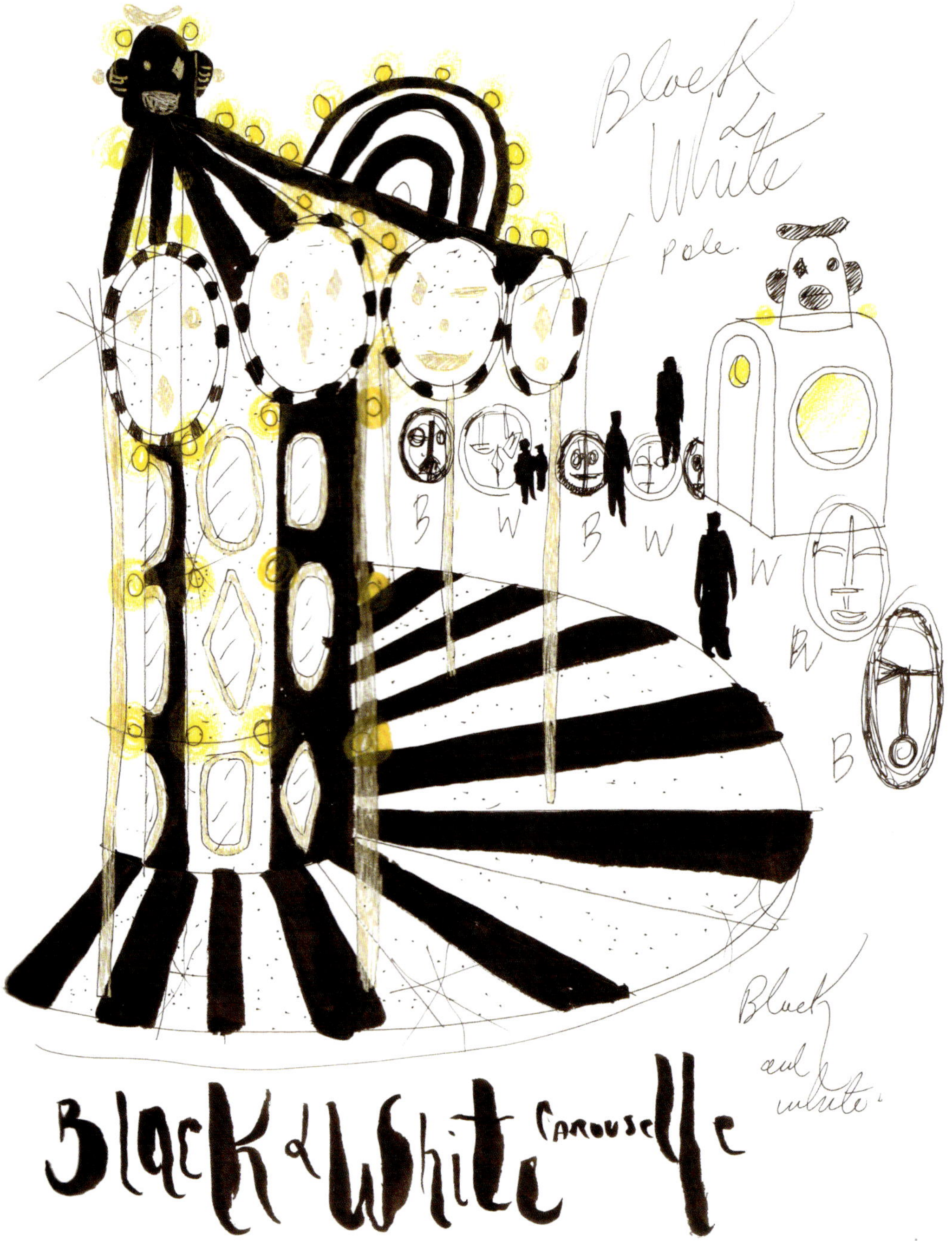

Black & White
pole.

Black
and
white.

Black & White Carouselle

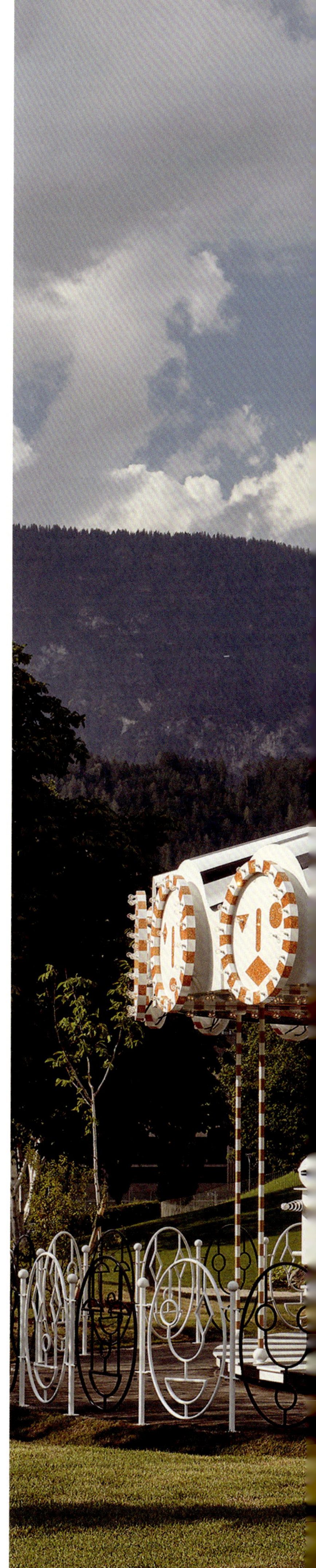

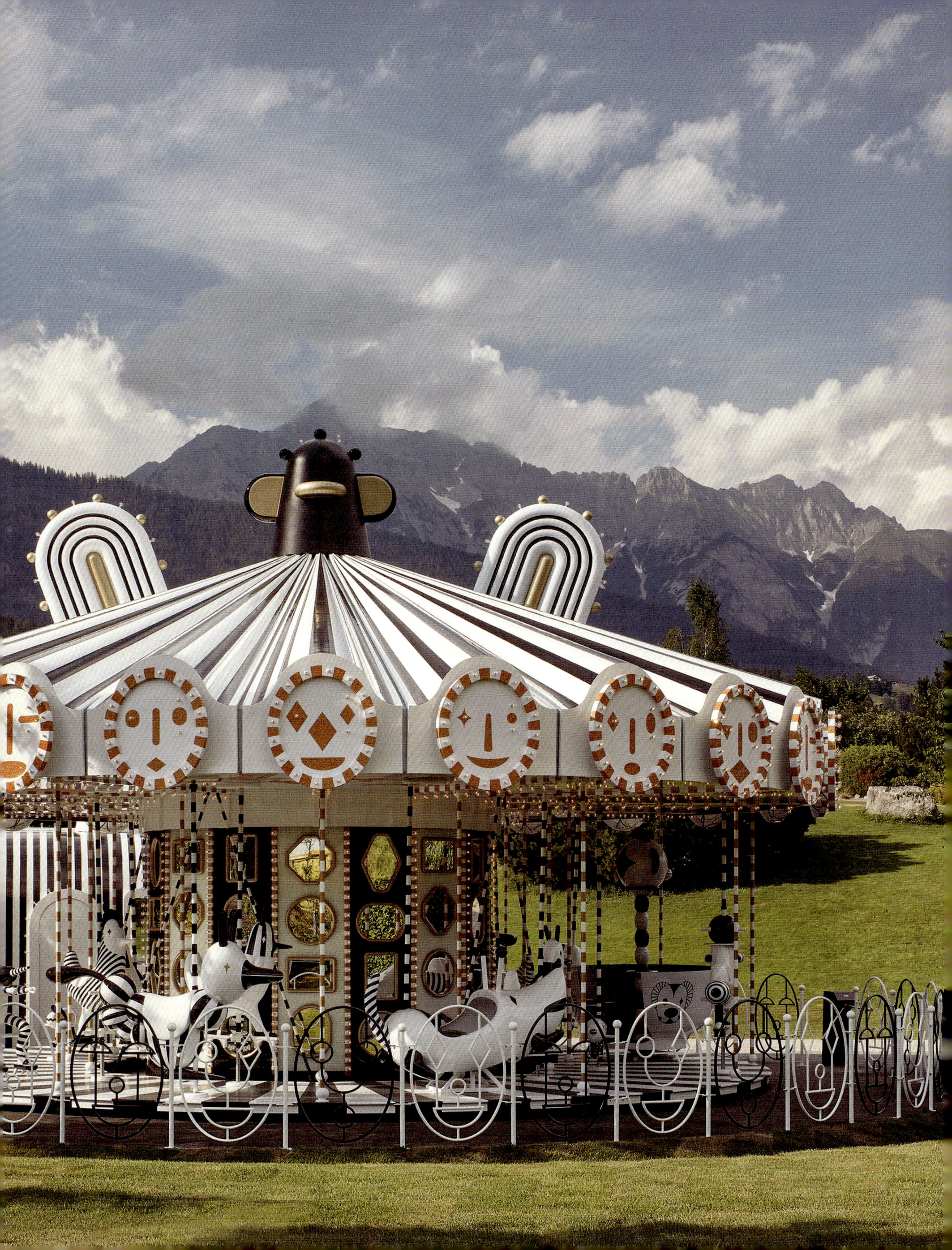

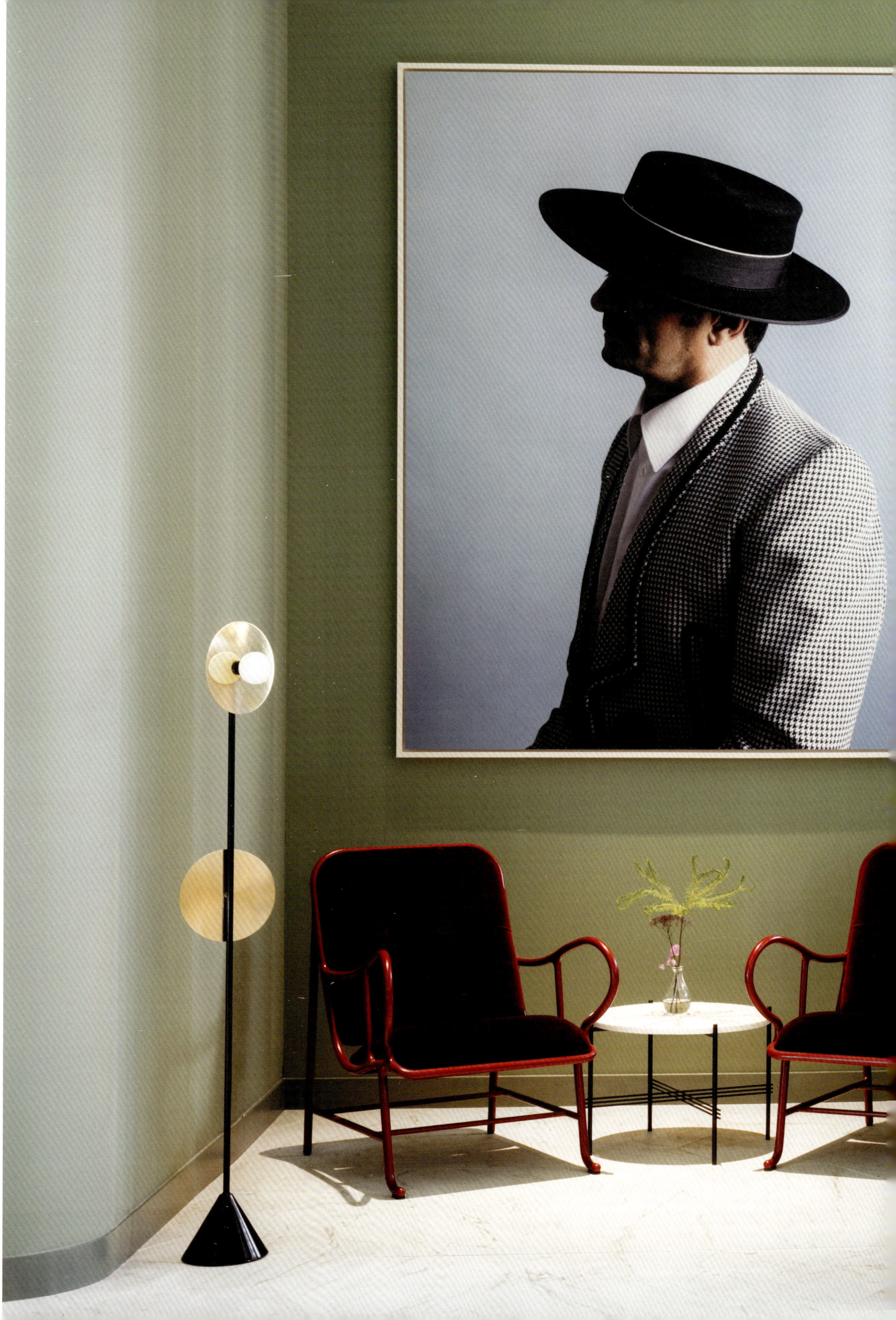

↓ Barceló Torre de Madrid Hotel—Interior design featuring Gardenias armchair and Scuba lamps, 2016

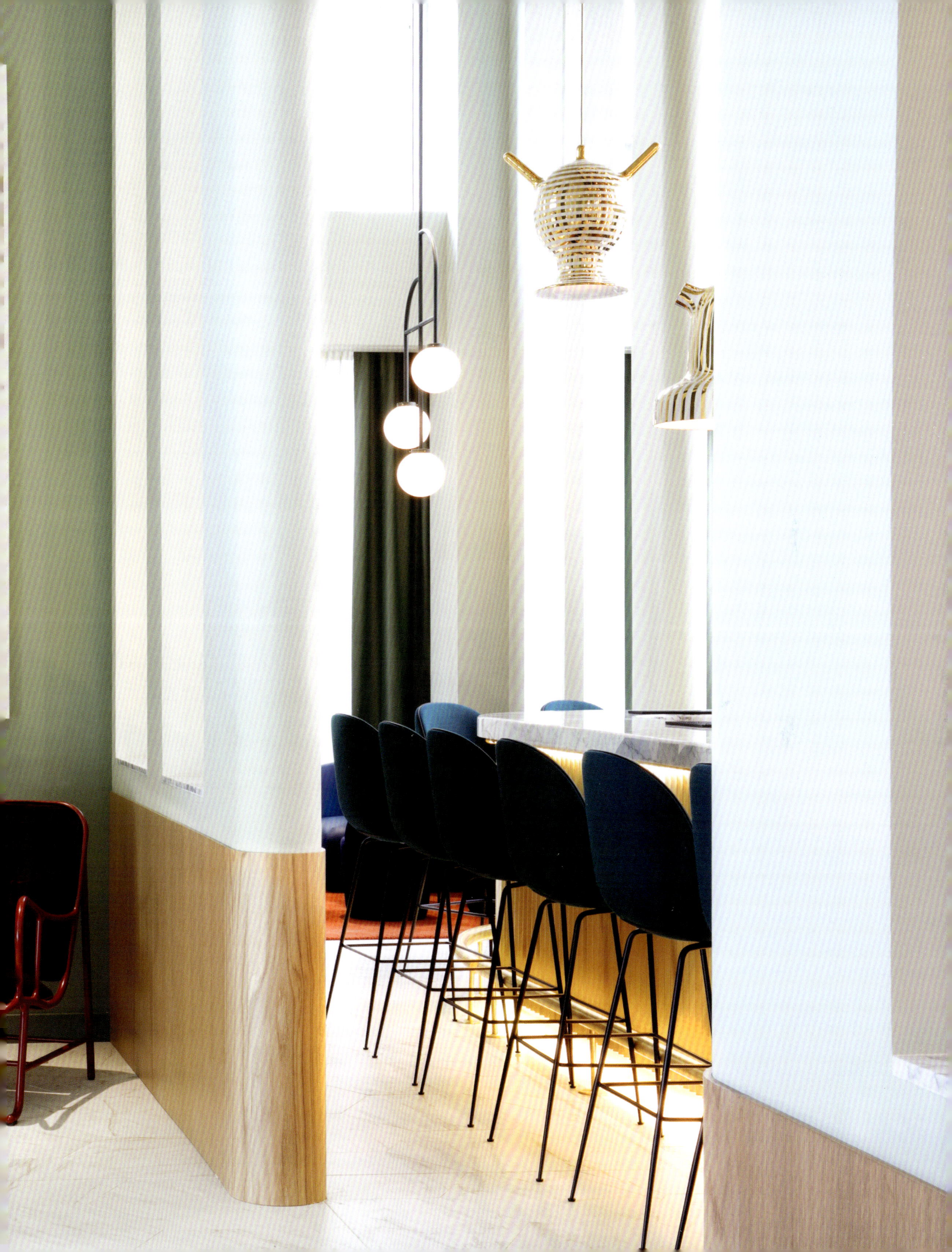

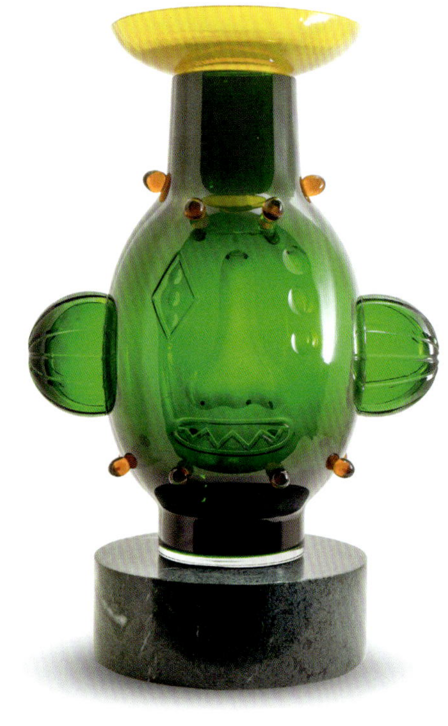

↑ Verdino — Limited-edition vase made in Murano for Galerie Kreo, 2018
↓ Portrait of Sir Jon Animal — Acrylic on canvas, 120 × 180 cm, 2022

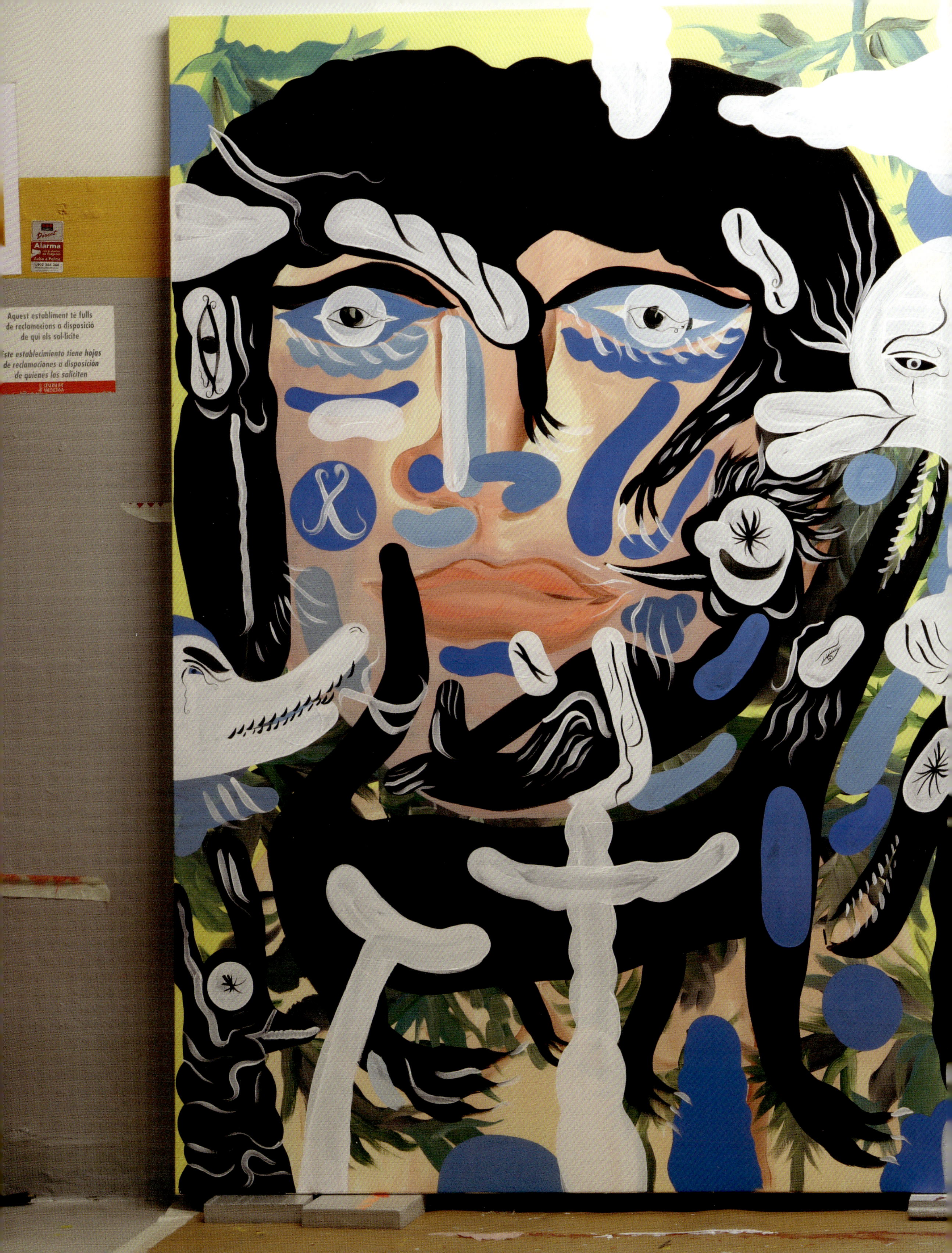
Aquest establiment té fulls
de reclamacions a disposició
de qui els sol·liciti
Este establecimiento tiene hojas
de reclamaciones a disposición
de quienes las soliciten

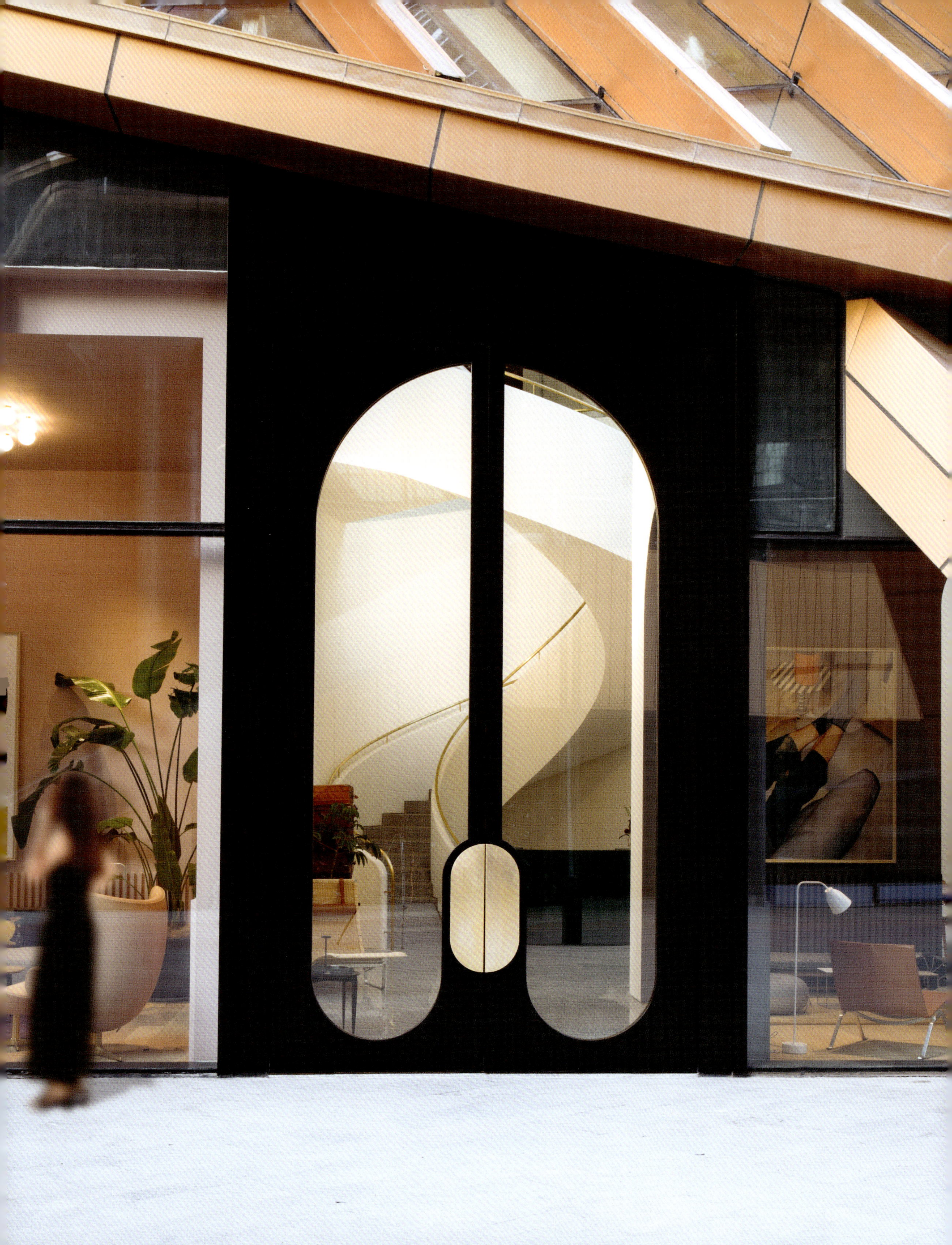

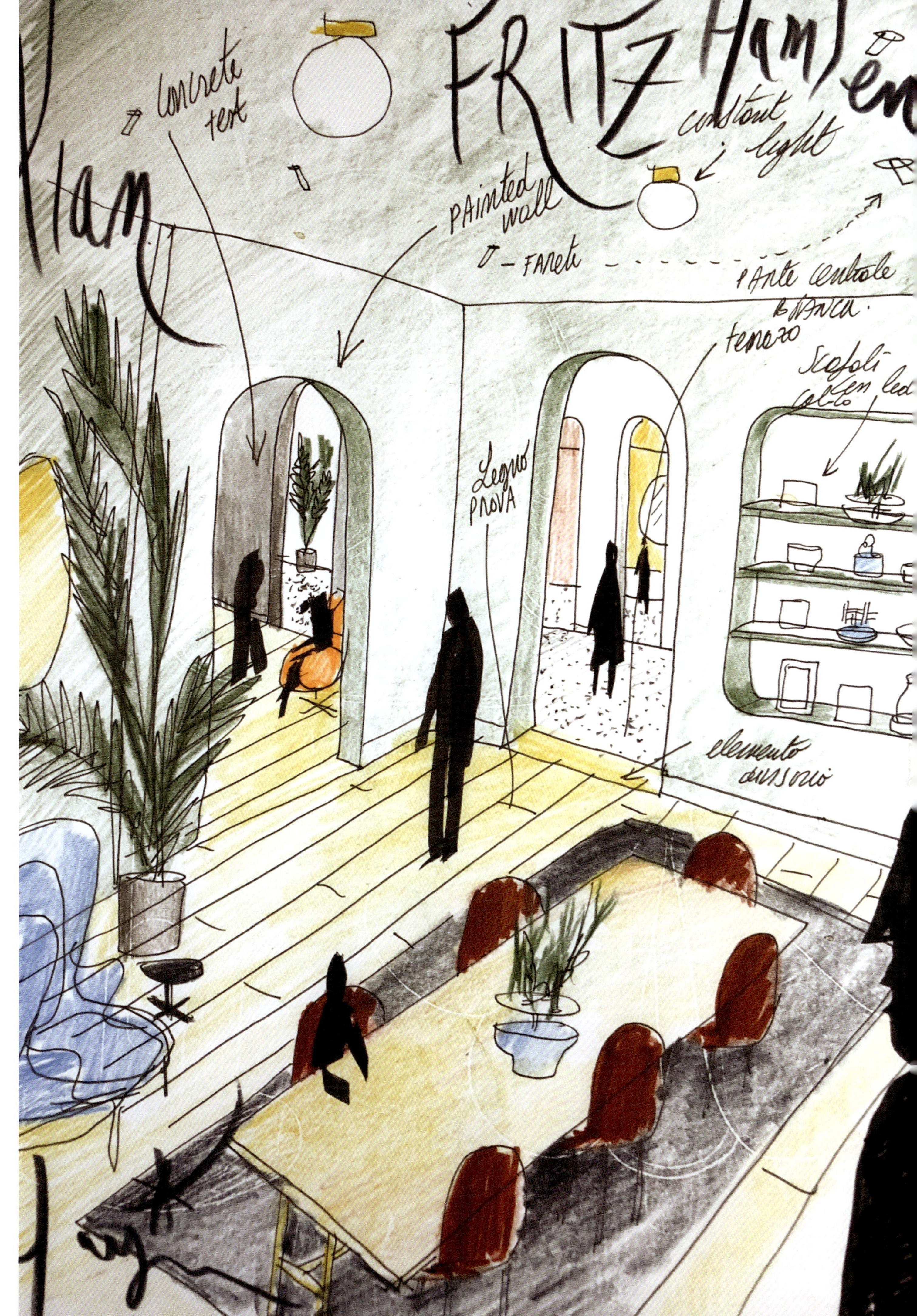

Plan
concrete text
FRITZ Hansen
PAinted wall
constant light
FAreti
pAnte centrale bianca
terrazo
Scafali
Legno PROVA
elemento divisorio

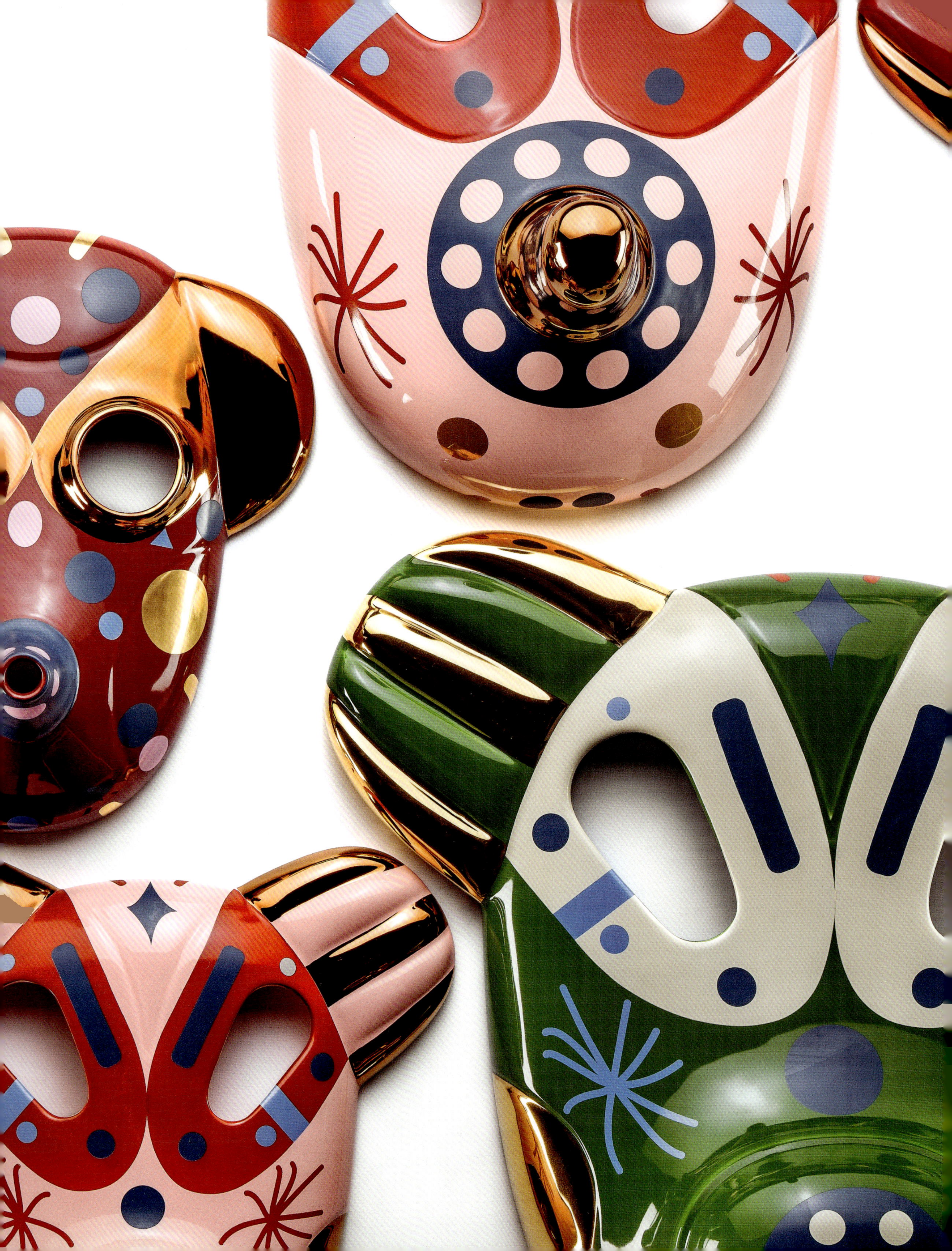

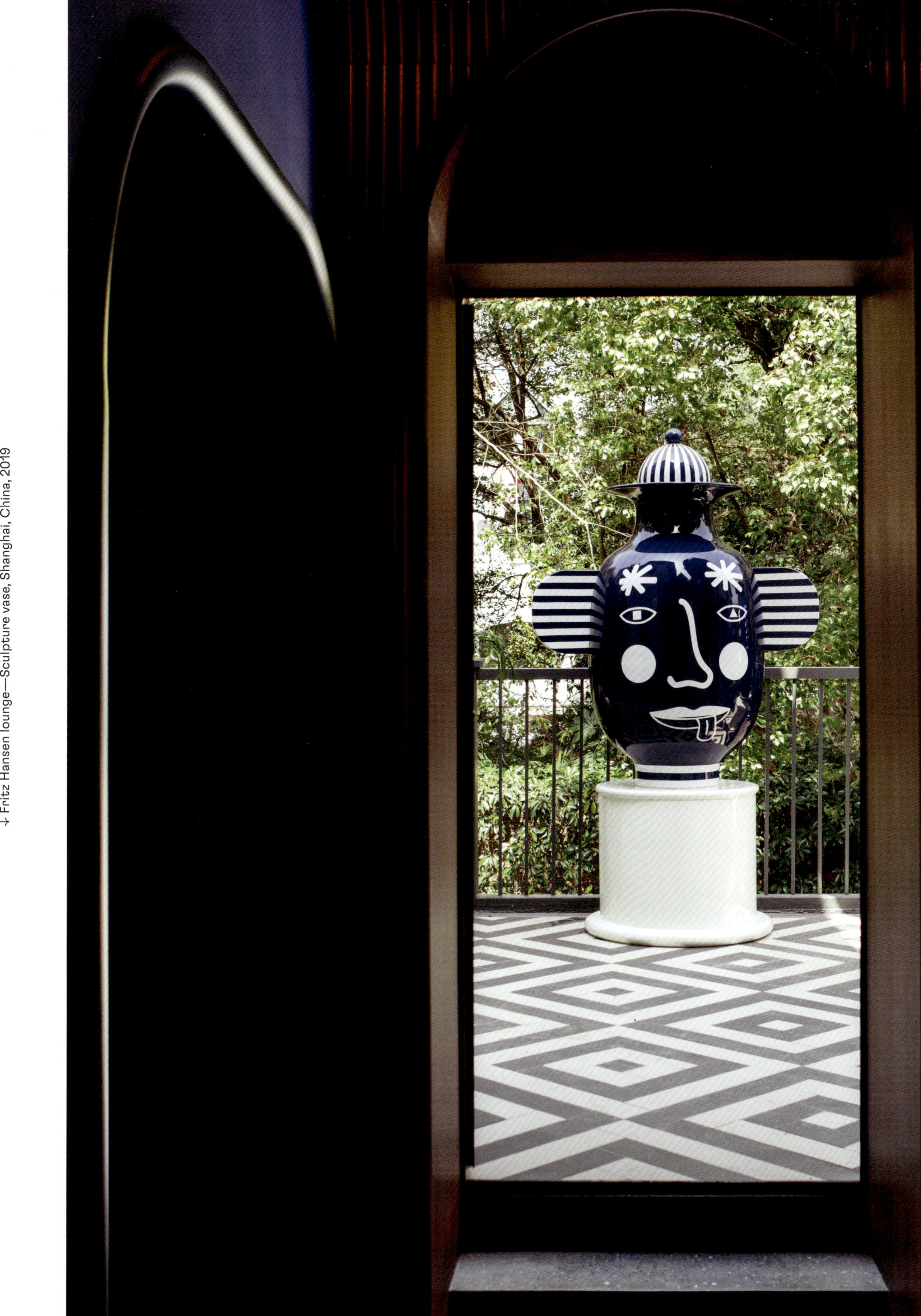

↑ Baile—Ceramic masks for Bosa, 2020
↓ Fritz Hansen lounge—Sculpture vase, Shanghai, China, 2019

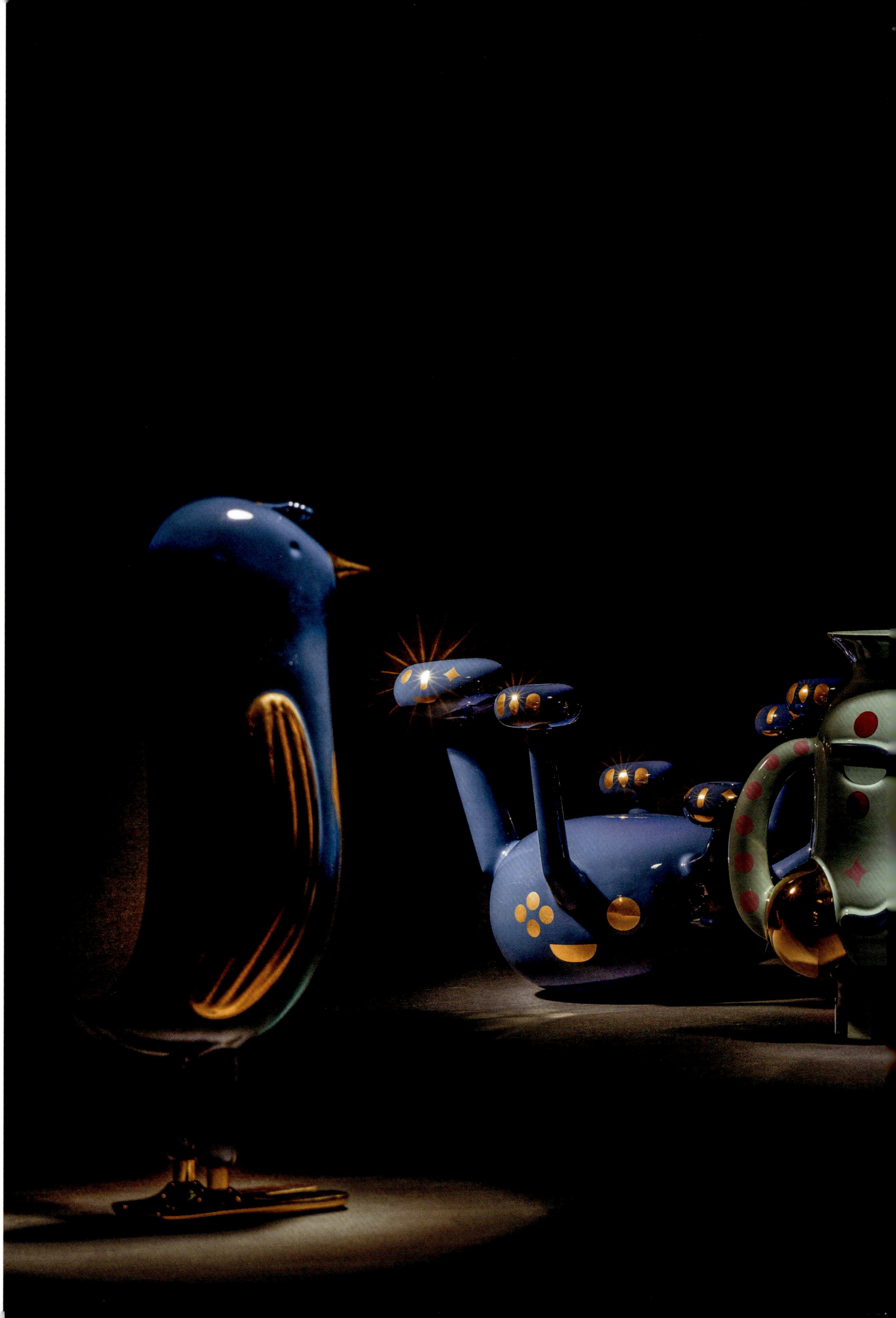

↓ Baile—Ceramic vases, candle holder, sculpture, mask and table for Bosa, 2020

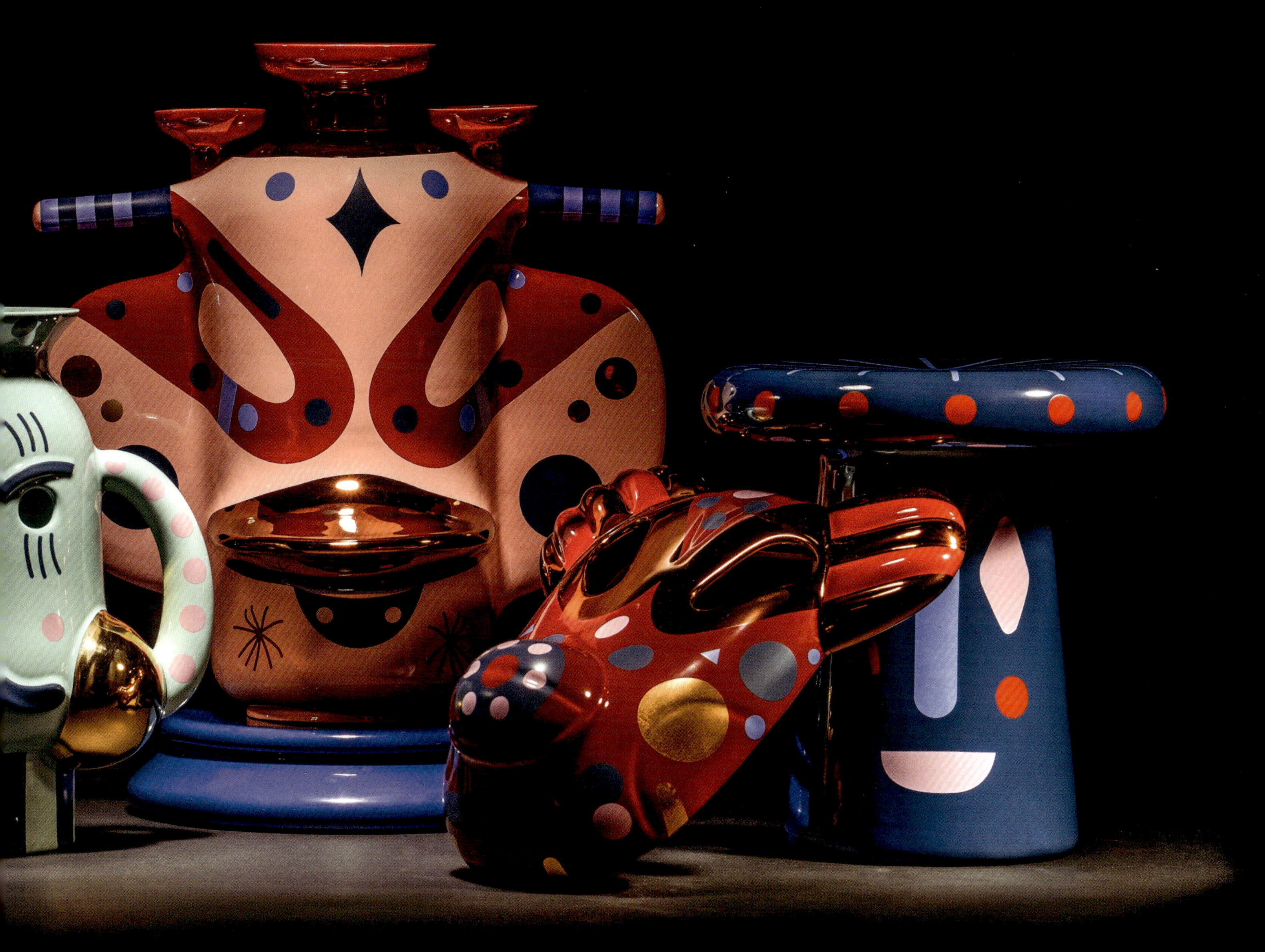

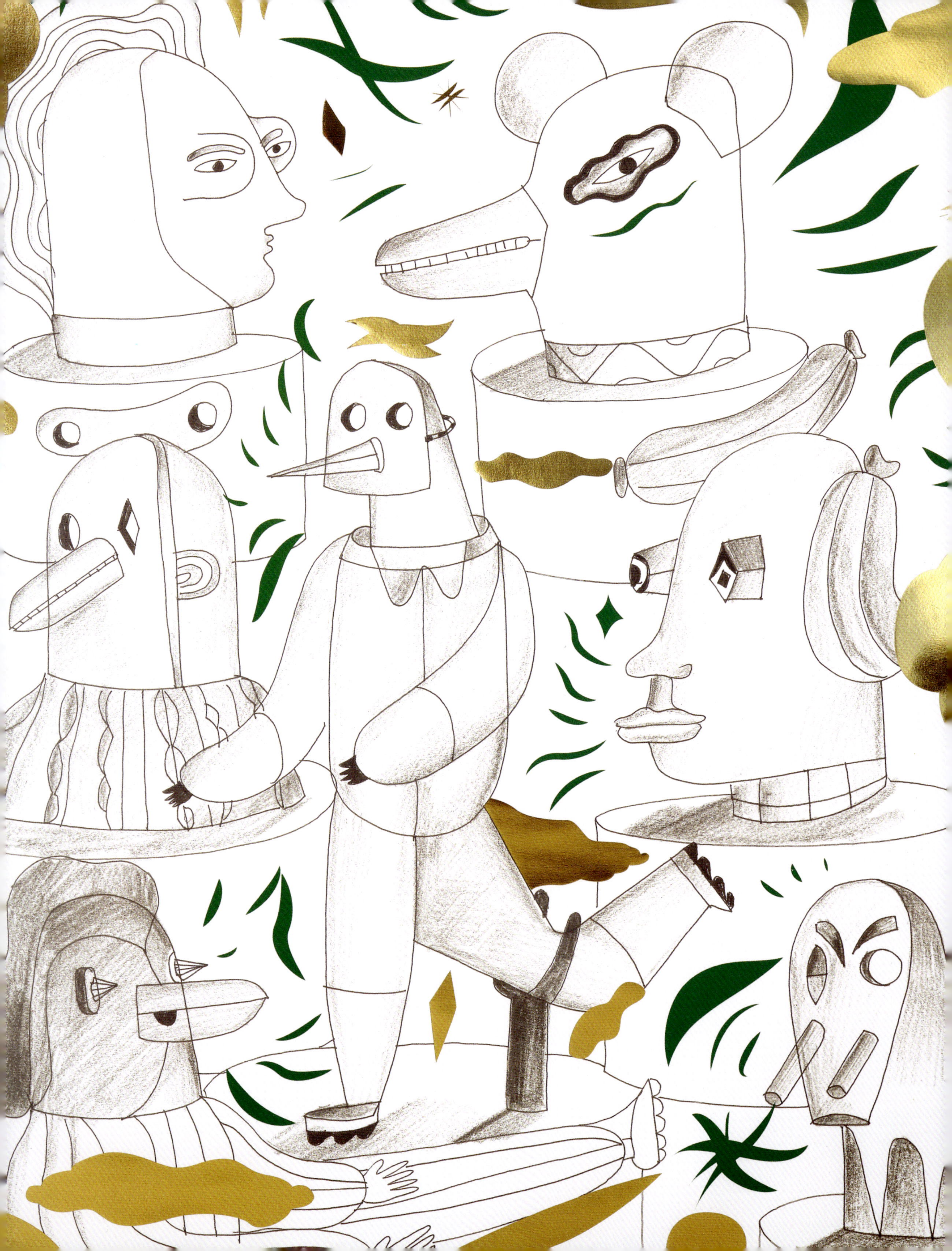

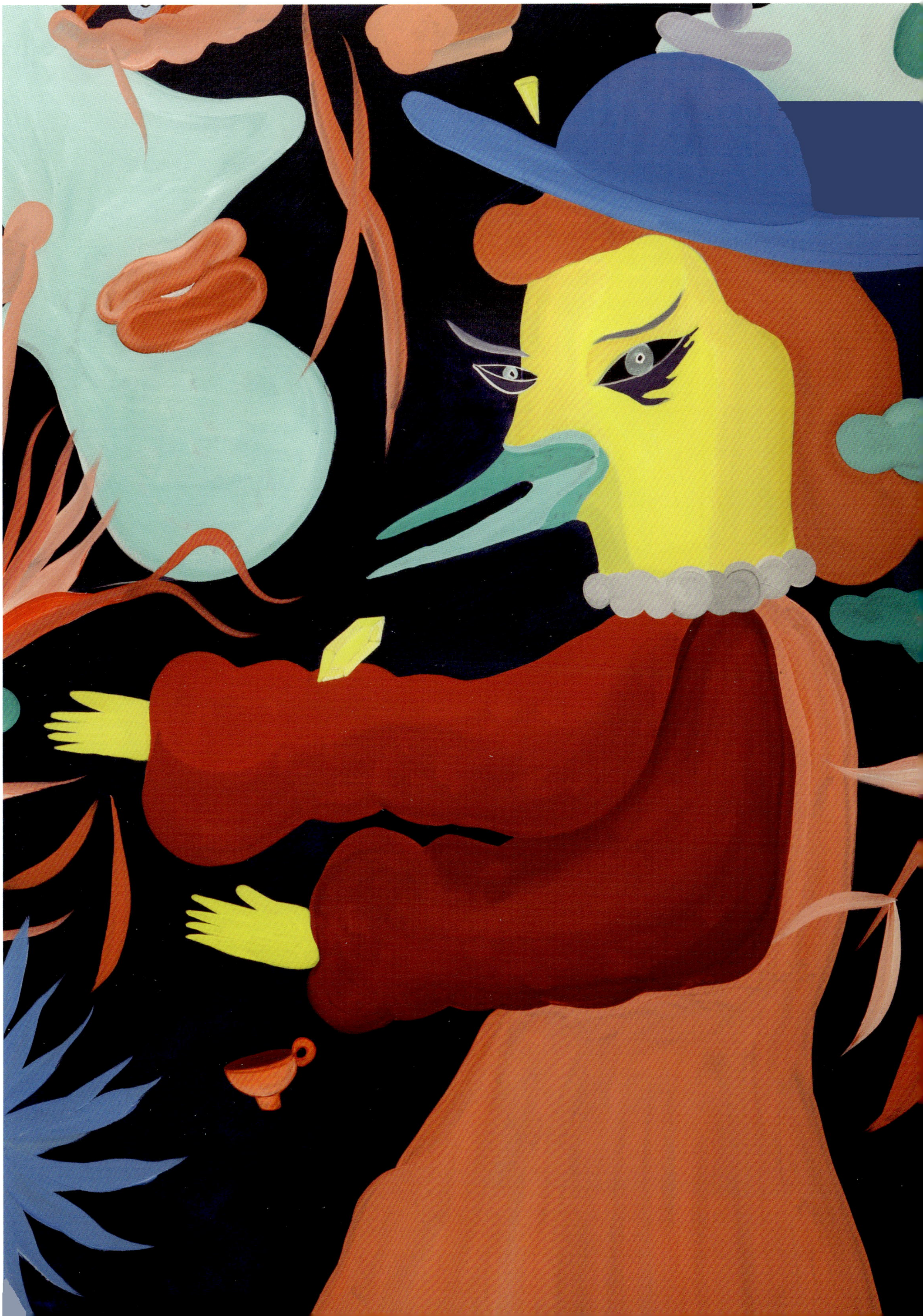

↑ Animalotèque—Limited-edition print for Wrong Shop, 2022
↓ Thimea—Acrylic painting, detail, 2022

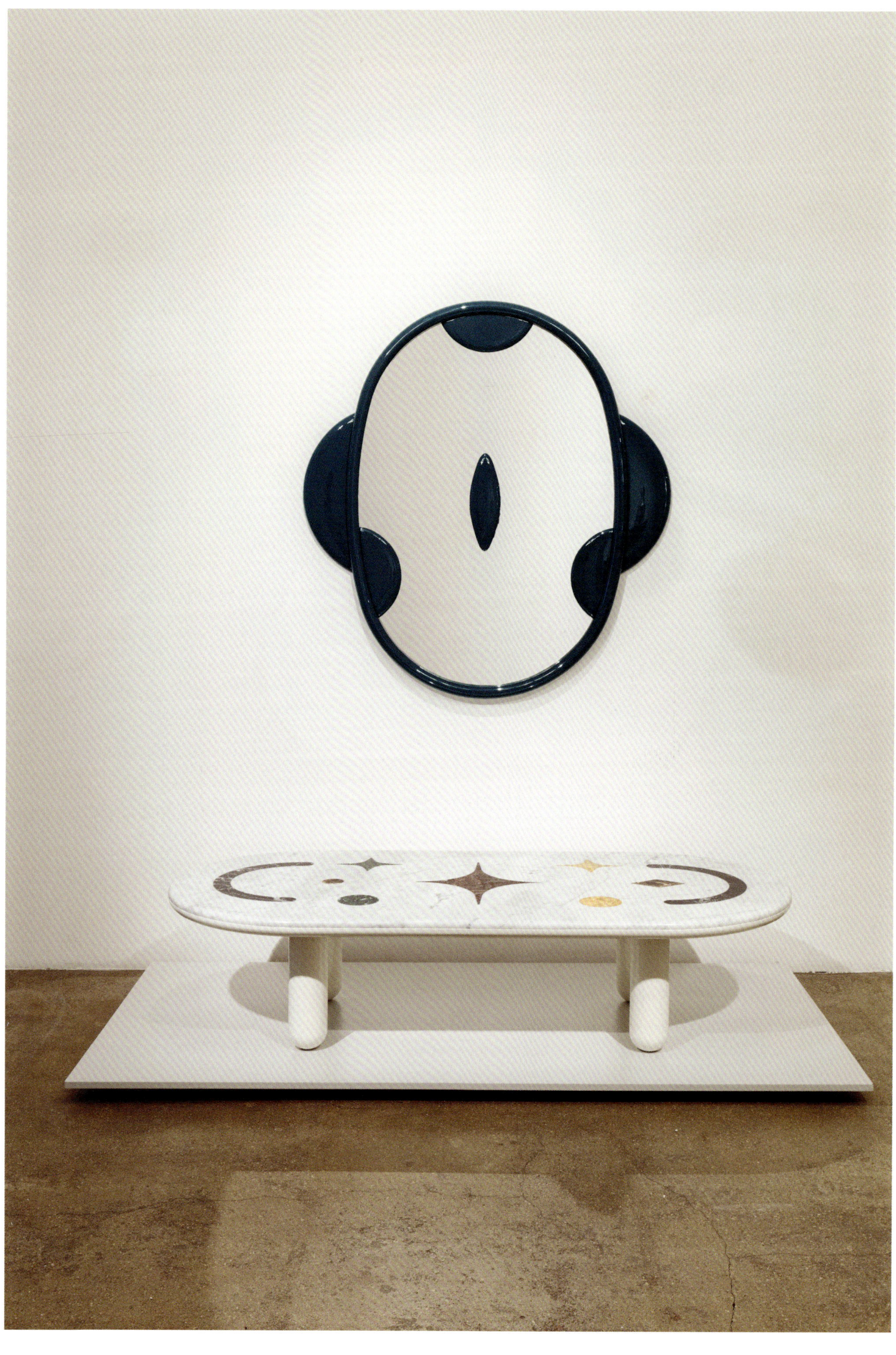

↓ Chromatico—Limited-edition mirror and table from the exhibition at Galerie Kreo, Paris, France, 2018
↳ Sketch for Aleta chair for Viccarbe, 2017

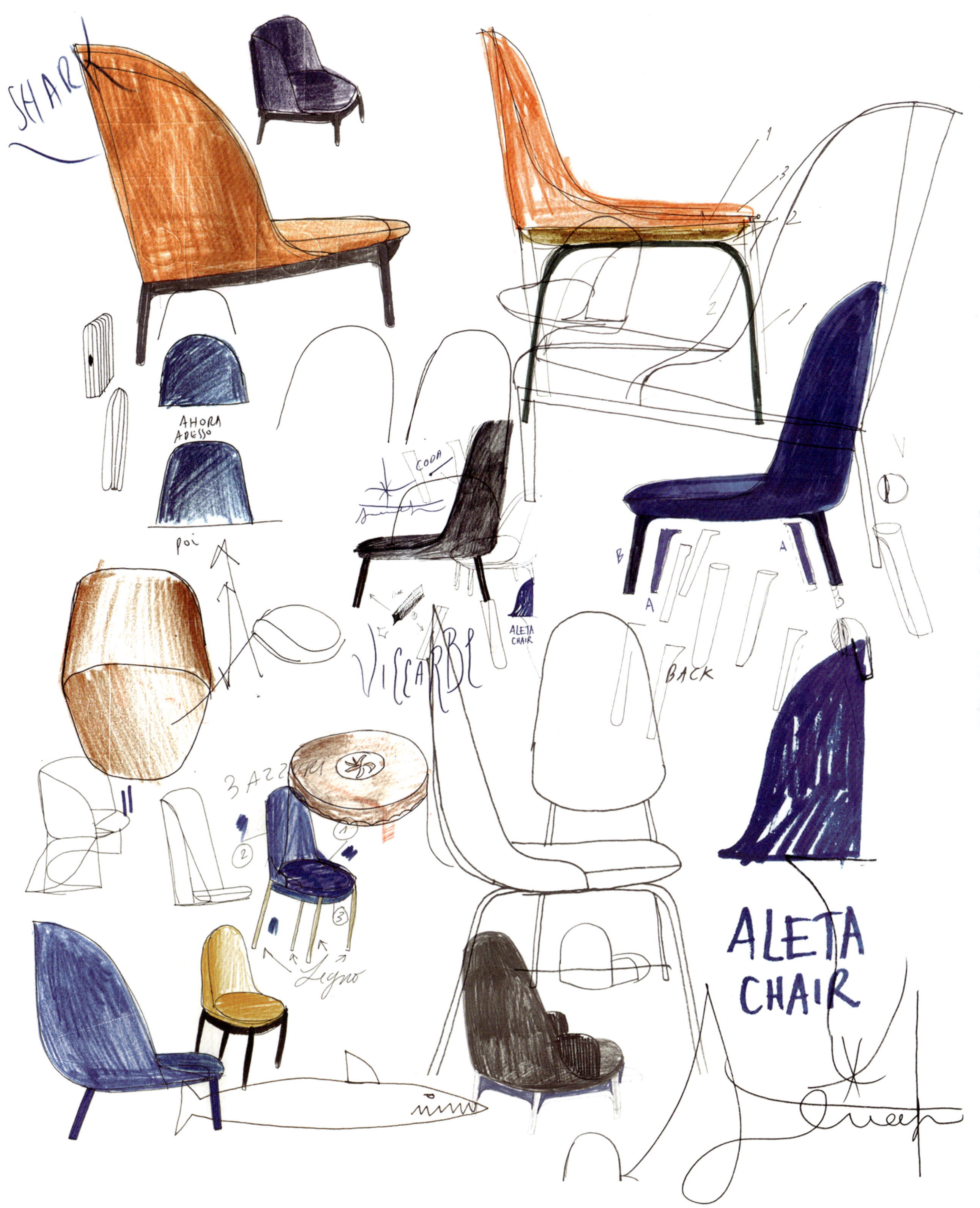

SHARK
AHORA ADESSO
poi
CODA
VICCARBE
ALETA CHAIR
BACK
3AZZURI
Legno
ALETA CHAIR

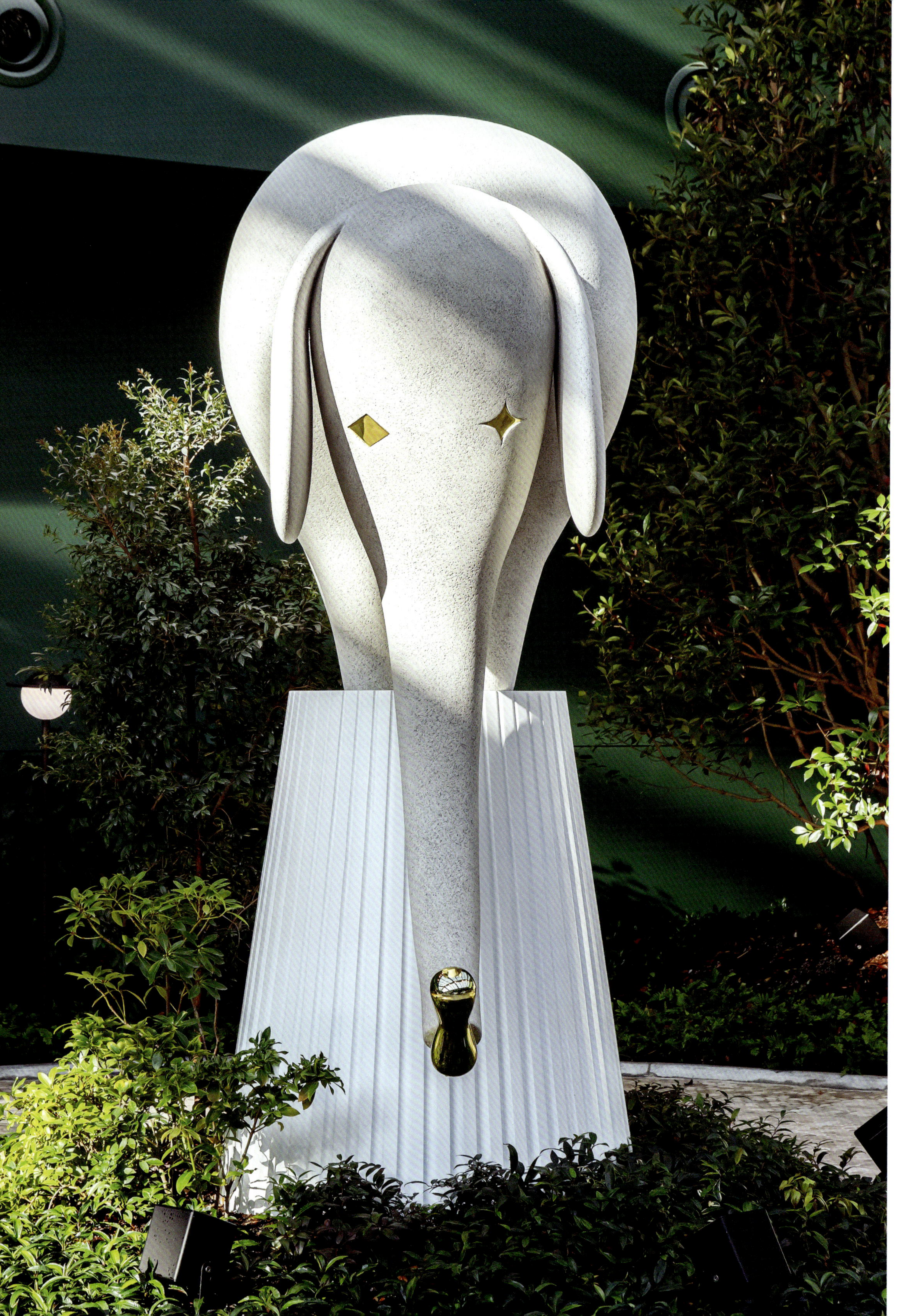

↑ Sharing Elephant—Sculpture at MOKA Garden, Seoul, South Korea, 2020
↓ Fountain Head—Sculpture at MOKA Garden, Seoul, South Korea, 2020

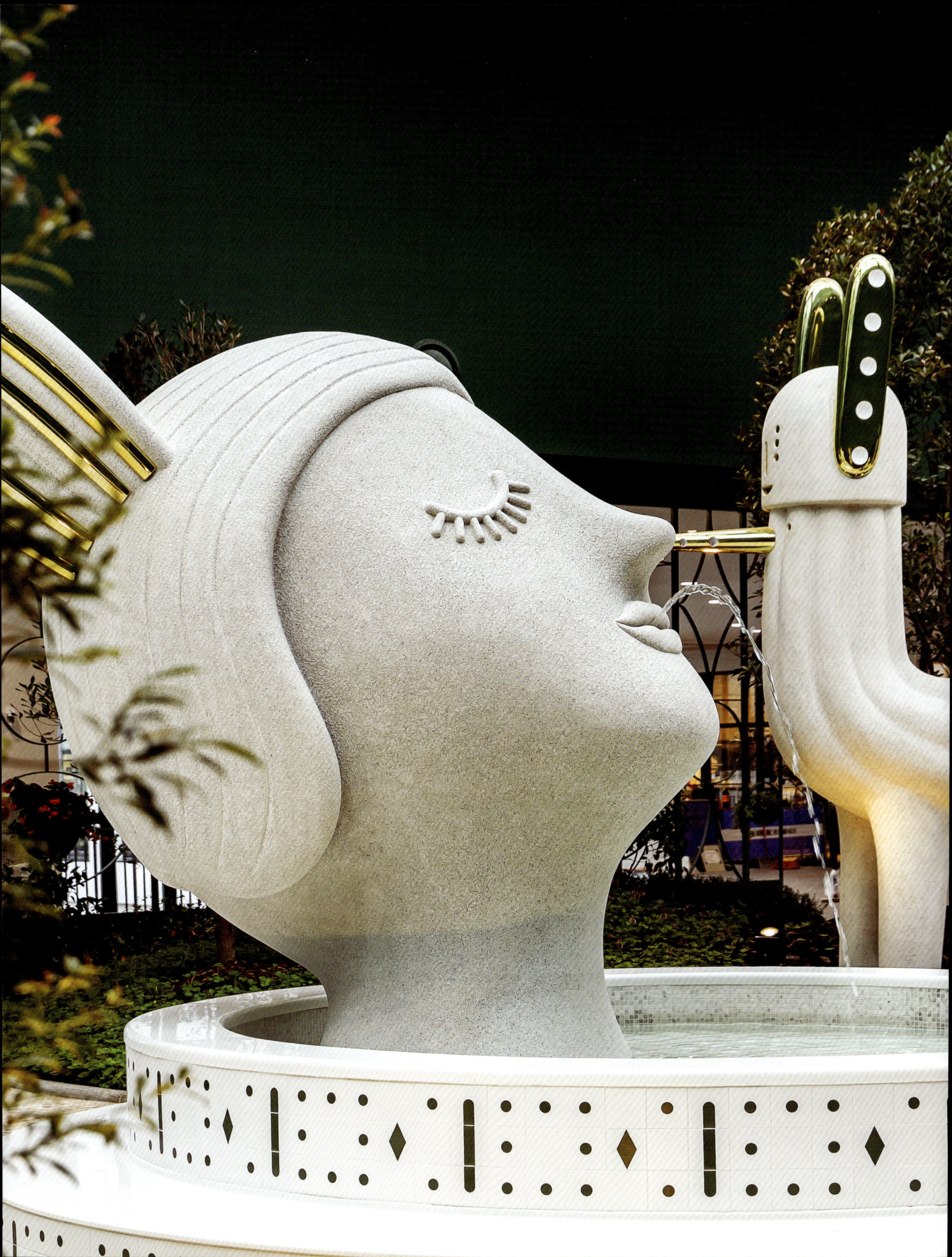

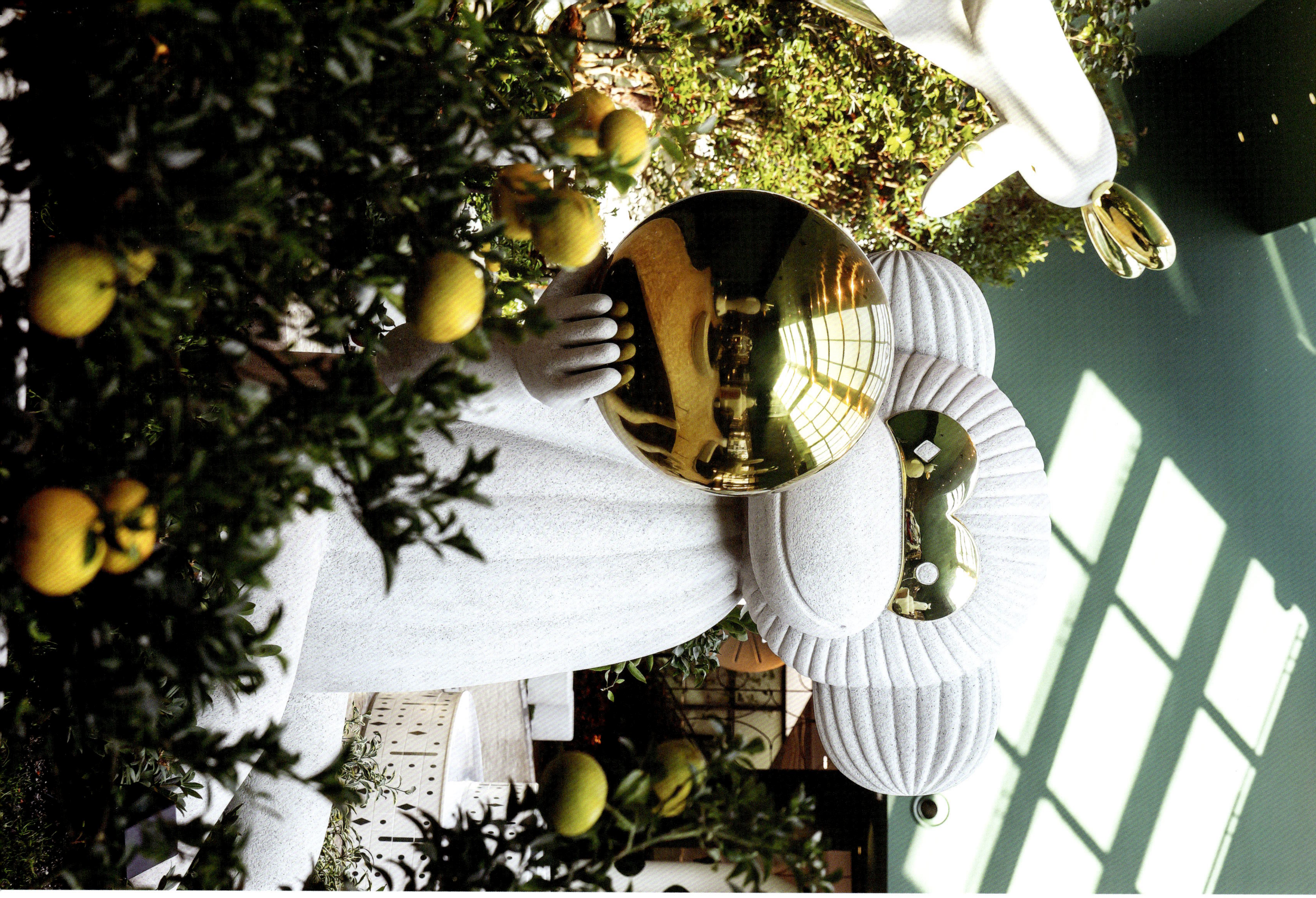

↑ Thinking Monkey—Sculpture at MOKA Garden, Seoul, South Korea, 2020
↓ Wide-angle view of MOKA Garden, Seoul, South Korea, 2020

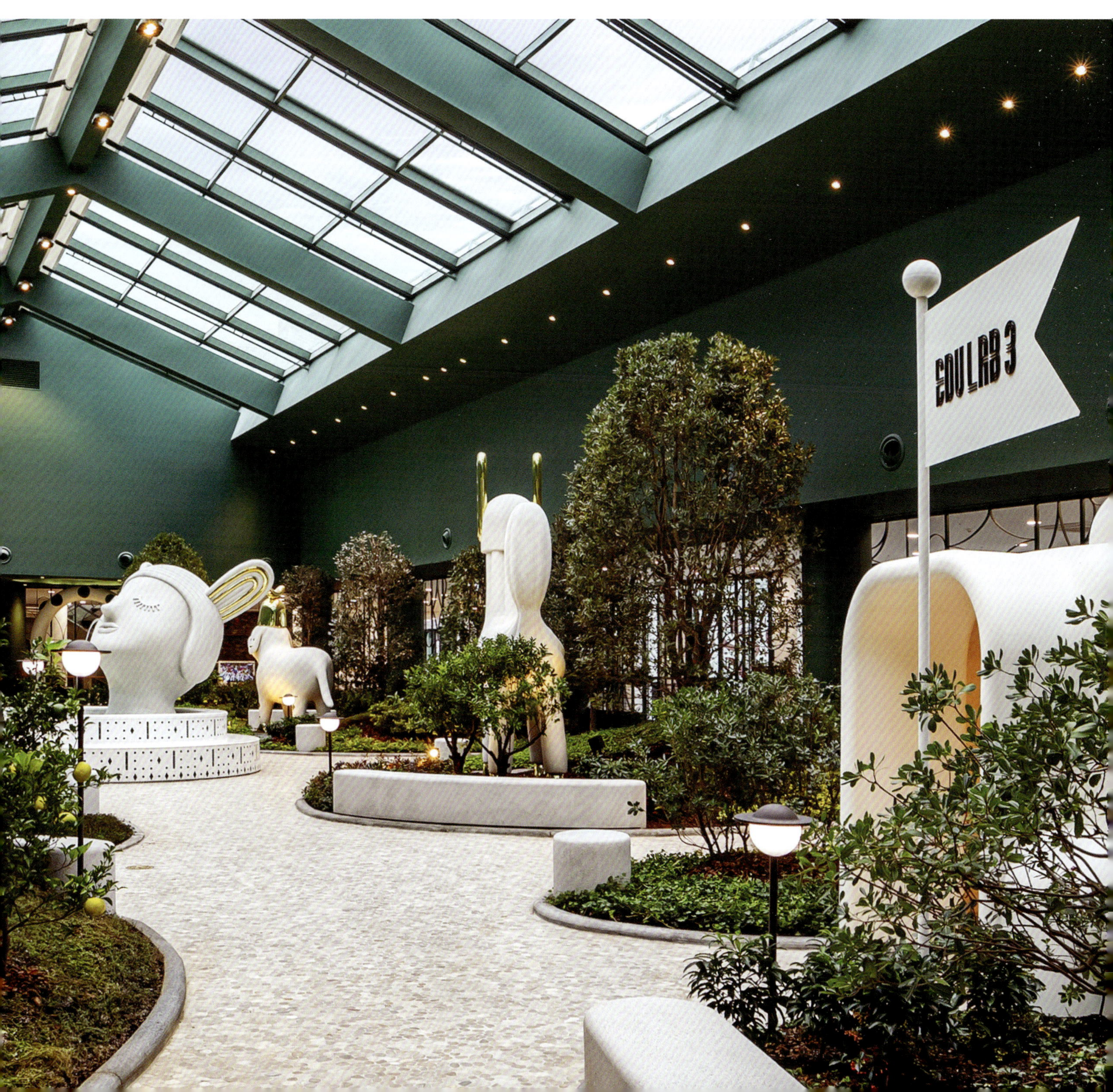
EDU LAB 3

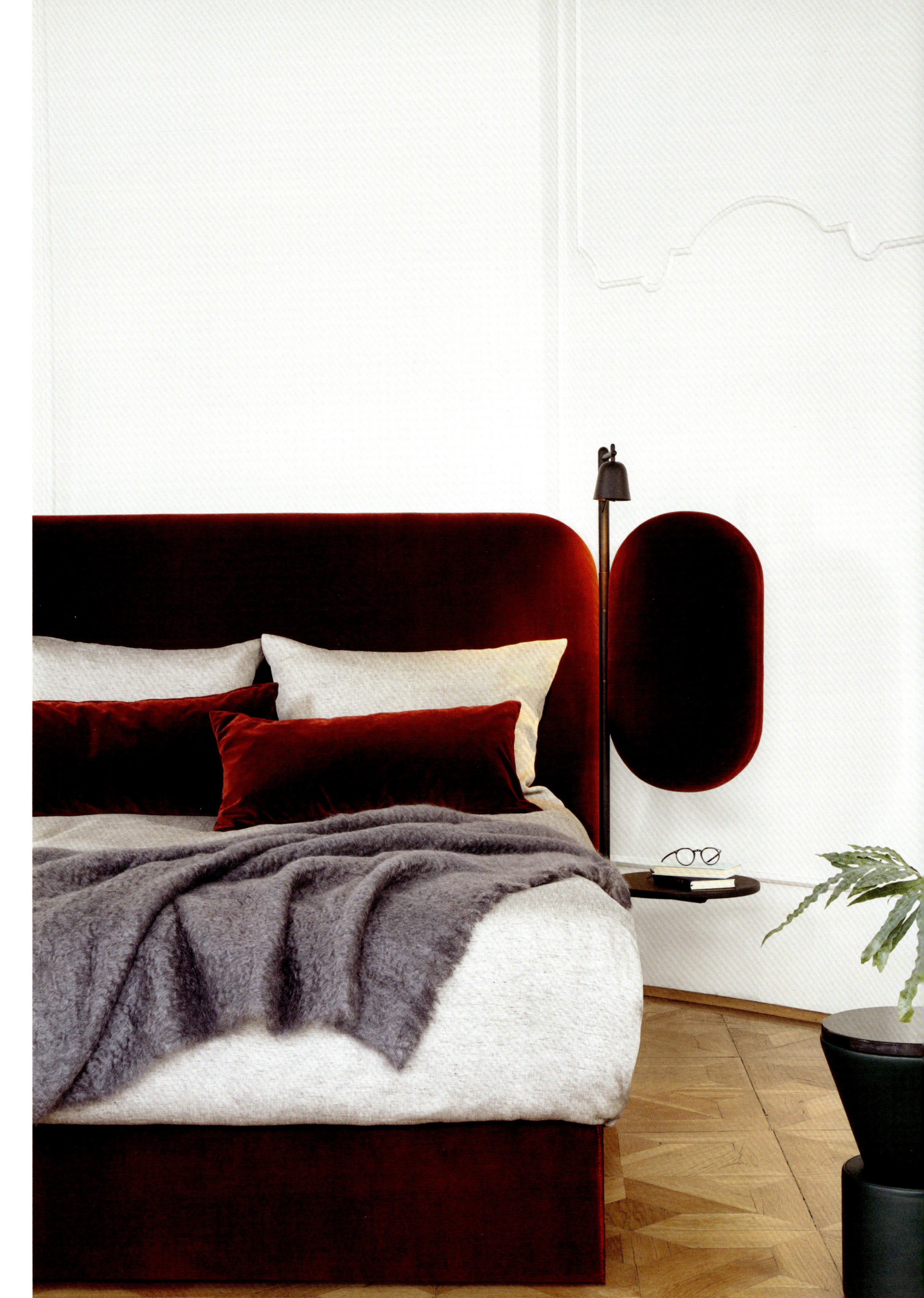

↓ Wings—Bed for Wittmann, 2017
↓ Twenty Two—Handmade wooden chair for Ceccotti Collezioni, 2009

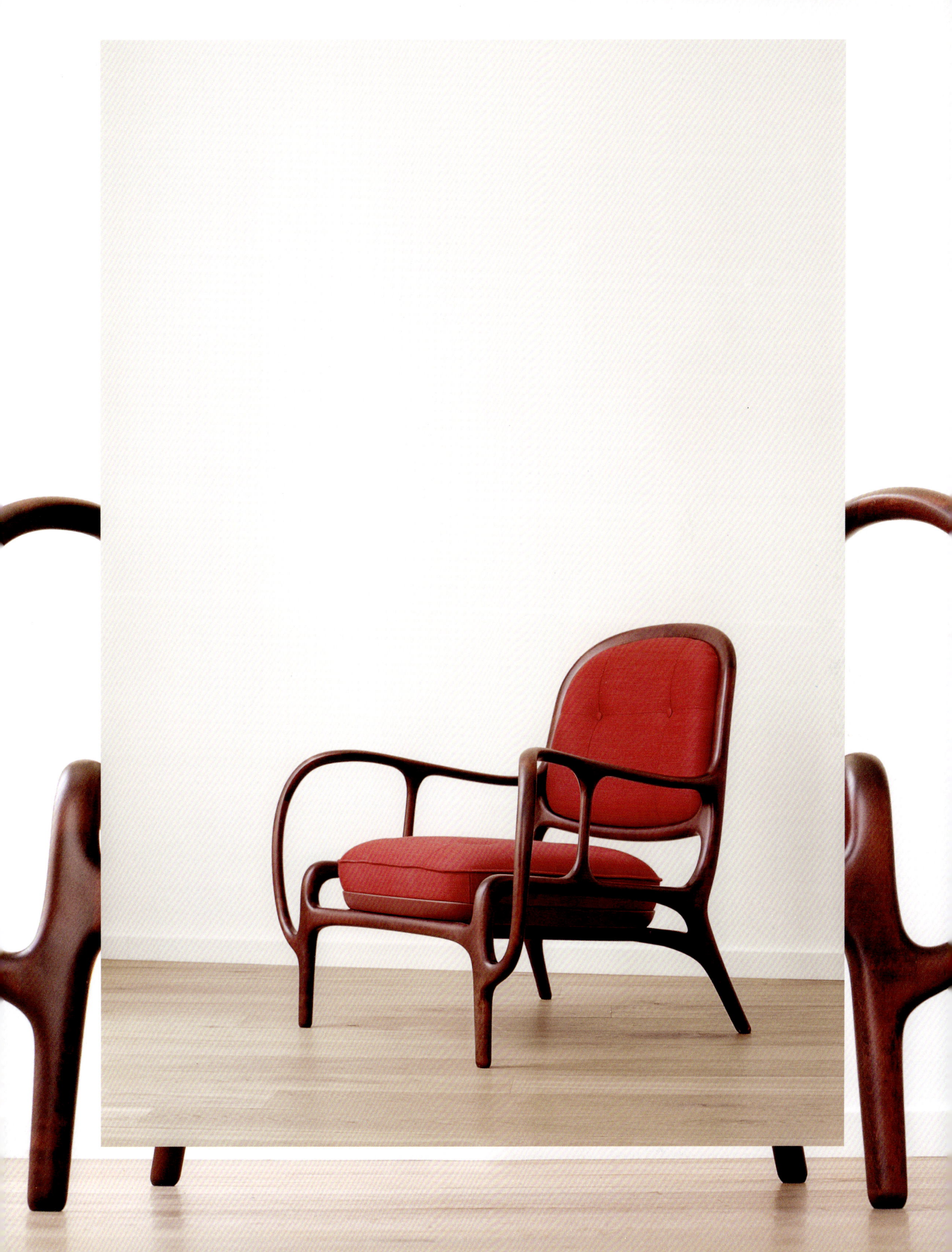

METAL

Wood

* inesto dentro el legno

* inside THE WOOD

TUBE ENTER THE WOOD.

1

PLASTIC SHELL
Scocca plastica.

2

inside VERSION

metal on tone.

APOLSTHER.
SCOCCA
EMBOTITA.

HOLES IN SAME AREA AS TUBULAR IDEA

stule

no

in joinery

side VIEW.

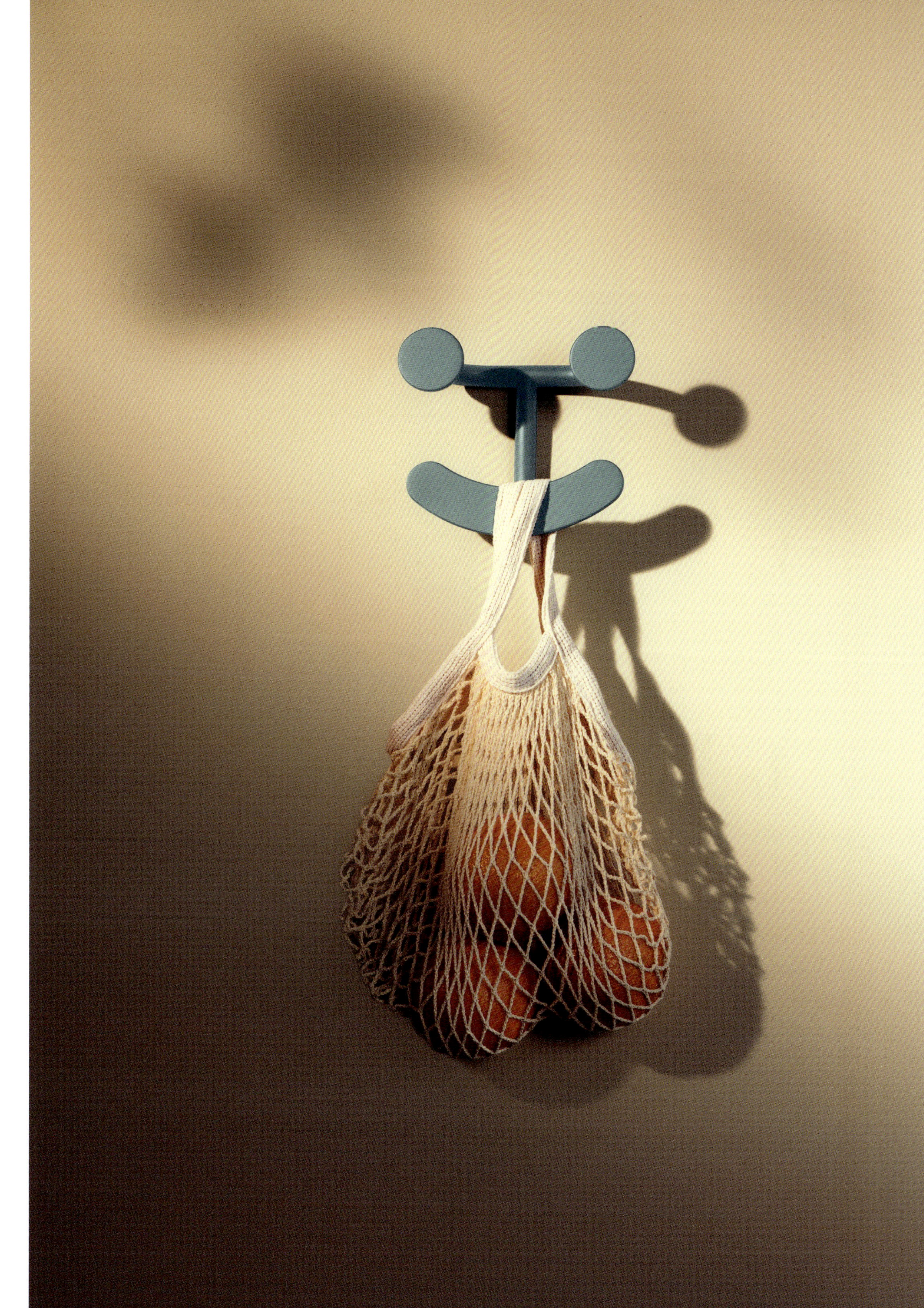

† Sketches for the Catch JH1 Chair for &Tradition, 2013
↓ Happy Hook—Hanger for Fritz Hansen, 2020

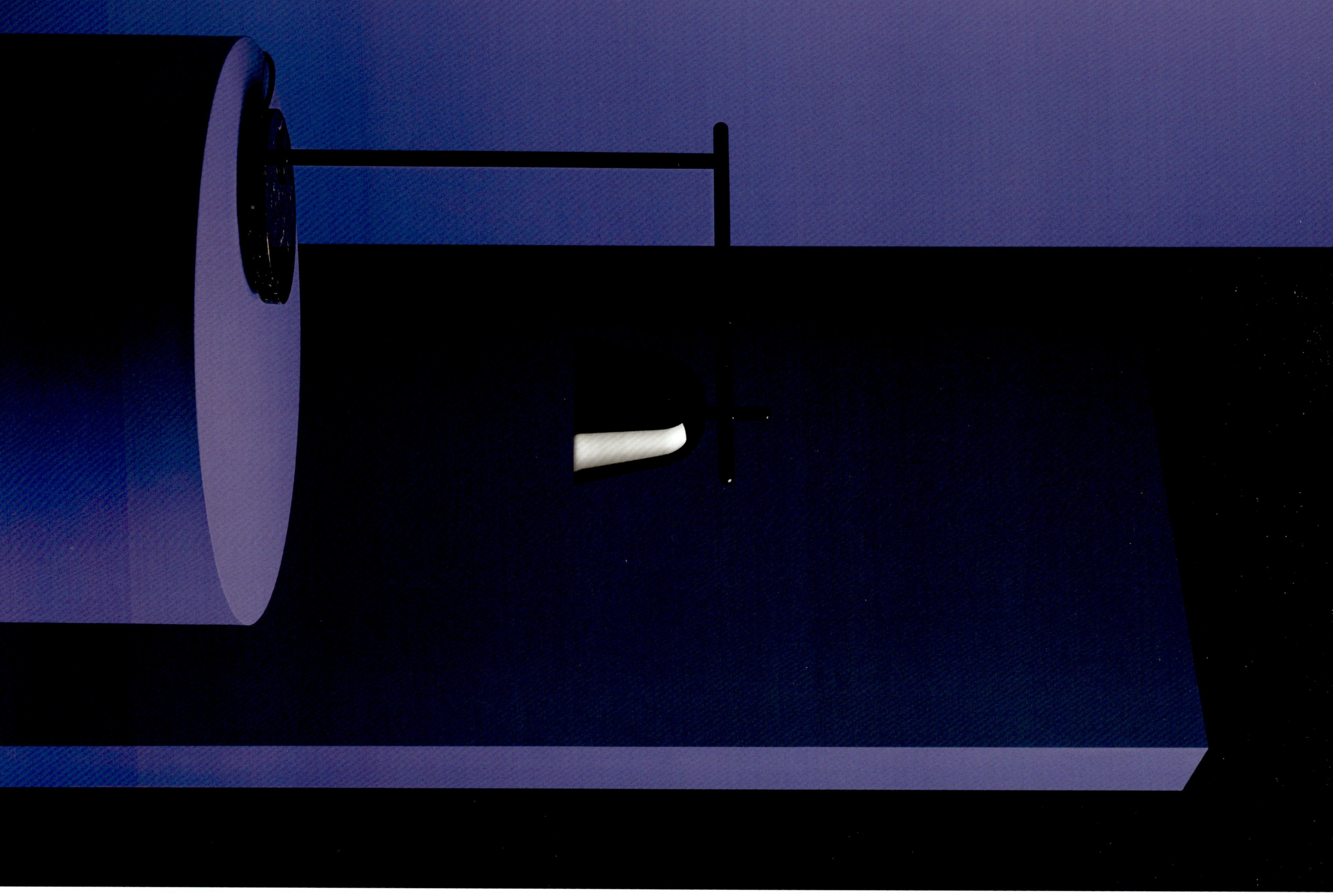

↑ Lightoread—Table lamp for Parachilna, 2018
↓ Milà—Plastic chair for Magis, 2015

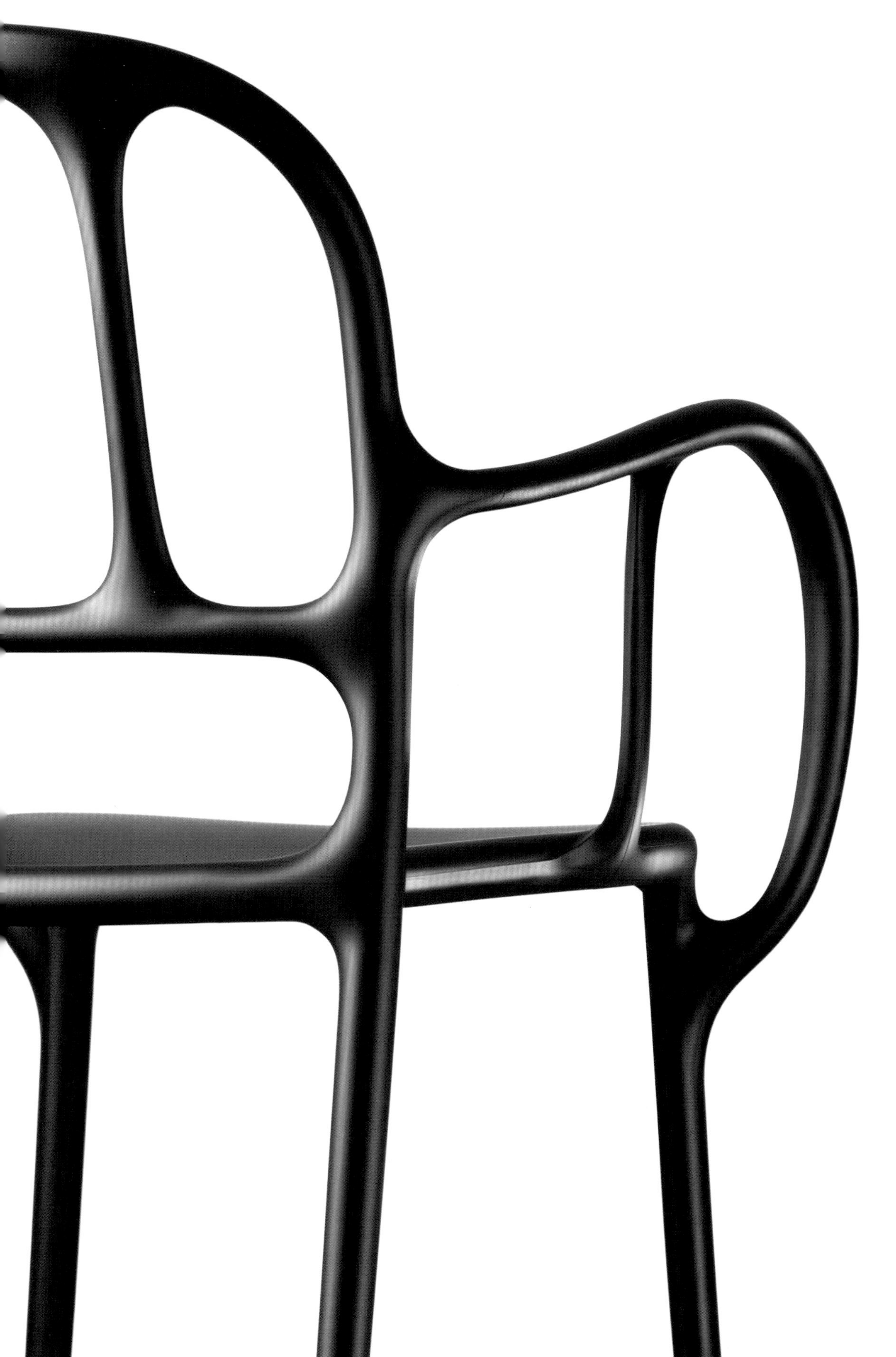

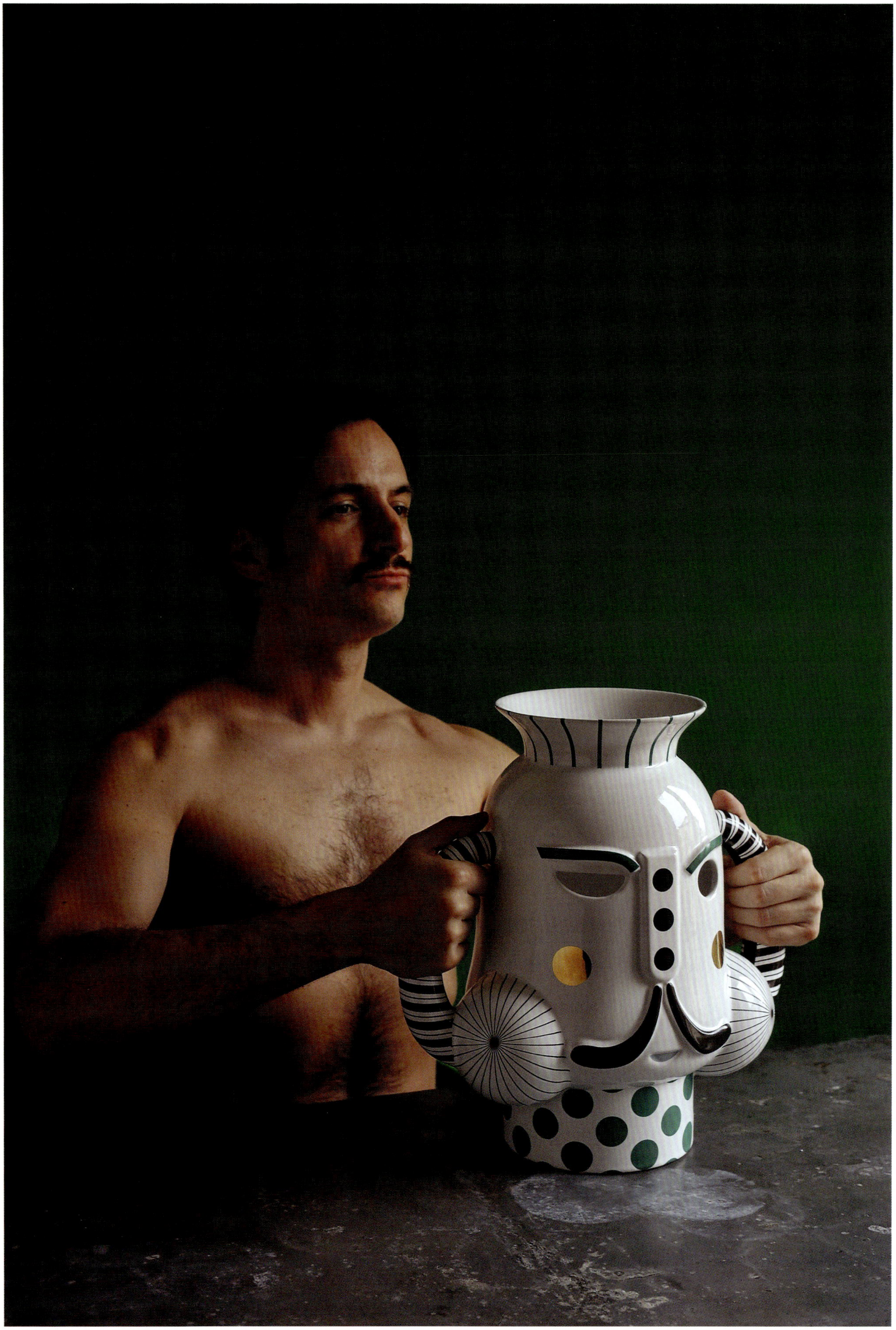

↑ King Vase—Ceramic, part of the Theatre Hayon collection for Bosa, 2019
↓ Masquemask—Exhibition at the Central Museum of Textiles, Łódź, Poland, 2019

54

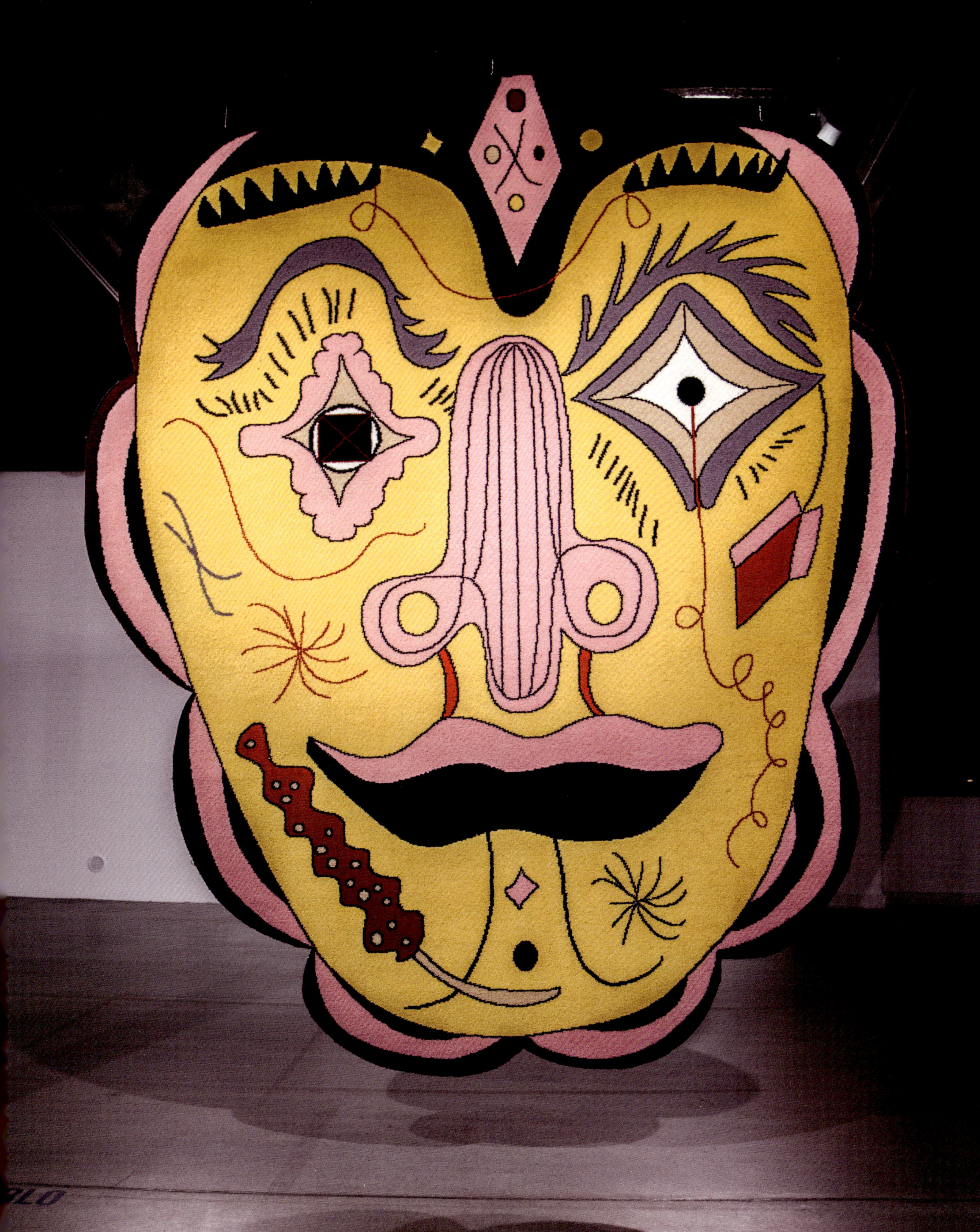

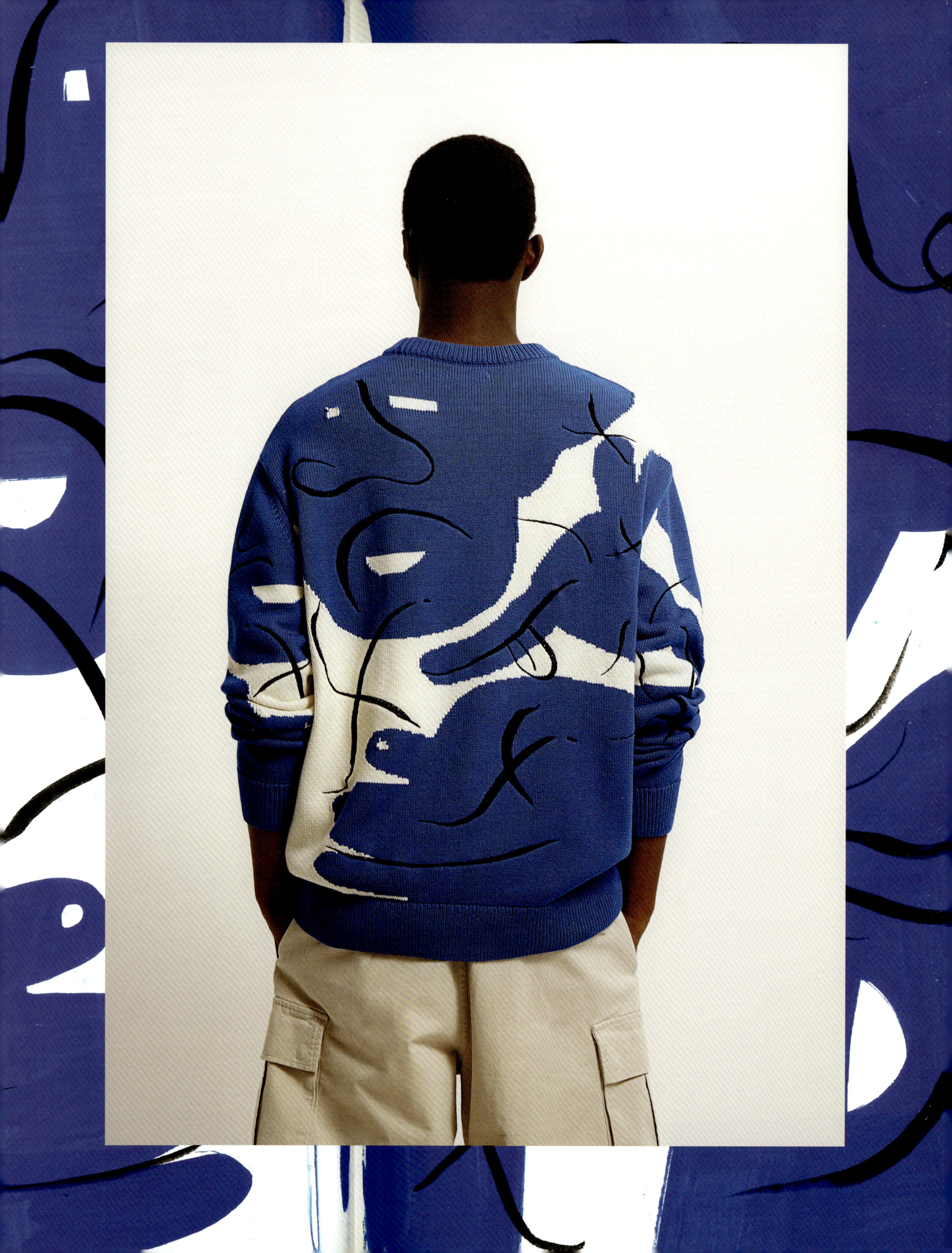

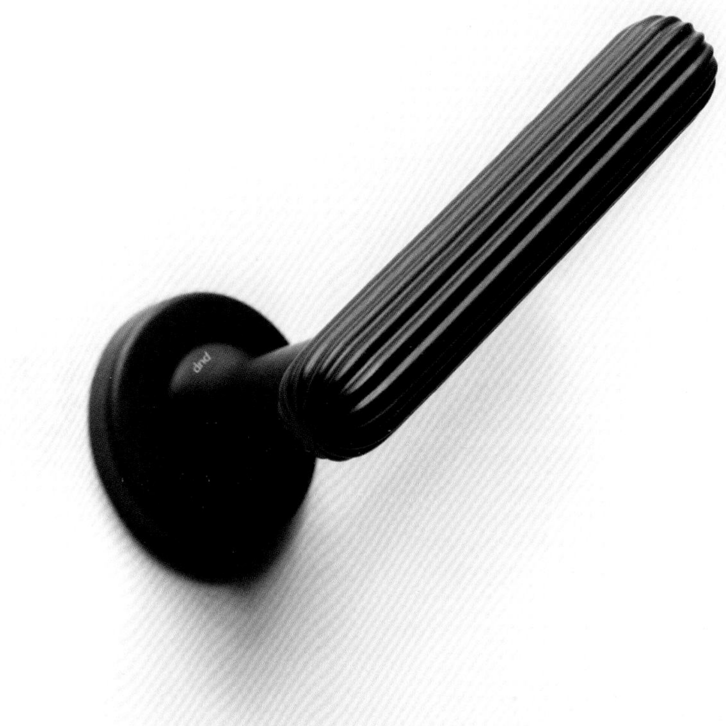

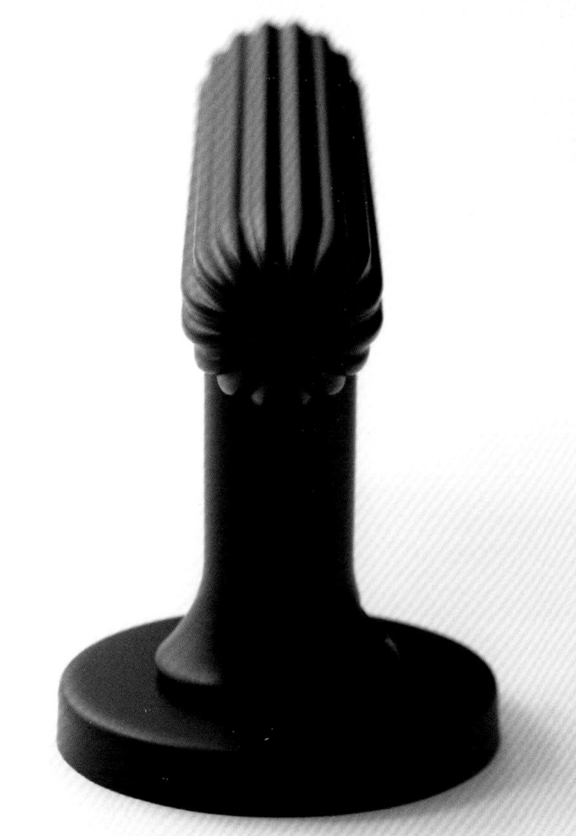

↑ Jaime Hayon × Zara—Jacquard sweater, 2021
↓ Zeppelin—Metal door handle for DND Handles, 2018

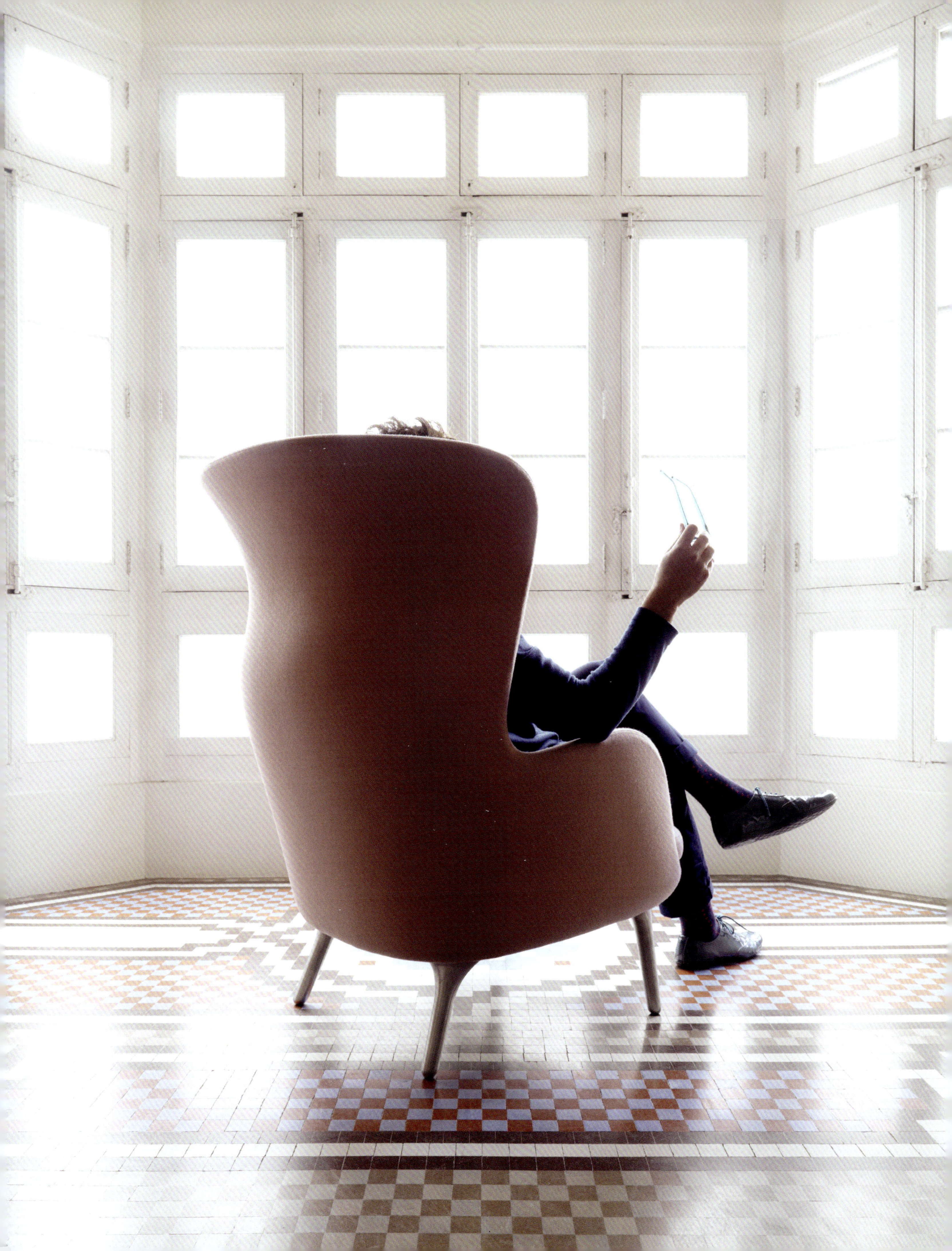

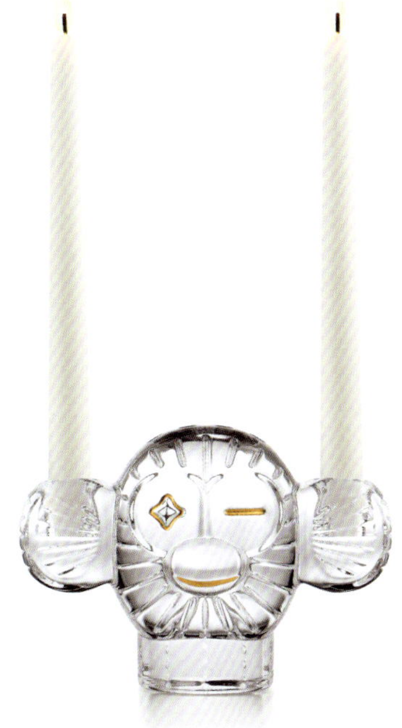

↑ Ro—Lounge chair for Fritz Hansen, 2013

↓ Faunacrystopolis Monkey Candlestick—Candle holder for Baccarat, part of the Carnival of the Animals, 2020

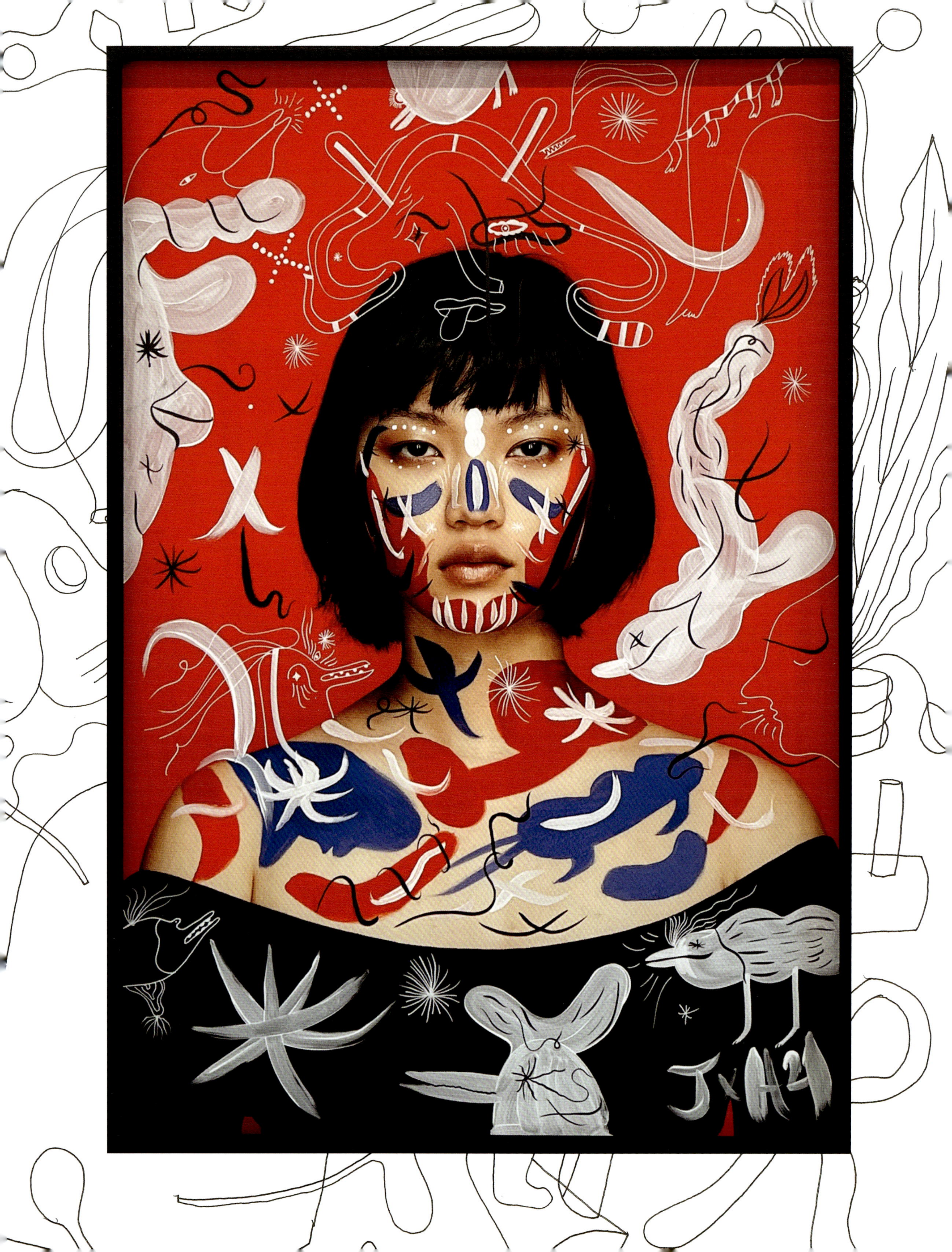

JxH21

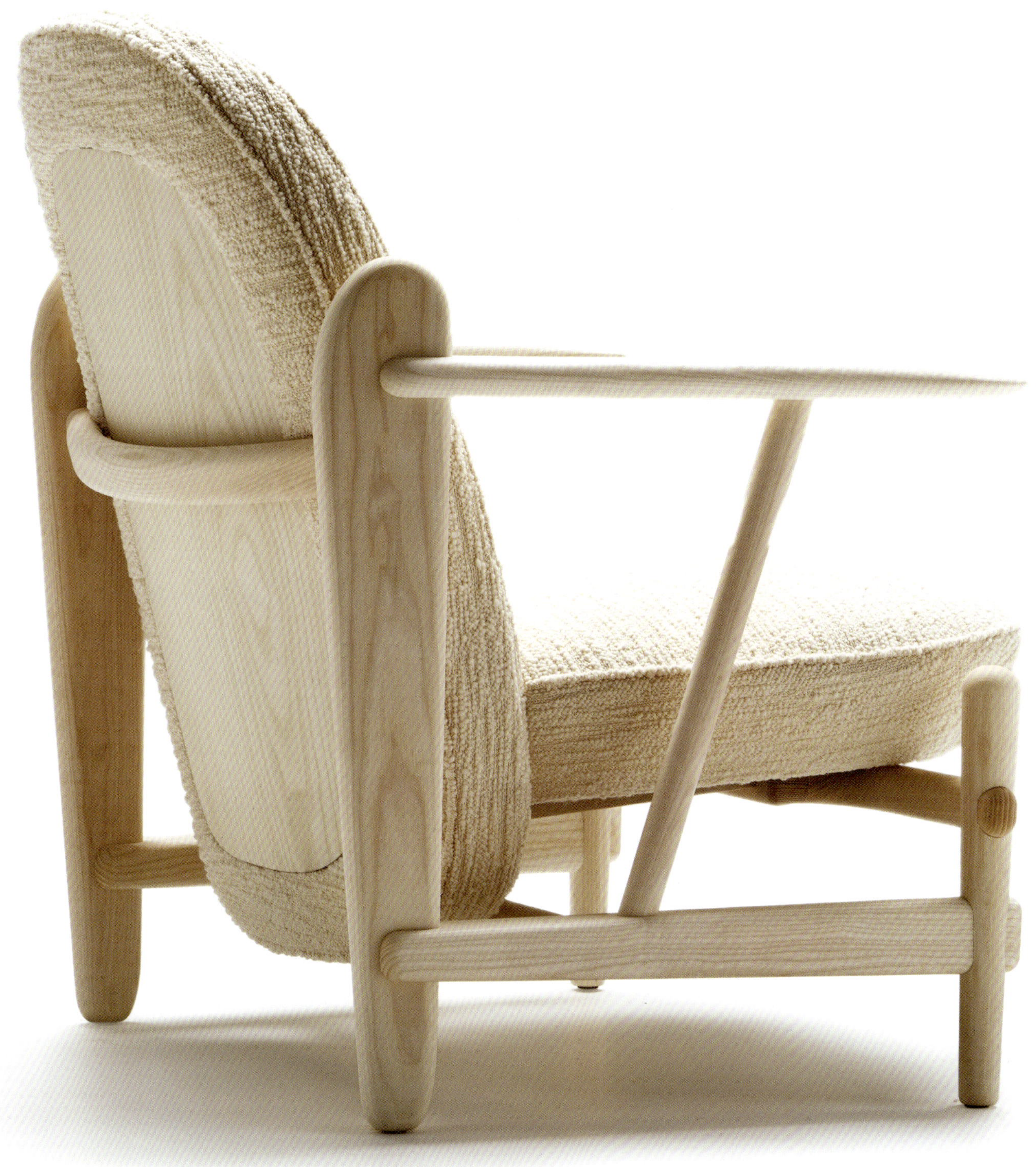

↑ Gene—Hand-painted photograph, 2021
↑ T-Bone—Armchair for Ceccotti Collezioni, 2021

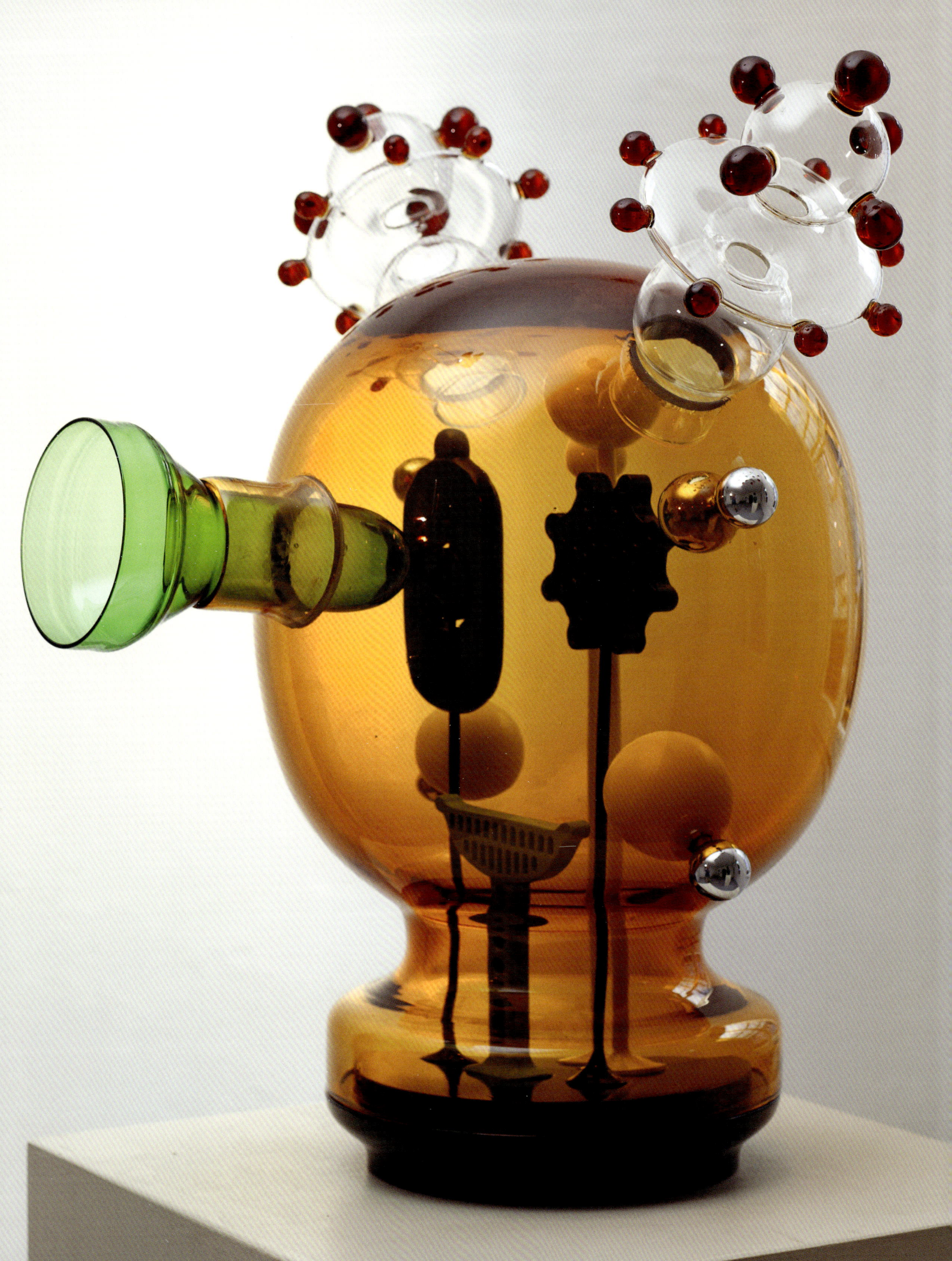

→ Opposites, extremes, and boundaries are all part of a game of levels where information and the way it is absurdly turned upside down become the basis of my artistic process.

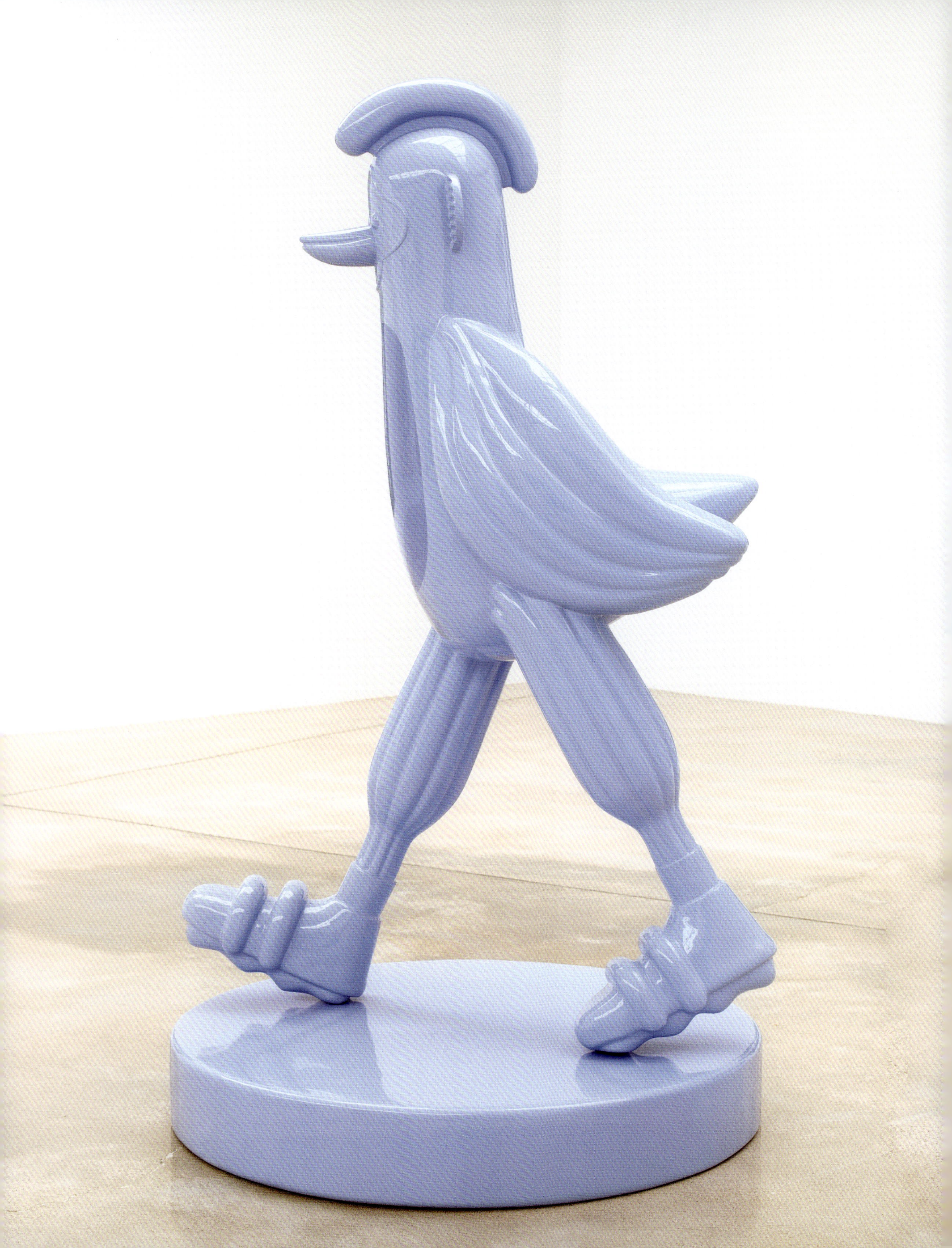

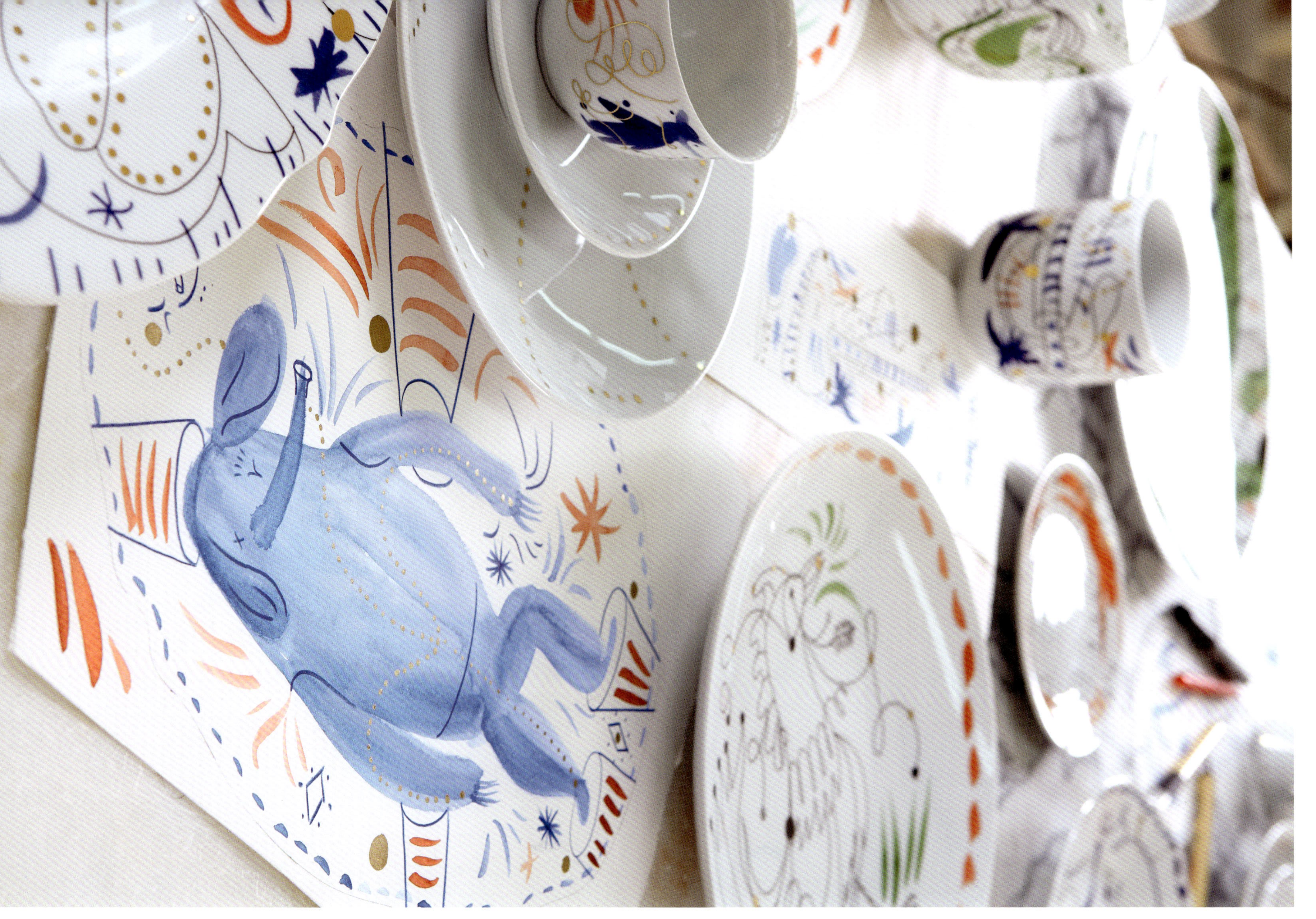

↑ Walking Punk Bird—Fiberglass sculpture, part of Cosmotik Jungle exhibition at L21 Gallery, Mallorca, Spain, 2021
↑ Sketches and prototypes of the Folkifunki ceramic tableware collection for Vista Alegre, 2016

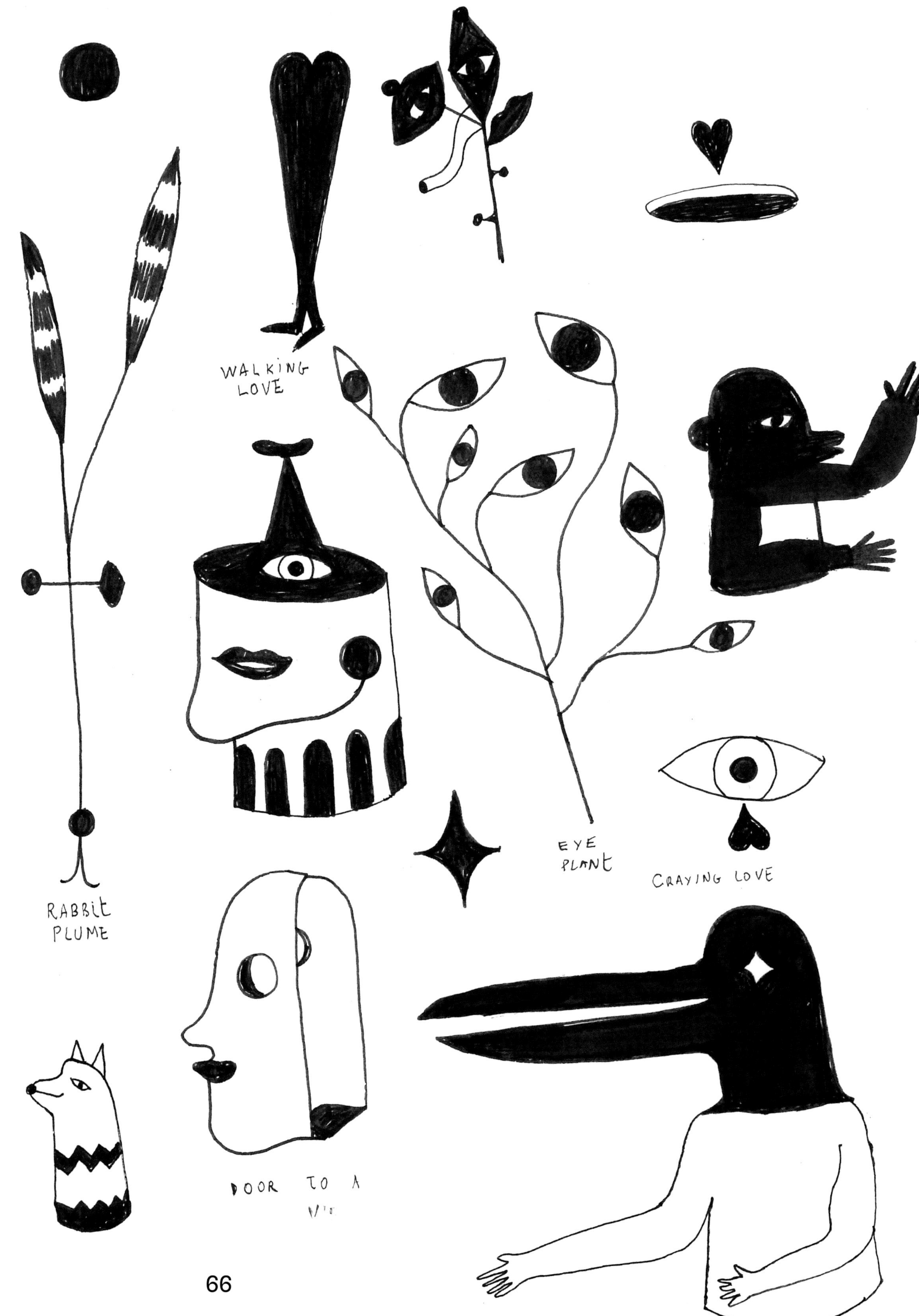
WALKING
LOVE
RABBIT
PLUME
EYE
PLANT
CRAYING LOVE
DOOR TO A
V/18

↑ Study for tattoo
↓ Dino and Explorer—Armchair and side table for BD Barcelona Design, 2019

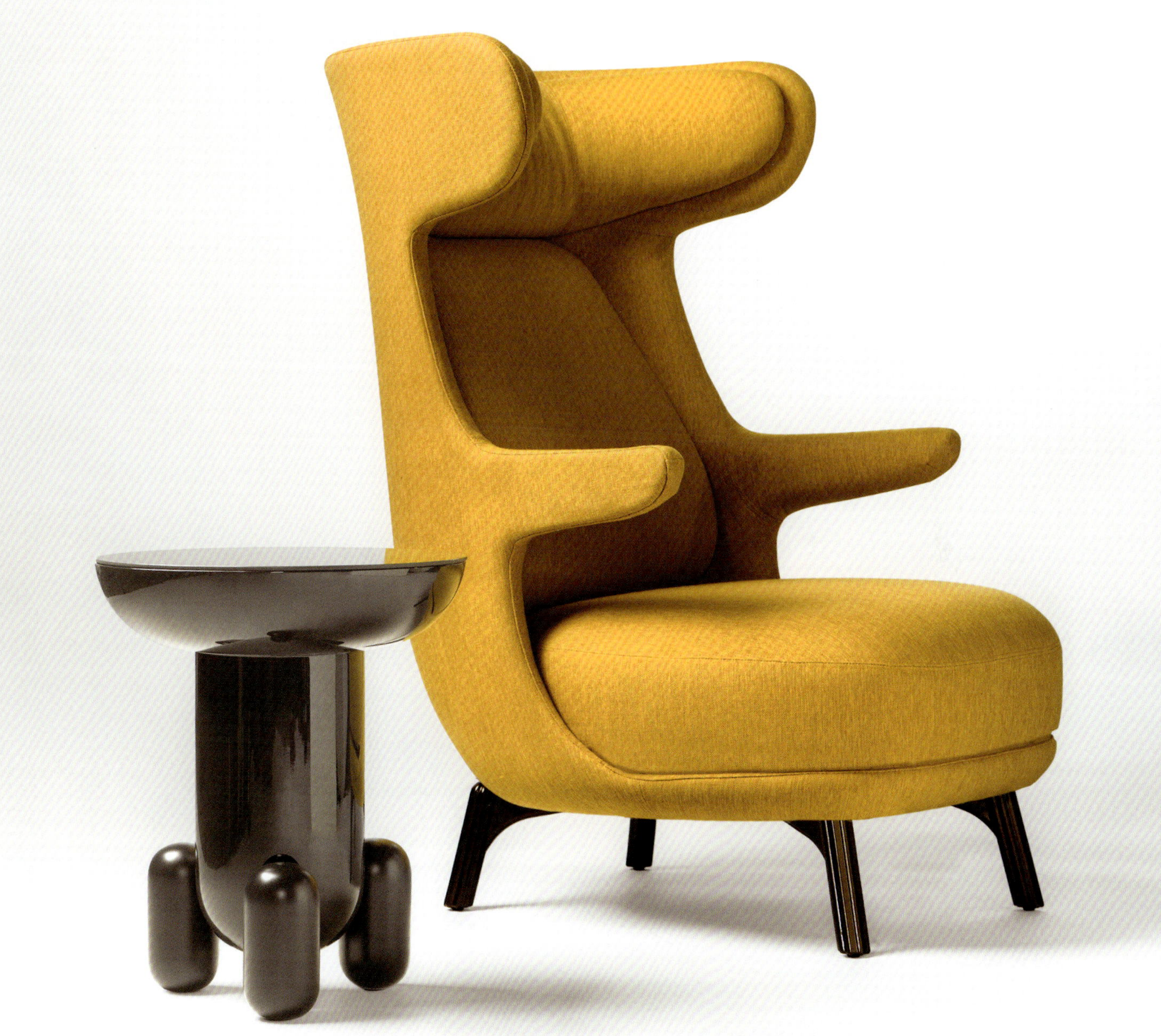

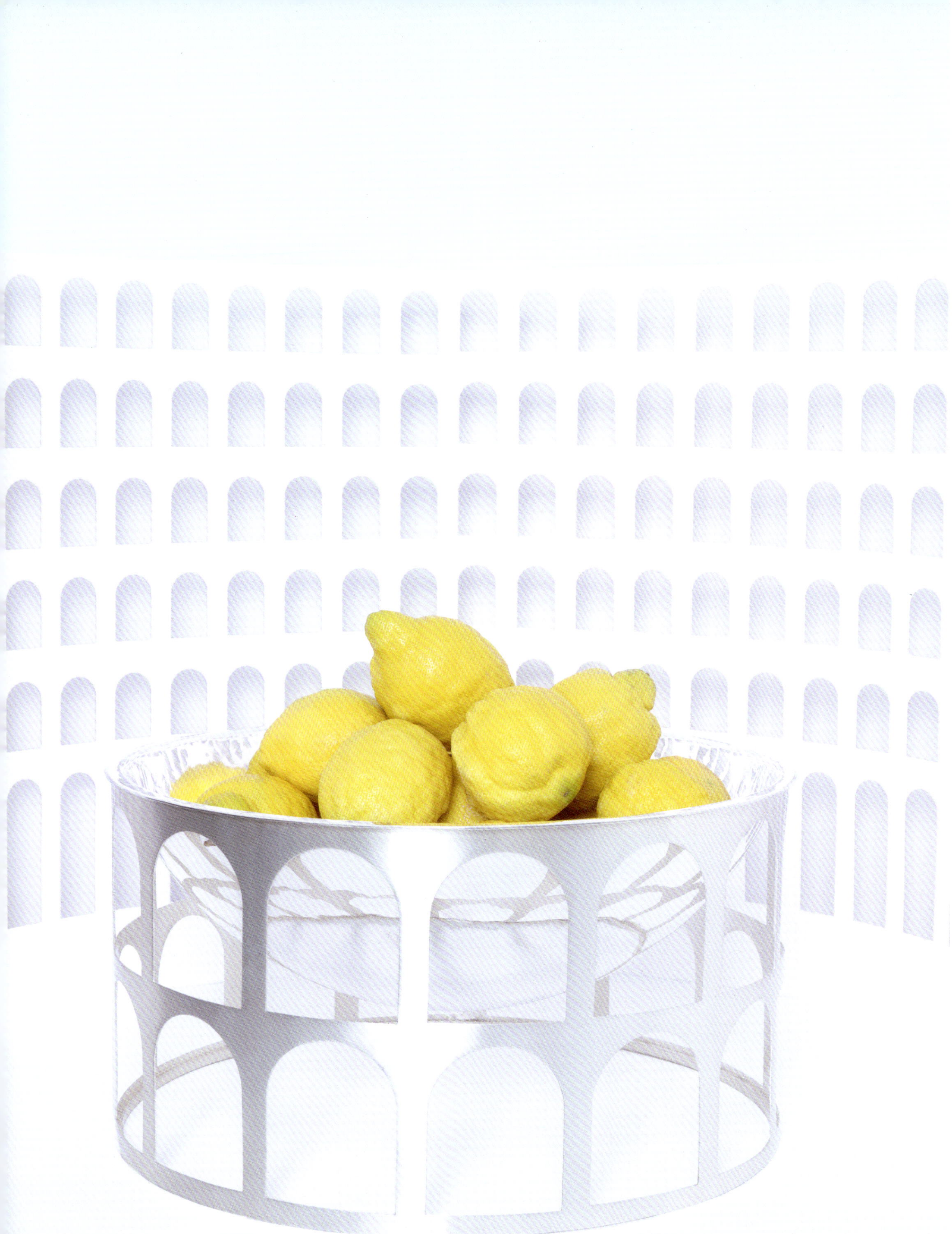

↑ Colosseum—Centerpiece from New Roman Collection for Paola C, 2014
↓ Custom-made cabinet for home with elements from the New Roman Collection for Paola C

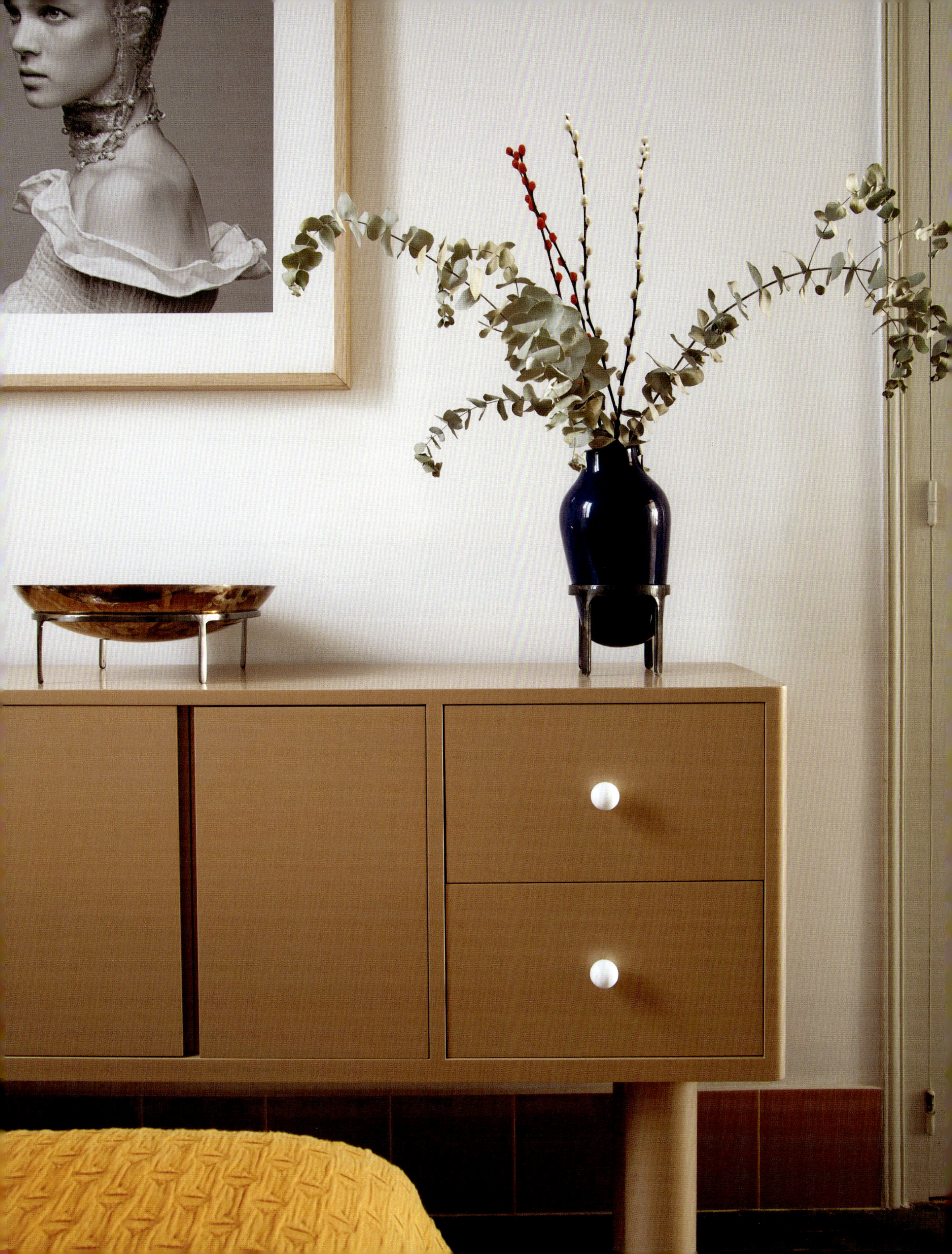

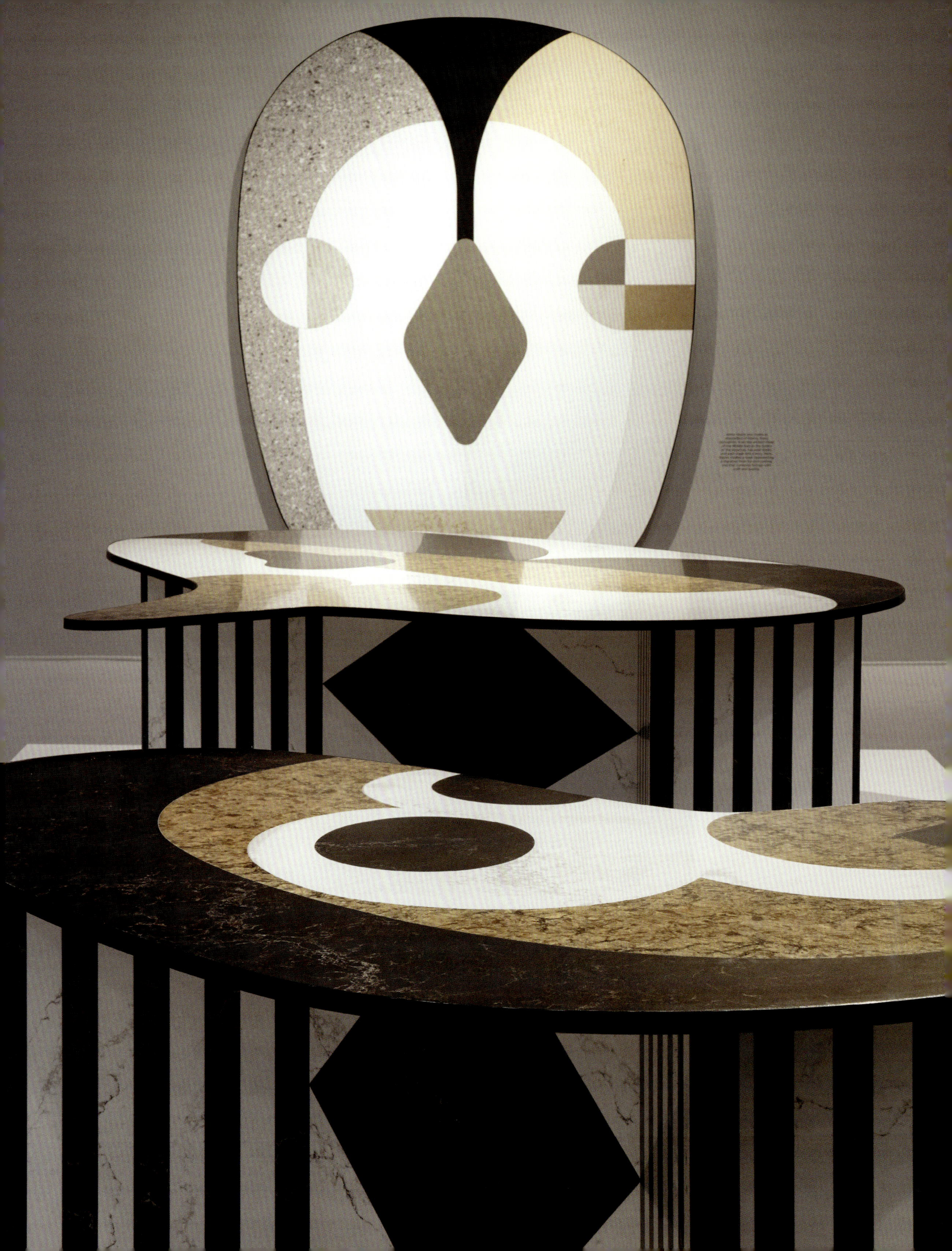

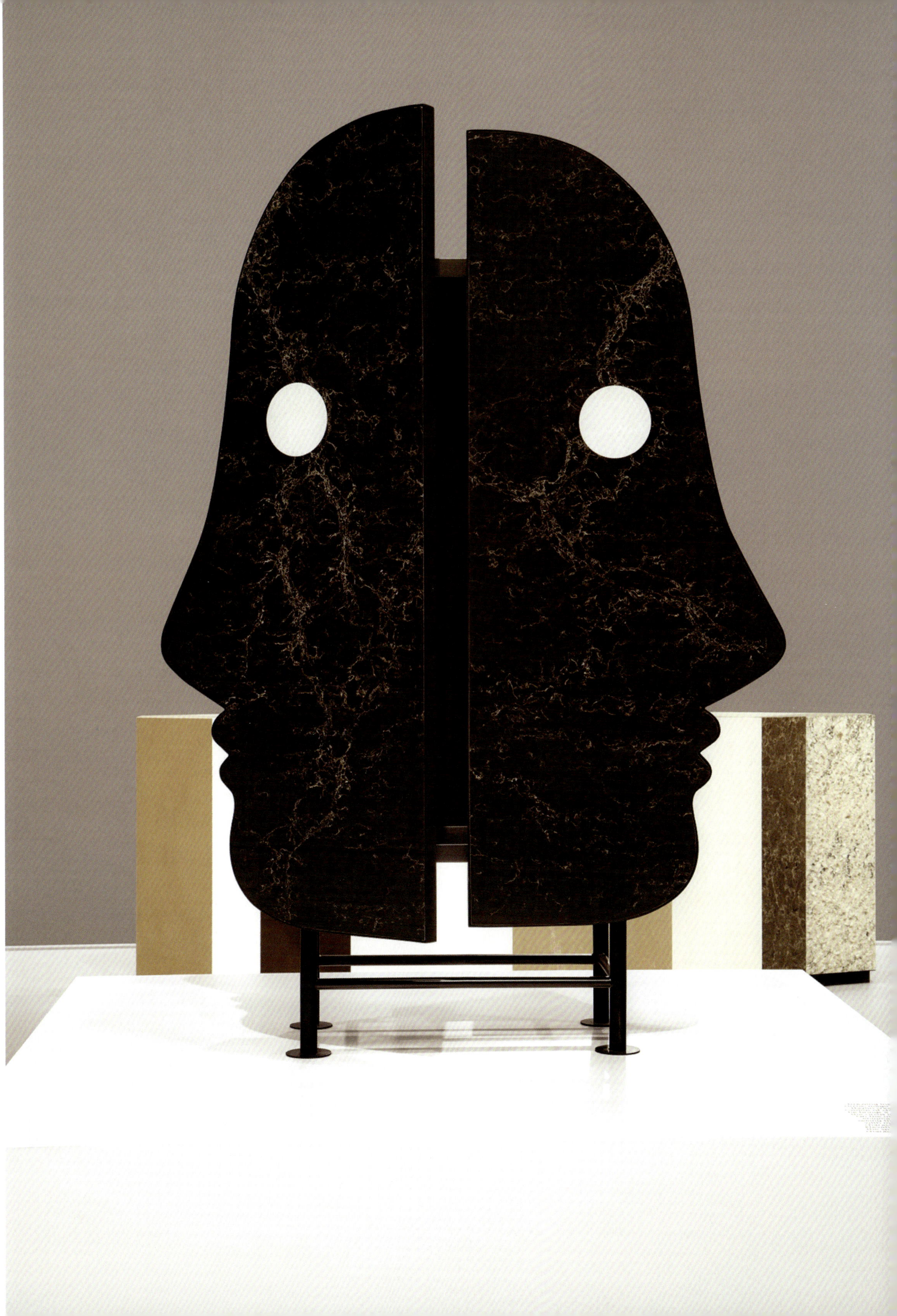

↑ Mask—Bird and Monkey Tables from the Stone Age Folk installation at Palazzo Serbelloni for Caesarstone, Milan, Italy, 2017
↓ Face Cabinet from the Stone Age Folk installation at Palazzo Serbelloni for Caesarstone, Milan, Italy, 2017

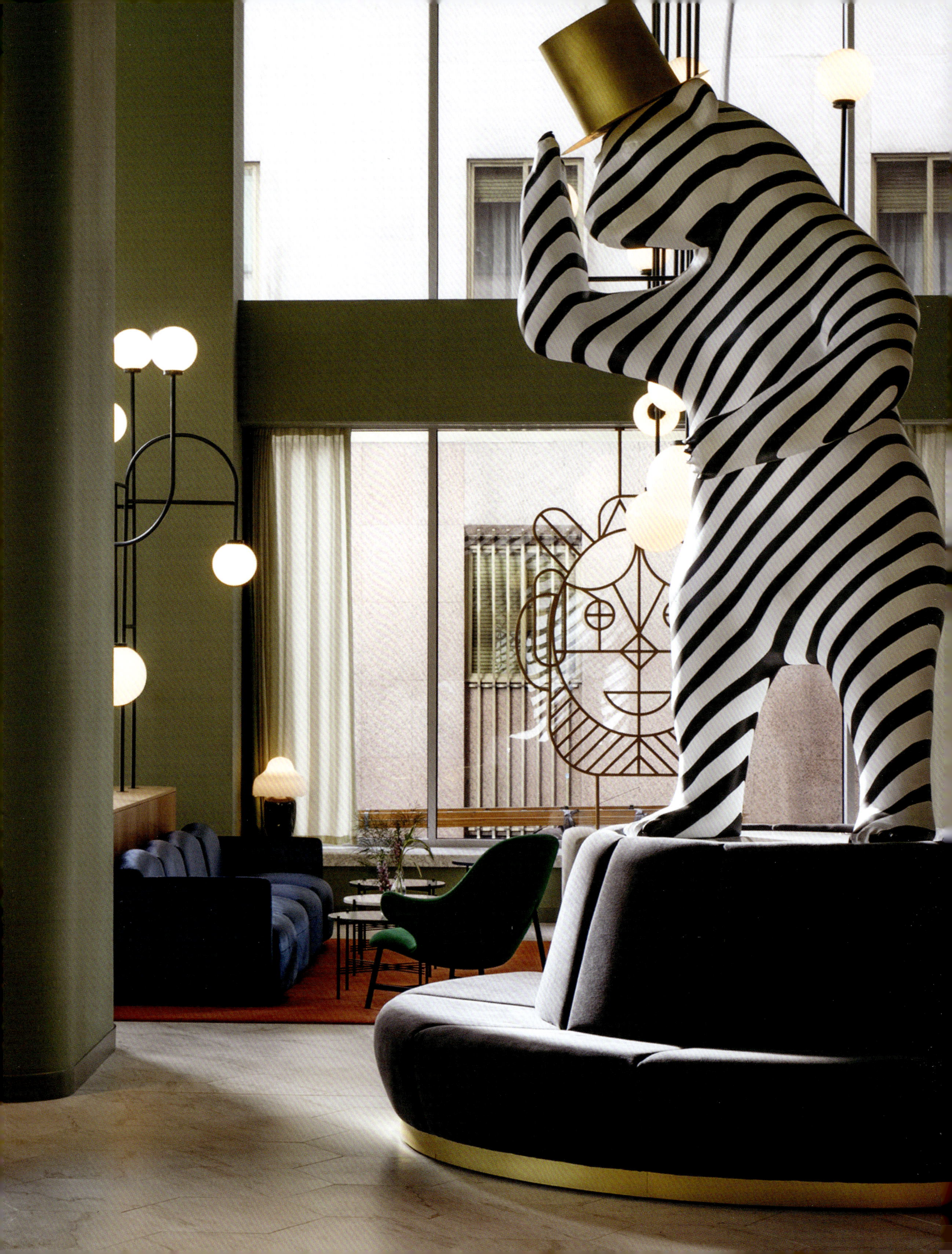

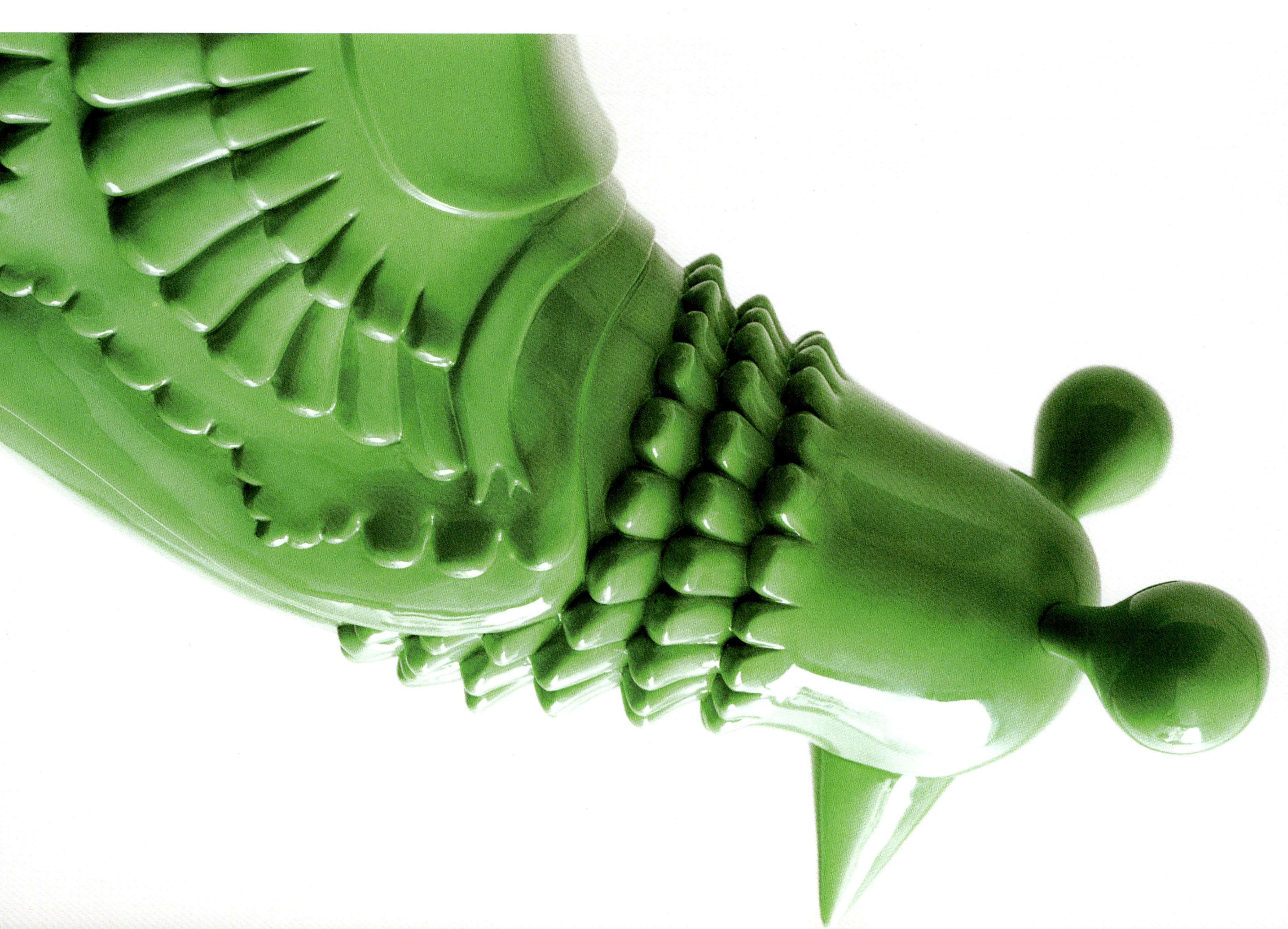

↑ Barceló Torre de Madrid Hotel—Bear sculpture at the entrance, interior design project, 2016
↓ Green Chicken—Sculpture shown at Contrasts Gallery, Shanghai, China, 2006

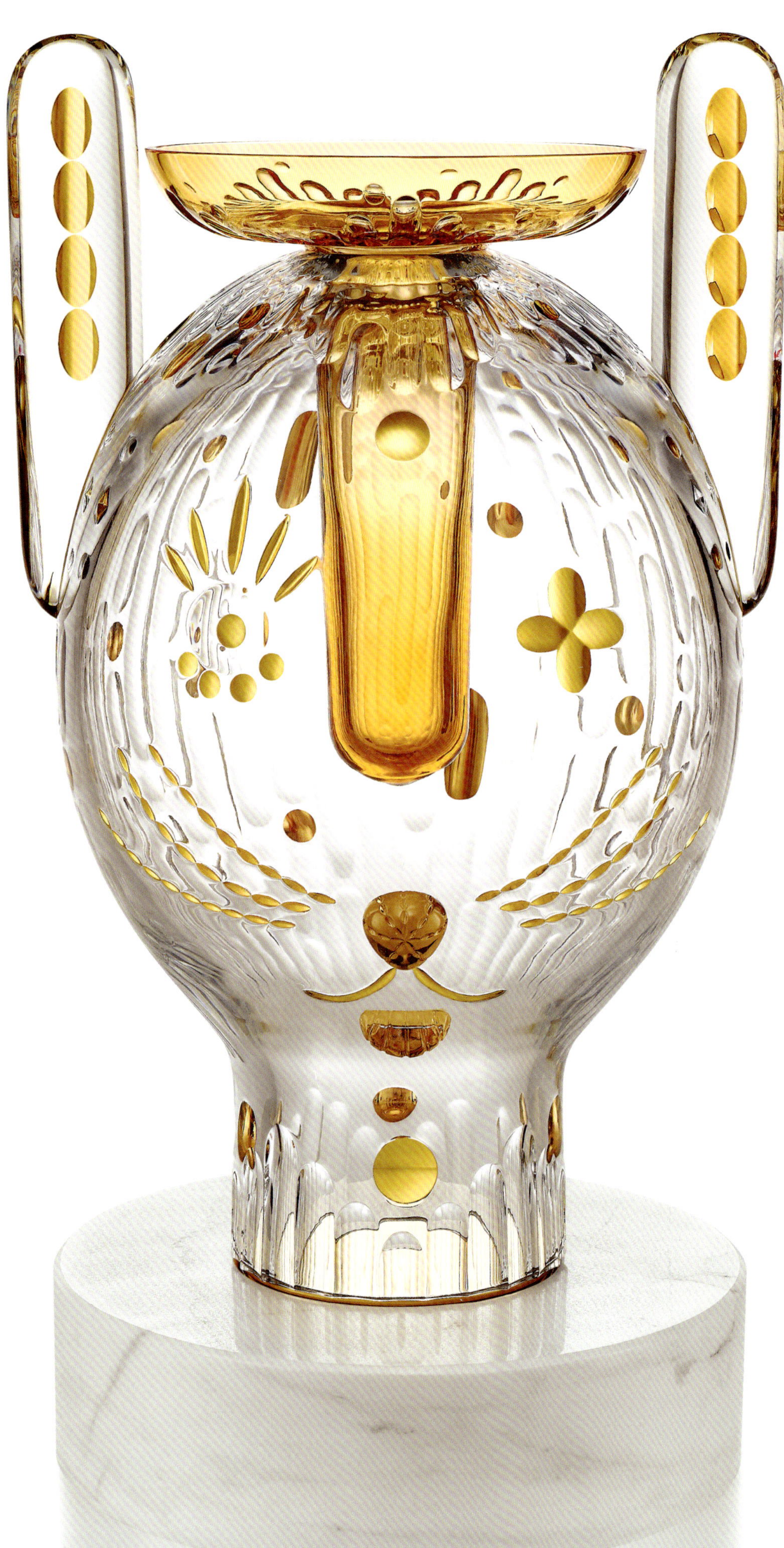

↑ Rabbit—Limited-edition collection from Baccarat Faunacrystopolis, Carnival of Animals, 2020
↓ Sketch for Baccarat

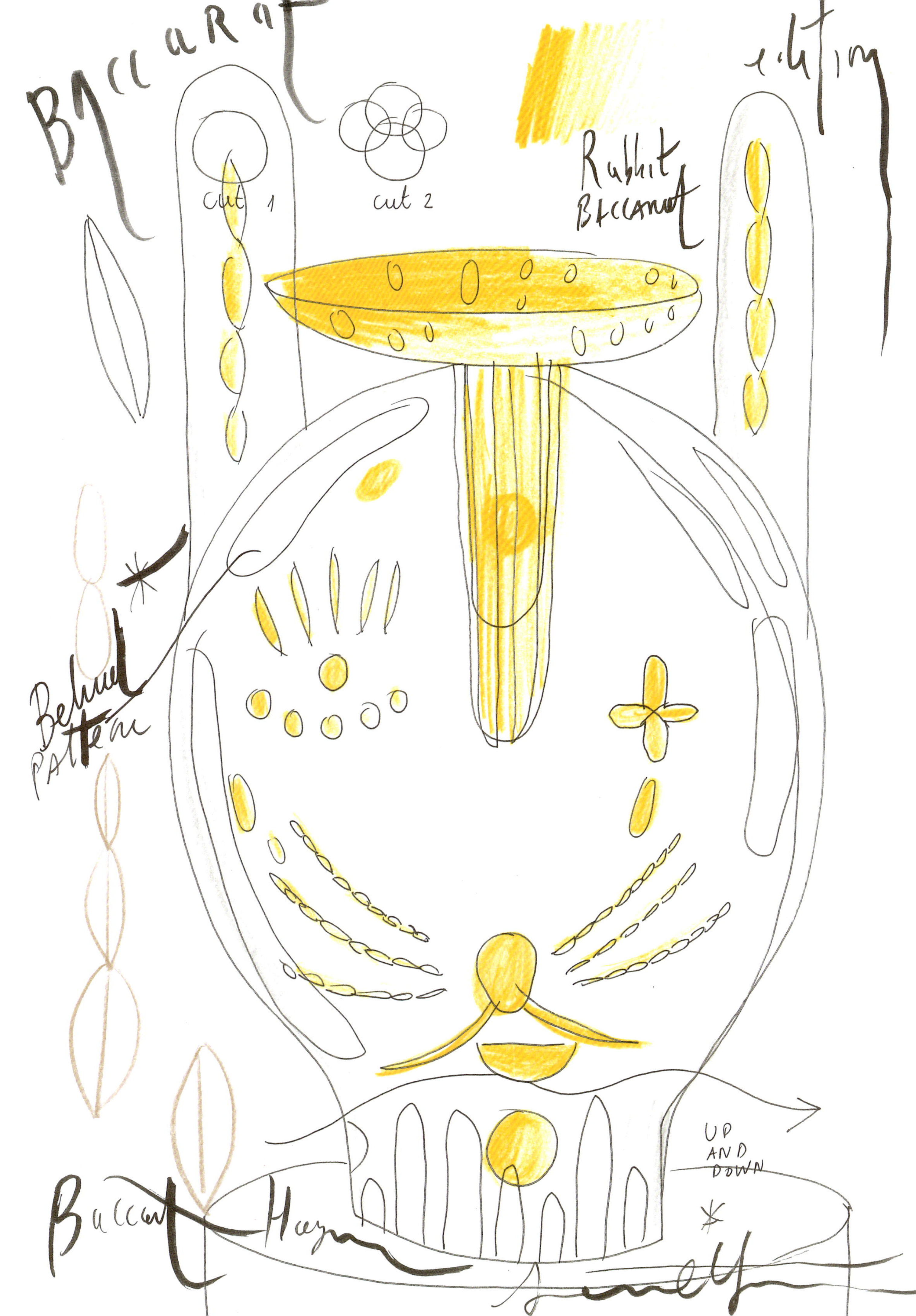
BACCARAT
edition
cut 1
cut 2
Rabbit
BACCARAT
Behual
PATTERN
UP
AND
DOWN
Baccarat Hazar

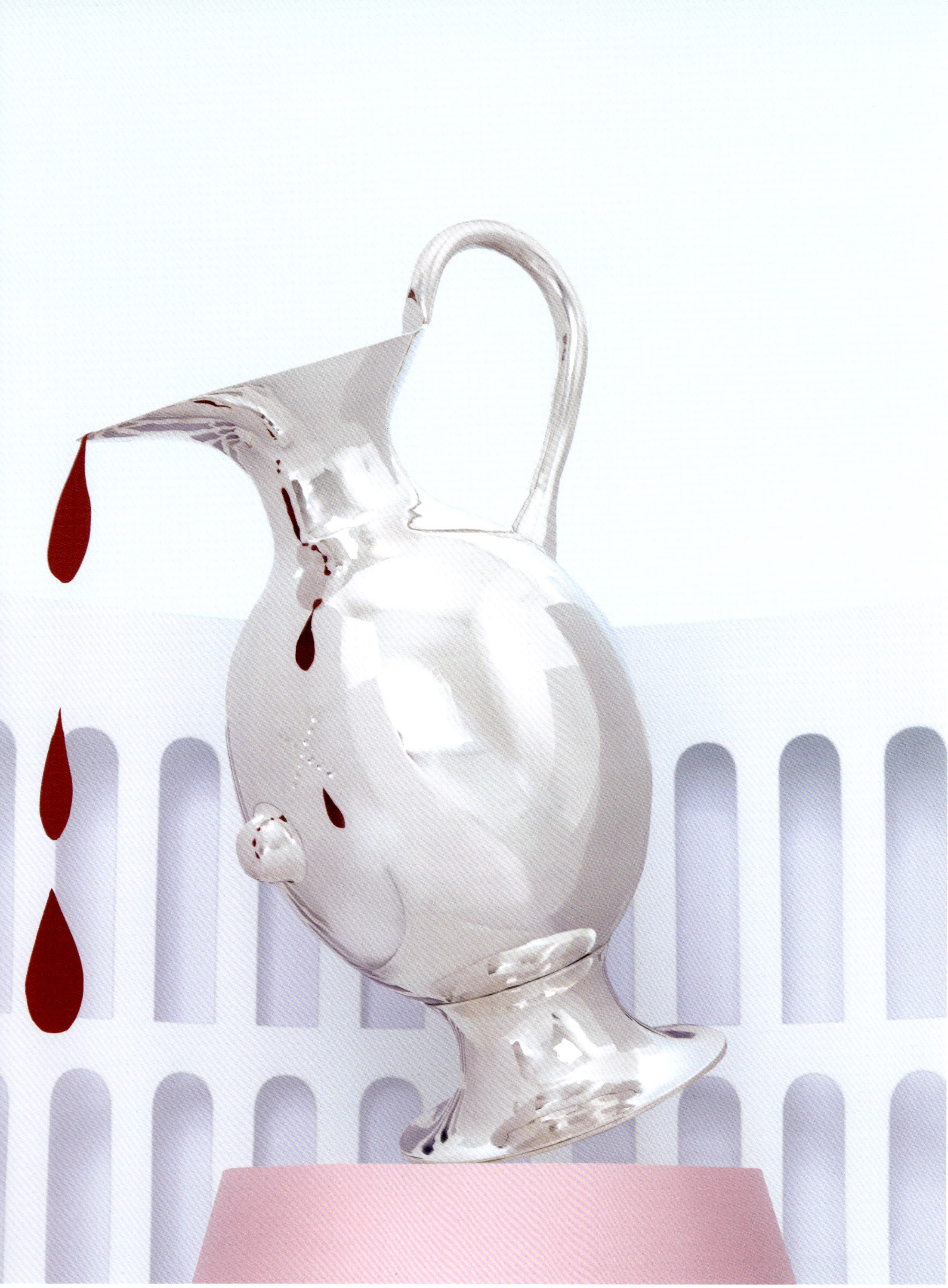

↑ Augustus—Silver-plated carafe from New Roman Collection for Paola C, 2014
↓ Graphnight, Aeromaticolor, and Oceanographic—Limited-edition ceramic vases for Maison Matisse, 2019

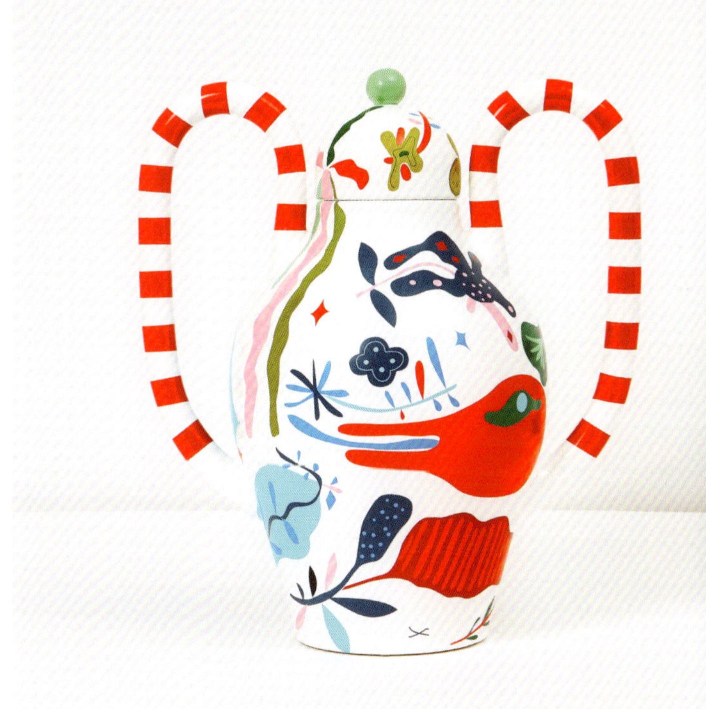

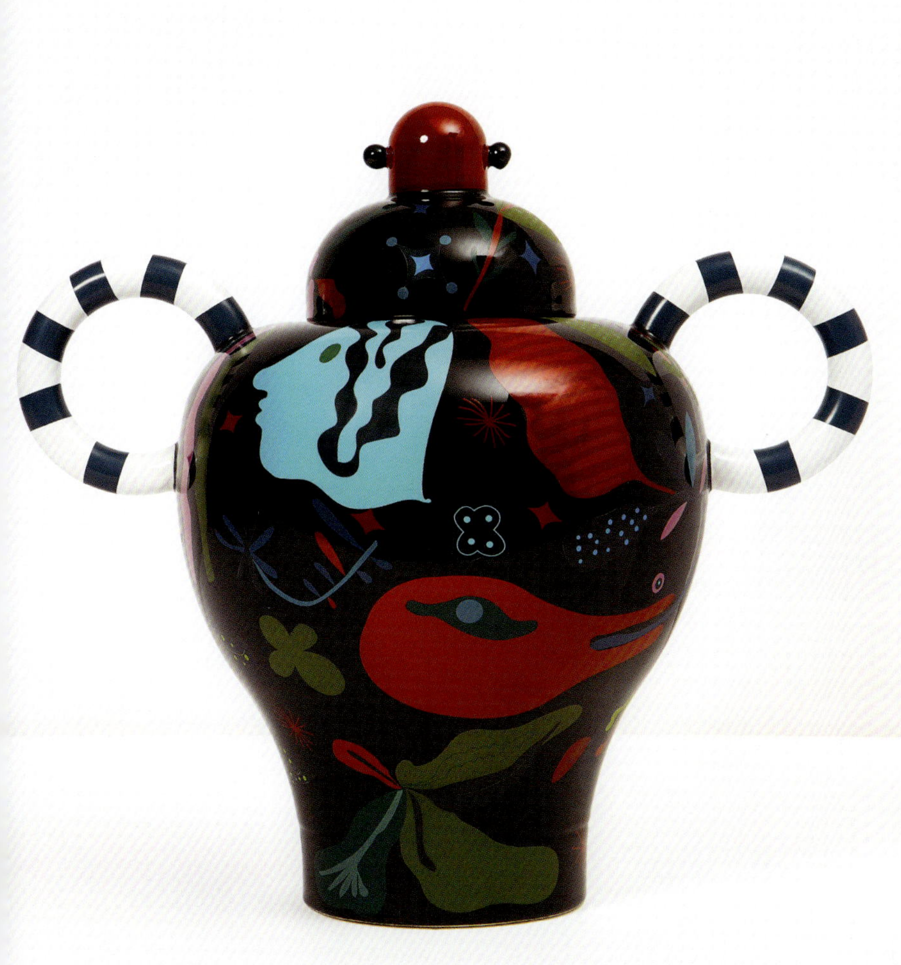

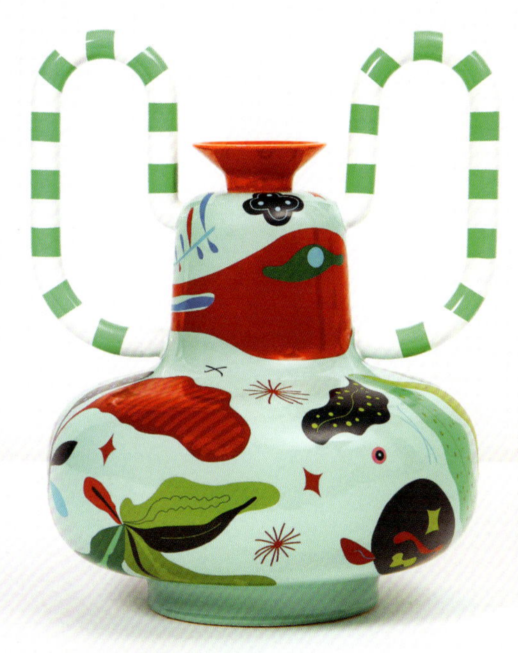

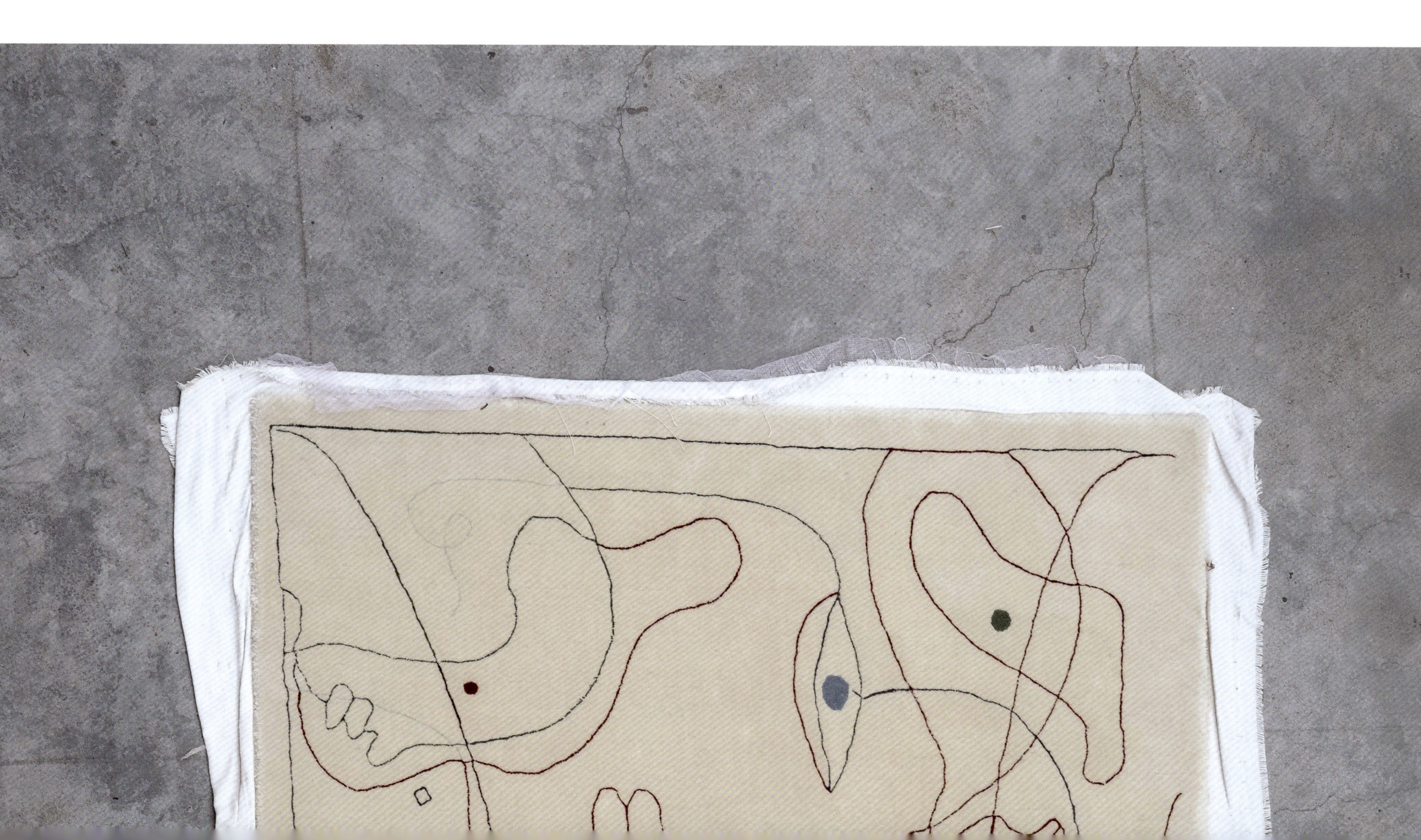

↓ Silhouette—Collection of rugs designed for Nanimarquina for indoor and outdoor use.
Embroidery on kilim technique, a laborious process, handmade in Pakistan, 2020

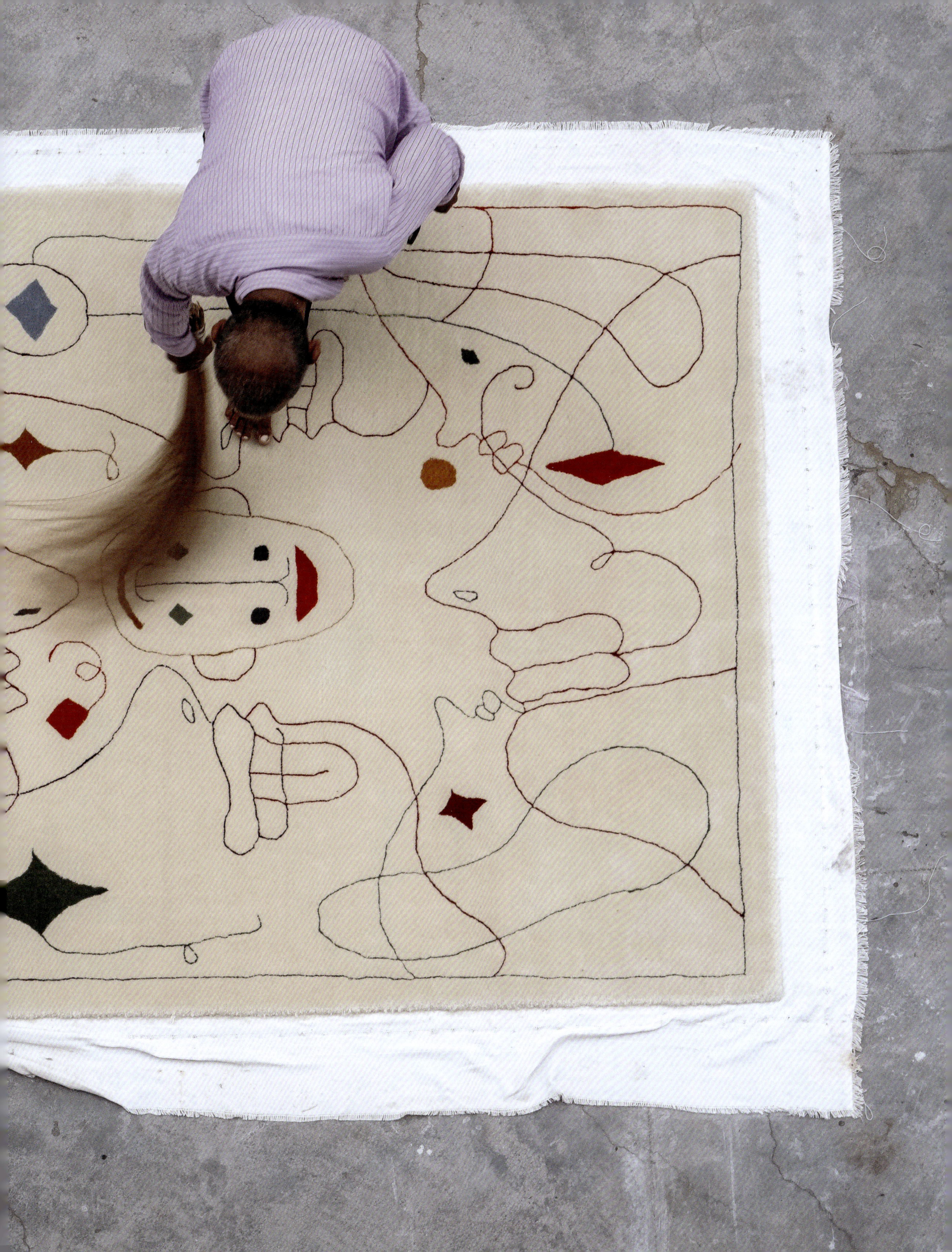

→ I look at the world with a third eye, and this feeds my vitality. In my dreams, through my research, and during my travels I meet cultures and come across new perspectives that reveal to me who I am.

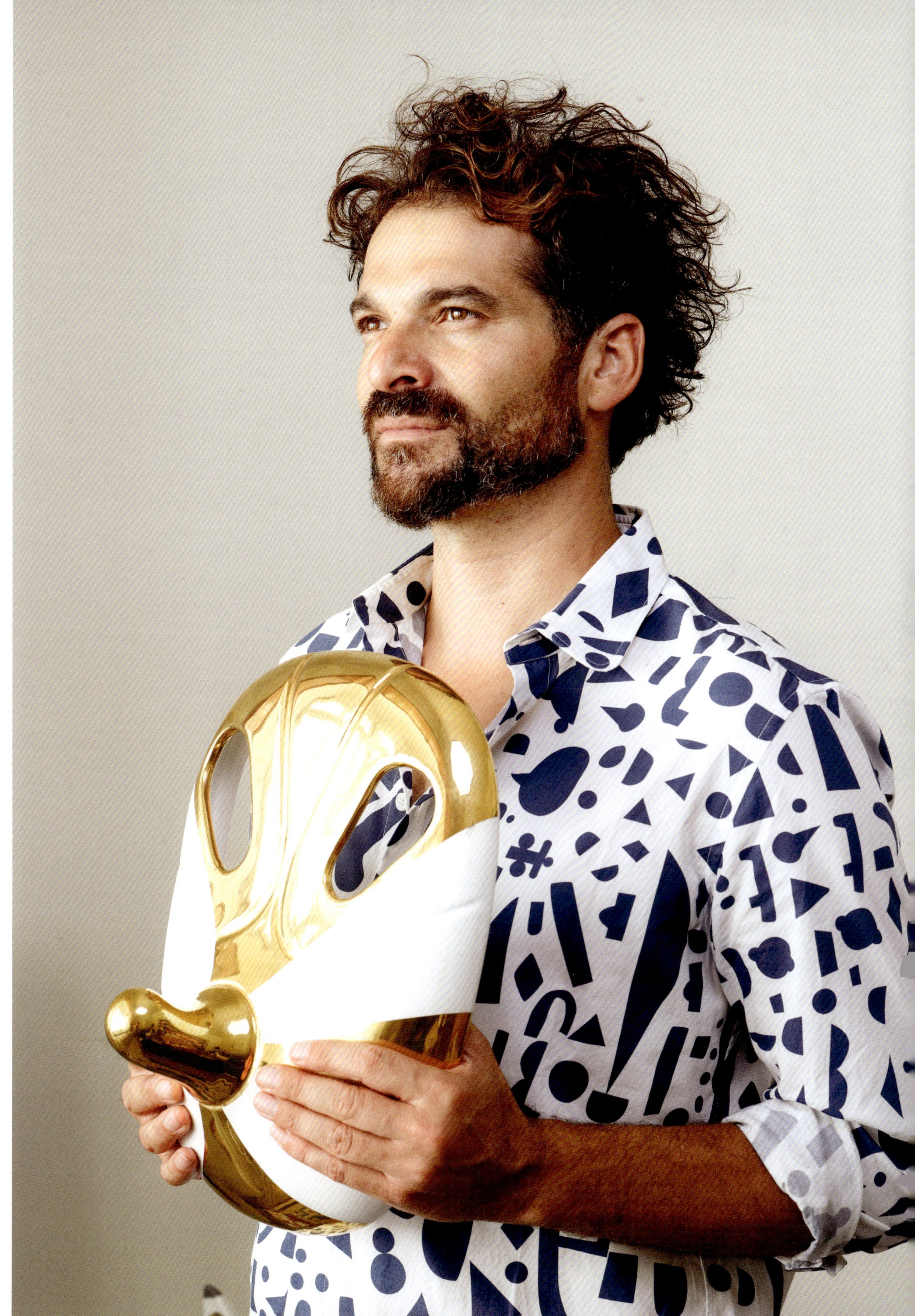

↓ Jaime Hayon with ceramic mask by Bosa

↑ Monkey Side Table—for BD Barcelona Design, made of solid architectural concrete, 2015
↓ Mediterranean Digital Baroque—Ceramic cactus sculptures at the Ritz Carlton, South Beach, Miami, USA, 2006

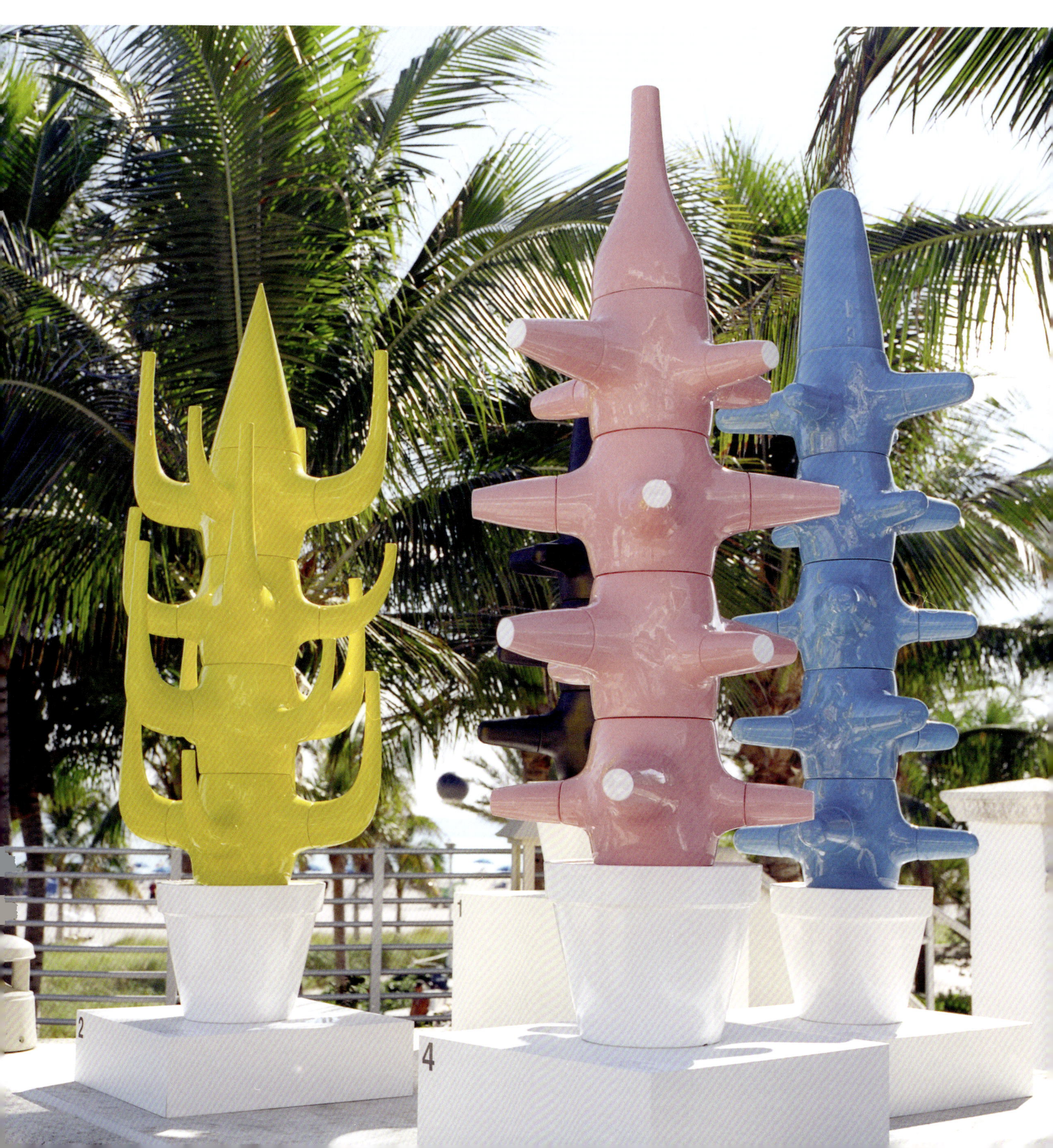

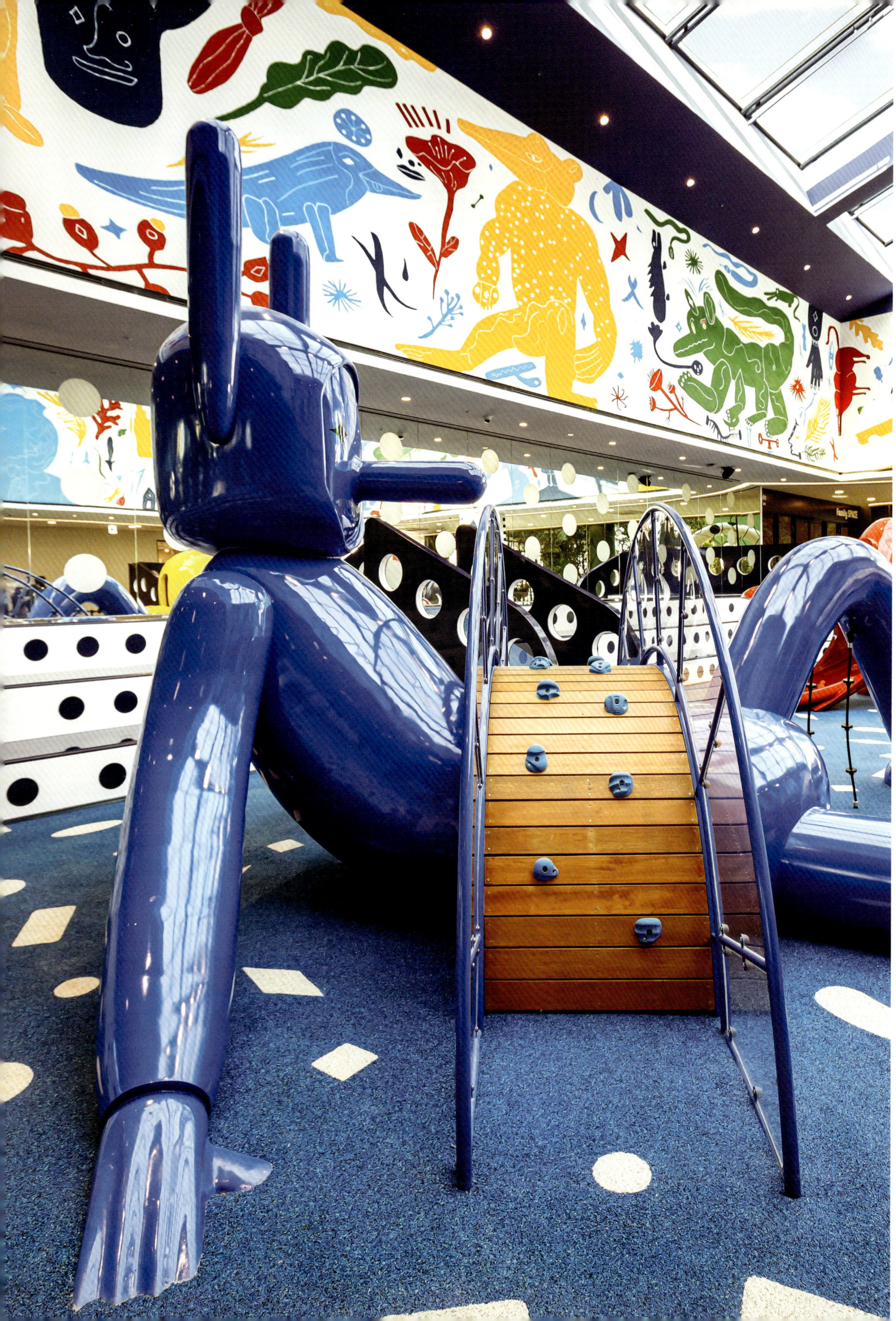

↓↑ MOKA Play—Children's playground at Hyundai Space 1, Namyangju, South Korea, 2020

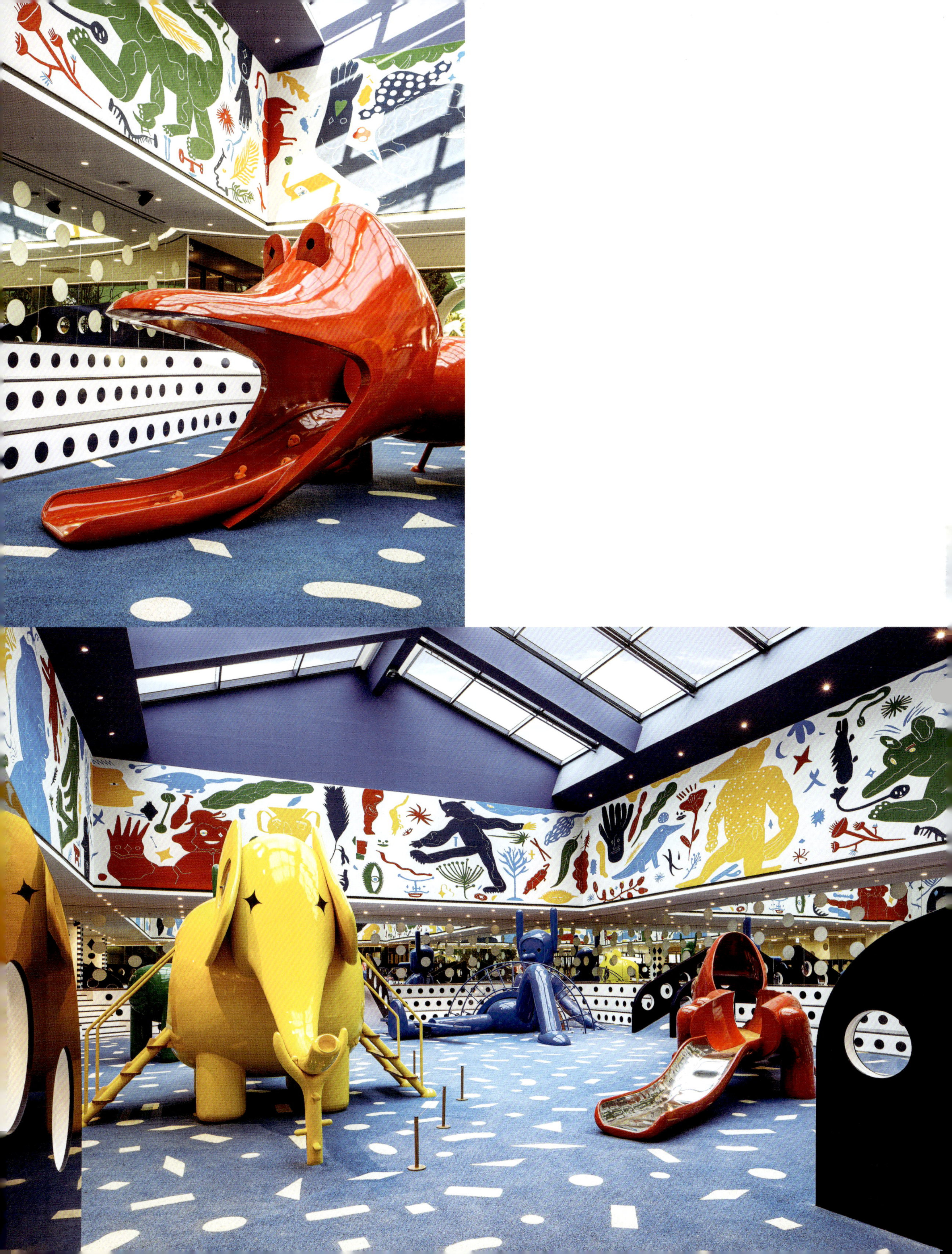

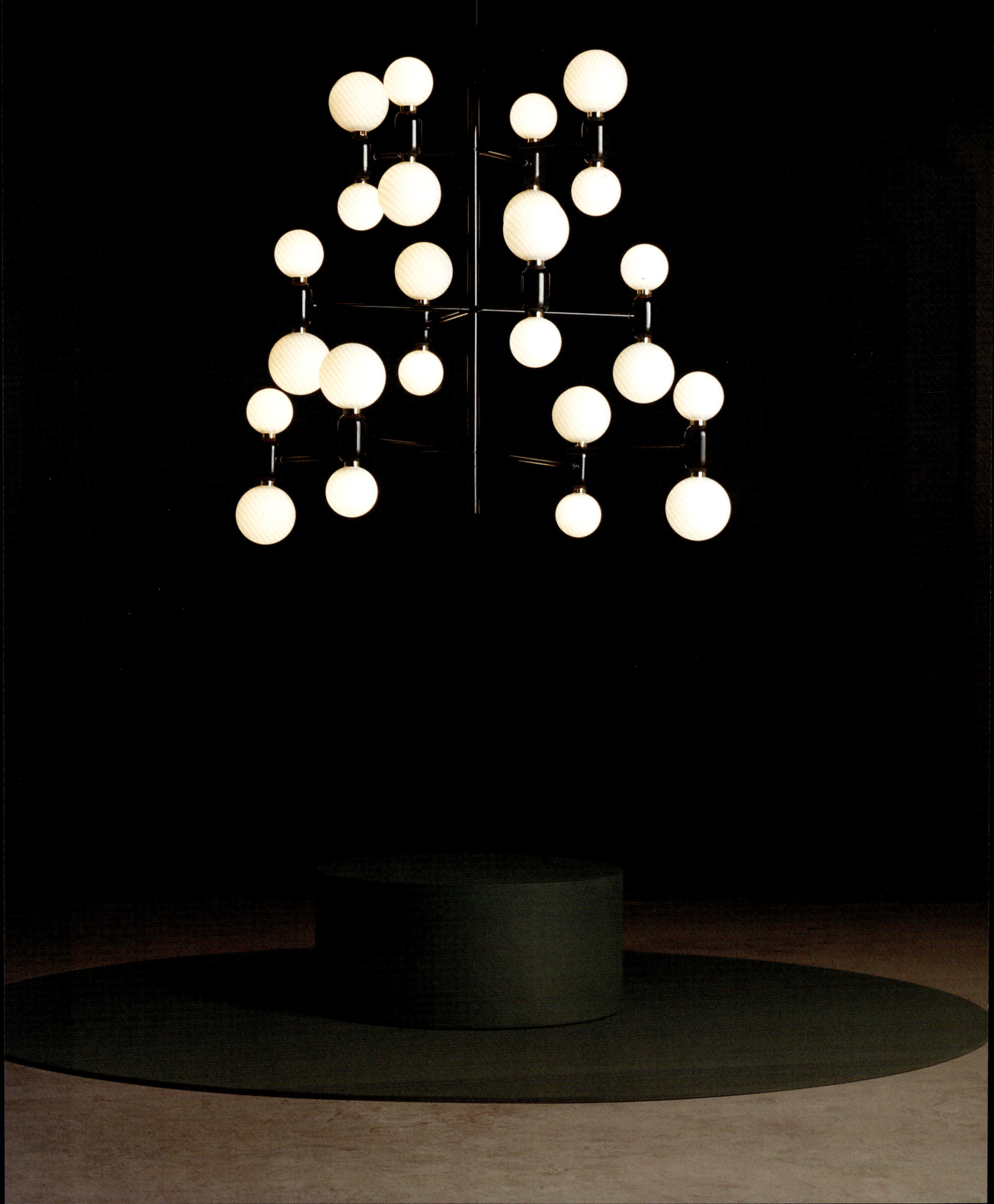

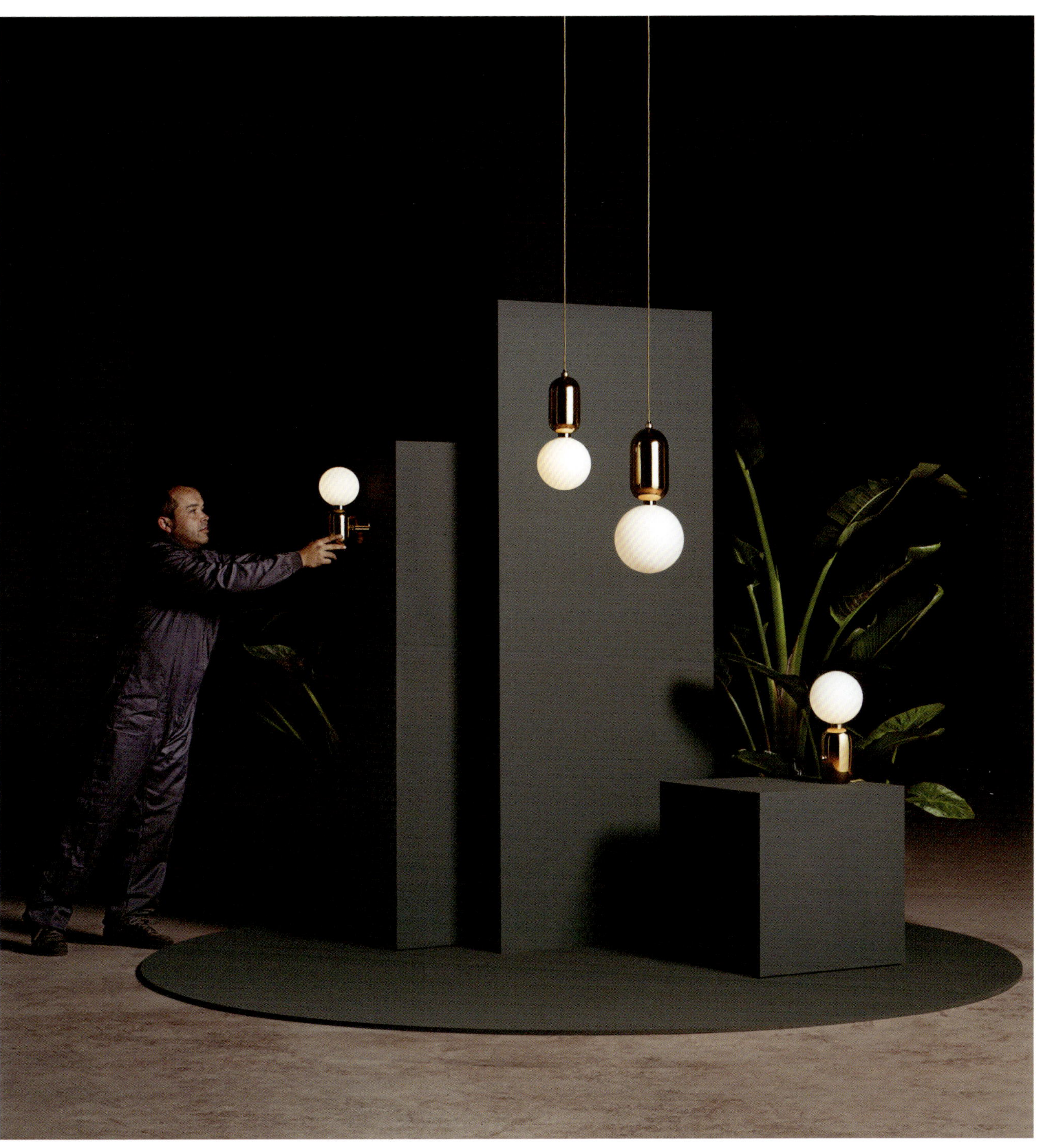

↓↑ Aballs—Ceramic, glass, and metal chandelier, wall appliqué, and hanging lights for Parachilna, 2015

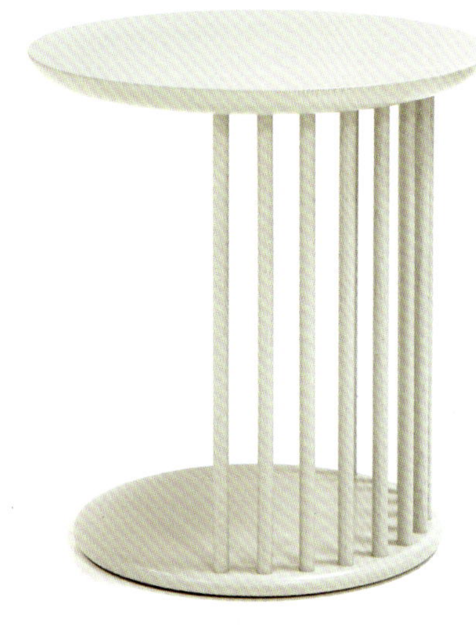

↓ Sticks Table—for Wittmann, Hayon Workshop IV, 2019

↓ Primates—From the Fauna by Hayon tapestry series, created for the exhibition at TextielMuseum, Tilburg, Netherlands, 2013

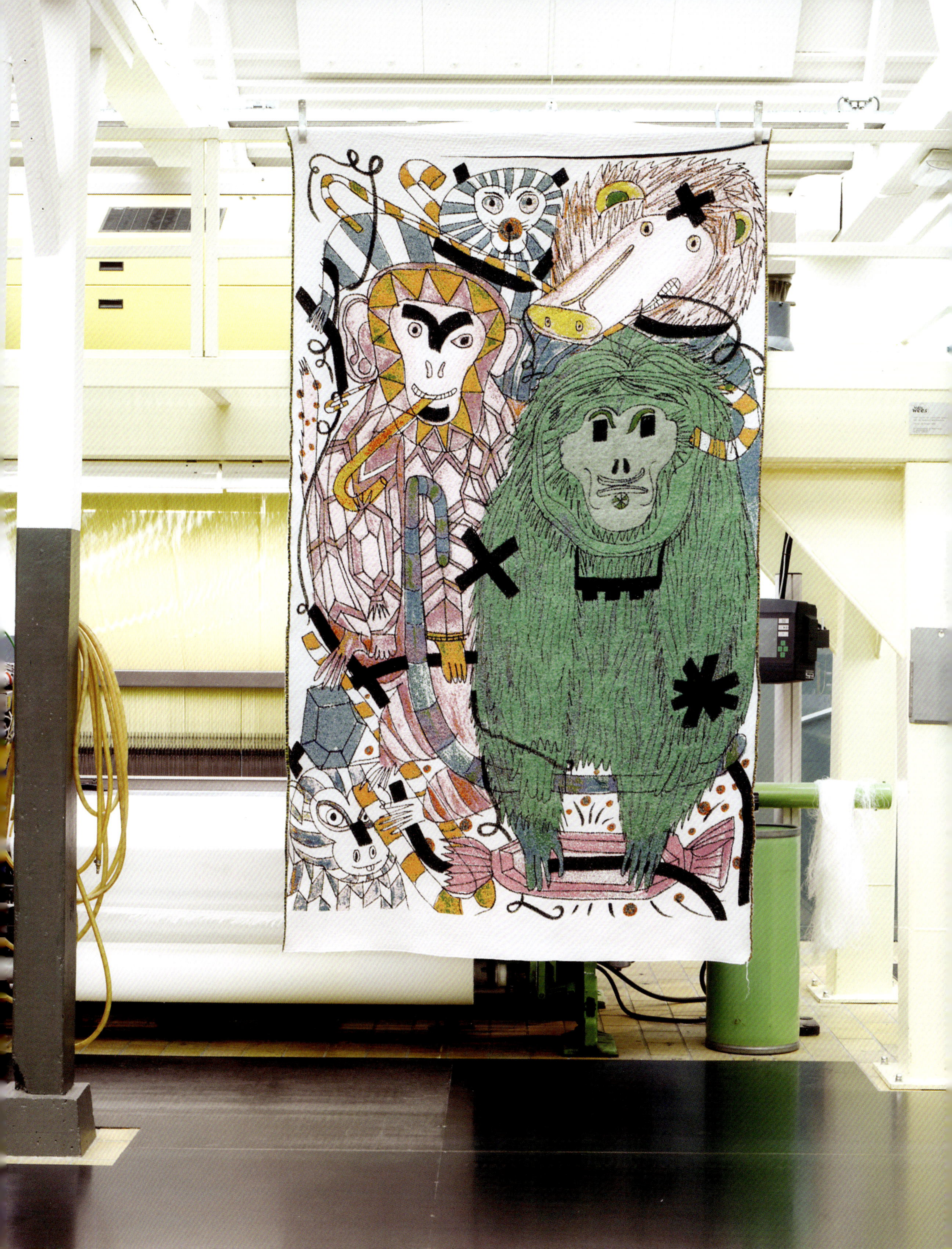

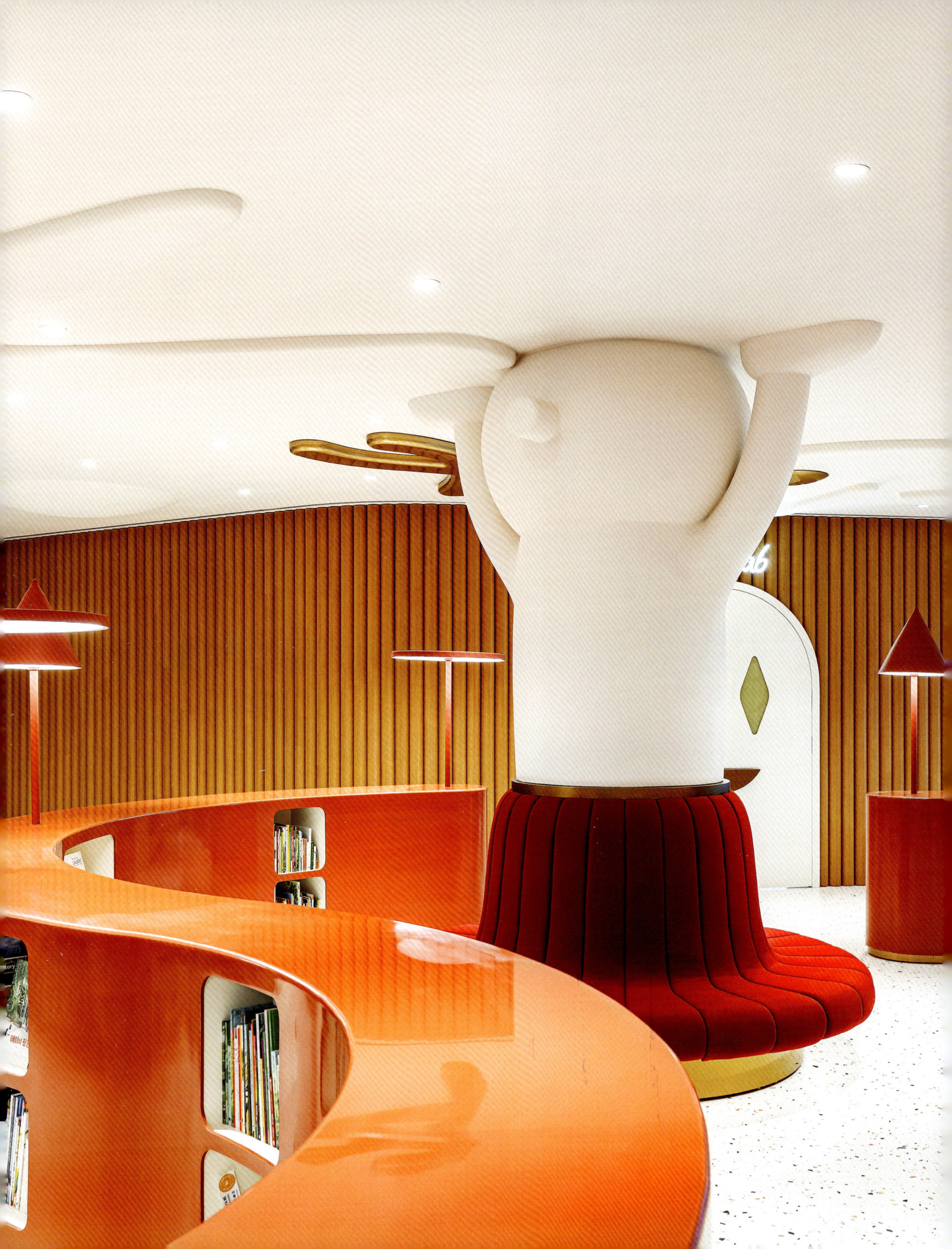

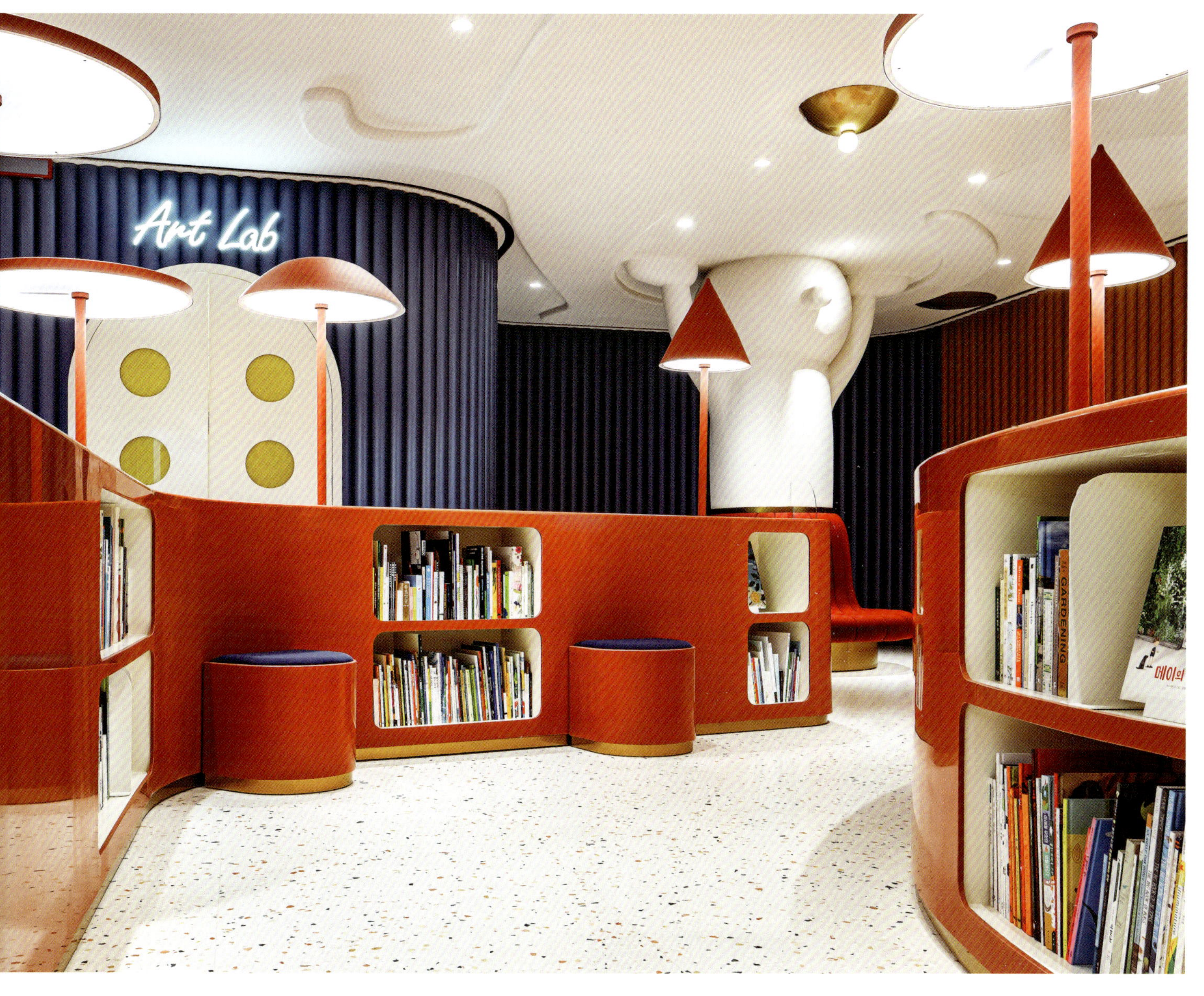

↑ MOKA Library—Interior design, Seoul, South Korea, 2020

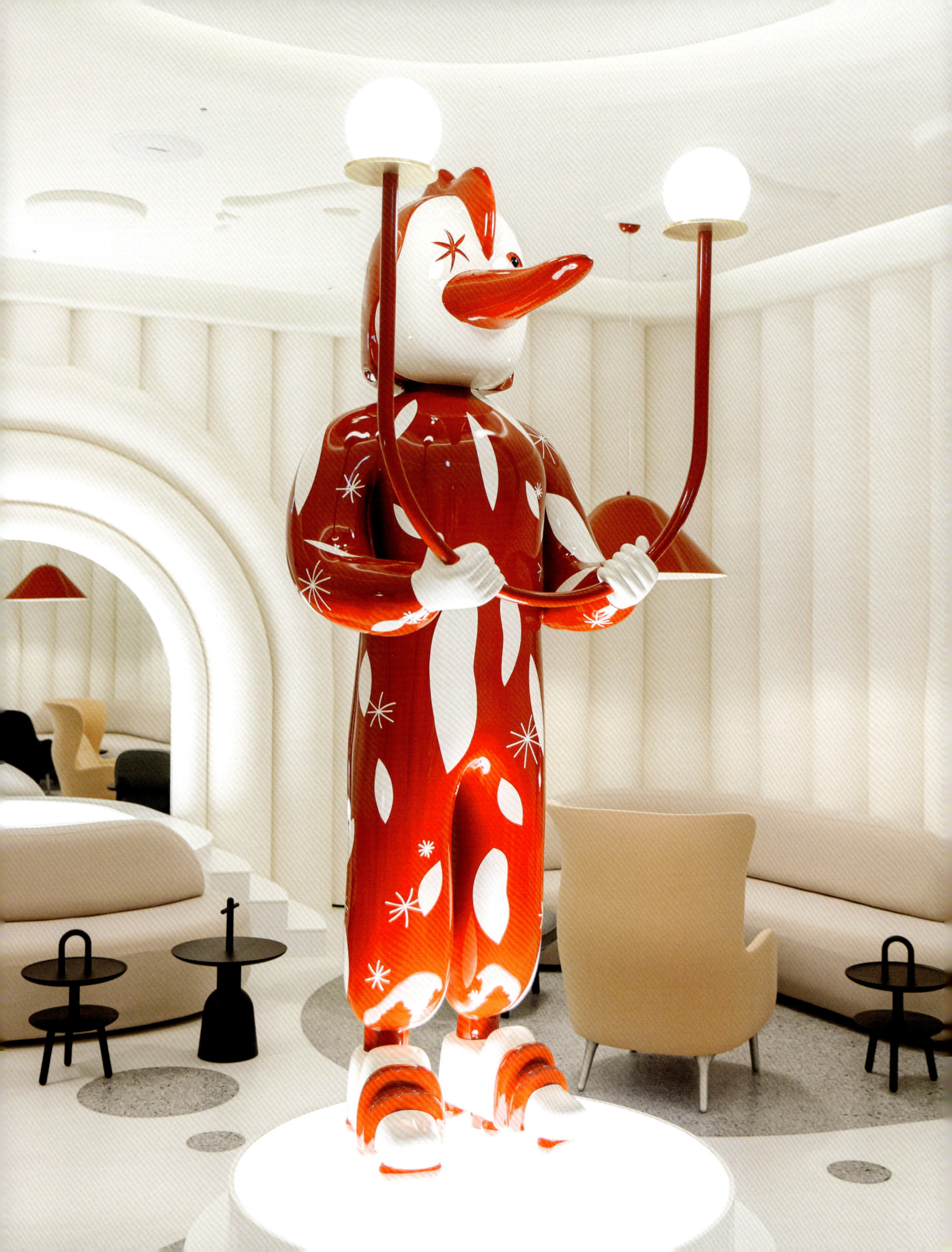

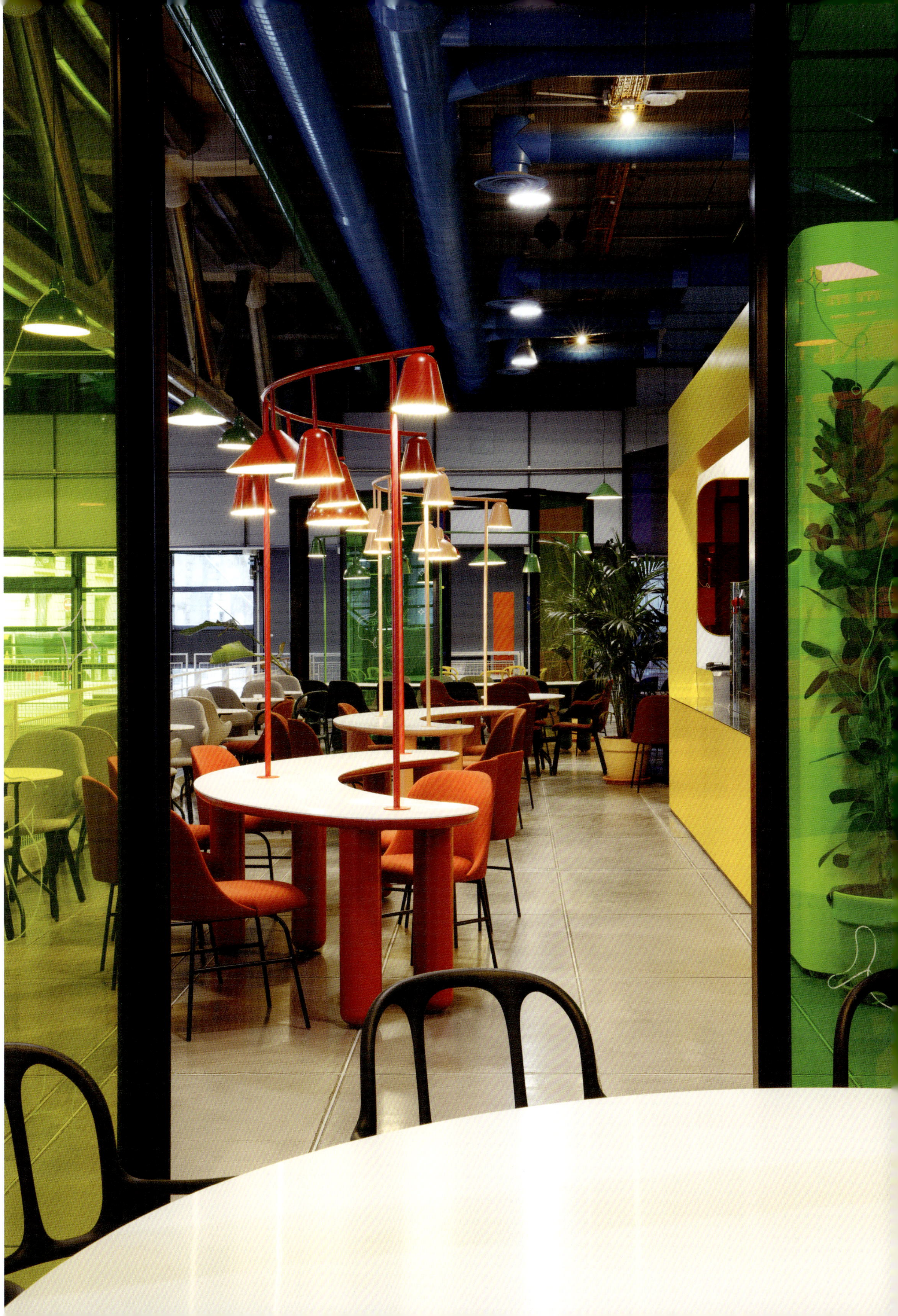

↑ The Hyundai YP Haus—Sculpture detail, Seoul, South Korea, 2021
↓ Le Central—Cafe at the Centre Pompidou, Paris, France, 2019

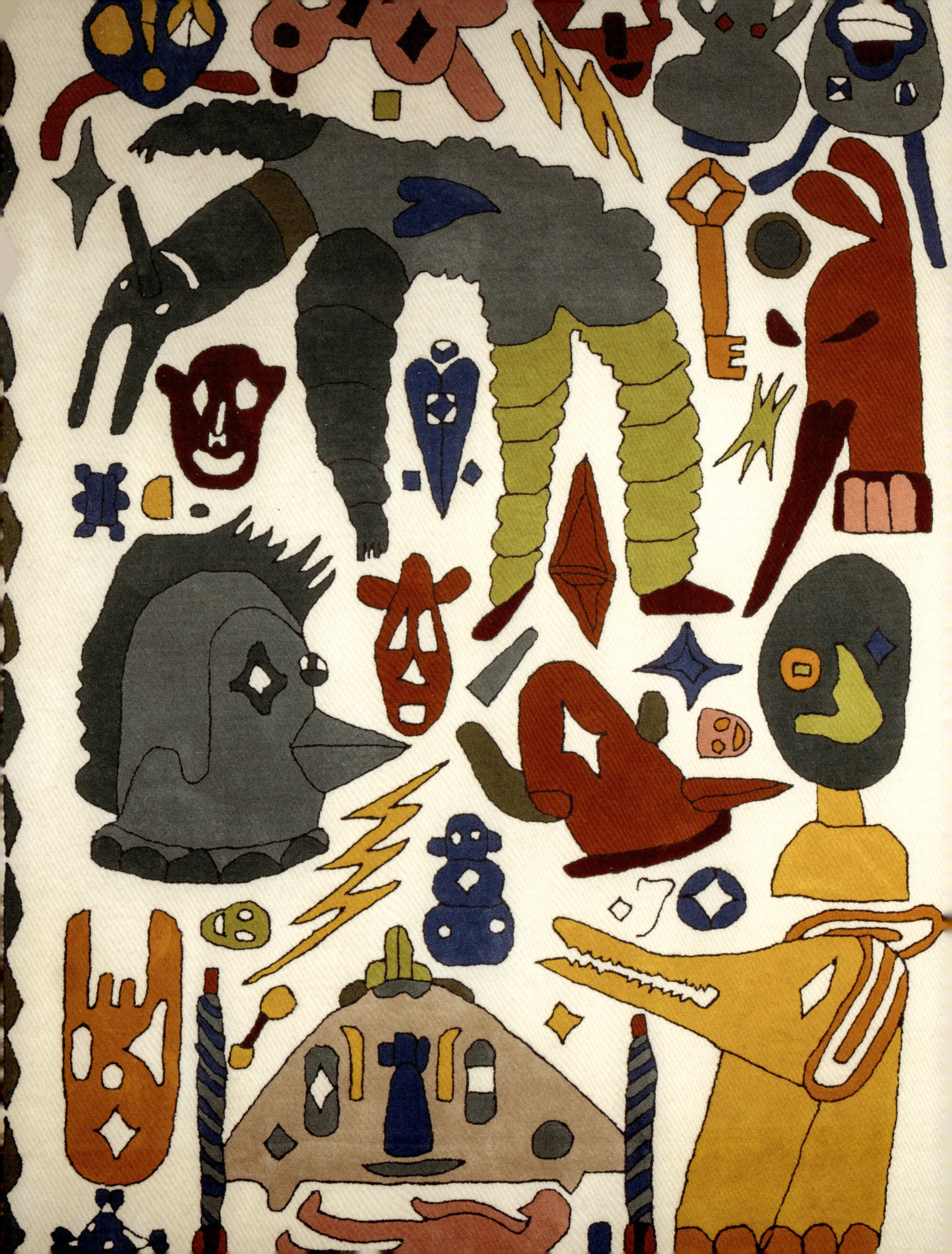

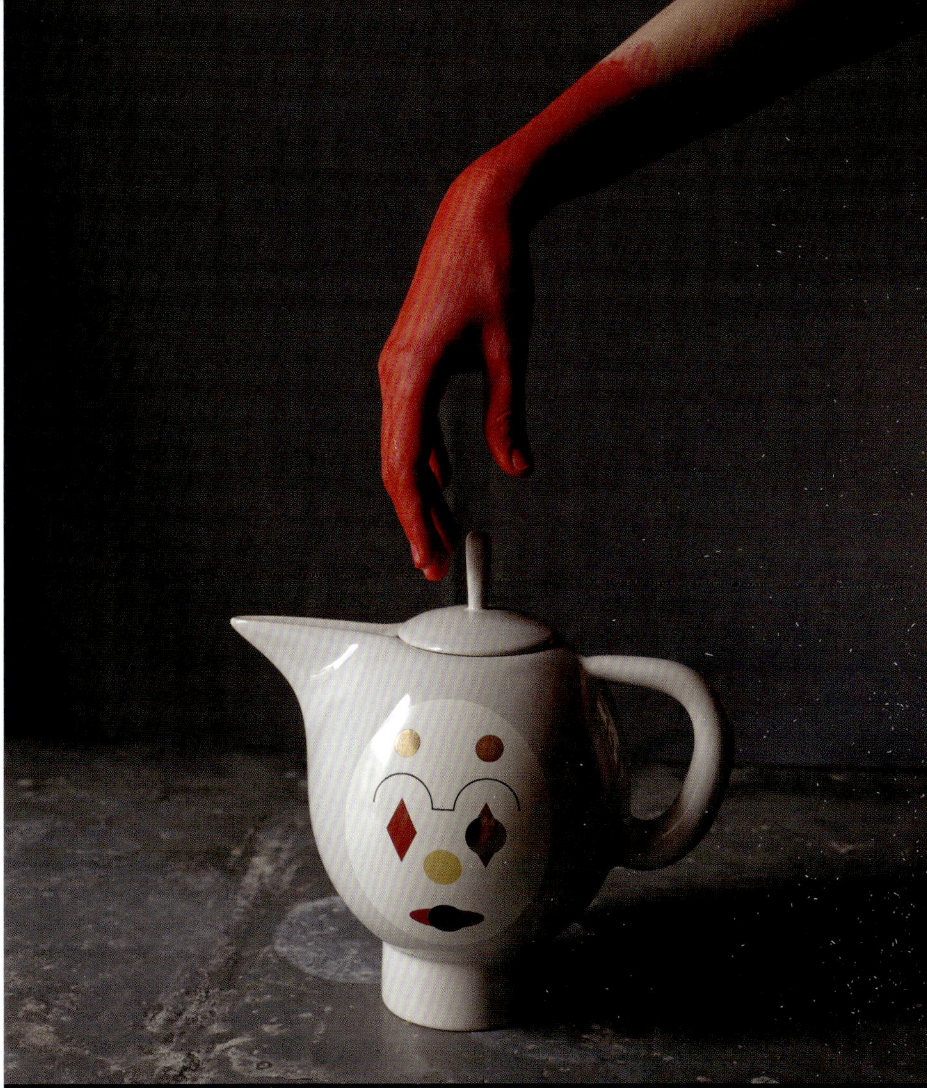

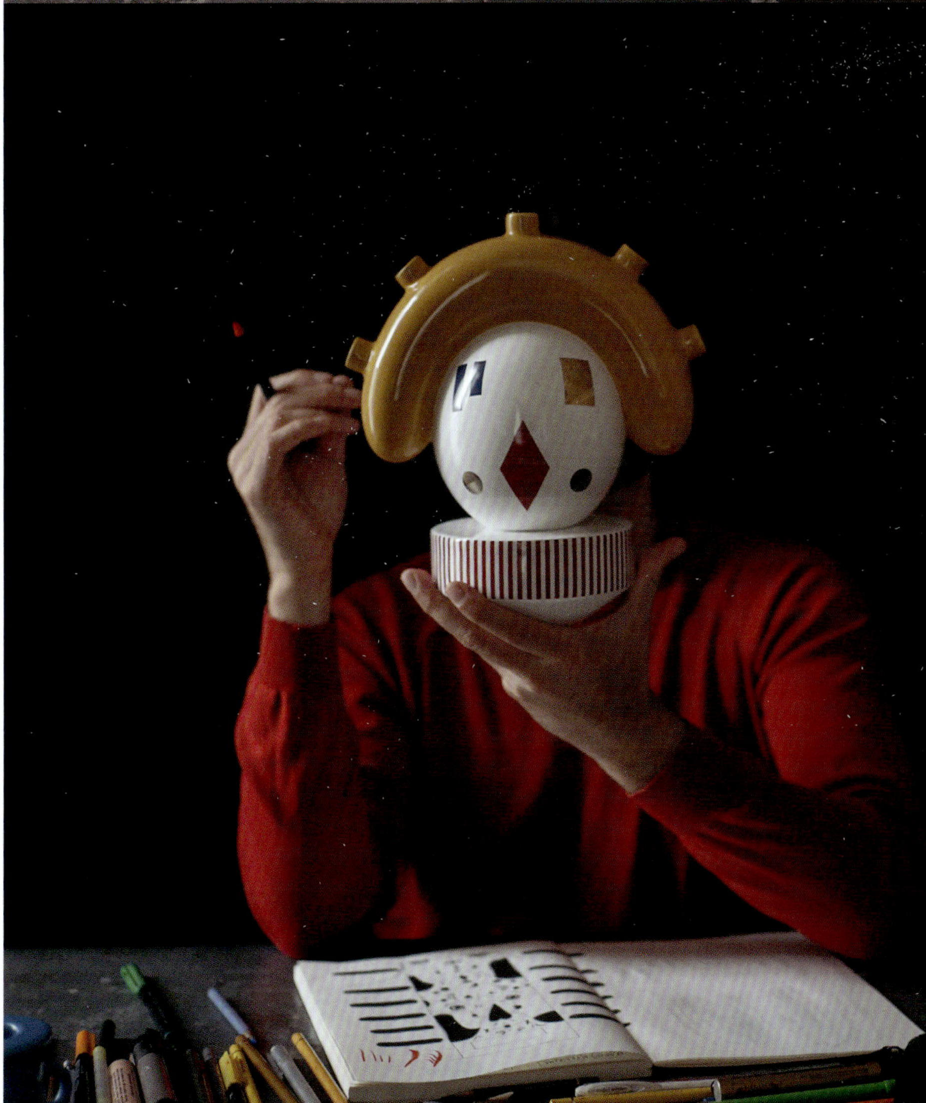

↑ Troupe—Rug for Nanimarquina, 2022

↓ David and Georgi Tulip—Teapot and vase, ceramic tableware pieces part of the Theatre Hayon collection for Bosa, 2019

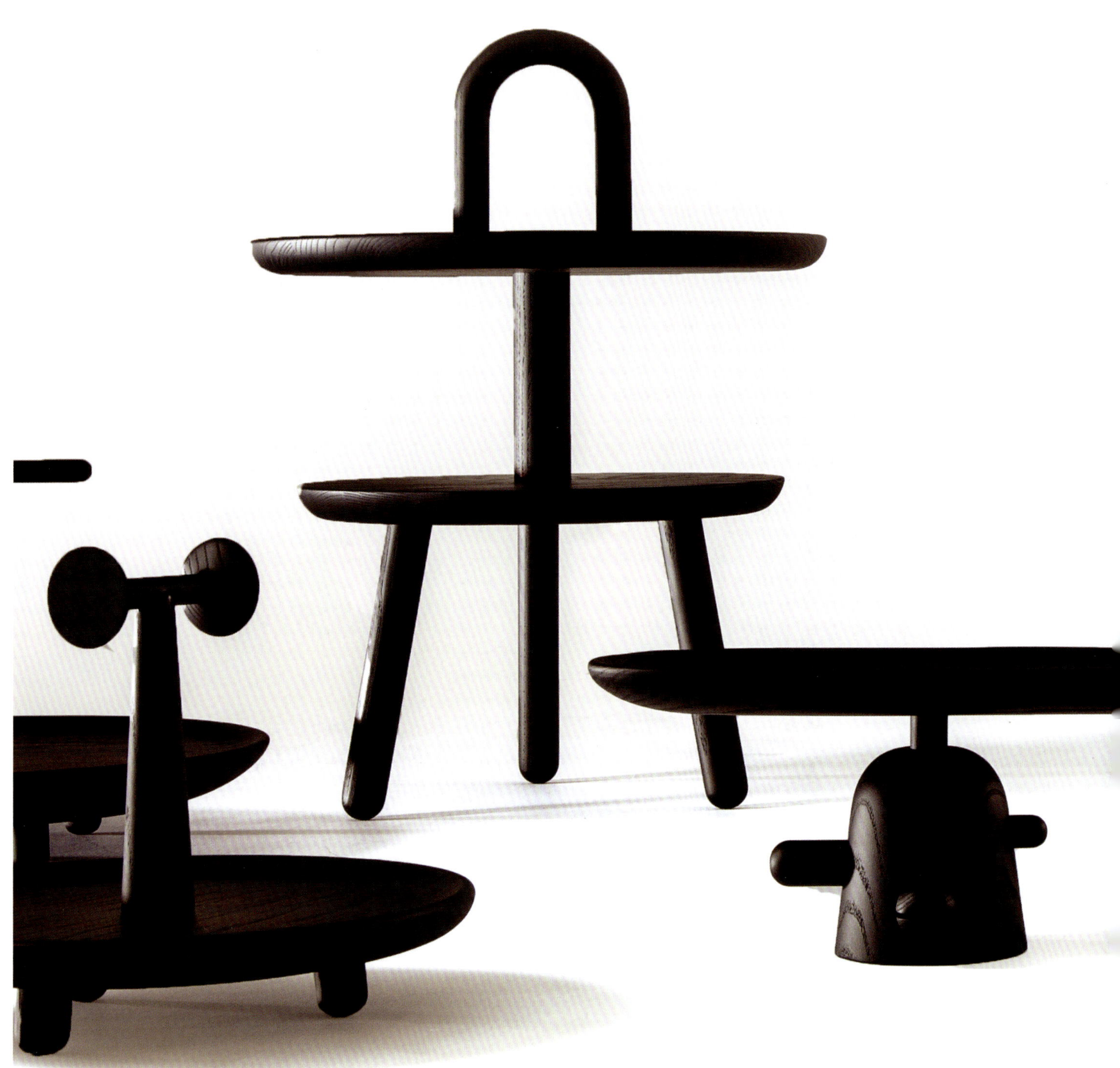

↓ Réaction Poétique—Collection of functional objects in solid ash for Cassina, 2015

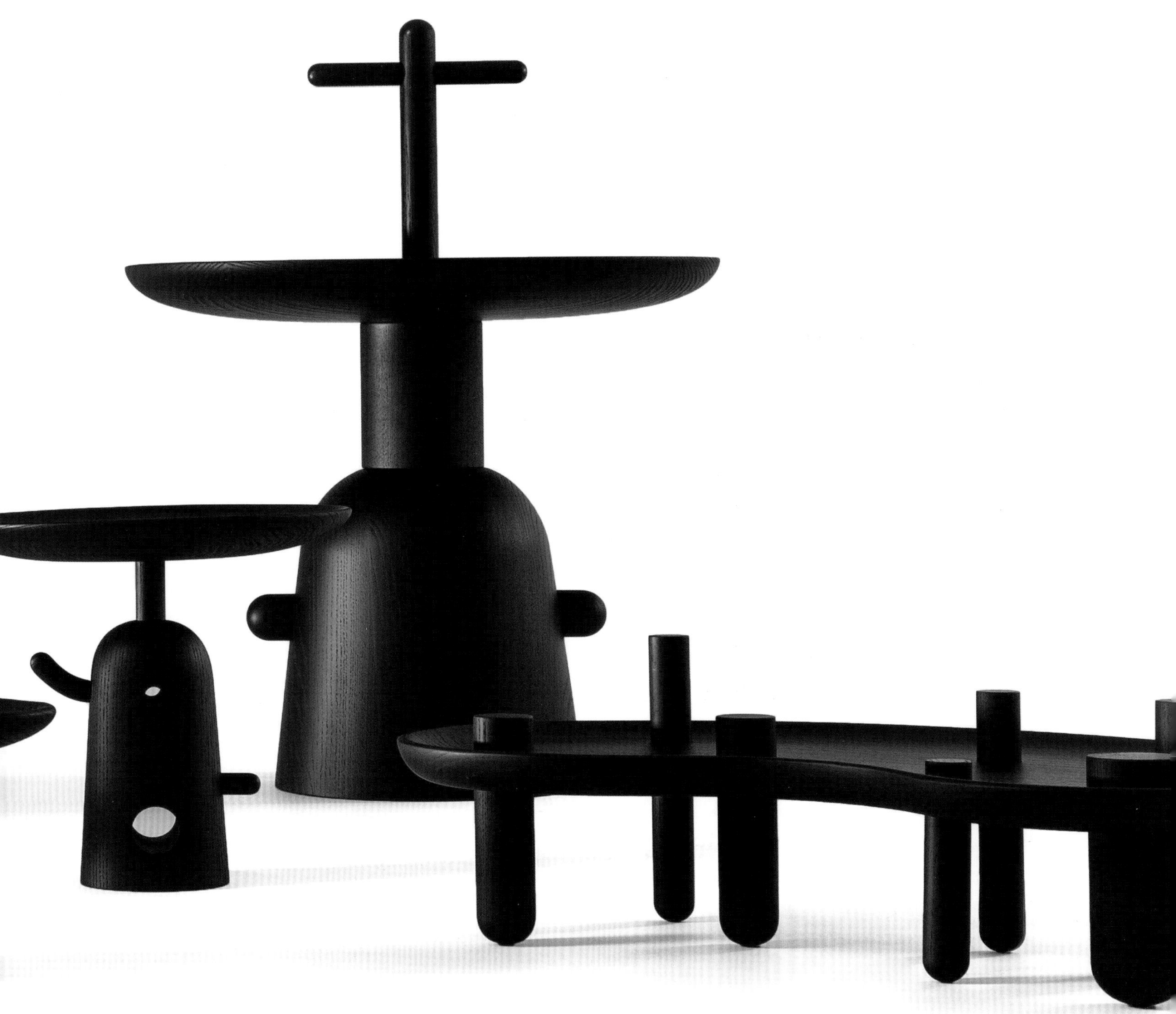

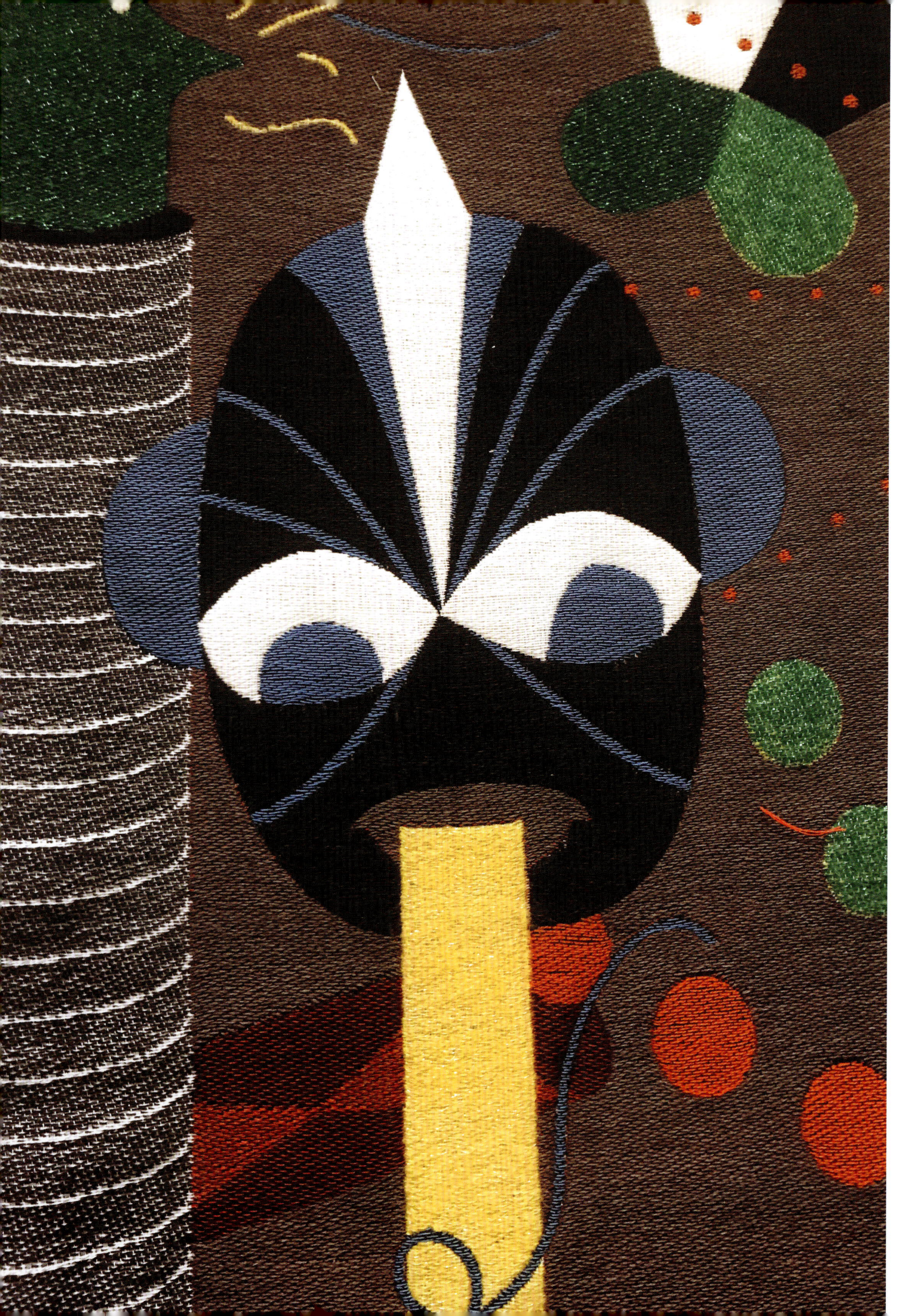

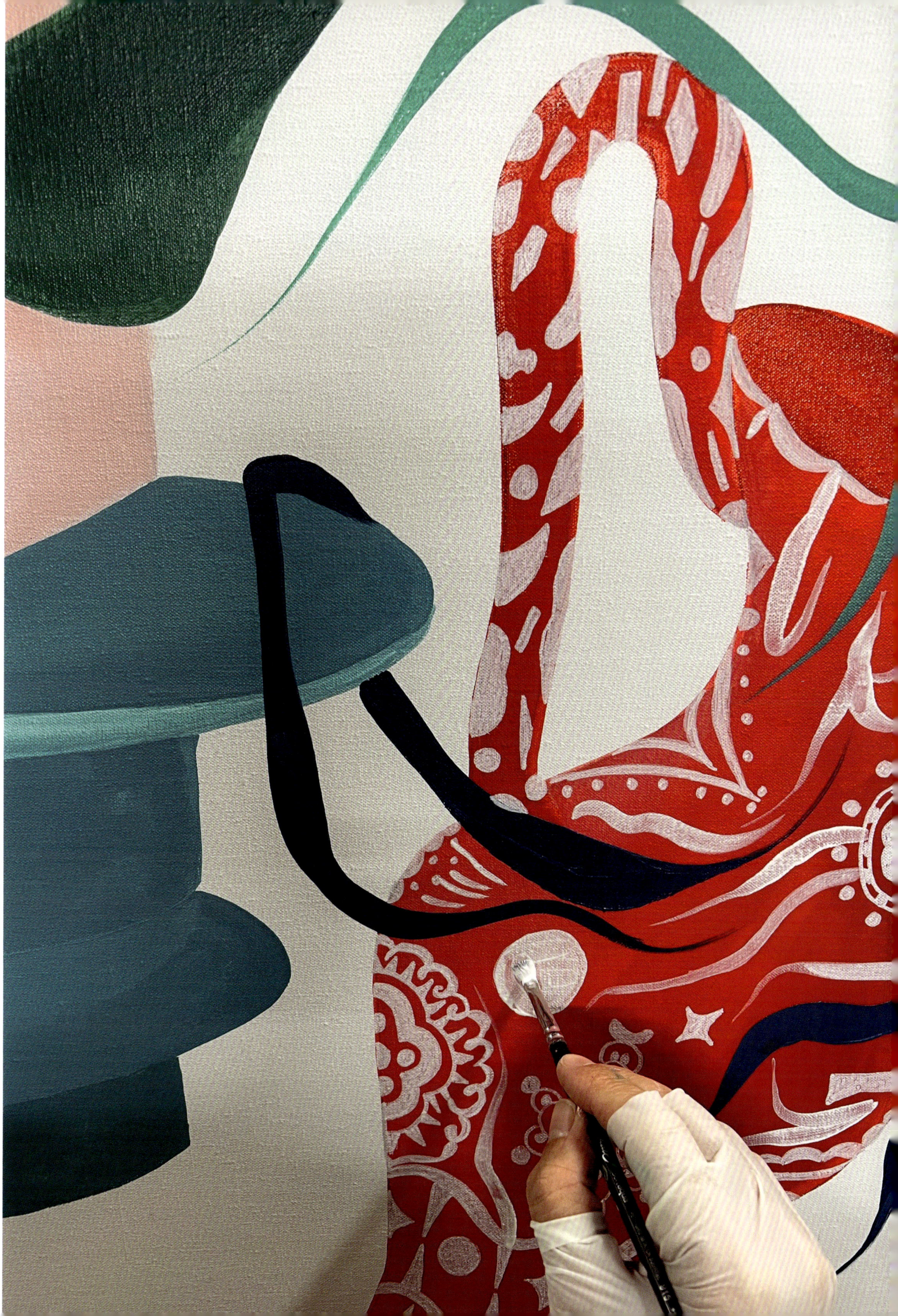

↑ Technicolor—Tapestry detail of the installation at the High Museum of Art, Atlanta, USA, 2017
↓ Acrylic on canvas, detail, 2022

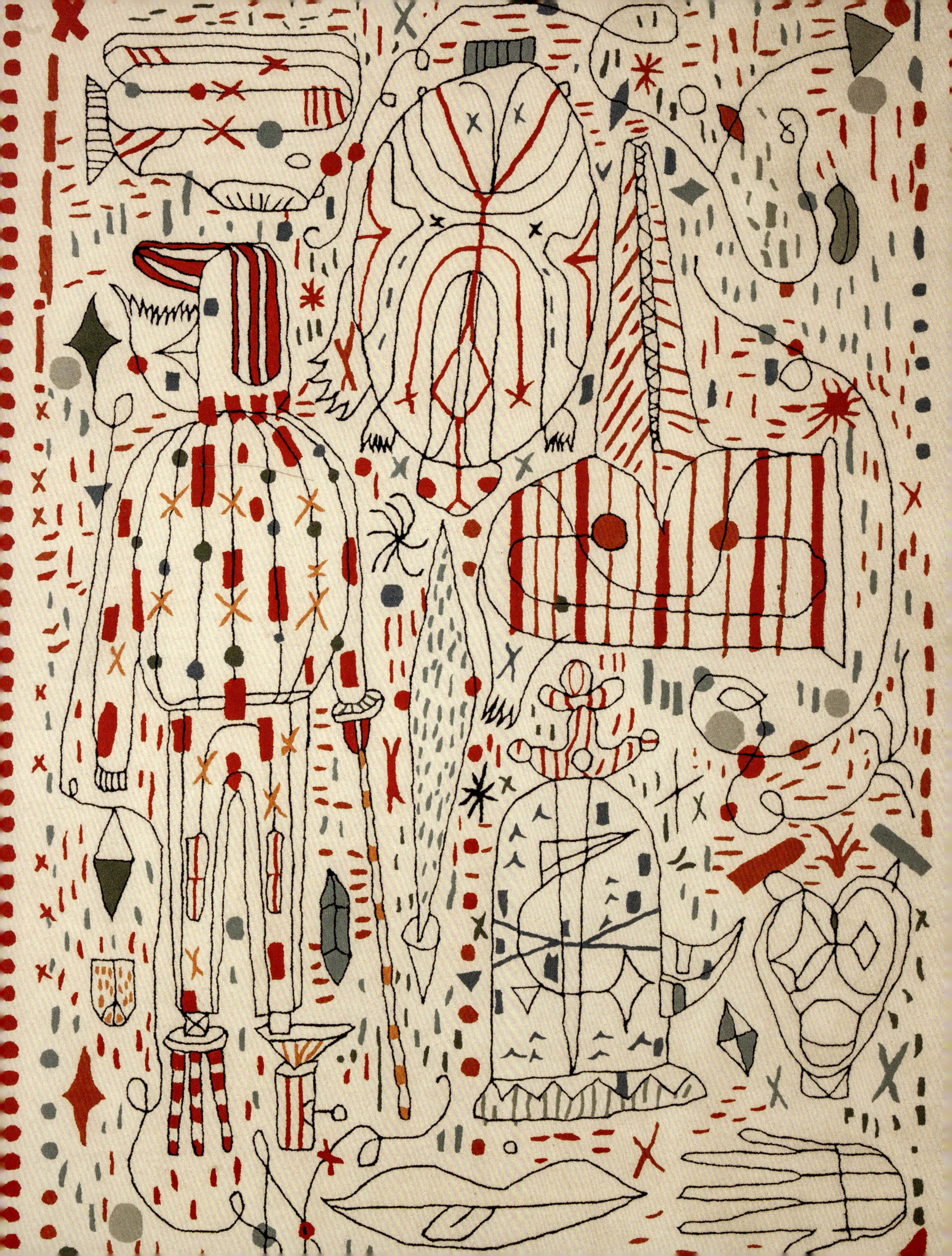

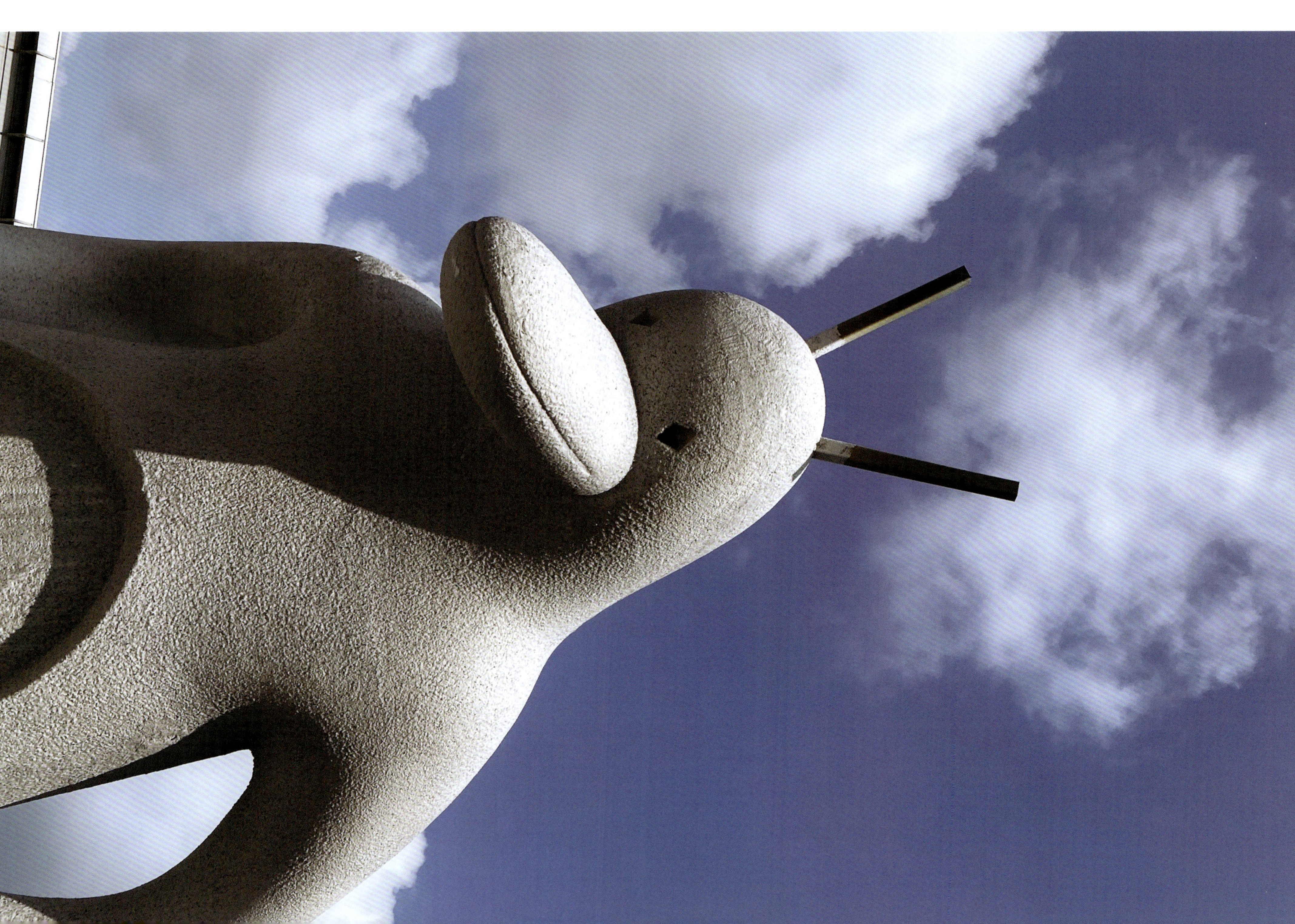

↑ Hayon × Nani—Rectangular hand-tufted rug for Nanimarquina, 2017
↓ Process for Curious Morpho sculpture for MOKA Garden, Seoul, South Korea, 2020

→ My idea of elegance is fine craftsmanship and cutting-edge technology. Together they generate a story that has its own niche outside everyday reality.

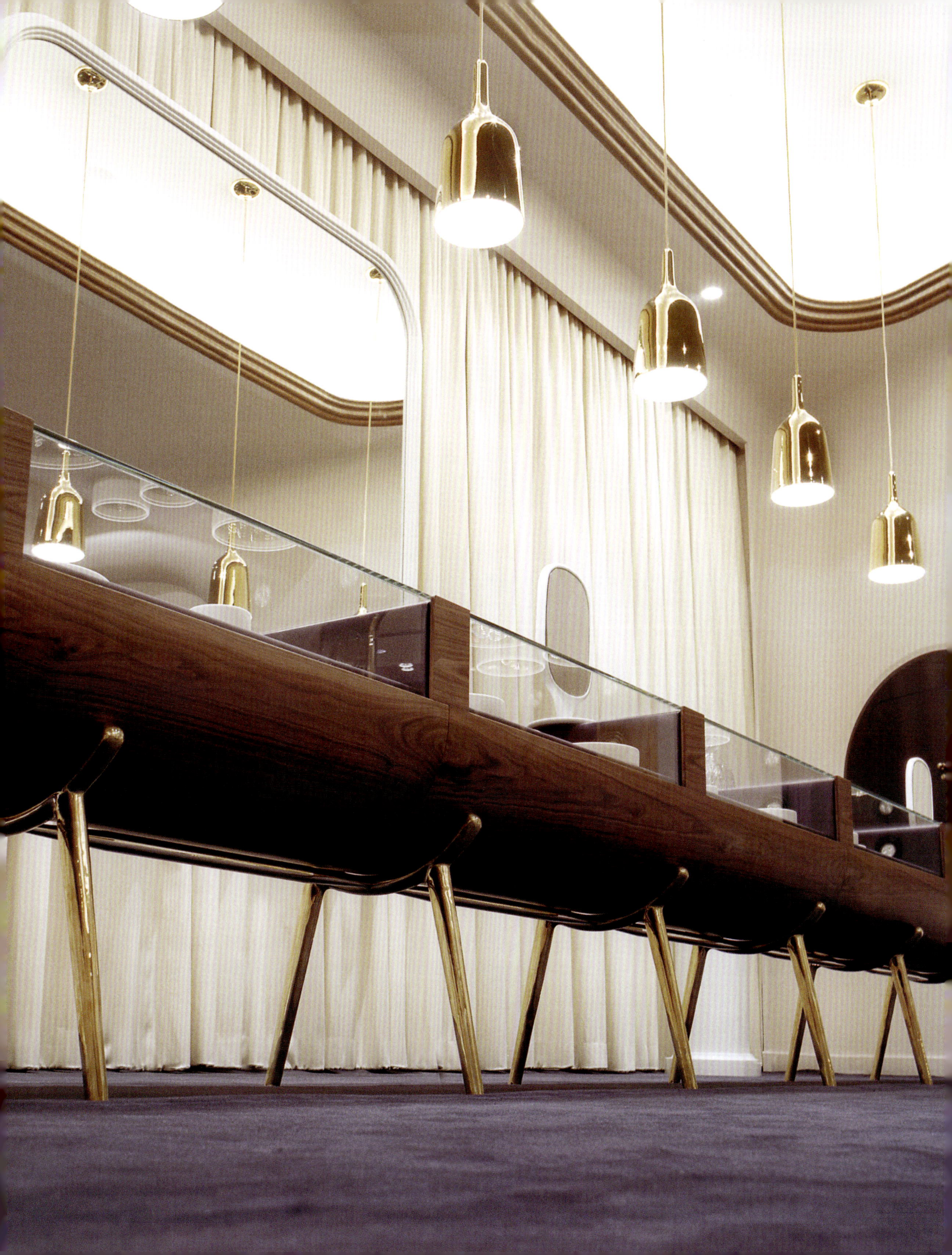

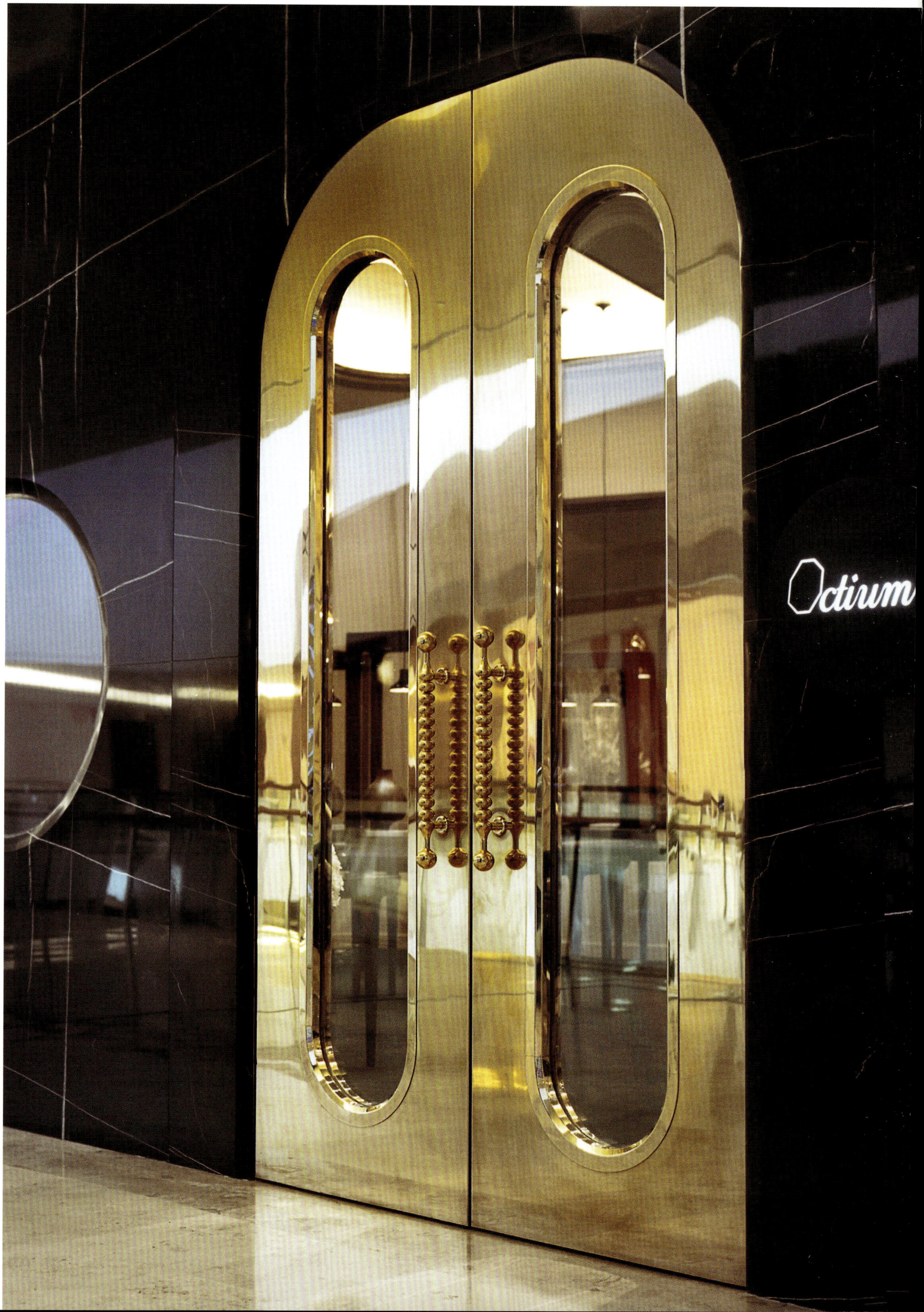

↓ Octium Jewelry—Interior design, Kuwait, 2009
↓ Smile stool—Stool in American cherry wood for Benchmark, 2020

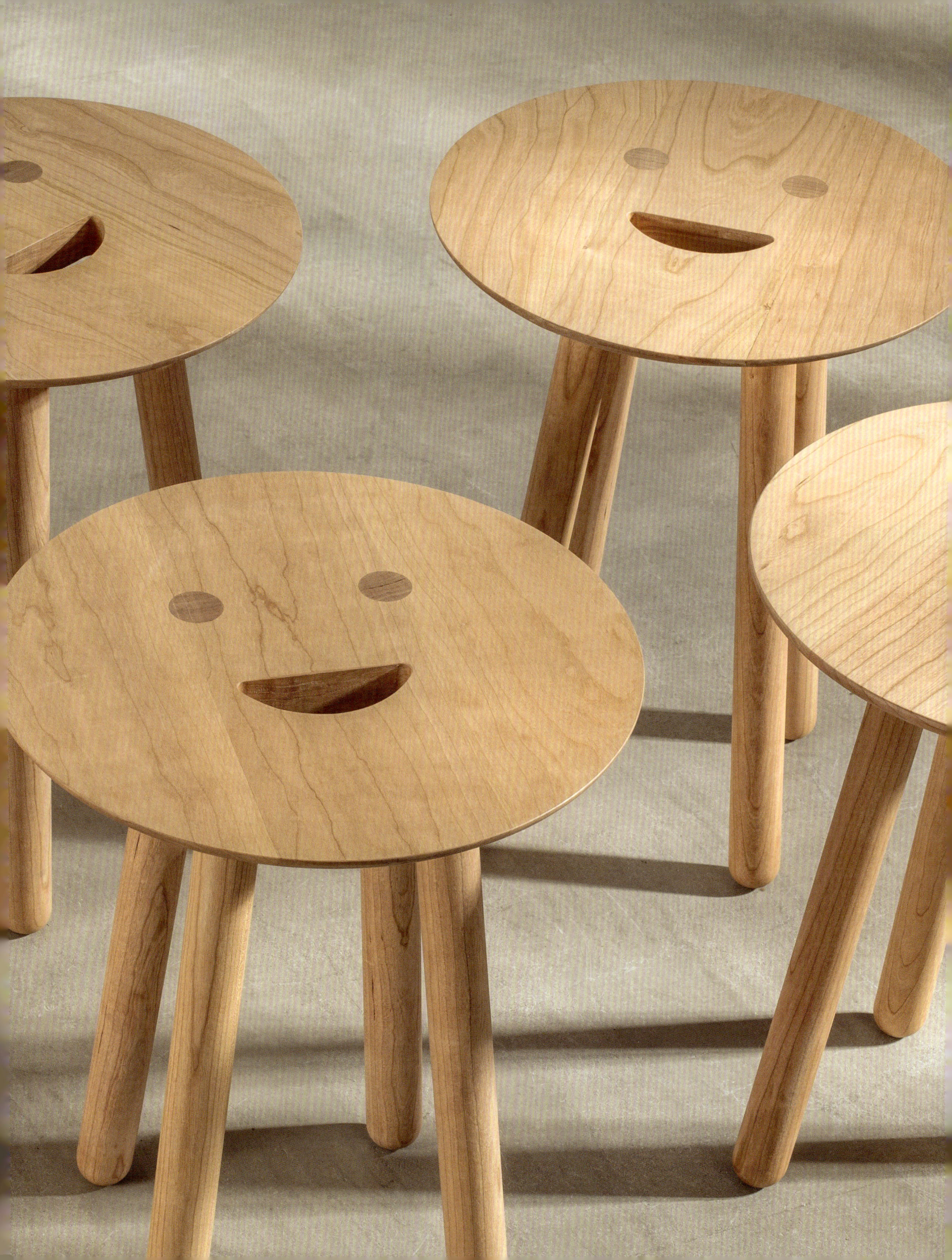

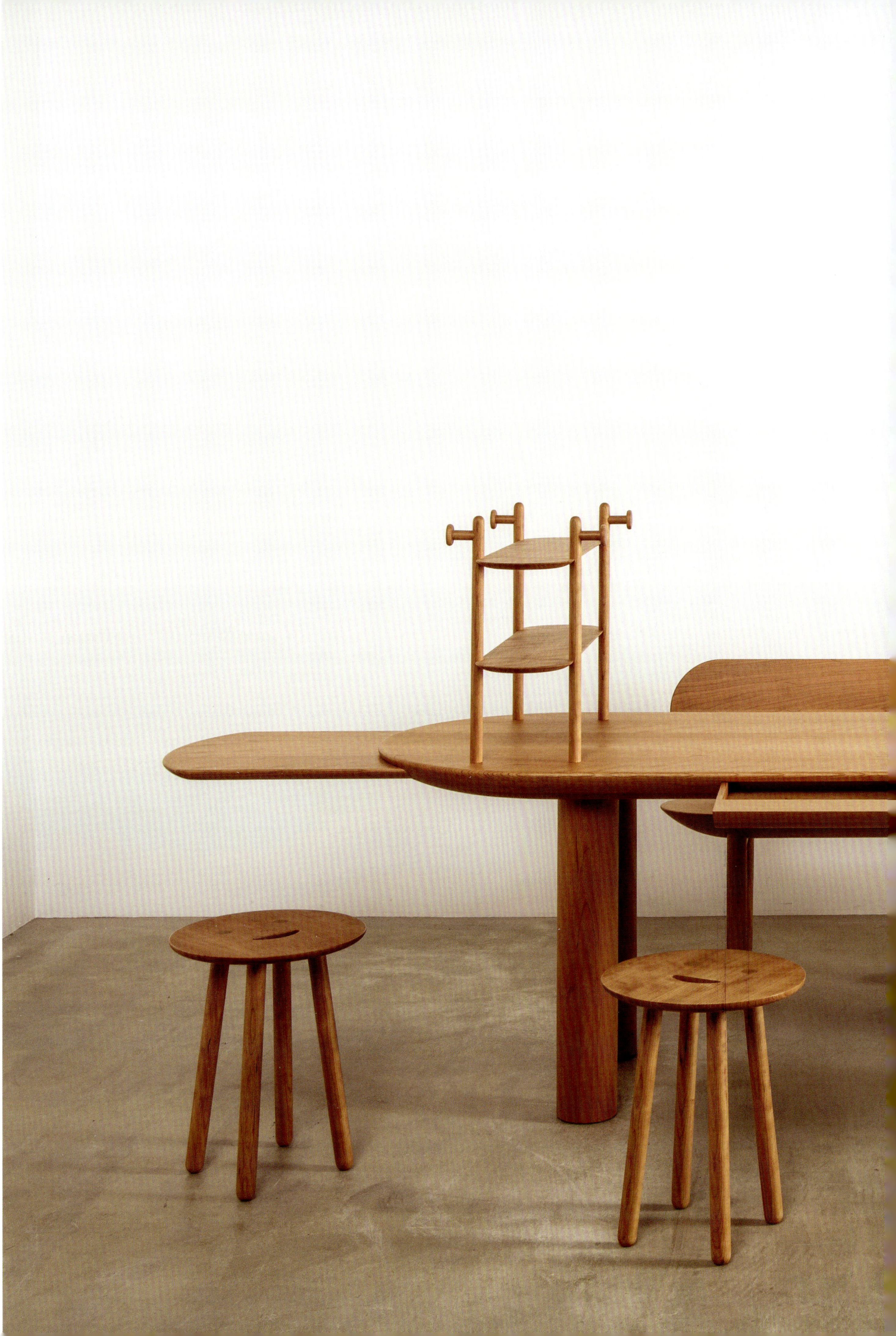

↳ Mesamachine—One-off piece, table, bench and stools in American cherry wood, 2020

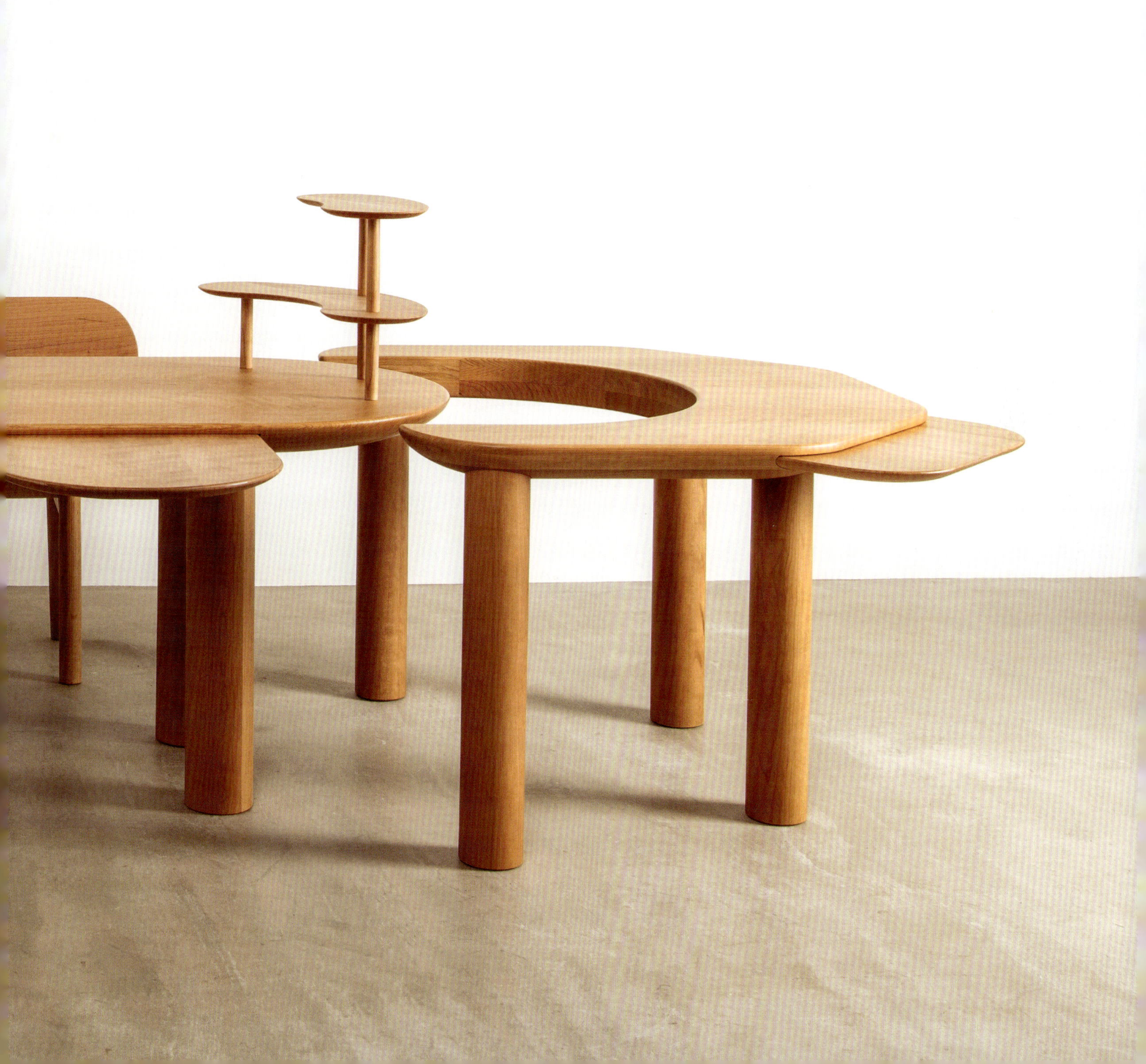

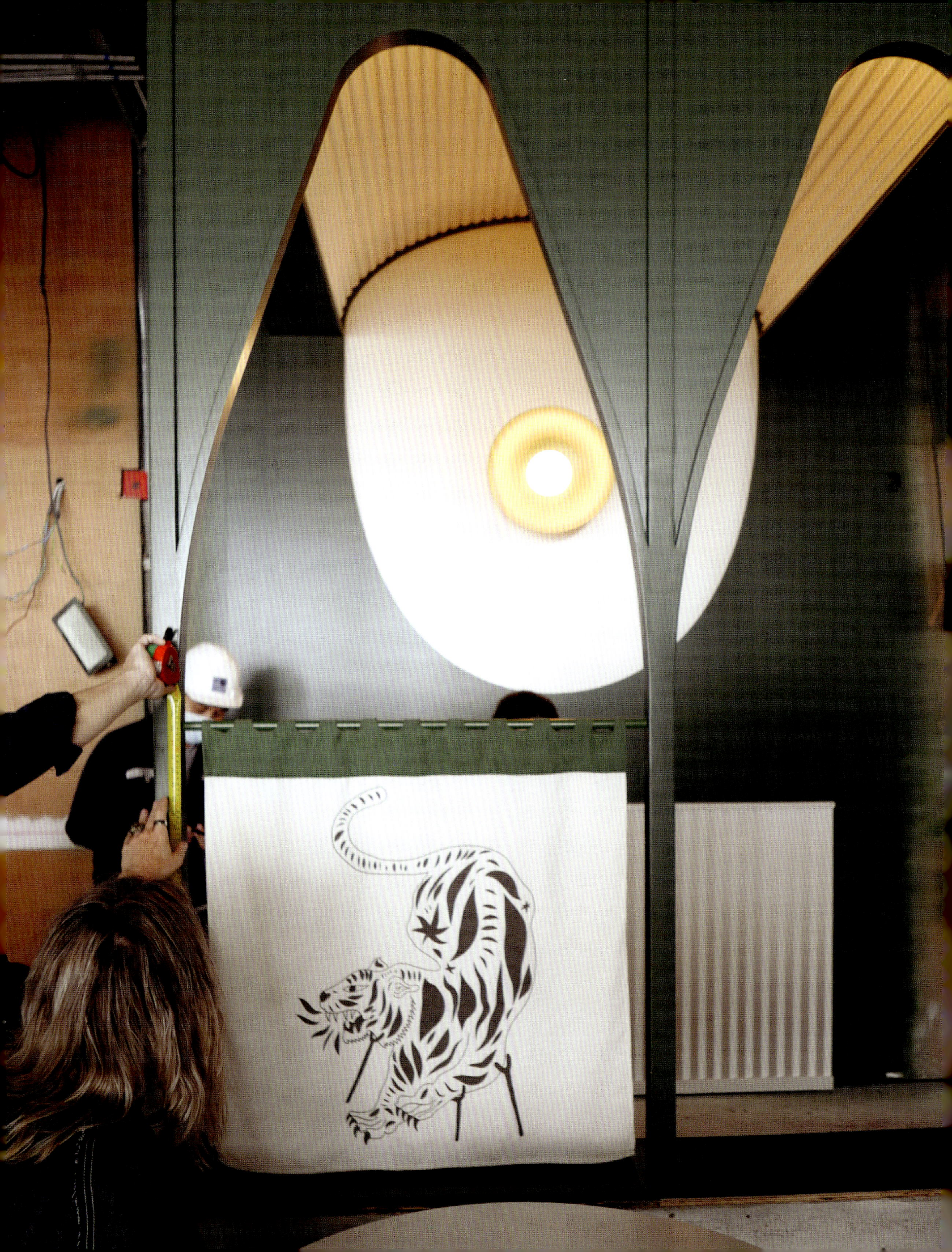

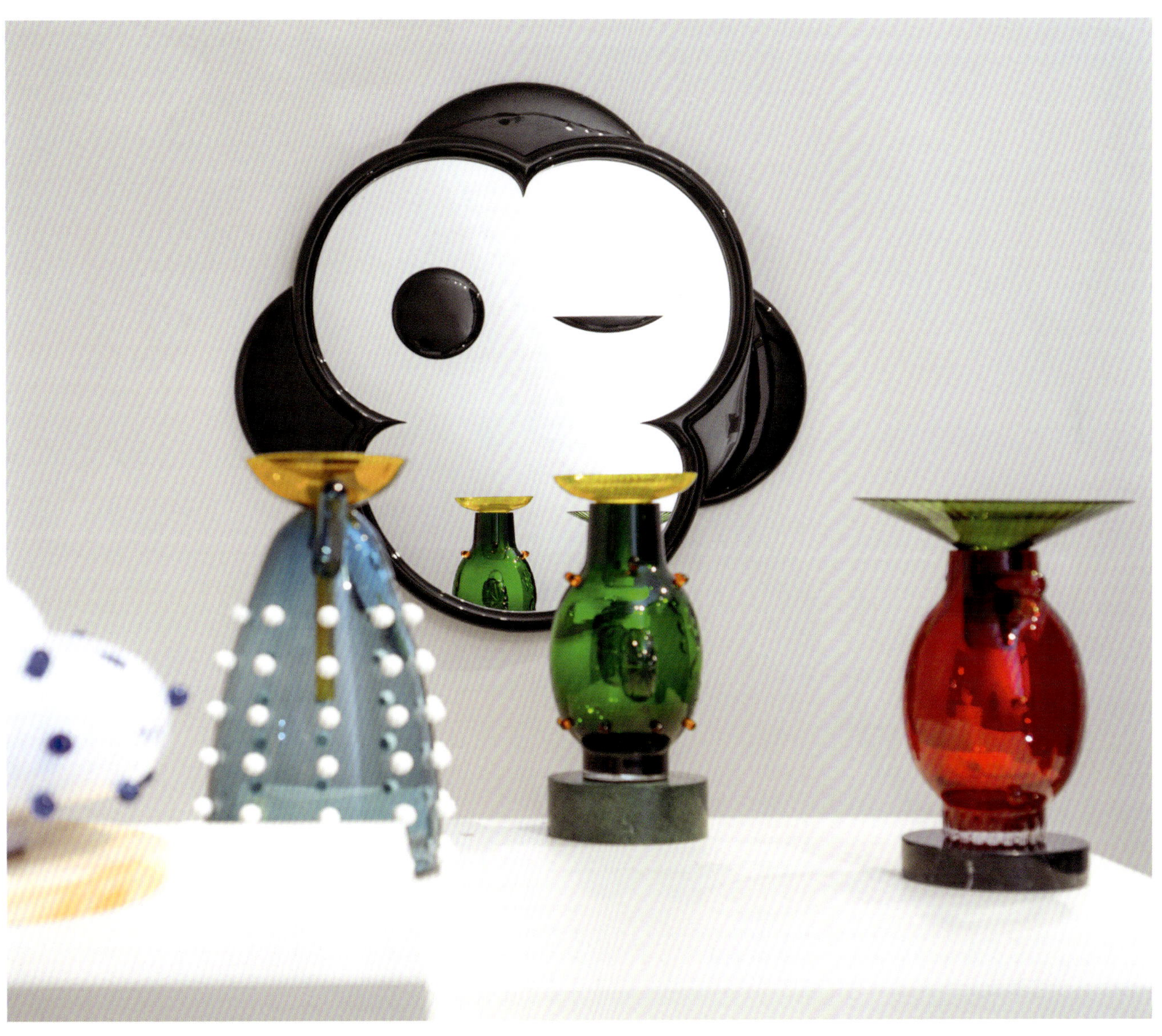

↑ The Standard Hotel—Restaurant and interior design, Bangkok, Thailand, 2022
↓ Cheeky, Oceanoz, Mentolato, and Rojopom—Mirror and vases for Chromatico exhibition at Galerie kreo, Paris, France, 2018

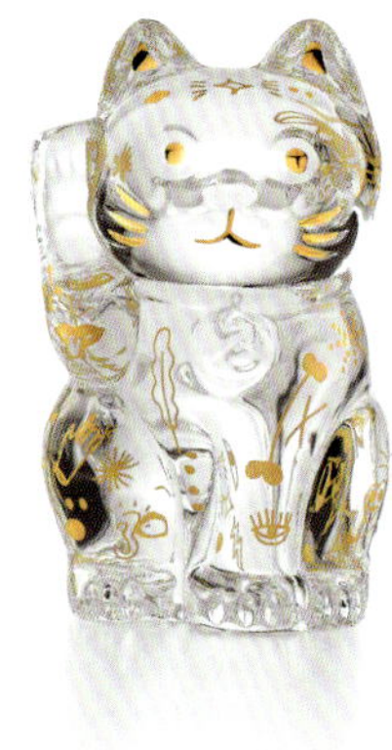

→ Maneki Neko—Figurine for Baccarat, part of the Carnival of the Animals, 2020
→ Fritz Hansen Showroom—Interior design, Xi'an, China, 2019

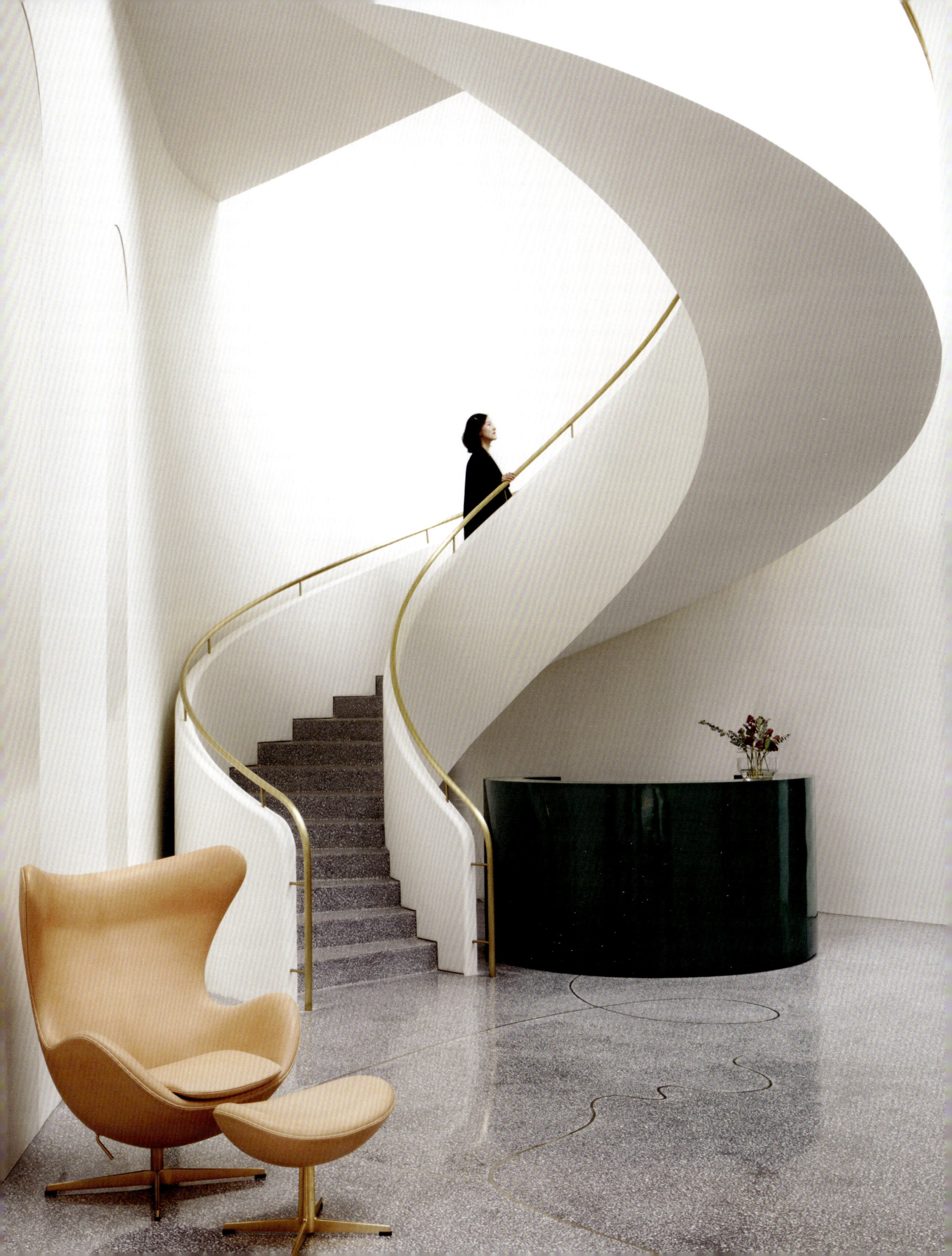

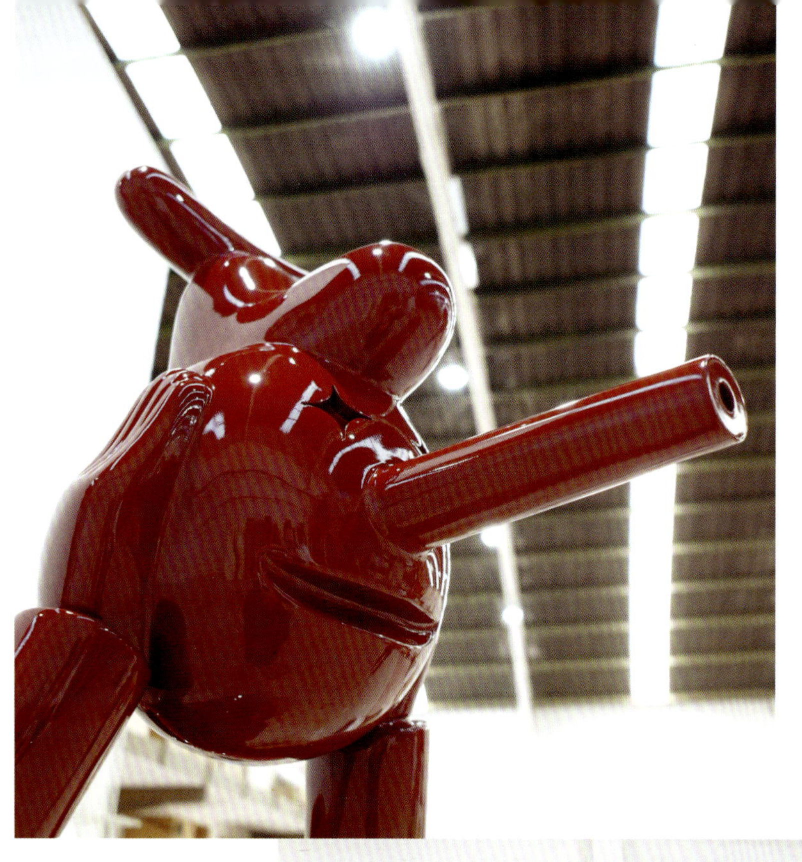

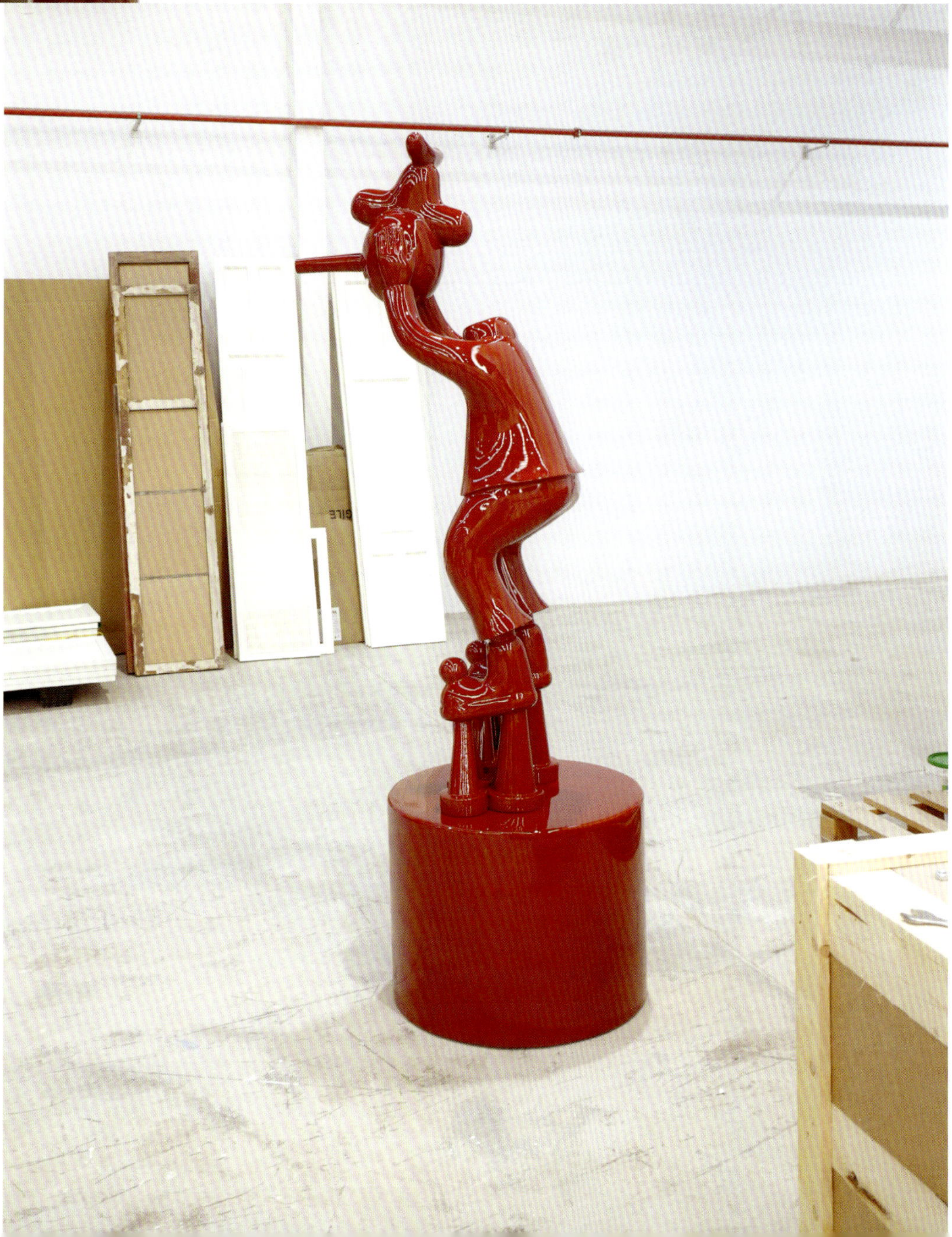

↑ Lose it—Lacquered fiberglass sculpture, 2022

→ Painting takes me to the very root of creation. It is the core of my work where composition is an extraction from my inner world—it really is an act of extraction.

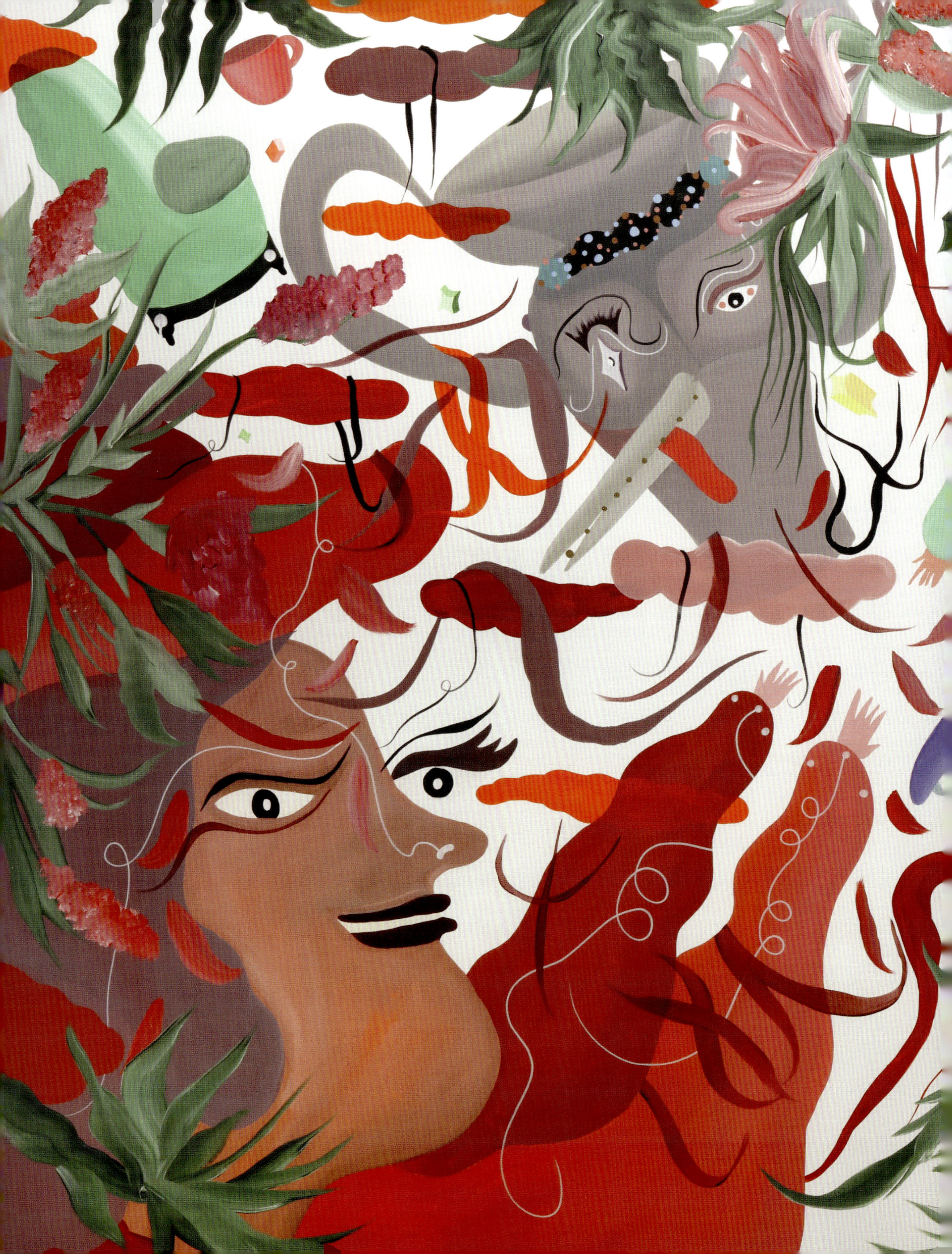

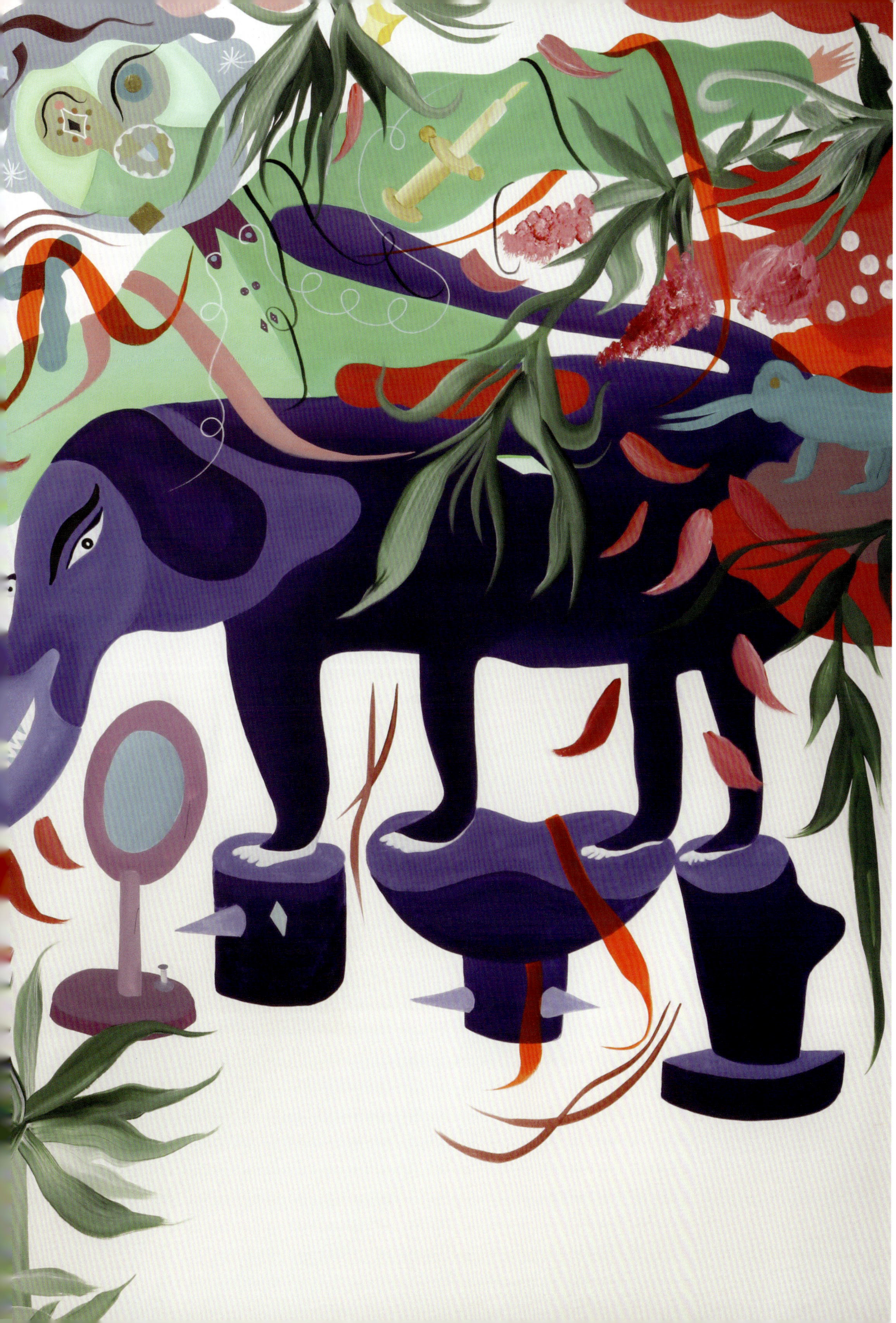

↑ The Harmony of the Rescue—Acrylic on canvas, 250 ×180 cm, 2022

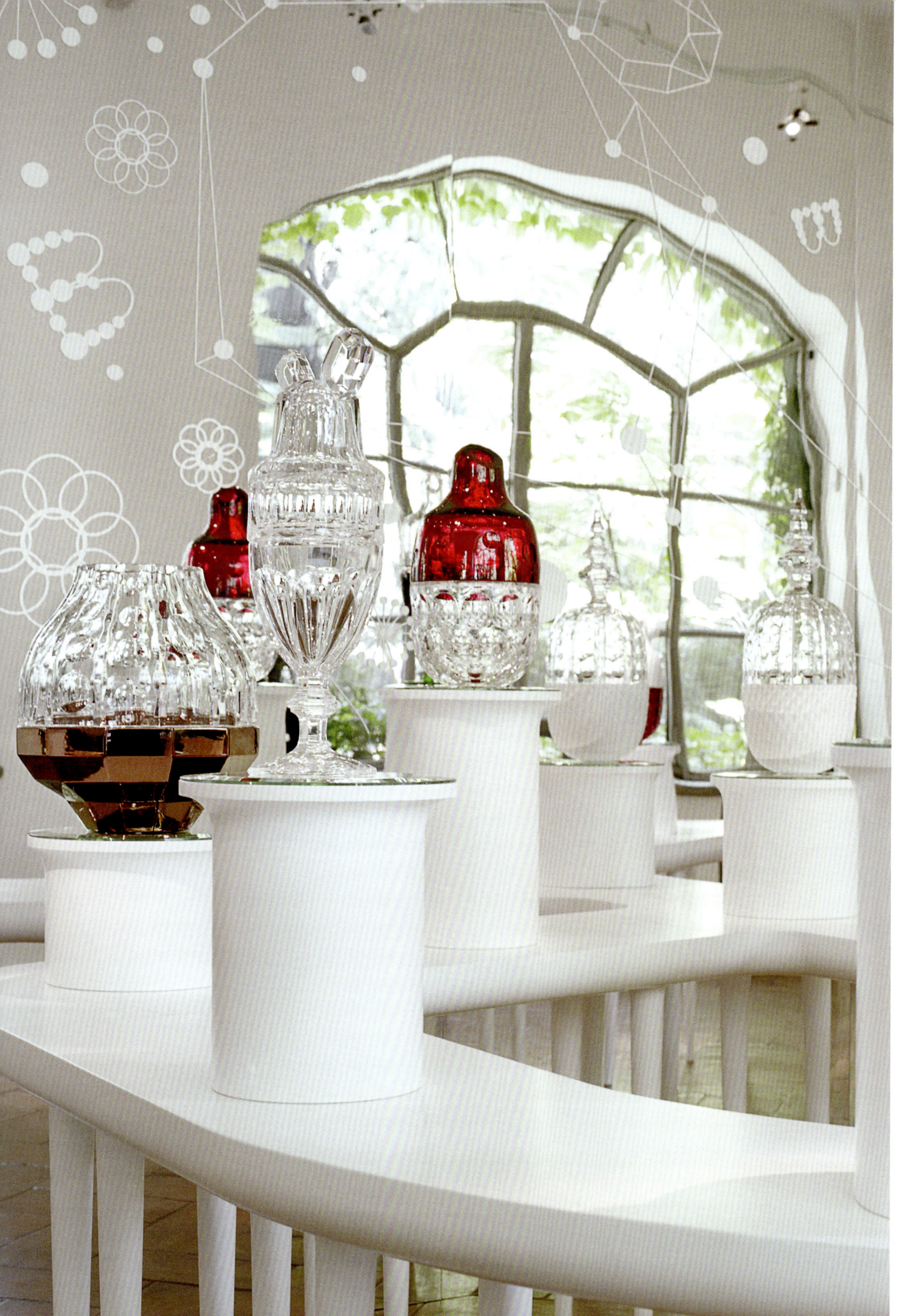

↑ Crystal Candy Set—Limited-edition vases at Rossana Orlandi Gallery, Milan, Italy, 2009
↓ Sketch for tumblers and wine glasses for Baccarat collection, 2018

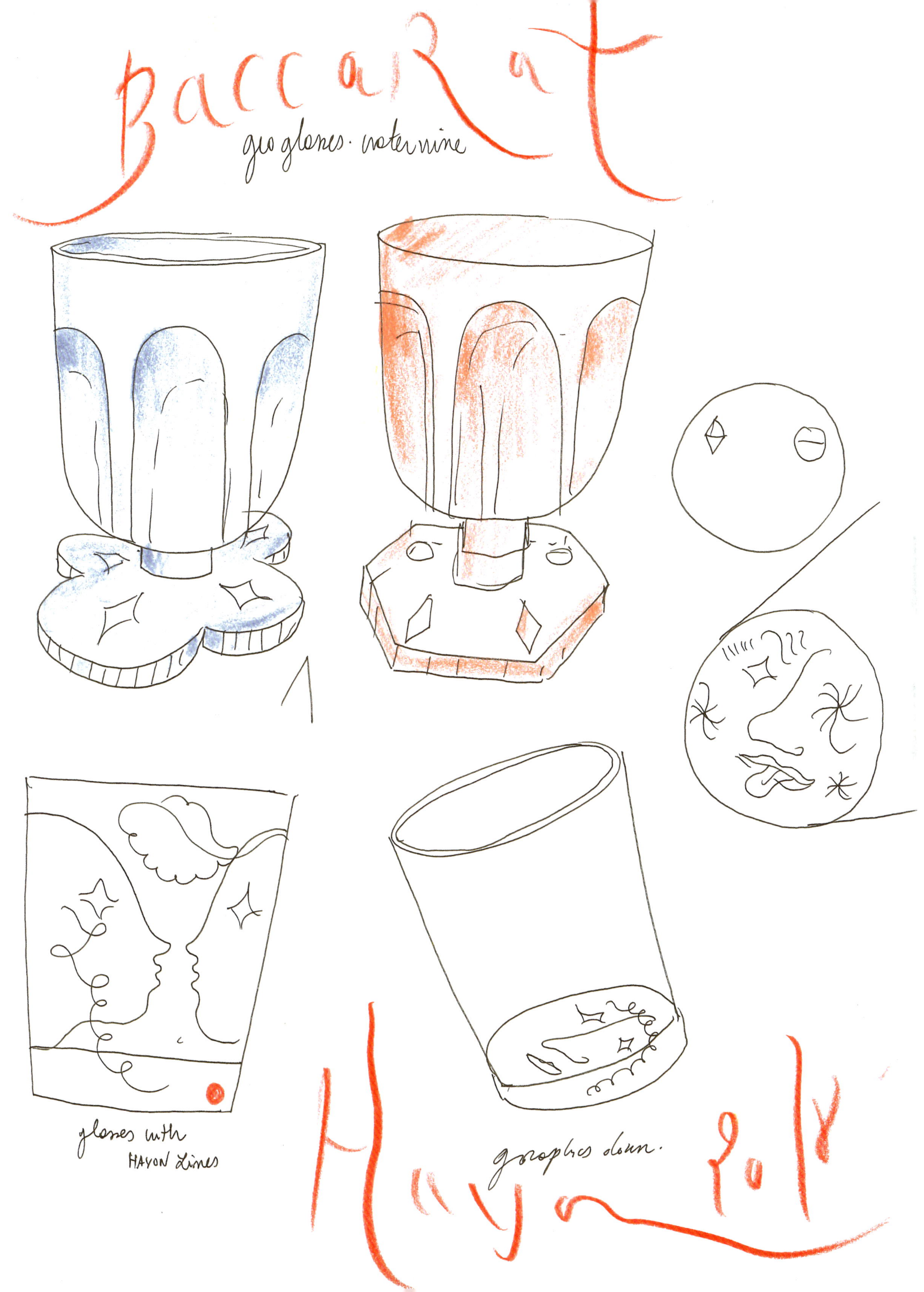

BaccaRat

geo glases. watermine

glases with
HAYON Lines

graphics down.

Hayon 2018

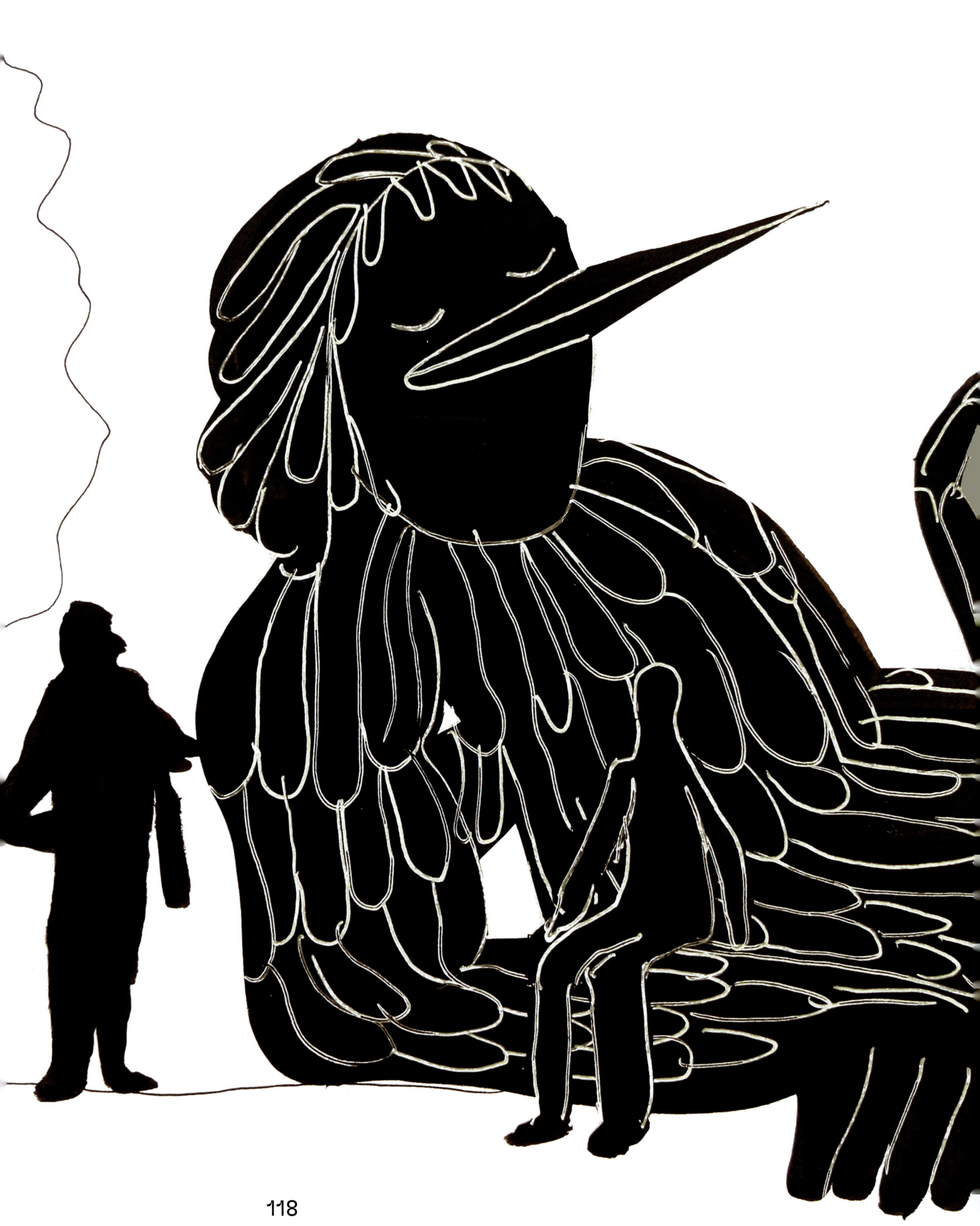

↑ Sketch for sculpture
↓ The Moustache Man—Lithography, 68 × 55 cm, Edition 55, 2022

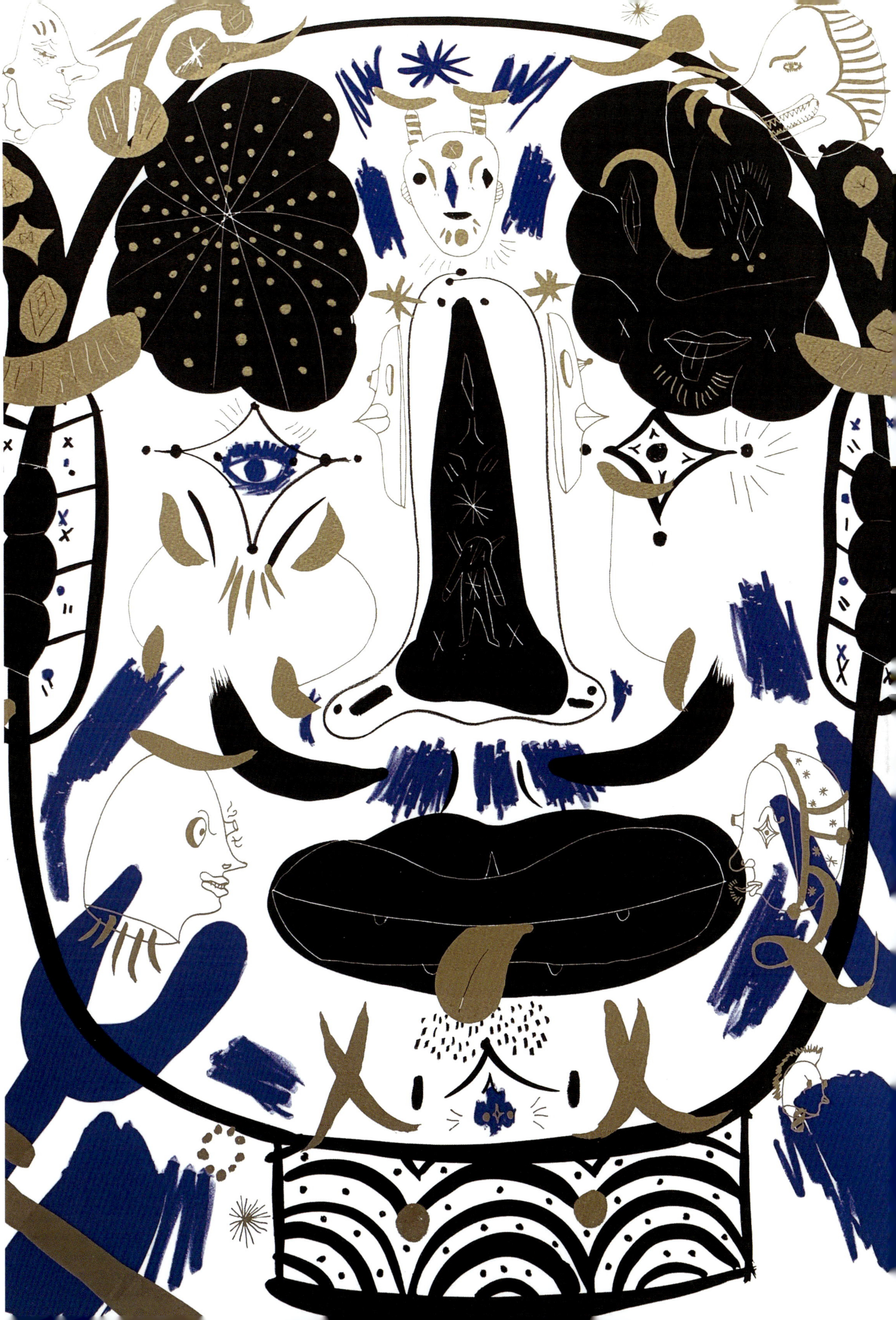

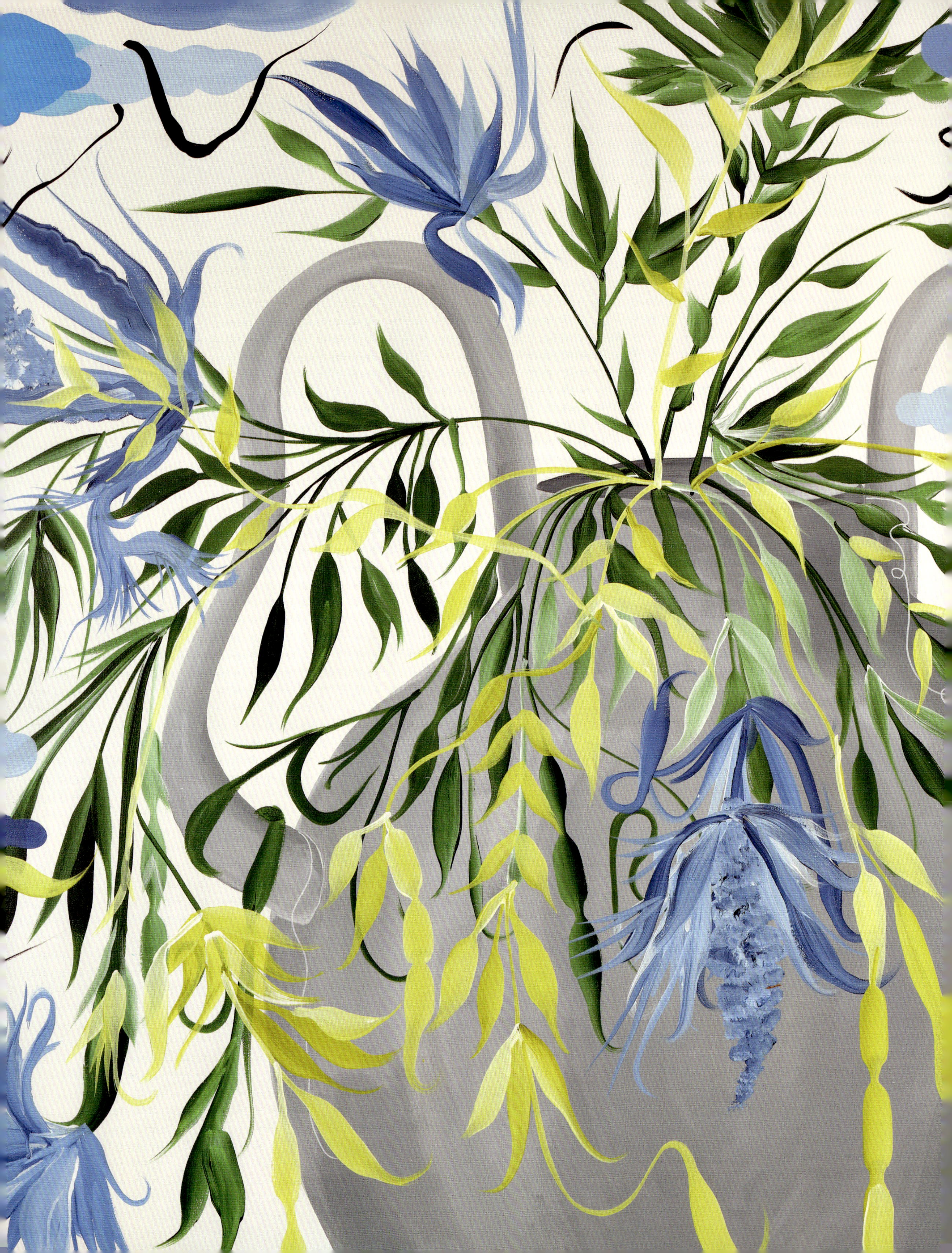

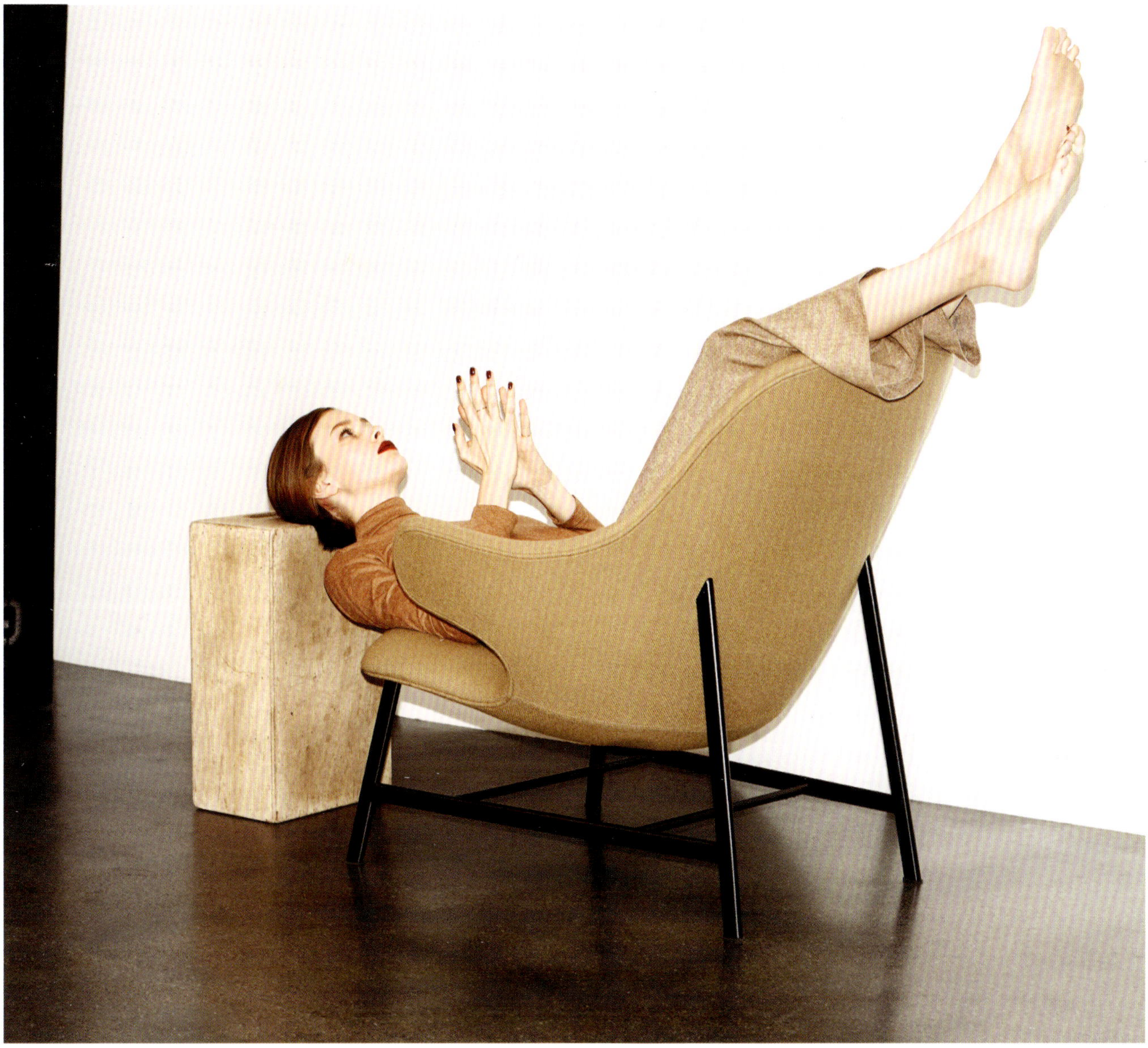

↑ Vase and Clouds—Acrylic on canvas, detail, 2022
↑ Catch JH13—Lounge chair for &Tradition, 2017

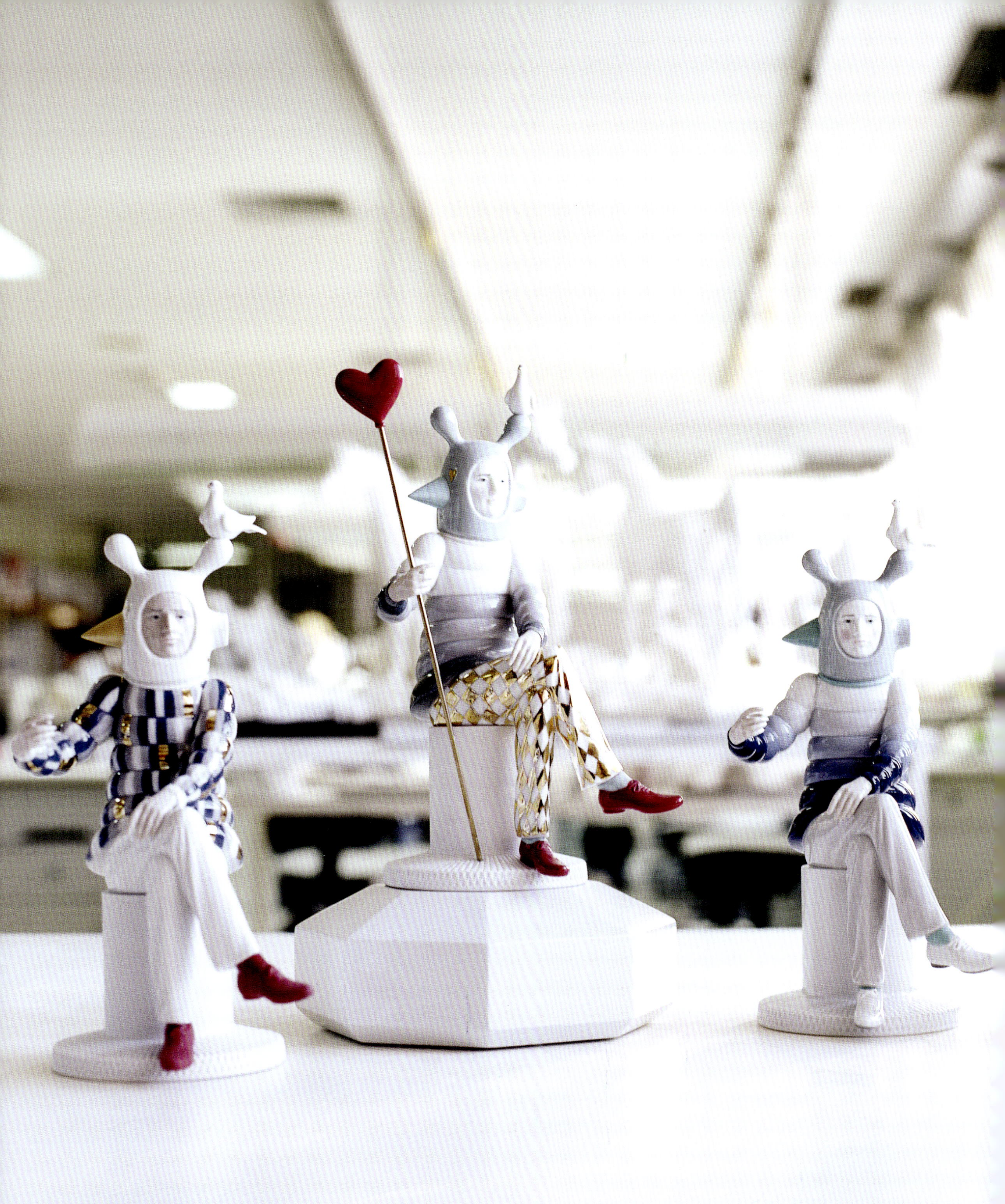

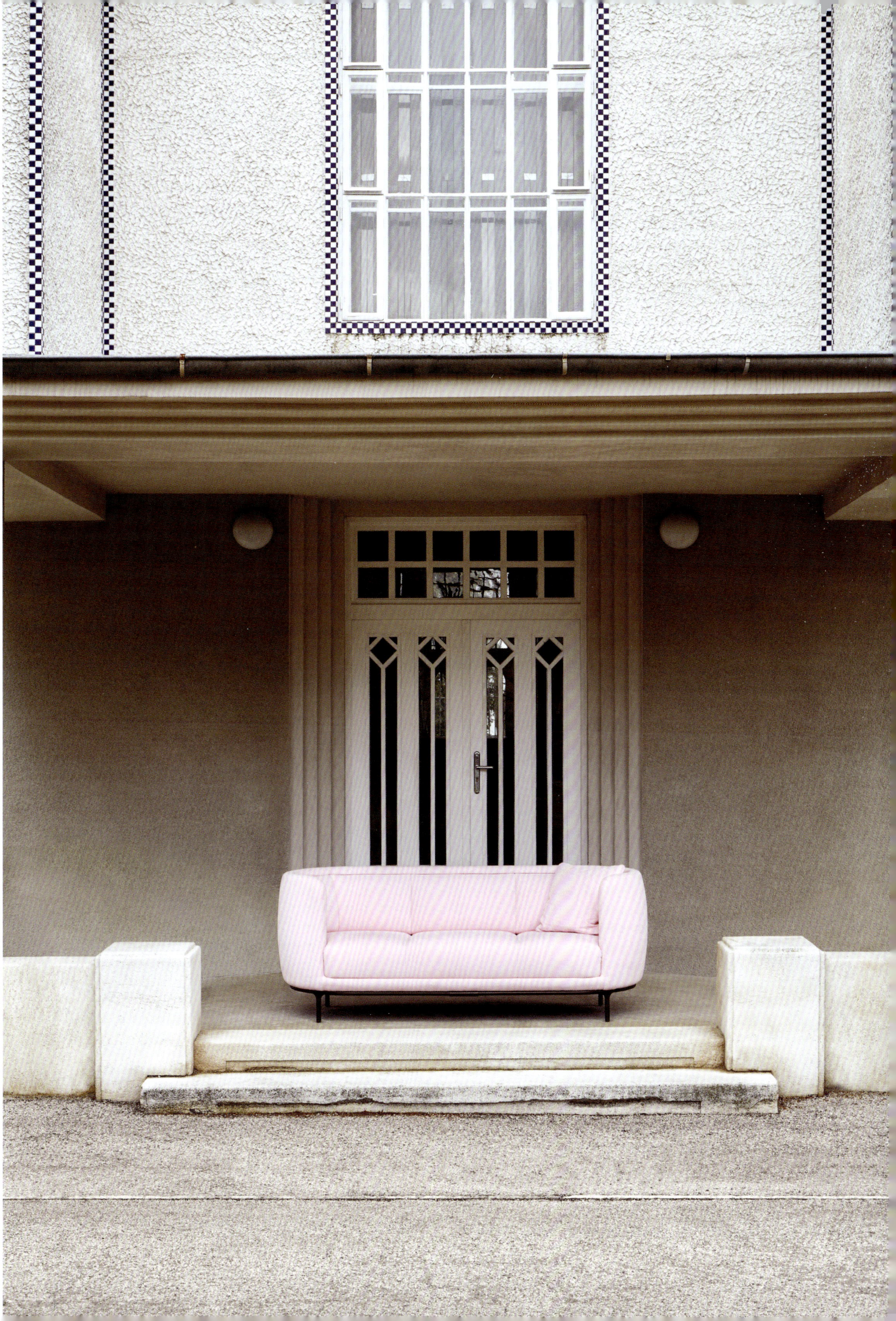

↑ The Lover—Variations from the Fantasy Collection, ceramic products for Lladró, 2008
↓ Vuelta—Sofa for Wittmann, 2020

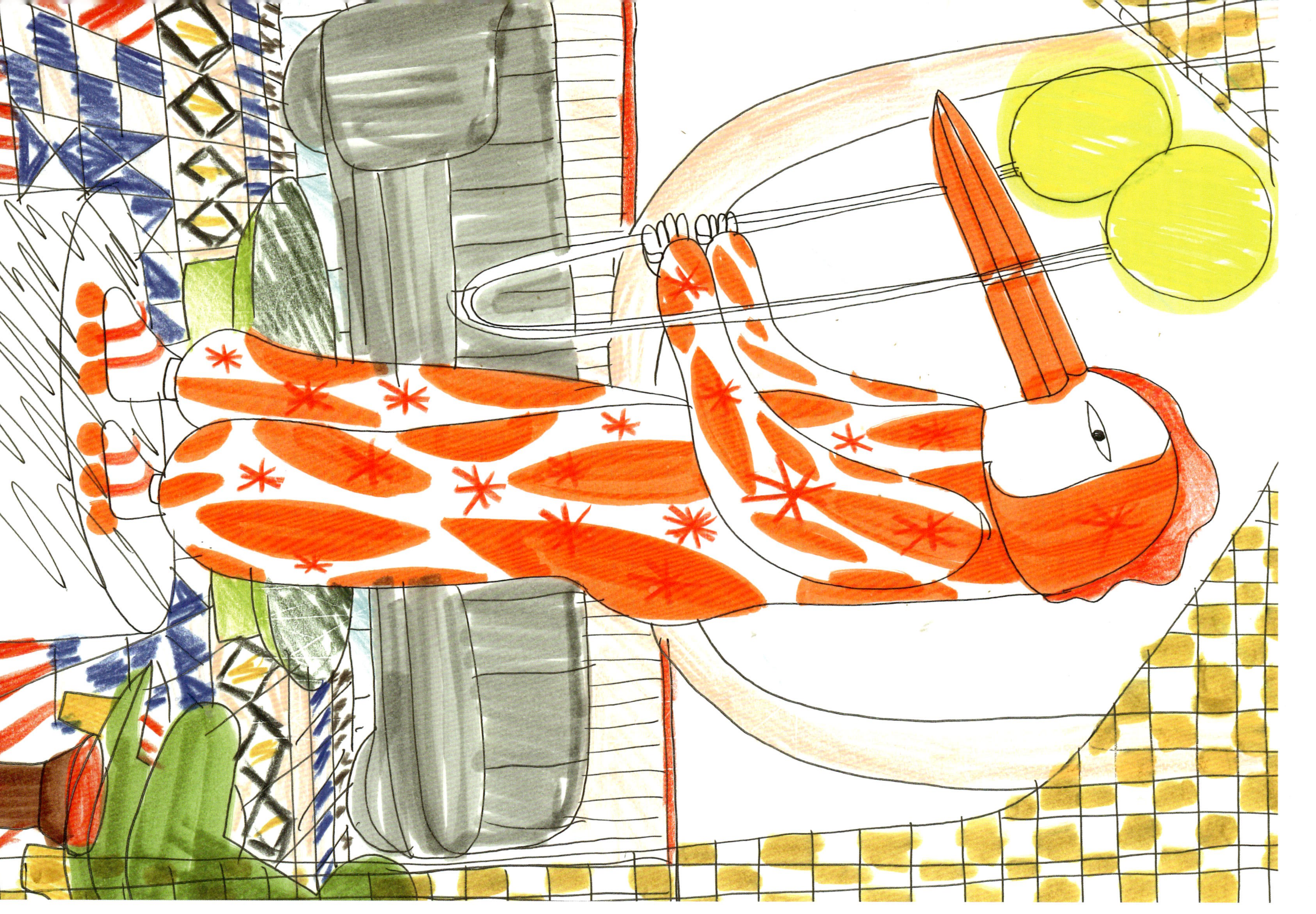

↑ Sculpture sketch for the Hyundai YP Haus
↓ Pangyo VIP Lounge—Mirror and detail, interior design for Hyundai Department Store, Seoul, South Korea, 2021

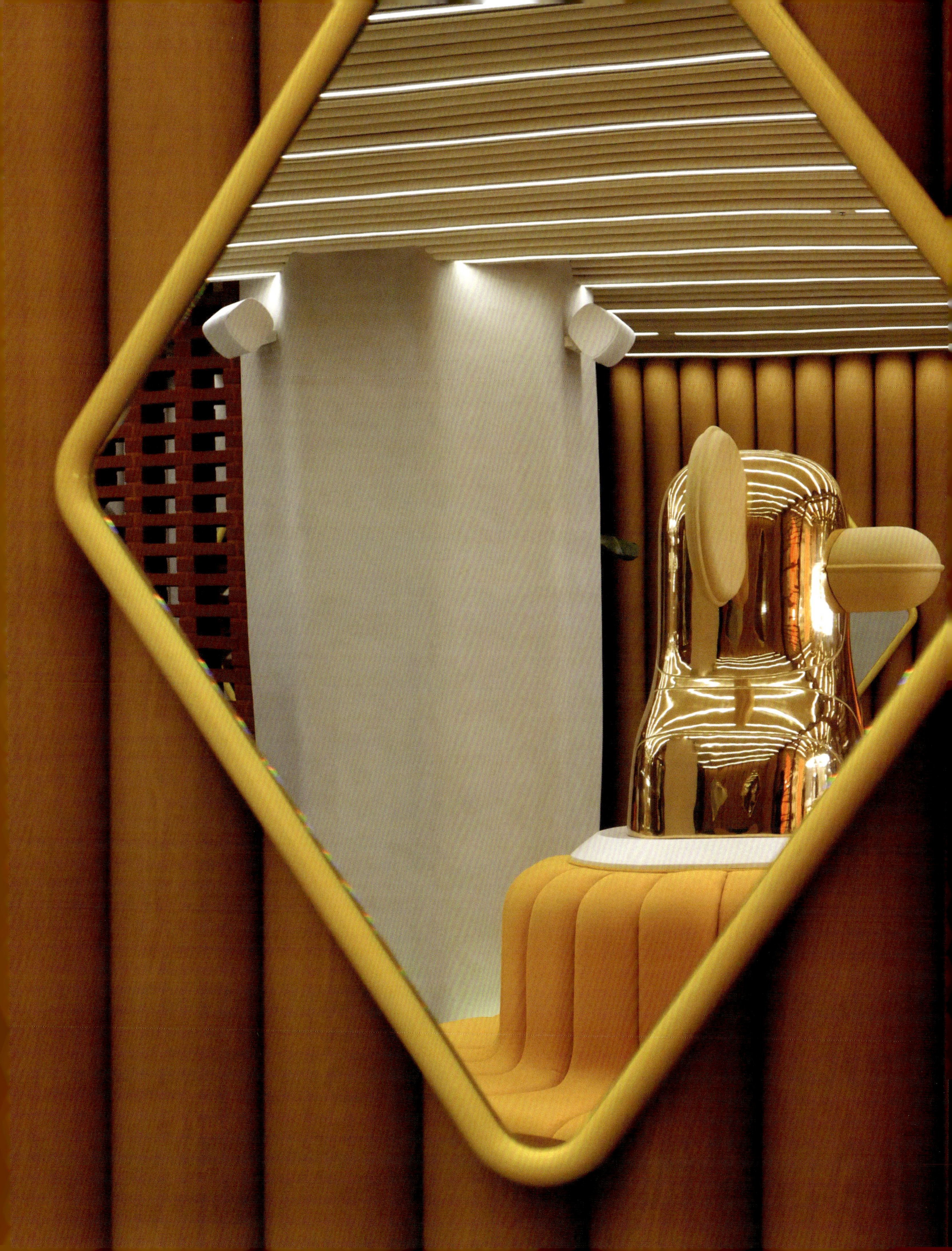

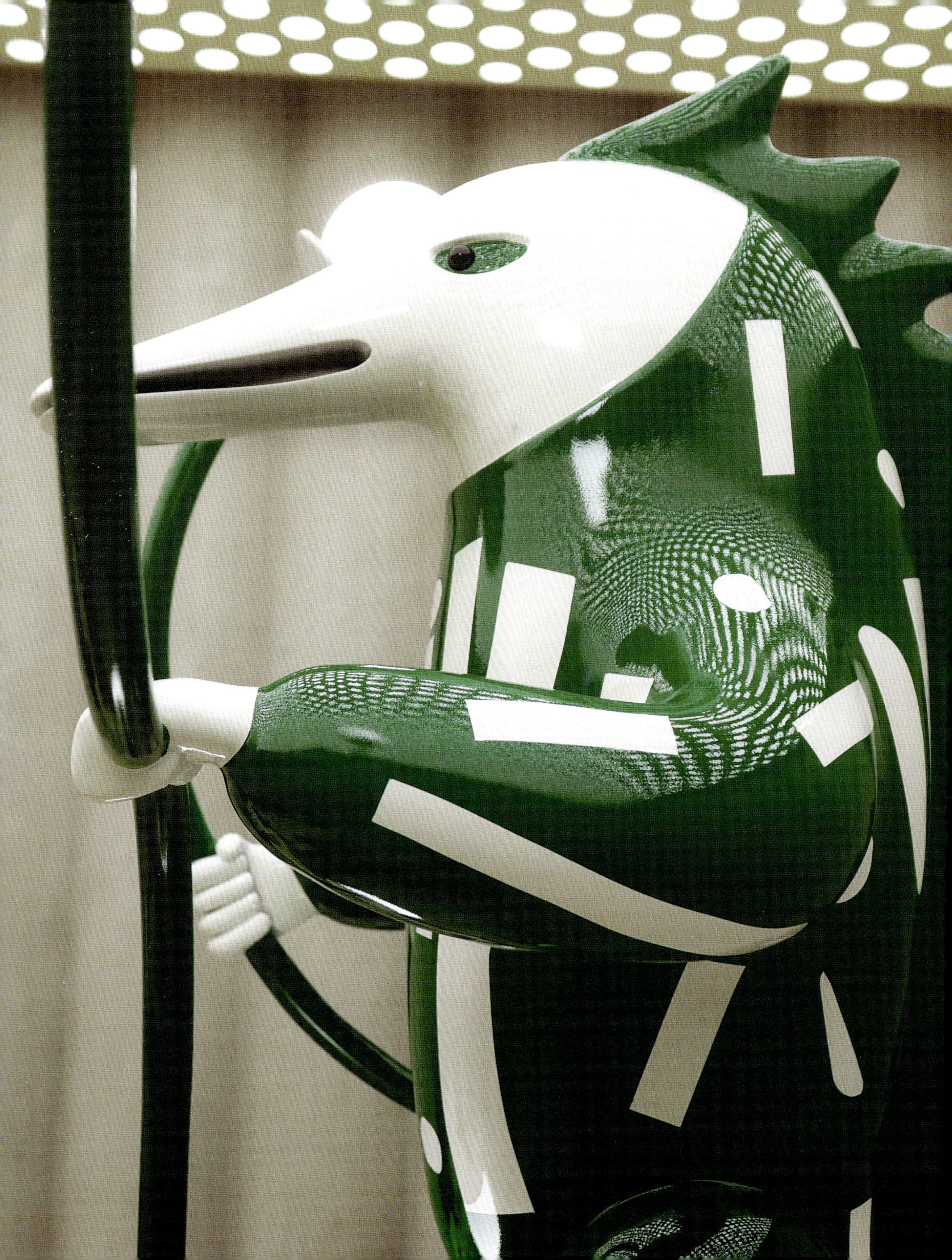

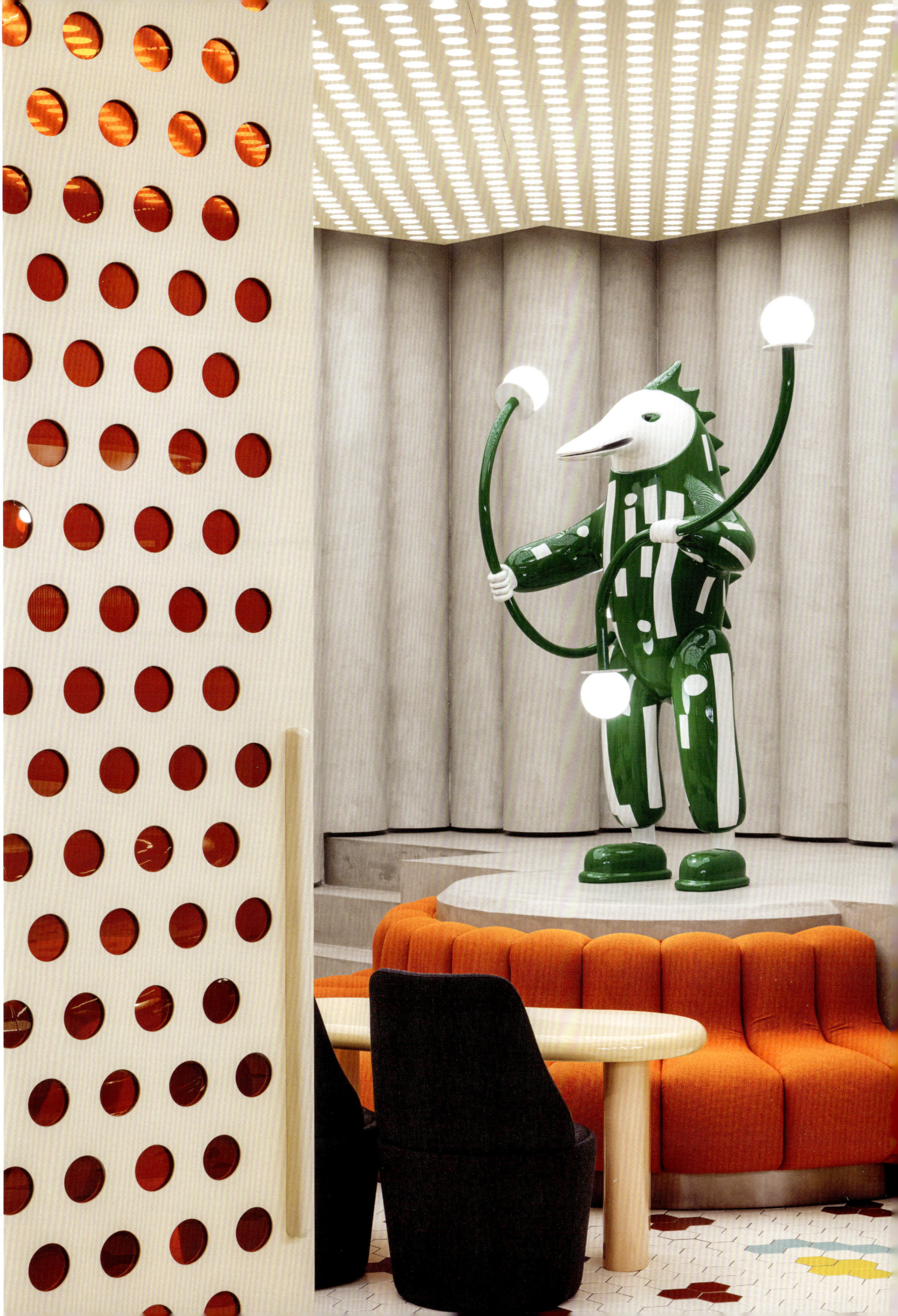

↑↓ Pangyo VIP Lounge—Sculpture and special event area detail for Hyundai Department Store, Seoul, South Korea, 2021

JAIME HAYON

GESTALTEN

Art is at the root of everything Jaime Hayon does. The various texts in this book attempt to convey the maturity and relevance of Hayon's work, taking an intimate look at Hayon's methods, professional approach, and visual research as he weaves effortlessly across several disciplines, including product design, sculpture, and painting. In addition to showcasing the milestones that have distinguished his twenty-year-long career, this book features an extensive collection of images that demonstrates the impressive scope and variety of his work. Particular attention has been paid to his public art, interior and exhibition design, monumental installations, and special projects ranging from collectible editions to contemporary art.

Hayon's relationship with specific materials, his theory of color, his drawing technique, and his ethnographic curiosity in studying cultural and productive contexts all show the proximity between his art and the contemporary debate on cultural appropriation and inclusivity. Ultimately his curiosity leads him to adopt arts, crafts, and techniques from different backgrounds and countries, propelling him into an ongoing process of aesthetic development.

AMIDST THE SEA OF DOING LIES THE LAND OF BEING

MARCO SAMMICHELI

Jaime Hayon started producing his substantial body of work around 20 years ago. It was talked about in the media right from the word go as critics considered him an interpreter capable of transmitting the spirit of his time. Hayon has never been afraid of colour. He chooses to use figurative shapes, and he has never shied away from the media machine—quite the opposite in fact, as he offered himself up as an empathic and versatile product. From the outset he looked on the world as a field of action where he could practice the profession of designer, artist, performer, and all-round communicator.

World Geography

Spanish by birth, Hayon comes from a family that has lived through all different kinds of travel for generations: discovery, escape, exile, rescue, conquest, relocation, commuting, missions, assimilation, leaving no tracks but then discovering them again in order to find the way home. Morocco, Italy, the Netherlands, Israel, China, South Korea, the United States of America, Austria, Thailand, and Great Britain are just some of the countries in which Hayon has set down roots through his work with the opening of professional studios, the inauguration of permanent installations, and the development of cultural and commercial projects that have had a strong impact on local society, thanks to the involvement of museums, universities, companies, and communities. But most notably, every time Hayon visited one of these countries, the things that happened did not come about in a unilateral way. In fact, each context is completely different and should be analyzed in terms of what Jaime did or lived through while there to understand the extent to which the place influenced both his artistic personality and his life on the whole. The people he met, the places he visited, the different cultures he experienced—from the artisanal to the gastronomical, from the artistic to the anthropological, from the natural ecosystem of flora and fauna to the light-heartedness of entertainment and nightlife, every setting has played its part and has been absorbed into his imagination.

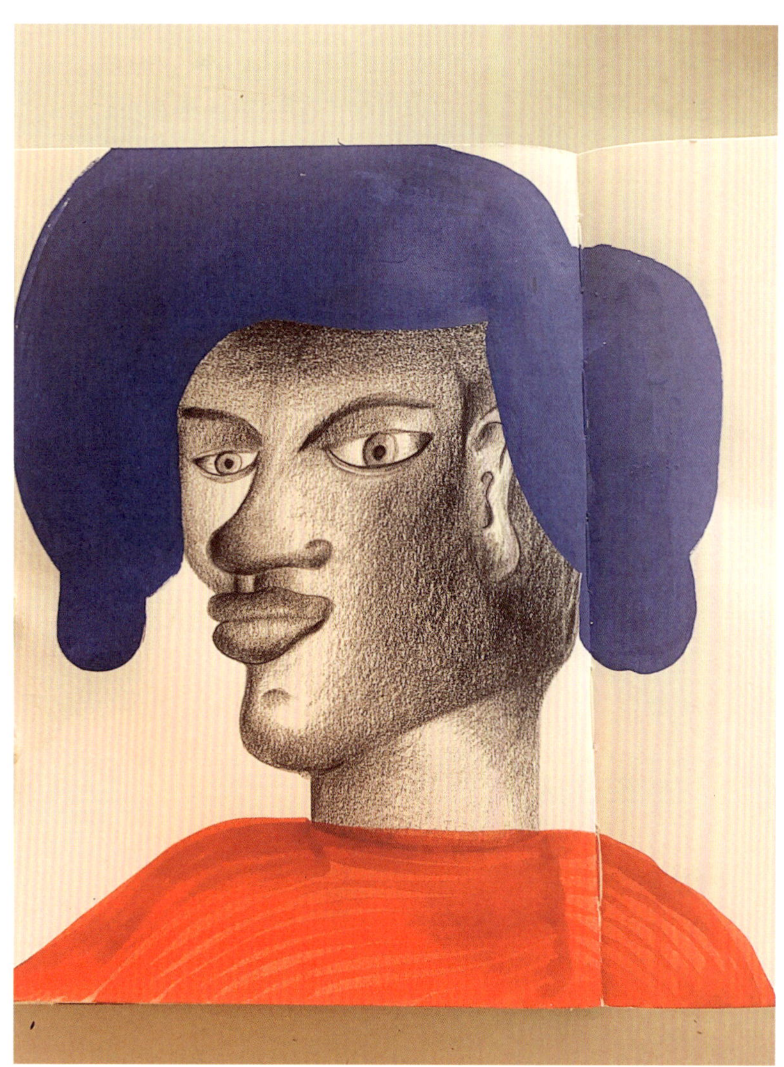

Pencil drawings

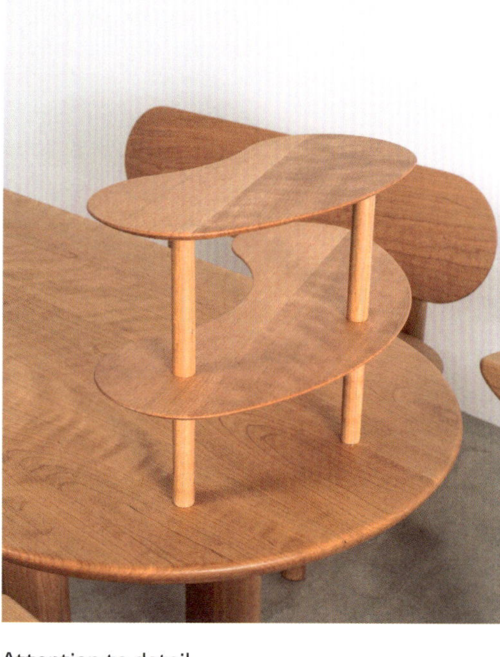

Attention to detail

Like a geographer, like an ethnographer, like an explorer, he lived these worlds to the full. He fed off them and learned from them, drawing on their strength, integrating his experience into his creative vision. Jaime Hayon produced thousands of drawings in hundreds of sketchbooks that contain an untidy and authentic map of inspiration and references sifted from that happy kind of anxiety that every human being has inside. Here the really strong point is his style of drawing. His graphic representations are a powerful visual tool and their openness and generosity allow people to identify and connect with them. Through his drawings Hayon has rendered what was private public, what was particular universal, and what was real-life fantastic.

Body Sketching

The world of Hayon's sketchbooks is very lively. It is inhabited by figures and faces, by citizens of a detailed cosmogony made up of humans and animals, masks, myths, and anthropomorphic characters almost all of which have faces drawn by Hayon. Sometimes it is just a mouth, or a tongue, an eyebrow, a nose, a mole—everything becomes a body. This is a recurring theme in the work of the Spanish artist and designer, who has an urgency to humanize the landscape of objects that he creates, an interesting trait coming from someone who, for a long time, used his own face and body as a tool for communication, often being photographed for the publicity campaigns for the products that he designed. This trait should not be misconstrued as mere revelling in the media limelight but as a precise performative code. Often decorated, made-up, or disguised, Hayon used his body as if it were a blank sheet of paper to draw on. Almost a psychoanalytical transfer, a strategic spell, an allegorical version of a demiurge that creates, moulds, exchanges.

In metaphorical terms it is as if Hayon's world slips in and out of the material substance it is made of, as if the different souls that host his artistic personality have a vast zodiacal spectrum, as if it holds within it all twelve signs, planets, and moons. His talent and multidisciplinary

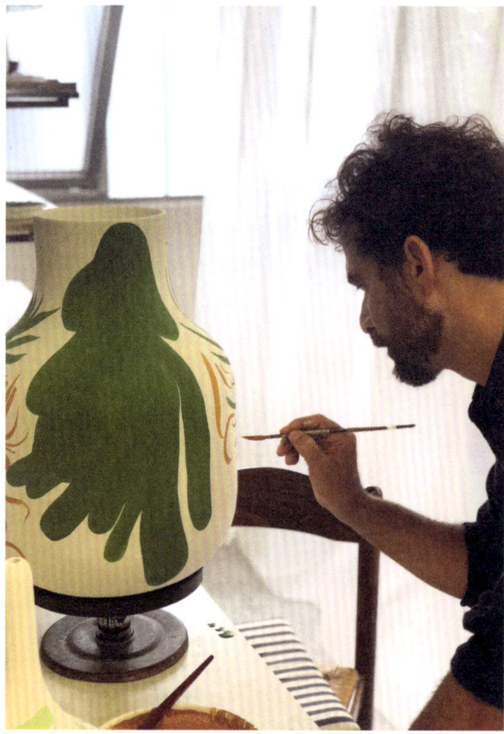
Drawing ceramics
in Veneto at Bosa

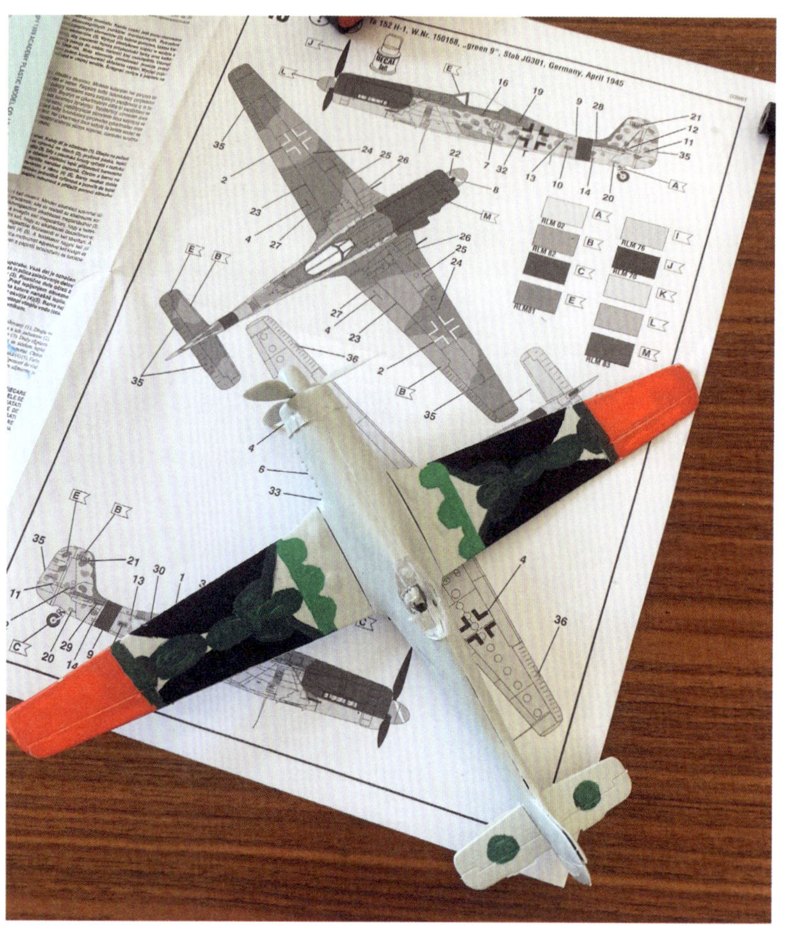
Game time
with Hayon's children

138

approach can easily be applied to different forms of expression. A body made up of several imaginary bodies that are projected into objects and projects. A body that today is also a page, a new space, a place for writing in tattoos, as if there were no limits of what material or format to work on. For Hayon the body is a canvas, a tool, a unit to measure space; the body in movement is mechanics and connections, transgression and care, limit and challenge. It is no coincidence that Hayon designs starting from the study of the body, he designs onto his body, he designs clothes for the body.

One of the first sports that Hayon ever practiced was skateboarding, a physical passion that is not only interesting because of the thousands of references to street culture in his work, but for the discipline the sport requires. Skateboarding is an example of how, just by adding a simple mechanical device to self-discipline, the body can multiply its potential and physical performance. The speed, acrobatics, and personal interpretative style, which is typical of skateboarding, can also be found in Hayon's approach to life and work. What started out as a disobedient subculture on the outskirts of our cities now takes centre stage as an Olympic sport—just like Hayon himself, oscillating between the outskirts and centre stage, never really one nor the other. It is like the theory of cultural anthropology of Masao Yamaguchi, professor at the University of Sapporo. He talked about a tribal figure that connects, chooses, generates, resolves, and is at ease in different social situations. Yamaguchi called this figure the "trickster" and identified it in many civilizations from the strongly hierarchical cultures in Asia to the communities of Native North Americans. The Italian carnival characters stand out as "tricksters" among the European cultures, in particular the characters from Venice and even more specifically the quick and agile figure of Harlequin with his multicoloured costume and various talents that range from rhetoric and creativity to mediation and compassion. This is a bizarre coincidence if we think about how important the Italian region of Veneto has been in the development of Hayon's career. He built a fundamental part of his practice between the provinces of Treviso and Venice thanks to meetings and

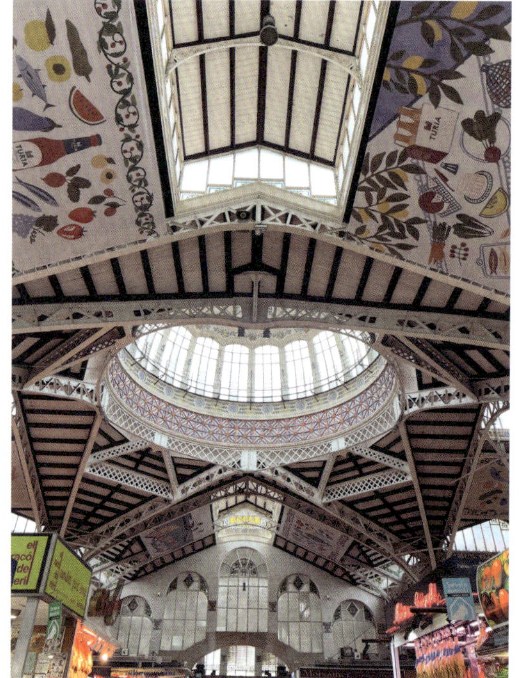

Valencia Central
Market

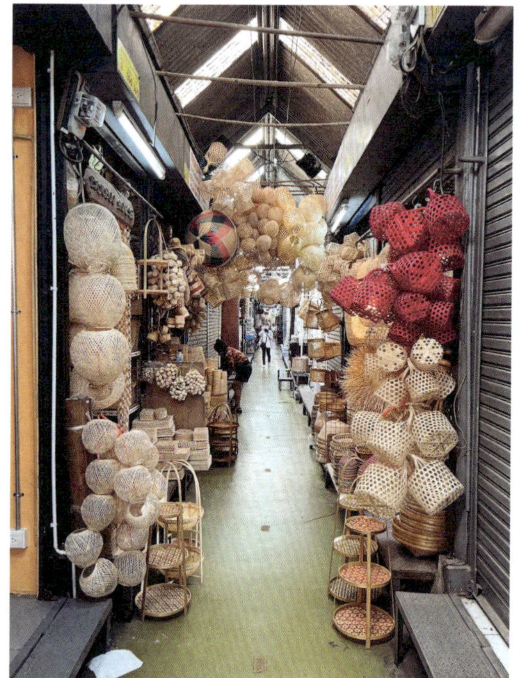

The passion
of shopping
and discovering,
here in a market
in Bangkok

collaborations with local companies and producers. He still has a professional base in the region today with a level of production parallel to that of his Spanish studio.

Citizenship

Years of skateboarding paired with his Iberian rootsmean that Hayon is not only familiar with certain urban cultures but is also used to an outdoor way of life in which socialising and interacting in spaces like the town square is perfectly natural. For this reason, Hayon is drawn to public spaces and nurtures an almost tribal sense of belonging. This tendency is not just due to a Mediterranean attitude but has been ingrained in him by his travels around the world. By assiduously spending time in cities and public spaces Hayon came to understand the generative or regenerative potential of art, infra-structure, and the dialogue between the inside and outside of public interventions.

It is in these spaces that he chooses to set some of his large-scale sculptures. Although commissioned, rather than being purely spontaneous like much of his other work, the public sculptures have evolved over the last few years, providing a number of functions and becoming ever more woven into the urban fabric of the cities they are in. This is public art with a strong sense of social service, because it creates relationships with its surroundings, makes changes to the landscape, and includes a high dose of social inclusivity as it evokes the idea of dynamic free time full of wonder and experiences. The park, whether outdoors or inside, is a concept in which Hayon freely explores his long-standing inspirational obsessions: play, the body, the home, nature.

Hayon does not skimp on colour or materials. In fact his projects are often characterised by the use of large volumes that interact with the surrounding architecture to promote the proximity between places and functions. Once again, this method is the result of his ongoing process of cultural assimilation. Due to his origins, he has a Mediterranean spirit that, with time, has expanded to make space for a variety of new elements and attitudes

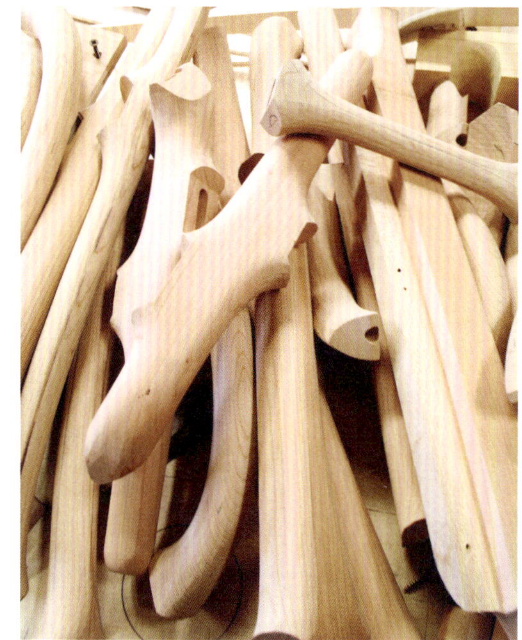

22 pieces of wood
used to create chair

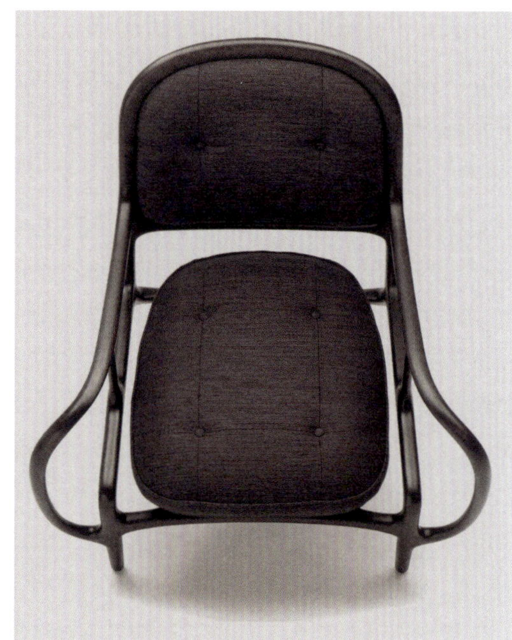

Twenty Two Chair
for Ceccotti Collezioni

from around the world: from northern Europe he has
absorbed the idea of a highly functional space full of
infrastructure; from Latin America the traditions of colour
and texture that represent environments and functions;
from Asia the custom of a space in which the commercial
nature of the market coexists side-by-side with politics
and social exchange; from Africa the tendency to use
height, floors, light, and shade to make the most of every
available portion of space.

Nature & Creation

Two clear tendencies are hidden within Hayon's
relationship with nature. If on the one hand there is the
desire to save something that previously lived in peaceful
automatism, on the other there is the sheer wonder at
a world that is an indispensable and inexhaustible source
of shapes and images. There is also another aspect
of creation that piques Hayon's curiosity and that is the
diversity, the metamorphosis, the hybridization, the
defiance of the endangered ecosystems that have been
subjected to such violent and unchecked transformations.
What was once an object of study for artists and writers
for its mythical and metaphorical meaning is now a
subject of introspection, desire, and fear. Plants, animals,
skies, oceans, and grasslands are no longer just stories
for nature documentaries. They are deep concerns that,
starting with the ancient tradition of zoomorphic
masks, enter Hayon's work to play the dreamlike part
of a "creation gone crazy" made up of binary species
and dual beings.
The nature that Hayon depicts in his paintings,
decorative objects, furniture, parks, and fountains is
mainly that of Aesop, Melville, and Bosch, but recently,
with a strong sense of irony and scandal, he has
started to address the monstrous imbalance created
by humankind's actions by depicting a nature that
explodes, mutates, annihilates itself, incapable of holding
it all together.

ART, NATURE, AND THE BODY. A CHRONICLE OF THINKING WITH YOUR HANDS

JAIME HAYON

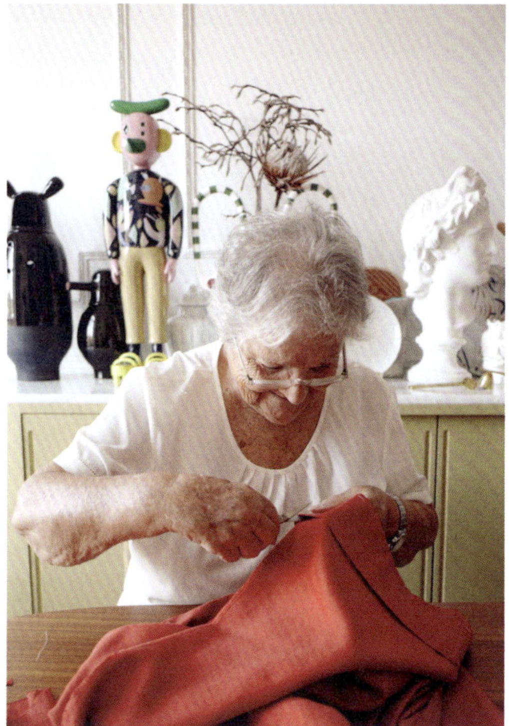

Hayon's mother

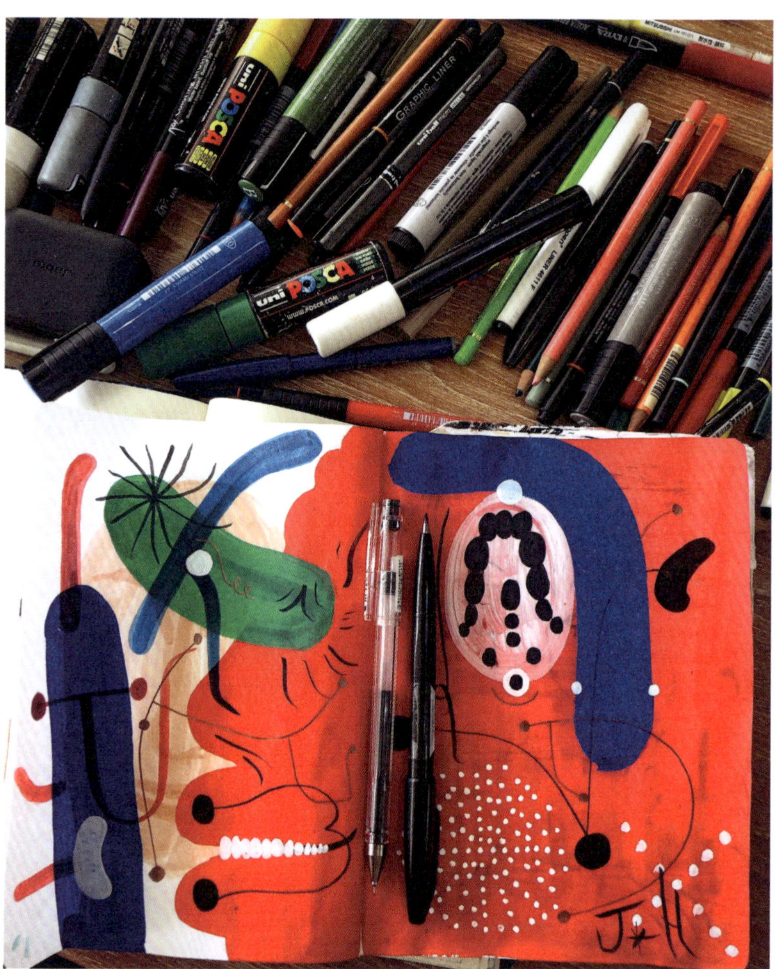

Drawing and sketching
all the time

"For me, skateboarding has always been a way of interpreting the street. The physical obstacles I encountered were excuses for practicing the sport. The dips for jumping, a hole in a flower bed with a tree sticking out of it were opportunities to fall in love with public space. A space of concrete curves interrupted by sudden breaks in the form of natural elements and public sculptures. I remember being a kid, around 1985 or 1986, going to the first skate parks—which, thinking about it now, remind me of Henry Moore's sculptures— and observing phenomena that would go on to become obsessions. I am referring to the texture of the surfaces, the shapes of what I see, the play of light and shadow. The unconscious awareness I had in feeling the road through the skateboard led me to imagine everything as soft, like a wave of the sea. At the end of the day, it is a sport that makes you think about one thing all the time: not getting hurt and not hurting anyone else.

Living the street in this way has always led me to look at public art, such as sculptures in public squares. They are pauses in the urban landscape, like a tree or a park. They are a bridge for urban integration between nature, art, and design. They offer a respite from the speed and aggressiveness of architectural development. Some of my favourite sculptors are Joan Mirò, Jean Tinguely, and Alexander Calder, and not just because of their masterful use of colour and volumes but for their ability to inhabit a space, to generate movement, and to activate a performance. Even if you do not move, these works of art mutate in the light, so you experience the same principle of the Earth in relation to the Sun— gravity, rotation, and transformation. This was another starting point for my public sculpture projects in Atlanta and Hong Kong, or even, going right back in time, at the Bisazza Foundation in Veneto. The transition from the two dimensions of drawing to the three dimensions of sculpture is based on a clear desire to reproportion elements and use scale in a different way every time. This is something that I believe I absorbed both from my fascination with surrealism and from Toy Art and its dramatization of play and of underground culture. Both cases, however, provide immediate enjoyment,

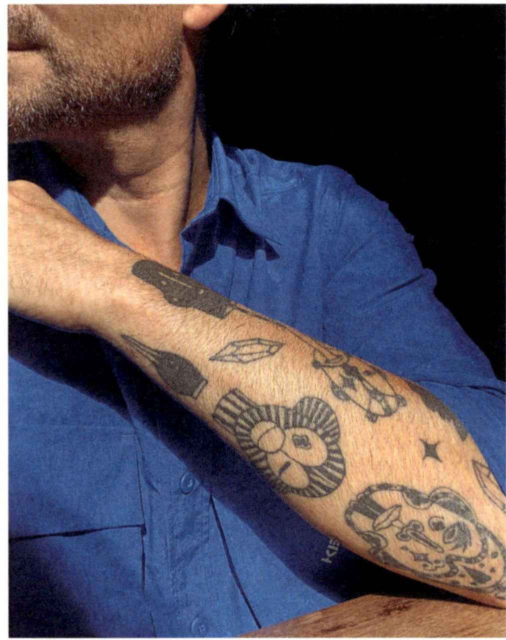

Body as a canvas

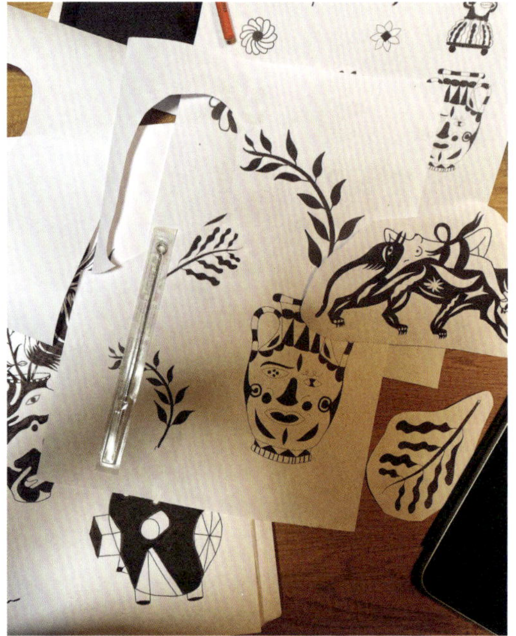

Research for tattoo

a fusion of different perceptions and allusions without a
hierarchy or priority, without categories. I believe in the
character of original forms, in inhabiting bodies, in evoking
anthropological, anthropomorphic, and zoomorphic
references. Inhabiting art makes me think of sculptures as
micro works of architecture for children who can really
experience them through play by using them as meeting,
places or dens, while adults might find the hyperbole of
an archaeological site that evokes the traditions of ancient
Egypt, Chinese literature, Korean customs, or Spanish
street culture. My world lives on art and it presents itself
as an open artwork because it allows the public that
experiences my design, my art, and the spaces I create,
absolute freedom of interpretation and experimentation
without any constrictions. **"**

" I am incredibly inspired by nature. After living the
last 25 years of my life without ever stopping, I have
come to realise that it is through nature that God exists
and expresses himself. I believe that the greatest creative
potential can be found in the force of nature. This is why
I never stop observing and depicting it. Flora and fauna are
a constant source of inspiration. Cats, cockerels, birds,
lions, elephants—they all lend themselves to creative
domestication, to becoming something else, even though
their relationships with humankind have been very clear
throughout history. In my world they become inhabitants,
ingredients that I mix together with absolute respect.
I look at their skin, the textures, how and what they eat,
where they live. Each environment comes into mine and
merges with a philosophy which is as much an approach to
life as it is an idea for the domestic space. It was not
by chance that I decided to move to Valencia, to a more
peripheral context compared to other large cities.
I wanted to experience the contrast between city, sea, and
countryside, feeling the sun on my skin, because I find
great inspiration in lands of contrast. Places like Lanzarote
and Thailand are where the genius of nature in relation
to the conditions of the surroundings creates colours and
shapes. When I am in nature, I open my third eye. **"**

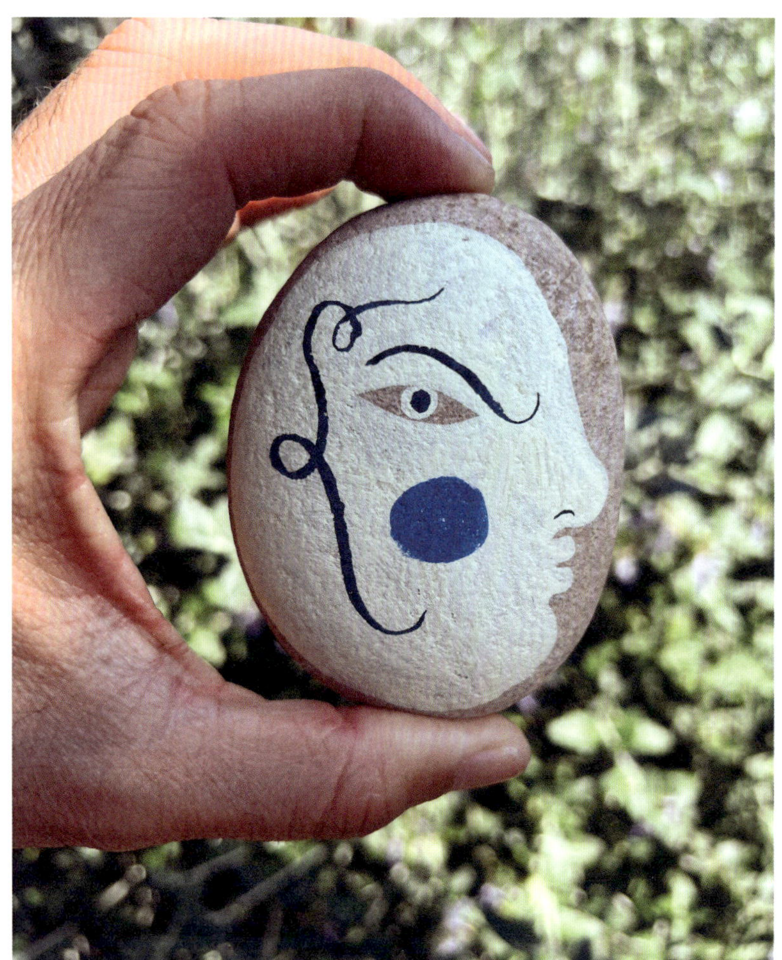

Silhouettes

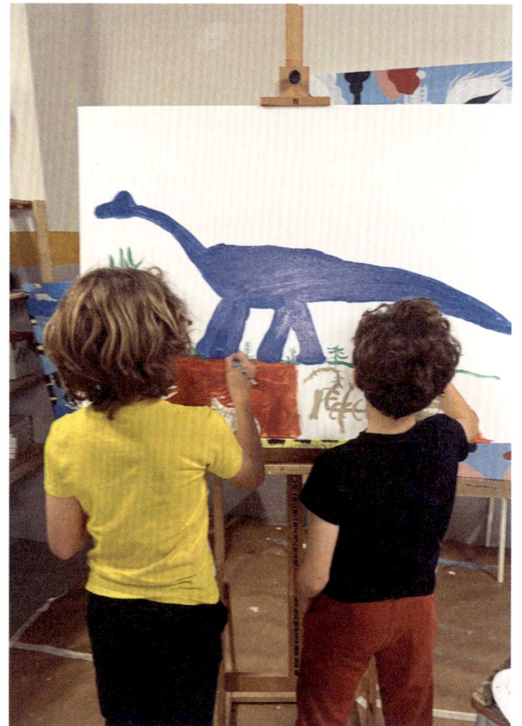

Hayon's children

"I actually find an equilibrium in nature that I try to bring back to my body through sport. In movement, especially gymnastics, there are strong connections between the parts, the mechanics and the relationship with light and shadow. The neck and spine are the perfect essence of femininity, softness, unity, and the transition between geometries and levers. Just think about dance and the moment in which the leg and foot of a dancer touch the ground. The artistic expression that passes through the body, with or without the aid of a costume, is close to perfection, a correlation between body, space, and objects. For me, the body contains a myriad of solutions that, when combined with language, become a universal code. This is what I look for with my work, for ways to leave a mark, in any expressive field, without distinction. It is no coincidence that, with the strong limits that contemporary society imposes on us, I have also chosen to express myself through tattoos. I need to have my drawings on my body, to mark the moment, to look inside me. It is a way of trying to overcome a disparaging idea of yourself. Even so, through work, I strive for technical perfection, as if it were—every time—a date with a woman, who in this case, with humility and courage, with risk and constancy, is a kind of absolute perfection."

HI-ME
HI-ON

NOTES
ON AN
ANTHOLOGY
OF VOICES

In 2006, in an article for the *Observer*, Dominic Lutyens voiced some very accurate considerations about Hayon's work. Through his own comments, quotations from the designer, and statements from critics, the journalist pinpointed the disruptive energy that would characterize the next two decades of the Spanish artist's career. The initial exuberance of the costumes and masks Hayon used and the performative aspect of the presentations of his furniture collections 20 years ago were all part of a strategy that brought together aesthetics, poetry, marketing, and identity.

For the curator Emily Campbell, "Jaime is a big personality who builds a culture around himself. But I'd never describe him as egocentric. He's one of those intellectually fearless, energetic people who dives right into the debate and is as fluent with language as he is confident with form." His neo-baroque design, maximalist ethos, and his unique way of mixing different historic styles have all brought Hayon closer to an international audience.

Aram Zeev, of London's historic Aram shop and gallery, said: "One could easily interpret Hayon's work as merely fashion-oriented, but his work is of a very high quality. There's a really imaginative mind there, coupled with a brilliant sense of humour."

Writer and critic Alice Rawsthorn is of the same idea: "In the early nineties, design was dominated by fairytale romanticism. Since then, a group of European designers has emerged with an exuberant, neo-baroque visual language that mixes product, interior, and graphic design. We live in a post-industrial culture in which most objects have been reinvented so often that it's becoming harder for designers to improve upon existing types. That's why product designers, like Jaime, are increasingly using graphic design to make their work seem fresh. They don't accept the old-fashioned, rationalist distinction between product and graphic design. Looking at Jaime's dolls, it's impossible to tell the difference, and it doesn't matter."

In the summer of 2007, *TIME* magazine included Hayon in its list of the World's 100 most influential designers. In the statement he released to Betsy Kroll,

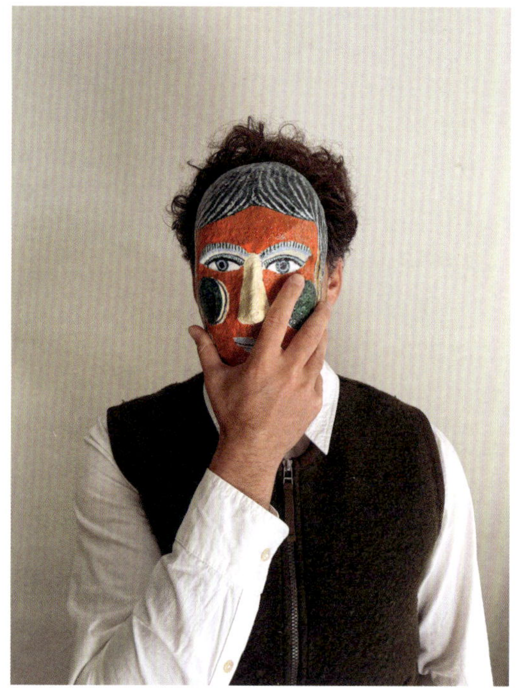

Mask by Parkpardon

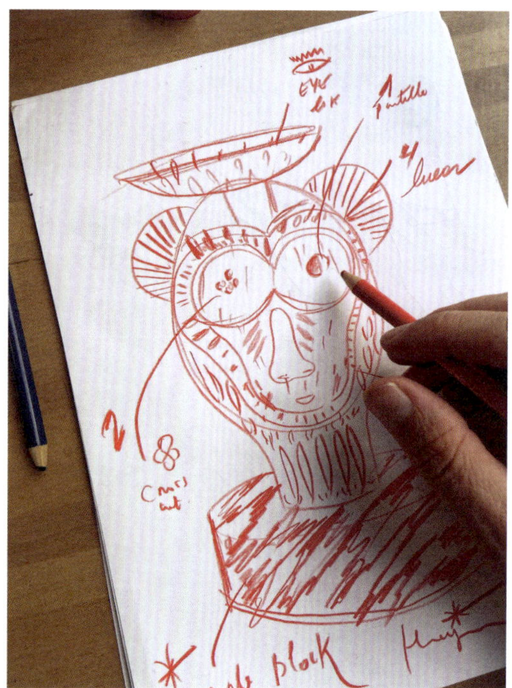

Sketching nonstop
for projects

Hayon said: "I think design can be much more than art. I work with intuition. If they say white, then I go black. And maybe in that black, there's a little bit of white." More than 15 years later, I am not sure how much Hayon would relate to this declaration, but there is certainly still a trace of its essence in his work, which shows the boldness of creative choices that are based on instinct, on an intuitive approach that is nourished by a constant, all-encompassing search for new ideas.

Just a year later in 2008, Armand Limnander, in an almost arrogant way, attempted to fit Hayon into a specific conceptual box in an article published in the *New York Times Magazine*. He talked about "visual extravaganza" and underlined how "Hayon's trajectory is as unconventional as his work". Hayon's unclassifiable spirit and refusal to conform to the canons of society have led him to believe in self-taught knowledge and experimentation by osmosis. "I'm a big believer in learning by doing, and I have ideas to last me a lifetime. I'm not an architect, but not knowing everything can be an asset when you're creating, because you're not limited by what you think is impossible. Plus, you can always find someone to help with practical details—what matters most in the 21st century is having a great concept."

In 2016, in the cover story of the magazine *OnOffice*, Helen Parton went over some of the aspects that, amongst the public and critics, have always created an attachment to Hayon's work. In Hayon's visual world, Parton argues, the viewer is taken on a narrative journey shaped by a combination of shapes, colours, and anthropo-zoomorphic references. It is a state of unpredictable excitement, where the boundaries between art and design evaporate as they merge into a single project. The Iberian press often refers to Hayon's world as a "mundo interior". Throughout his career this uniqueness has led him to coin a number of neologisms such as "Scandinavian tropical". For Hayon, it is just a way of approaching things: "Put together two words that don't match and you have something new. ... Inspiration comes from conversations—it comes from being open to new things. It's not hard for me to come up

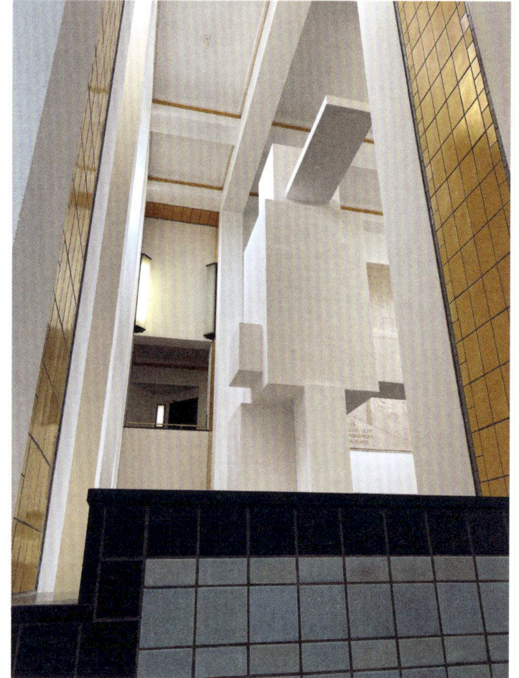

Kunstmuseum
Den Haag

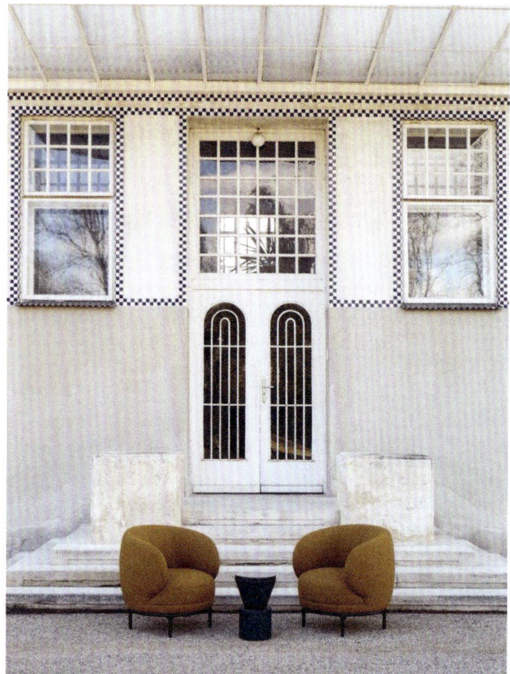

The importance
of history: outside
Josef Hoffmann's
Sanatorium
Purkersdorf with
Hayon's designs
for Wittmann

with new ideas. I look for shadows in the morning to sit out in my house in a village on the outskirts of Valencia where the people have no idea what I do."

Hayon's popularity amongst a vast and varied public is proved by the success of his exhibitions and museum installations. Hayon has worked with a long list of curators, including Galit Gaon, Sue-an van der Zijpp, Sarah Schleuning, Li Edelkoort, and Ana Dominguéz Siemens, and he has exhibited his work in China, South Korea, the United States, Israel, the Netherlands, and Italy, to name just a few. "Funtastico" at the Groninger Museum was definitely the first exhibition to bring Hayon's semiotic mosaic and characteristic approach to composition into a museum. Van der Zijpp wrote, "Apparently effortlessly and without any evident hesitation or second-guessing, he draws elegant lines with thick felt pens on the huge canvases. His efficiency, precision and speed are astonishing, evoking associations with automatic drawing, a technique practiced by the surrealist. Indeed, his work clearly displays stylistic correspondences with this movement. ... It is a cacophony of ideas, bizarre figures, jokes, stories and loose ends, events and fantasies. Subsequent sketchbooks have a longer format in which the drawings, now more precise and more elaborate, are grouped around a concrete project.

As for his source of inspiration, Hayon claims: "It's all about creating my own individual world and about improving things that already exist. Of course you can point to influences, but I am primarily myself. I take inspiration from objects for children, for example, such as toys—and even more so now I have children of my own. But I am also attracted to kitsch, nostalgic objects, forgotten corners, trashy alleyways, things that others often find ugly, bizarre, scary, or in bad taste—I find them marvelous! Regardless of how ugly we often consider them to be, there are also things that are part of our collective memory. I often see something, such as this, for instance," pointing at an image of a somewhat unfortunately modelled earthenware teapot in the form of a chicken, "and then I think, 'Hey, I can do something with this.'"

ARCHIVE
1993–2022

HAYONSTUDIO

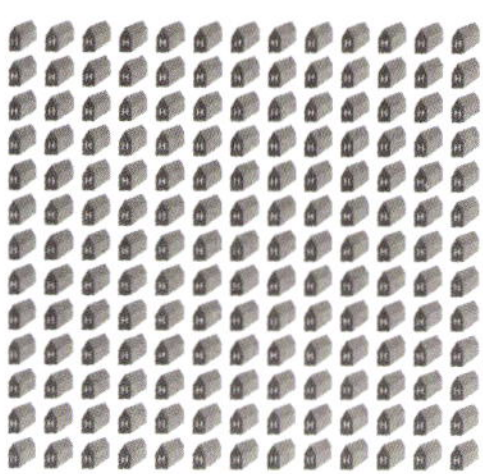

2000
Hayonstudio creation

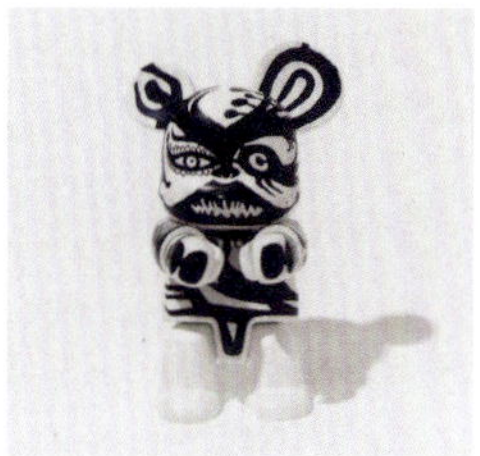

2002
Art Toyz collections
for Toy2

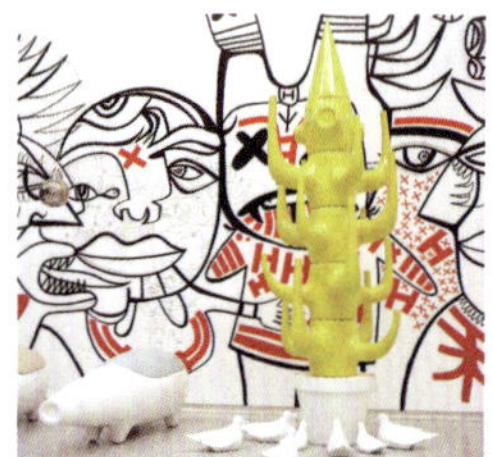

2003
Mediterranean Digital
Baroque exhibition
at David Gill Gallery,
London, U.K.

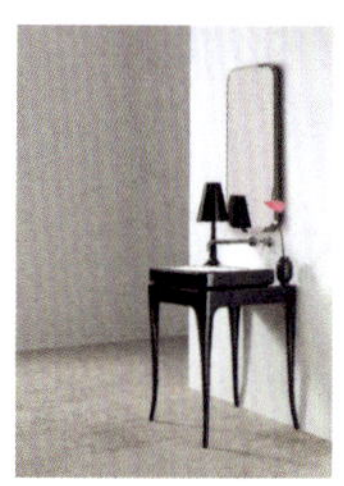

2004
AQHayon bathroom
collection, ArtQuitect
Editions

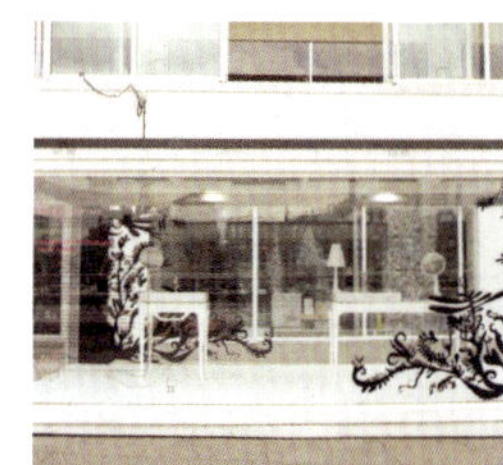

2004
AQHayon Collection
featured in the Tank
at the Design Museum,
London, U.K.

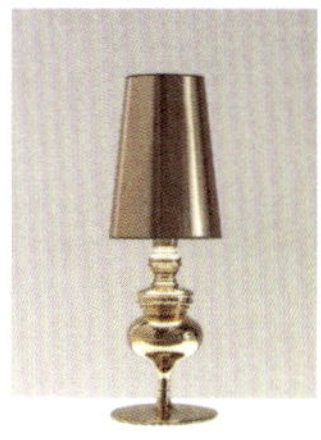

2005
Josephine table lamp
for Metalarte
P. 221

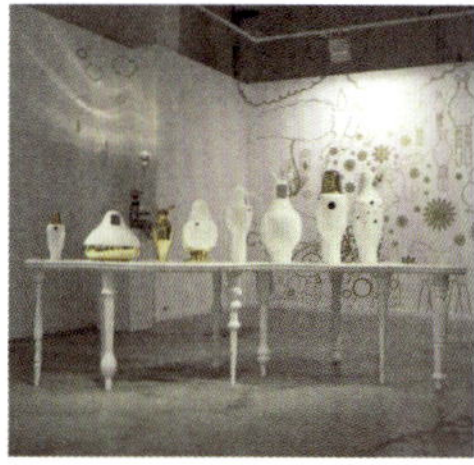

2005–2006
Mon Cirque exhibition
at Iguapop Gallery,
Barcelona, Lisbon,
Minneapolis, Paris,
Cologne & Kuala
Lumpur

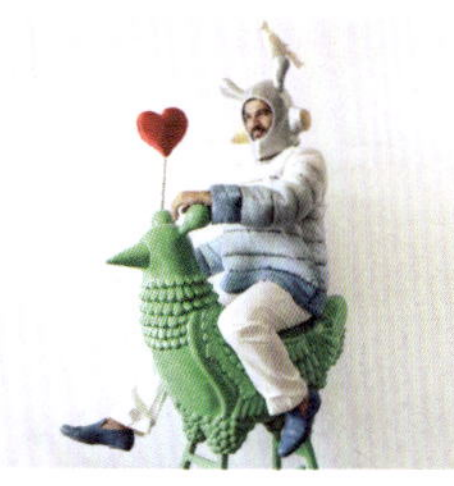

2006
Green Chicken,
sculpture for
Contrasts Gallery,
Shanghai, China
P. 73

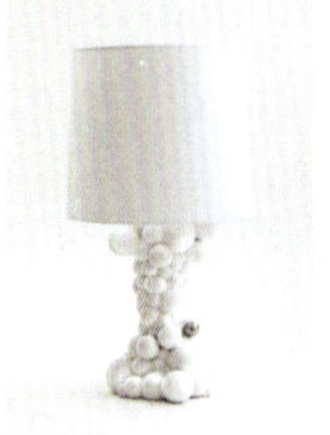

2006
Hayon Ceramics,
products for
Bosa Ceramiche

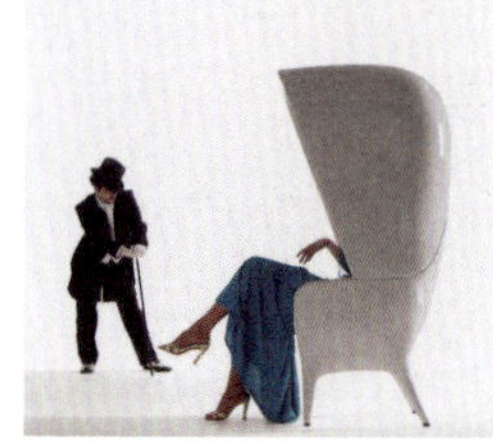

2006
Showtime Collection:
seating, cabinet, vases,
table, and chair for
BD Barcelona Design
P. 260

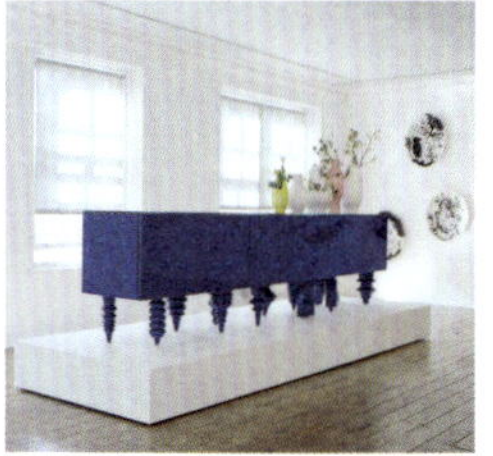

2006
Stage, installation
at Aram Gallery,
London, U.K.
P. 261

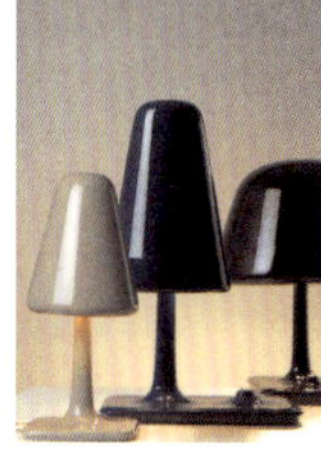

2006
Funghi Collection,
ceramic lamp family
for Metalarte

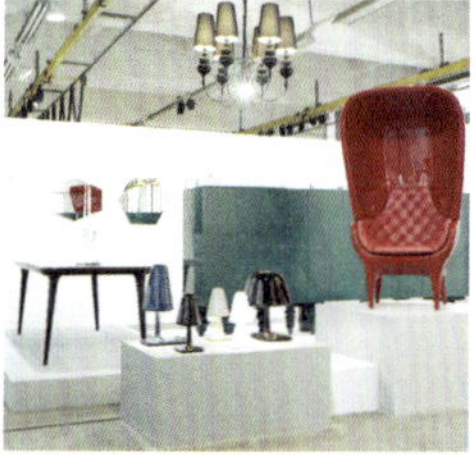

2007
J'aime, design
installation at Salone
del Mobile, Milan, Italy

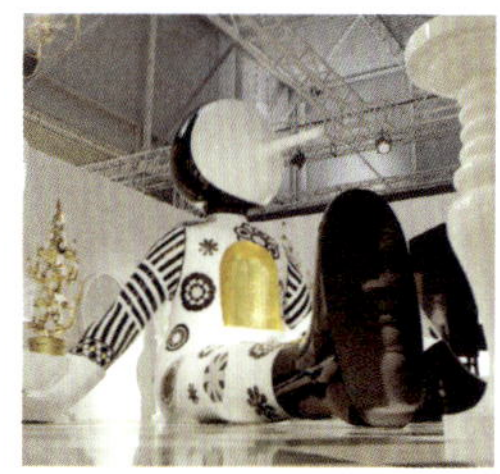

2007
Bisazza: Hayon Pixel-
Ballet, installation
& limited edition for
Bisazza, Milan, Italy

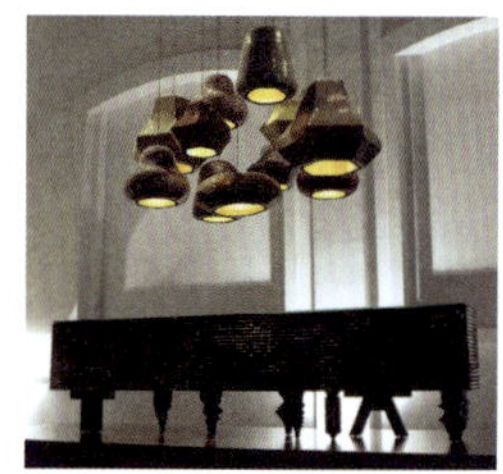

2007
Sparkle Shady, lights
& cabinet for Swarovski
Crystal Palace,
Milan, Italy

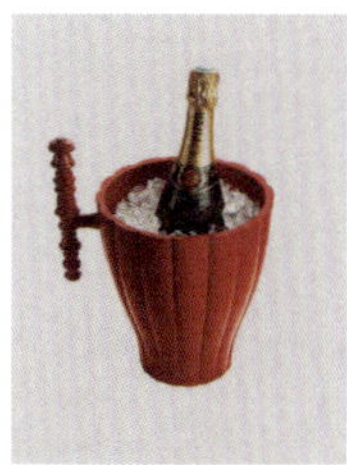

2007
The Seau & Vasque,
champagne containers
for Piper-Heidsieck

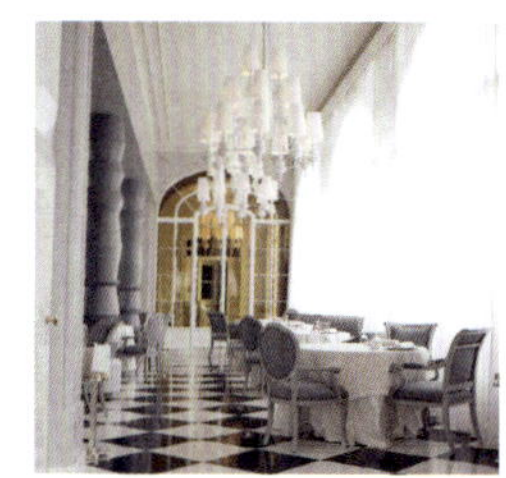

2007
La Terraza del Casino,
interior design for
a Michelin-star
restaurant, Madrid,
Spain

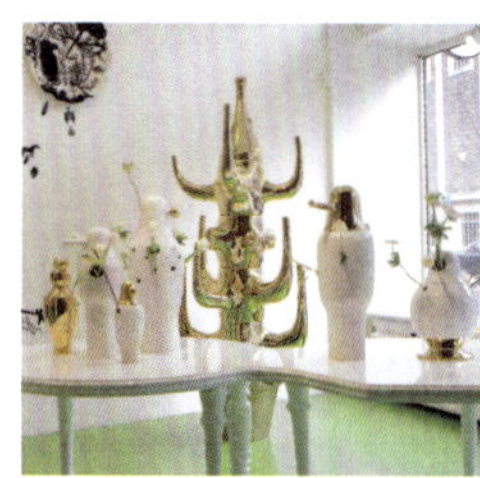

2007
Stage, installation
at Vivid Gallery,
Rotterdam,
Netherlands

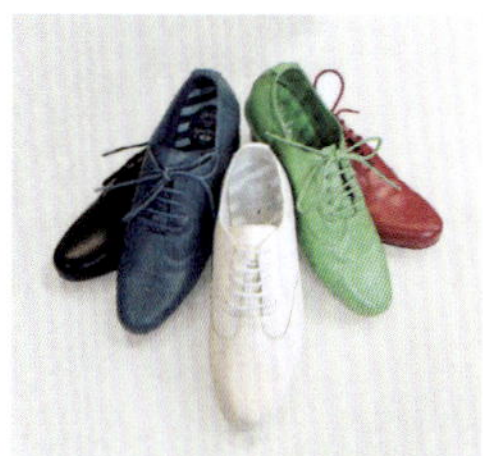

2008
Camper Shoe,
collection & interior
design for Camper
shop in Carnaby
Street, London, U.K.

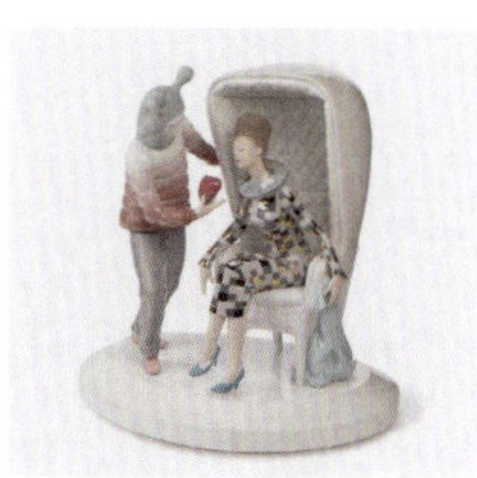

2008
The Fantasy Collection,
ceramic products
for Lladró. From
2007–2011 artistic
advisor for the brand

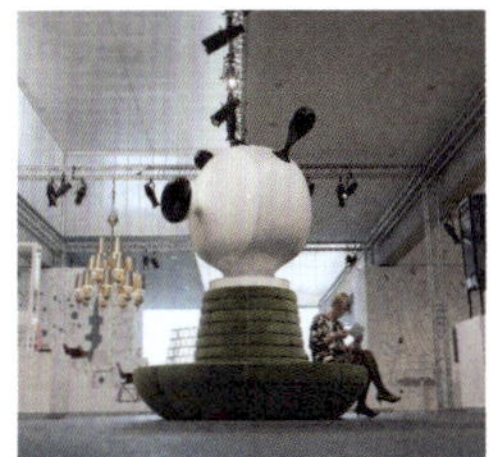

2008
Guest of honour,
installation for
Biennale Interieur,
Kortrijk, Belgium

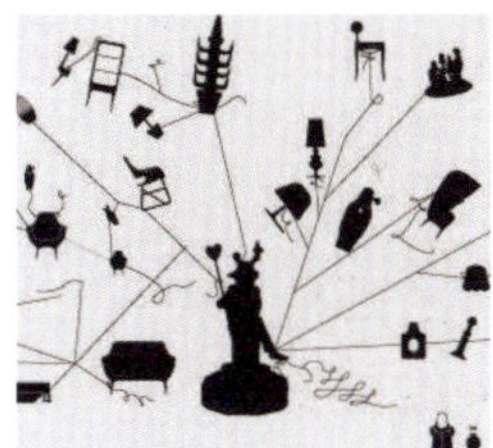

2008
Stage, installation
for Isetan,
Tokyo, Japan

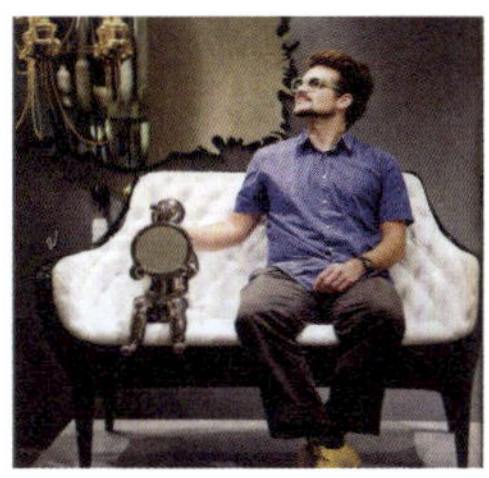

2008
Stage: Jaime Hayon,
installation at Lane
Crawford, Hong Kong

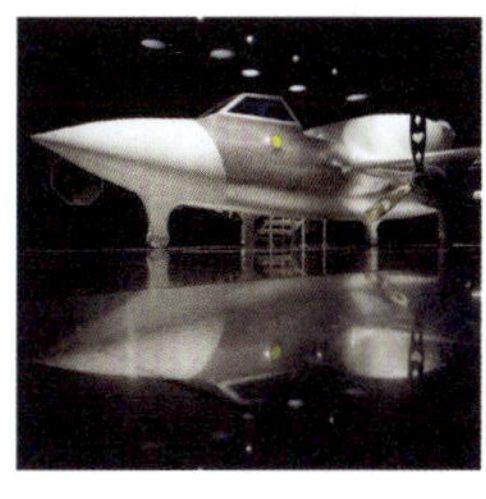

2008
Jet Set, installation
for Bisazza, Milan, Italy

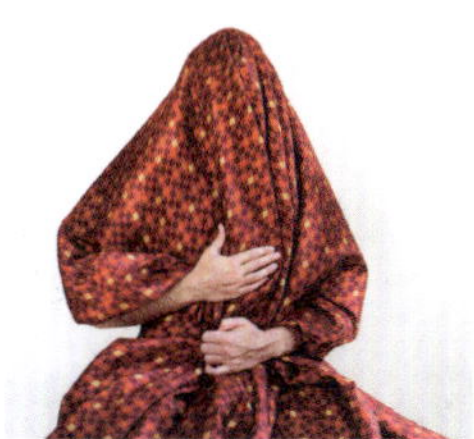

2008
Serious Fun, textile
collection for
Bernhardt Design

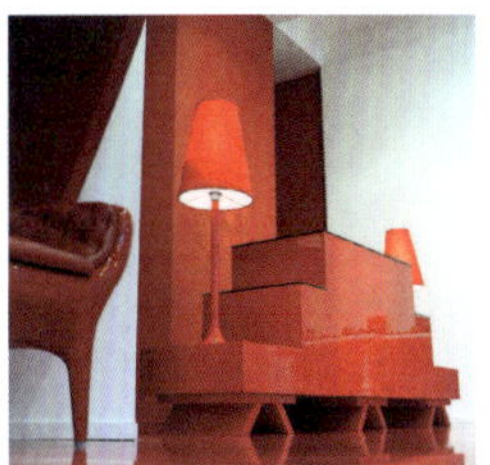

2008
Camper Shops,
interior design in
Barcelona, Mallorca,
Paris & Milan

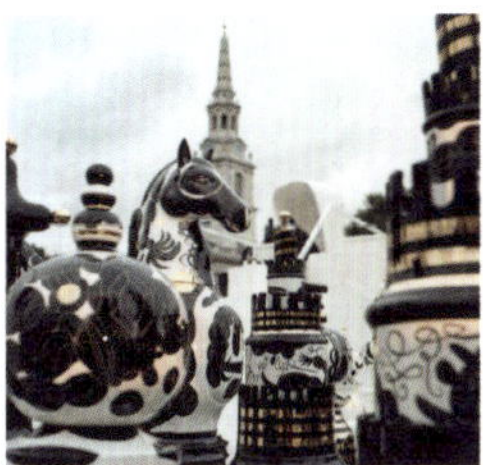

2009
The Tournament,
installation in Trafalgar
Square during
the London Design
Festival, U.K.
Pp. 9, 240–241

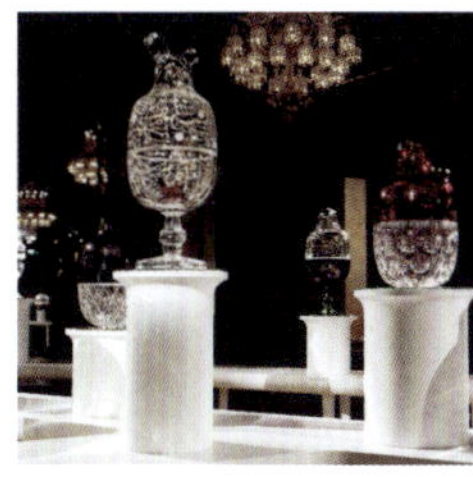

2009
Crystal Candy Set,
installation at Baccarat
Salle de Bal, Paris
& Rossana Orlandi
Gallery, Milan
Pp. 116, 266–267, 292

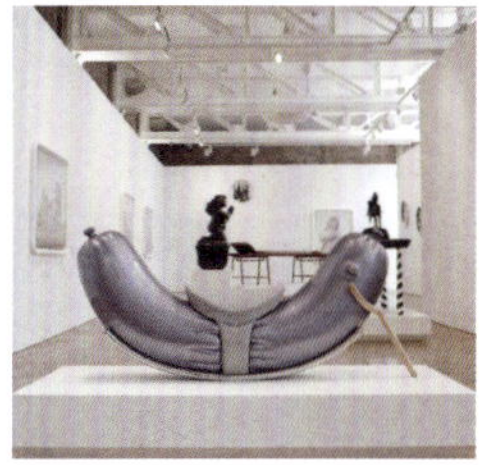

2009
American Chateau,
exhibition at Spring
Projects Gallery
London, U.K.

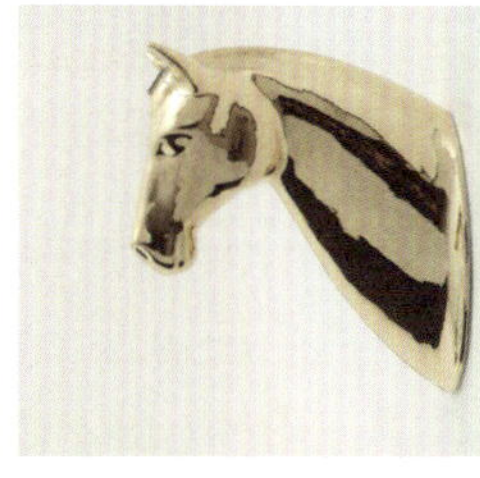

2009
Jaime Hayon, ceramics
exhibition at British
Ceramics Biennial,
Stoke-on-Trent, U.K.

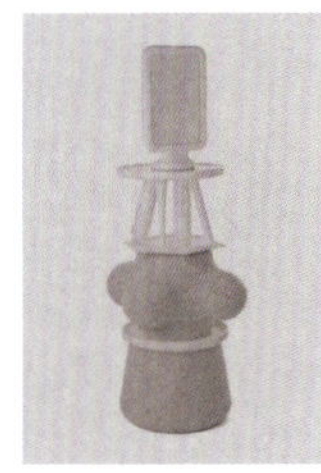

2009
Elements, stackable
table collection
for Moooi

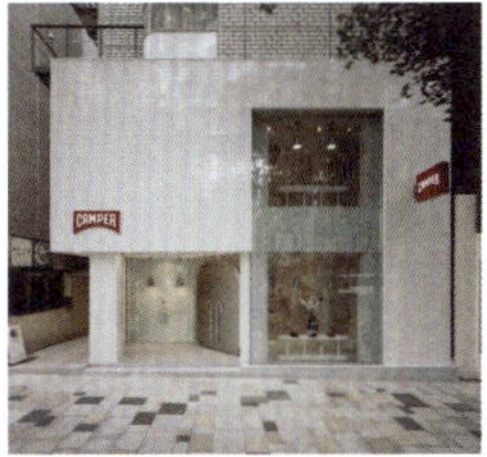

2009
Camper Store,
interior design,
Tokyo, Japan
P. 283

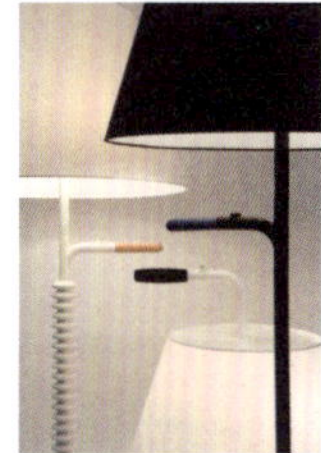

2009
Bastoni, floor lamp
collection
for Metalarte

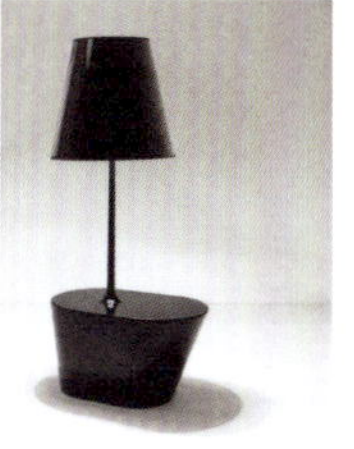

2009
América, floor lamp
collection
for Metalarte

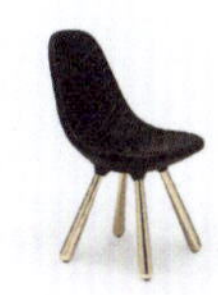

2009
Tudor, chair
& cabinet for
Established & Sons

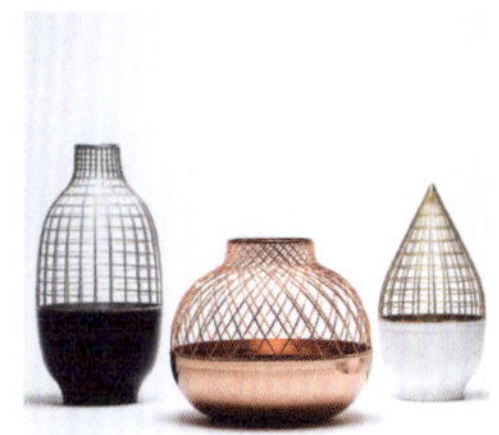

2009
Grid, metal vase
collection,
for Gaia & Gino

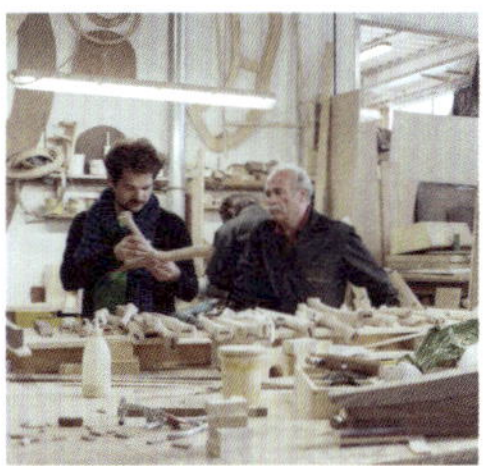

2009
Twenty Two,
chair for Ceccotti
Collezioni
P. 49

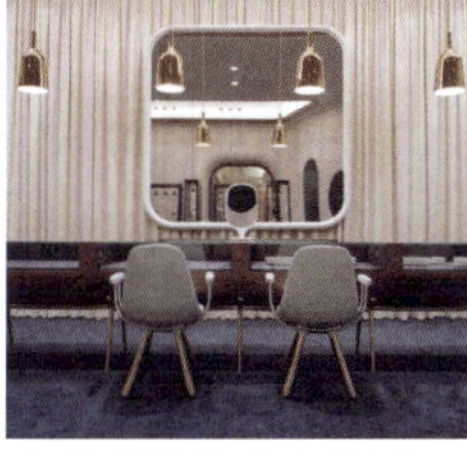

2009
Octium Jewelry,
interior design, Kuwait
Pp. 103–104

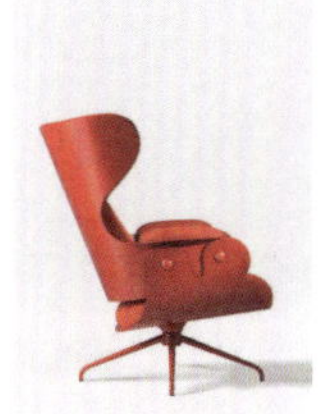

2010
Showtime Lounger,
for BD Barcelona
Design

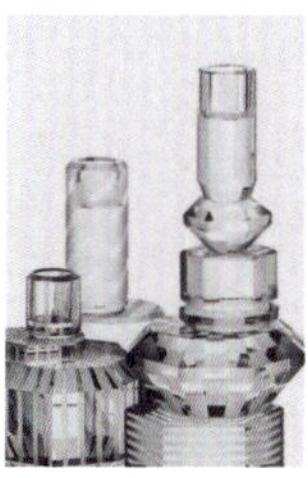

2010
Valencia, glass candle
holders for Gaia & Gino

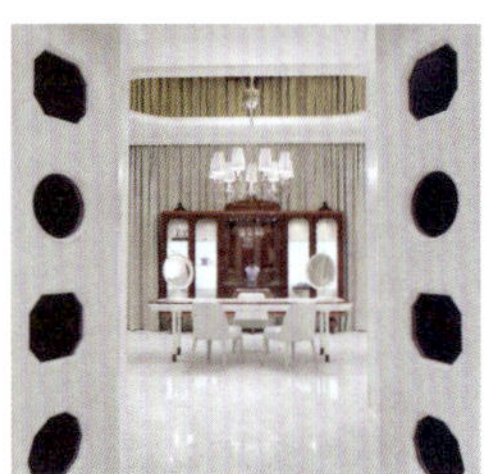

2010
Fabergé Salon,
interior design for
Fabergé boutique,
Geneva, Switzerland

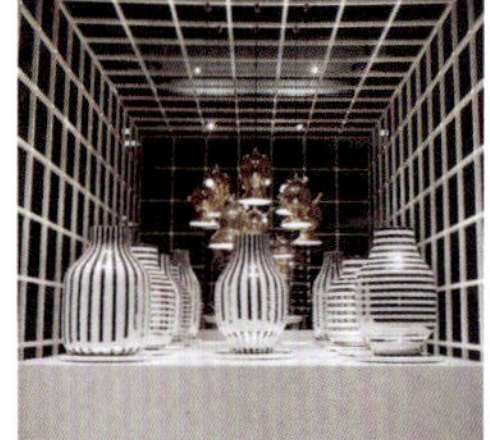

2010
Smart Grid Gallery,
installation for Enel
at Salone del Mobile,
Milan, Italy
P. 288

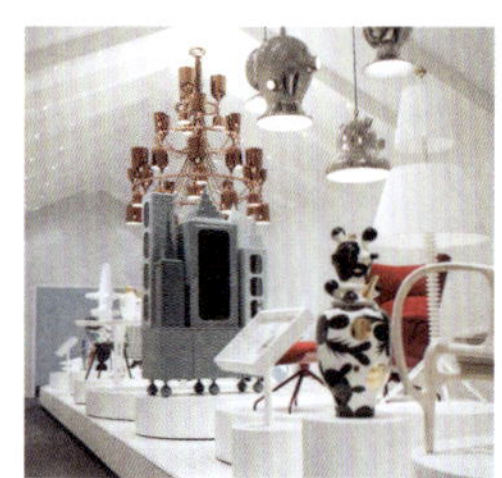

2010
Moving Ideas,
exhibition at
Maison&Objet
Designer of the Year
P. 260

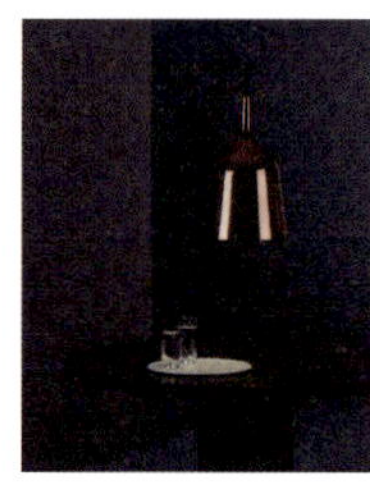

2010
Copa Cabana,
lighting collection
for Metalarte
P. 283

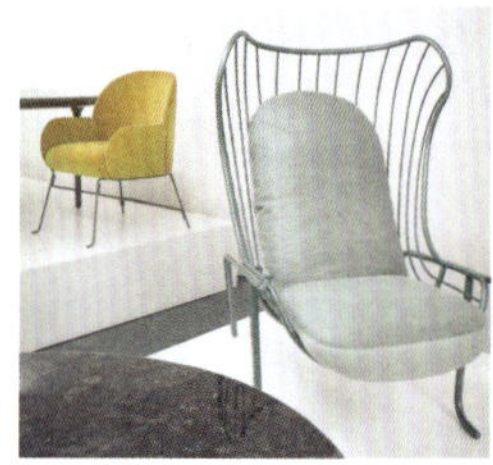

2010
Sé Collection II,
furniture for
Sé London

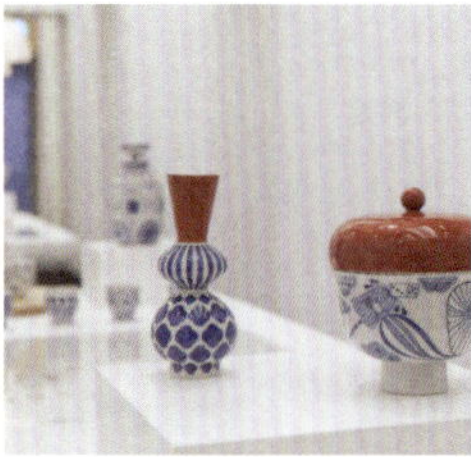

2010
Choemon Gamma,
porcelain collection
for Kutani Choemon
Pp. 214–215, 264

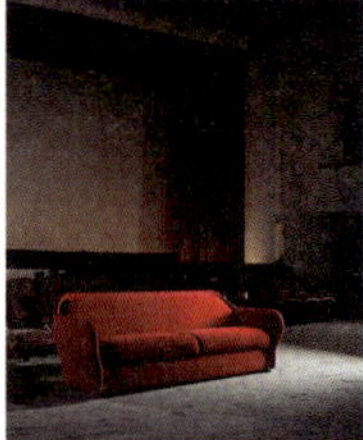

2010
Bardot, sofa & armchair
for Bernhardt Design
P. 191

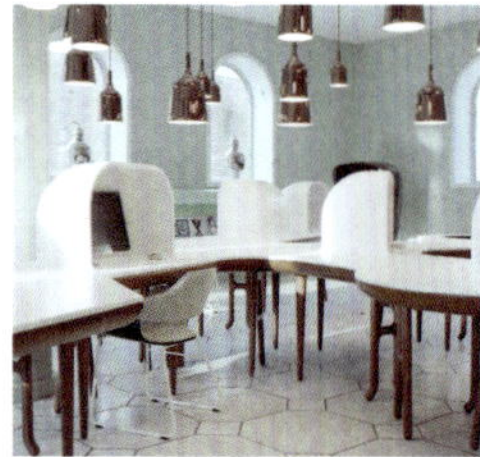

2011
Info Centre, interior
design, Groninger
Museum, Groningen,
Netherlands

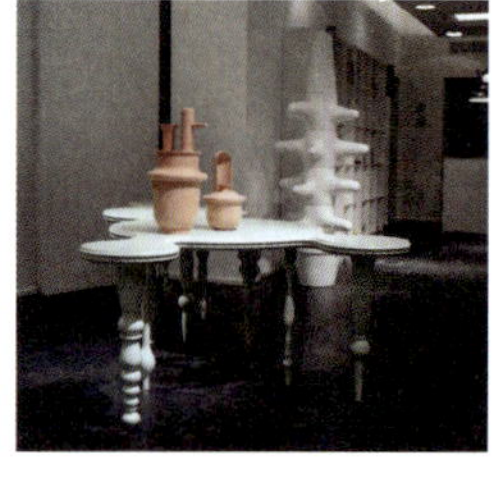

2011
Selection by Hayon,
exhibition at
OA Gallery, Madrid,
Spain

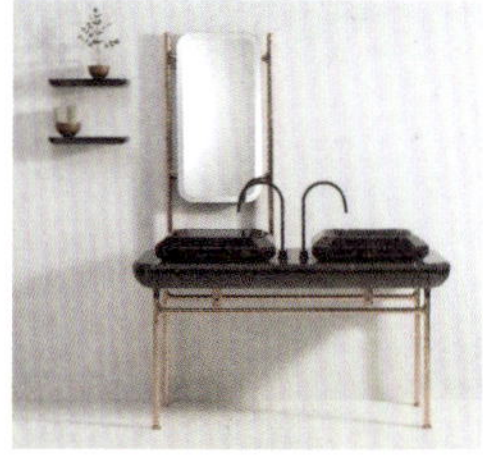

2011
Hayon Collection,
bathroom for Bisazza

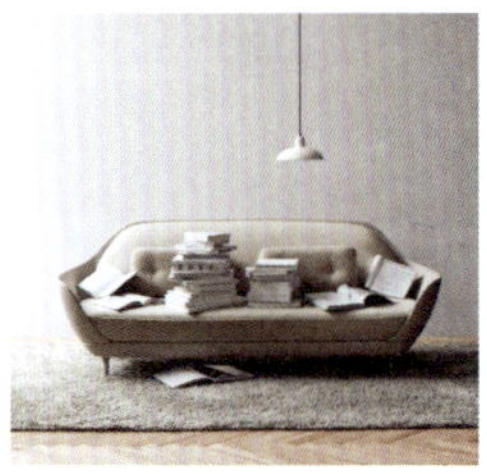

2011
Favn, sofa for
Fritz Hansen

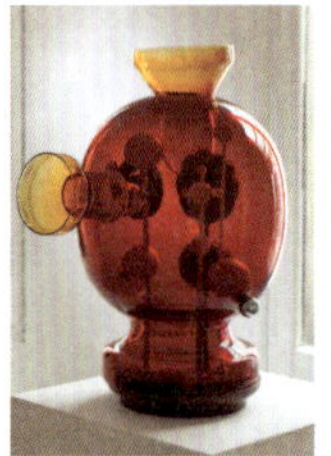

2011
Testa Mecanica,
exhibition at
Glasstress, Venice, Italy
P. 62

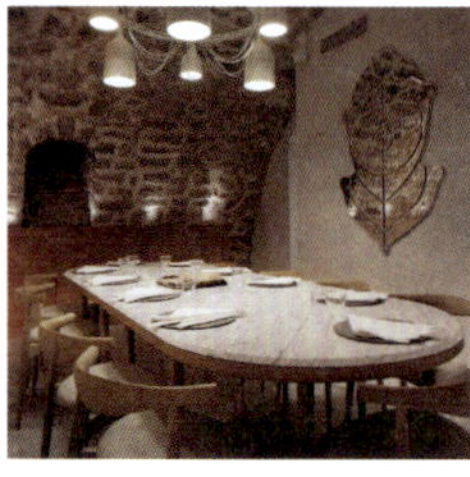

2012
Le Sergent Recruteur,
interior design
for a restaurant in
Paris, France

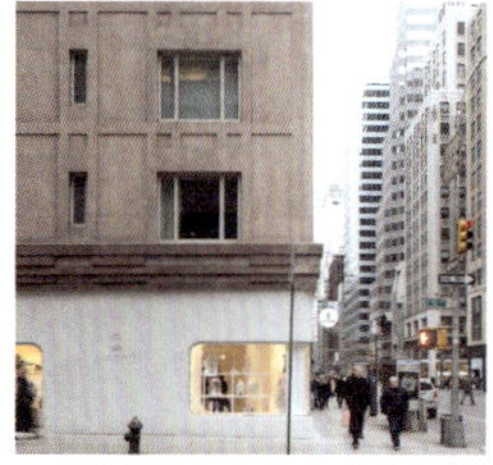

2012
Lladró store,
interior design,
New York, USA
P. 189

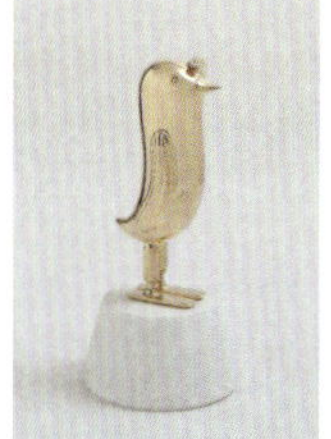

2012
Hope Bird,
ceramic sculpture
for Bosa
Pp. 1, 304

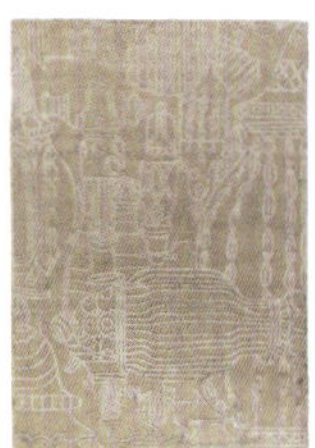

2012
Jaime Hayon Rug
Collection, for the
Rug Company

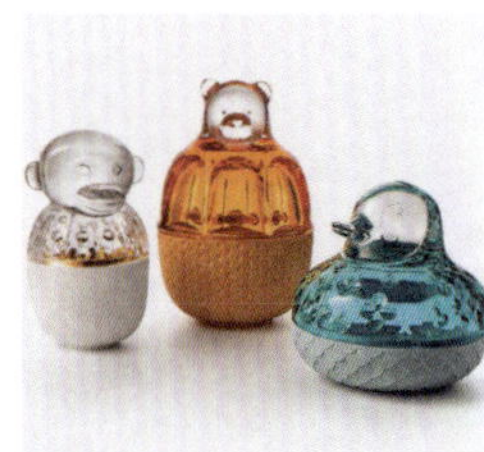

2012
The Baccarat Zoo
Collection, crystal
containers
for Baccarat

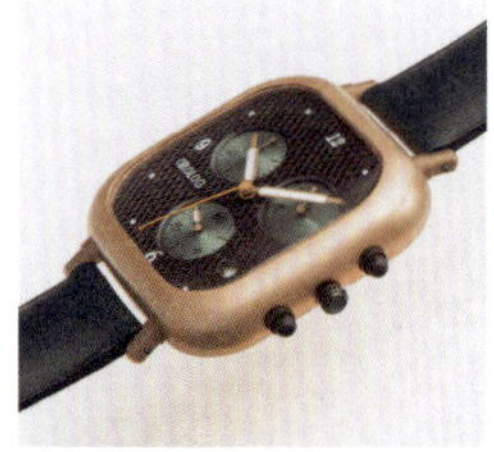

2012
Orolog, watch
collection for Orolog
P. 271

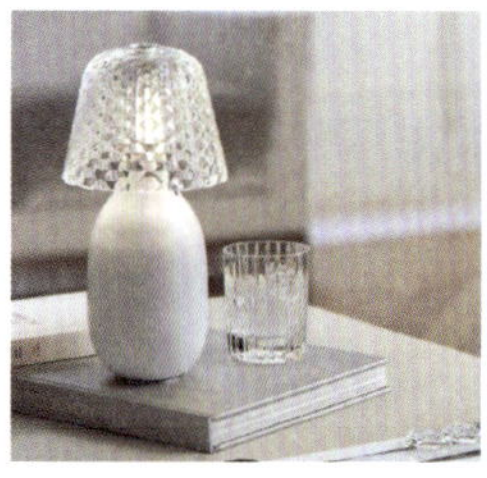

2013
Candy Lights,
lamps for Baccarat
P. 220

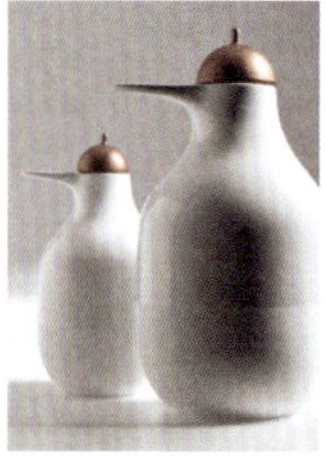

2013
Pellicani, ceramic
containers for Bosa

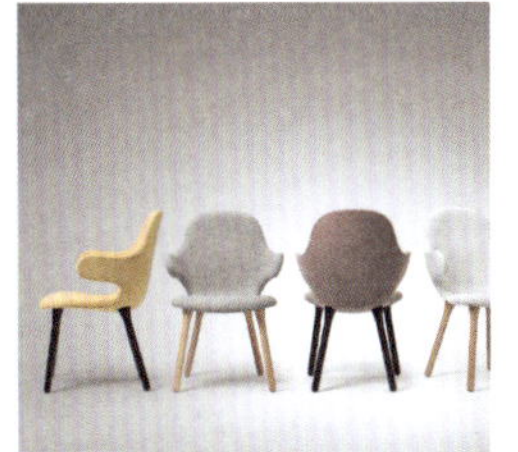

2013
Catch JH1, chair
for &Tradition
Pp. 50, 221, 275

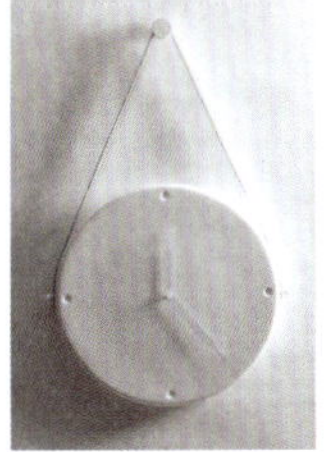

2013
Bosa by Hayon,
ceramic objects
for Bosa

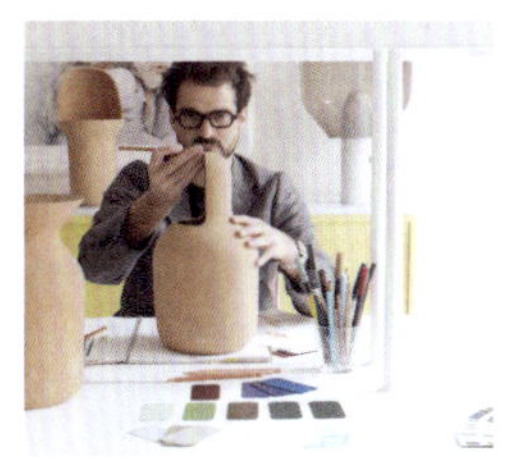

2013
Gardenias,
outdoor furniture
& accessories for
BD Barcelona Design
Pp. 221, 290

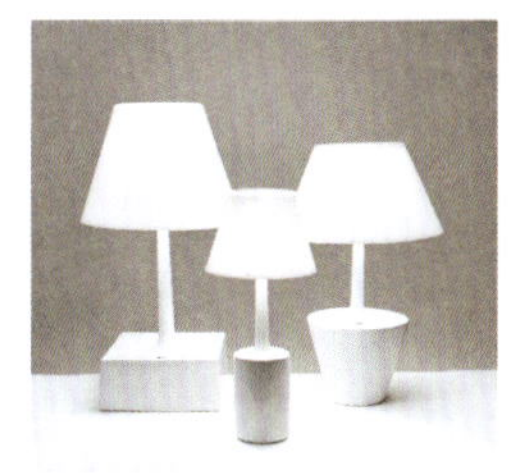

2013
Santas, lighting
for Metalarte

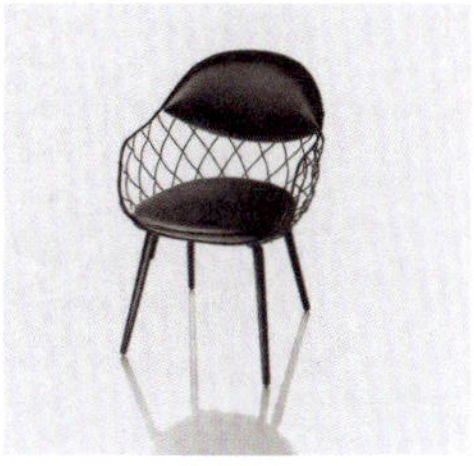

2013
Piña, chair for Magis

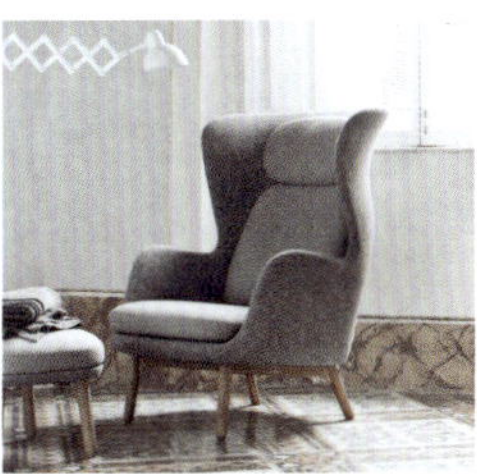

2013
Ro, lounge chair
for Fritz Hansen
Pp. 58, 287

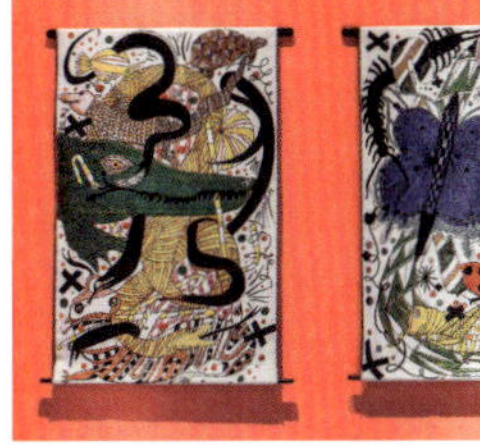

2013
Fauna by Hayon,
exhibition at
TextielMuseum,
Tilburg, Netherlands
Pp. 89, 262

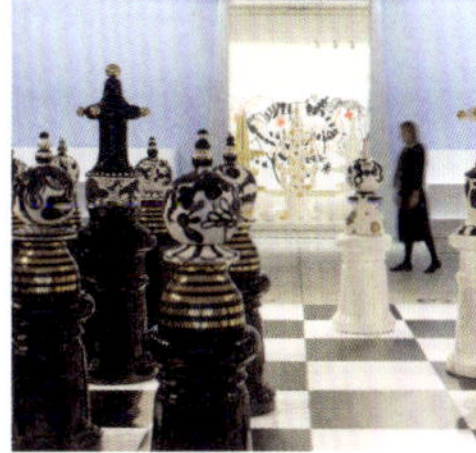

2013
Funtastico,
retrospective
exhibition at Groninger
Museum, Groningen,
Netherlands
P. 262

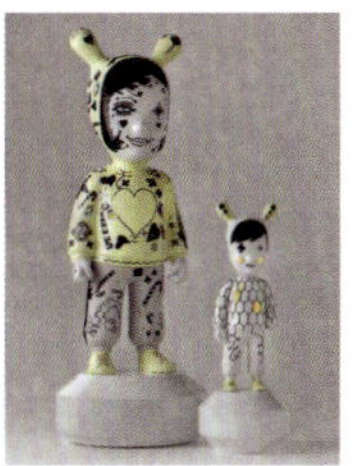

2013
The Guest, porcelain
figurines for Lladró
P. 238

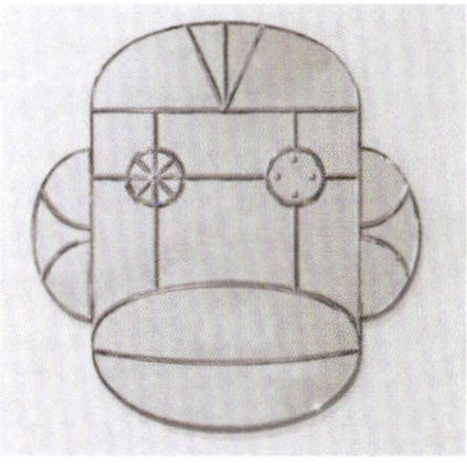

2014
Carnival Series,
limited-edition
mirror collection
for Galerie Kreo

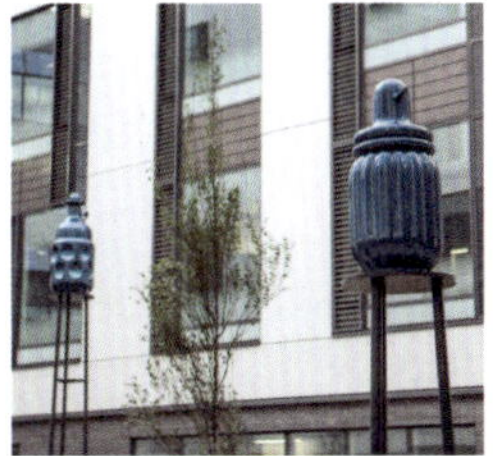

2014
Mon Cirque, public
sculptures at
Southmead Hospital
in Bristol, U.K.
P. 27

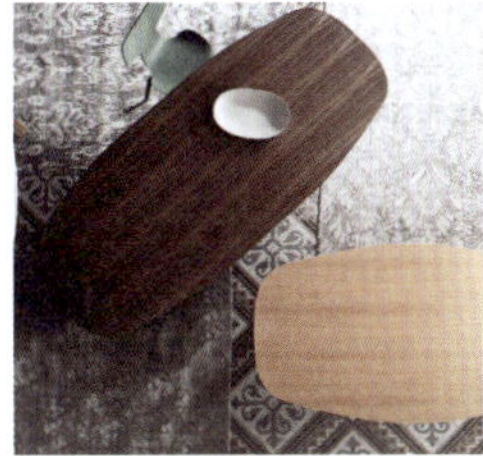

2014
Analog, table
for Fritz Hansen

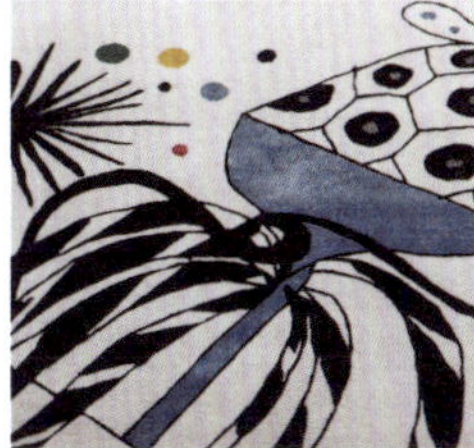

2014
Japanese Folklore,
rug for Nodus

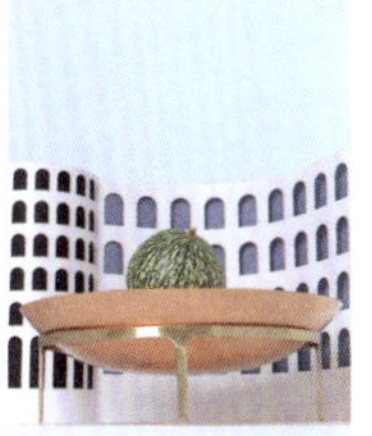

2014
New Roman,
tableware collection
for Paola C
Pp. 68–69, 76

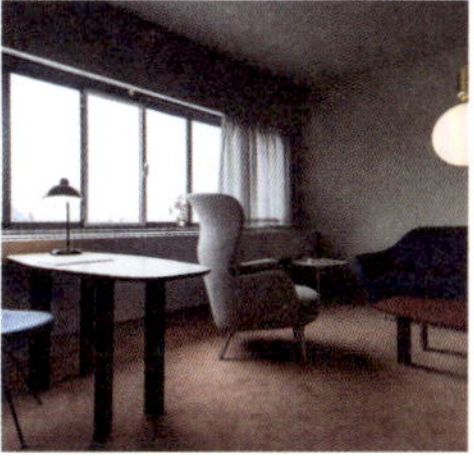

2014
Room 506, interior
design for Radisson
Collection Royal
Hotel in Copenhagen,
Denmark

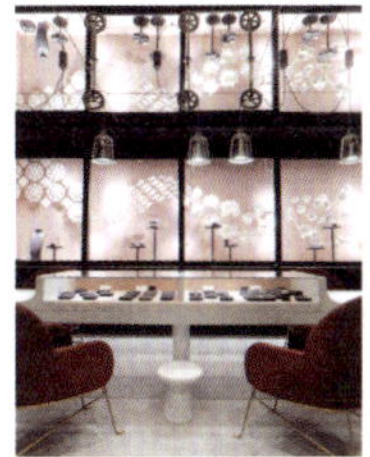

2014–2015
Nirav Modi Boutiques,
interior design,
New Delhi, Mumbai
& New York
Pp. 194, 196

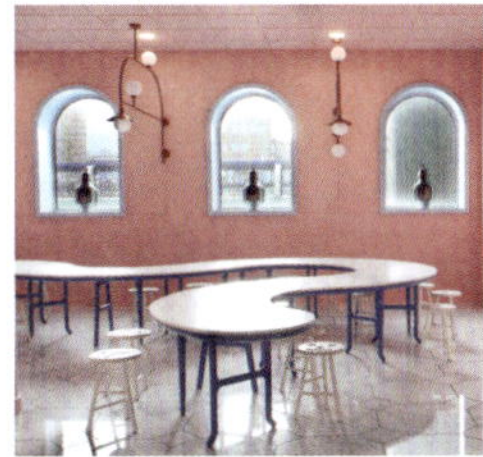

2015
Family Lab, interior
design, Groninger
Museum, Groningen,
Netherlands
Pp. 286, 293

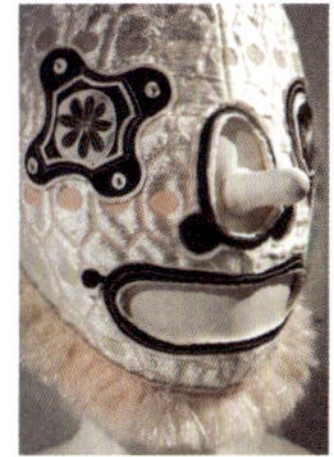

2014–2015
¿Qué Pasa Guey?
exhibition at
TextielMuseum,
Tilburg, Netherlands

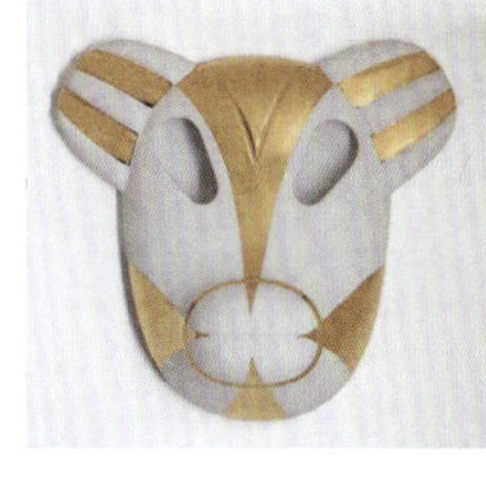

2014
Hayon × Bosa,
ceramic objects
for Bosa
P. 81

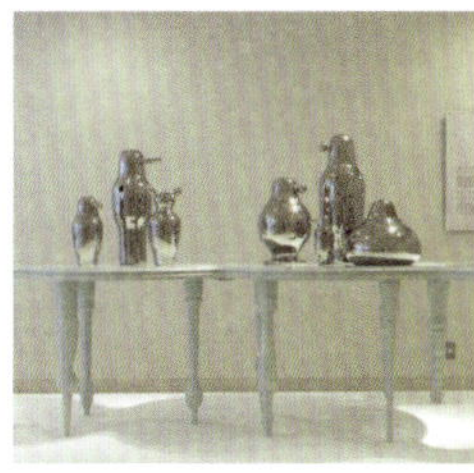

2014–2015
Backstage Tokyo,
installation at Spanish
Embassy, Tokyo, Japan

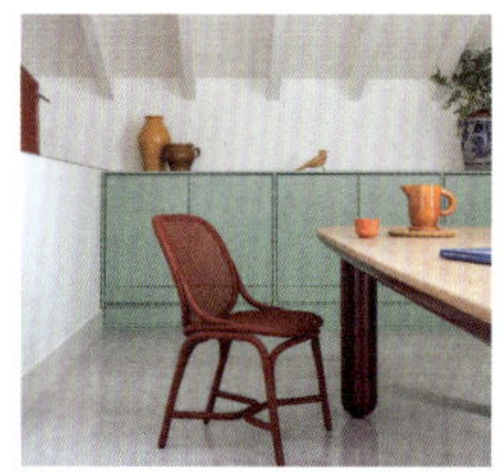

2014
Frames, chair
for Expormim
Pp. 219, 233

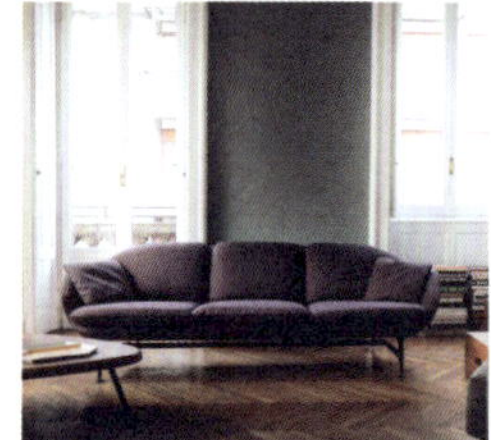

2014
Vico, sofa
for Cassina

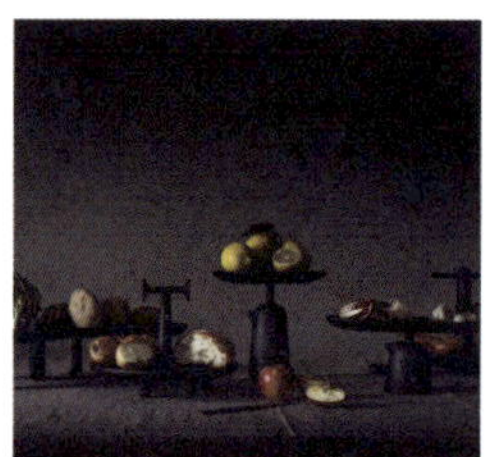

2015
Réaction Poétique,
wood accessories
for Cassina
Pp. 96–97

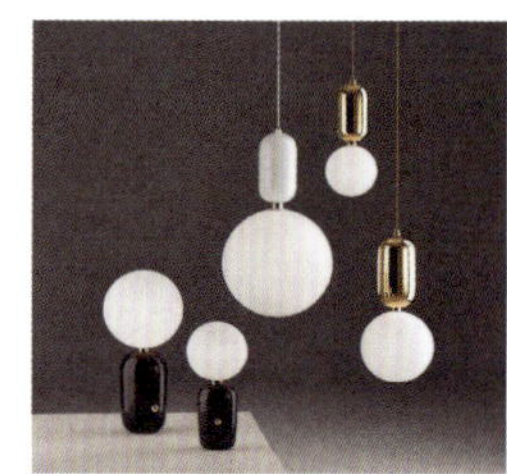

2015
Aballs, lights
collection for
Parachilna
Pp. 86–87, 229

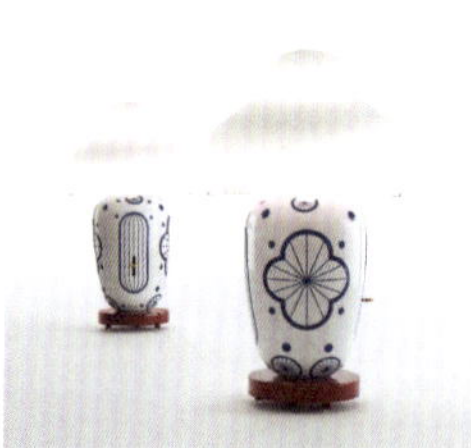

2015
Chinoz, lamps
for Parachilna
P. 212

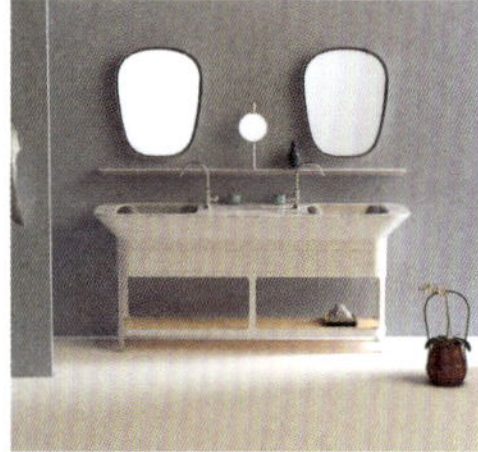

2015
Materico, bathroom
collection for Toyo

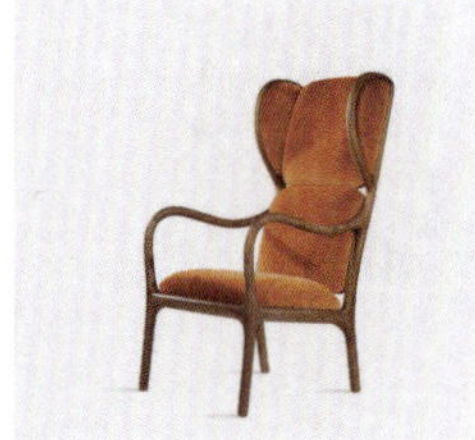

2015
Bergère 30, armchair
for Ceccotti Collezioni

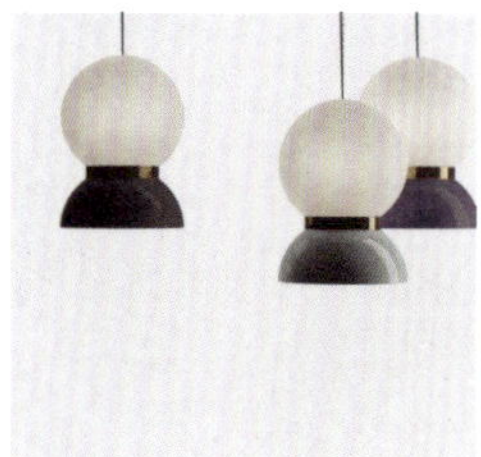

2015
Saint Louis, lighting
for Ceccotti Collezioni

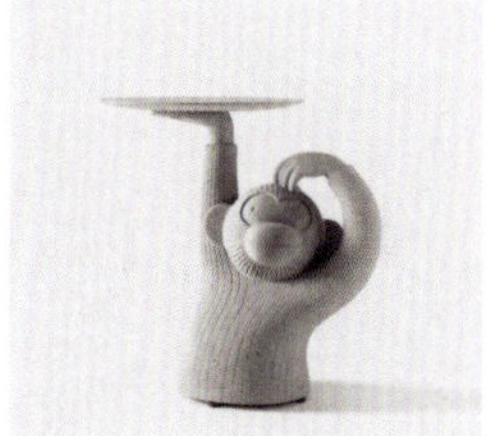

2015
Monkey Side Table, for
BD Barcelona Design
P. 82

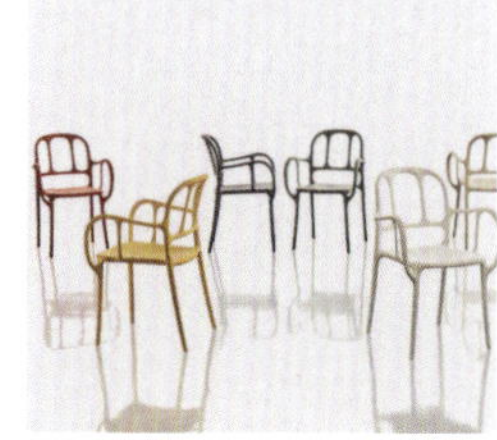

2015
Milà, chair for Magis
P. 53

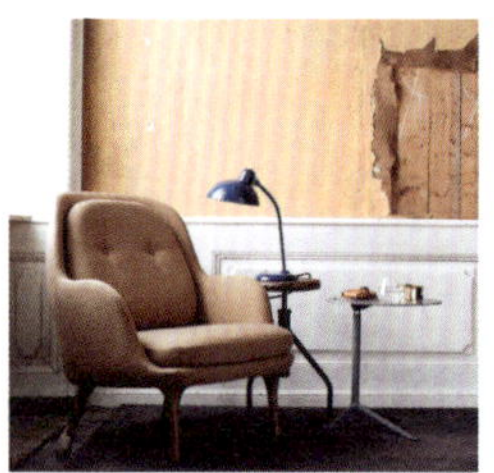

2015
Fri, lounge chair
for Fritz Hansen

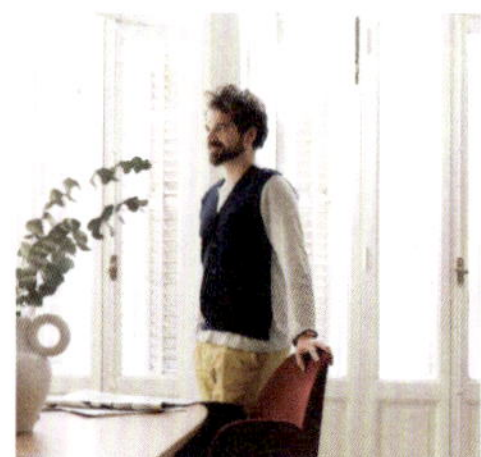

2015
Sammen, chair
for Fritz Hansen

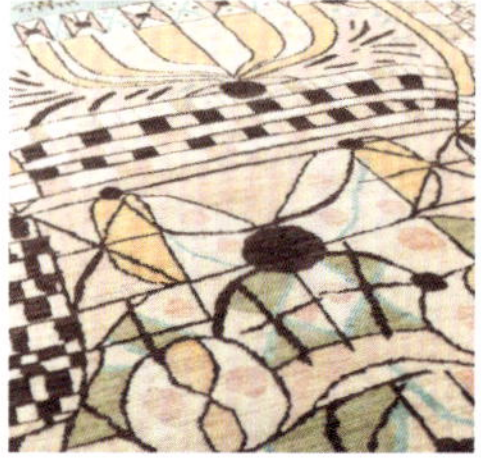

2015
Afghan Folklore,
rug for Nodus

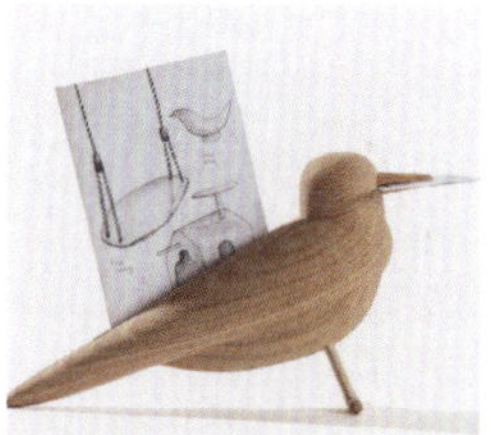

2015
Villa Le Lac Paulownia,
for Cassina

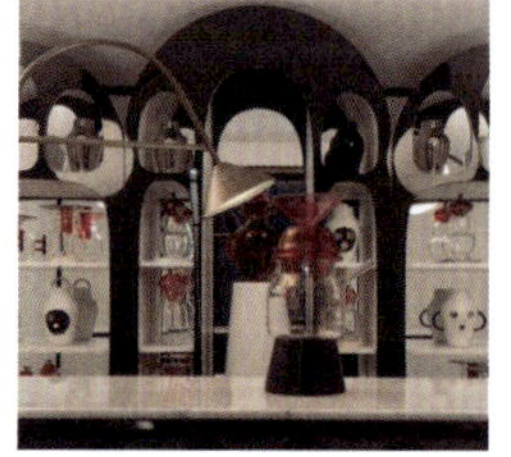

2015
Kuriopotec, exhibition
at the Garden of
Wonders, Milan, Italy
Pp. 226–227

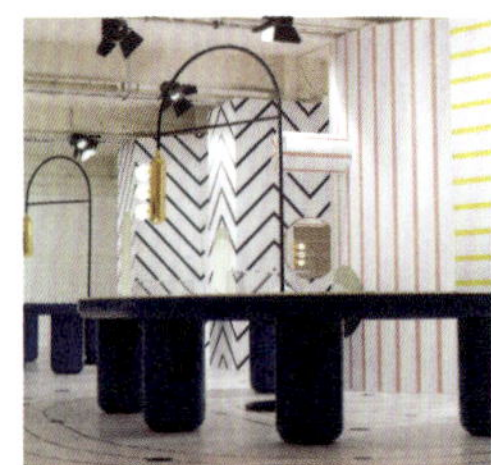

2015
Urban Perspectives
for MINI, installation,
Milan, Italy
P. 187

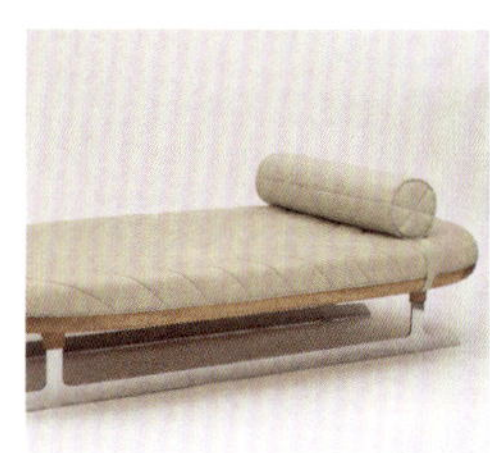

2015
Game On, exhibition
at Galerie Kreo,
Paris & London
P. 210

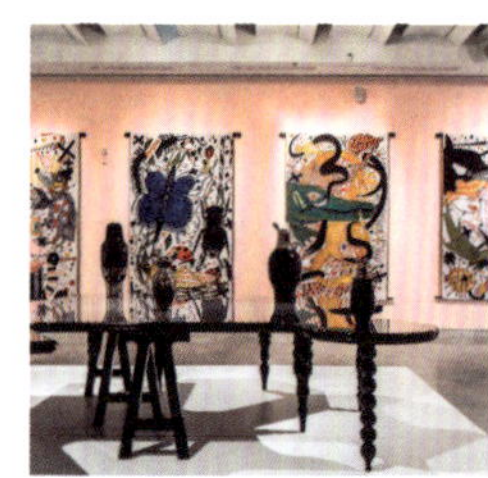

2015–2016
Funtastico,
exhibition at Holon
Design Museum,
Holon, Israel

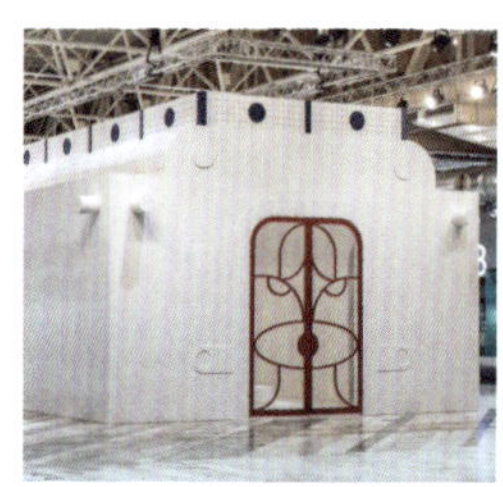

2016
Hayon DNA Gallery,
exhibition at
Stockholm Furniture
& Light Fair, Sweden
Pp. 24–25

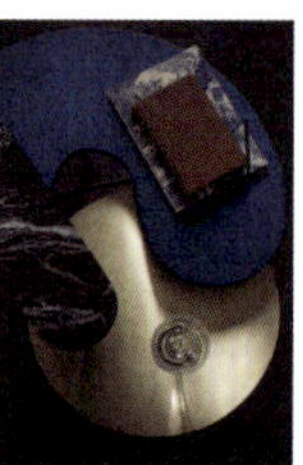

2016
Palette, table
collection
for &Tradition
P. 275

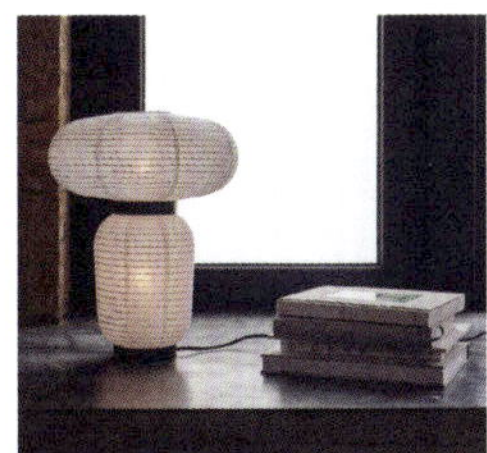

2016
Formakami, lighting
for &Tradition
P. 11, 250

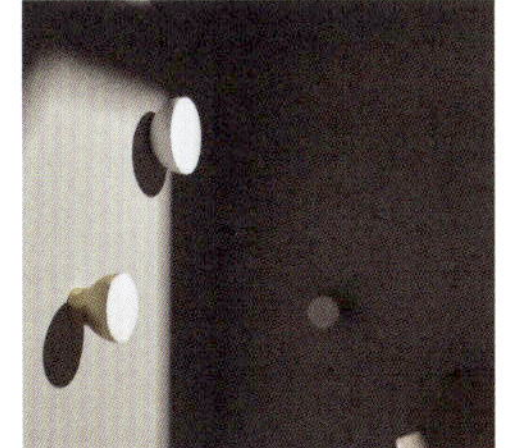

2016
Passepartout, lighting
for &Tradition

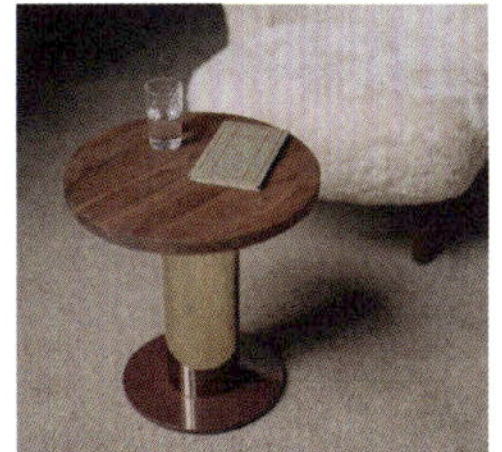

2016
Mezcla, table
collection
for &Tradition

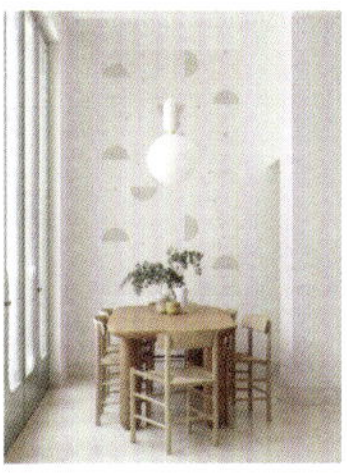

2016
Eco Wallpaper,
for Boråstapeter

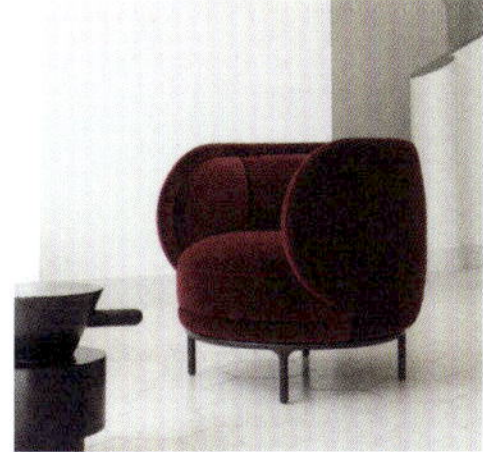

2016
Hayon Workshop I,
furniture collection
for Wittmann

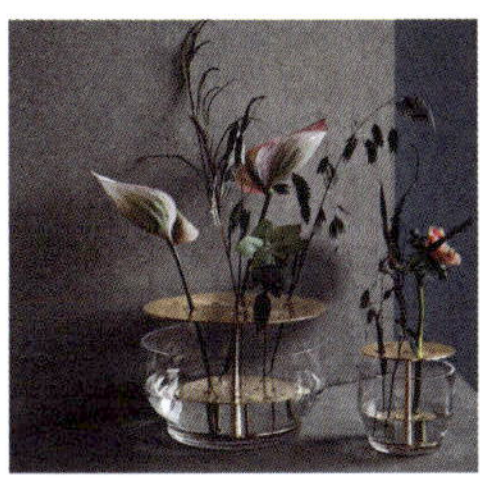

2016
Accessories,
for Fritz Hansen
P. 274

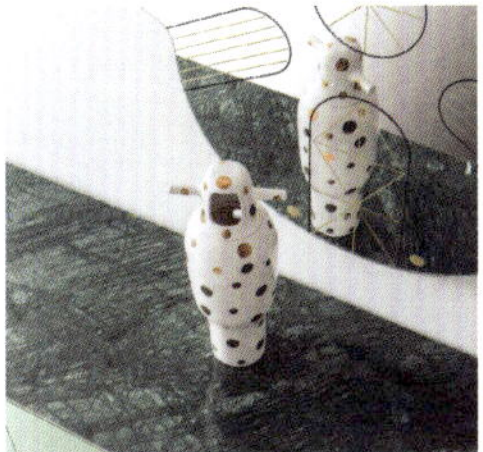

2016
10th Anniversary
Collection, limited-
edition furniture
for BD Barcelona
Design

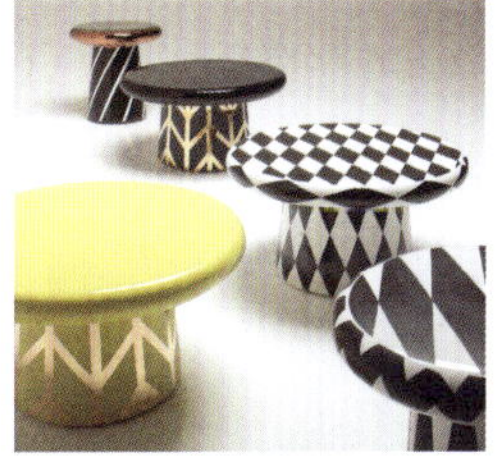

2016
T-Table, table
collection for Bosa
P. 24

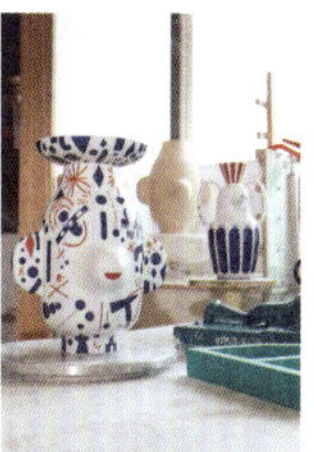

2016
Folkifunki, ceramic
collection
for Vista Alegre
Pp. 65, 258

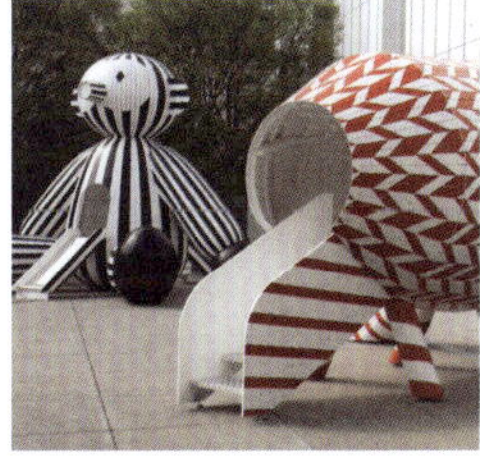

2016
Tiovivo, installation
at High Museum
of Art, Atlanta, USA
Pp. 12–13

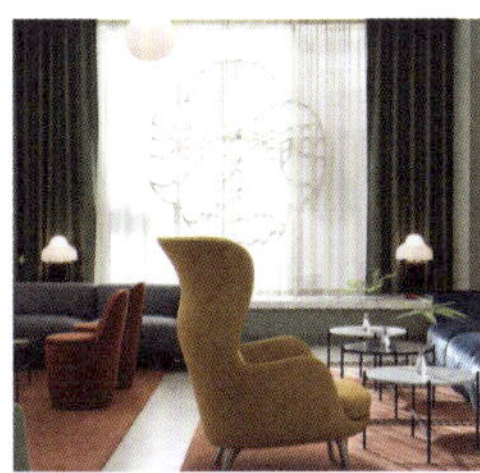

2016
Barceló Torre
de Madrid Hotel,
interior design,
Madrid, Spain
Pp. 30–31, 72, 239, 282,
294, 296–297

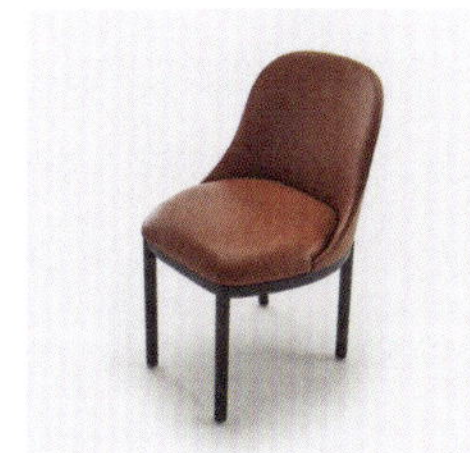

2017
Aleta, chair
for Viccarbe
P. 43

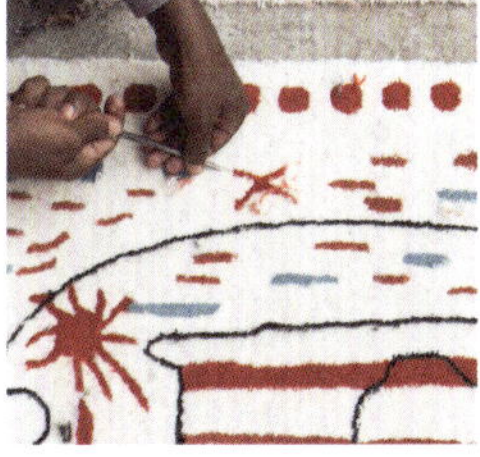

2017
Hayon × Nani, rug
for Nanimarquina
P. 100

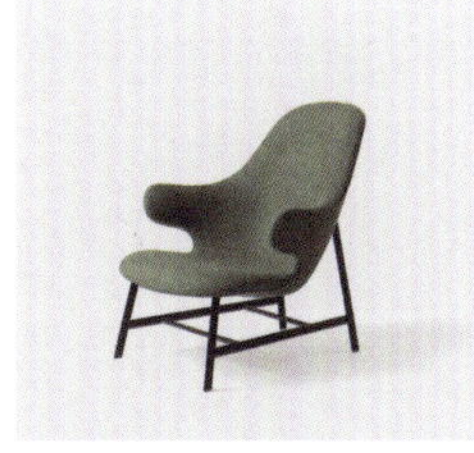

2017
Catch JH13, lounge
chair for &Tradition
Pp. 121, 297

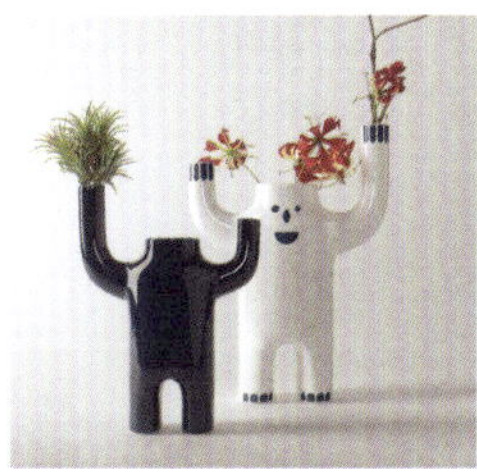

2017
Happy Susto,
ceramic vases for
BD Barcelona Design
P. 285

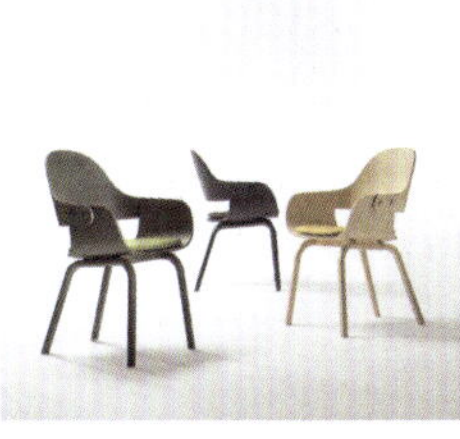

2017
Showtime Nude,
chairsfor BD
Barcelona Design

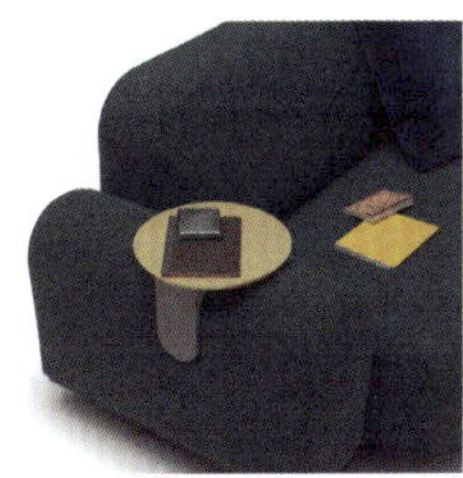

2017
Arcolor & Leafo,
living room collection
for Arflex
P. 207

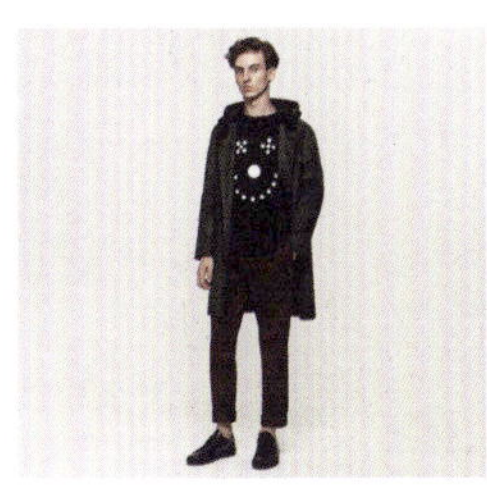

2017
Hayon × Jijibaba,
fashion collection
for Jijibaba
Pp. 195, 252, 265

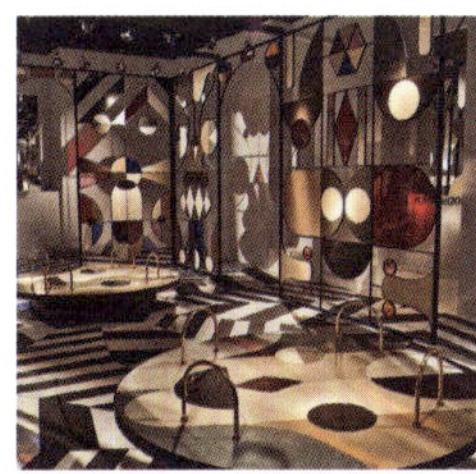

2017
Stone Age Folk,
installation at
Palazzo Serbelloni
for Caesarstone,
Milan, Italy
Pp. 14–15, 70–71

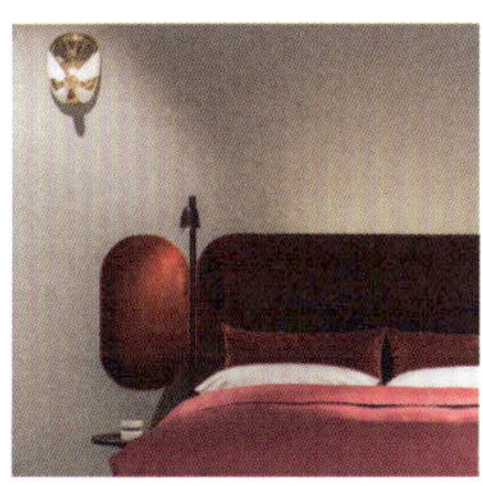

2017
Hayon Workshop II,
furniture collection
for Wittmann
P. 48

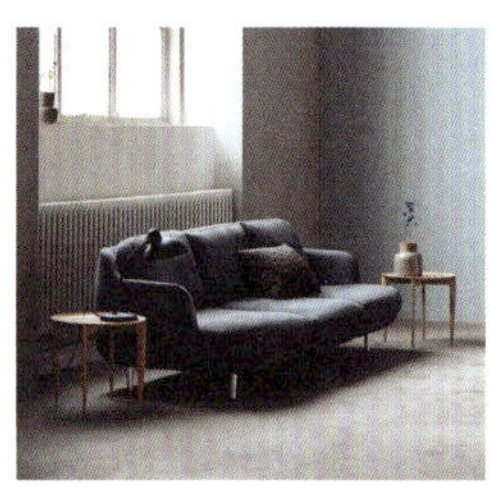

2017
Lune, sofa
for Fritz Hansen
P. 289

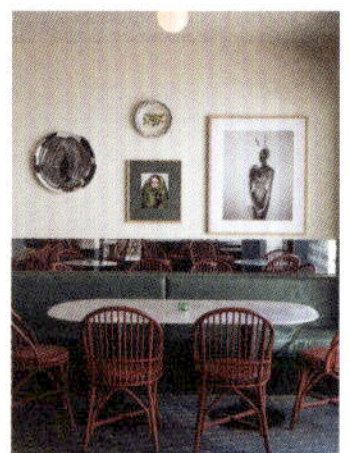

2017
Mar de Avellanas,
interior design,
Valencia, Spain
Pp. 228, 272

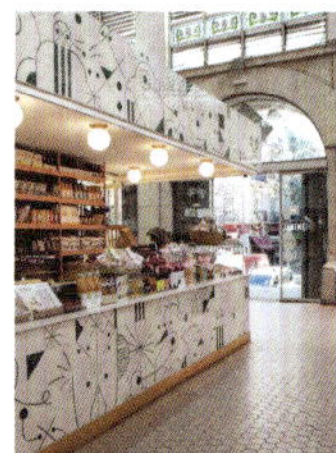

2017
UNO market booth,
interior design,
Central Market,
Valencia, Spain
P. 235

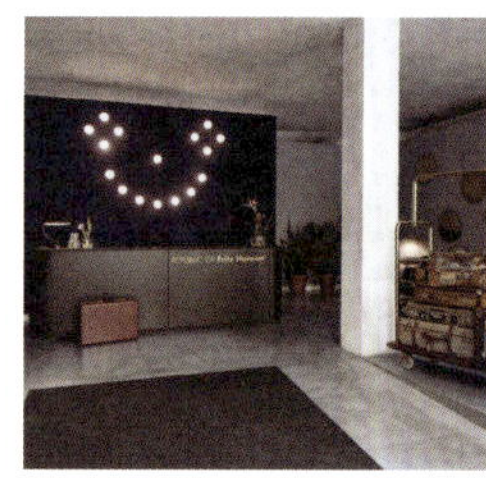

2017
Fritz Hotel,
installation at
Fuorisalone,
Milan, Italy

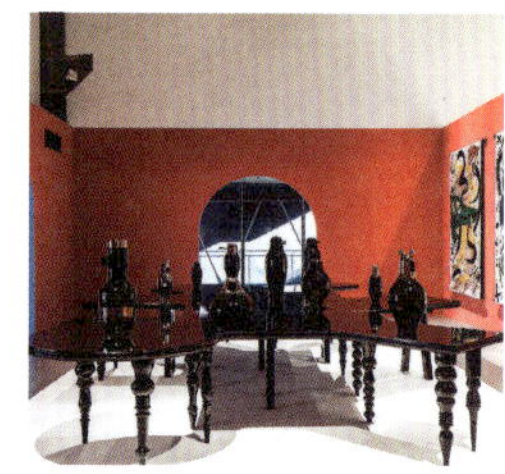

2017
Funtastico, exhibition
at Modern Art
Museum, Shanghai,
China

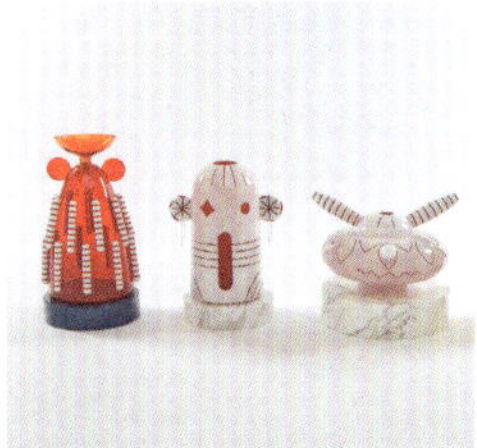

2017
Afrikando, exhibition
at Milwaukee
Art Museum,
Milwaukee, USA
P. 184

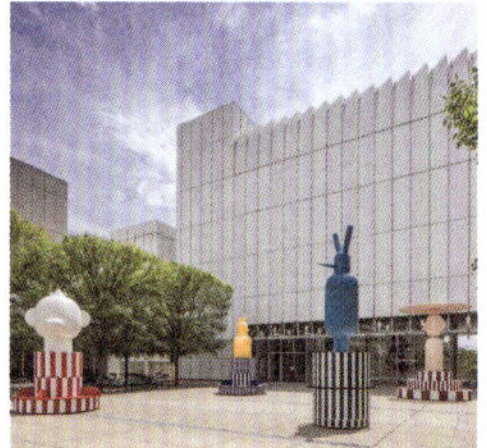

2017
Merry Go Zoo,
installation at High
Museum of Art,
Atlanta, USA
Pp. 2–3, 5

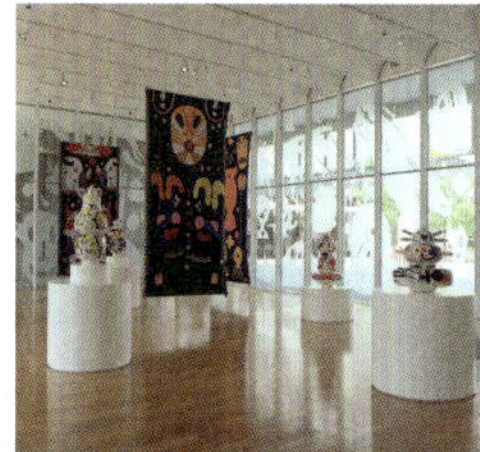

2017
Technicolor, exhibition
at High Museum
of Art, Atlanta, USA
Pp. 6–7, 98

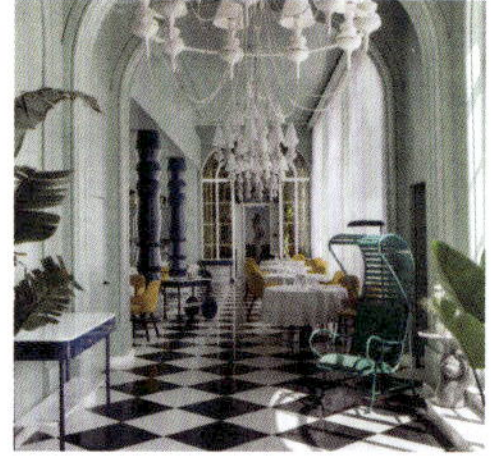

2018
La Terraza del Casino,
restaurant interior
design, Madrid, Spain
Pp. 183, 221

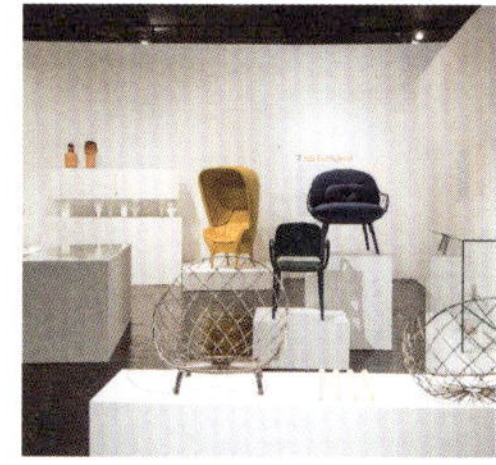

2018
Backstage, exhibition
at Fernán Gómez
Cultural centre,
Madrid, Spain

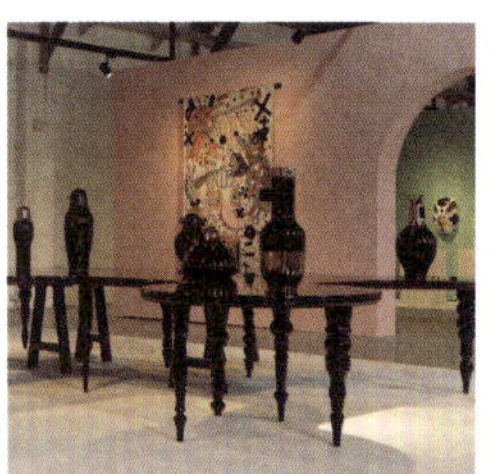

2018
Funtastico, exhibition
at Songshan Cultural
Park, Taipei, Taiwan

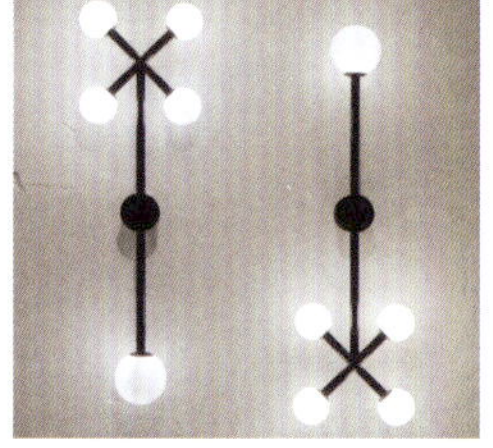

2018
Chromatico, exhibition
at Galerie Kreo,
Paris and London
Pp. 42, 60, 109, 185, 222

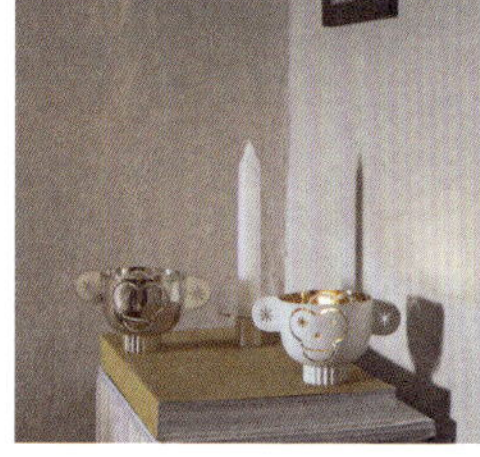

2018
Monkos & Pipoz,
candleholders
for Paola C
P. 202

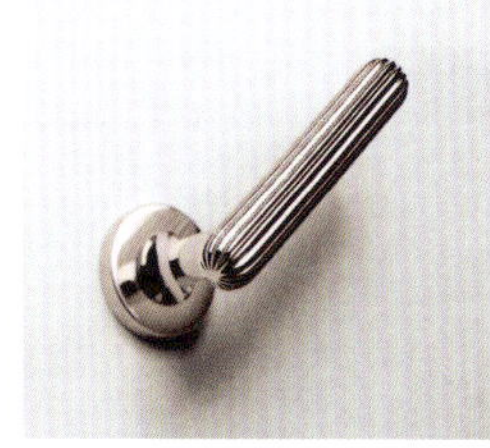

2018
Zeppelin, door handle
for DND Handles
P. 57

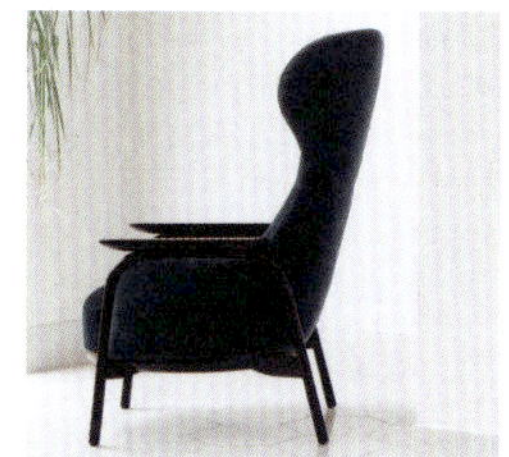

2018
Hayon Workshop III,
furniture collection
for Wittmann

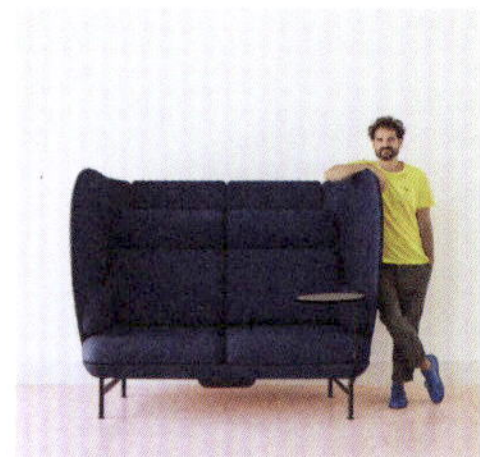

2018
Plenum, sofa
for Fritz Hansen

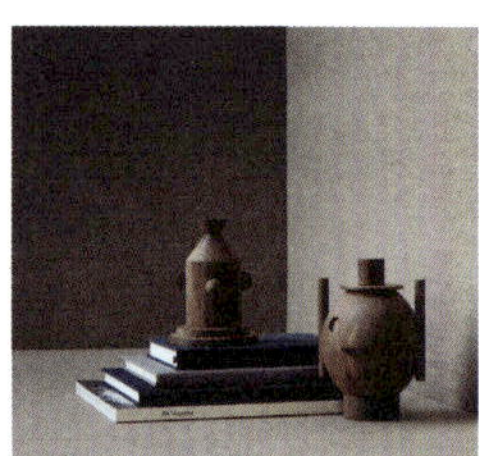

2018
Geosculptures, wooden
accessories,
for Fritz Hansen

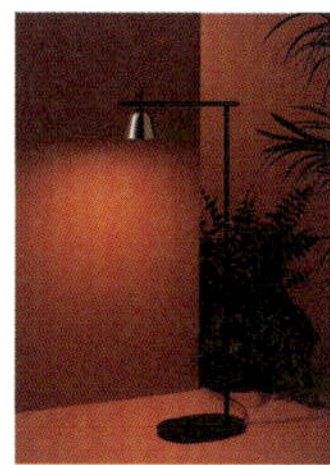

2018
Lightoread
& Lightolight,
lighting for Parachilna
Pp. 17, 52

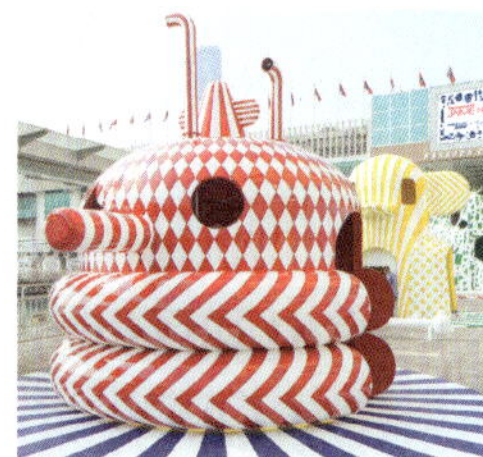

2018
Archisculptures &
Jaime Hayon Cosmos,
installation and
exhibition, Harbour
City, Hong Kong
p. 18–19

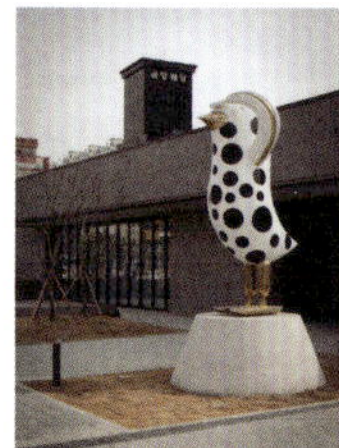

2018
Hope Bird,
public sculpture
at Ehwa Women's
Hospital, Seoul,
South Korea
P. 304

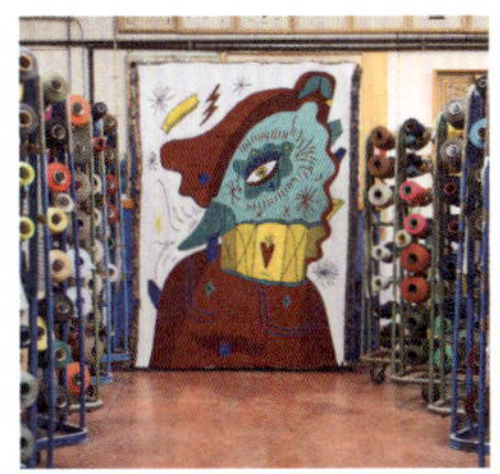

2019
Tugo—Tapestry,
exhibition at Rossana
Orlandi Gallery,
Milan, Italy.
Produced by Bonotto
P. 182

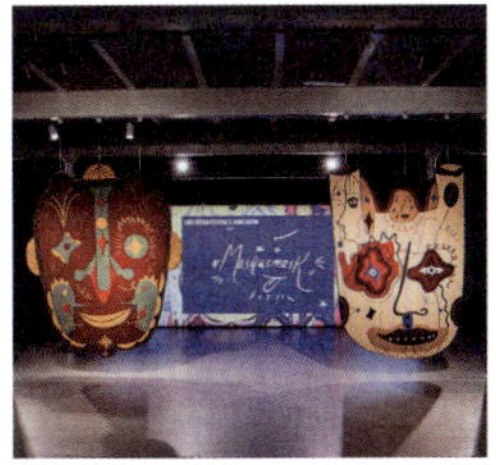

2019
Masquemask,
installation at Central
Museum of Textiles,
Łódź, Poland
P. 55

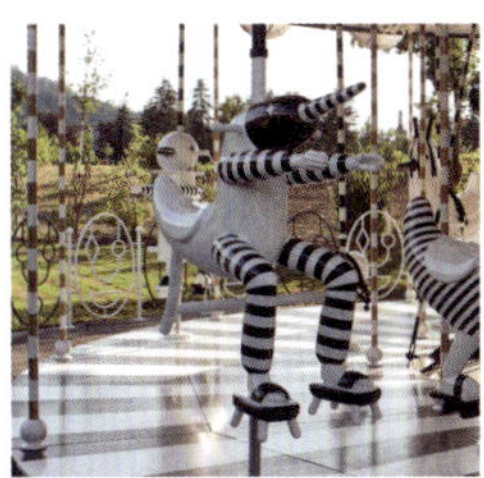

2019
Carousel, installation
at Swarovski
Kristallwelten,
Wattens, Austria
Pp. 28–29, 232, 251

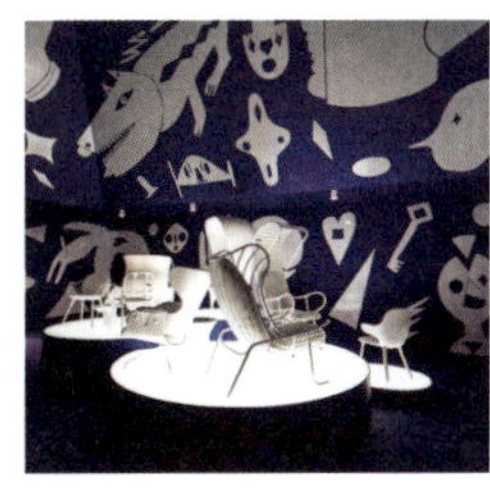

2019
Serious Fun, exhibition
at Daelim Museum,
Seoul, South Korea
Pp. 23, 255, 267

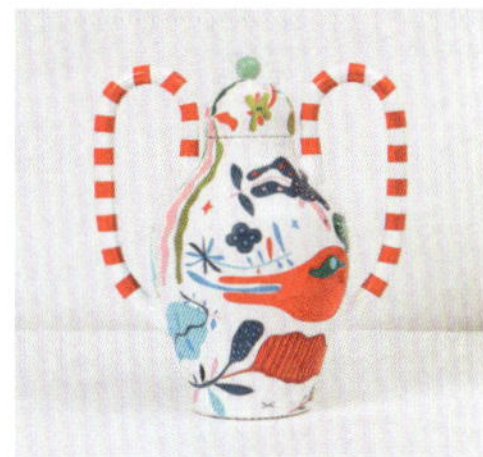

2019
Hayon × Maison
Matisse, limited-edition
vases for
Maison Matisse
Pp. 26, 77

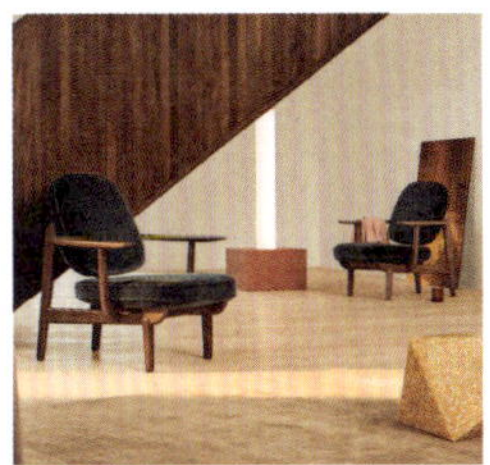

2019
Fred, lounge chair
for Fritz Hansen

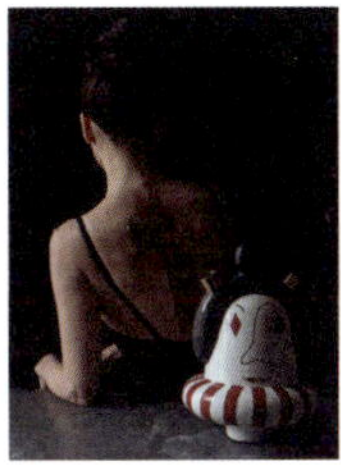

2019
Theatre Hayon,
ceramic collection
for Bosa
Pp. 54, 95, 183

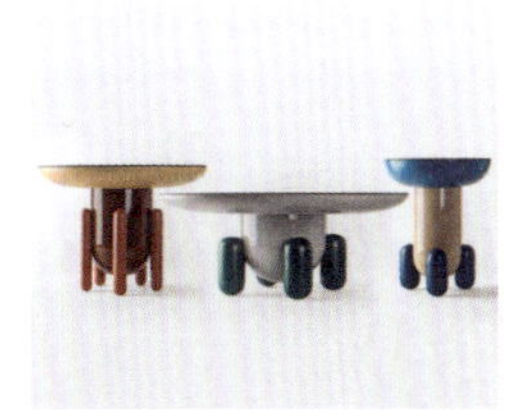

2019
Explorer,
side tables for BD
Barcelona Design
P. 217

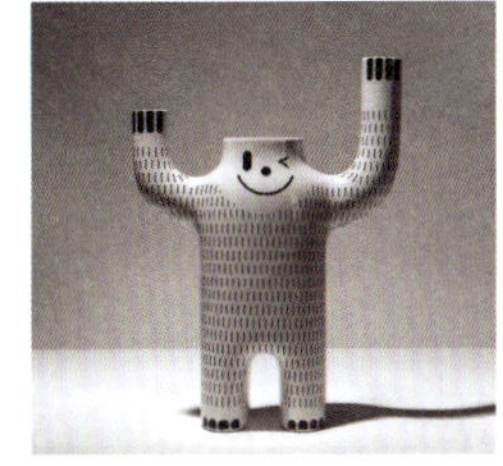

2019
Happy Yeti,
ceramic vases for BD
Barcelona Design

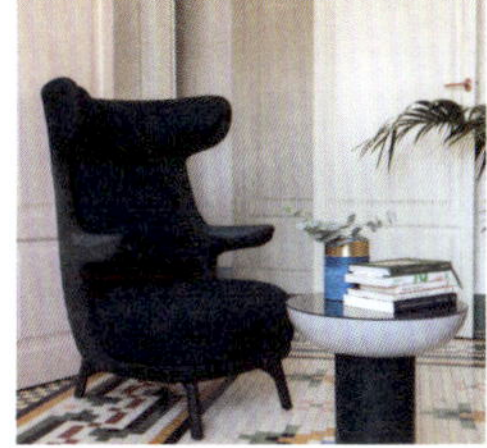

2019
Dino,
lounge chair for BD
Barcelona Design
P. 67

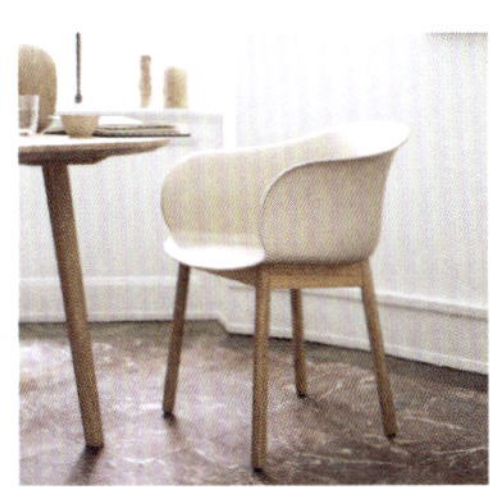

2019
Elefy, chair
for &Tradition
P. 284

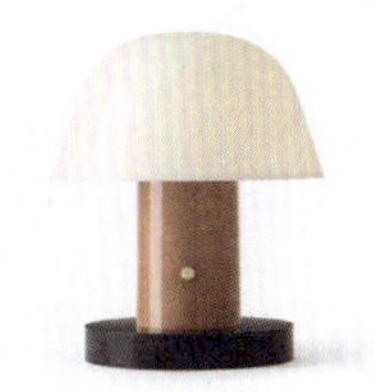

2019
Setago, lamp
for &Tradition
P. 206

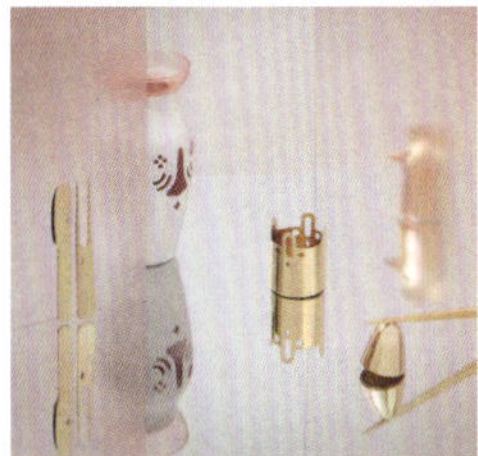

2019
FUN-tional, tableware
collection for Paola C
Pp. 202–203

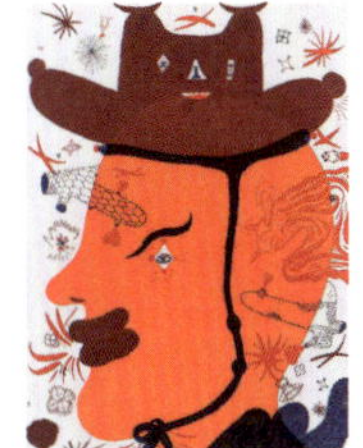

2019
Lithograph Series,
with Edition
Copenhagen, Denmark
P. 280

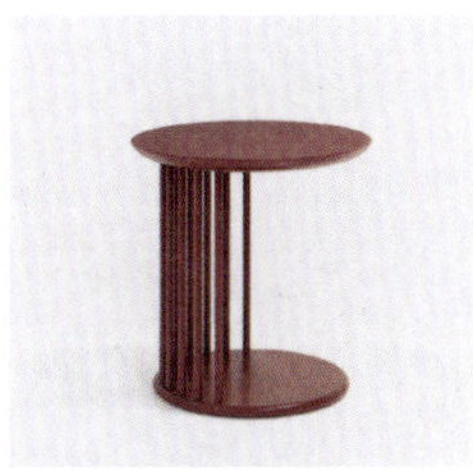

2019
Hayon Workshop IV,
furniture collection
for Wittmann
P. 88

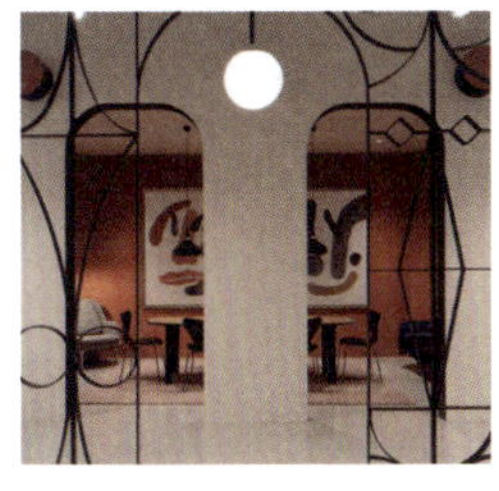

2019
Fritz Hansen
Showrooms, interior
design in Bangkok,
Xi'an, Singapore
& Shanghai
Pp. 34–35, 37, 111, 193,
197, 268–269

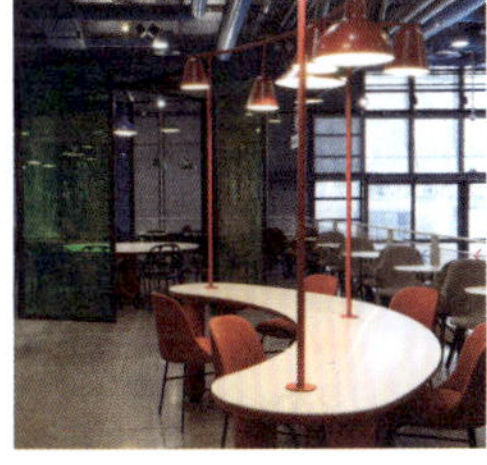

2019
Le Central, interior
design, Centre
Pompidou, Paris,
France
Pp. 93, 270

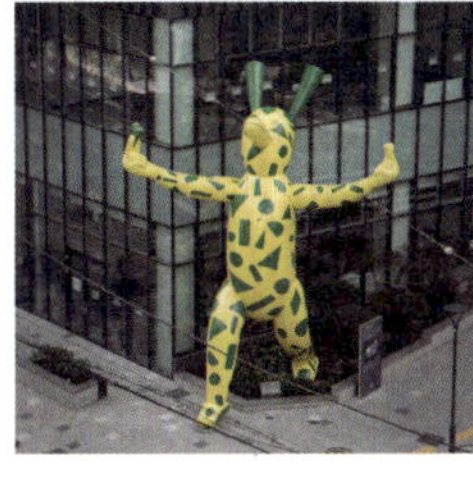

2020
Love, public sculpture,
Seoul, South Korea
Pp. 298–299

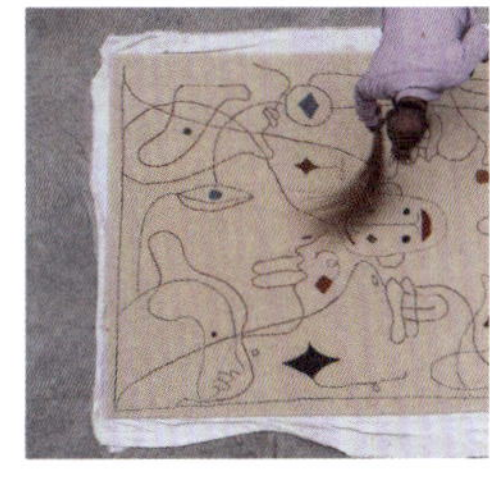

2020
Silhouette, rug
collection for
Nanimarquina
Pp. 78–79

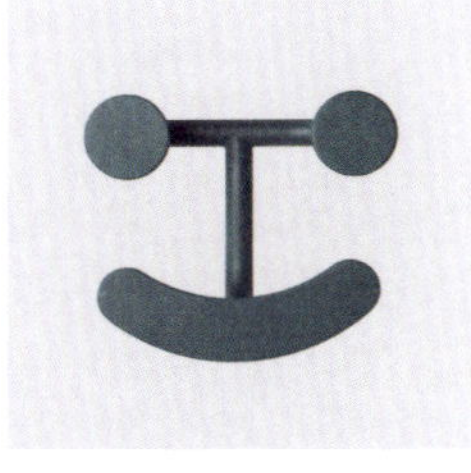

2020
Happy Hook, hanger
for Fritz Hansen
P. 51

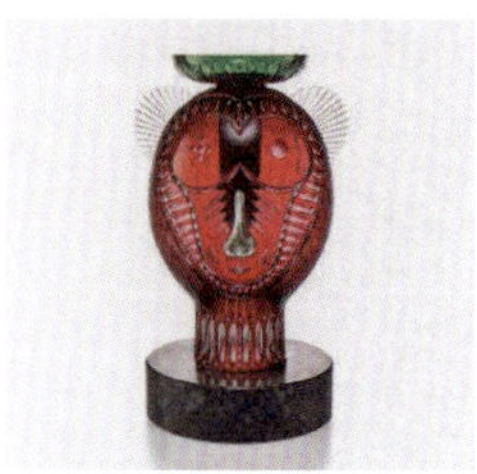

2020
Faunacrystopolis,
collection for Baccarat
Pp. 59, 74–75, 110, 117

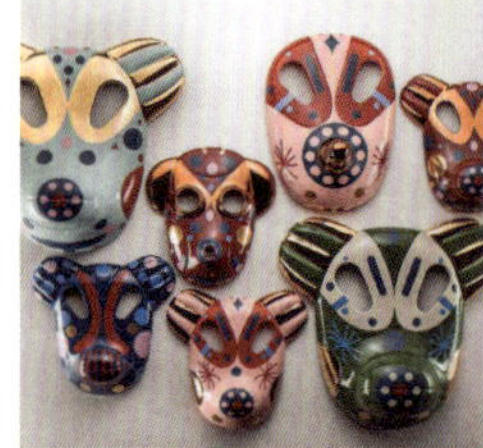

2020
Baile, ceramic
collection for Bosa
Pp. 36, 38–39

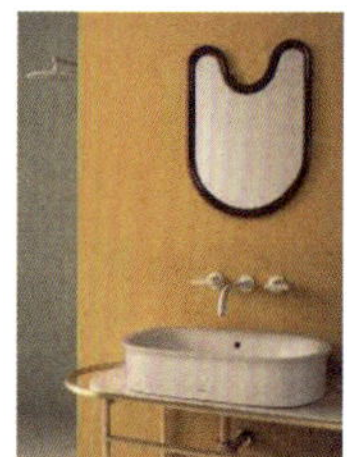

2020
Toto by Hayon,
bathroom collection
for Toto
P. 279

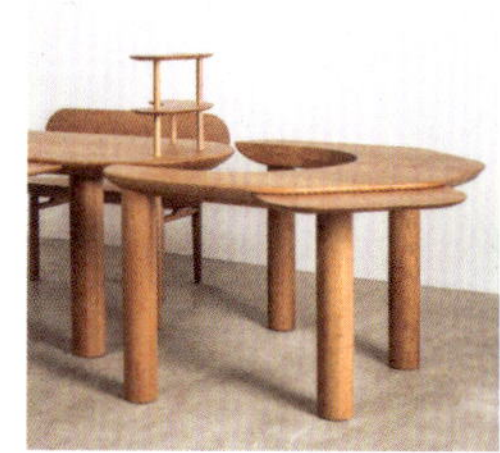

2020
Mesamachine, for
Connected, Design
Museum, London, U.K.,
and Madrid Design
Festival, Madrid, Spain
Pp. 105–107

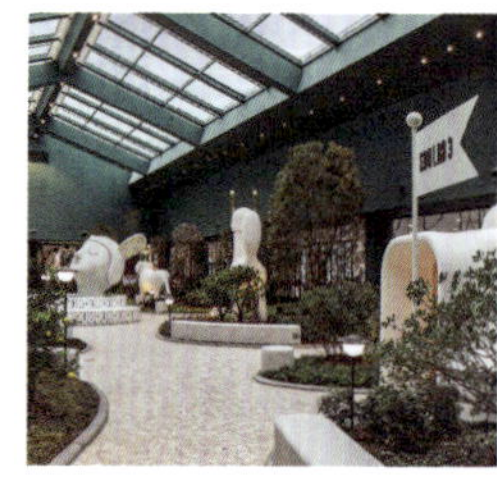

2020
Garden, Children's
Library & Playground,
Hyundai MOKA, Seoul,
South Korea
Pp. 44–47, 84–85, 90–91,
101, 231, 244, 249, 259

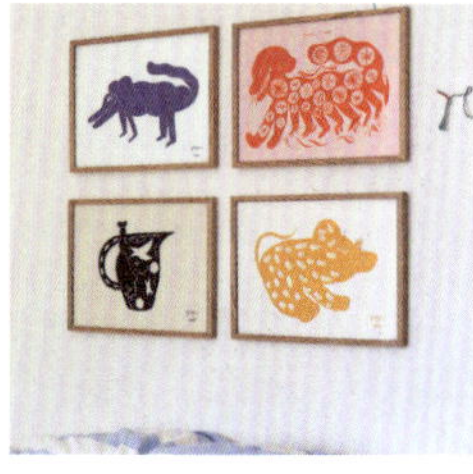

2021
Jaime Hayon × MADO,
graphic prints
for MADO

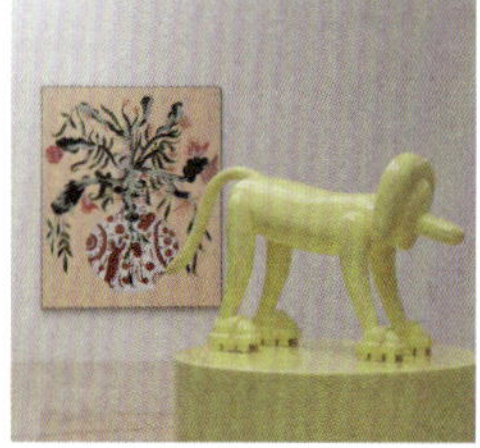

2021
Cosmotik Jungle,
exhibition at L21
Gallery, Mallorca, Spain
Pp. 20–21, 64, 256, 291

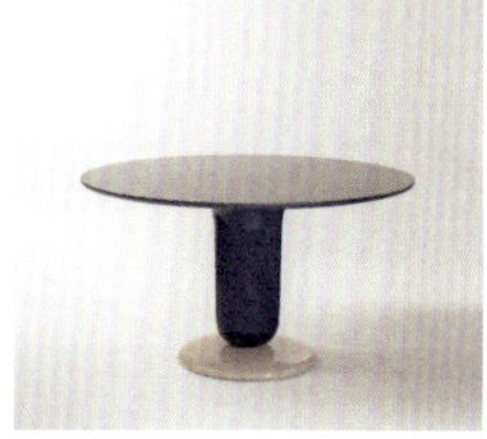

2021
Explorer,
dining table for BD
Barcelona Design
P. 186

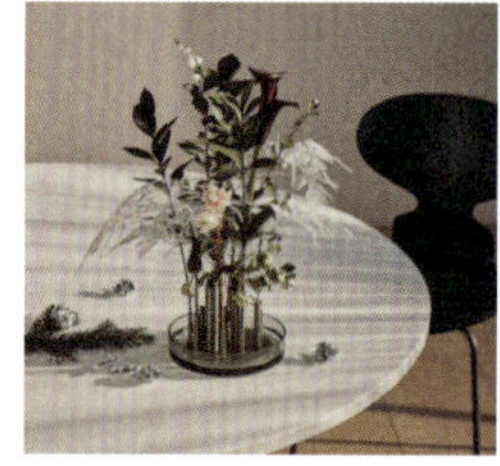

2021
Ikeru, vase
for Fritz Hansen

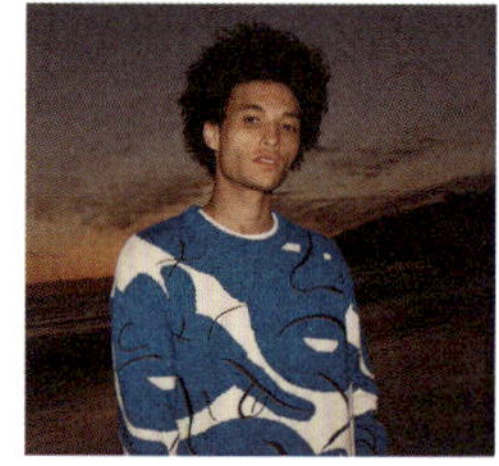

2021
Jaime Hayon × Zara,
streetwear collection
for Zara
Pp. 56, 213

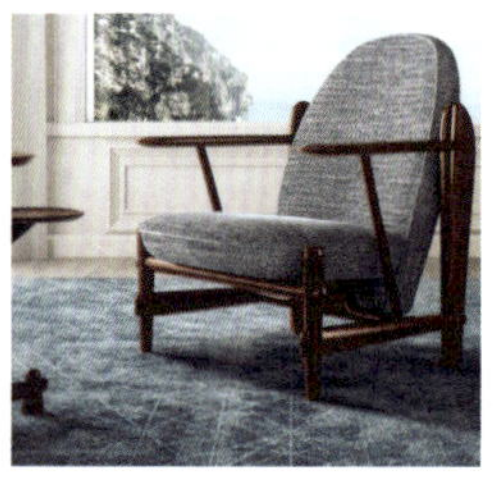

2021
T-bone & Árbol,
armchair and side table
for Ceccotti Collezioni
P. 61

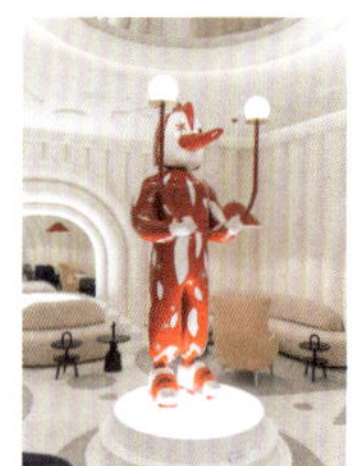

2021
The Hyundai YP Haus,
interior design for
Hyundai Department
Store, Seoul,
South Korea
Pp. 92, 124, 178–181

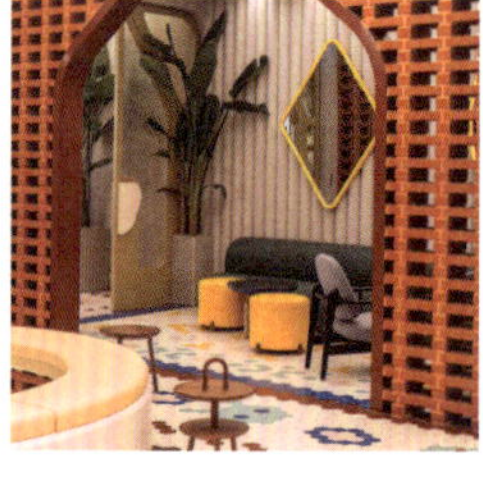

2021
Pangyo VIP Lounge,
interior design for
Hyundai Department
Store, Seoul,
South Korea
Pp. 125–127, 208

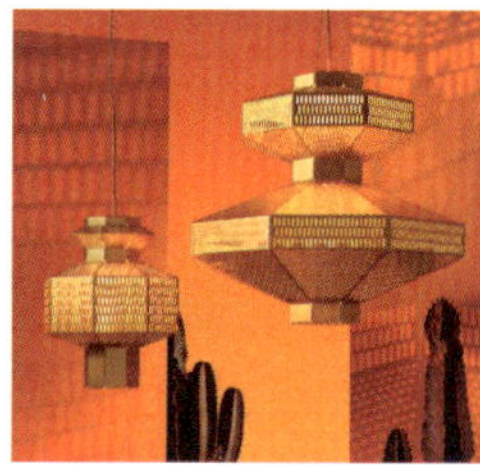

2022
Ma-Rock, lighting
for Parachilna
P. 209

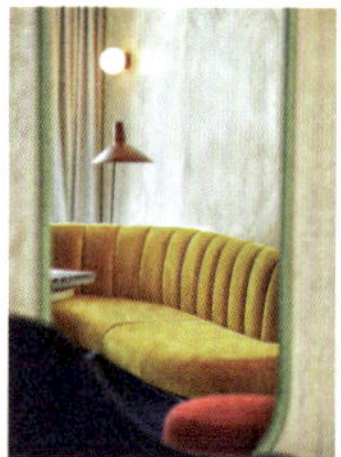

2022
The Standard Hotel,
interior design,
Bangkok, Thailand
Pp. 108, 234, 242,
245, 248

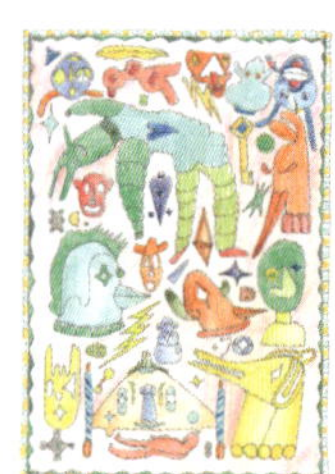

2022
Troupe, rug
for Nanimarquina
P. 94

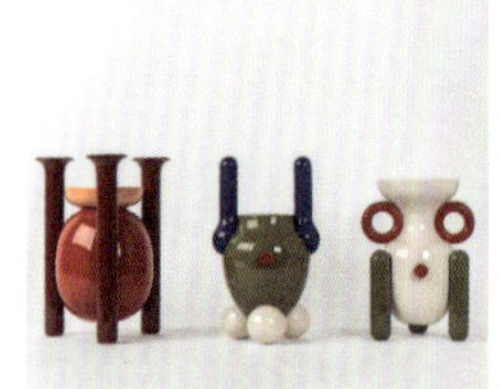

2022
Explorer,
vases for BD
Barcelona Design
P. 22

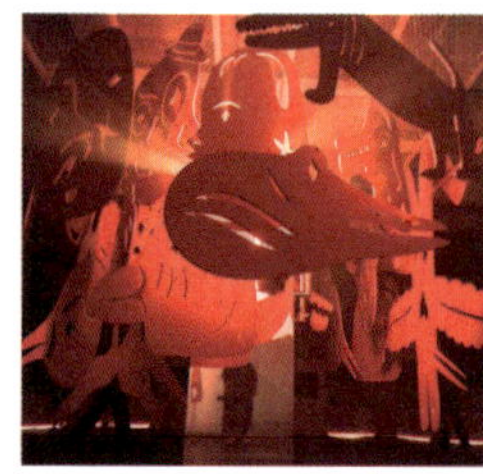

2022
Shadow Theater,
installation at the
Bangkok Design Week,
Bangkok, Thailand
P. 281

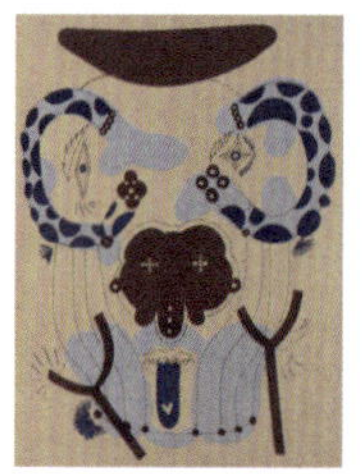

2022
Polígrafa
Lithograph Series
P. 236

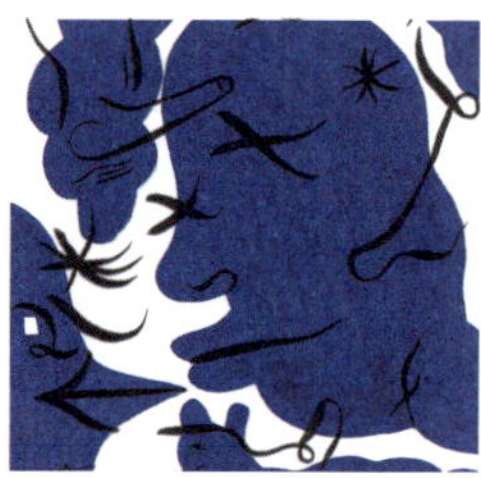

2022
Limited-edition prints
for Wrong Shop
Pp. 16, 40

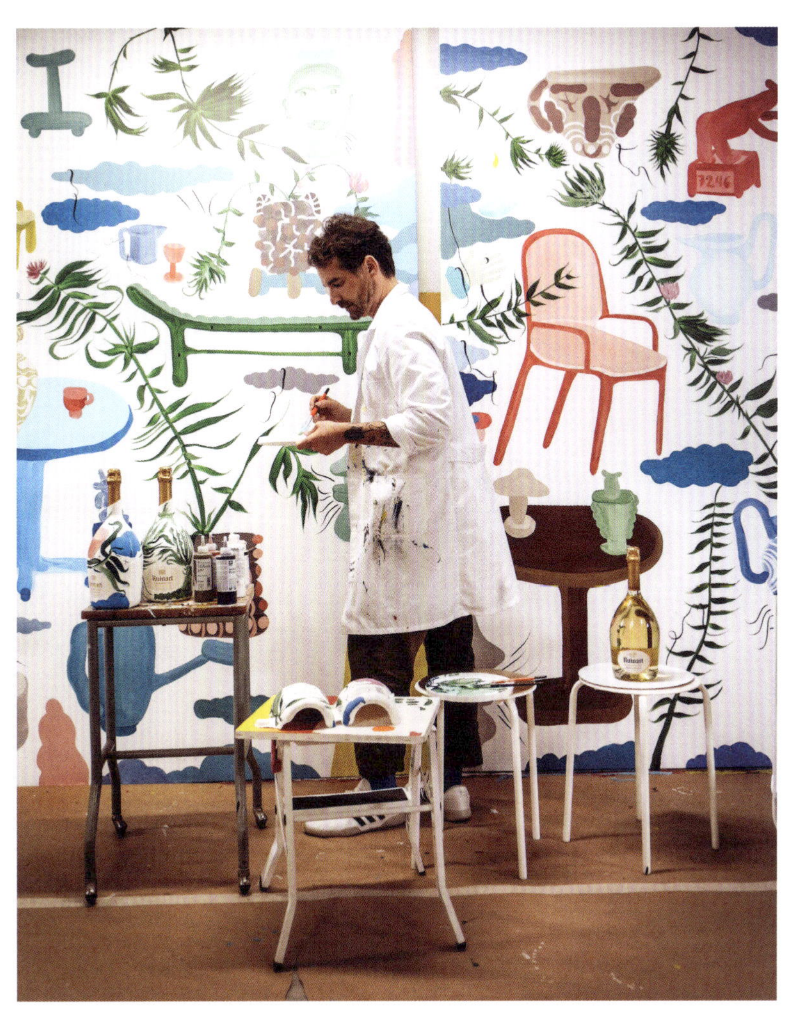

HISTORY OF
AN OPTIMISTIC
AESTHETIC

EXHIBITIONS

2021
Cosmotik Jungle, exhibition at L21 Gallery, Mallorca, Spain

2020
Connected, Design Museum, London, U.K., and Madrid Design Festival, Madrid, Spain

2019
Serious Fun, exhibition at Daelim Museum, Seoul, South Korea

Swarovski Carousel, installation at Swarovski Kristallwelten, Wattens, Austria

Masquemask, installation at Central Museum of Textiles, Łódź, Poland

2018
Jaime Hayon Cosmos, exhibition at Ocean Terminal Forecourt, Harbour City, Hong Kong

Funtastico, exhibition at Songshan Cultural Park, Taipei, Taiwan

Chromatico, exhibition at Galerie Kreo, Paris and London

Backstage, exhibition at Fernán Gómez Cultural Centre, Madrid, Spain

2017
Merry Go Zoo, installation at High Museum of Art, Atlanta, USA

Technicolor, exhibition at High Museum of Art, Atlanta, USA

Afrikando, exhibition at Milwaukee Art Museum, Milwaukee, USA

Funtastico, exhibition at Modern Art Museum, Shanghai, China

Stone Age Folk, installation at Palazzo Serbelloni for Caesarstone, Milan, Italy

2016
Tiovivo, installation at High Museum of Art, Atlanta, USA

Hayon DNA Gallery, Guest of Honor exhibition at Stockholm Furniture & Light Fair, Sweden

2015
Funtastico, exhibition at Holon Design Museum, Holon, Israel

Game On, exhibition at Galerie Kreo, Paris and London

Kuriopotec, exhibition at the Garden of Wonders, Milan, Italy

Urban Perspectives, installation, Milan, Italy

2014
Backstage, installation at Spanish Embassy, Tokyo, Japan

¿Qué Pasa Guey? exhibition at TextielMuseum, Tilburg, Netherlands

2013
Funtastico, retrospective exhibition at Groninger Museum, Groningen, Netherlands

Fauna by Hayon, exhibition at TextielMuseum, Tilburg, Netherlands

2011
Testa Mecanica, exhibition at Glasstress, Venice, Italy

Selection by Hayon, exhibition at OA Gallery, Madrid, Spain

2010
Moving Ideas, Designer of the Year exhibition at Maison&Objet Paris, France

Smart Grid Gallery, installation for Enel at Salone del Mobile, Milan, Italy

2009
Crystal Candy Set, installation at Baccarat Salle de Bal, Paris, & Rossana Orlandi Gallery, Milan

The Tournament, installation in Trafalgar square during the London Design Festival, U.K.

Jaime Hayon, ceramics exhibition at British Ceramics Biennial, Stoke-on-Trent, U.K.

American Chateau, exhibition at Spring Projects Gallery London, U.K.

2008
Guest of honour, installation for Biennale Interieur, Kortrijk, Belgium

Jet Set, installation for Bisazza, Milan, Italy

Stage: Jaime Hayon, installation at Lane Crawford, Hong Kong

Stage, installation for Isetan, Tokyo, Japan

2007
Stage, installation at Vivid Gallery, Rotterdam, Netherlands

Bisazza: Hayon Pixel-Ballet, installation for Bisazza, Milan, Italy

J'aime, design installation at Salone del Mobile, Milan, Italy

2006
Stage, installation at Aram Gallery, London, U.K.

2005–2006
Mon Cirque, exhibition in Barcelona, Lisbon, Minneapolis, Paris, Cologne & Kuala Lumpur

2004
AQHayon Collection featured in the Tank at the Design Museum, London, U.K.

2003
Mediterranean Digital Baroque, exhibition at David Gill Gallery, London, U.K.

AWARDS

2021
Spanish National Design Award, Designer of the Year

Wallpaper Design Awards, MOKA Playground

Madrid Design Festival Award, Designer of the Year

2020
Elle Decoration Spain Design Awards, Art Designer of the Year

2019
Wallpaper Design Awards, Swarovski Carousel

Wallpaper Awards, Lightolight & Lightoread for Parachilna

2018
Elle Decoration International Design Award, Hayon × Nani for Nanimarquina

Elle Decoration International Design Award, Wing Bed for Wittmann

Ad Spain, Designer of the Year

2017
Stockholm Furniture Fair, Guest of Honor

2016
Elle Deco International Design Awards, Designer of the Year

German Design Awards, Frames Collection for Expormim

2015
Wallpaper Design Awards, Villa Le Lac Paulownia

2014
Fuera De Serie Best Interior

Elle Deco International Design Awards, Ro lounge chair for Fritz Hansen

Adi Fad Silver Delta Award, Gardenias Collection for BD Barcelona Design

2013
Wallpaper Design Awards, Restaurant Le Sergent Recruteur

2012
Elle Decoration International Design Award, Bisazza Bath by Hayon

2011
Ad Spain, Designer of the Year

2010
Maison&Objet, Designer of the Year Scènes d'Intérieur

2009
Ad Russia, Designer of the Year

2008
Elle Deco Alemania, Designer of the Year

Intérieur Biennal, Guest of Honor—Designer of the Year

Elle Deco Japan, Designer of the Year

2007
Wallpaper Awards, The Tournament

2006
Elle Deco Awards, AQ Hayon Collection

Jaime Hayon (b. 1974), is a Spanish artist known for his designs, interiors, large urban installations, sculptures, and paintings. His optimistic aesthetics and bold visual language play with shapes, colours, and recurring motifs. His work has been displayed in monographic exhibitions in museums, galleries, and fairs in Europe, America, the Middle East, and Asia.

For the last two decades, Hayon has been the subject of multiple books and publications. He received the highest recognition in Spain—the national design award, as well as many more international media prizes and awards.

He trained at the European Institute of Design in Madrid and then specialized in industrial design at the École Nationale Supérieure des Arts Décoratifs (ENSAD) in Paris. He then joined Fabrica, a research centre of the Benetton group in Italy, where he headed the design department for four years.

In the field of design, some of the most renowned European and Asian companies have relied on Hayon to create design collections, spaces, shops, and exhibitions that interpret the spirit of his time.

Hayon's works are part of the collections of numerous museums, including the Groninger Museum in the Netherlands, the Museu del Disseny in Barcelona, the MAD in New York, the Design Museum in Holon, the High Museum in Atlanta, the Milan Triennale, the North Carolina Museum of Art, and the TextielMuseum in the Netherlands. He has been a visiting lecturer at the ECAL in Lausanne, the Domaine de Boisbuchet in Lessac, the Łódź Design Festival in Poland, the National Design Centre in Singapore, and the Design Indaba in Cape Town, amongst many others.

JAIME HAYON

This book was
conceived by
Hayonstudio

Edited by
Hayonstudio
and gestalten

Contributing Editors
Marco Sammicheli
for Hayonstudio
Robert Klanten
for gestalten

Text by
Marco Sammicheli

Captions by
Claudia Oliva

Editorial Management
Claudia Oliva
for Hayonstudio
Anna Diekmann
for gestalten

Graphic Design
Zaven

Typeface
GT Flexa Standard
by Dominik Huber
with Marc Kappeler

Printed by
Wilco Art Books
Netherlands,
Amersfoort
Made in Europe

Photo Credits

&Tradition
Aleksandra Pawłowska
American Hardwood
  Export Council
Arflex
Baccarat
Beaumarly
Bernhardt
Bisazza
Boråstapeter
Bosa
BD Barcelona Design
Camper
Cassina
Ceccotti Collezioni
Cristina Vaquero
Daelim Museum
Dnd Handles
Established & Sons
Expormim
Fabrice Gousset
Fritz Hansen
Gaia & Gino
Galerie Kreo
Groninger Museum
Harbour City
Hayonstudio
High Museum of Art
Hyundai Department
  Store
James Mollison
Jean Pierre Vailancourt
Jijibaba
Jonathan Hillyer
Kyungsub Shin
L21 Gallery
Lladró
Łódź Design Festival
KlunderBie
Kutani Choemon
Yves Drieghe
MADO
Maison Matisse
Magis
Mark Cocksedge
Metalarte
Milwaukee Art Museum
MINI
Moooi
Nanimarquina
Nienke Klunder
Nodus

Orolog
Parachilna
Paola C
Piper-Heidsieck
Polígrafa
Ruinart
Salva López
Sacha Maric
Sé London
Standard Hotels
Southmead Hospital
Susana Fialho Mota
Swarovski
The Ravestijn Gallery
The Rug Company
Tom Mannion
Toto
Toy
Vicky Lam
Viccarbe
Vista Alegre
Wittmann
WOORI
Wrong Shop
Zara

Published by gestalten
Berlin 2022

ISBN
978-3-96704-054-8

© Die Gestalten Verlag
GmbH & Co. KG,
Berlin 2022

All rights reserved.
No part of this
publication may
be reproduced
or transmitted in
any form or by any
means, electronic or
mechanical, including
photocopy or any
storage and retrieval
system, without
permission in writing
from the publisher.

Respect copyrights,
encourage creativity!

For more information,
and to order books,
please visit
www.gestalten.com

Bibliographic
information published
by the Deutsche
Nationalbibliothek.
The Deutsche
Nationalbibliothek
lists this publication
in the Deutsche
Nationalbibliografie;
detailed bibliographic
data is available
online at
www.dnb.de

Thanks to

Hayonstudio
Nienke Klunder
Massimo Parolin
Claudia Oliva
Matteo Zorzenoni
Marco Serena
Giulia Morrone
Giulia Marchetto
Angel Tausia
Luca Tresso
Claudia Ortega
Vicent Carbonell
Carla López
Kaii Tu
Angelika Seeschaaf
Danilo Morosin

Thank you to all
our clients and
collaborators who have
believed in creativity
and dared to take
on new challenges
together with us.

Special thanks to
Nienke Klunder for
many years of close
creative collaboration
and art direction.
Also a special mention
to KlunderBie who
have collaborated for
over a decade with
the photography of
our projects.

Thank you to friends
and family who I have
had the luck to share
this journey with.

↓ The Answers in the Clouds—Acrylic on canvas, detail, 2022

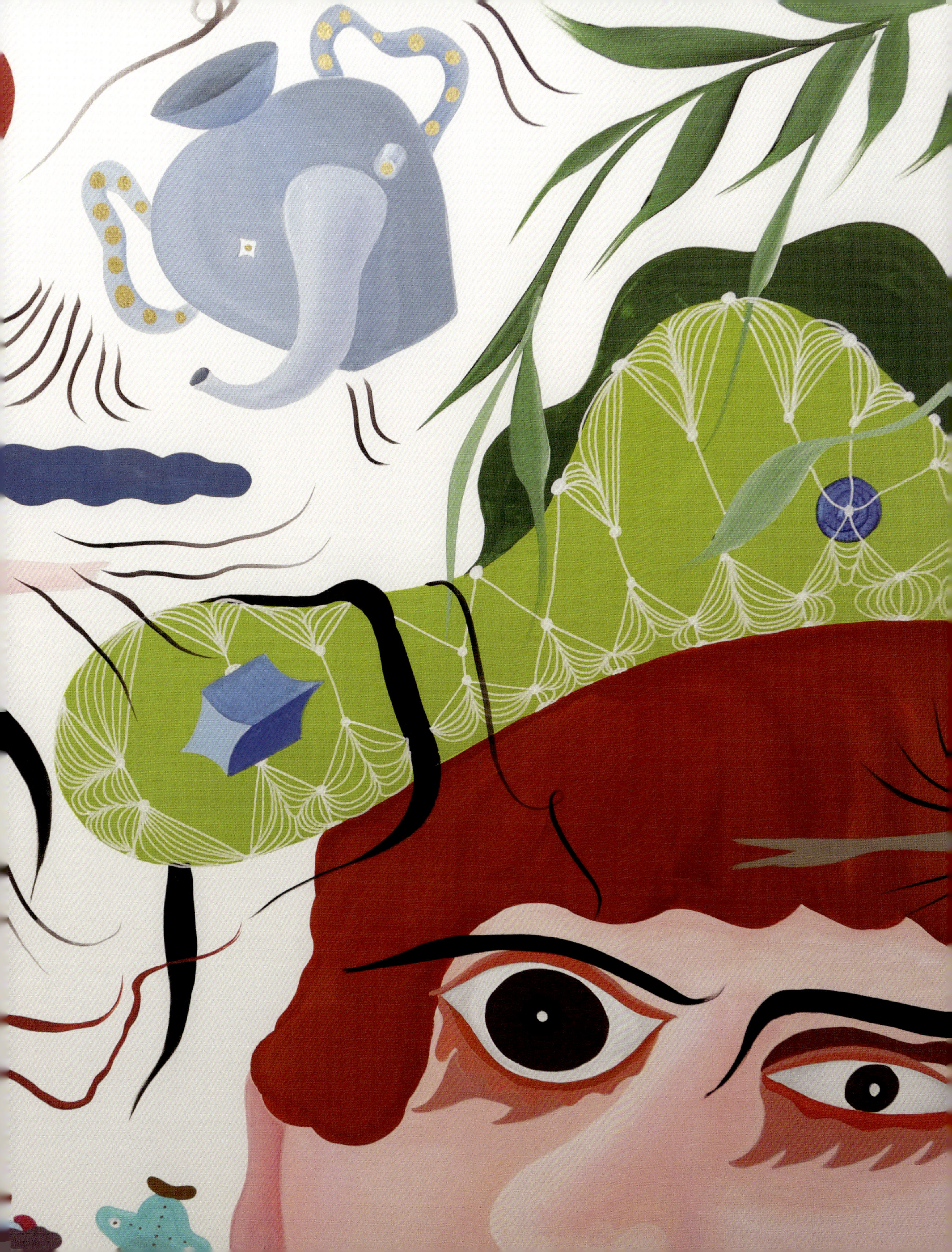

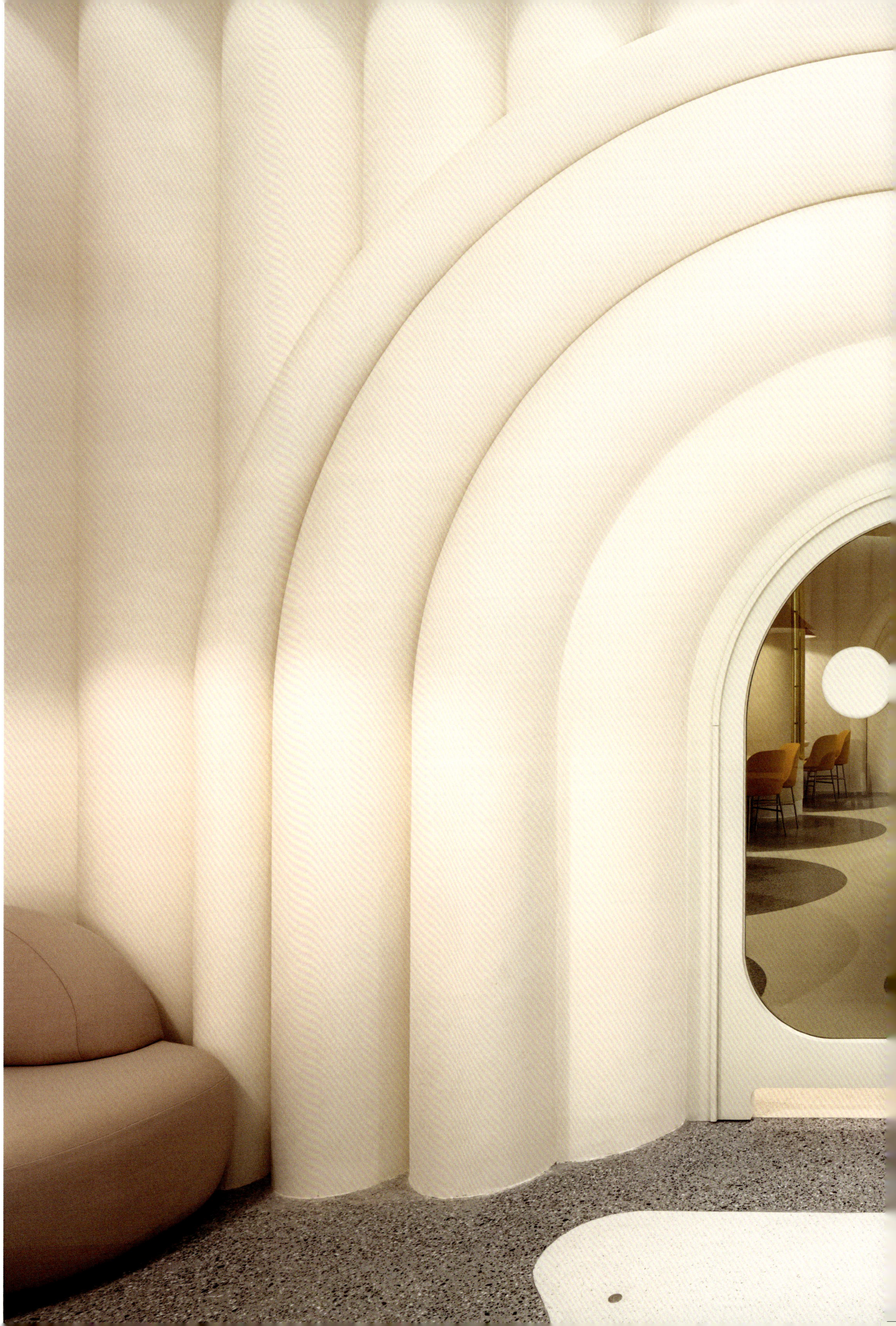

↓ The Hyundai YP Haus—Lounge entrance door and interior design for Hyundai Department Store, Seoul, South Korea, 2021

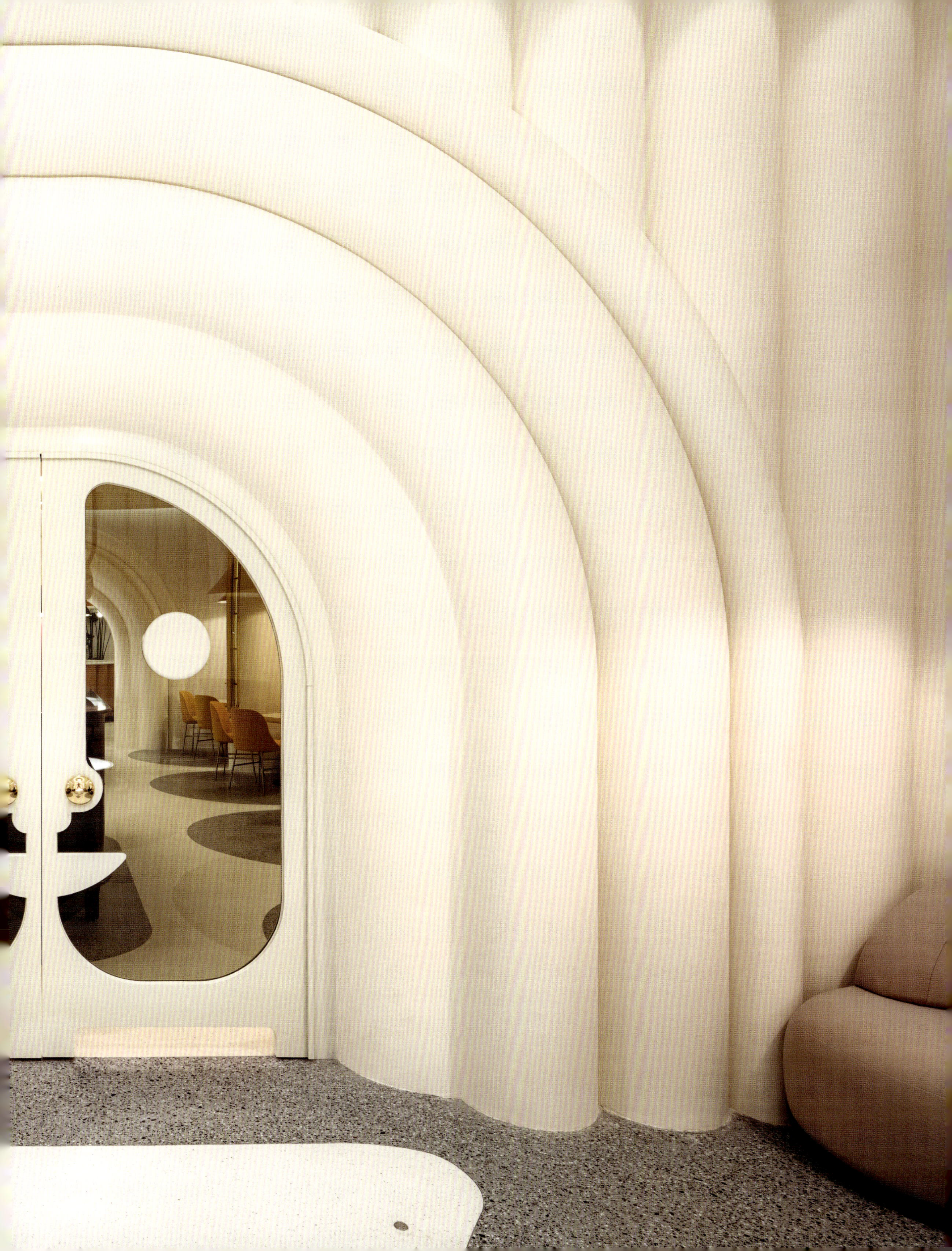

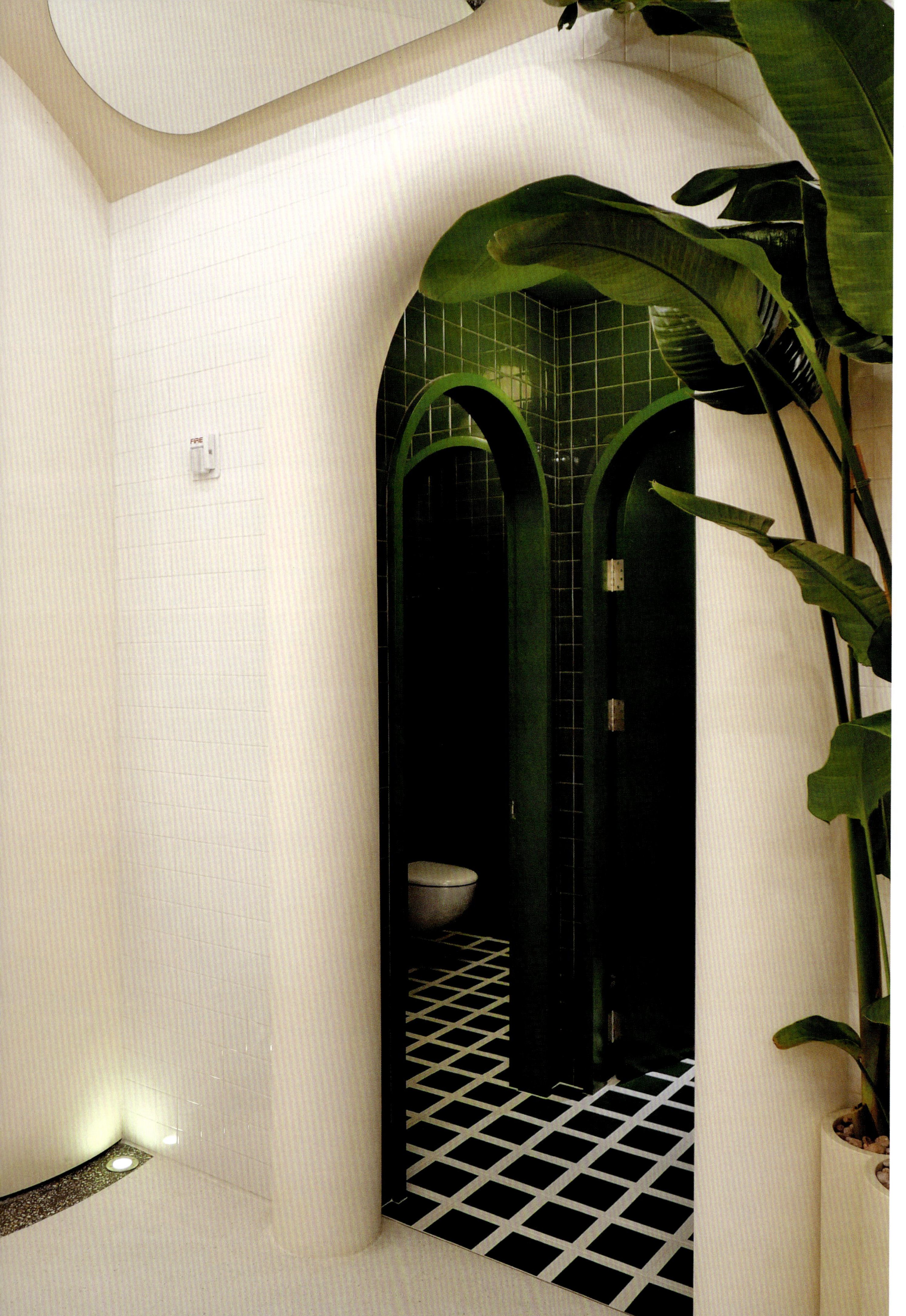

↑↓ The Hyundai YP Haus—Restrooms and lounge area and interior design for Hyundai Department Store, Seoul, South Korea, 2021

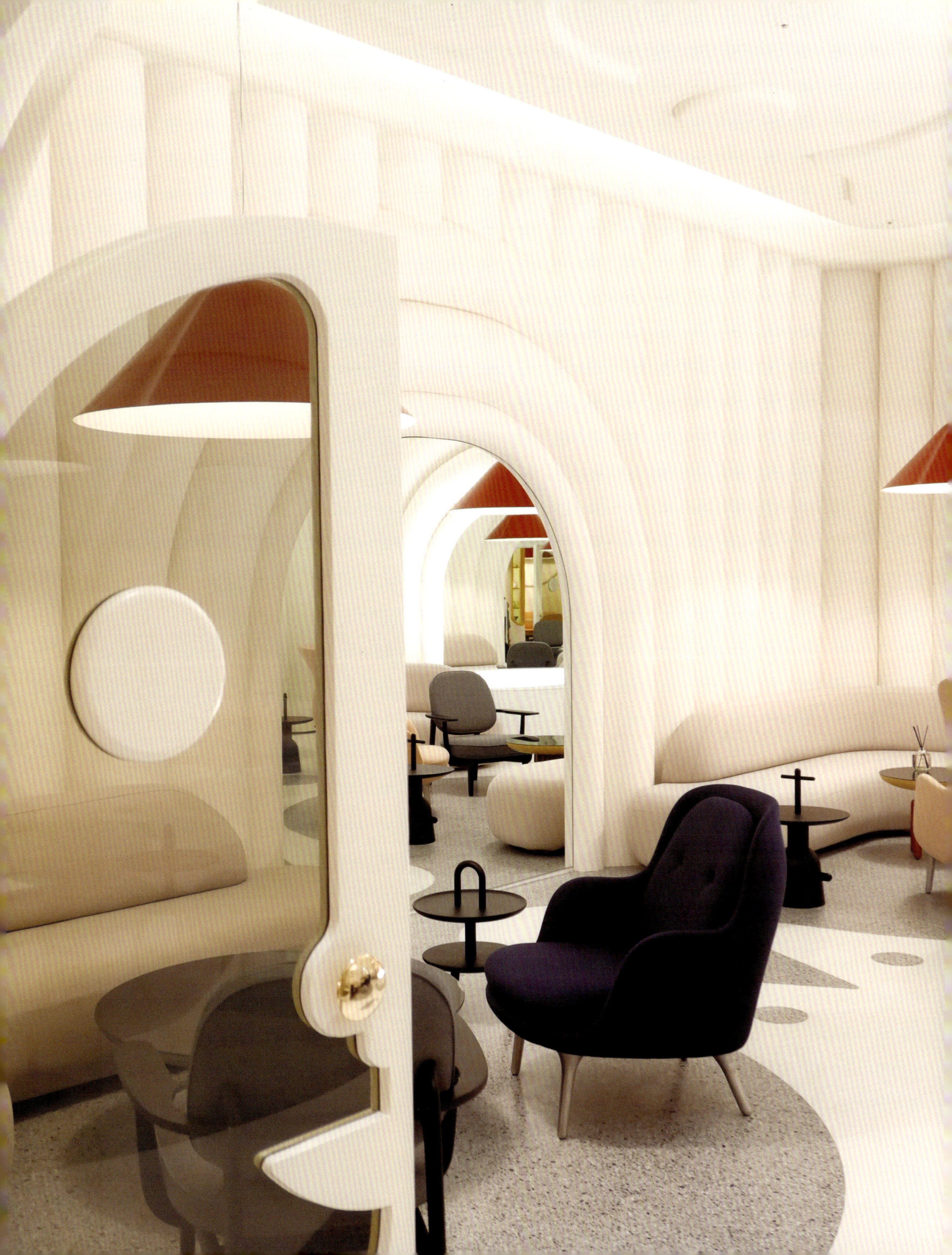

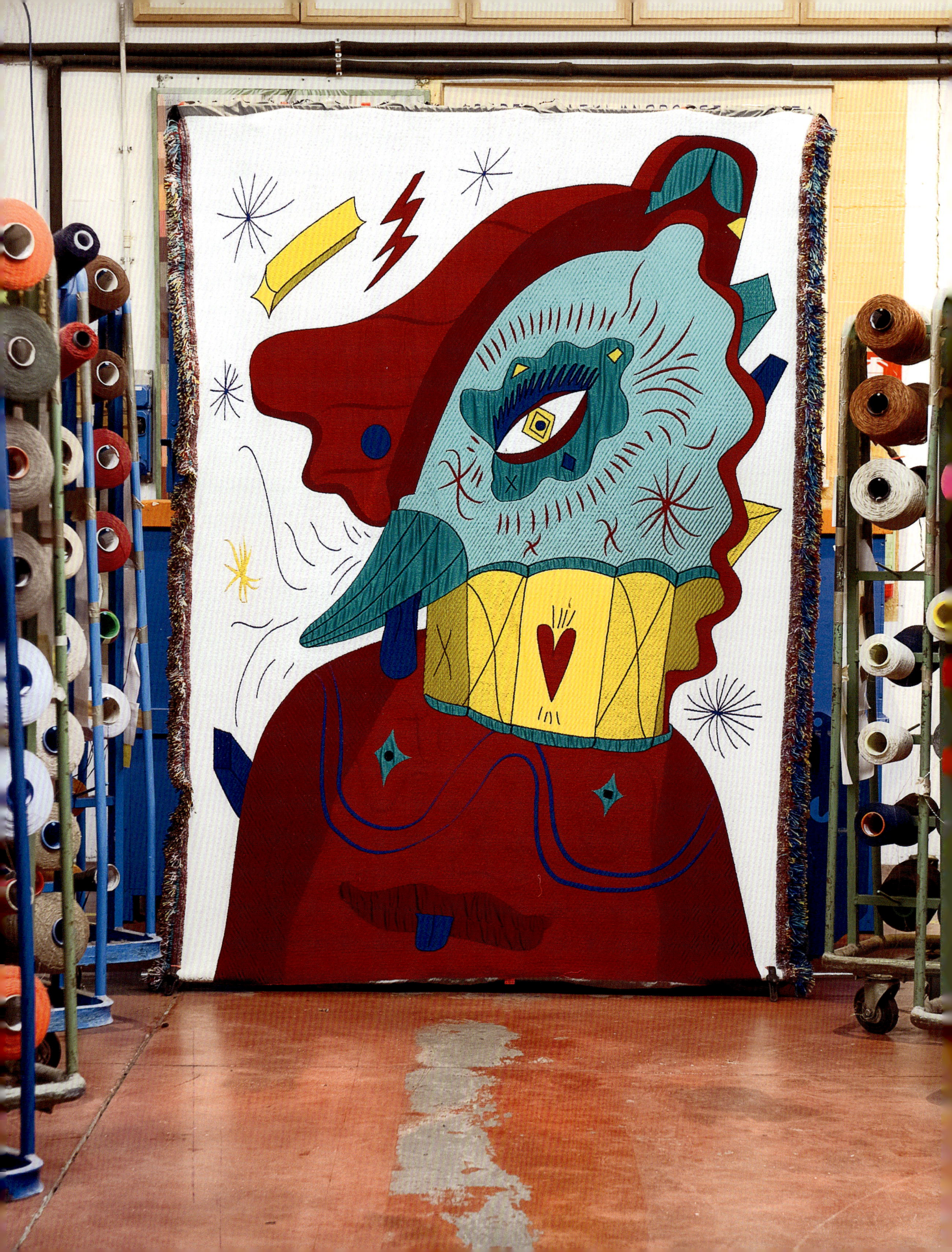

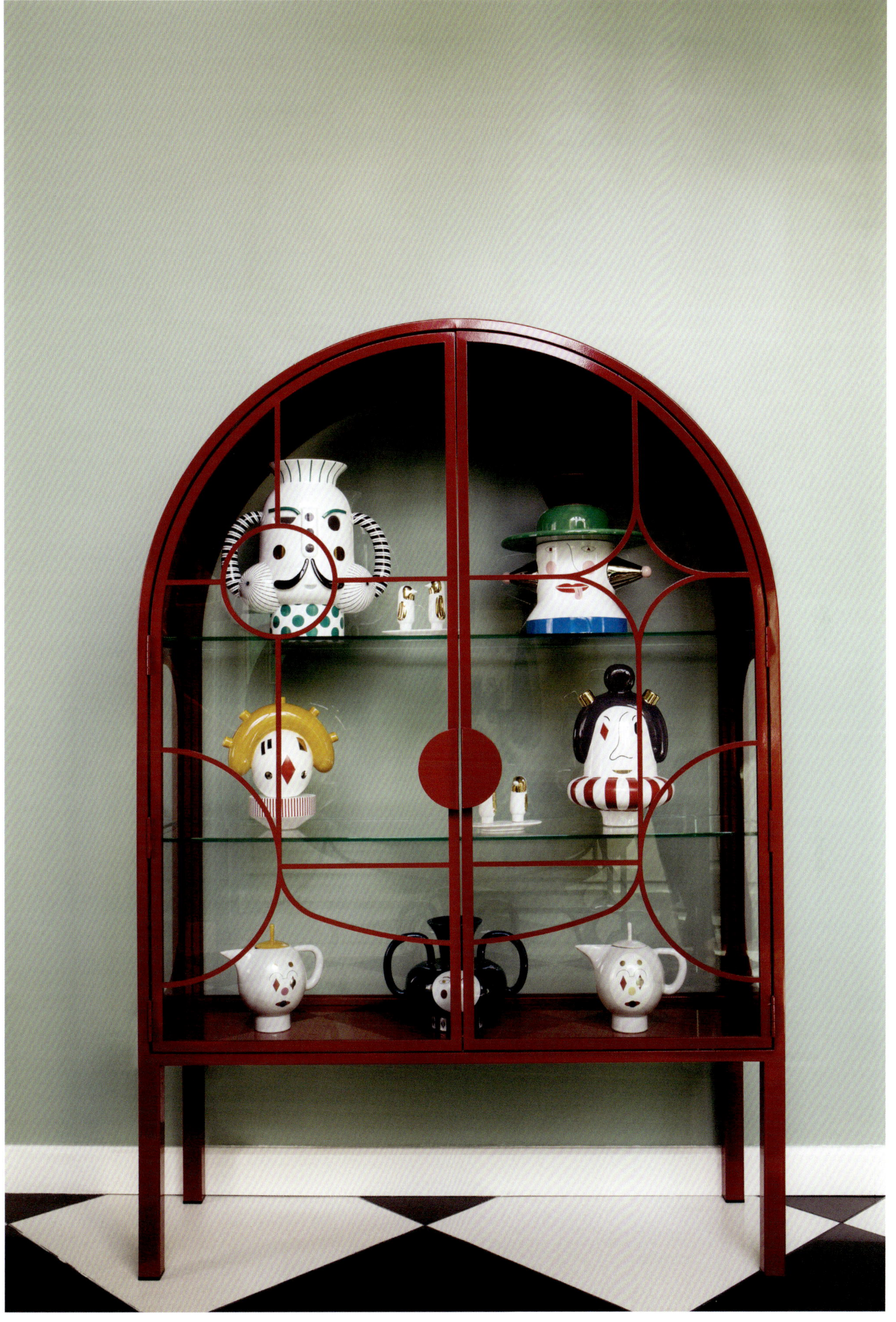

↑ Tugo—Recycled plastic tapestry at Bonotto atelier for Rossana Orlandi exhibition, Milan, Italy, 2019
↓ Custom-made cabinet with Theatre Hayon ceramic collection at La Terraza del Casino restaurant, Madrid, Spain, 2018

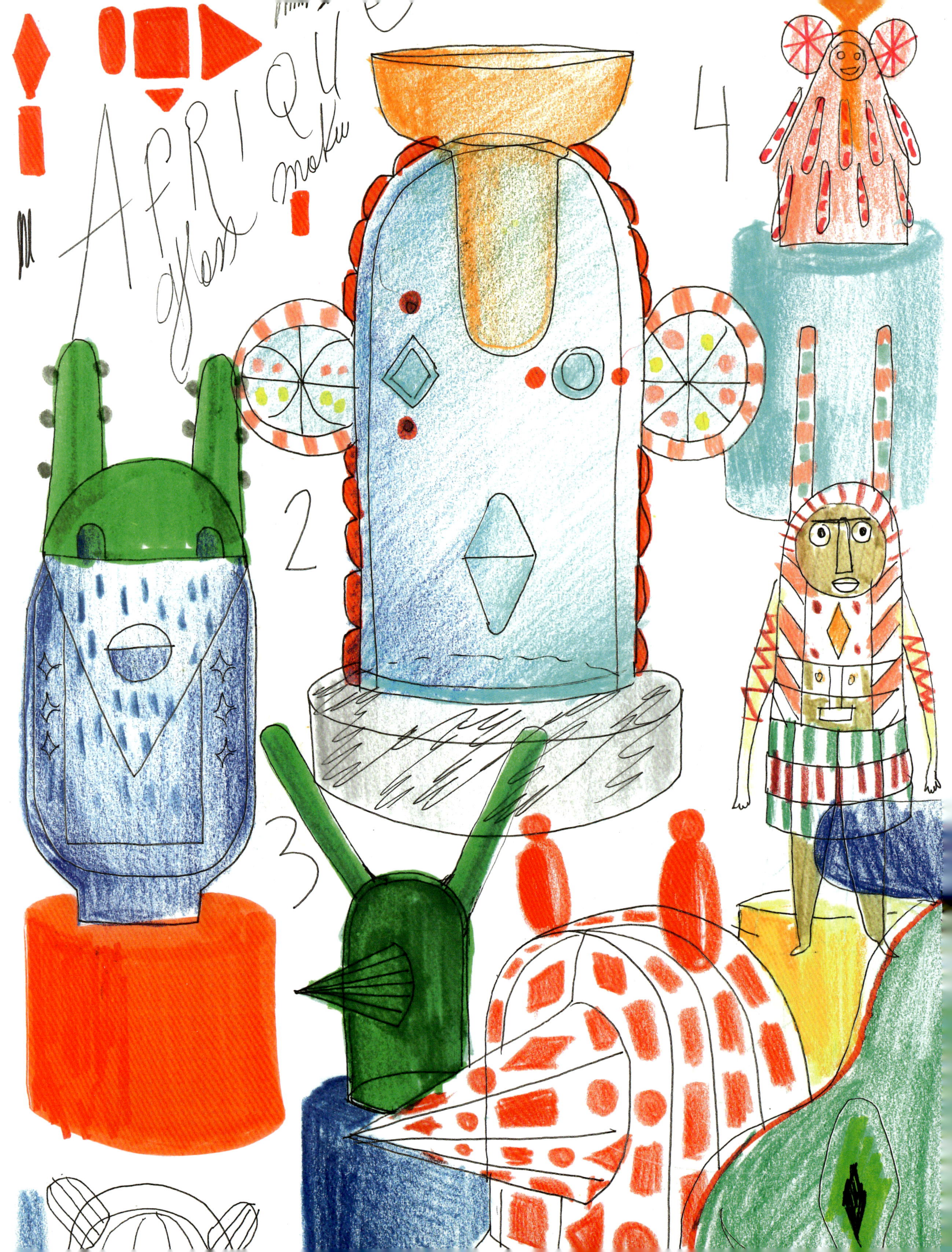

AFRIQUE
Hass moku
2
3
4

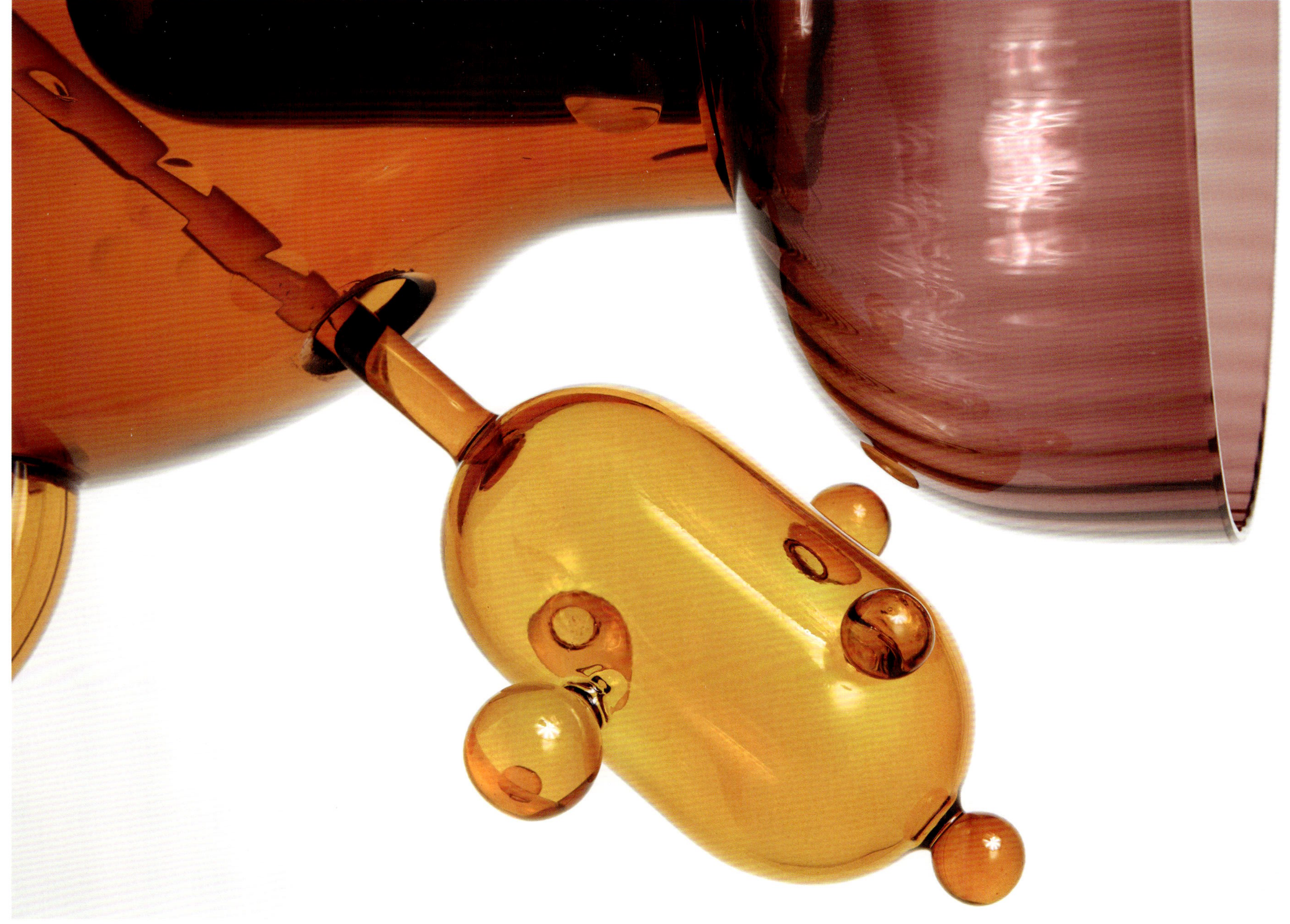
↑ Africa-inspired sketches for vases
↓ Rojopom—Handblown glass vase for Galerie Kreo Chromatico exhibition, 2018

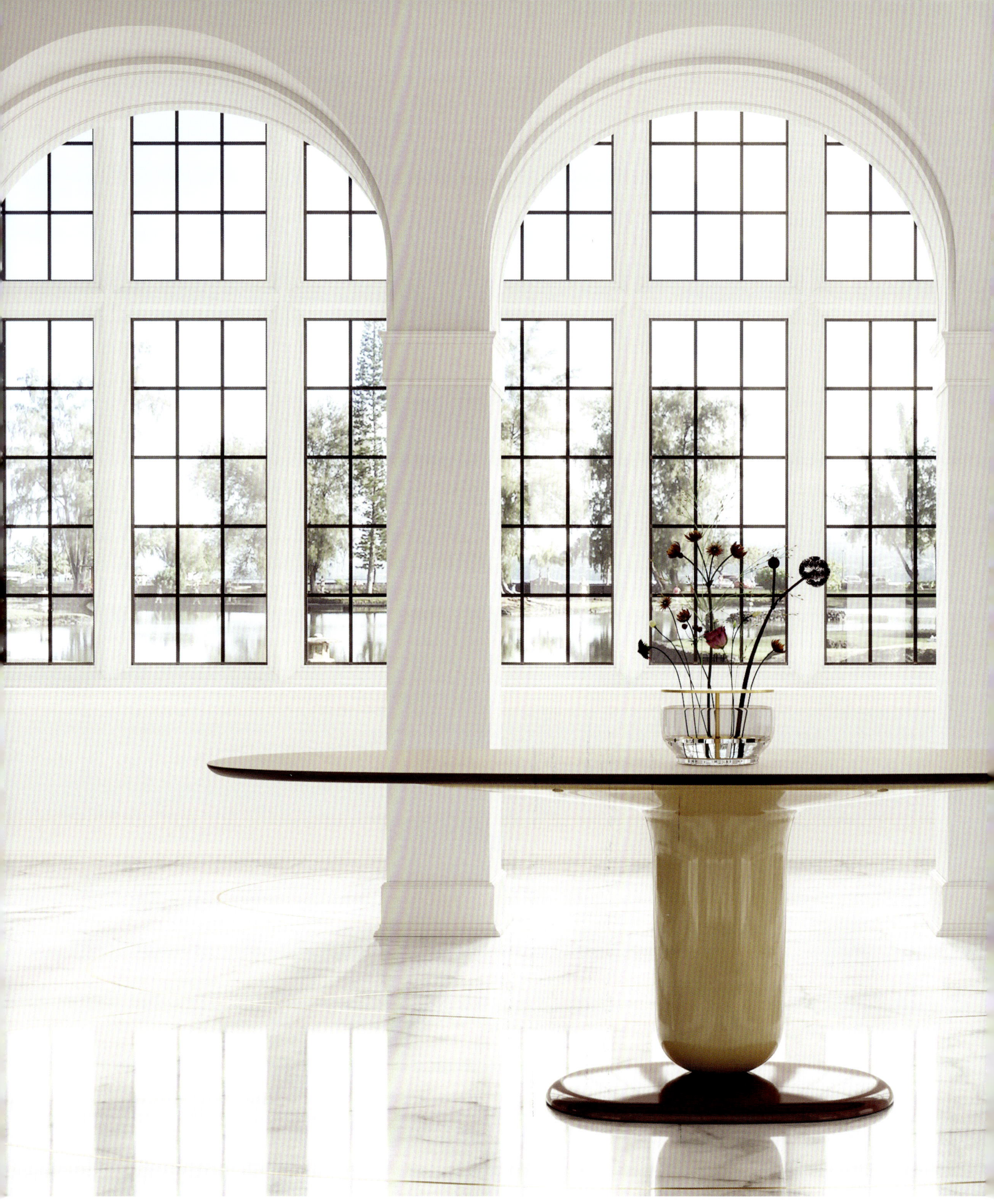

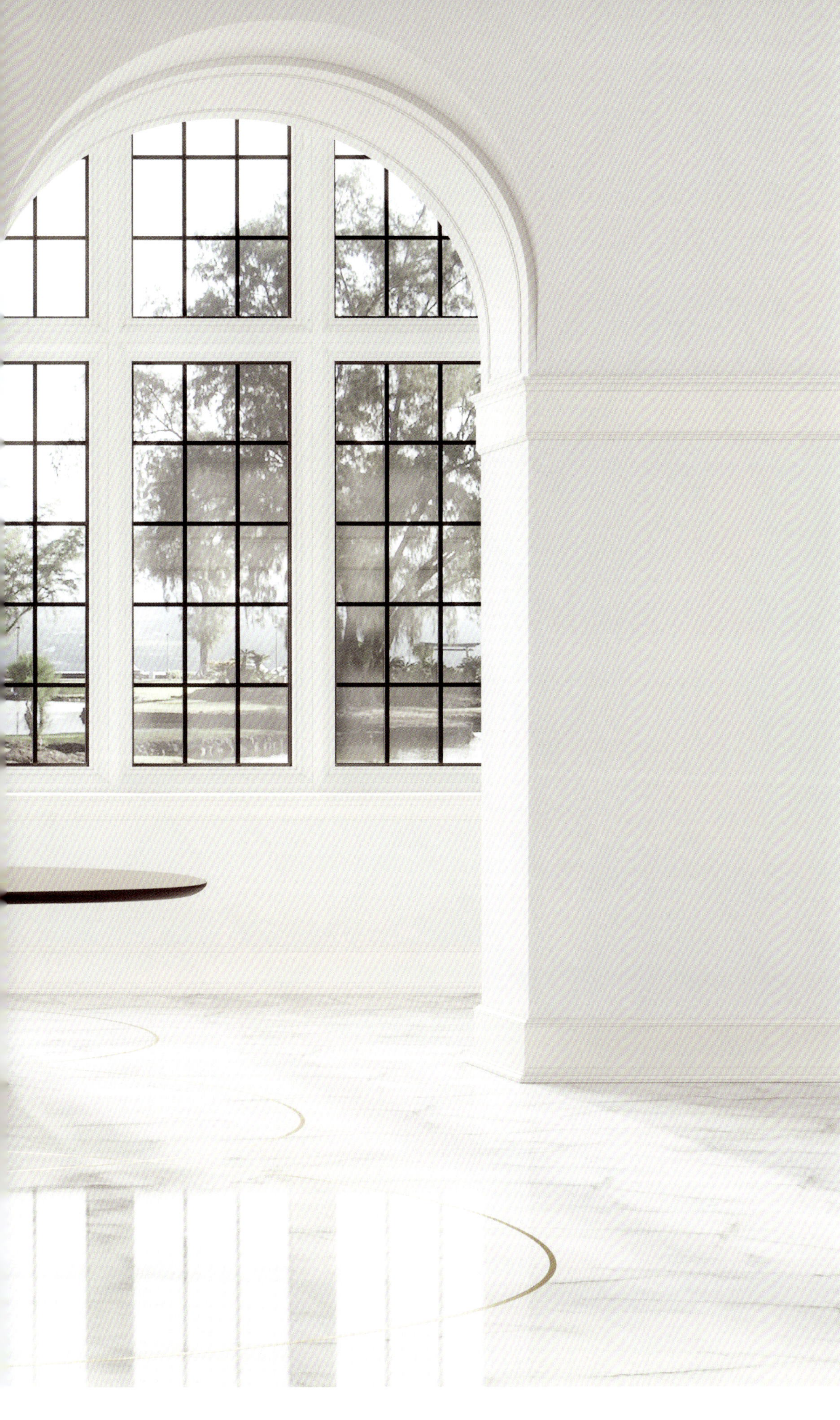

↑ Explorer—Dining table for BD Barcelona Design, 2021

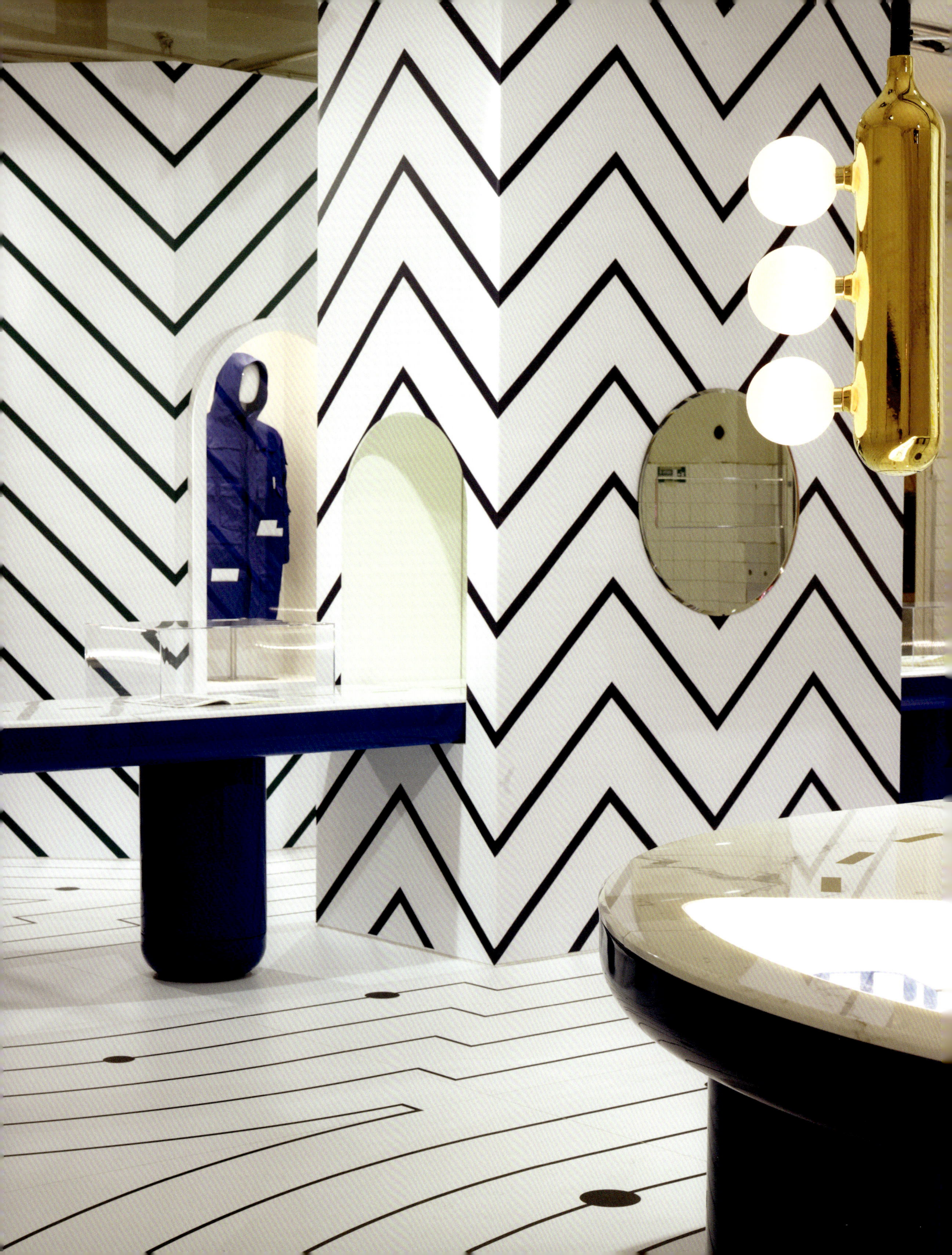

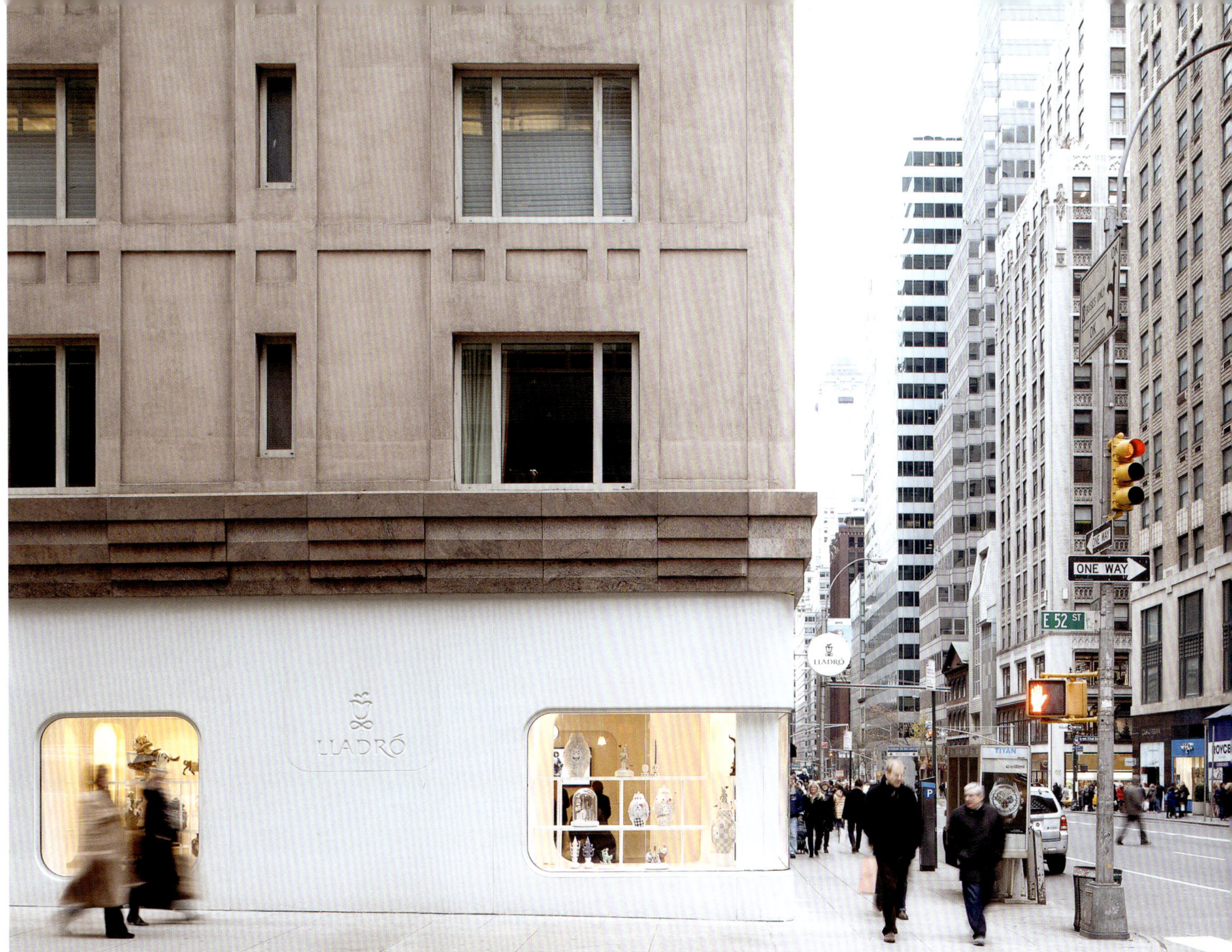

↑ Urban Perspectives—Installation for MINI, Milan, Italy, 2015
↓ Lladró store, Madison Avenue—Interior design project, New York, USA, 2012

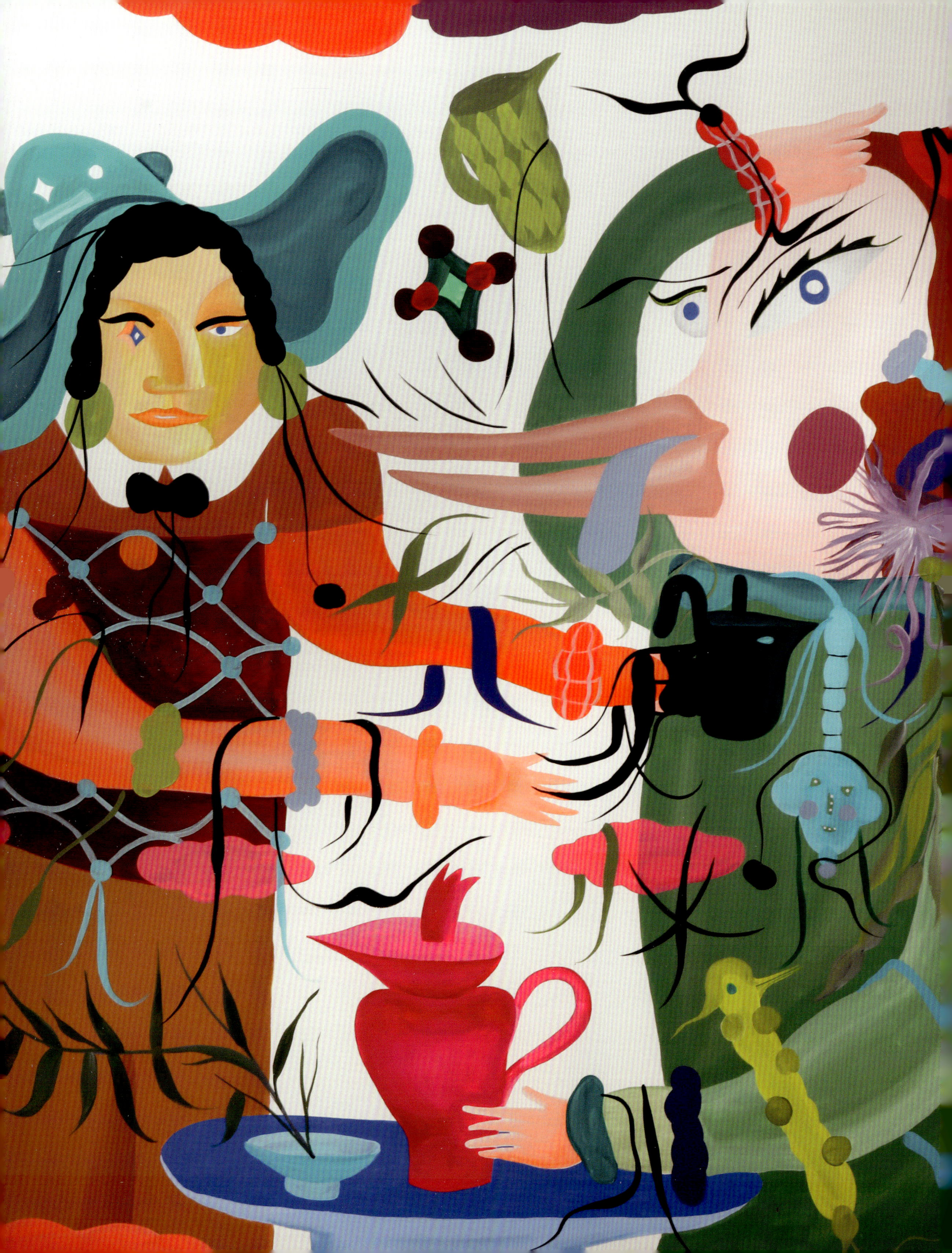

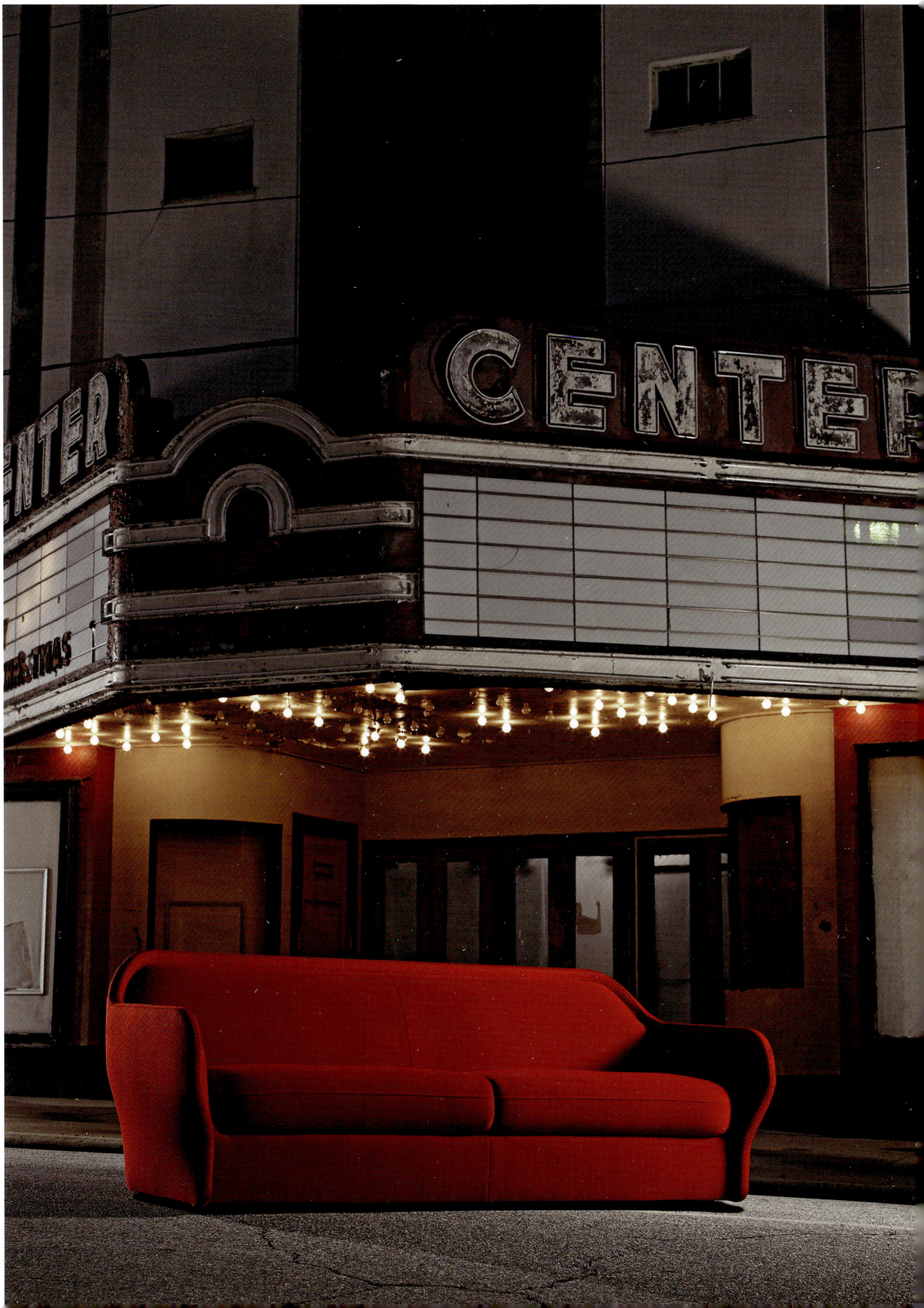

↑ The Tea Set—Acrylic on canvas, detail, 2022
↓ Bandot—Sofa for Bernhardt Design, 2010

→ For me space is tactile and my senses provide me with the unit of measurement I use when I design anything. Thanks to design, I can use my hands to think of objects that create relationships.

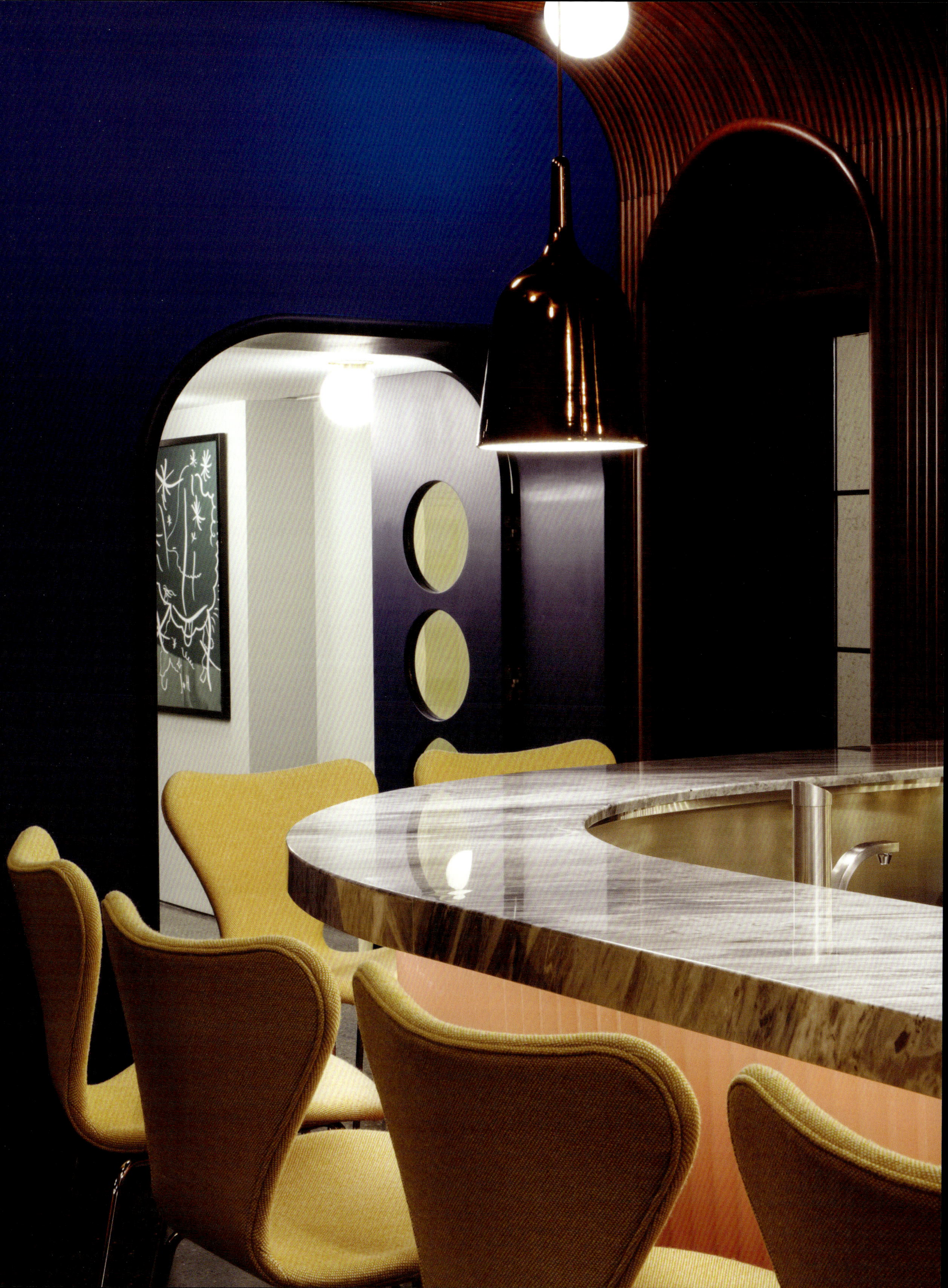

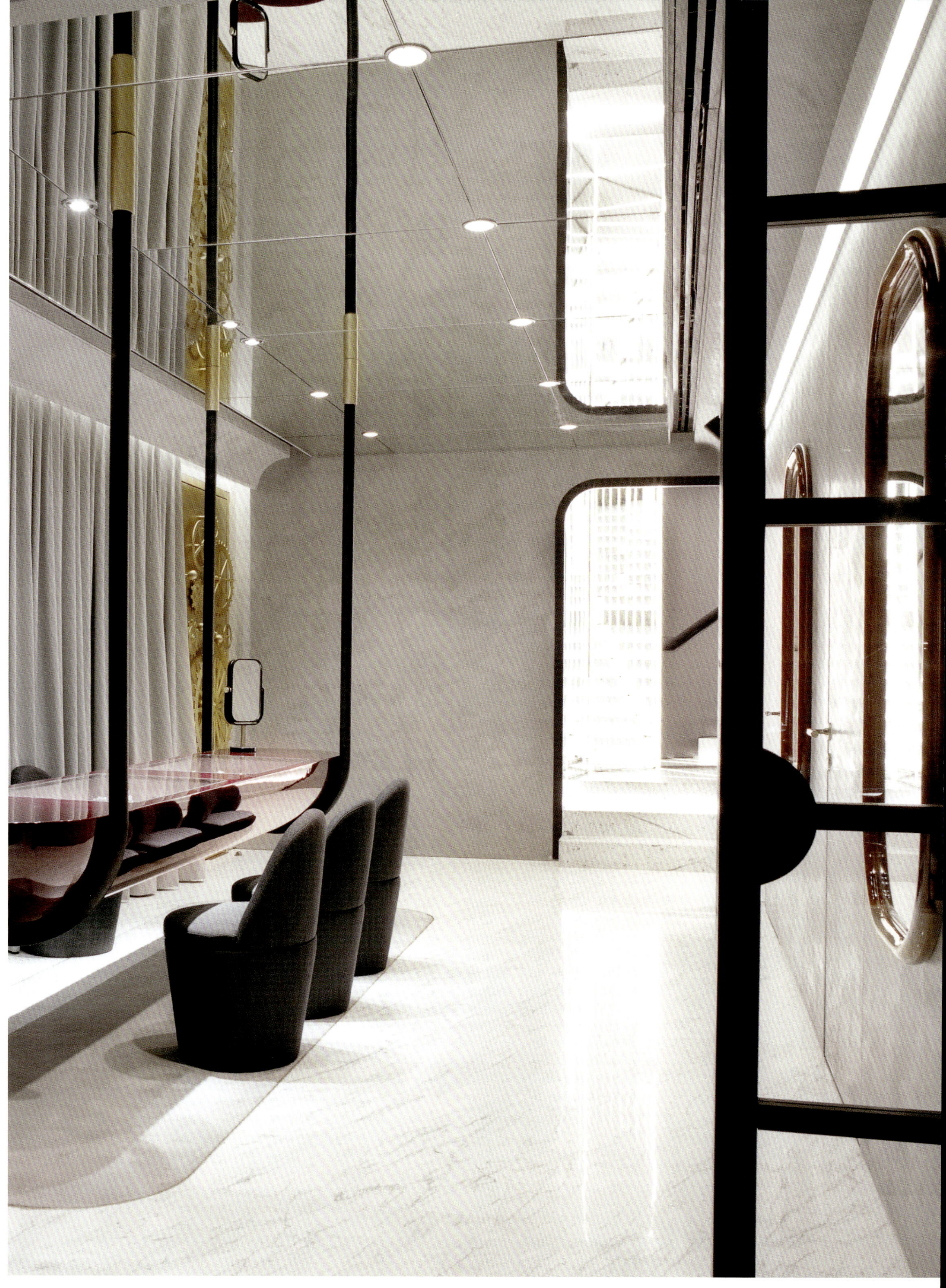

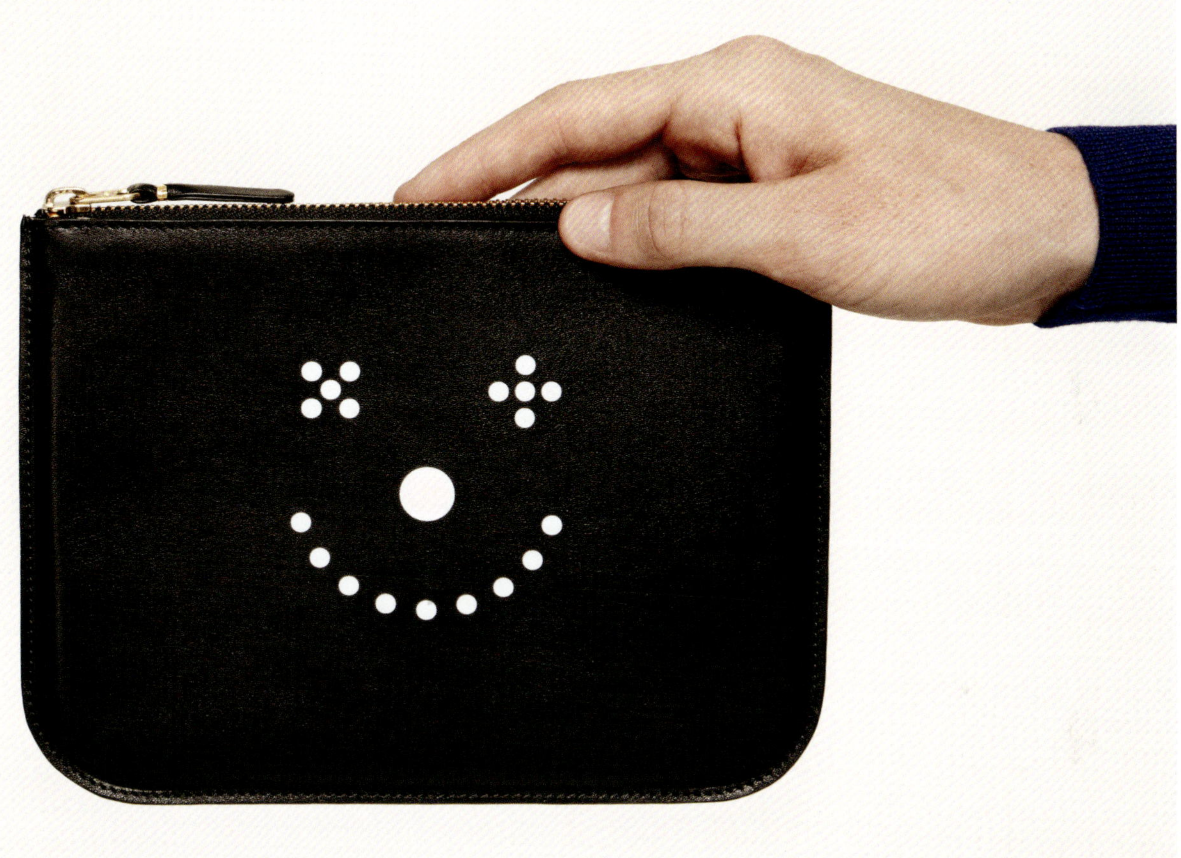

↑ Ninav Modi—Flagship jewelry boutique, New Delhi, India, 2014
↑ Hayon × Jijibaba—Fashion collection, black leather purse and white smiley print, 2017

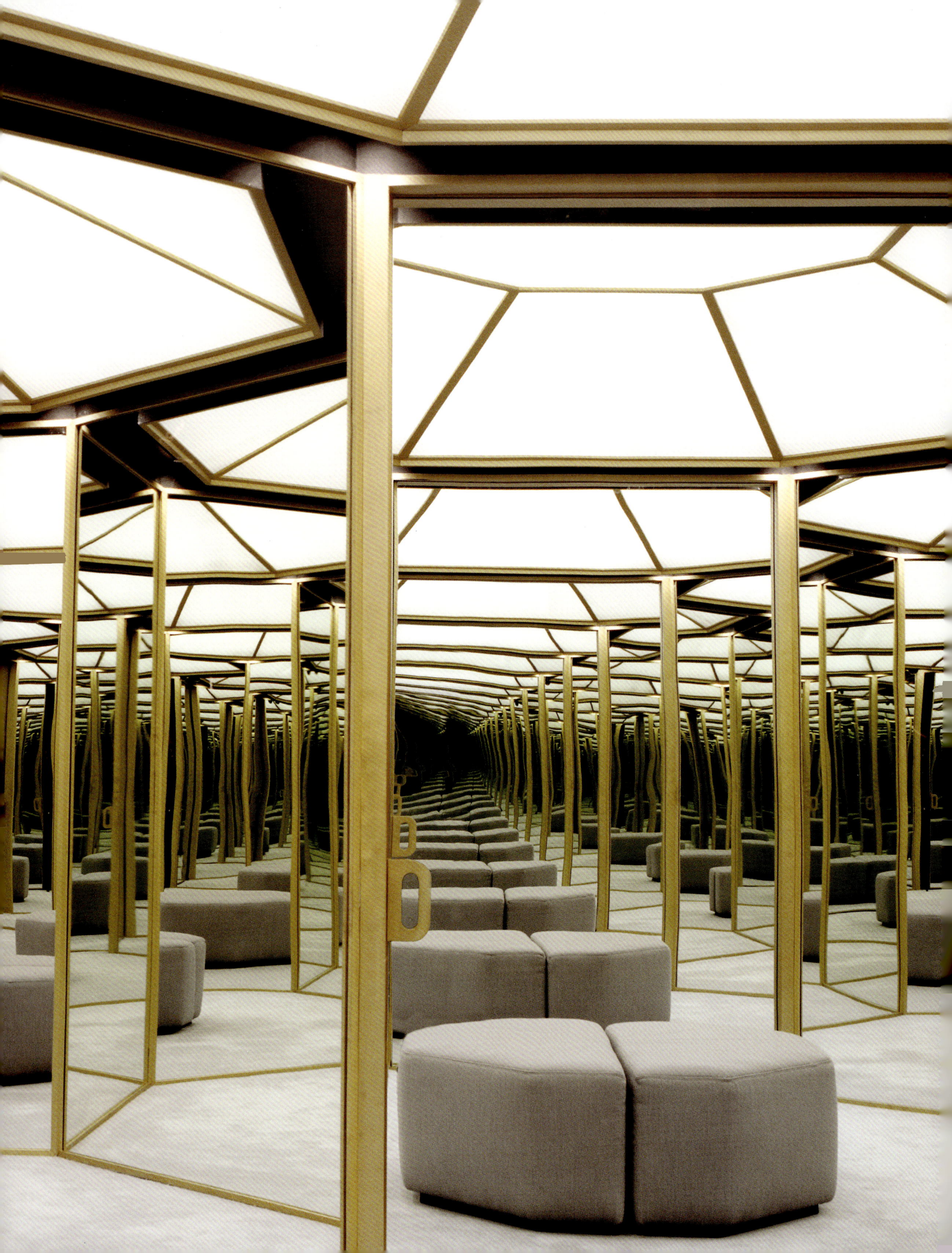

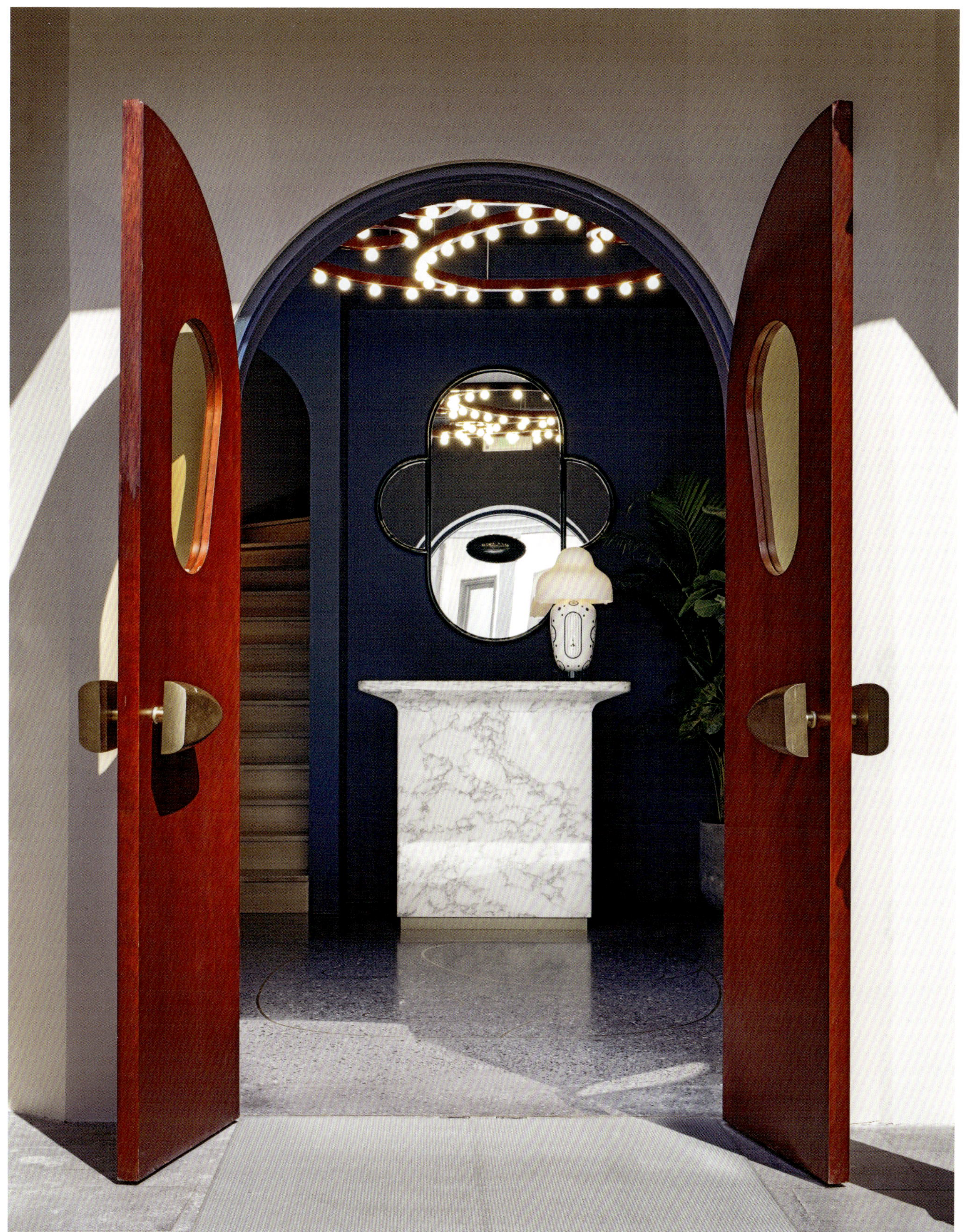

↑ Nirav Modi—Mirror room of the flagship jewelry boutique, New Delhi, India, 2014
↓ Fritz Hansen Lounge—Club entrance, Shanghai, China, 2019

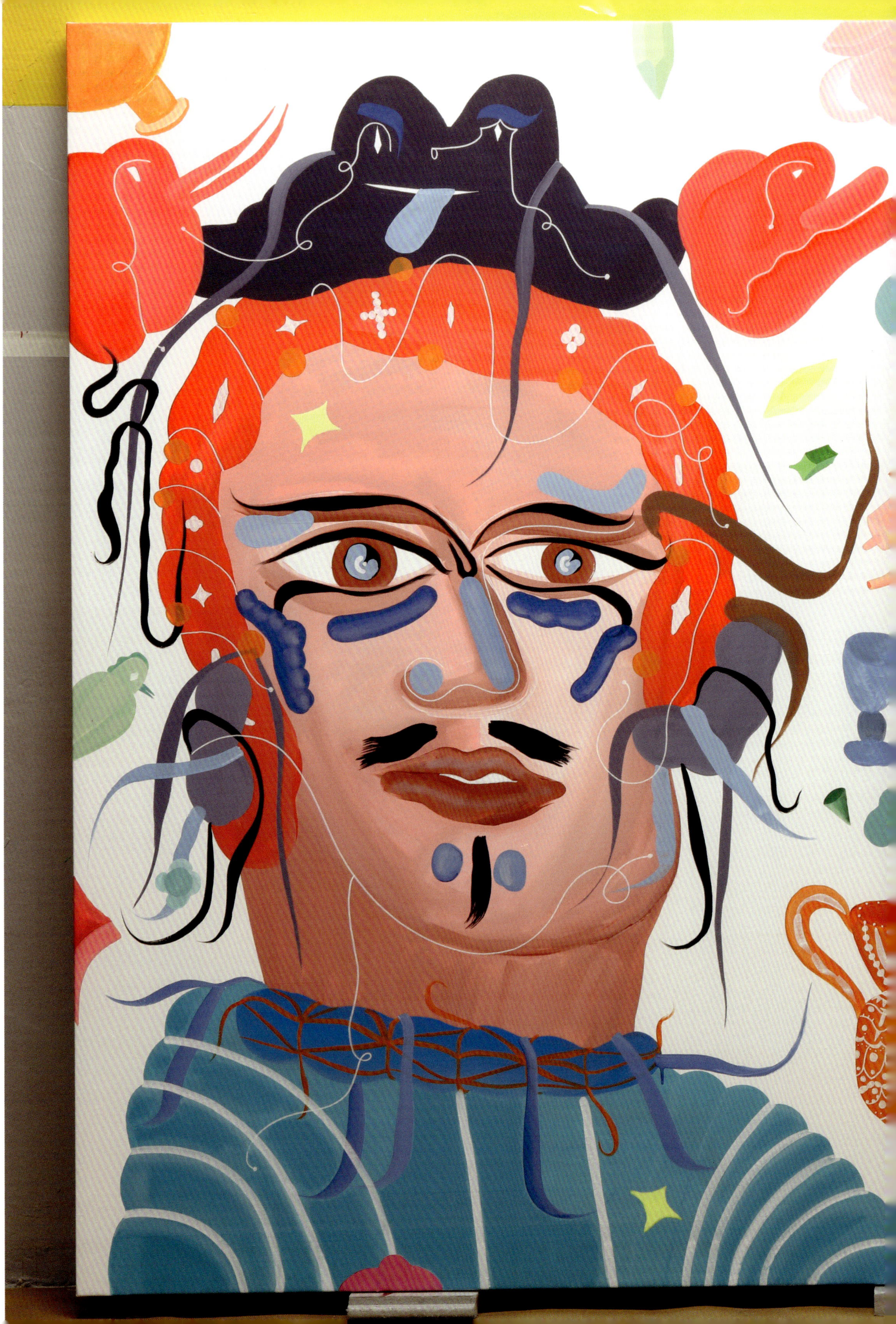

↓ Portrait of Sir David and Heady Thoughts—Acrylic on canvas, 120×180 cm, 2022

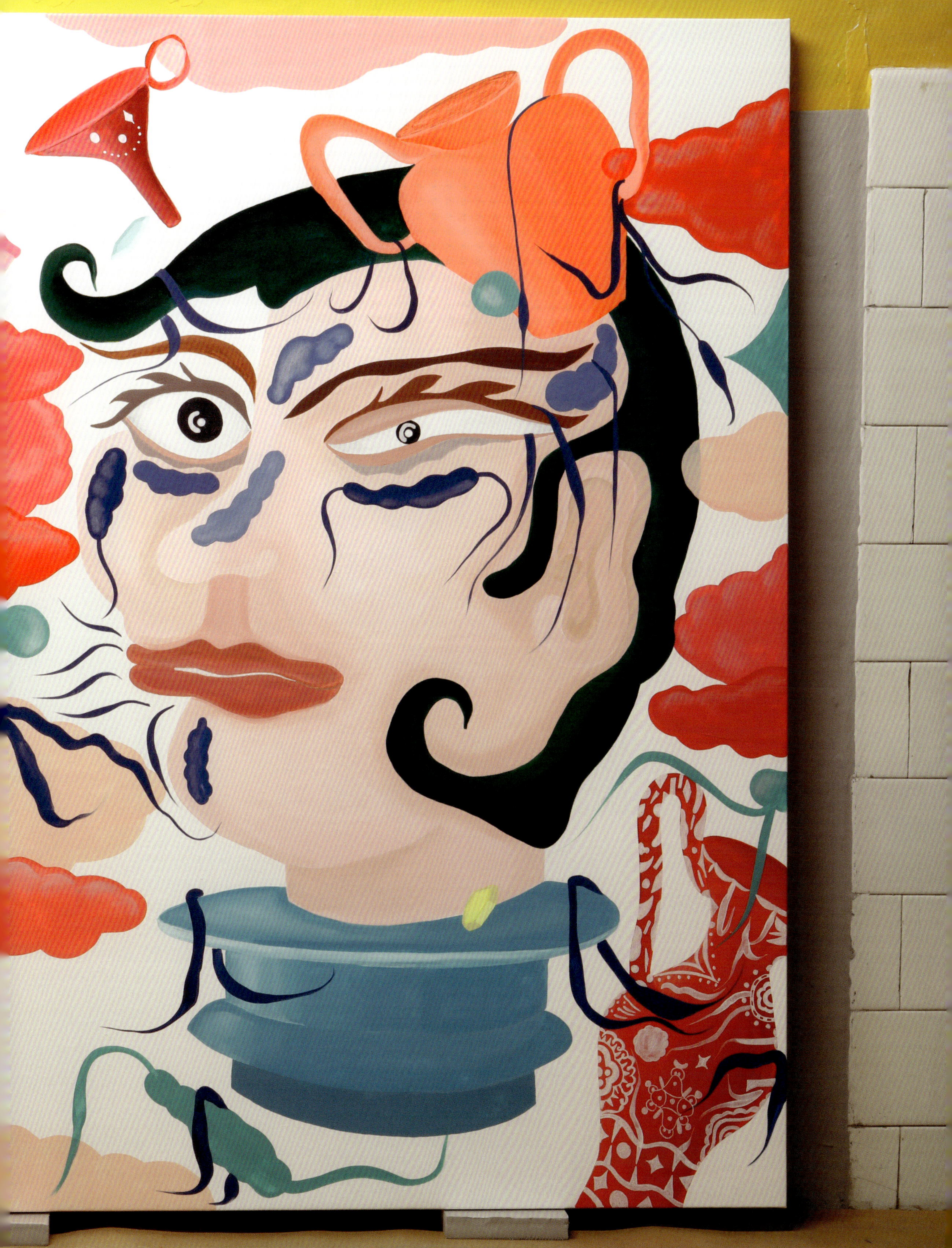

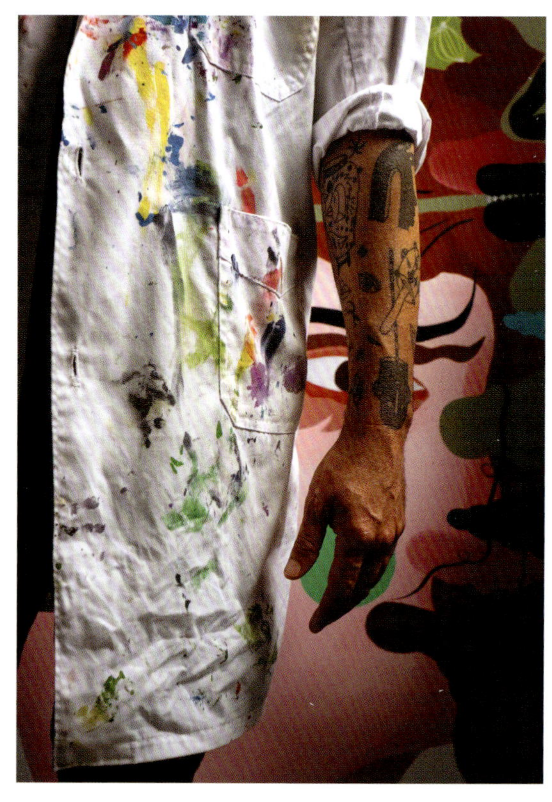

↑ Jaime Hayon at his atelier, Valencia, Spain
↓ Hayonstudio office in Valencia, Spain

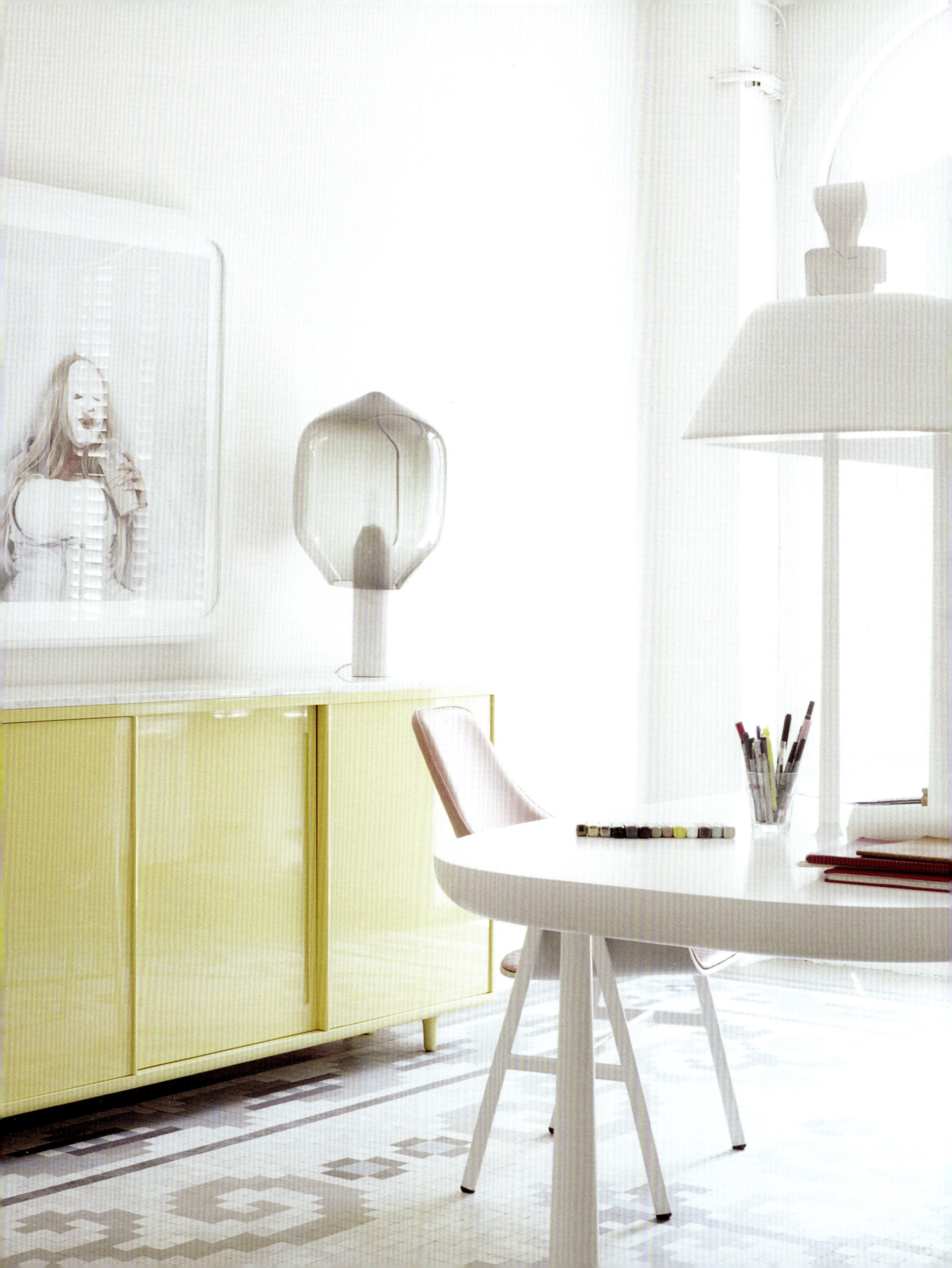

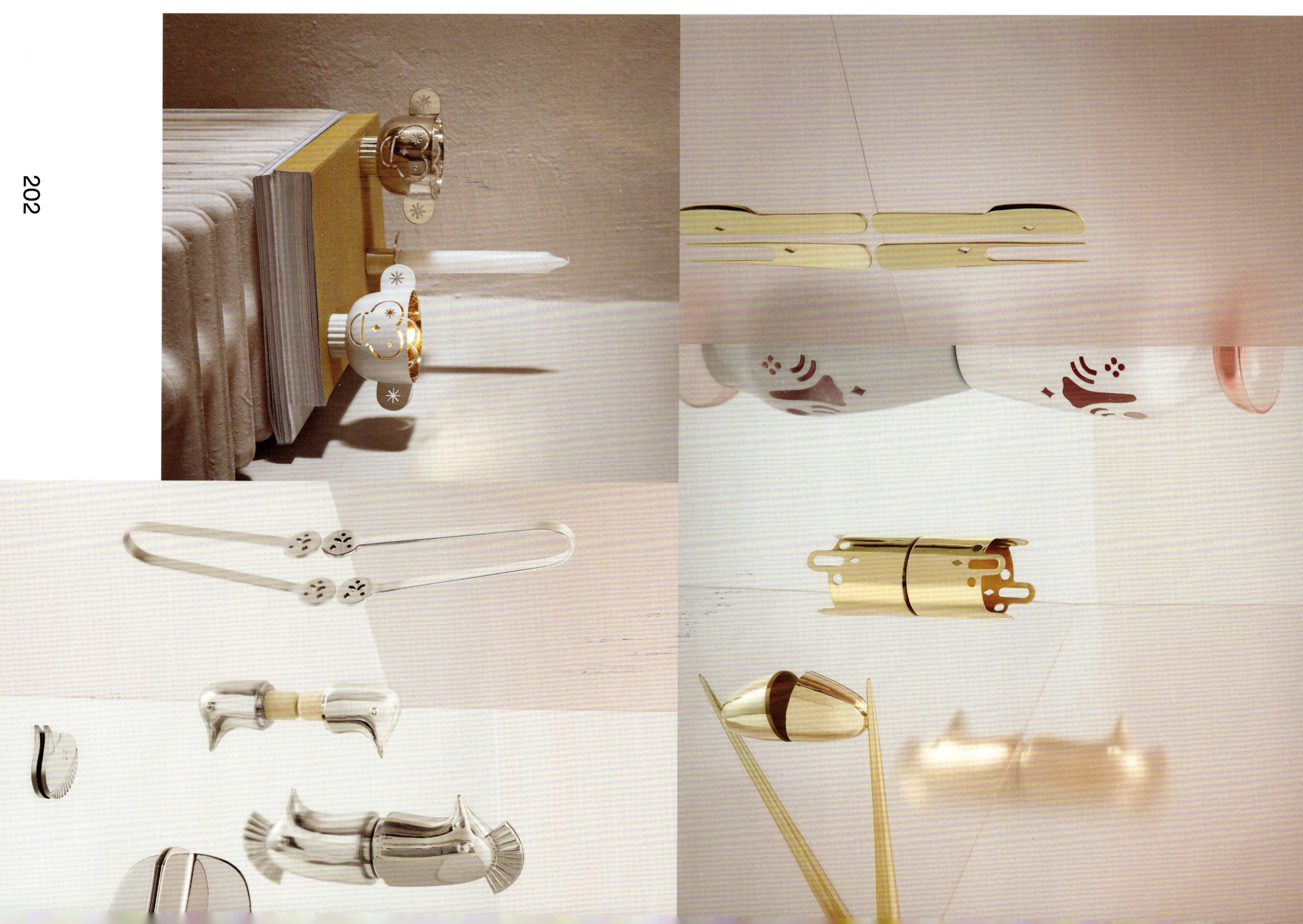

↓ FUN-tional and Monkos & Pipoz—Tableware objects and candle holders for Paola C, 2018–2019
↓ FUN-tional—Sketch for objects

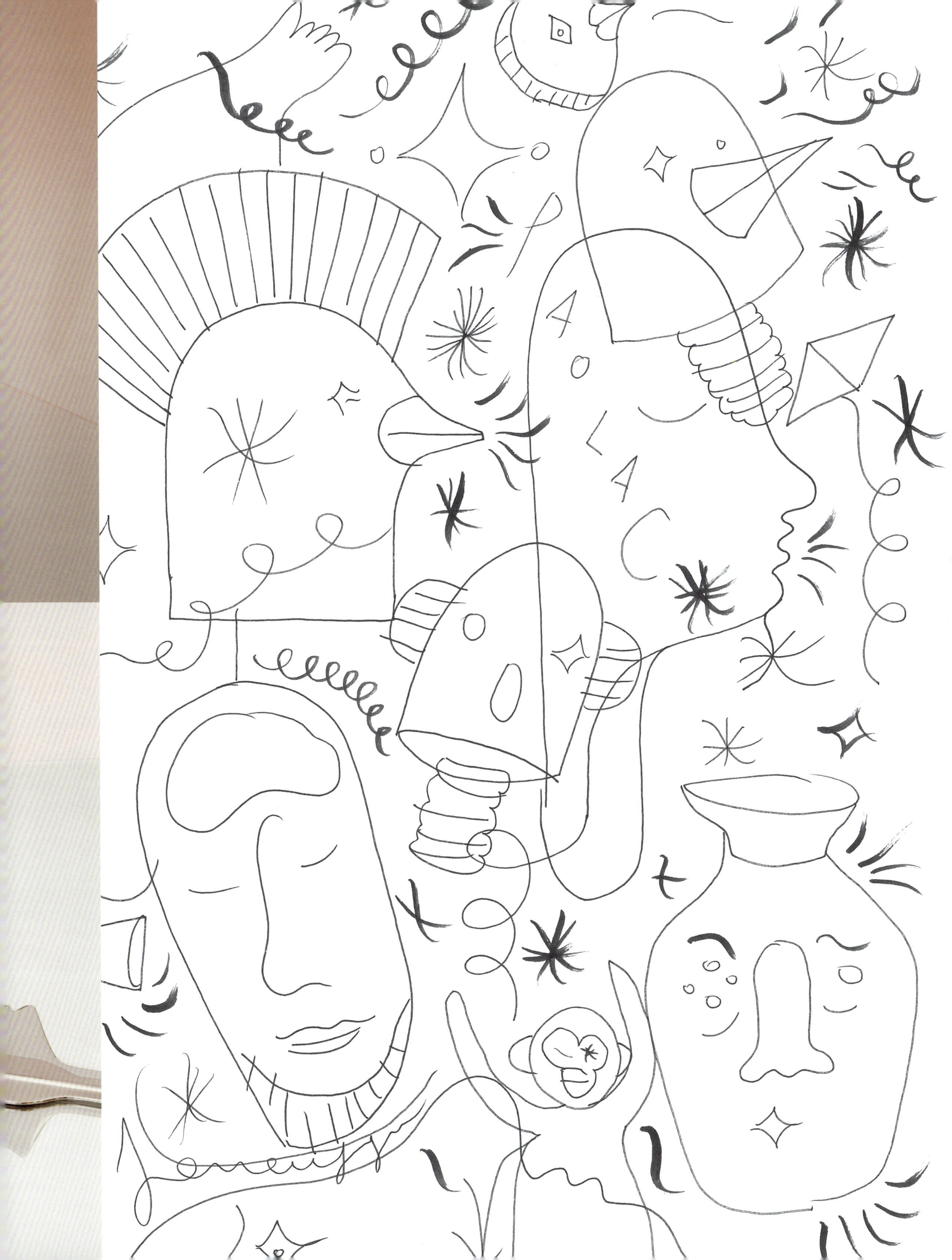

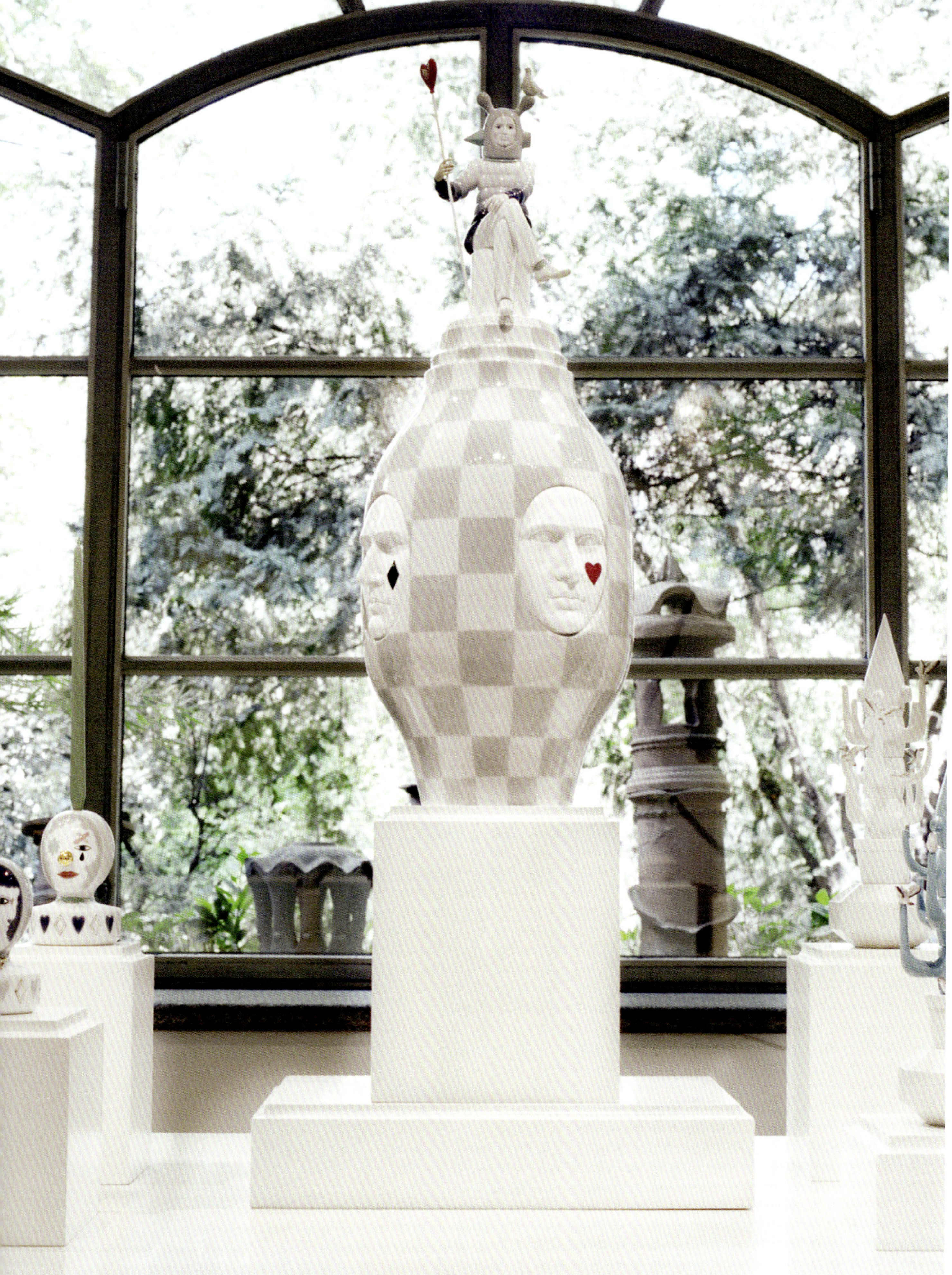

↑ Conversation vase with the Lover figurine—Part of the Fantasy Collection for Lladró, shown at Rossana Orlandi Gallery, Milan, Italy, 2008
↓ Vuelta—High-back armchair and sofa for Wittmann

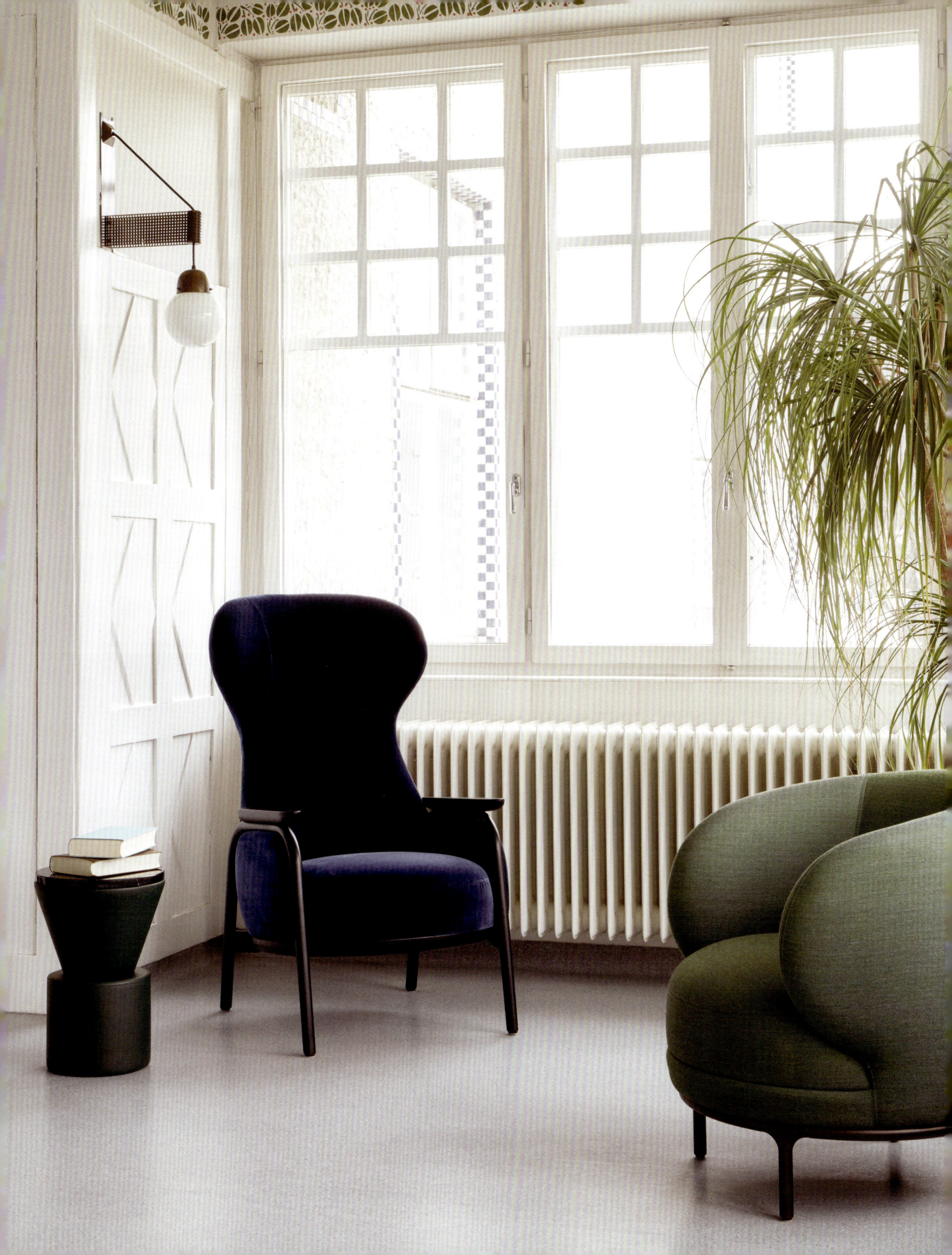

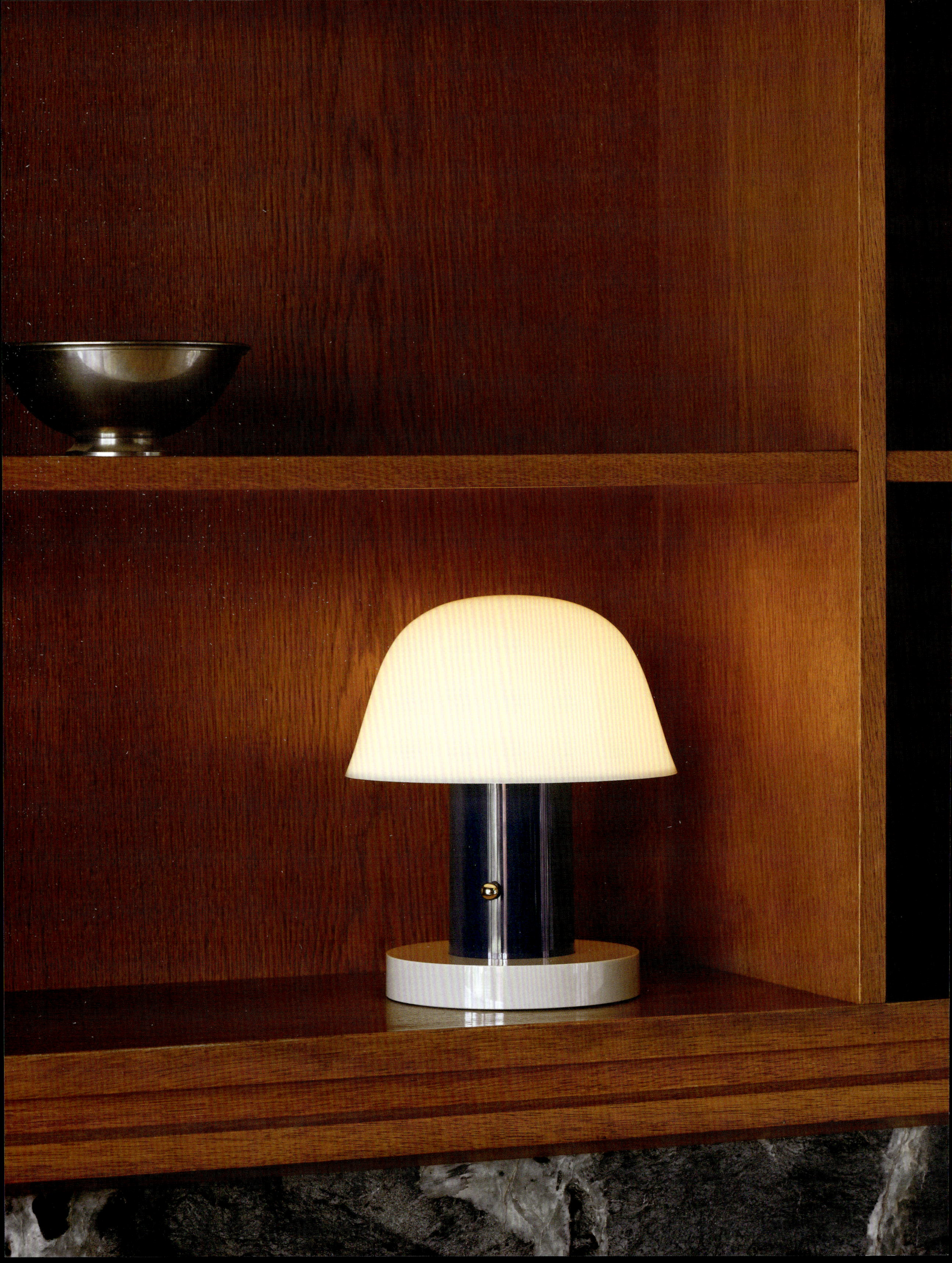

↑ Setago—Portable lamp for &Tradition, 2019
↑ Arcolor—Sofa and table for Arflex, 2017

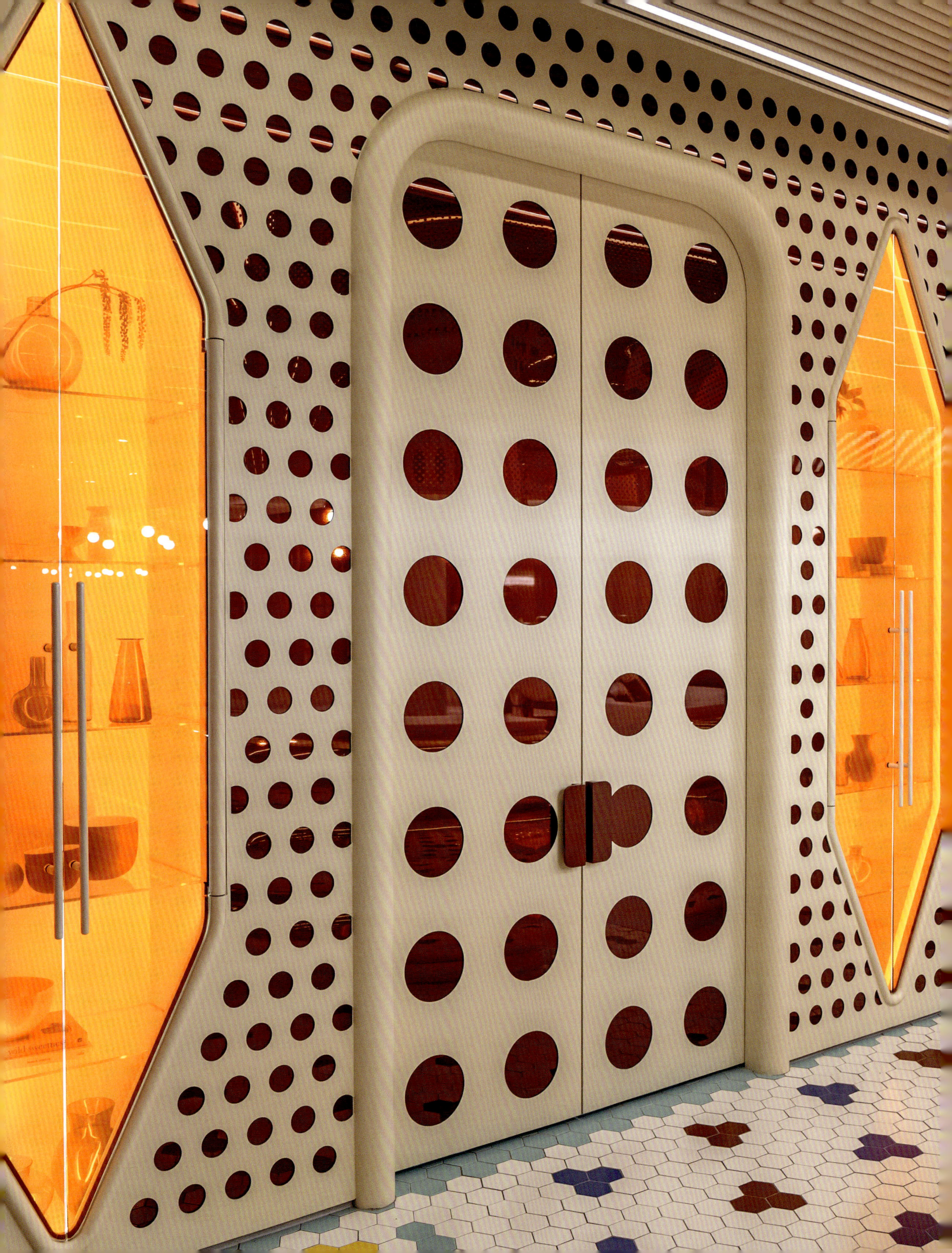

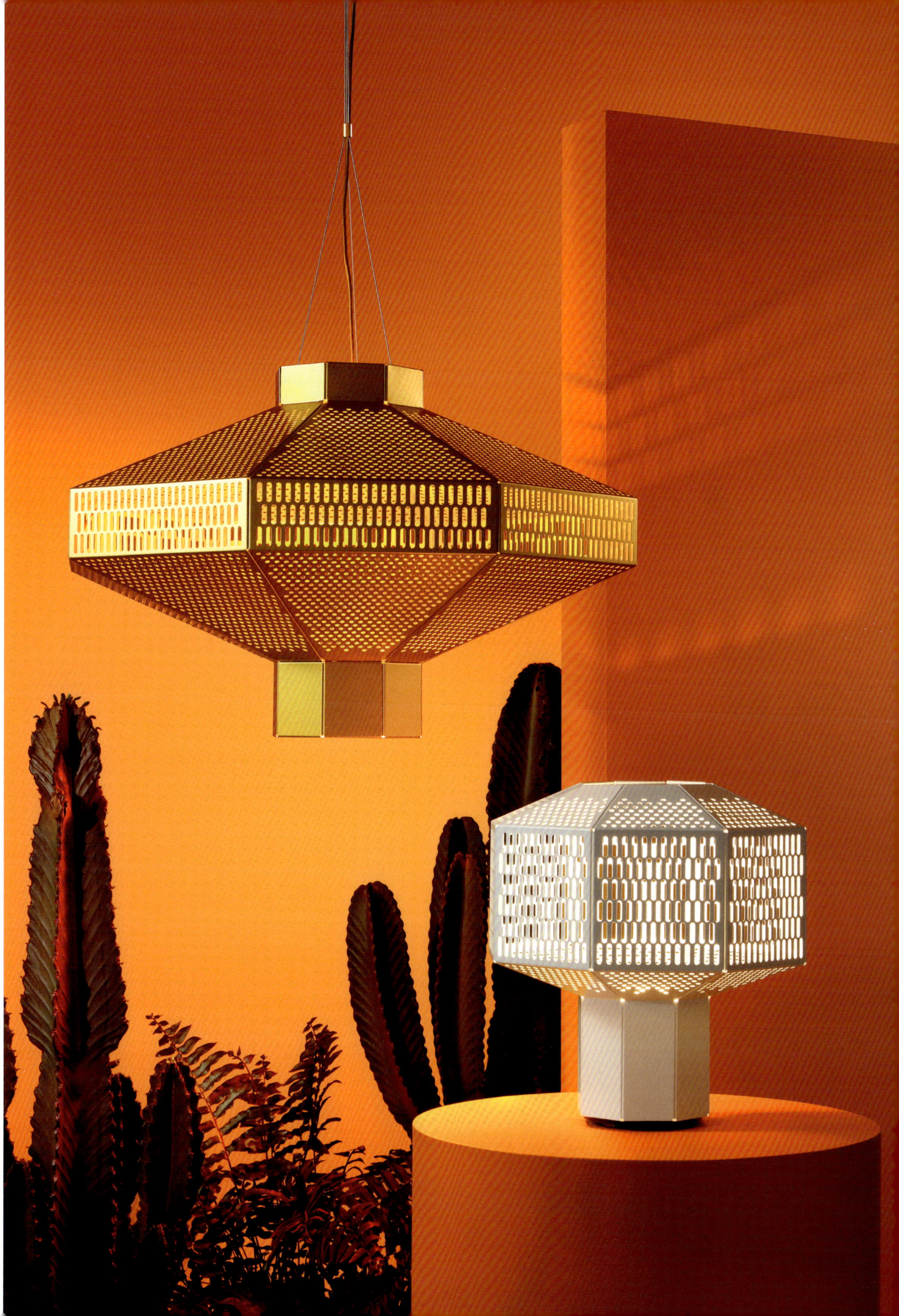

↑ Pangyo VIP Lounge—Interior design for Hyundai Department Store, Seoul, South Korea, 2021
↓ Ma-Rock—Metal lamps for Panachilna, 2022

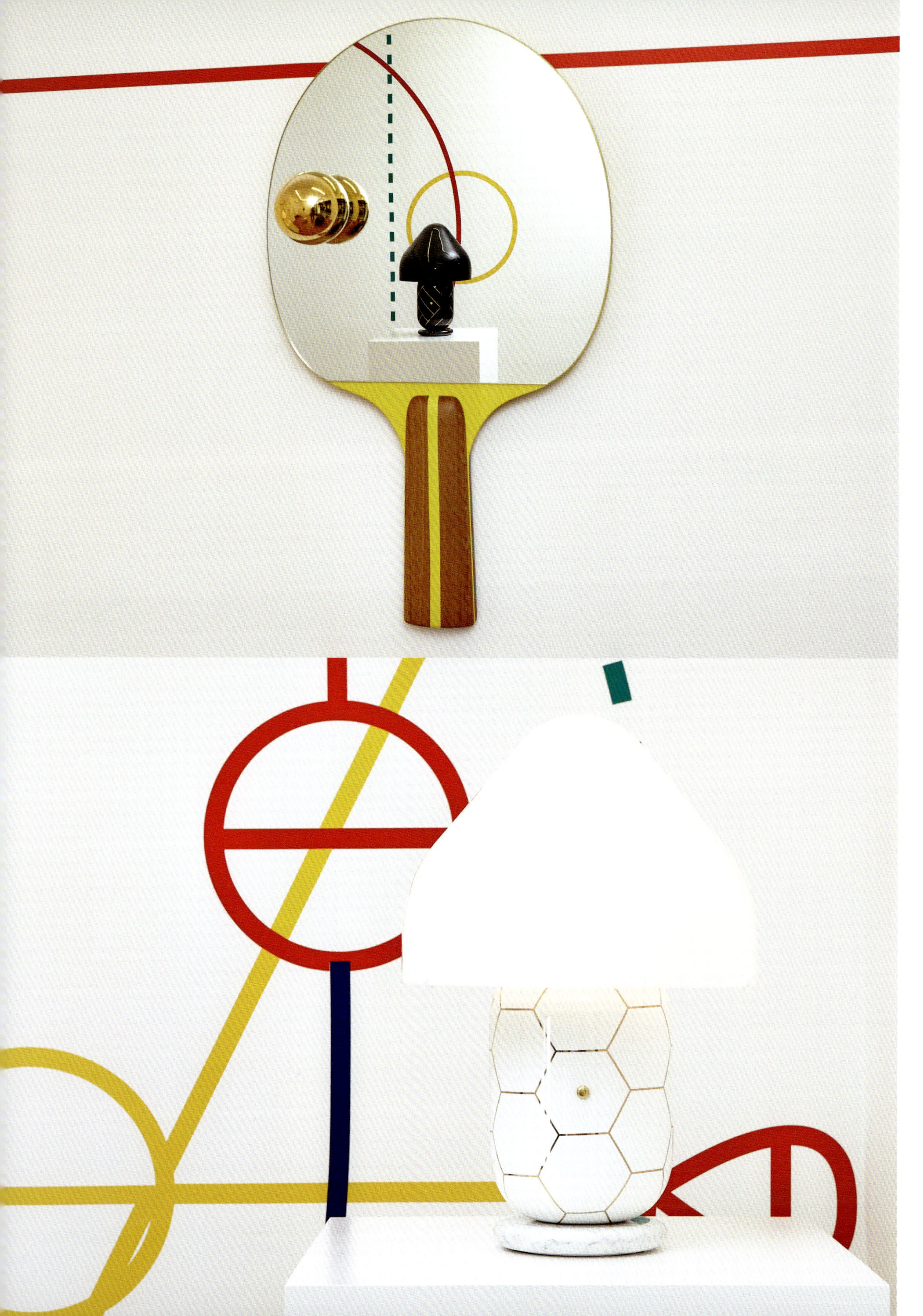

→ Even I myself cannot find a real logic in my actions, but the originality of my path is based on transverse relationships that are uncomfortable when forced into the categories of art and design.

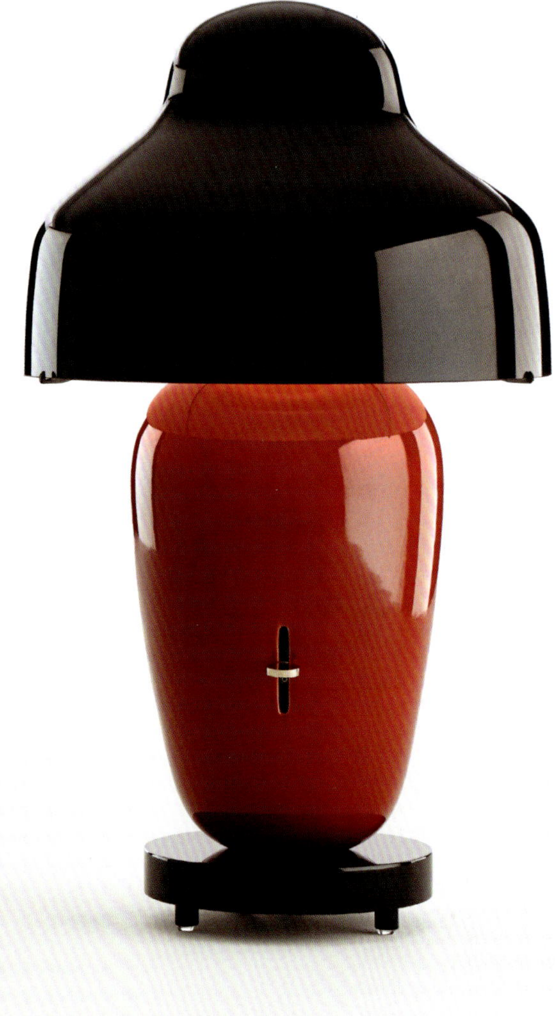

↑ Chinoz—Ceramic lamp for Parachilna, 2015
↓ Jaime Hayon × Zara—Streetwear collection, 2021

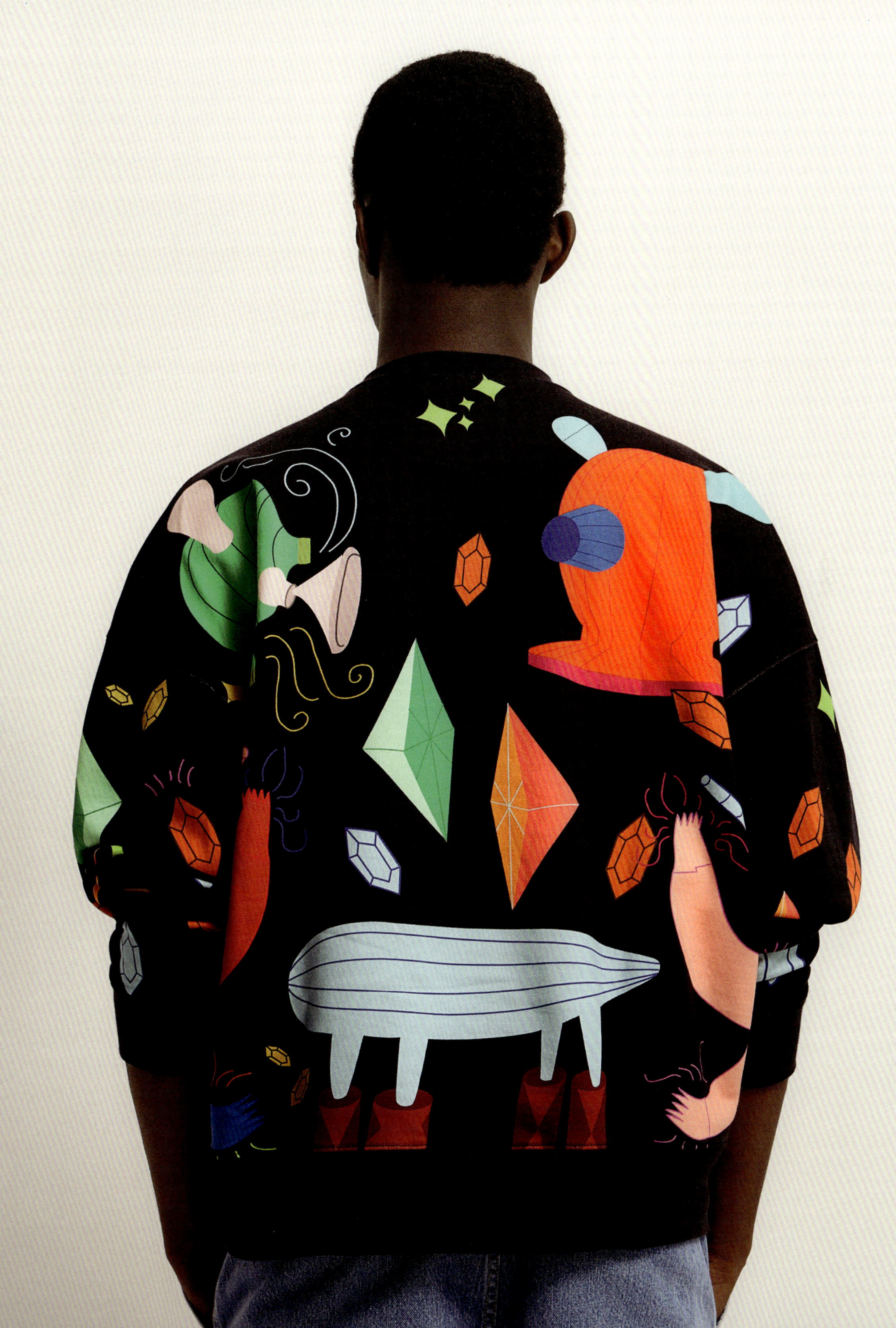

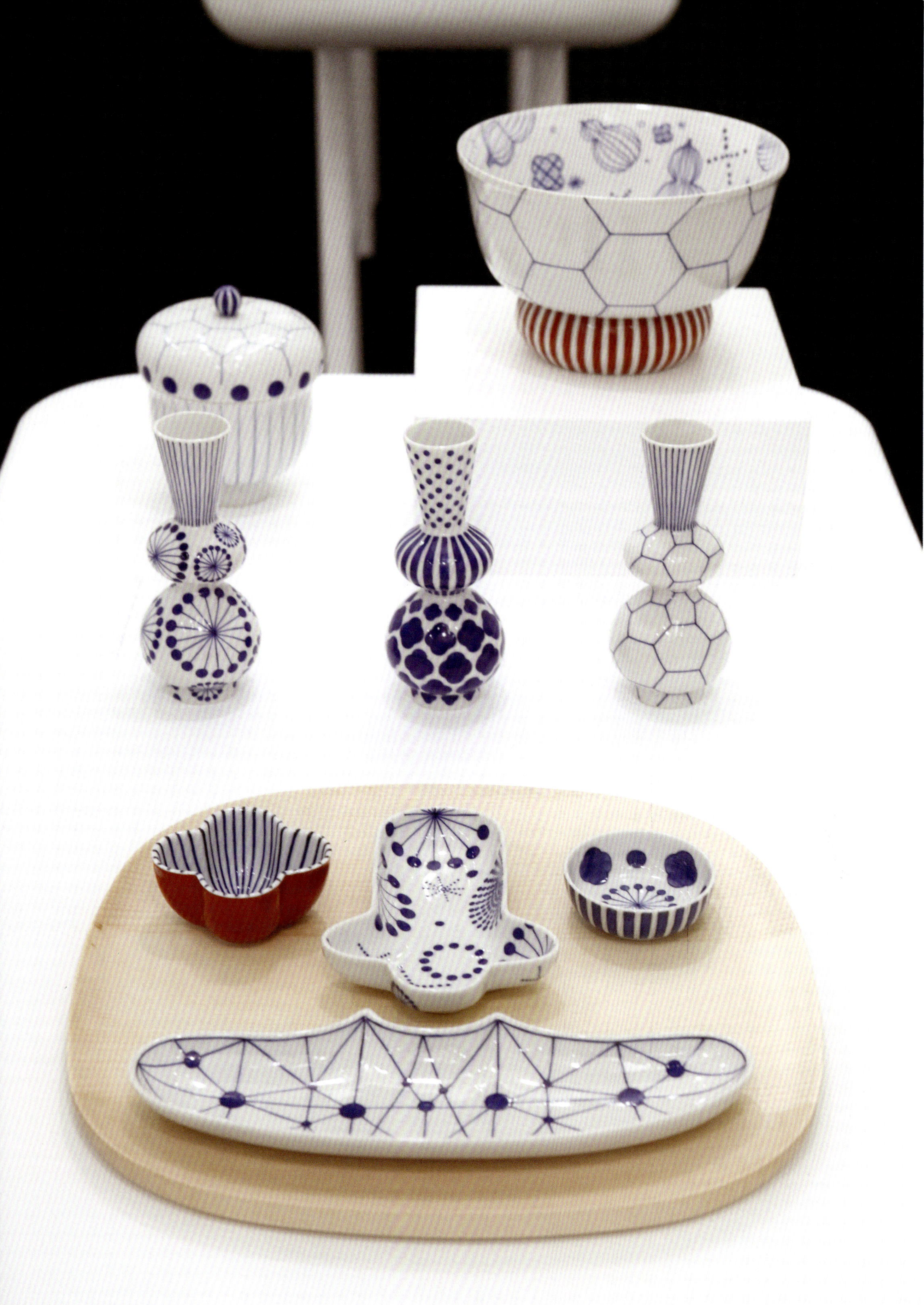

↑ Choemon Gamma—Japanese tableware porcelain collection, 2010
↓ Development of Choemon Gamma

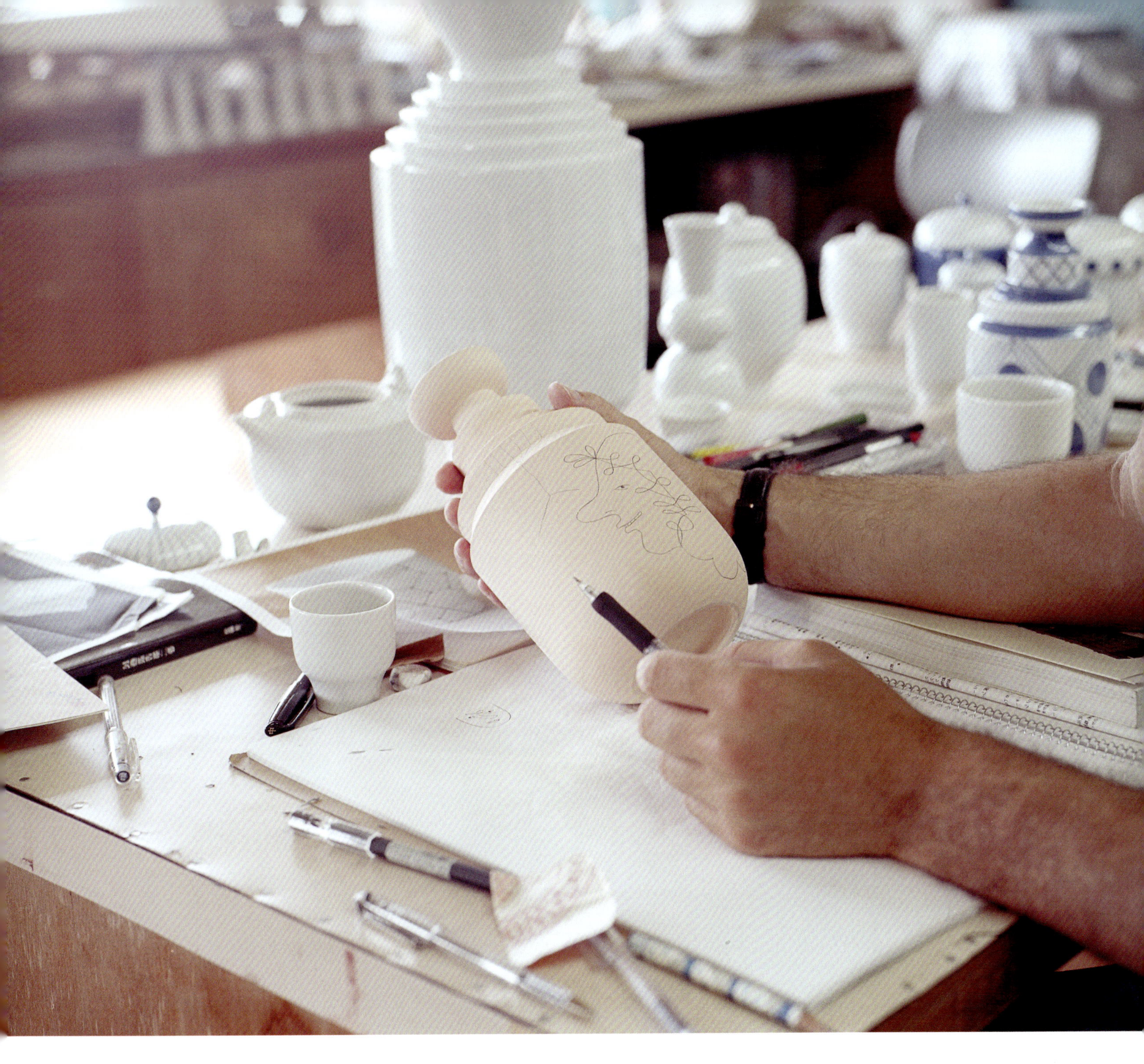

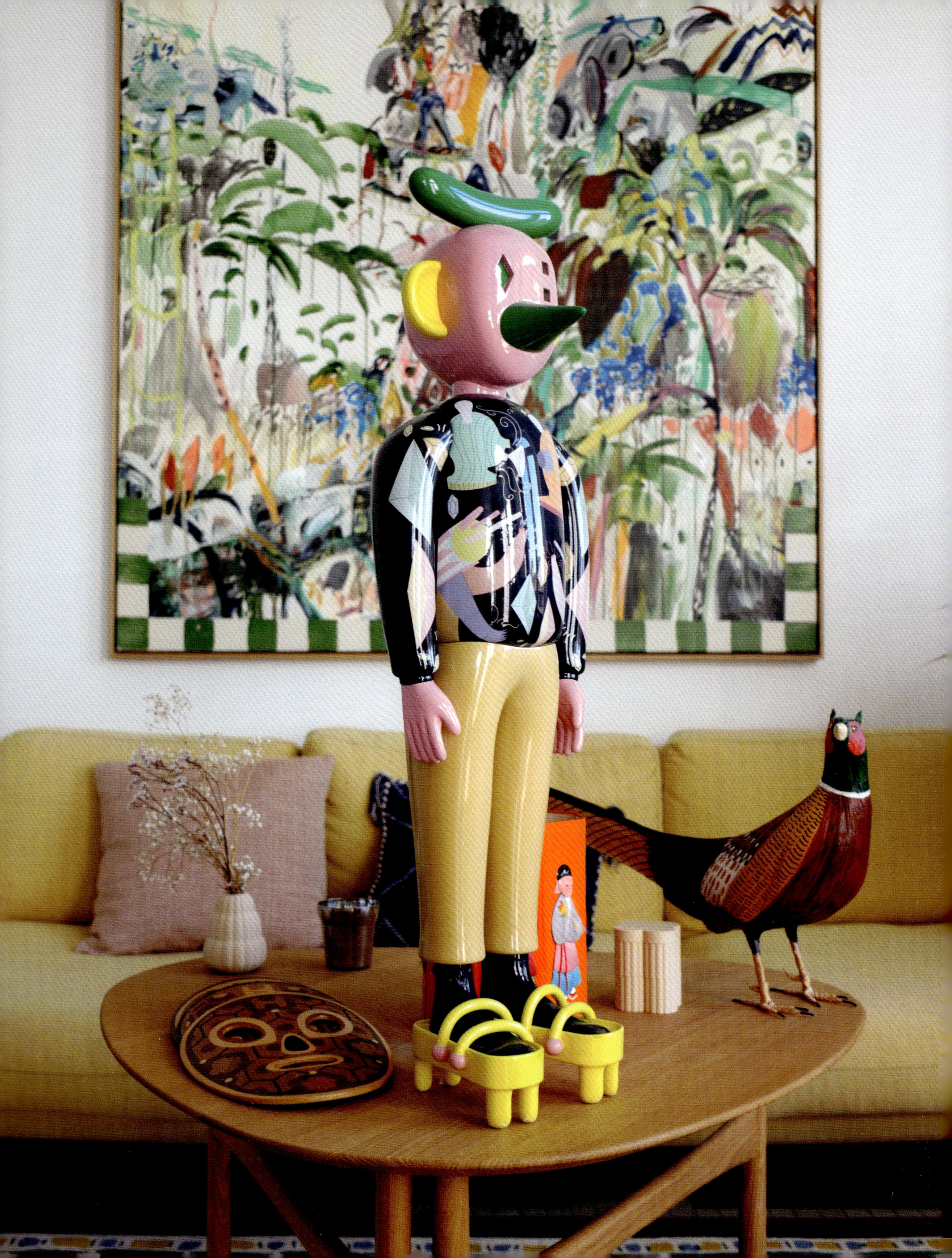

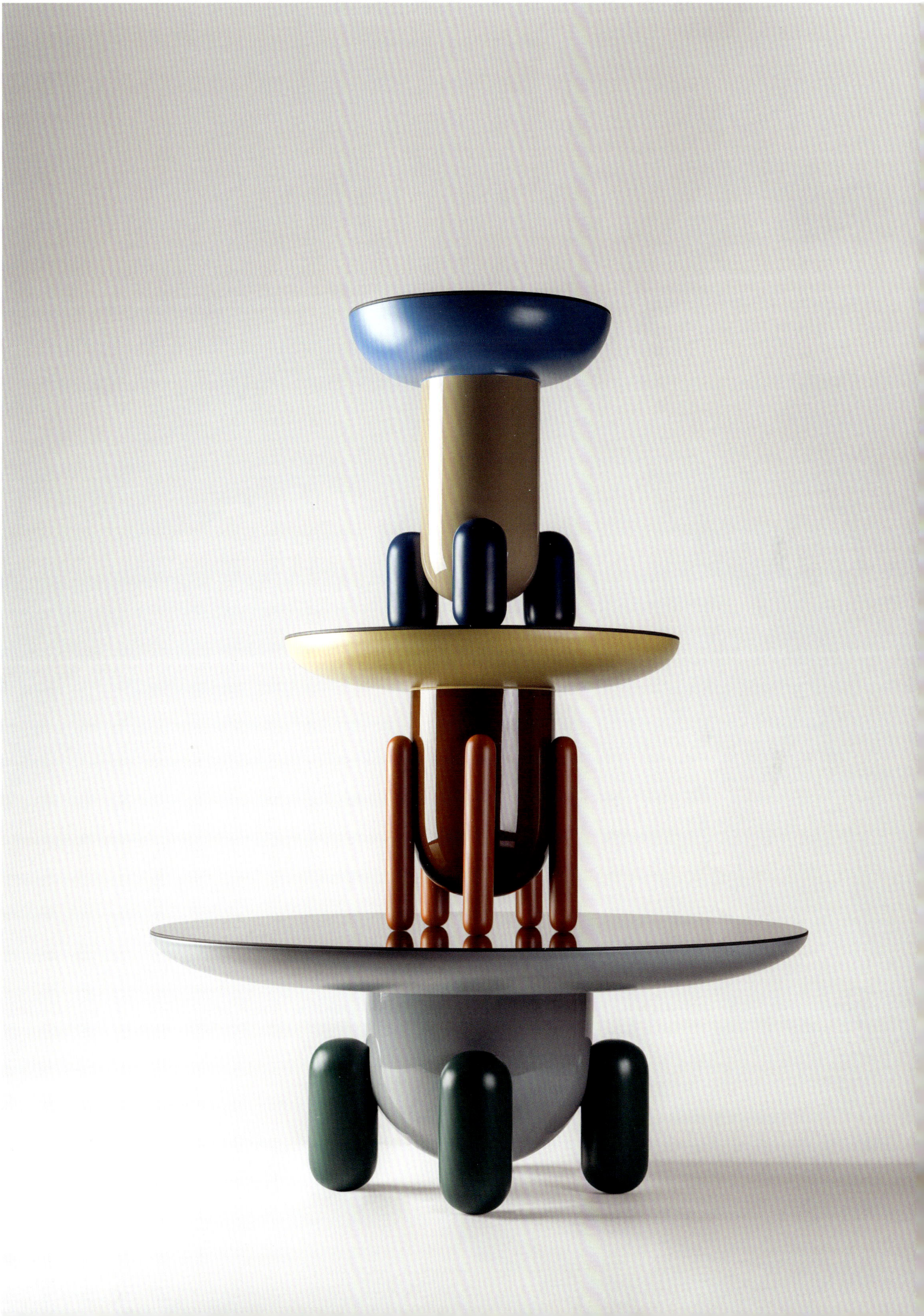

↑ Folkboy—Sculpture, 2021
↓ Explorer—Tables for BD Barcelona Design, 2019

→ I am excited by the idea of using ancient materials to sum up a new language. I transform objects so that they can talk and transmit unforgettable memories.

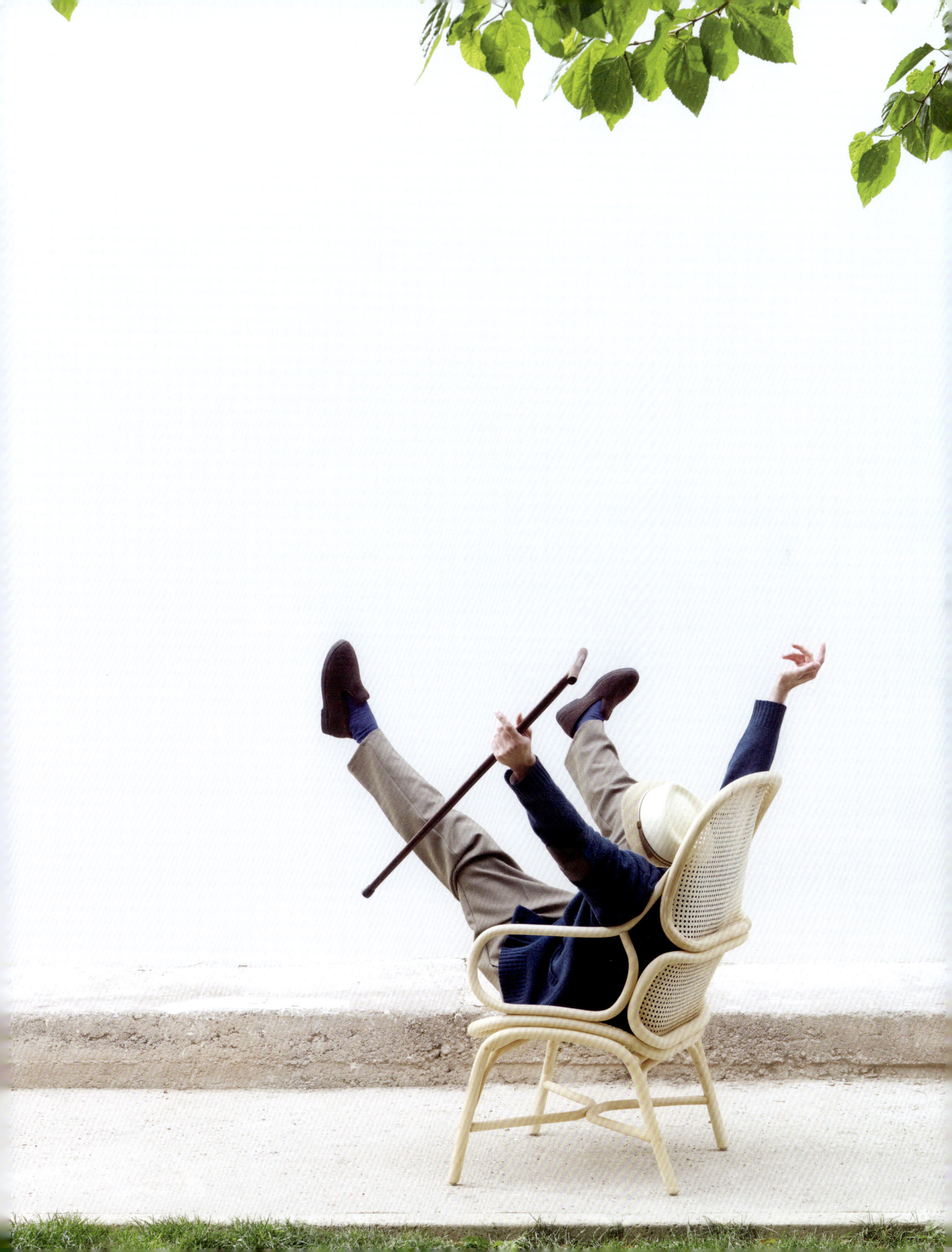

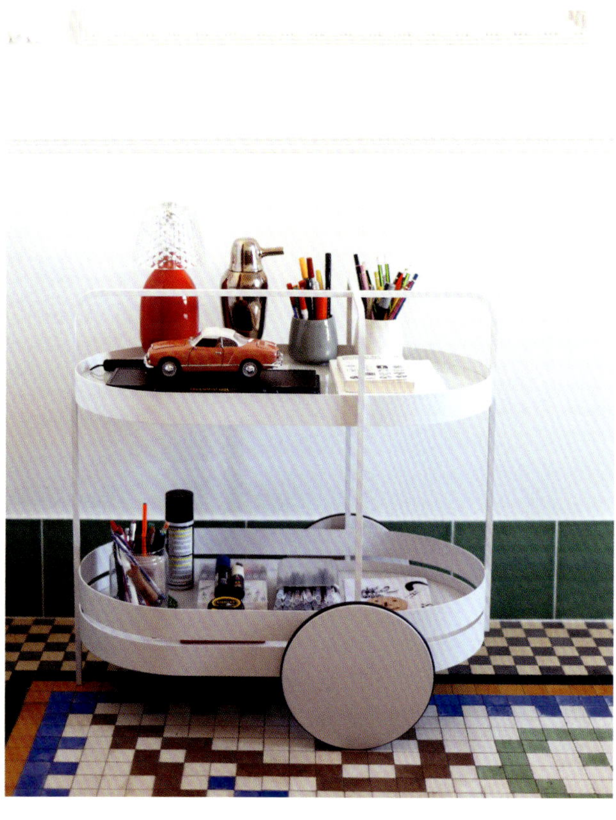

↓ Jaime Hayon residence featuring portable Crystal Candy light and Mon Cirque platinum vase
↓ La Terraza del Casino—Interior design of the restaurant, Madrid, Spain, 2018

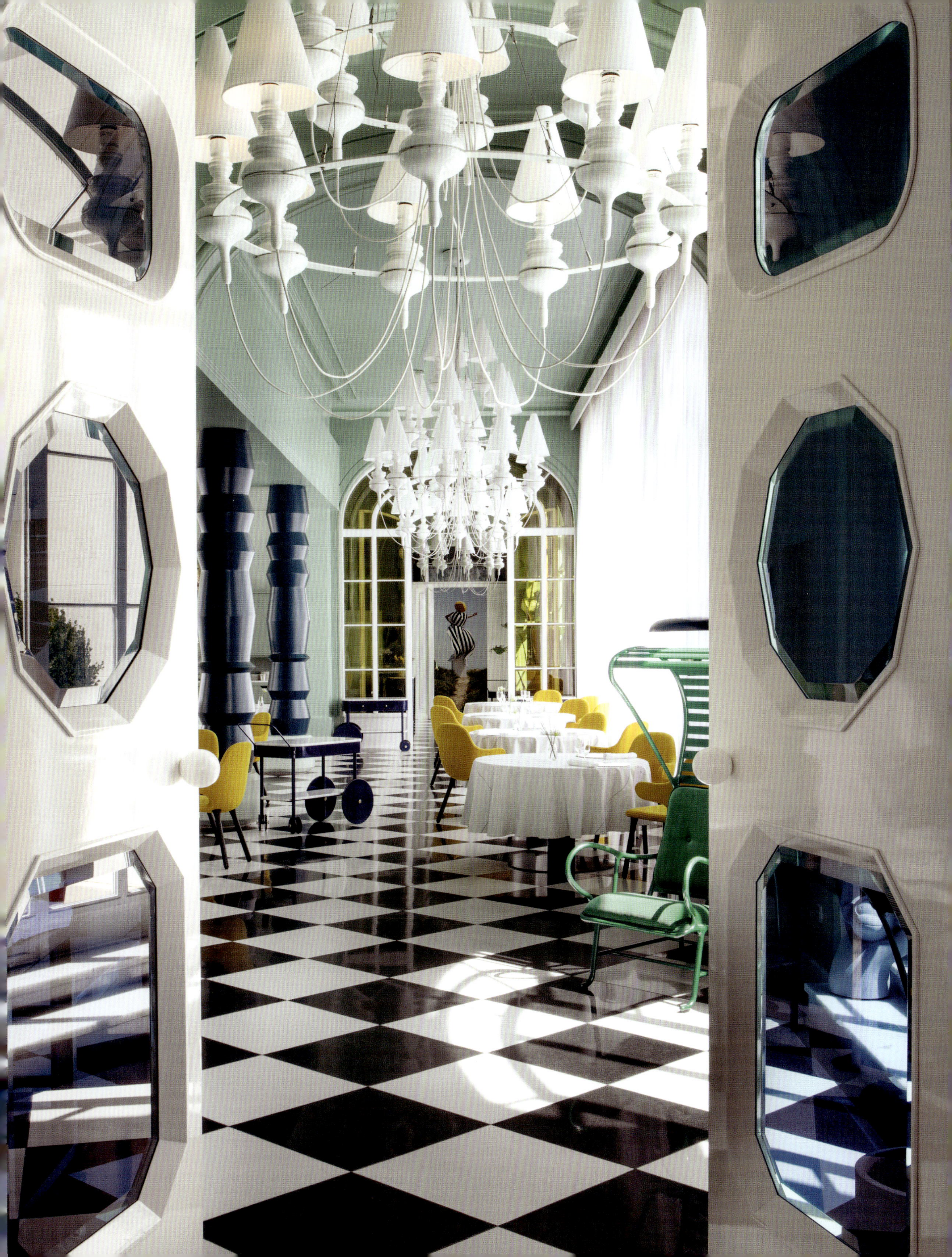

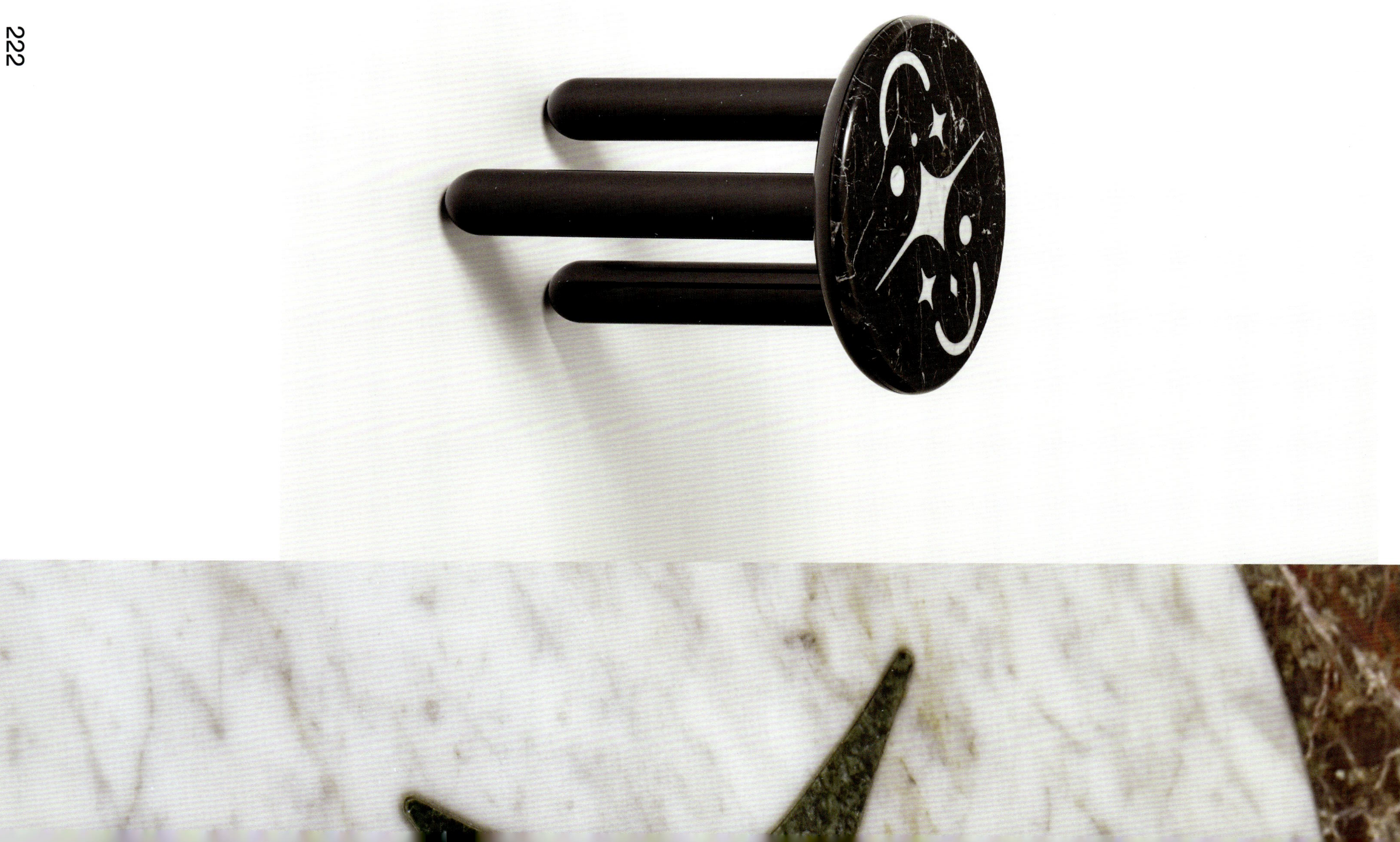

↓ Hymy—Limited-edition side table in wood and natural stone, from Chromatico exhibition at Galerie Kreo, Paris, France, 2018

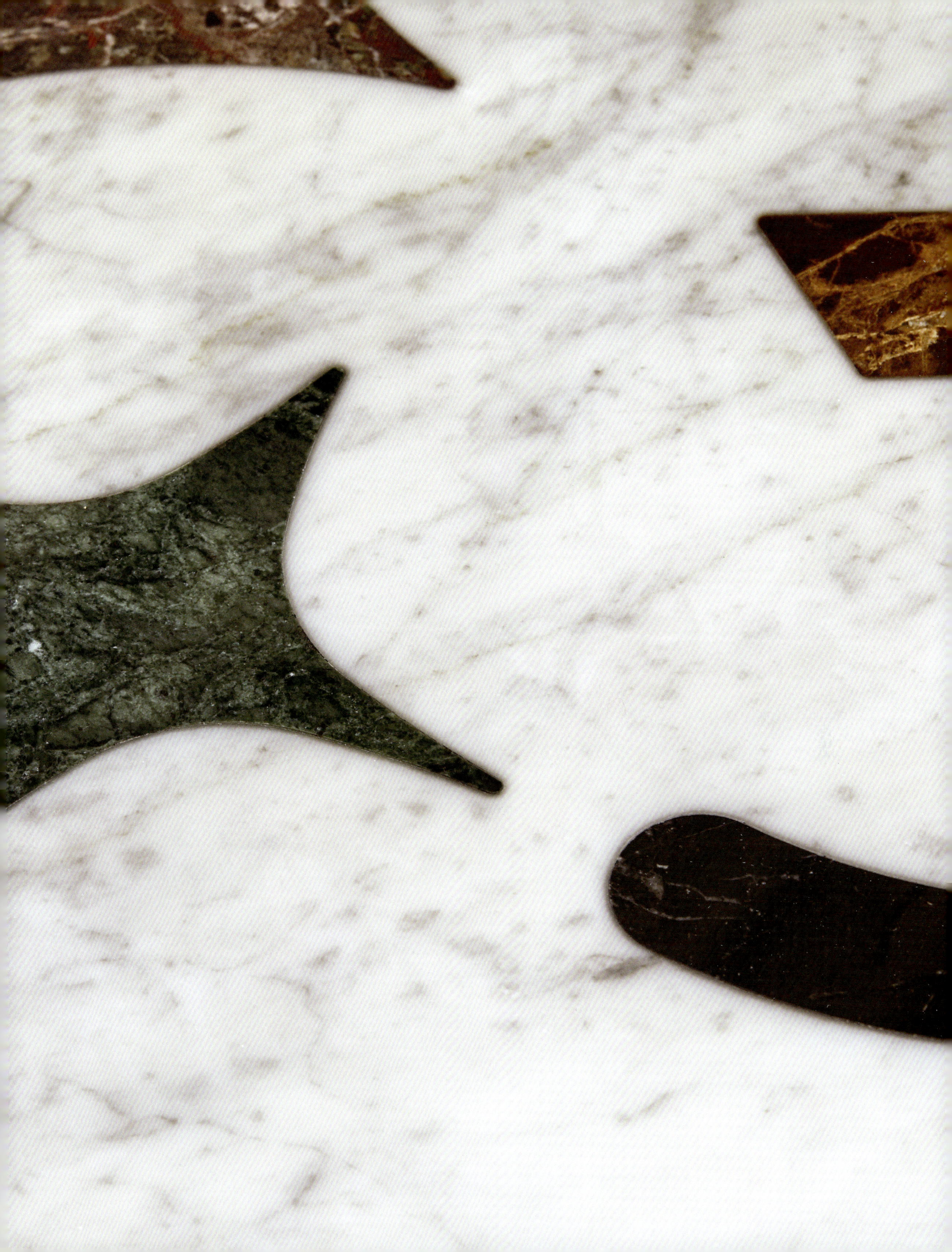

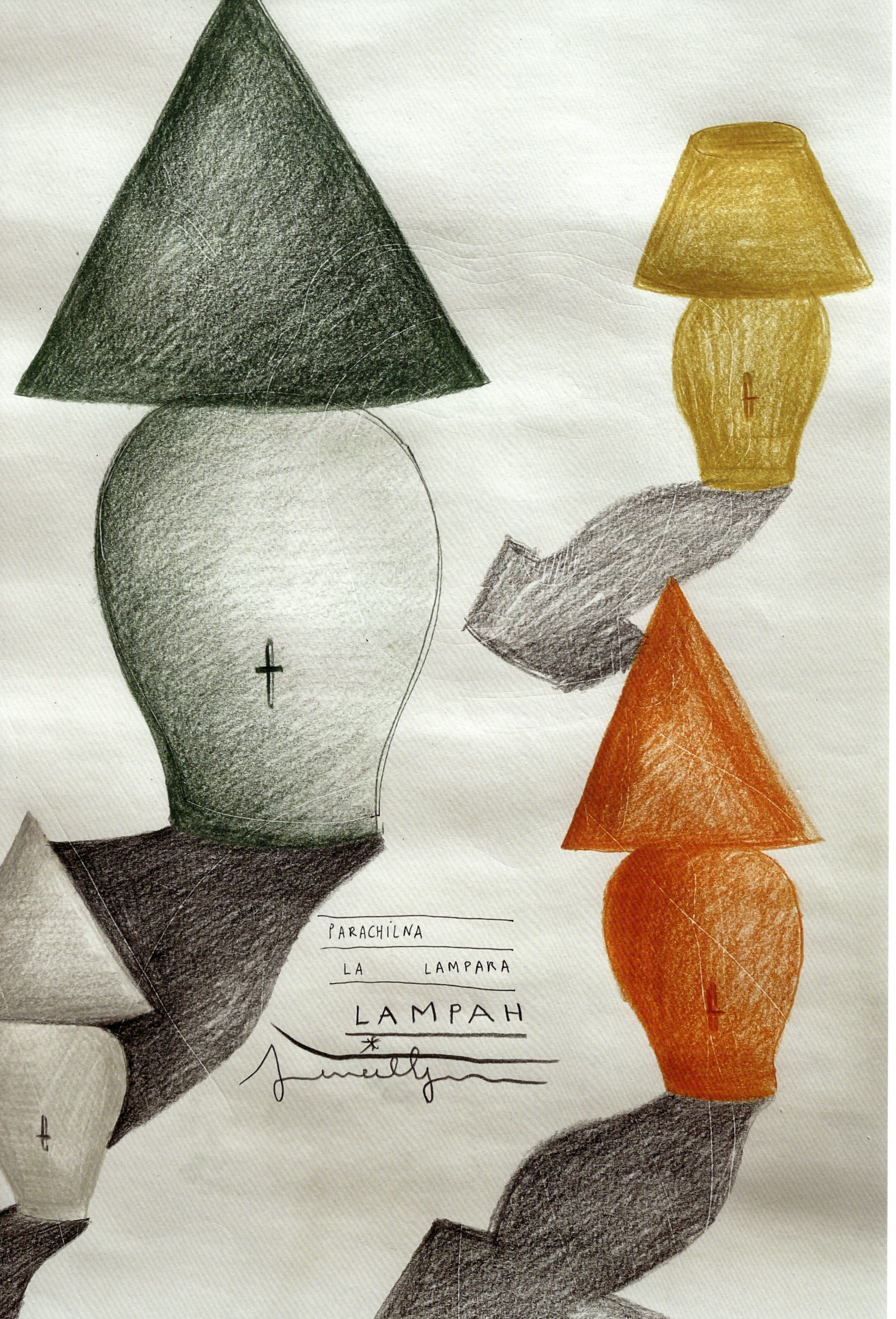

PARACHILNA
LA LAMPARA
LAMPAH

↑ Sketch for lamp collection
↓ Signature on hand-painted ceramic

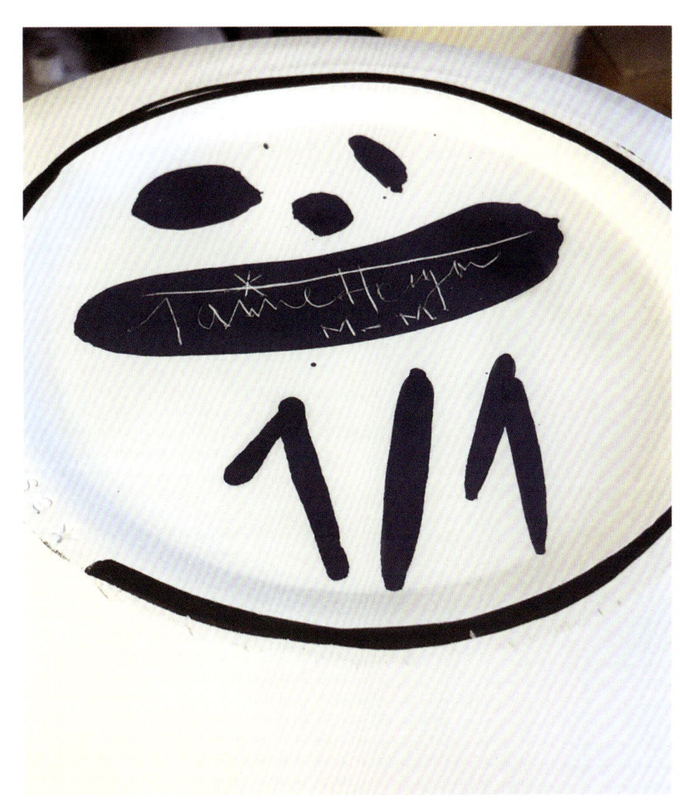

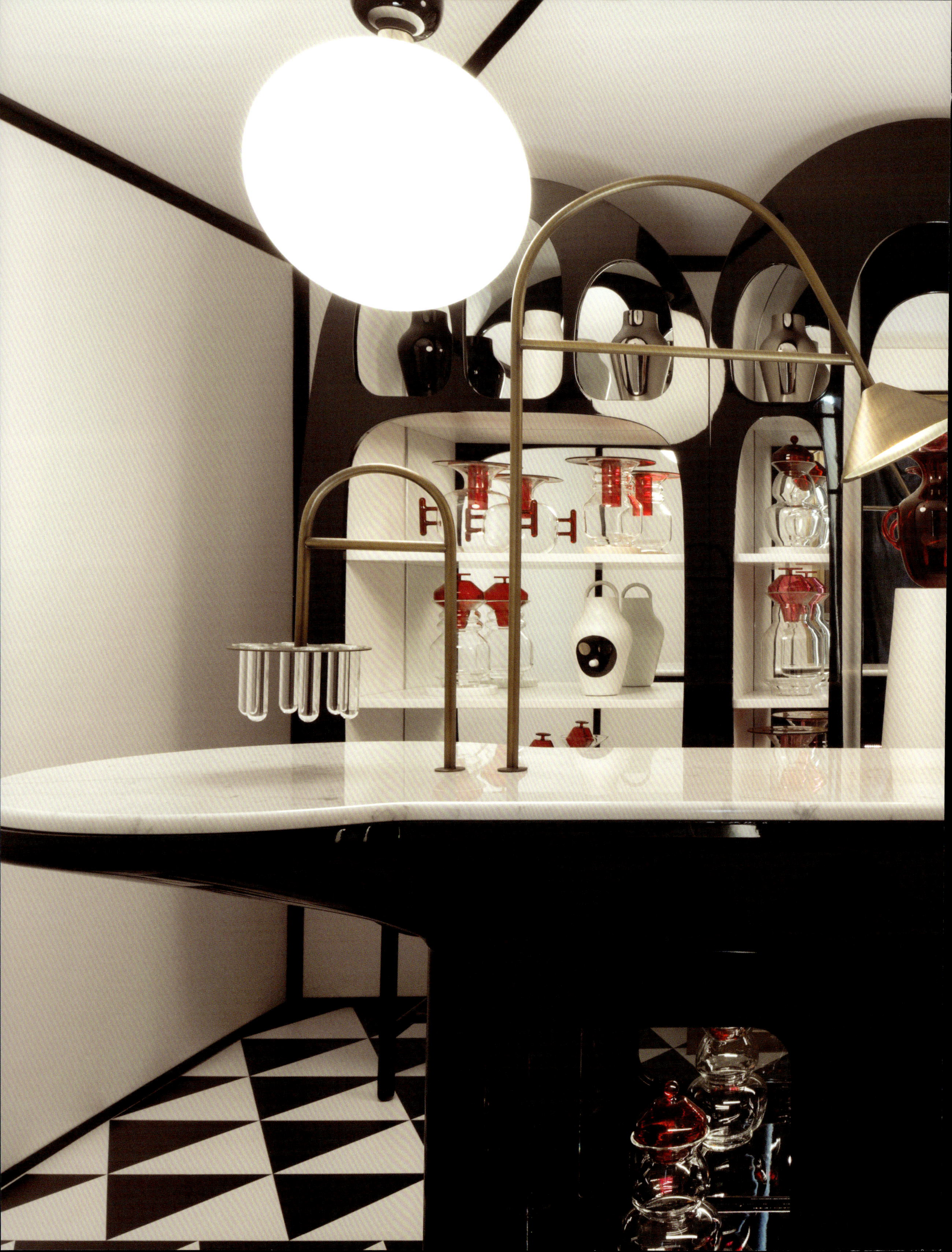

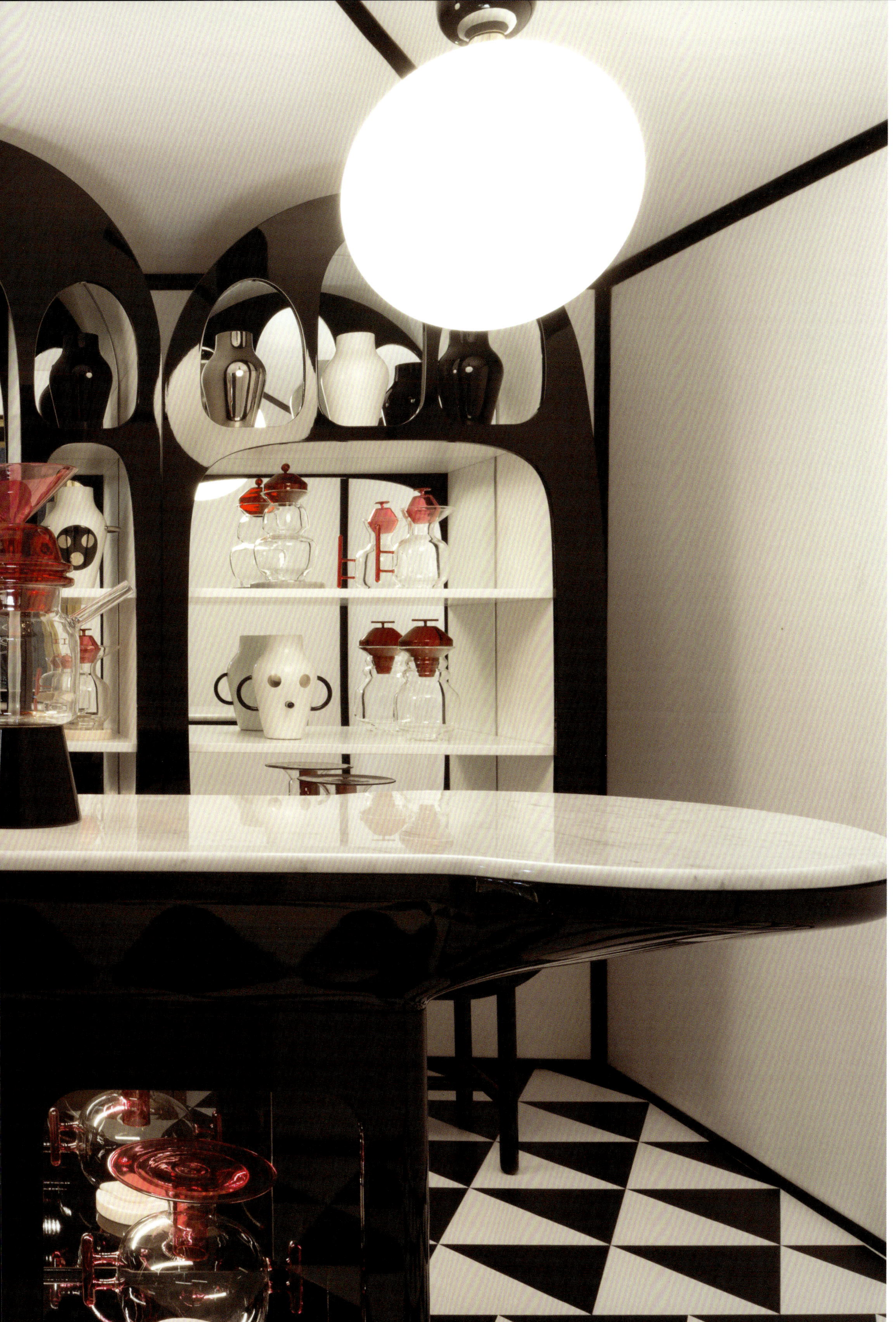

↑ Kuniopotec—Installation at the Garden of Wonders exhibition, Milan, Italy, 2015

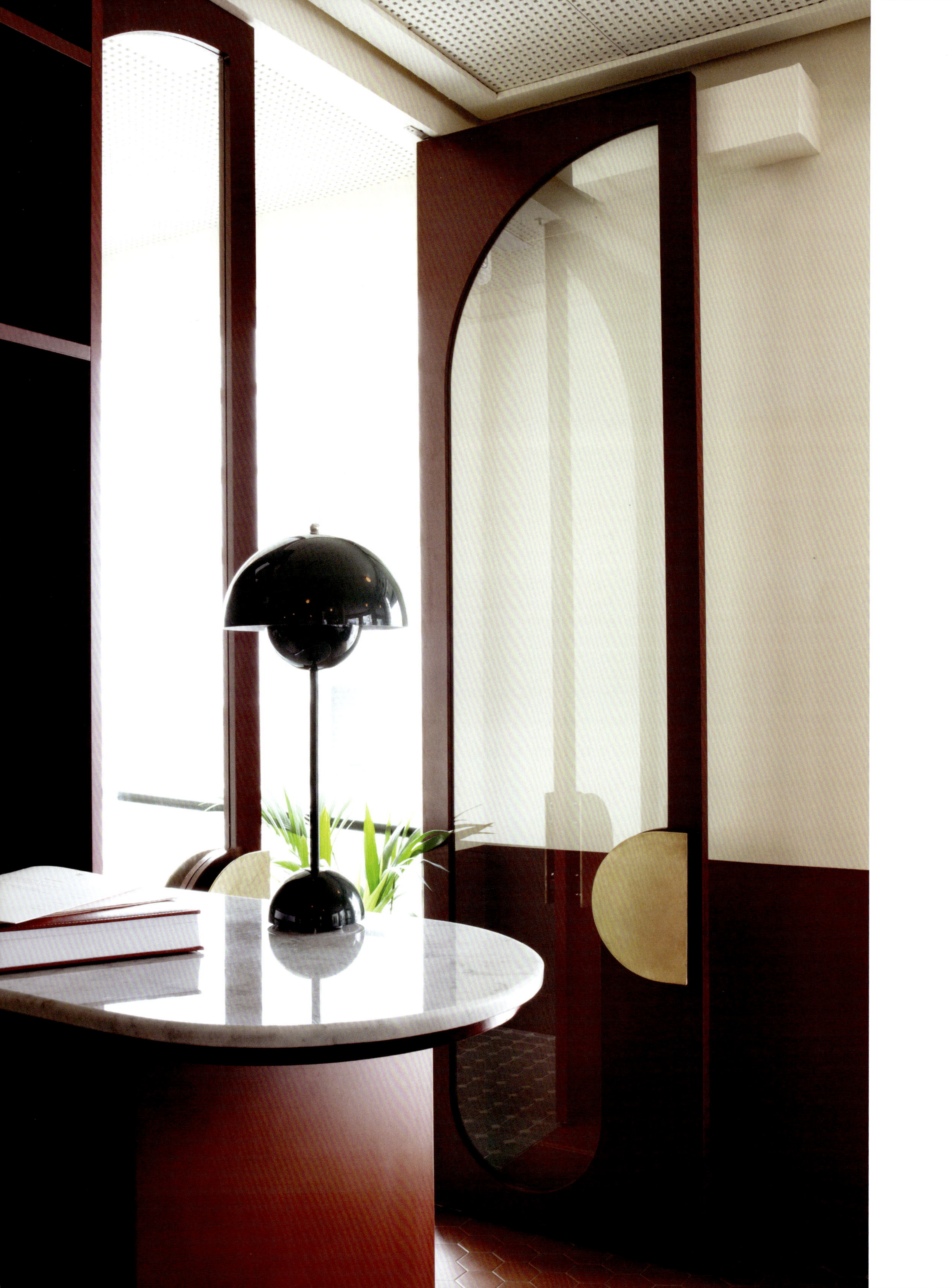

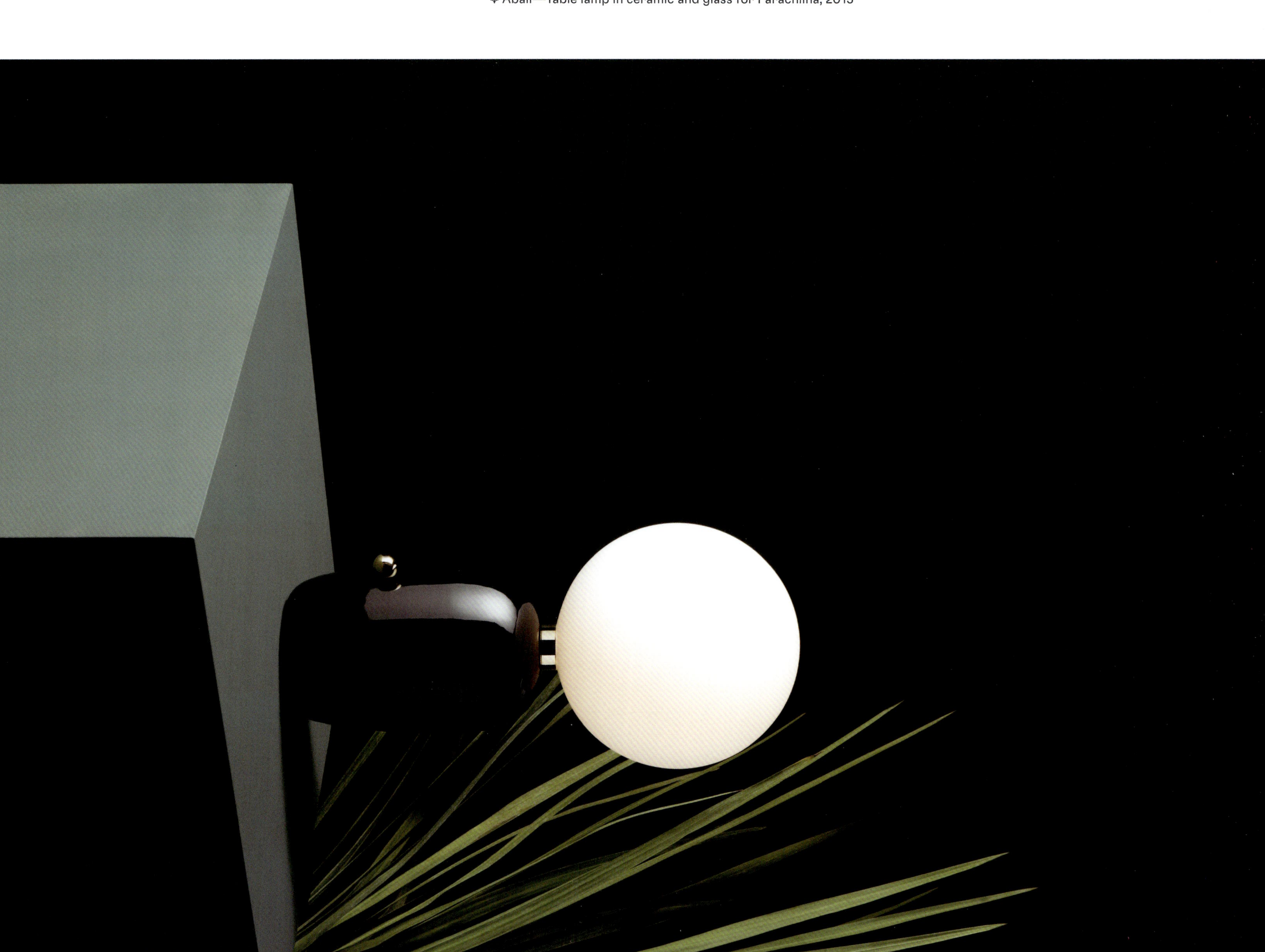

↑ Mar de Avellanas—Detail of restaurant interior design, Valencia, Spain, 2017
↓ Aball—Table lamp in ceramic and glass for Parachilna, 2015

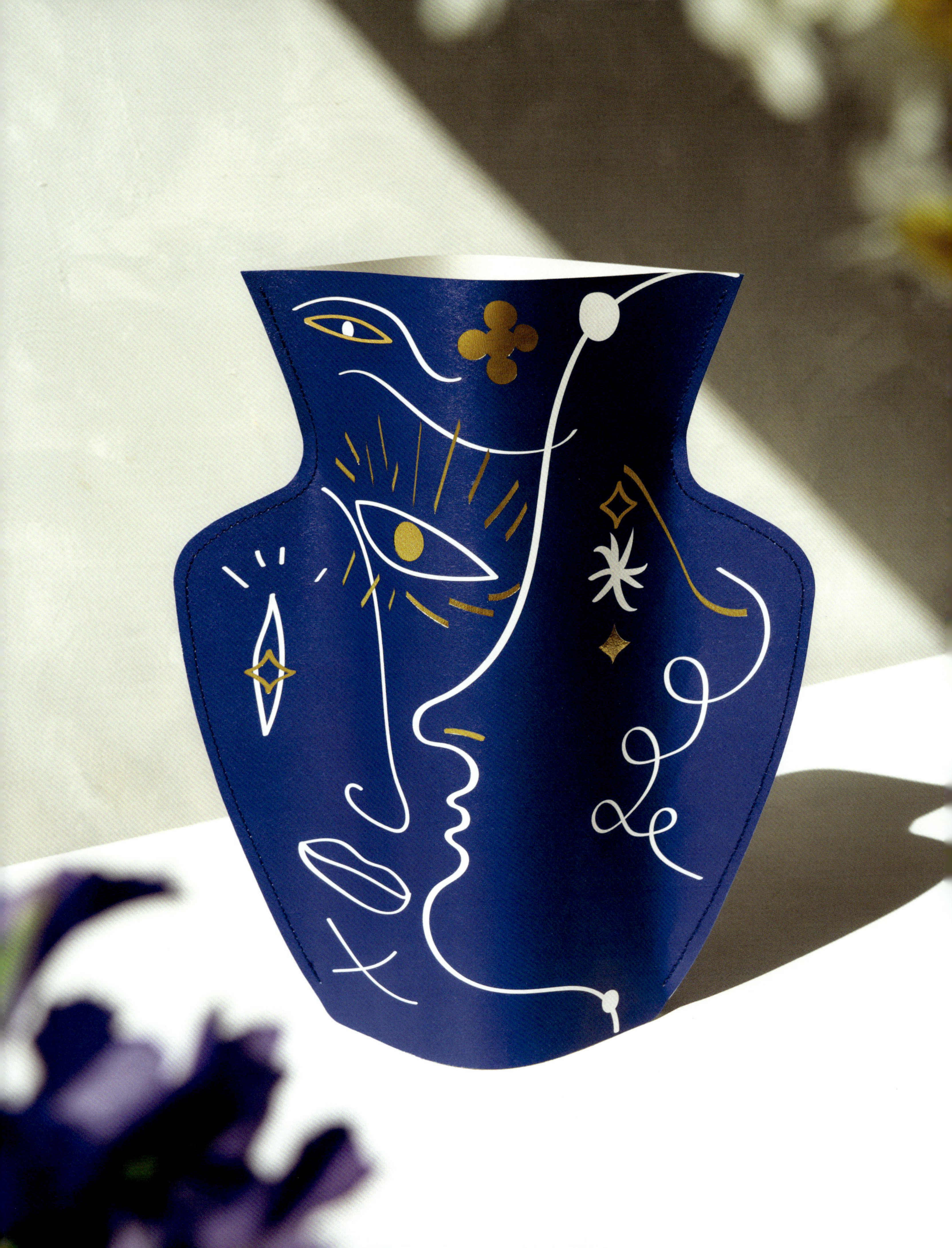

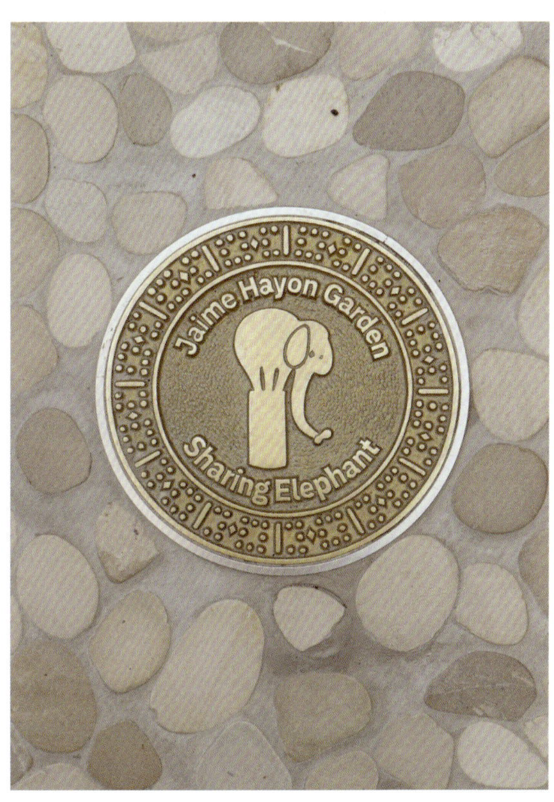

↑ Jaime Hayon Paper Vase—Vase for Octaevo, 2020
↓ Medallion detail from Jaime Hayon for MOKA Garden, Seoul, South Korea, 2020

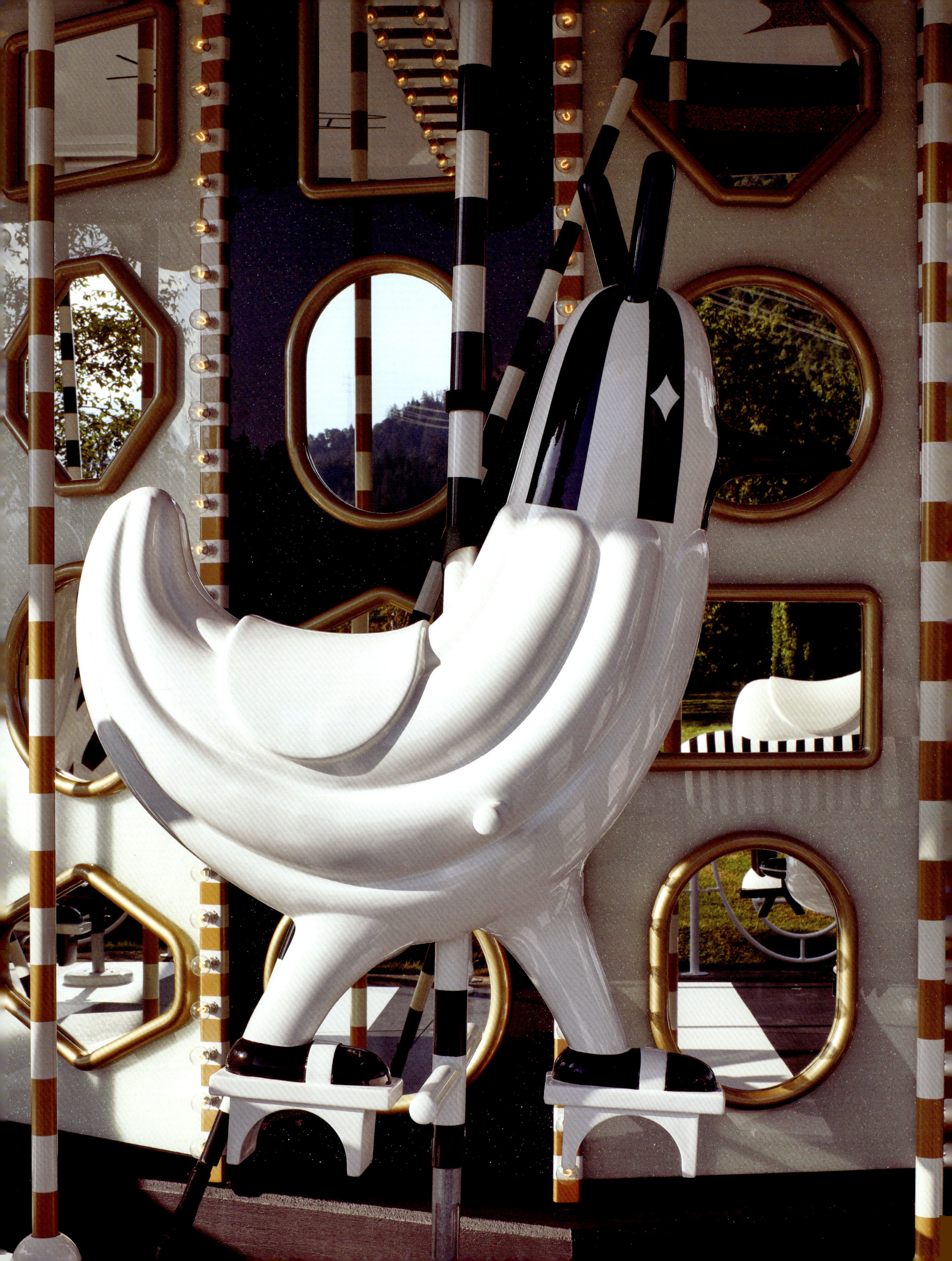

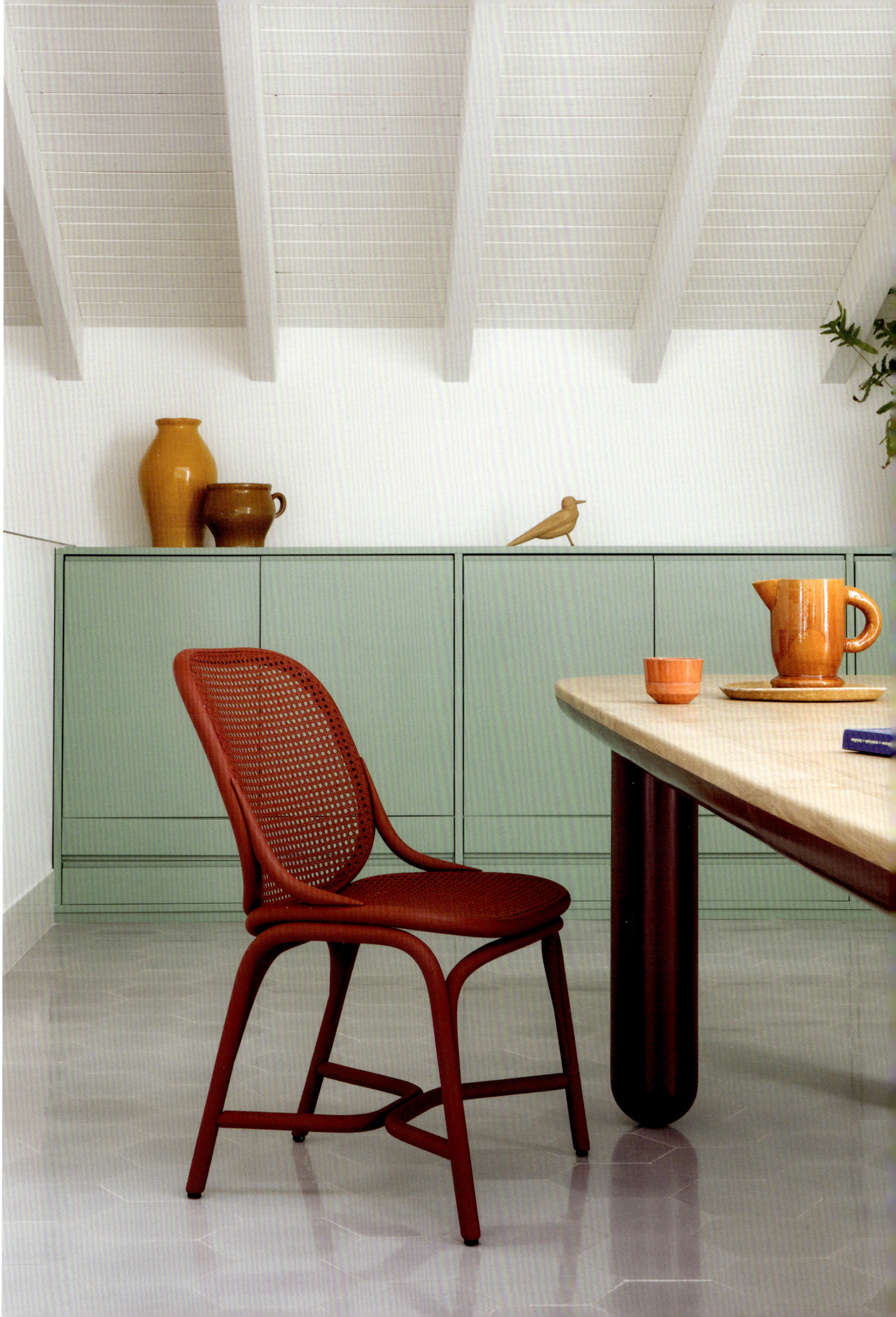

↑ Carousel—Swarovski Kristallwelten detail, Wattens, Austria, 2019
↓ Frames—Rattan dining chair for Expormim, 2014

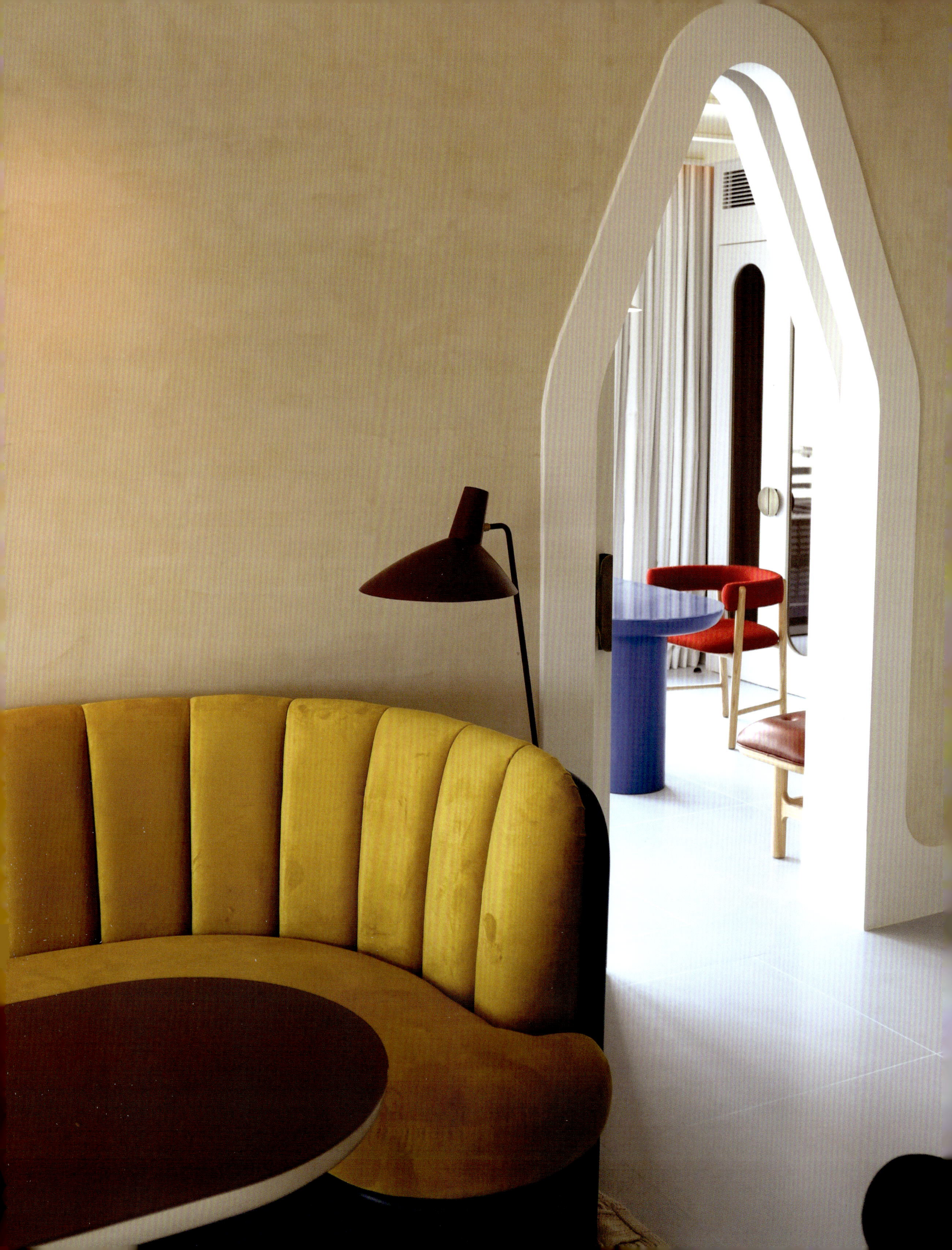

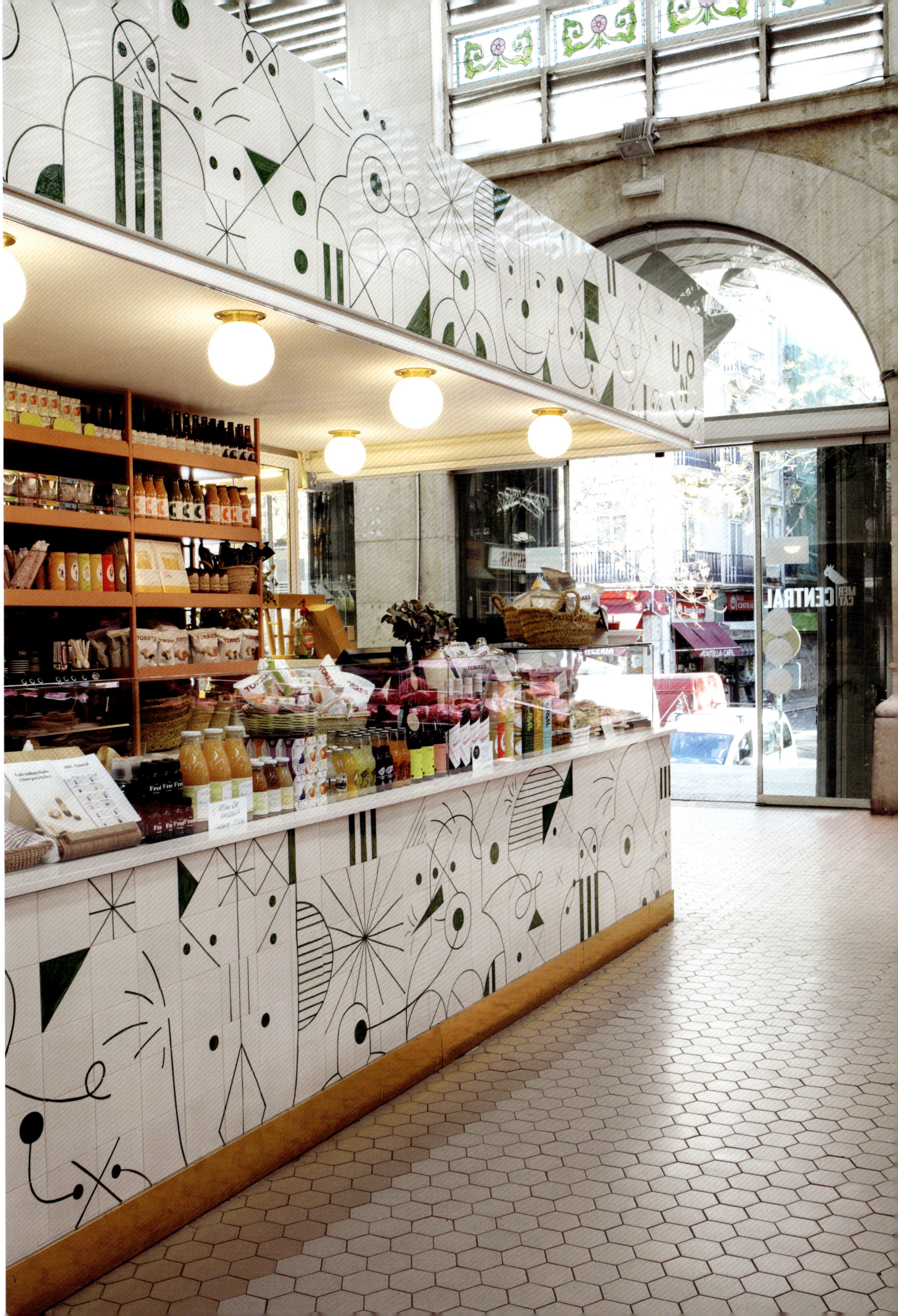

↑ The Standard Hotel—Guest suite, Bangkok, Thailand, 2022
↓ UNO—Food stand, Valencia Central Market, Spain, 2017

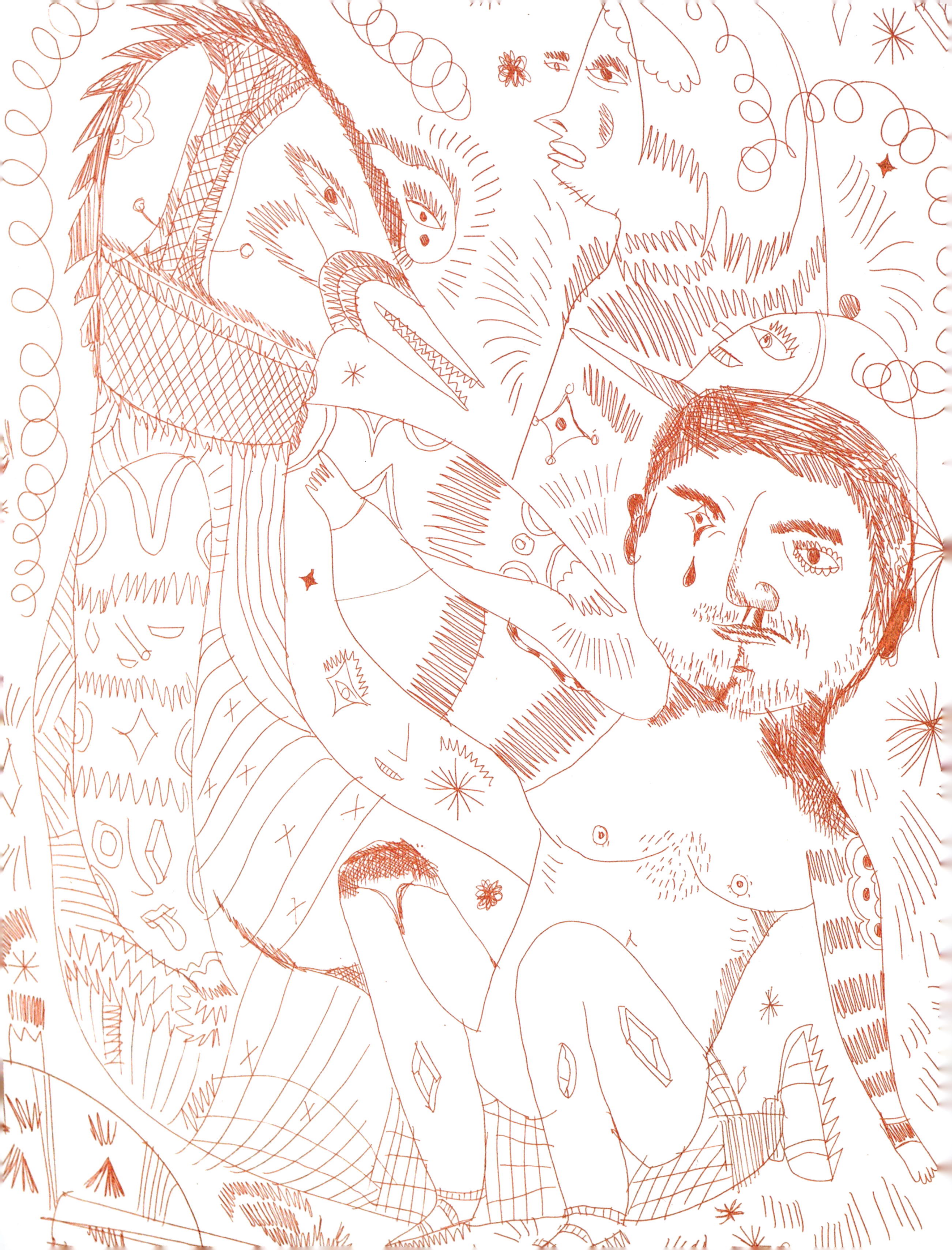

→ The coexistence of several different souls creates an untamable restlessness. When I am feeling reckless, I manage to summarize these many Jaimes into one or maybe two.

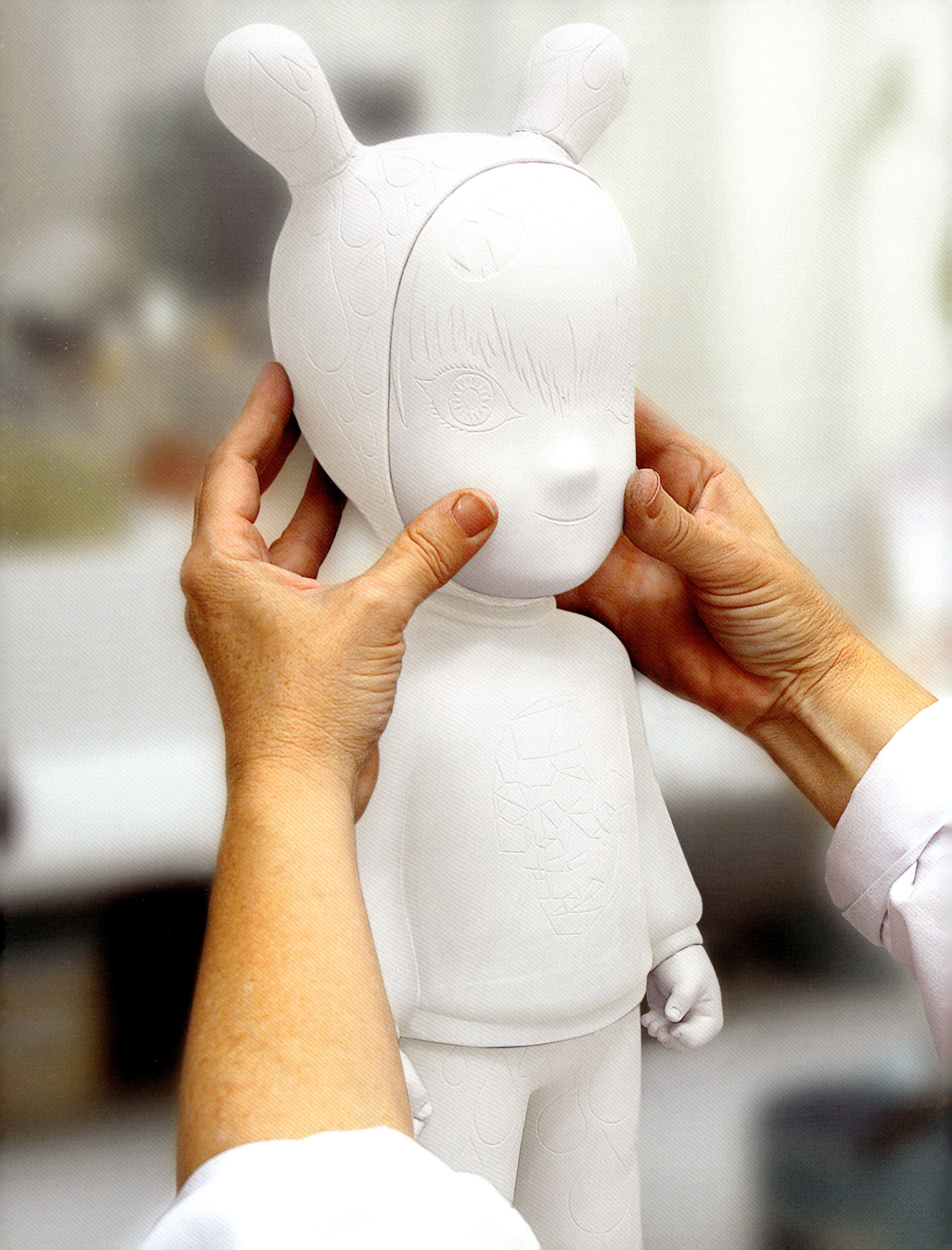

↑ The Guest—Porcelain sculpture for Lladró, 2016
↓ Barceló Torre de Madrid Hotel—Interior design, Madrid, Spain, 2016

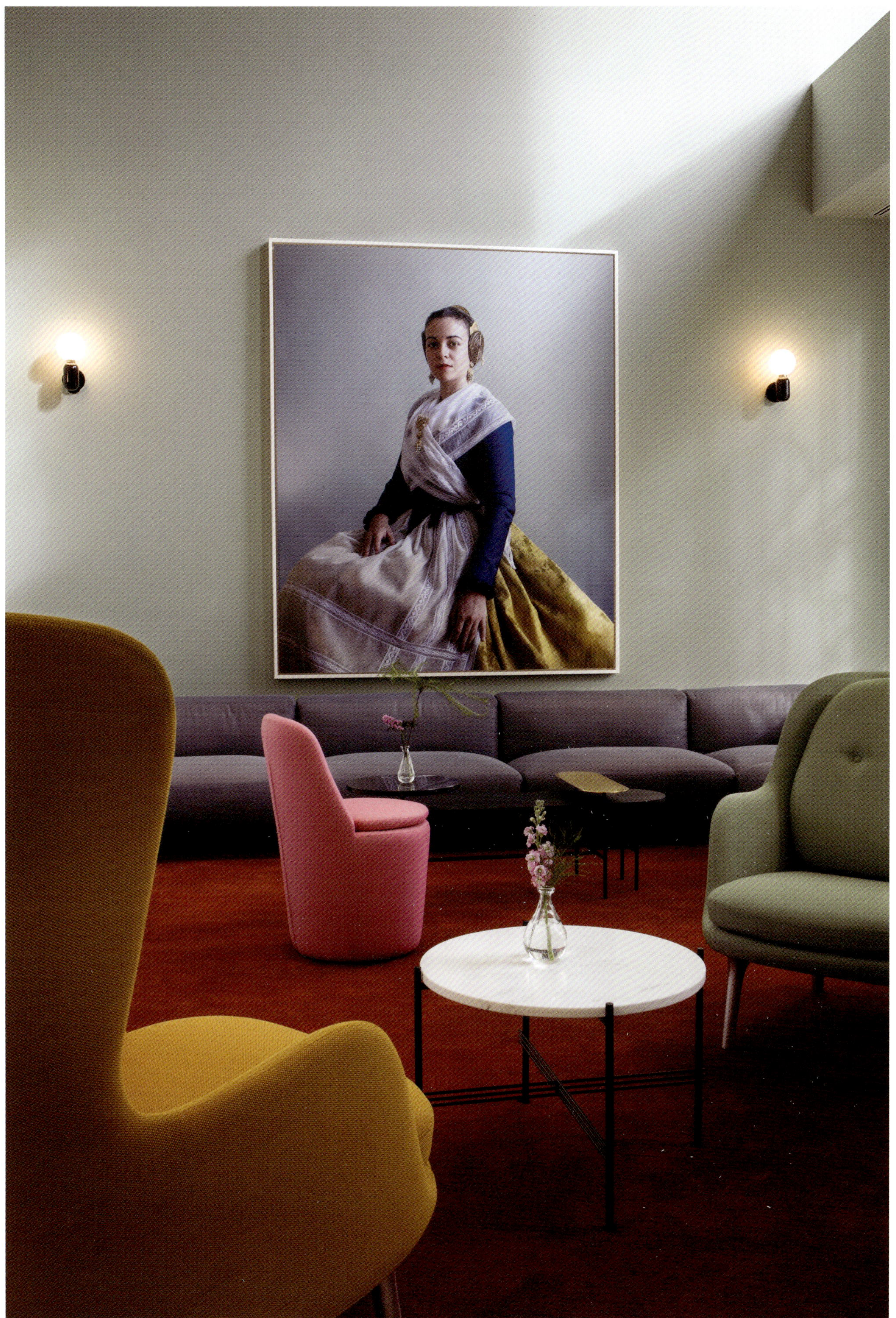

239

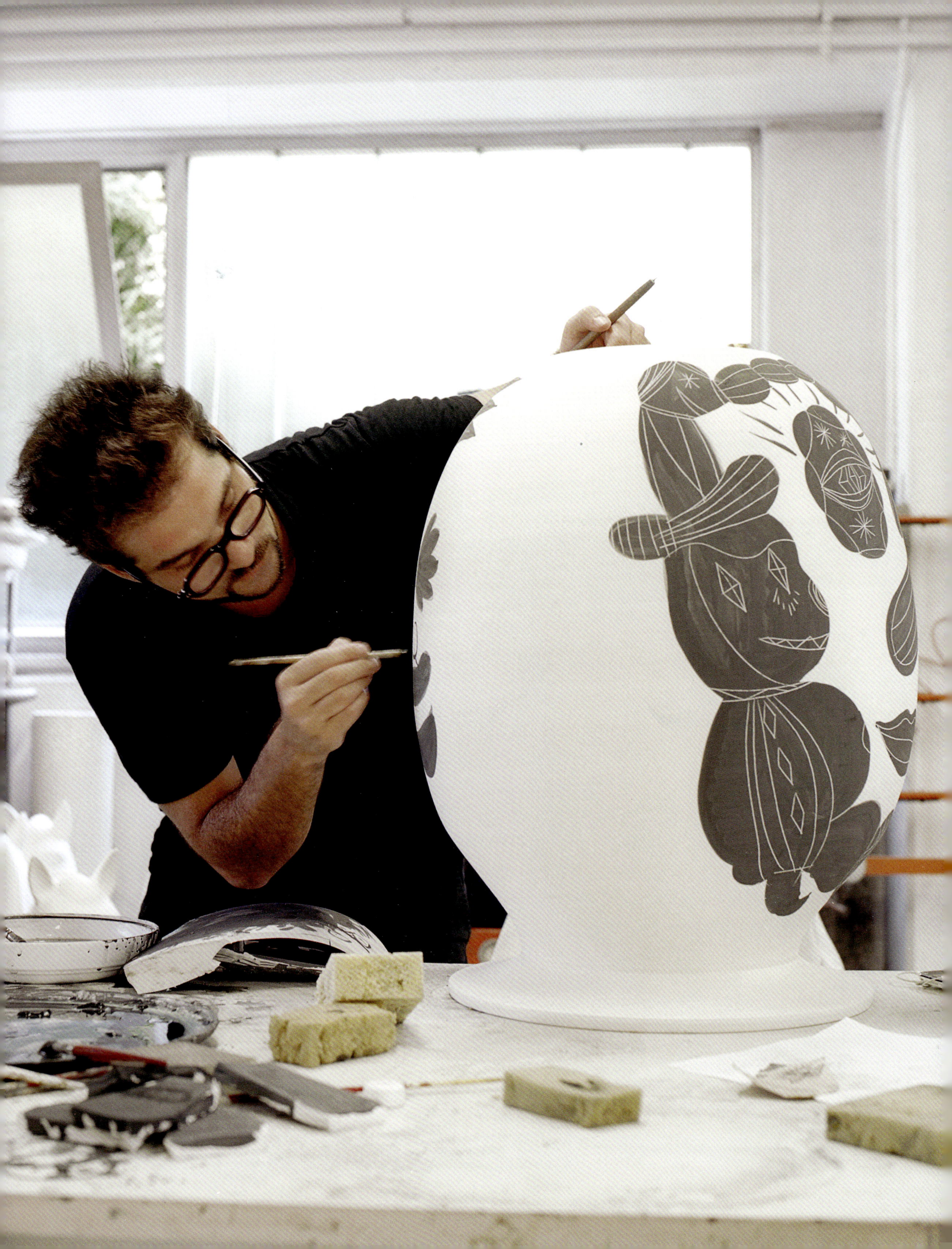

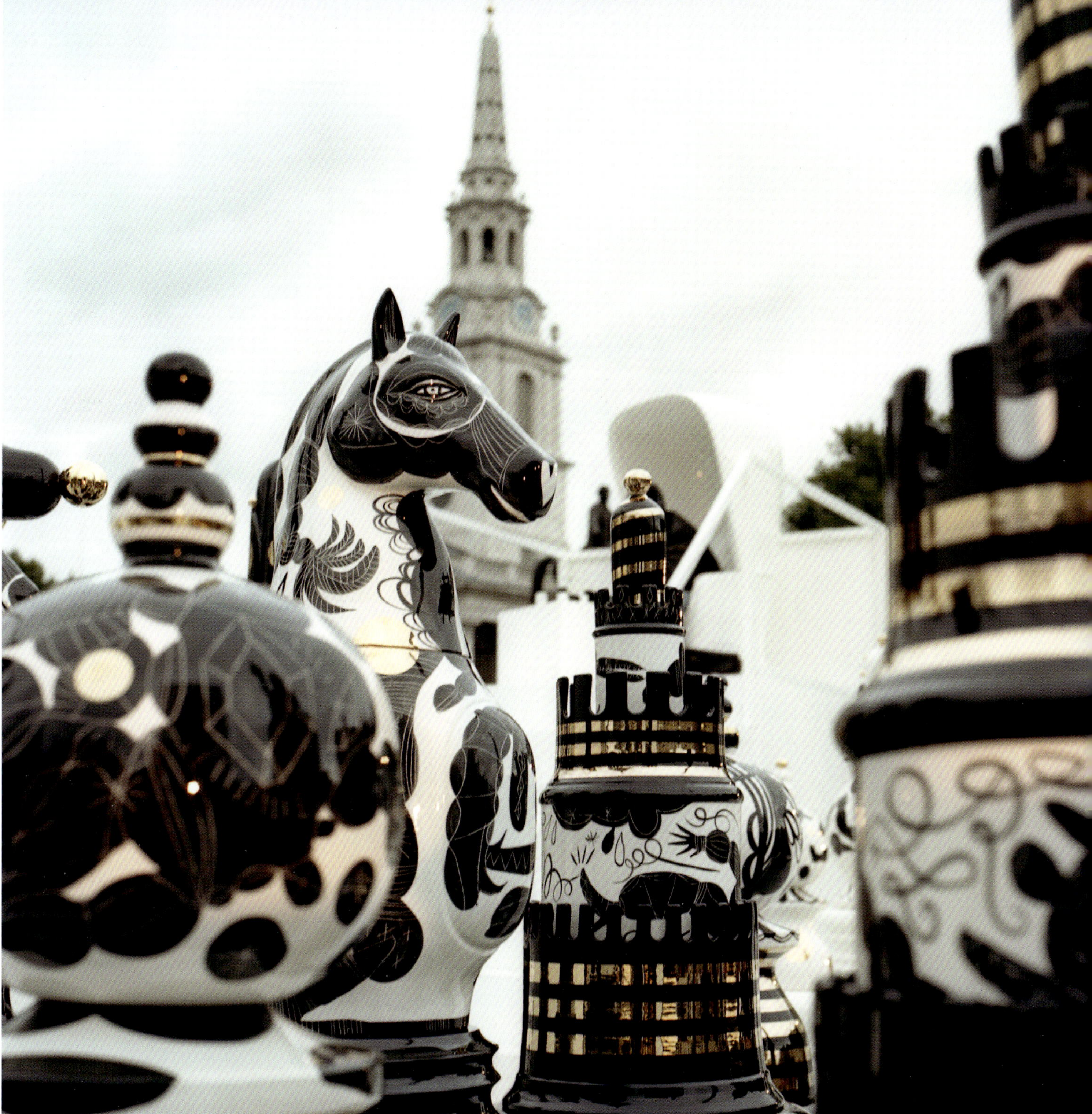

↑ The Tournament—Hand-painting ceramic pieces for installation
↓ The Tournament—Installation details, Trafalgar Square, London Design Festival, U.K., 2009

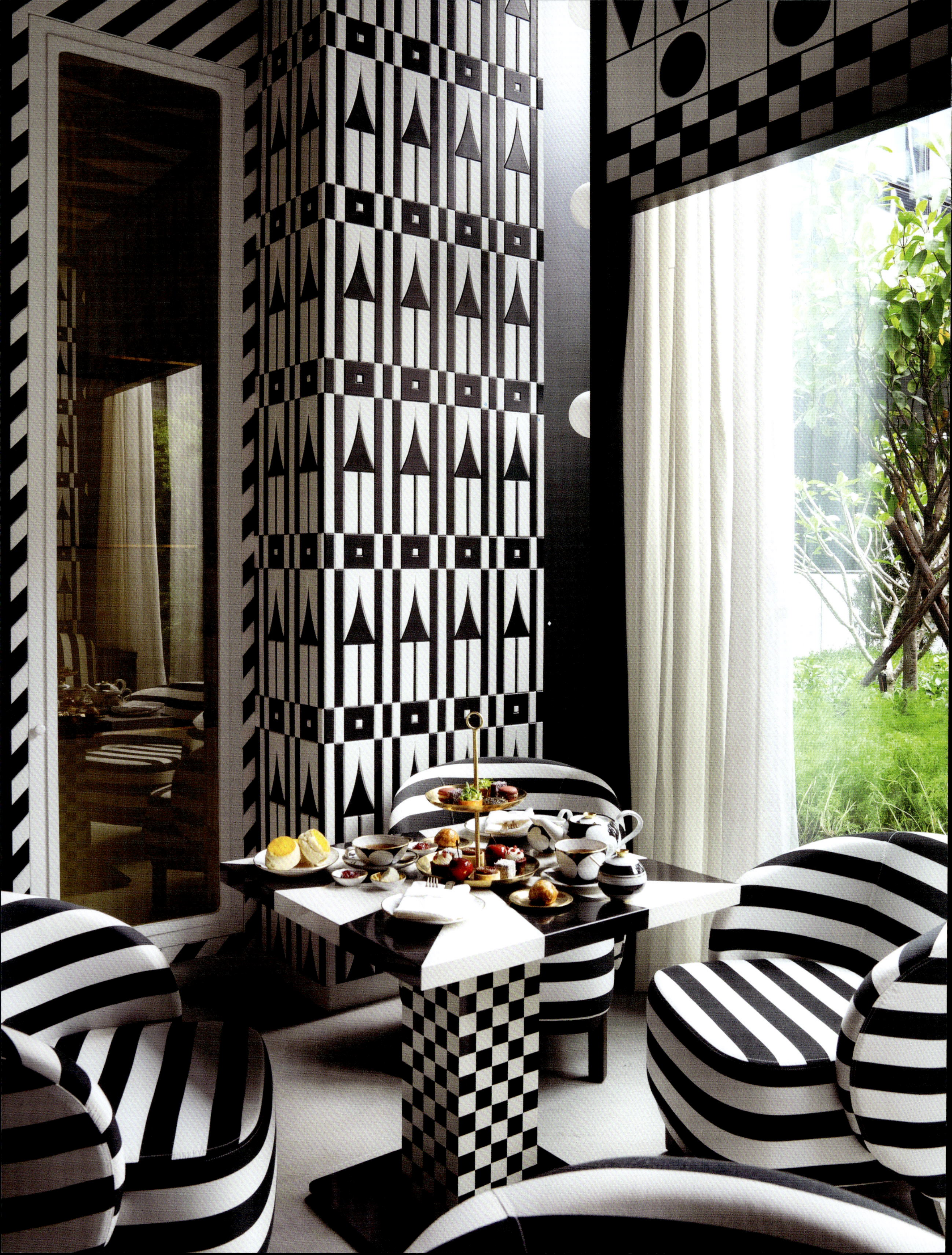

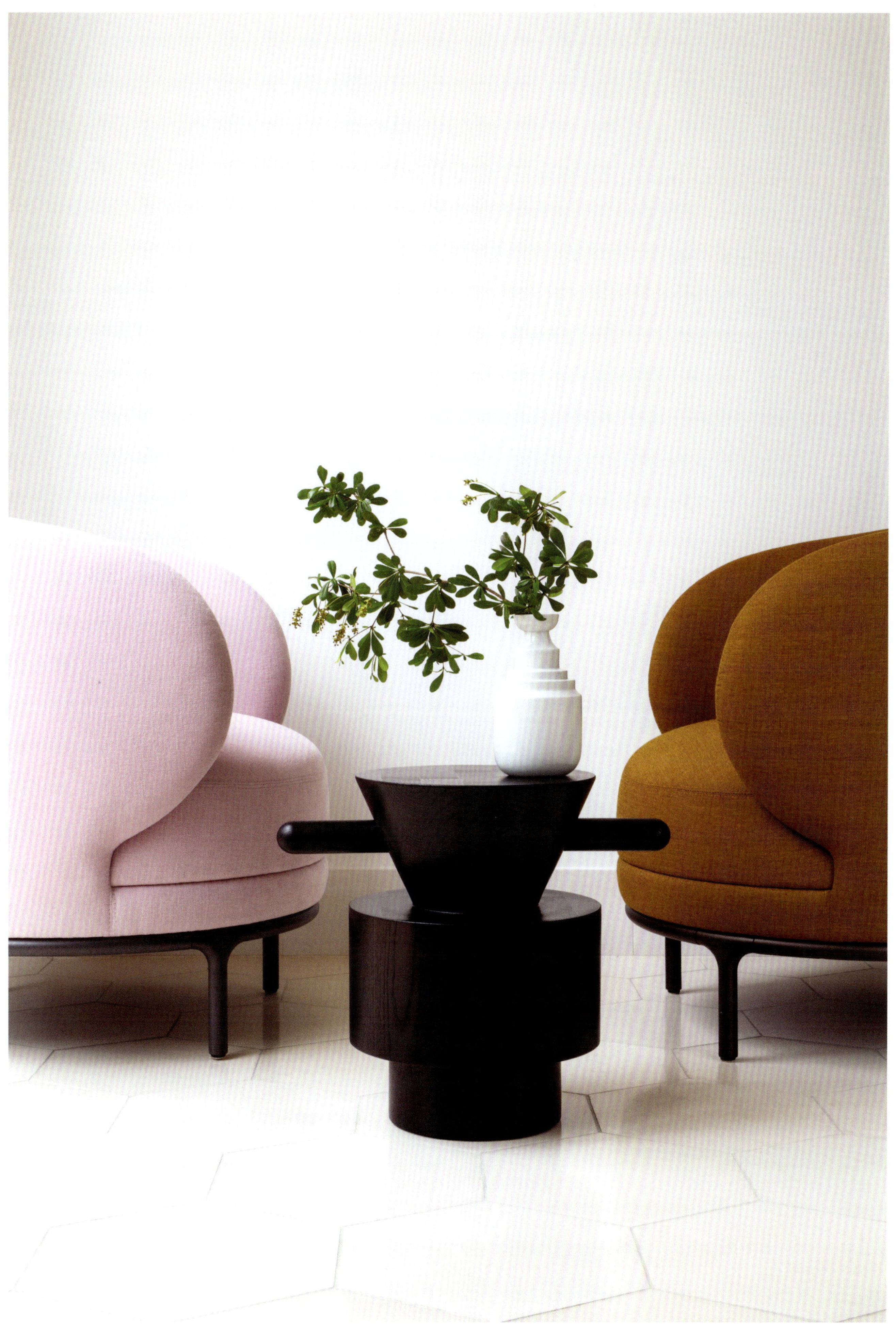

↑ The Standard Hotel—Interior design, Bangkok, Thailand, 2022
↓ Vuelta—Chair and table for Wittmann workshop, 2016

243

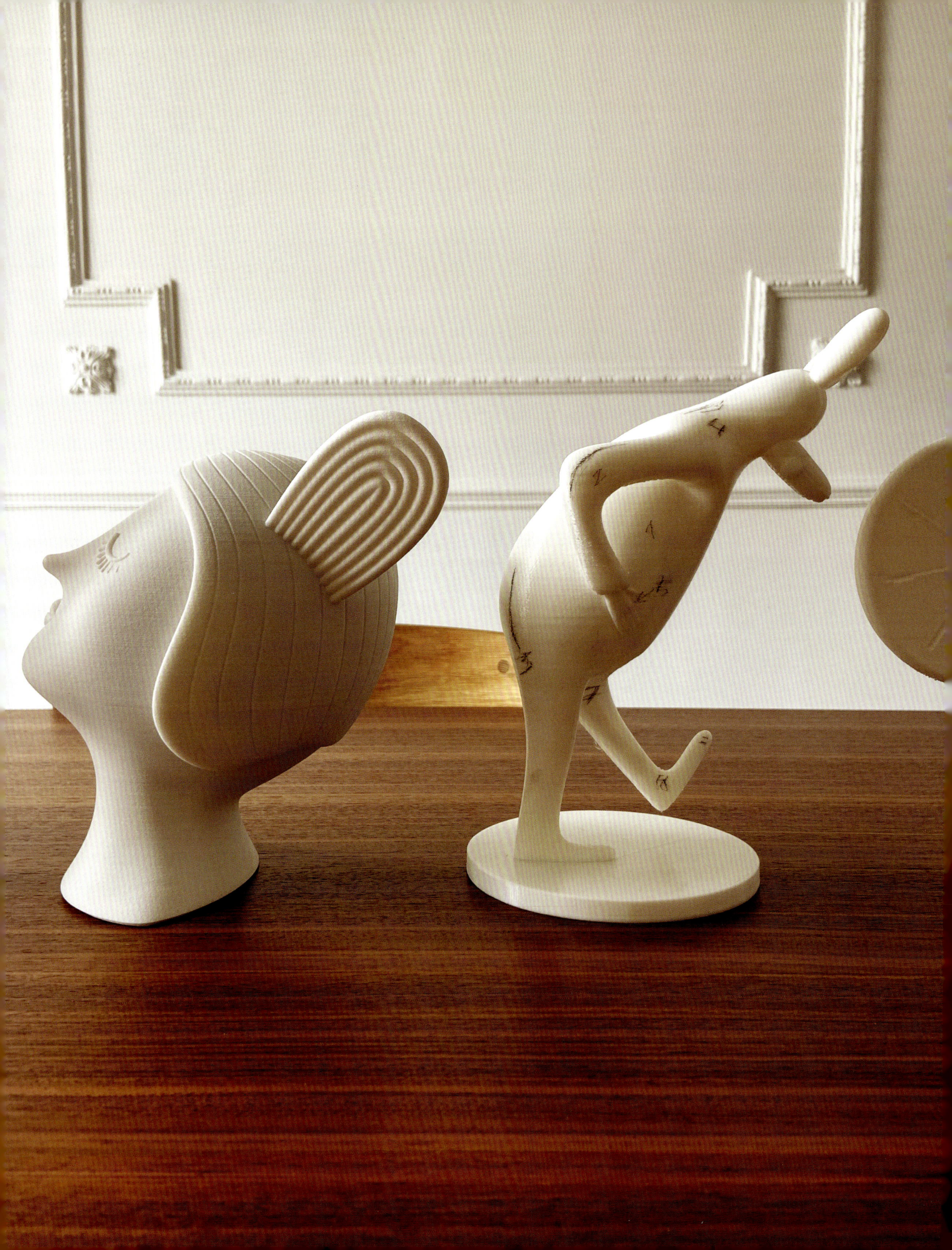

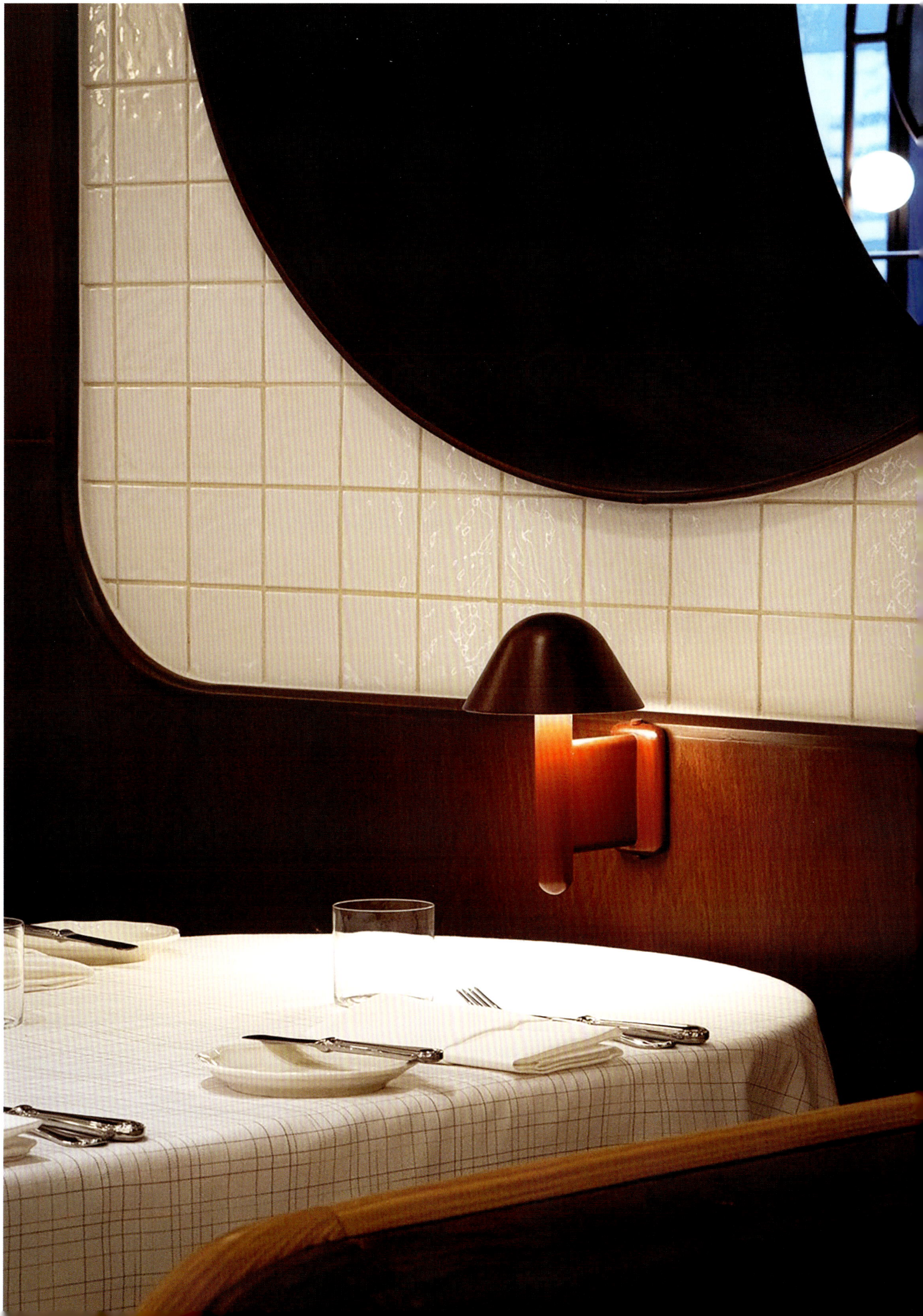

↑ Prototypes for MOKA Garden sculptures
↓ The Standard Hotel—Interior design, Bangkok, Thailand, 2022

→ I am not scared of bestial,
grotesque, or melancholy visions, on the
contrary I am attracted by them and
they create an expressive pathos where
my proverbial curvilinear mark becomes
sharpened perfection.

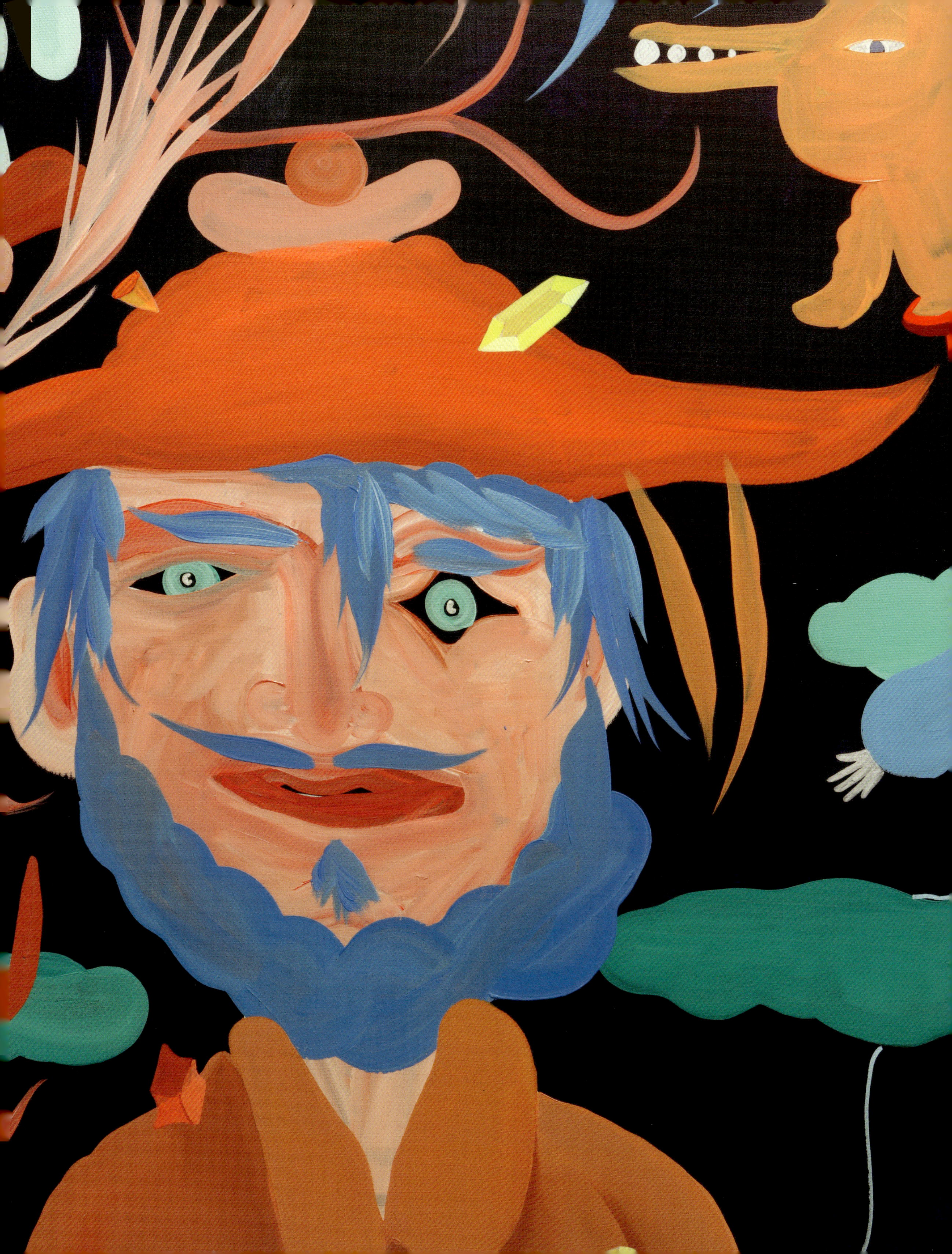

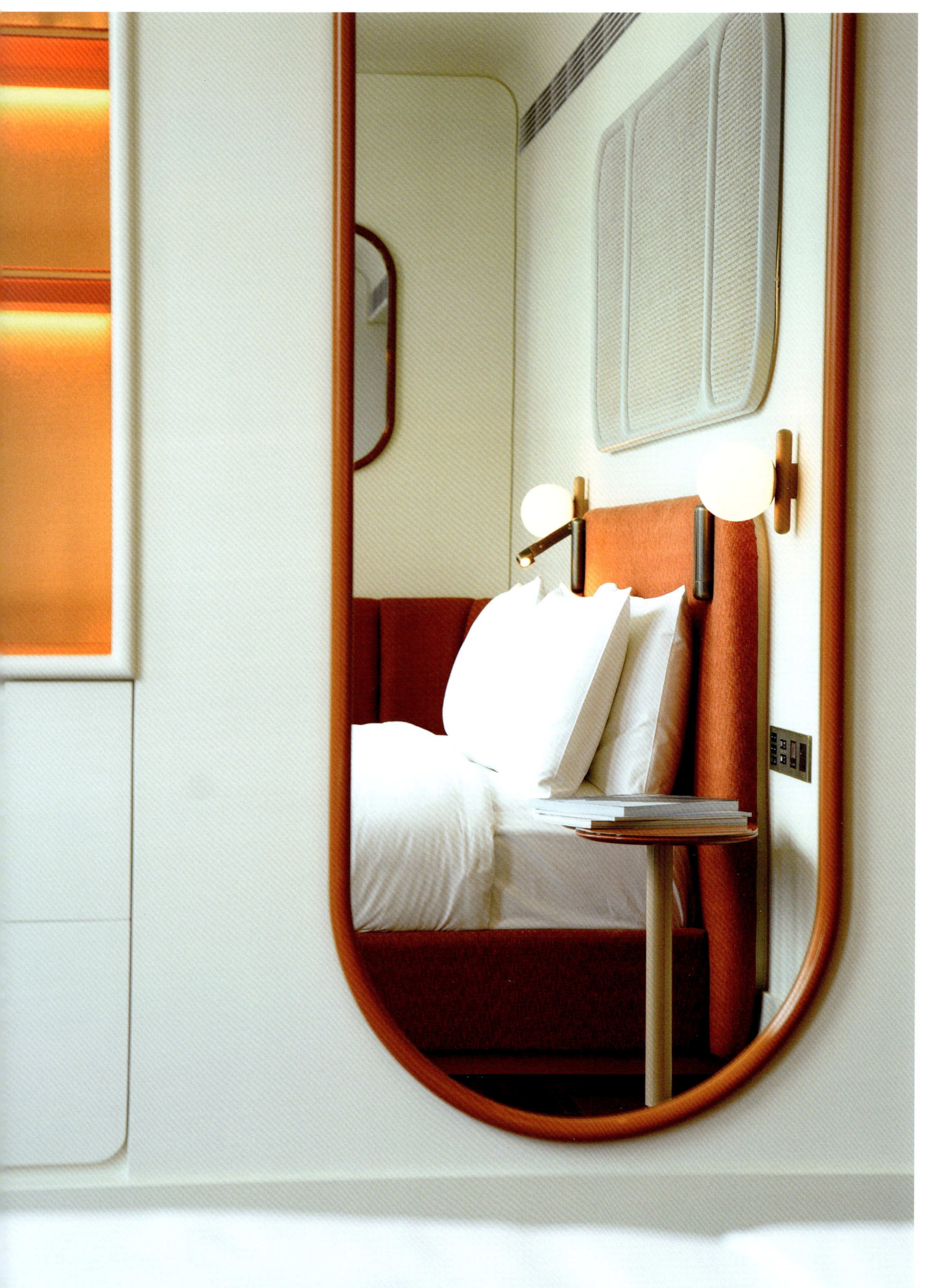

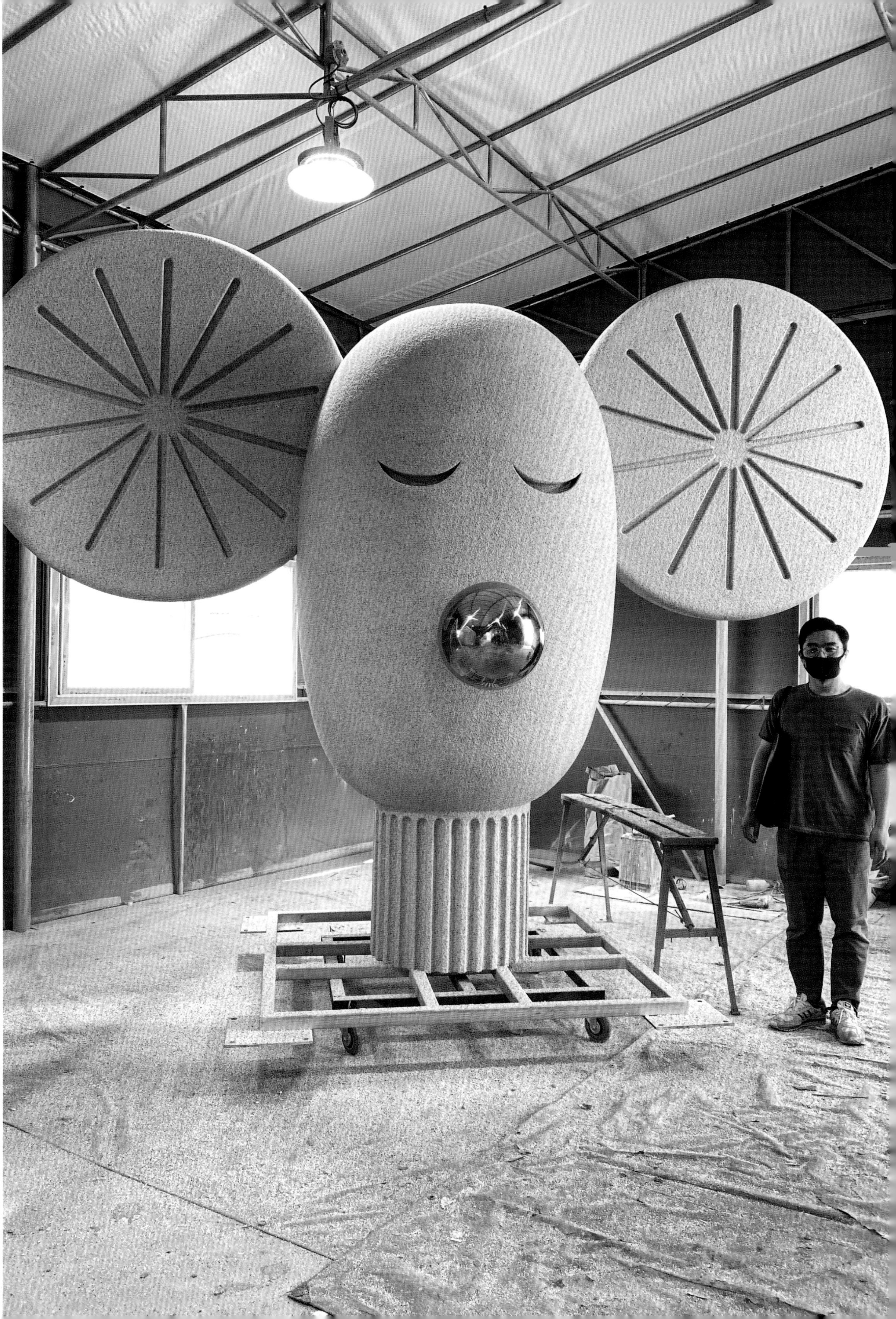

↑ The Standard Hotel—Interior design, Bangkok, Thailand, 2022
↓ The Listener—Sculpture for MOKA Garden, Seoul, South Korea, 2020

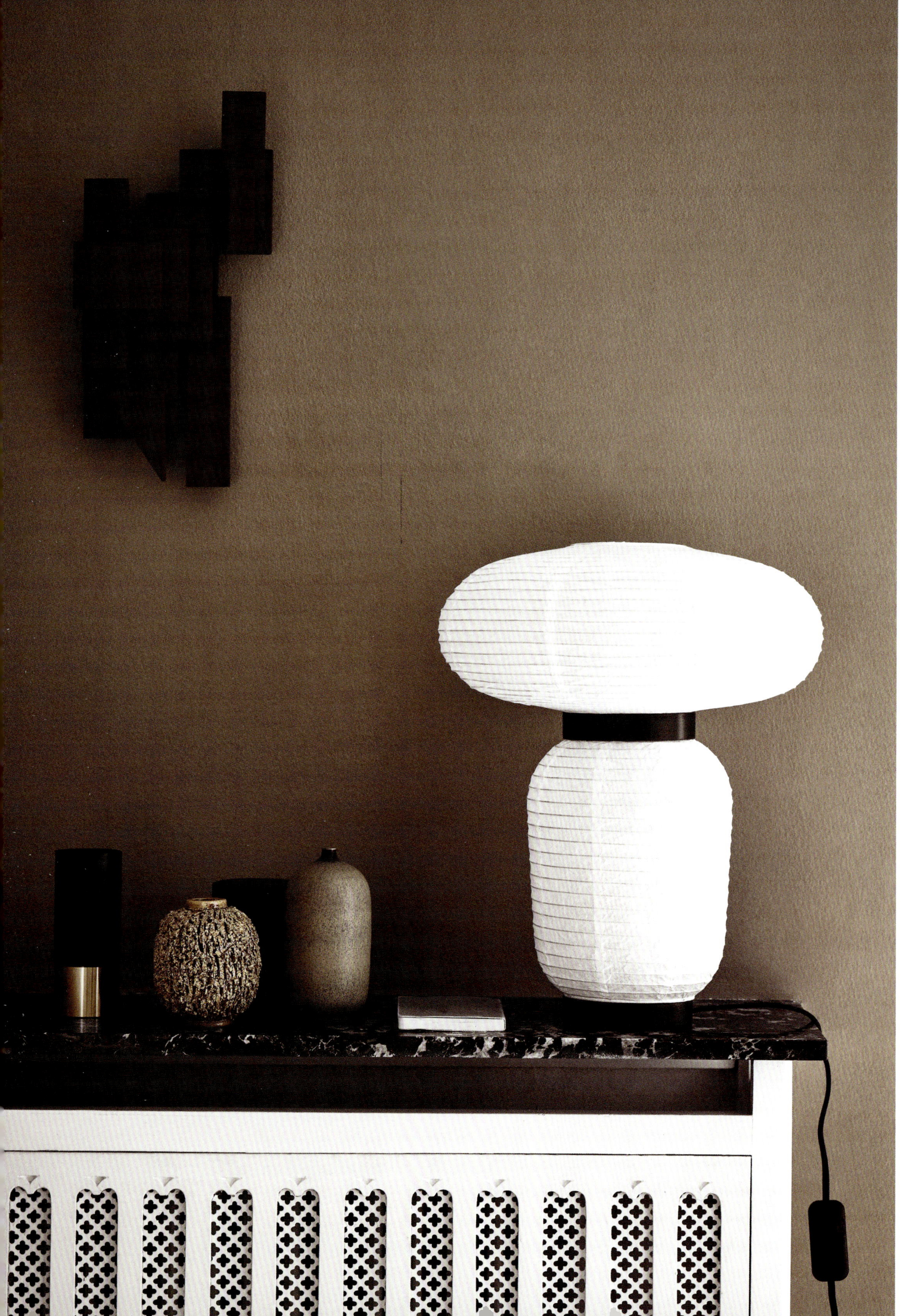

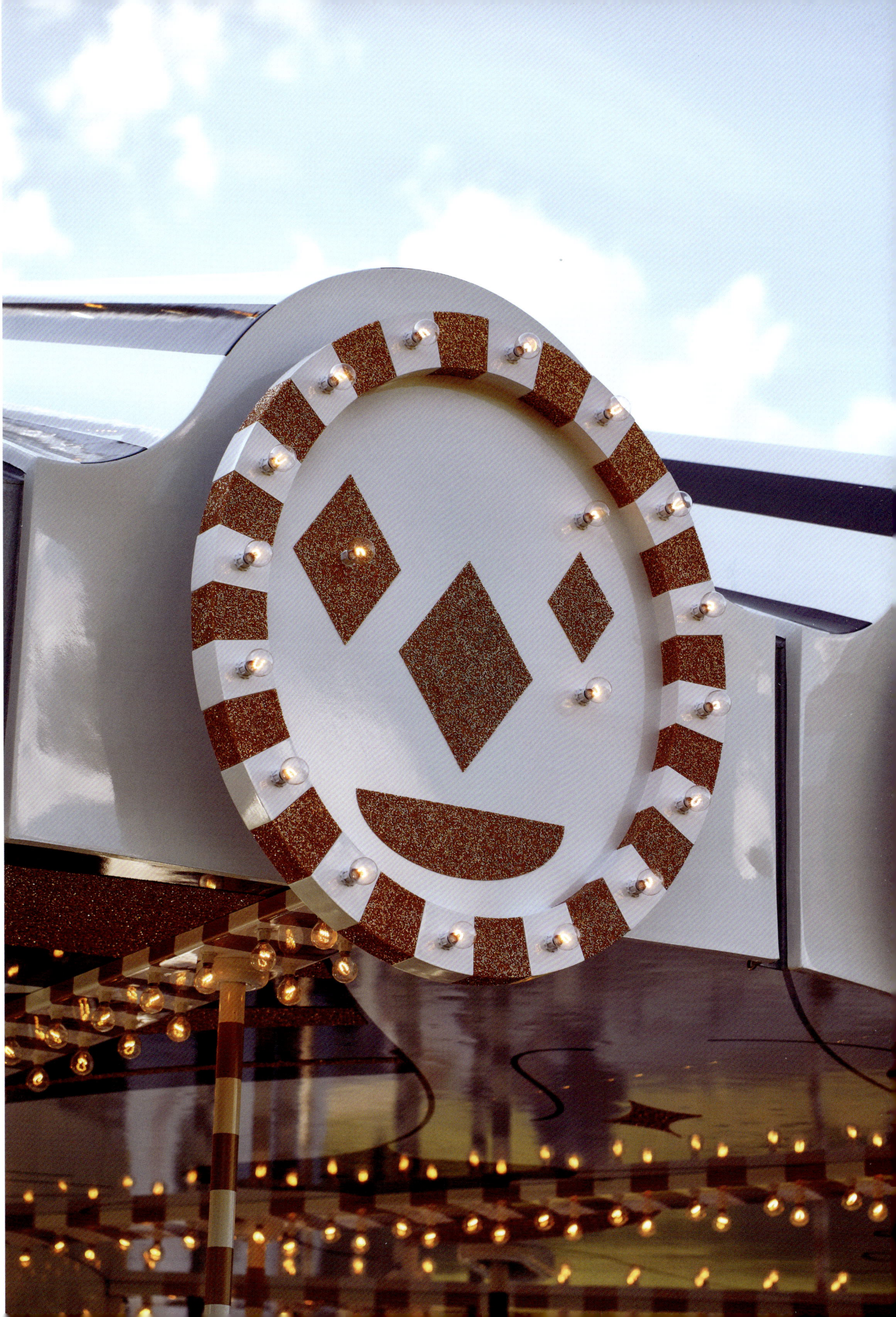

↑ Formakami—Table lamp for &Tradition, 2016
↓ Carousel—Swarovski Kristallwelten detail, Wattens, Austria, 2019

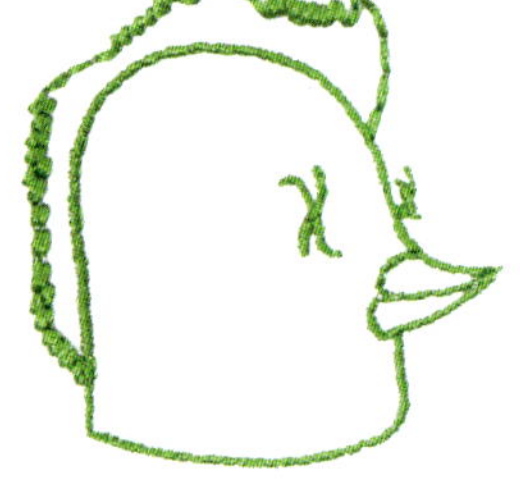

↑ Hayon × Jijibaba—Detail of stitching for a shirt from the fashion collection, 2017
↓ Vase and Clouds—Acrylic on canvas, detail, 2022

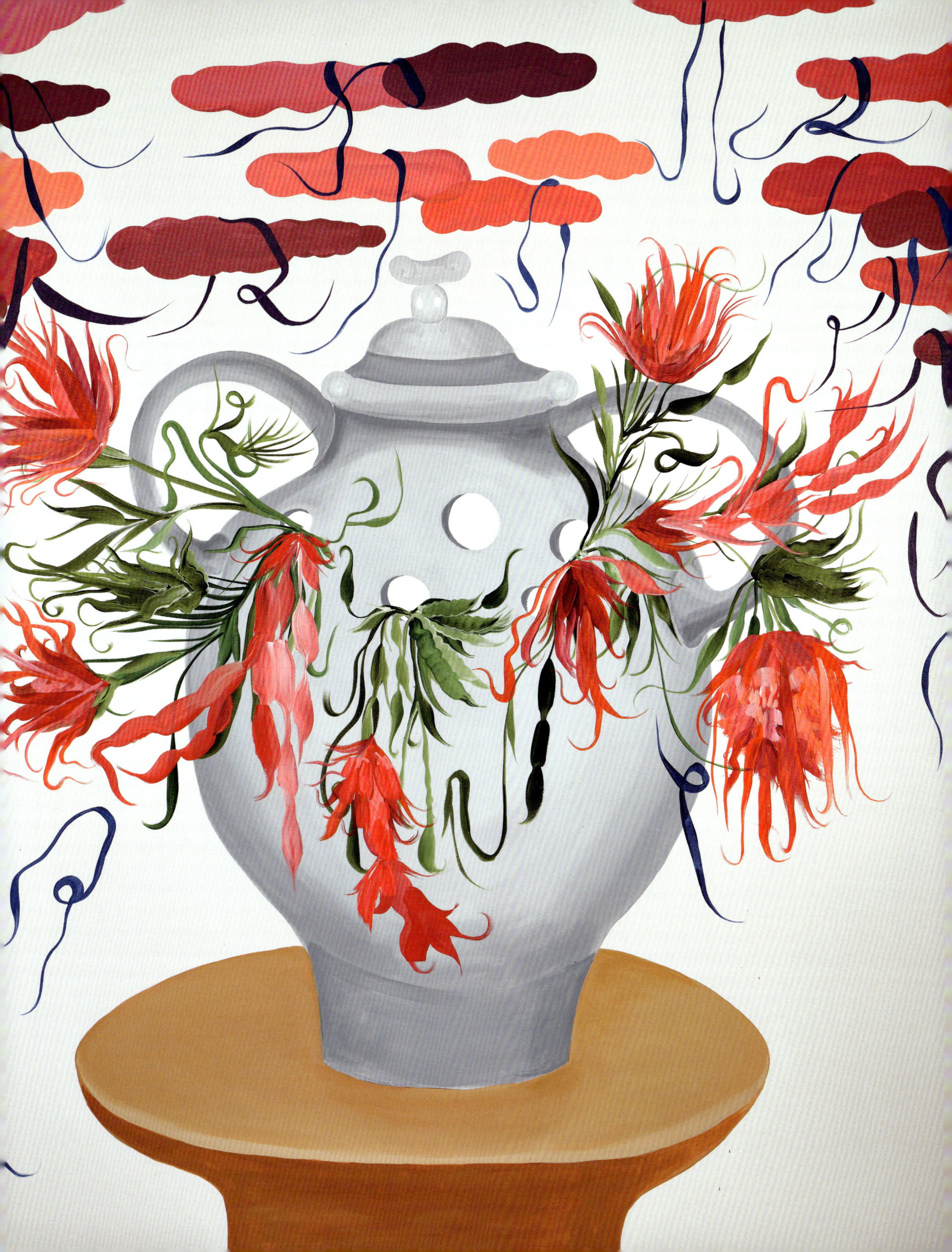

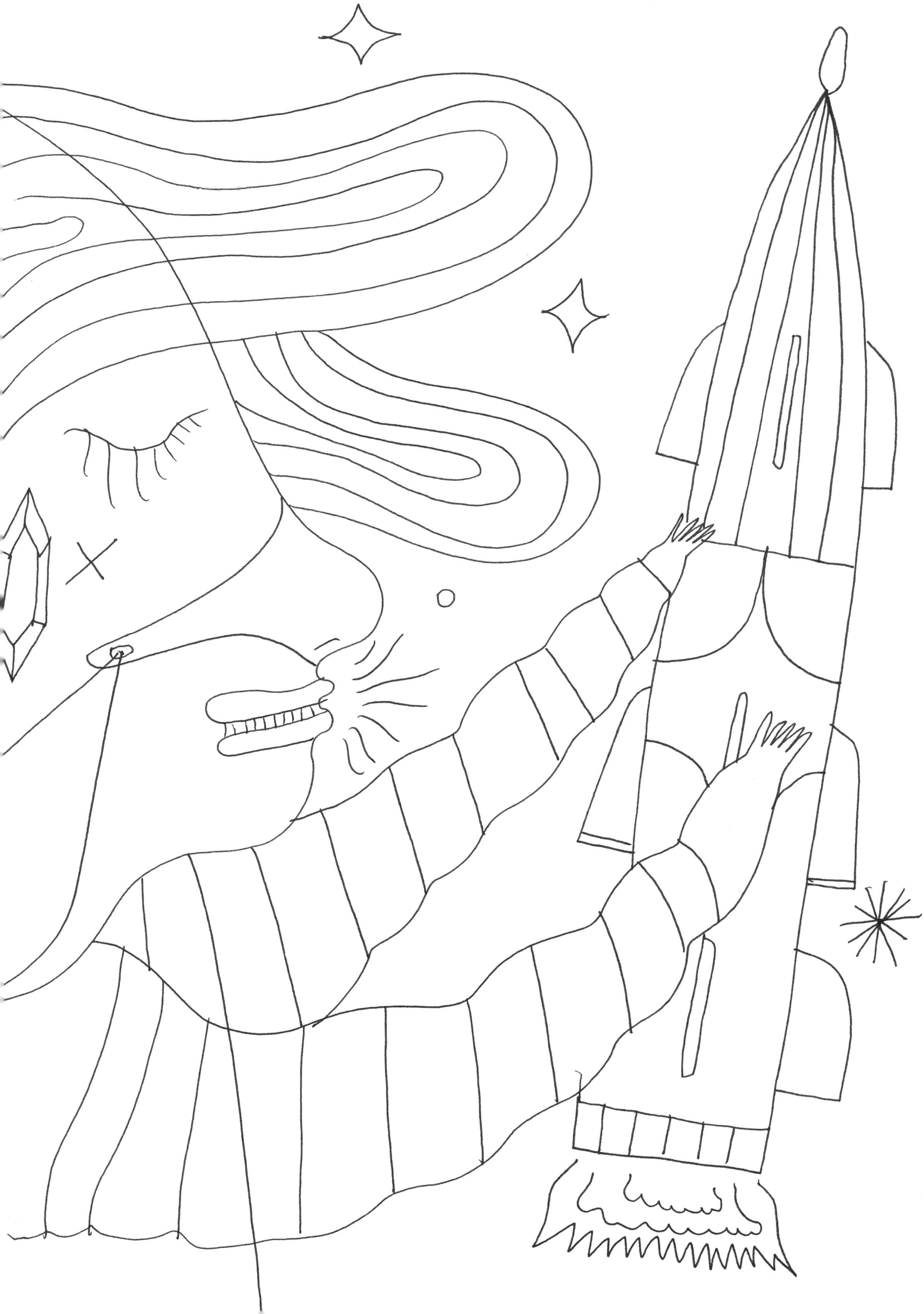

↑ Fantasy sketch, 2020

↳ Serious Fun exhibition—Furniture Galaxy room at the Daelim Museum, Seoul, South Korea, 2019

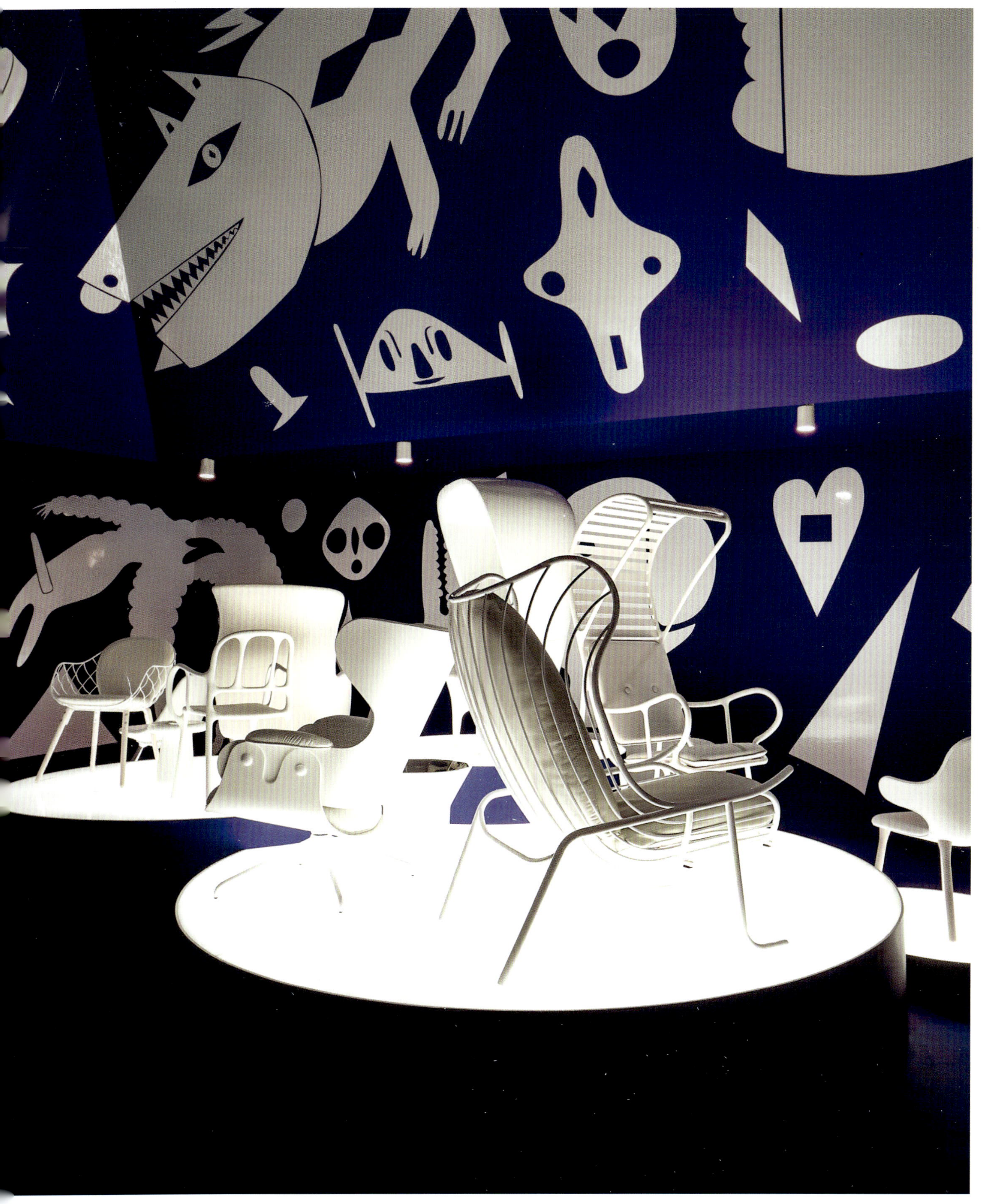

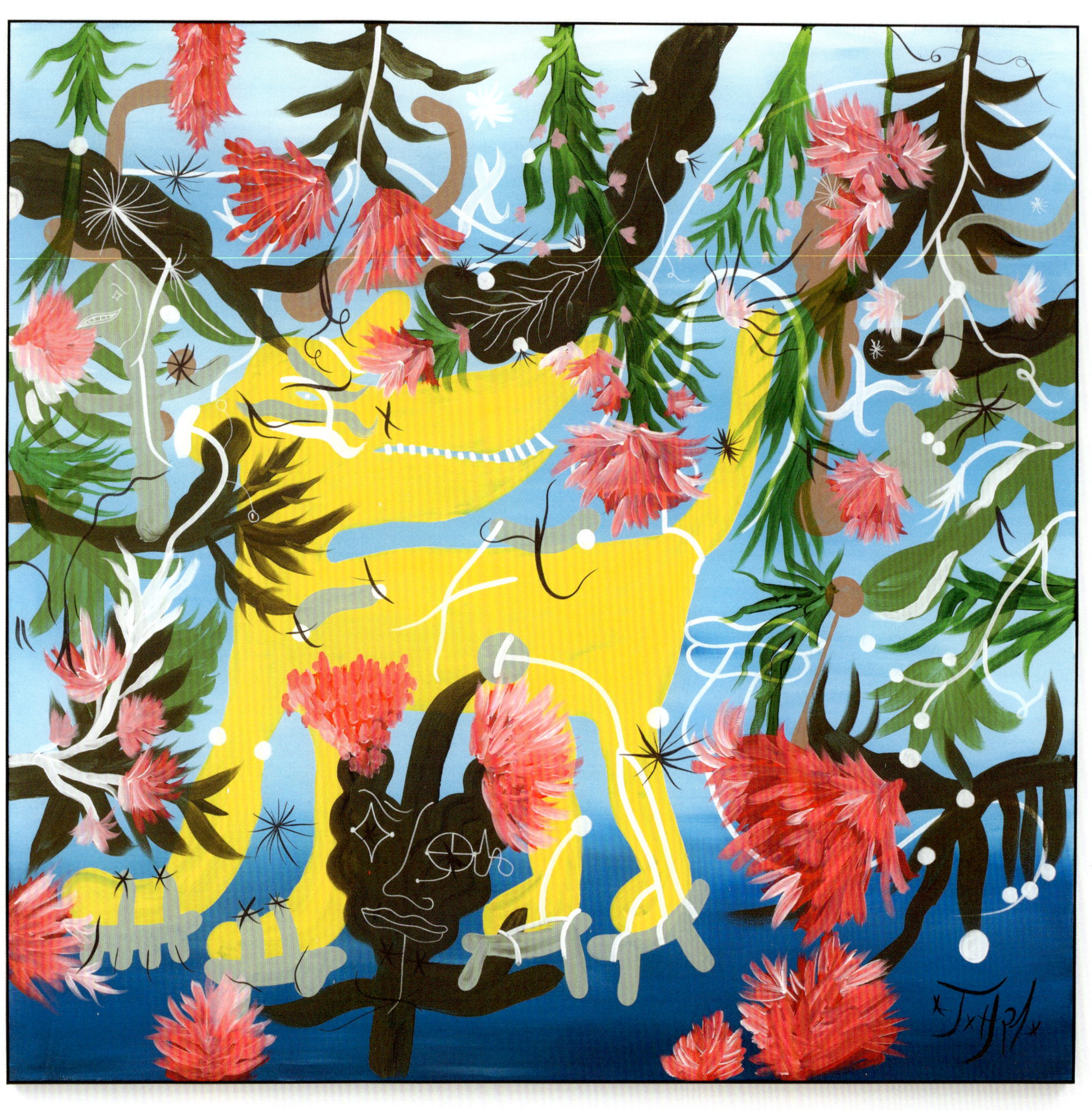

→ Everything is in the nature, the flowers and plants, the greenery, and in the geography of a landscape where I create the idea of a Mediterranean made of oil, bread, and fruit.

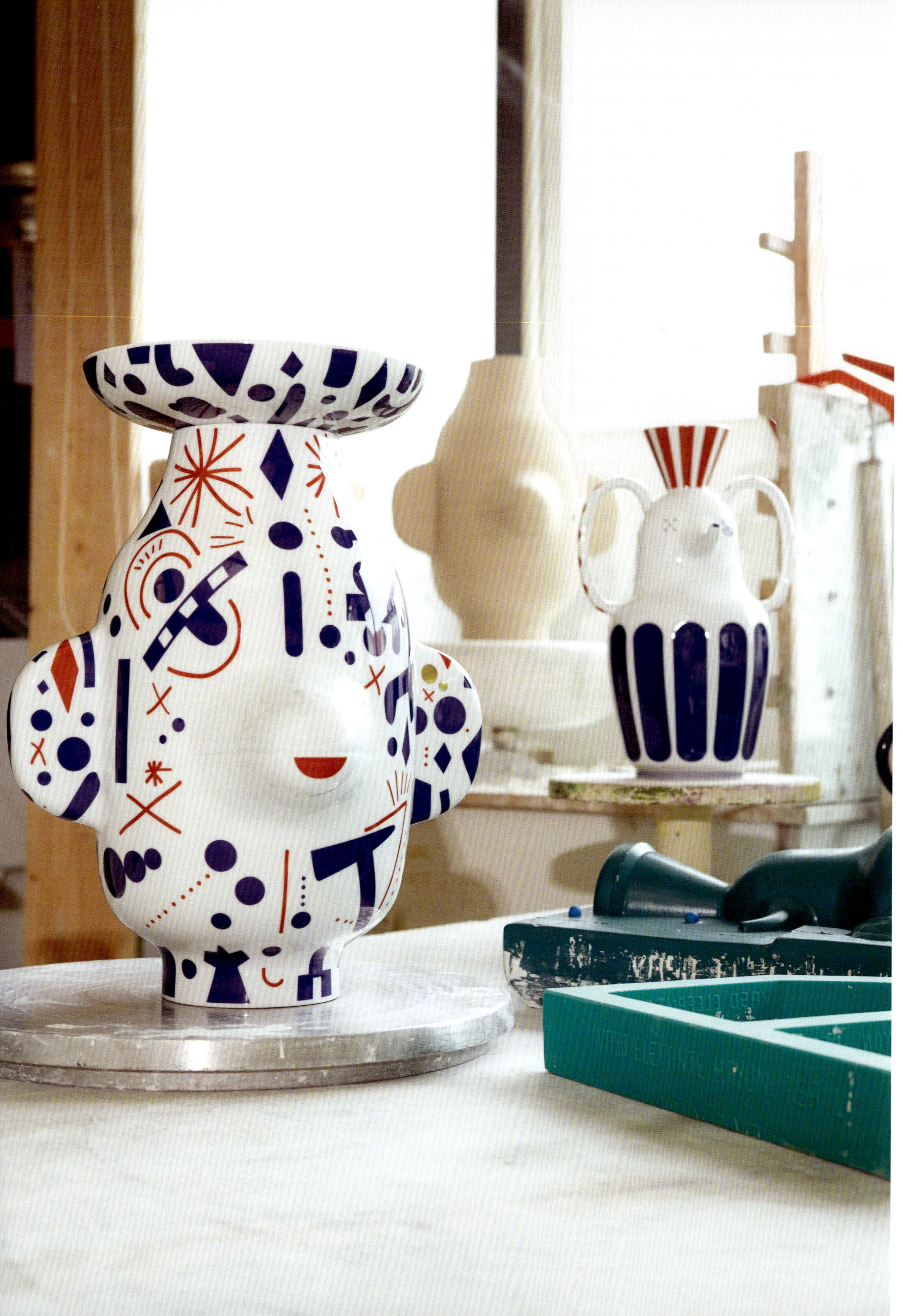

↑ Grimace—Vase with lid. Folkifunki collection for Vista Alegre, 2016
↓ Sketch for MOKA children's library, 2019

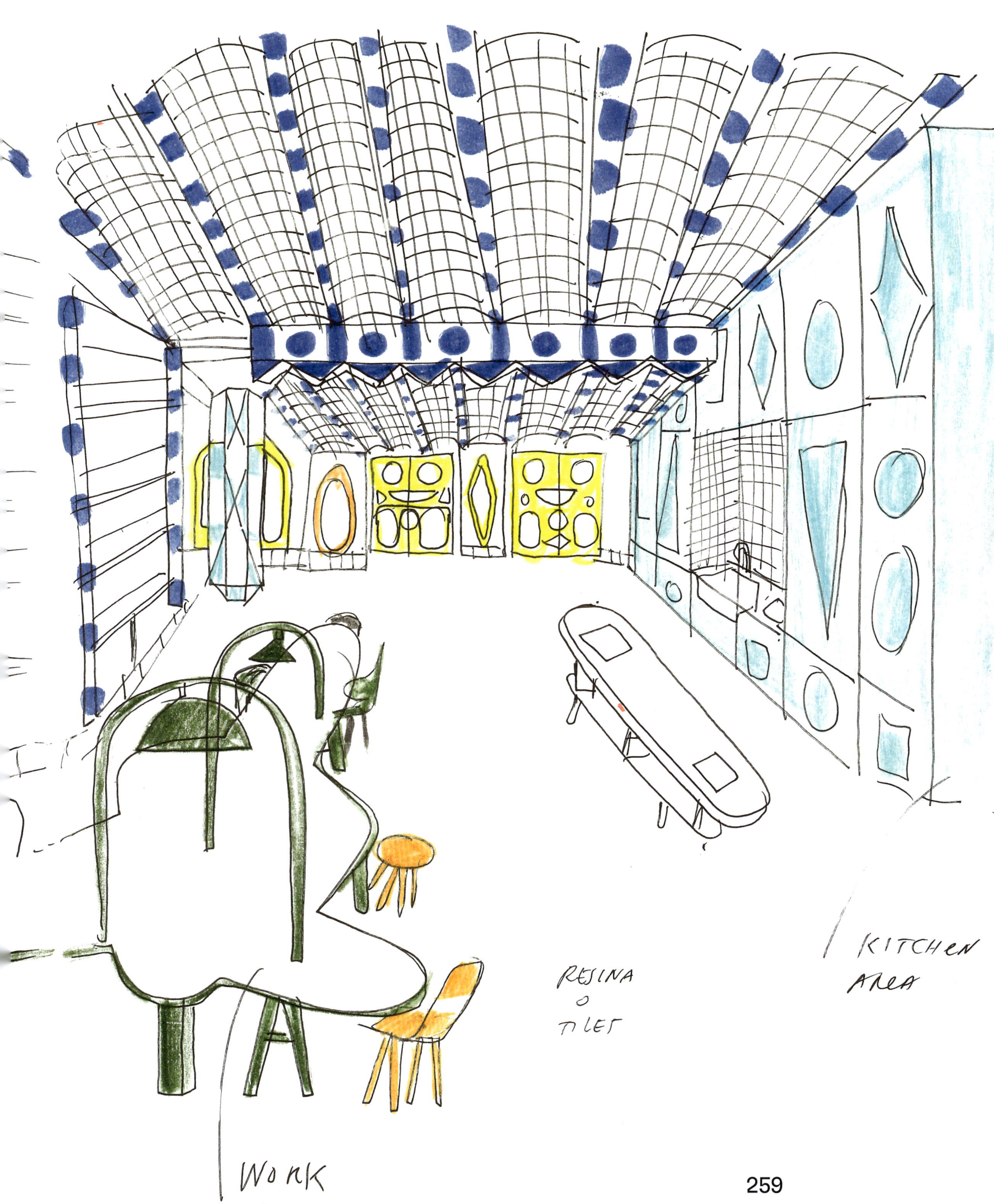

RESINA
O
TILES
KITCHEN
AREA
WORK
* DESK -
259

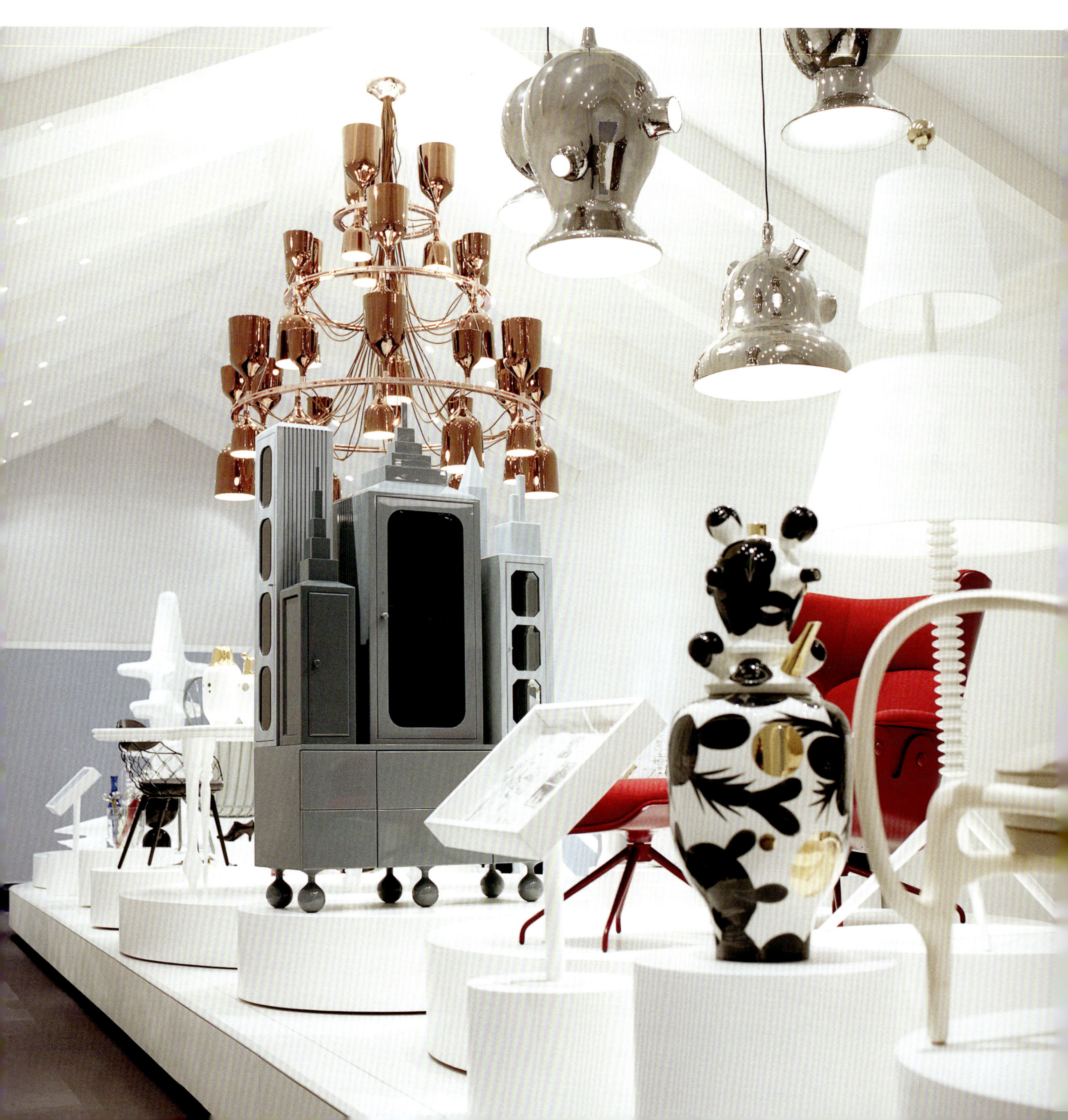

↑ Moving Ideas—Exhibition at Maison&Objet featuring: New York Is NY, cabinet—Copa Cabana, chandelier—
Vivid Basel, vase—BD Showtime Lounger—Scuba lamps in platinum, 2010
↓ Multileg and Showtime—Cabinet and vases for BD Barcelona Design, shown at Aram Gallery London at the Stage exhibition, 2006

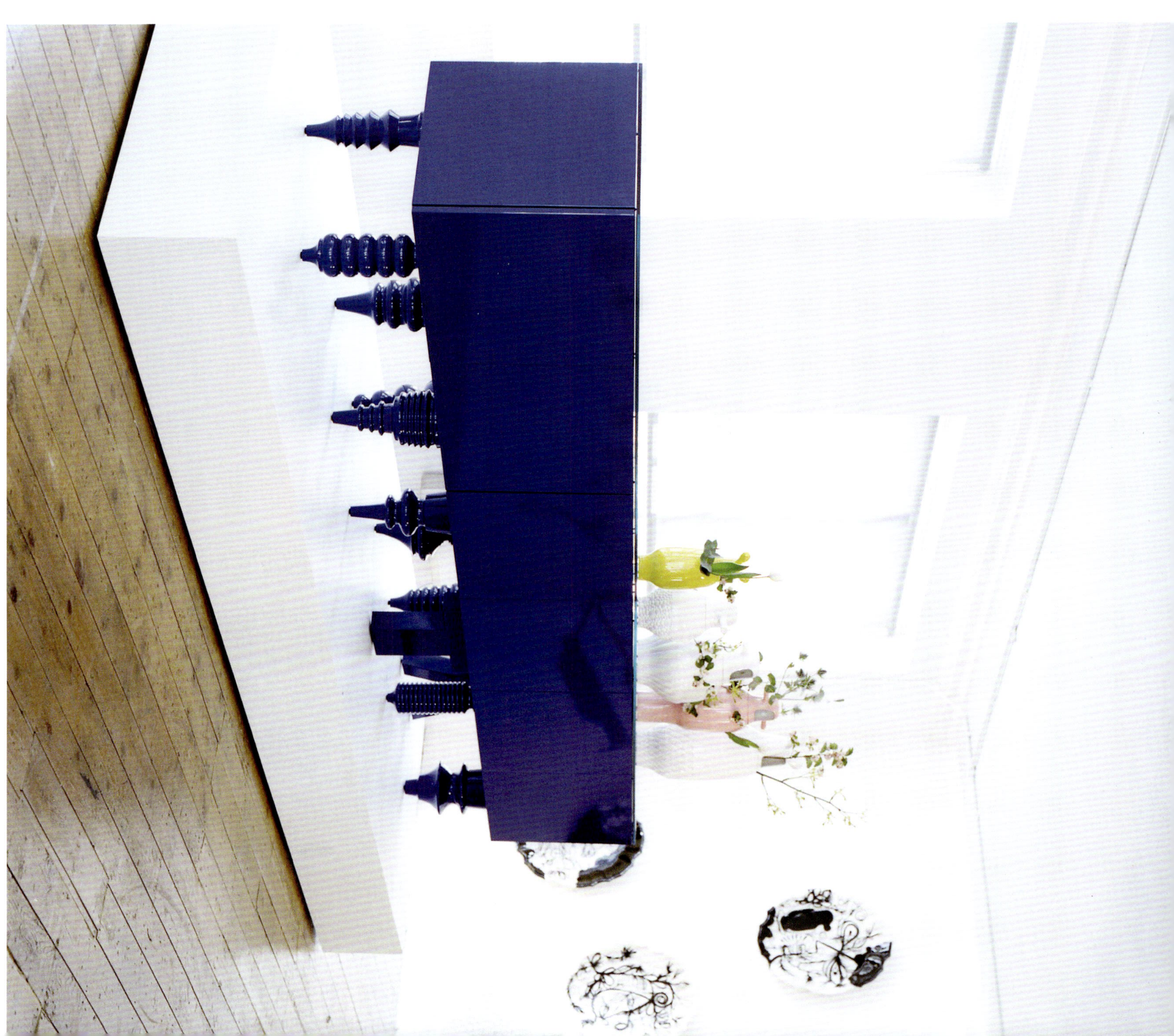

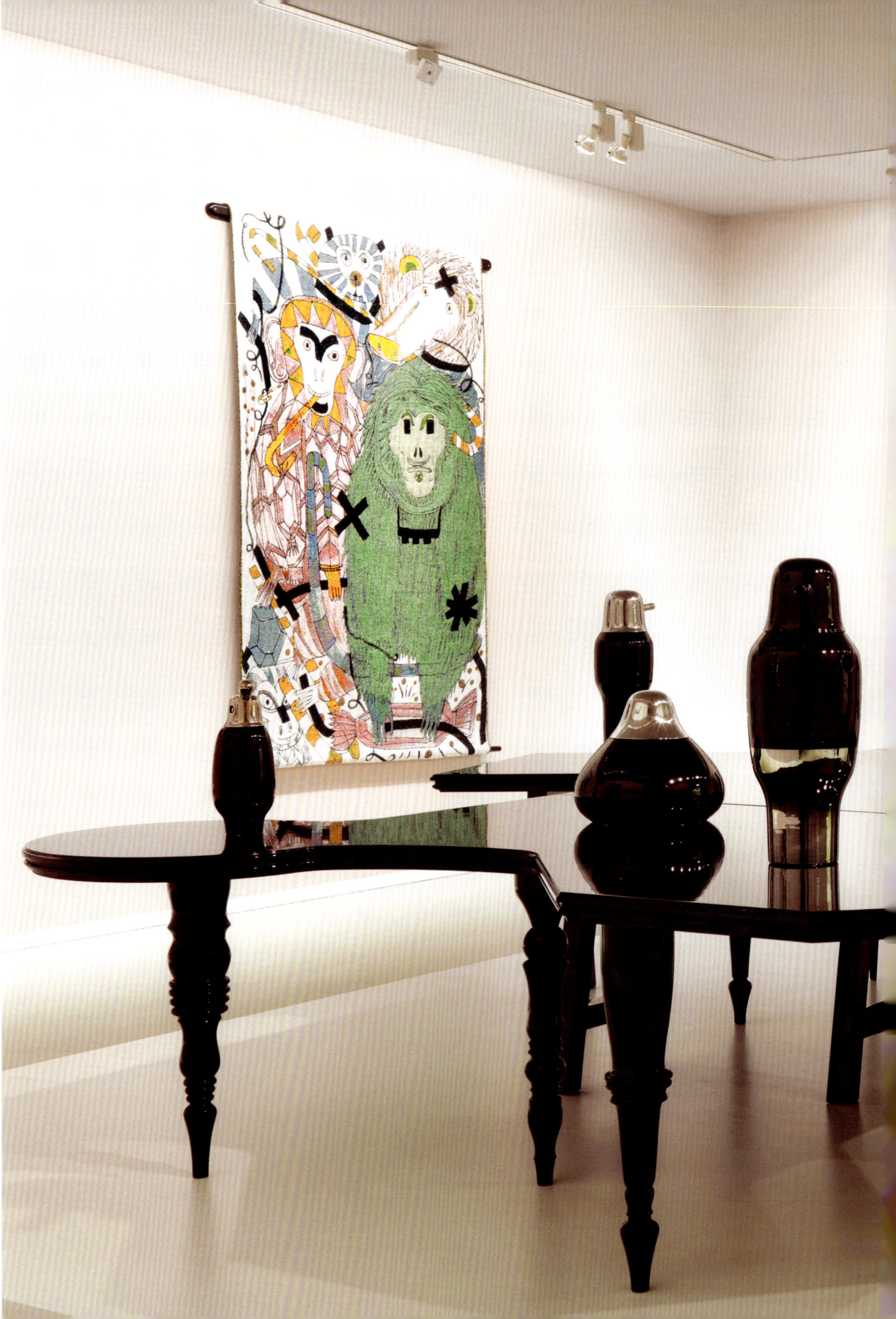

✛ Mon Cirque Black—Wood table and ceramic vases for the Groninger Museum. Fauna tapestries. Groningen, Netherlands, 2013

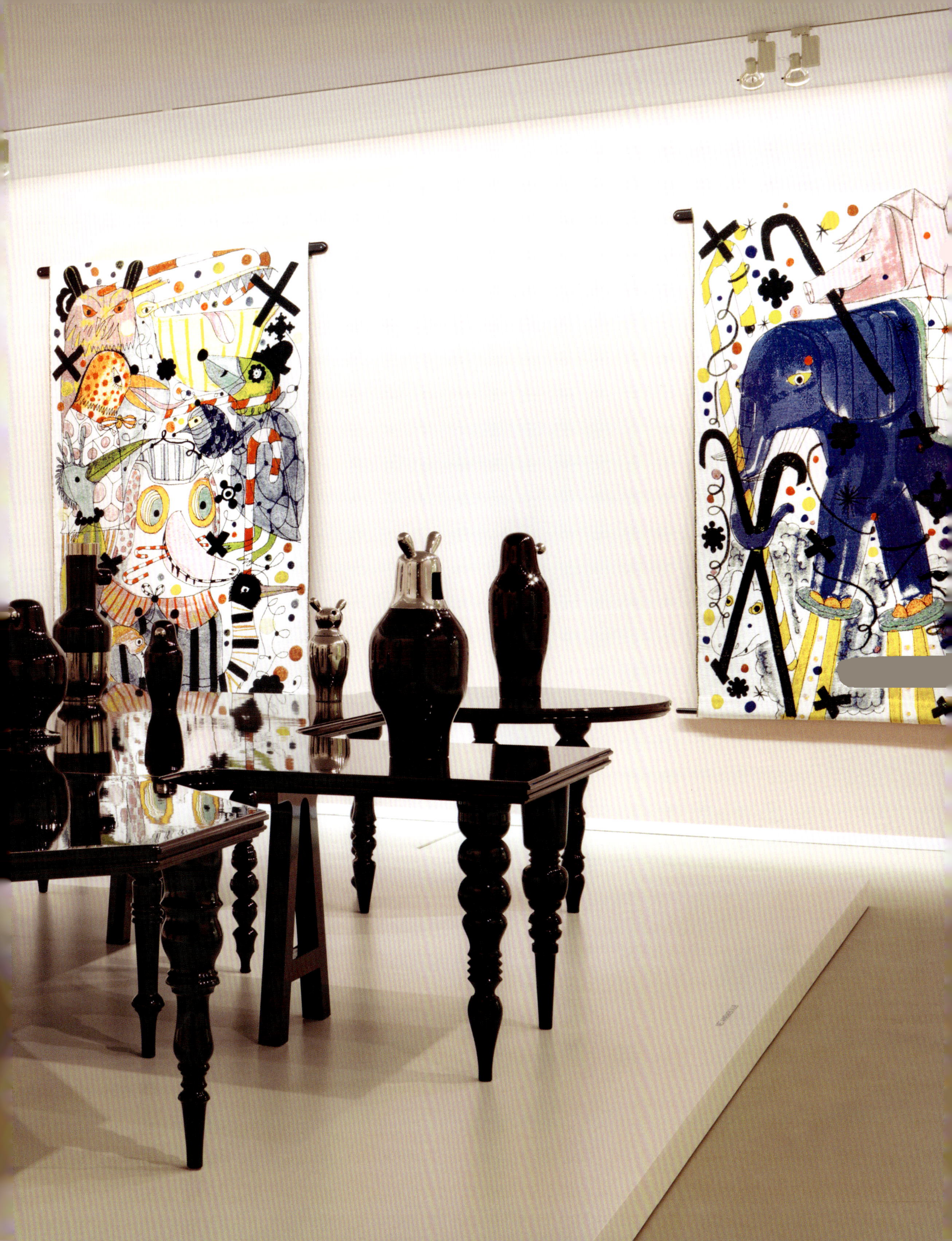

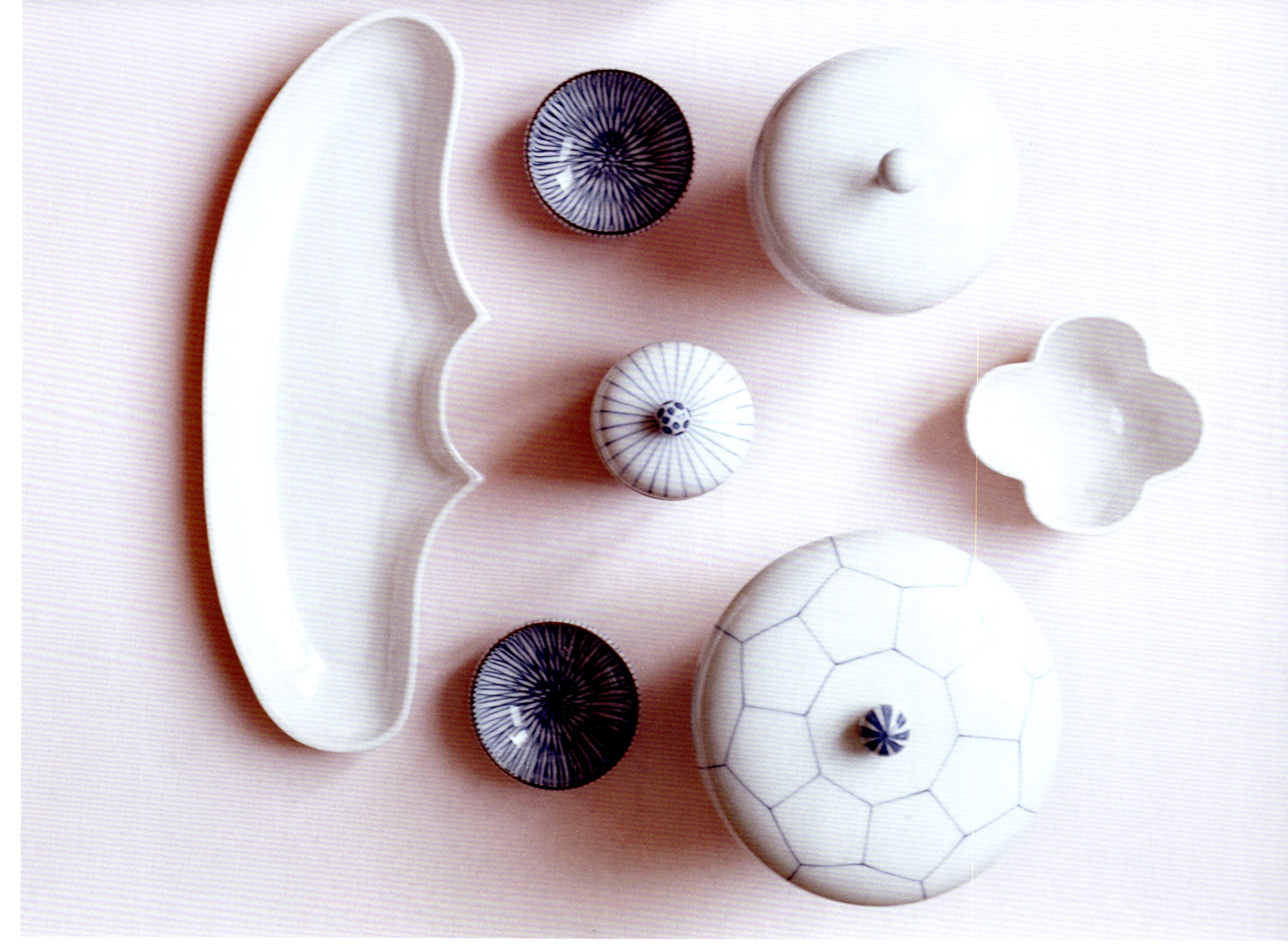

↑ Choemon Gamma—Detail of Japanese tableware porcelain collection, 2010
↓ Hayon × Jijibaba—Scarf for fashion collection, 2017

264

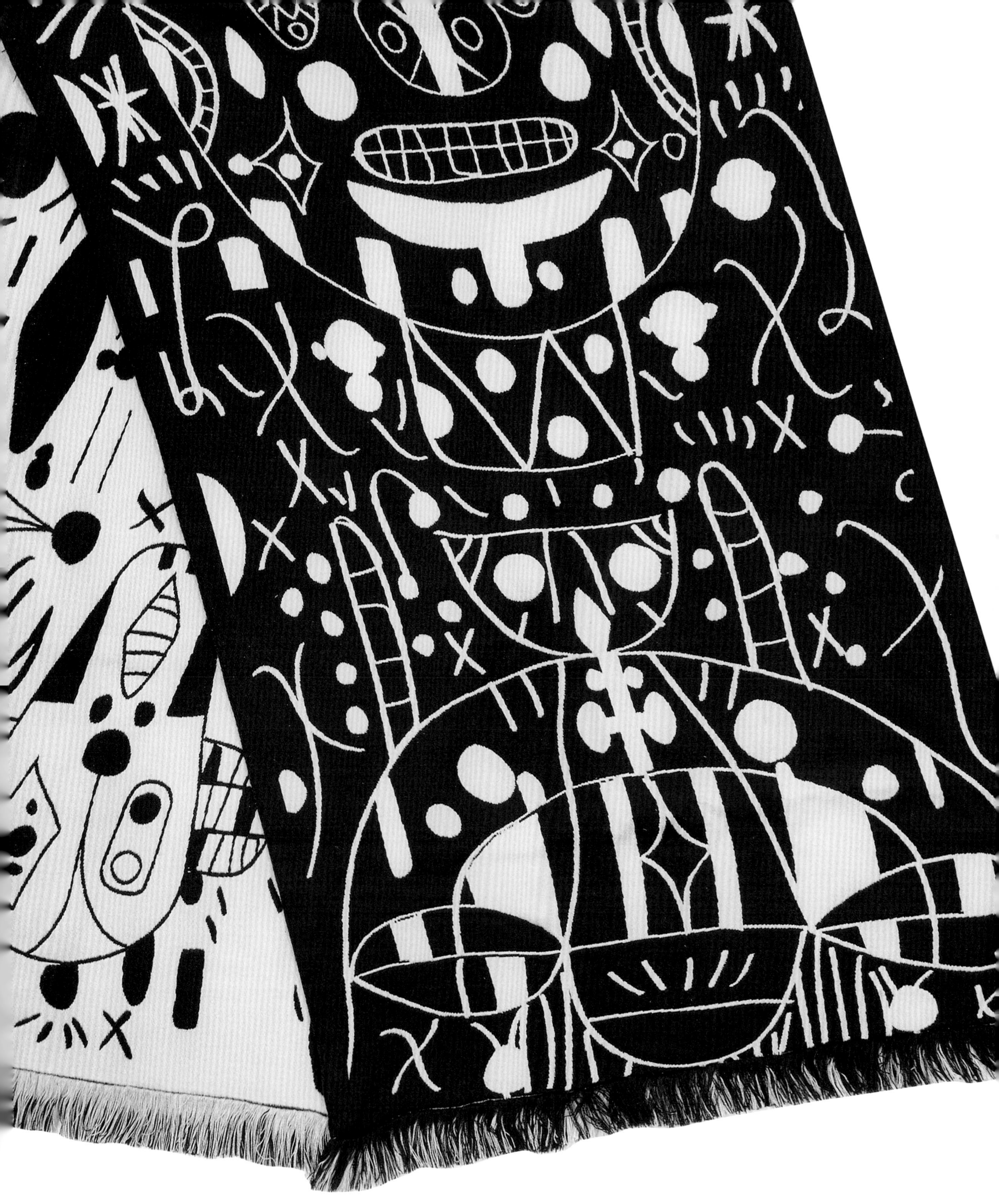

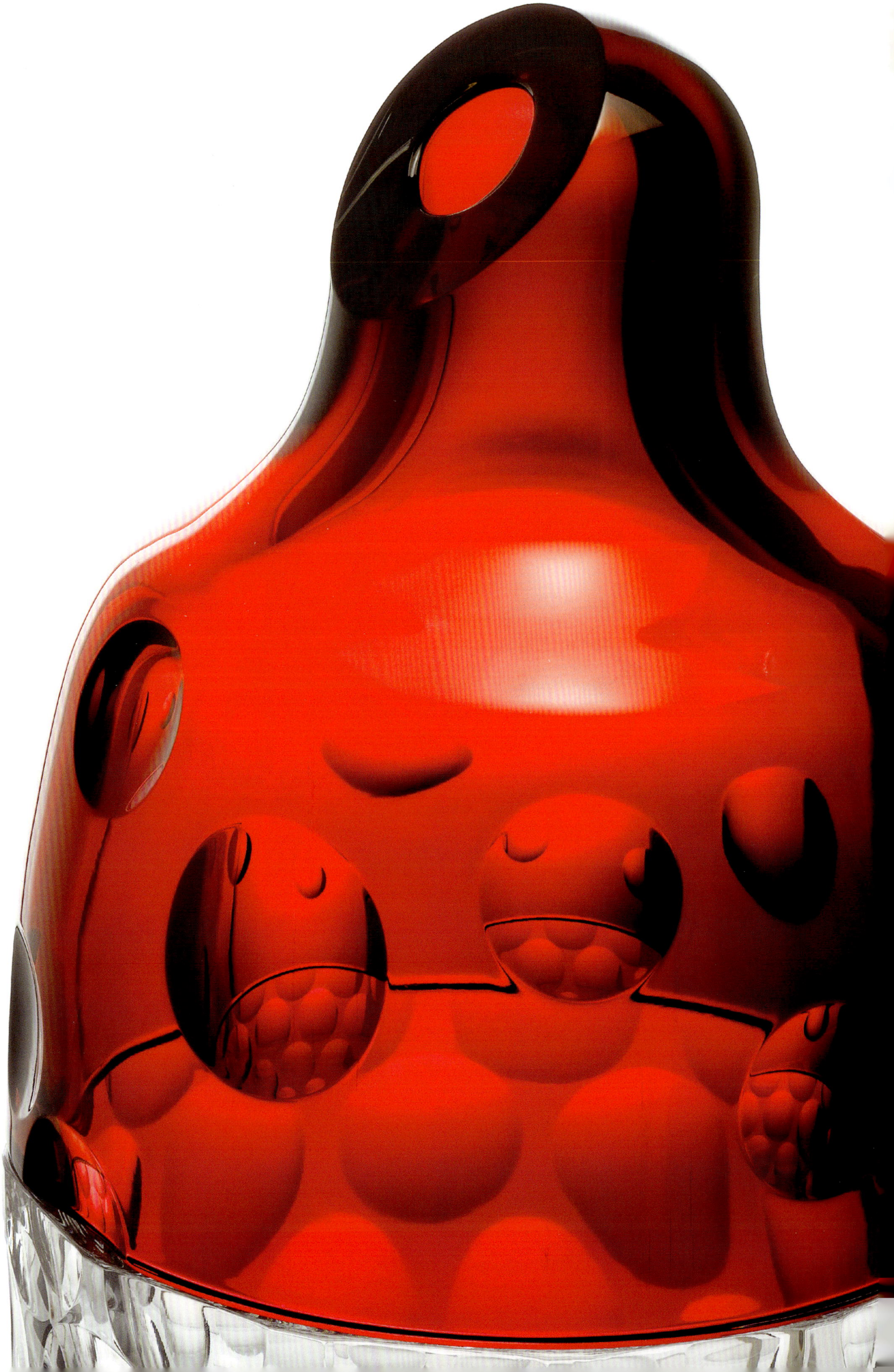

↓ Red Passion Golf vase, part of the Baccarat Crystal Candy set. Numbered and limited edition of 25
↓ Serious Fun exhibition—Crystal room at the Daelim Museum, Seoul, South Korea, 2019

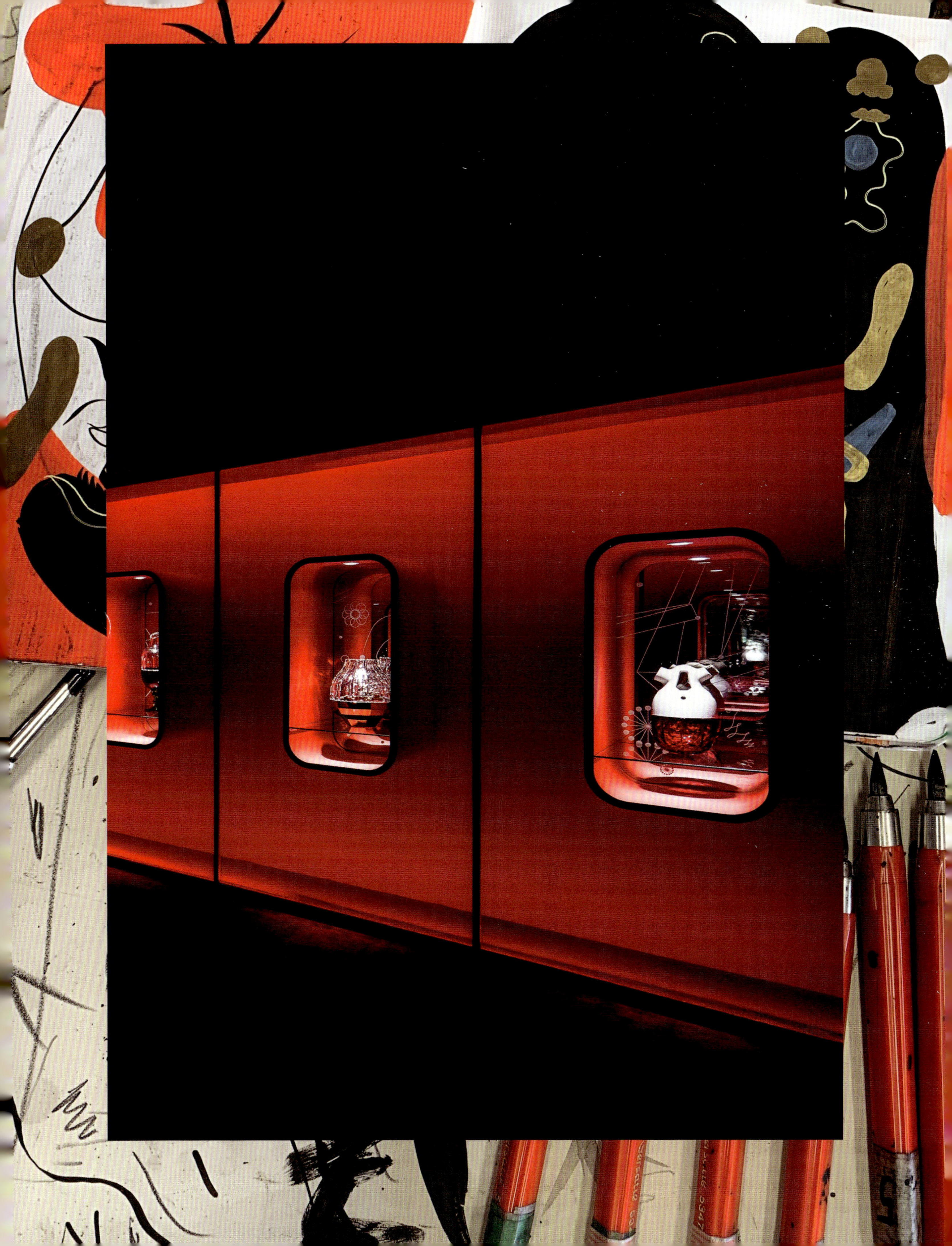

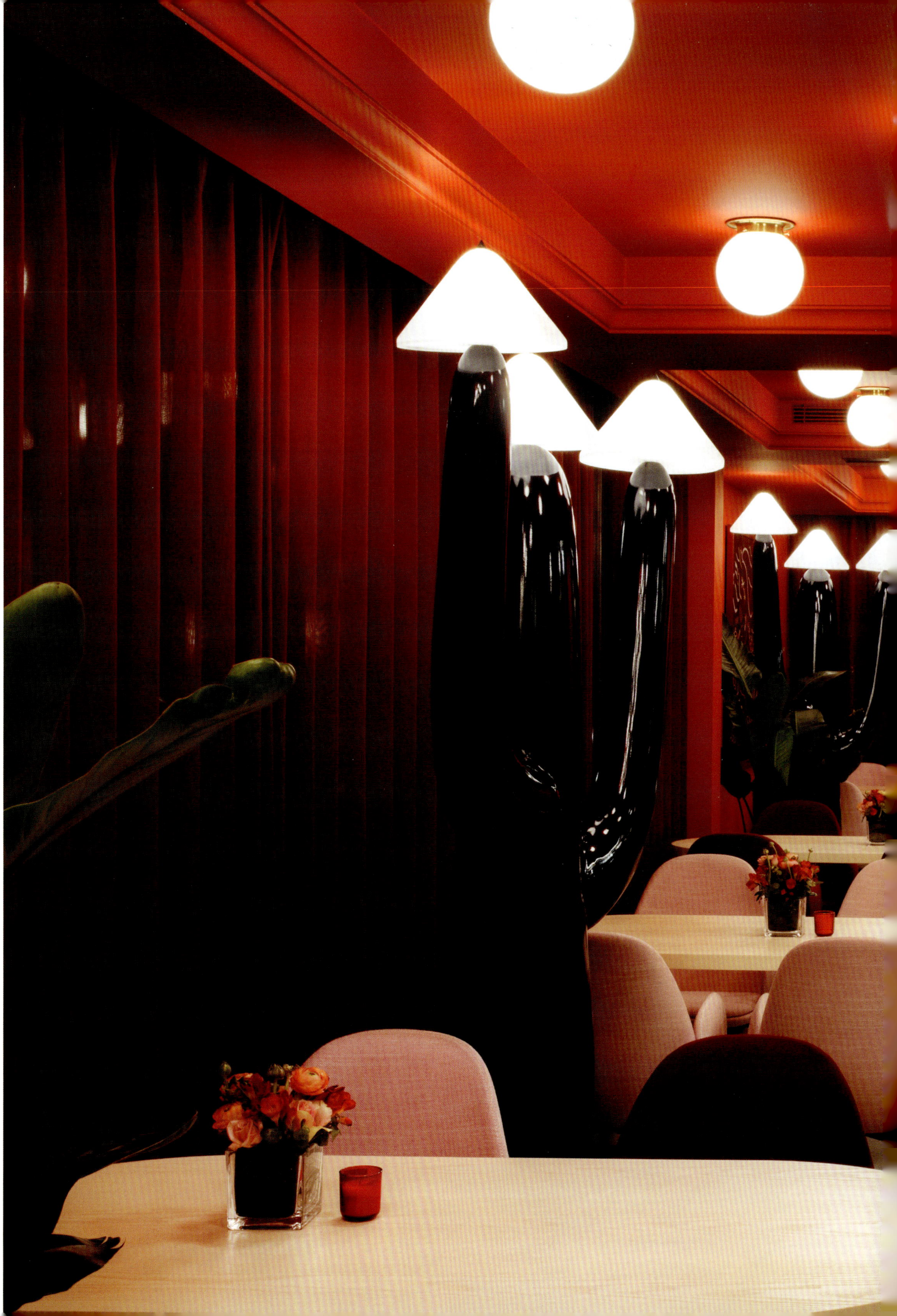

↓ Fritz Hansen Lounge Club—Interior design project, Shanghai, China, 2019

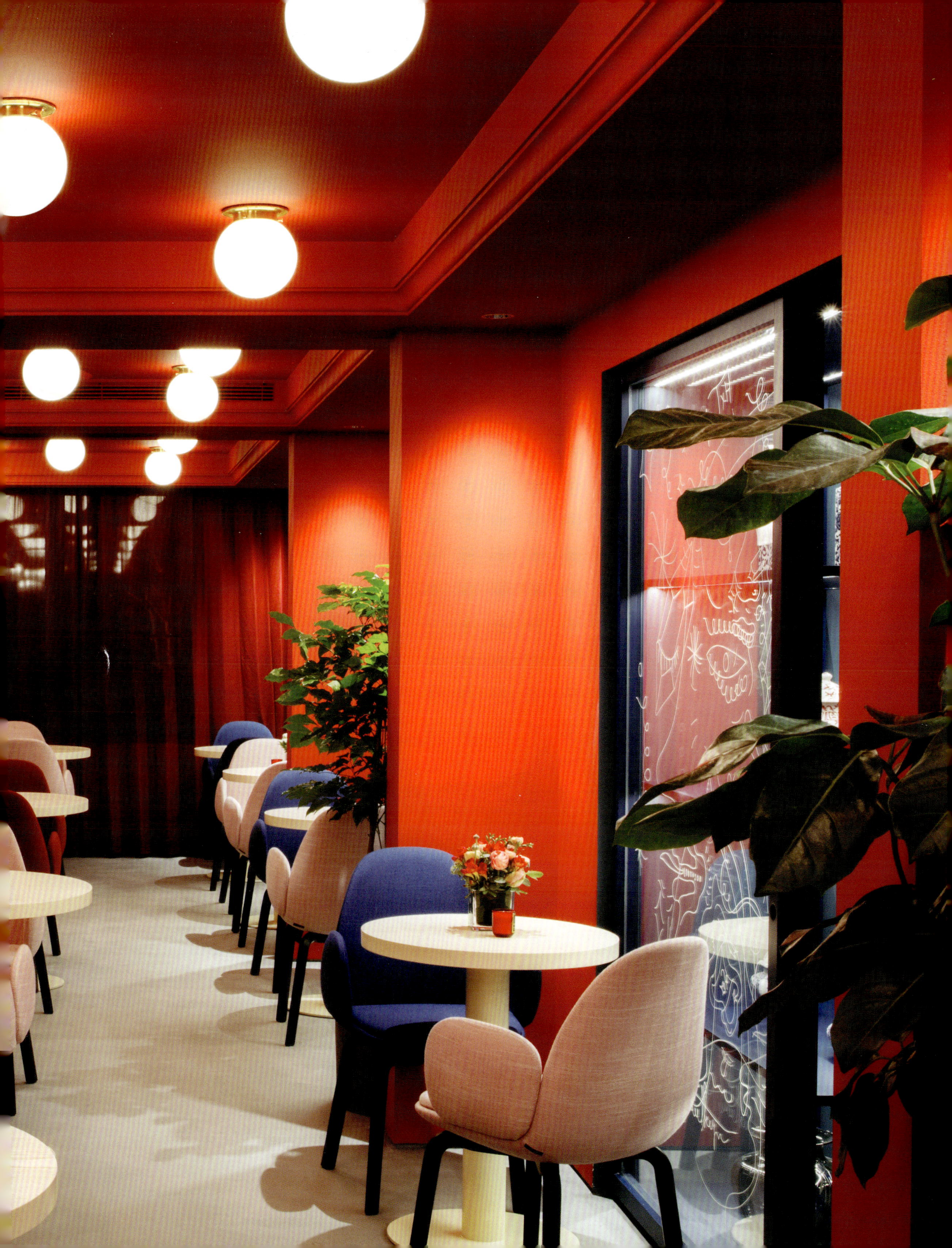

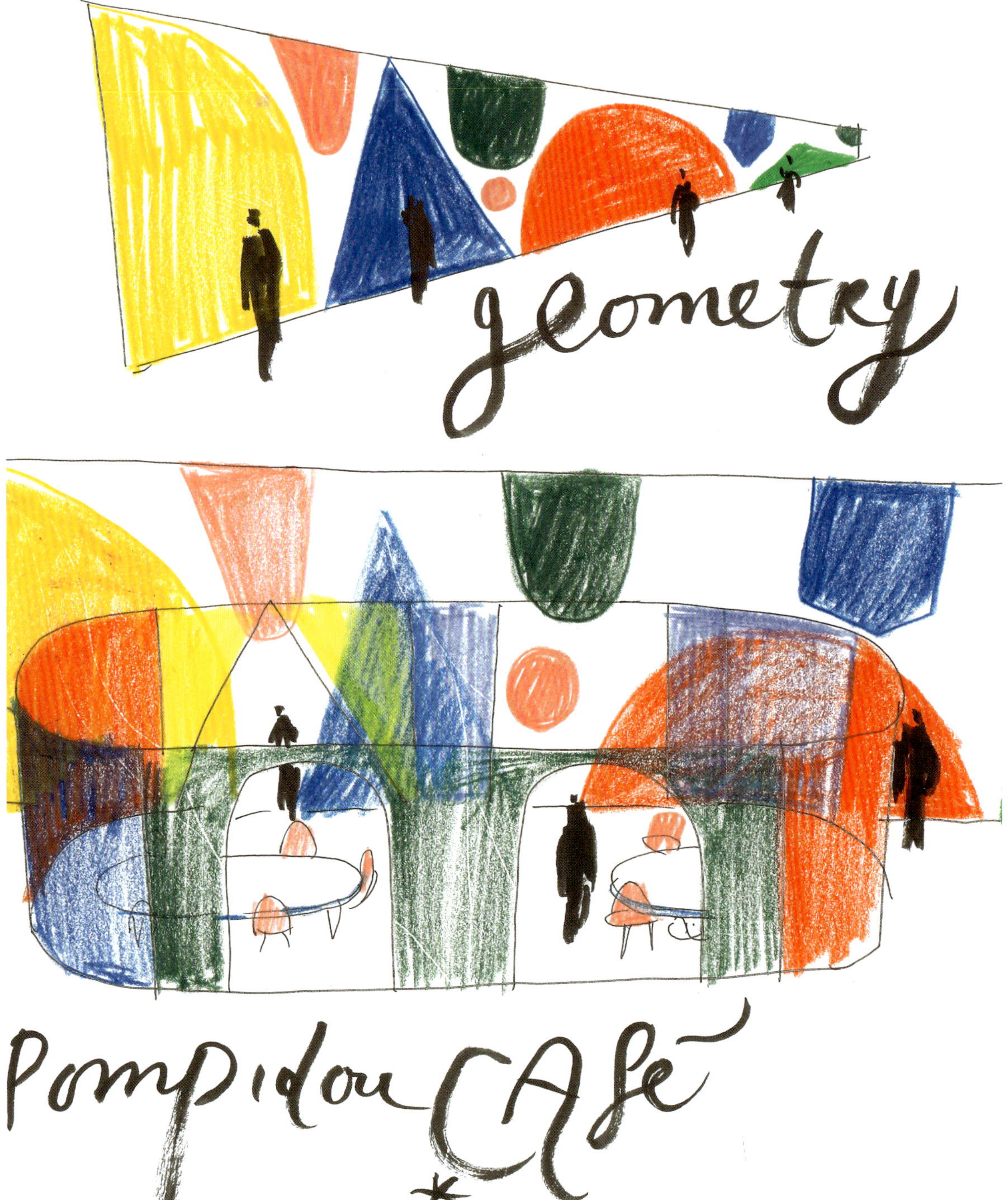

↑ Sketch for Le Central Café at the Centre Pompidou, interior design project
↓ Onolog—Wristwatch for Onolog, 2012

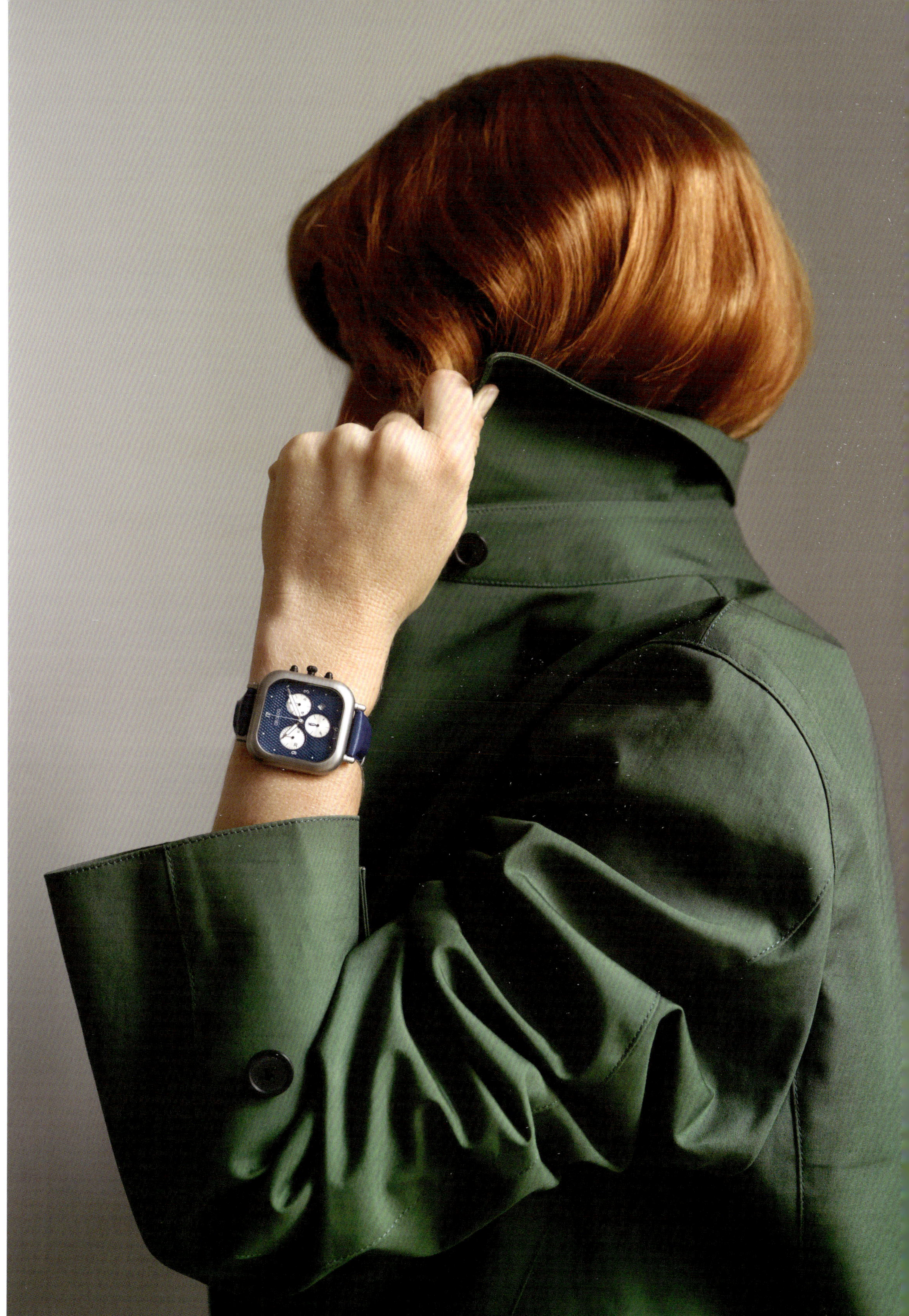

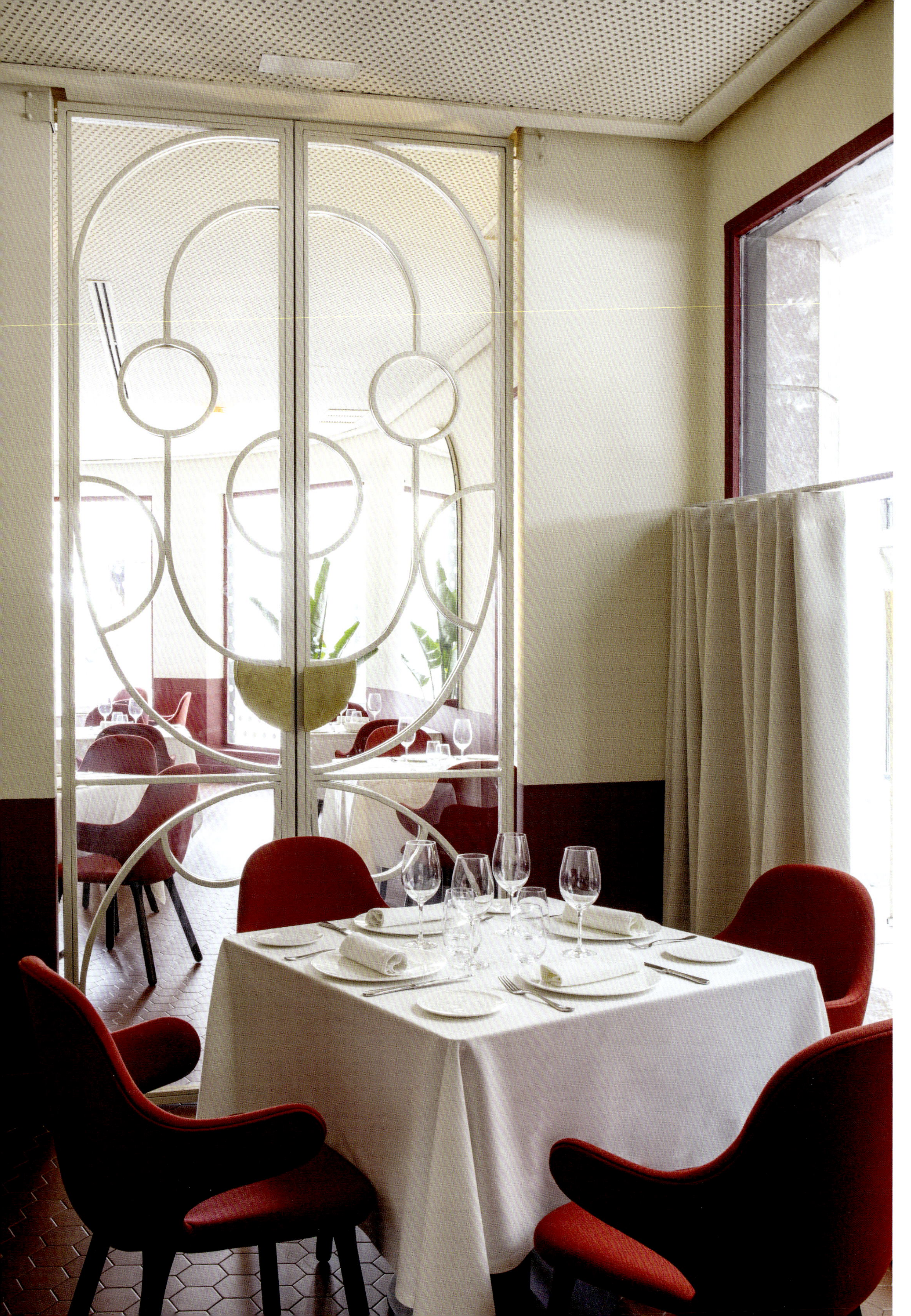

→ Building a family, being together, enthusiastically chasing an idea. Conviviality is everything—it is a dialogue made up of listening, learning, communication between craftsmen, collaborators, or special meetings.

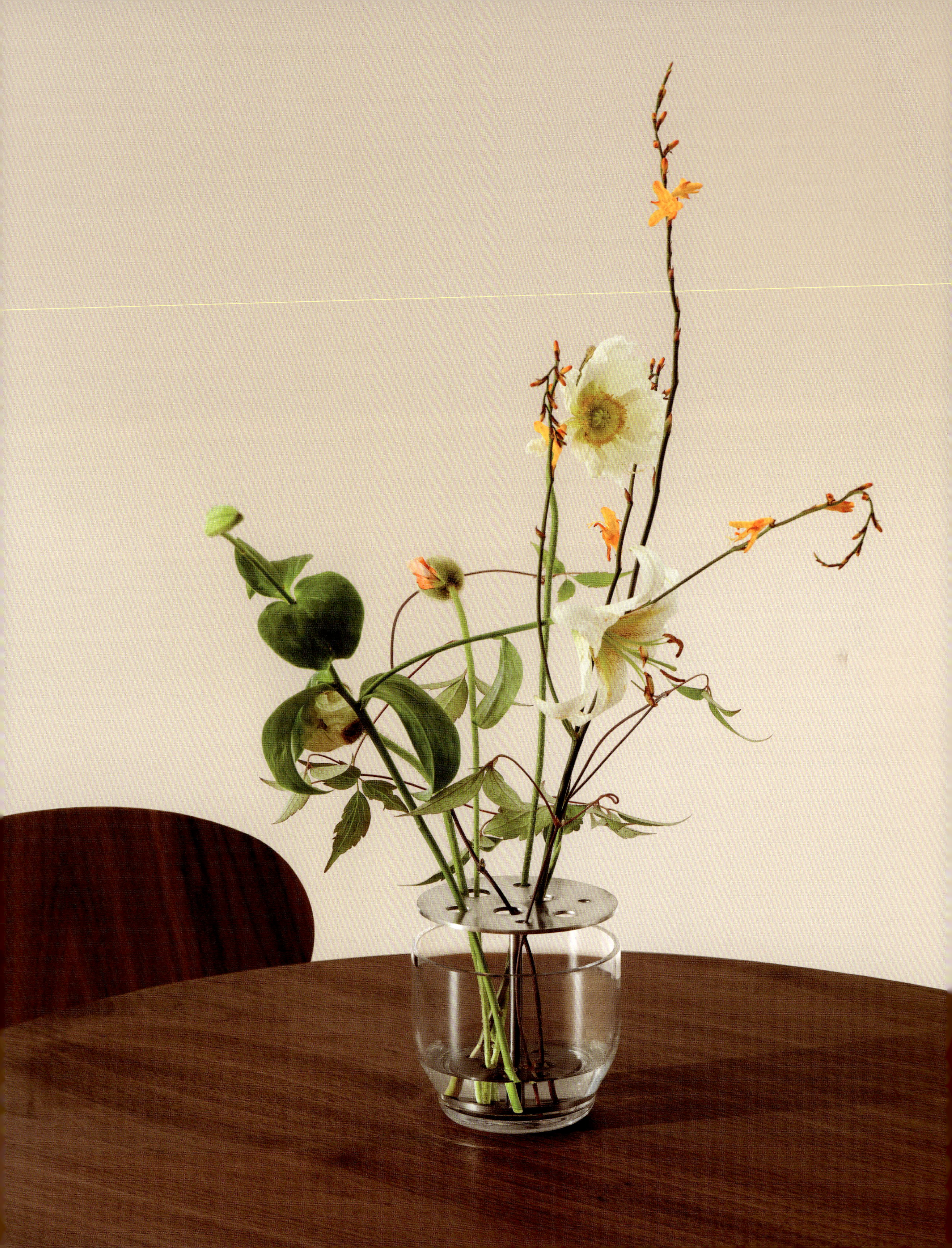

↑ Ikebana—Flower vase for Fritz Hansen, 2016
↓ Palette and Catch—JH9 Palette Desk and chair for &Tradition, 2016

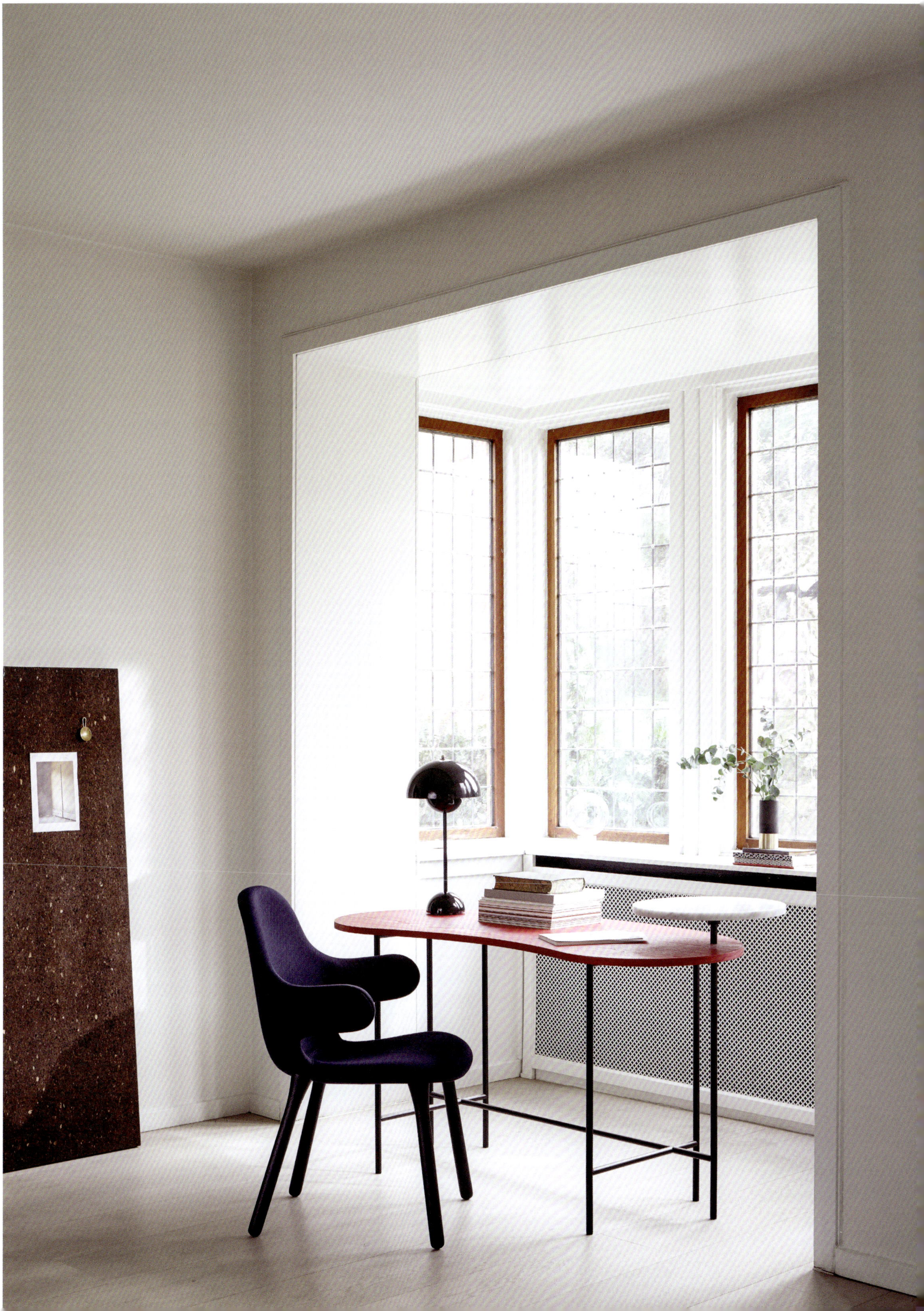

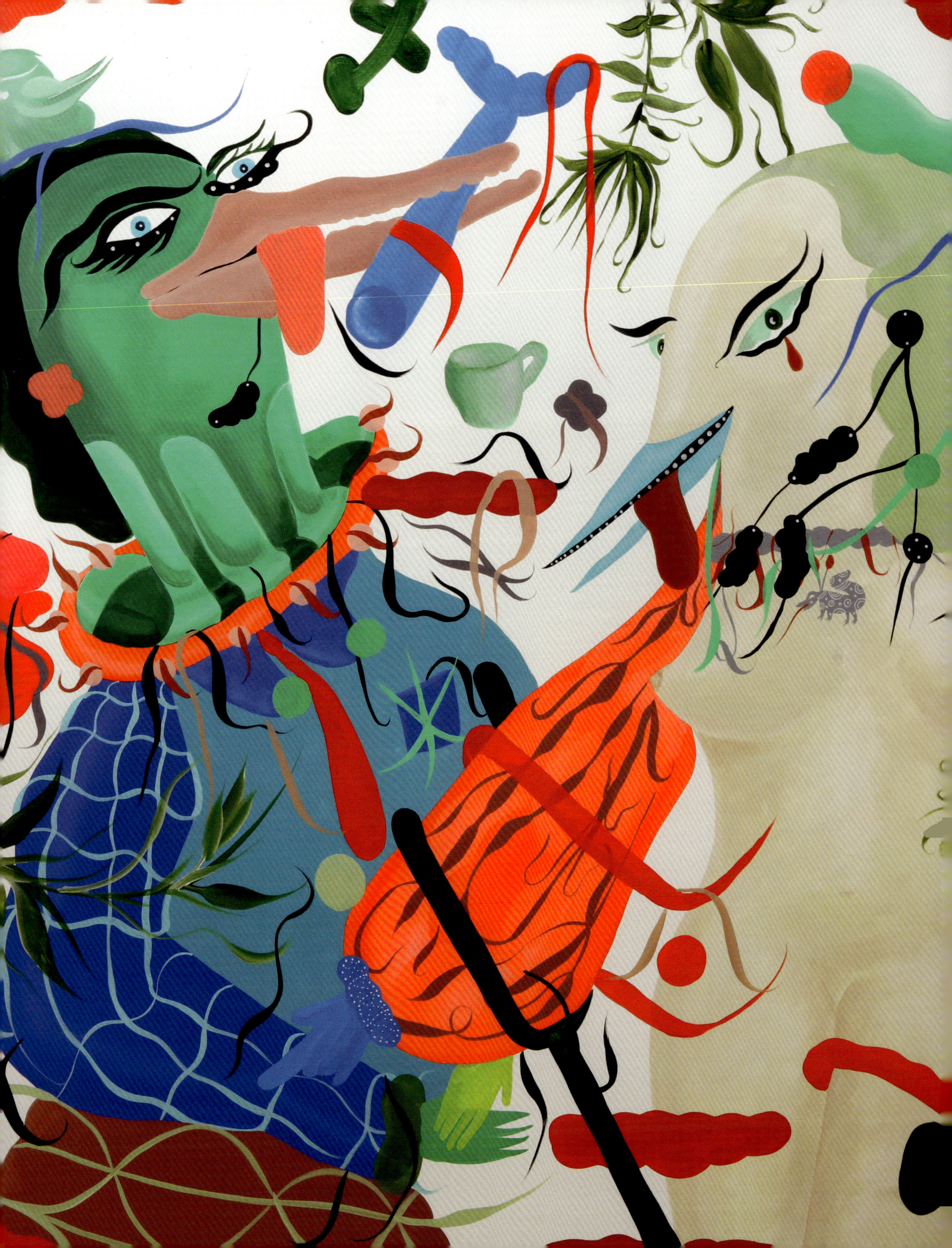

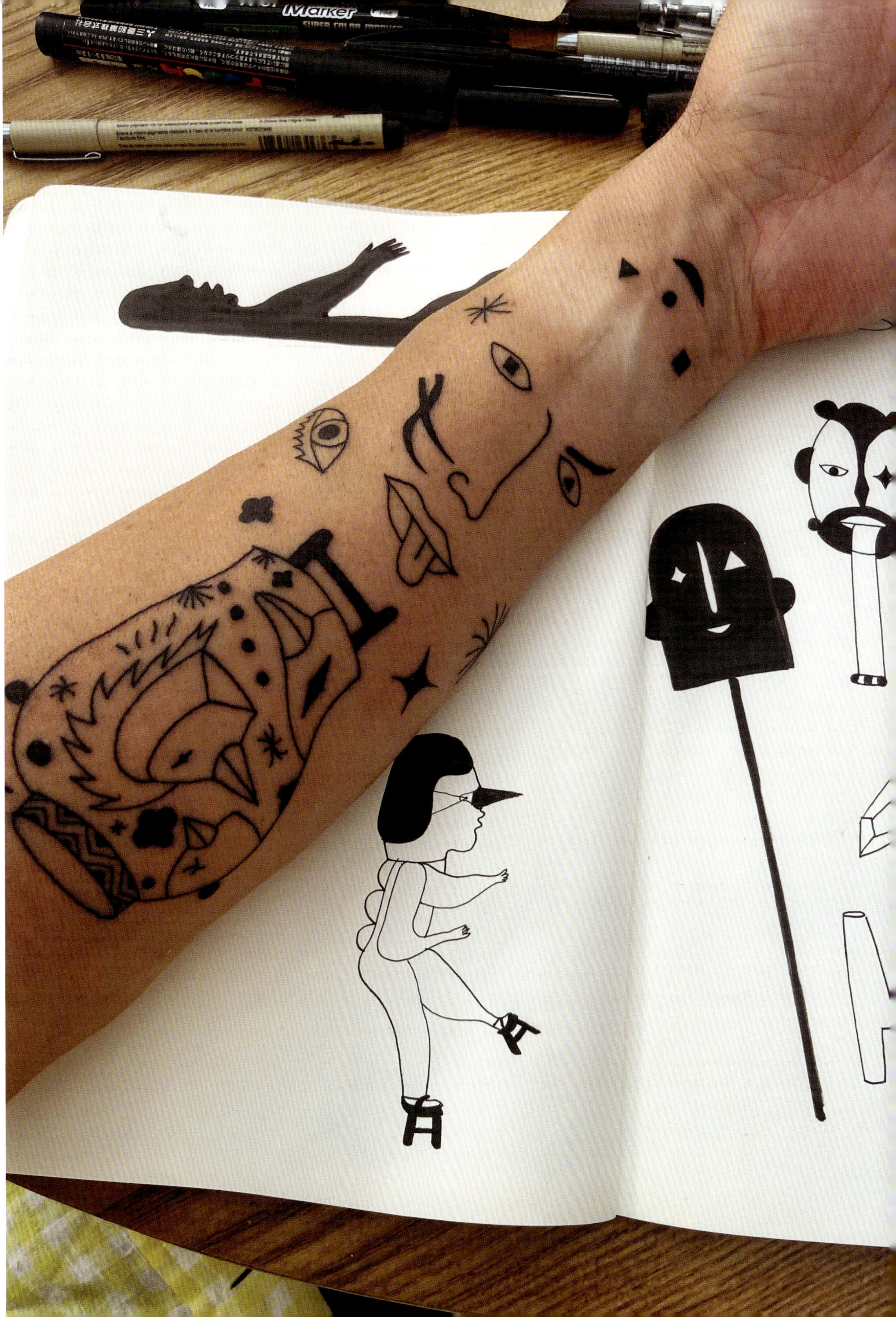

↑ Let's Start the Game—Acrylic on canvas, detail, 2022
↓ Sketches for tattoo project

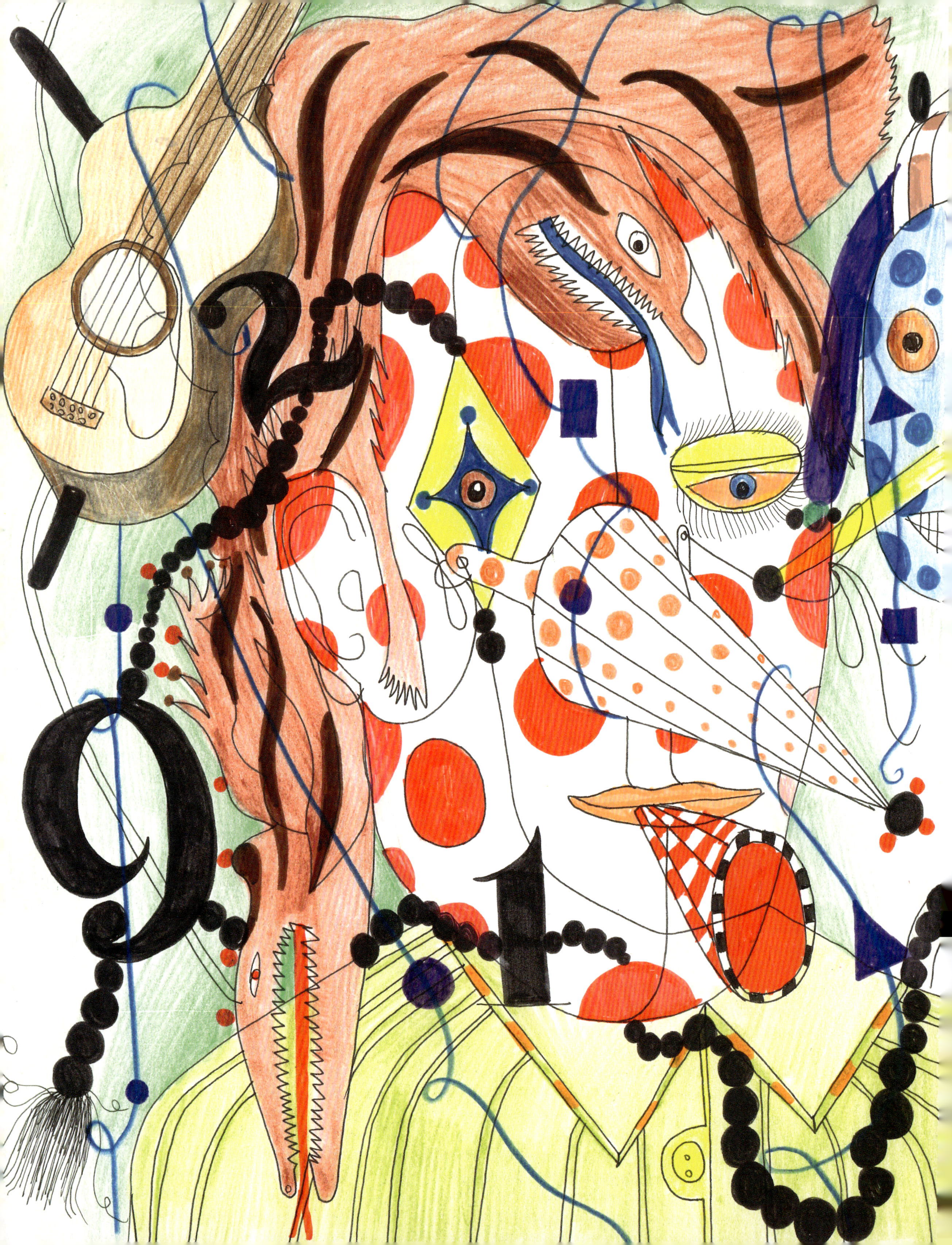

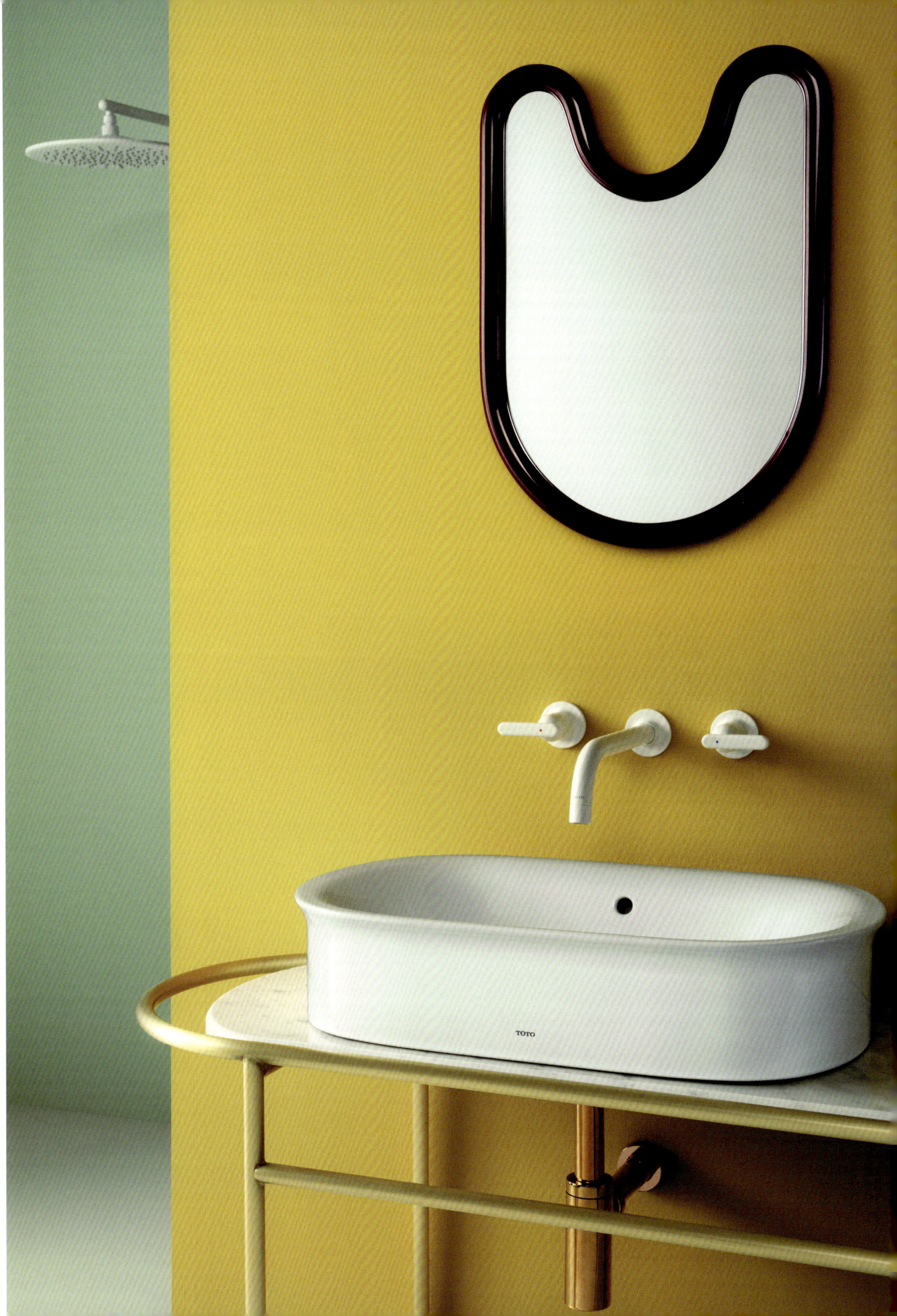

↑ Hand-drawing, pencil on paper
↓ Hayon series—Console, sink, faucet, and shower for Toto, 2020

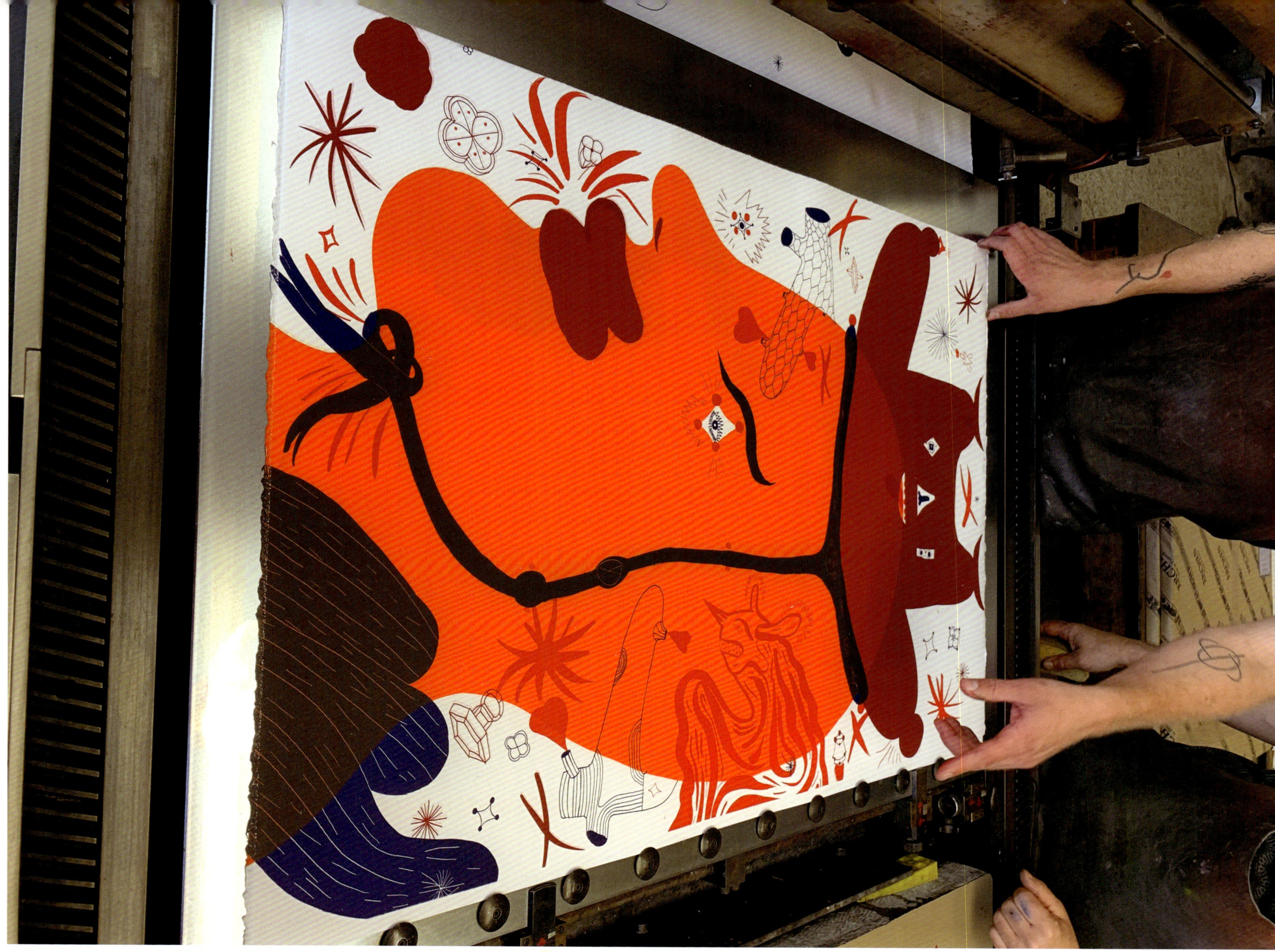

↑ Making of Hat Man—Lithography, Edition Copenhagen atelier, Denmark, 2019
↓ Shadow Theater—installation at the Bangkok Design Week, 2022

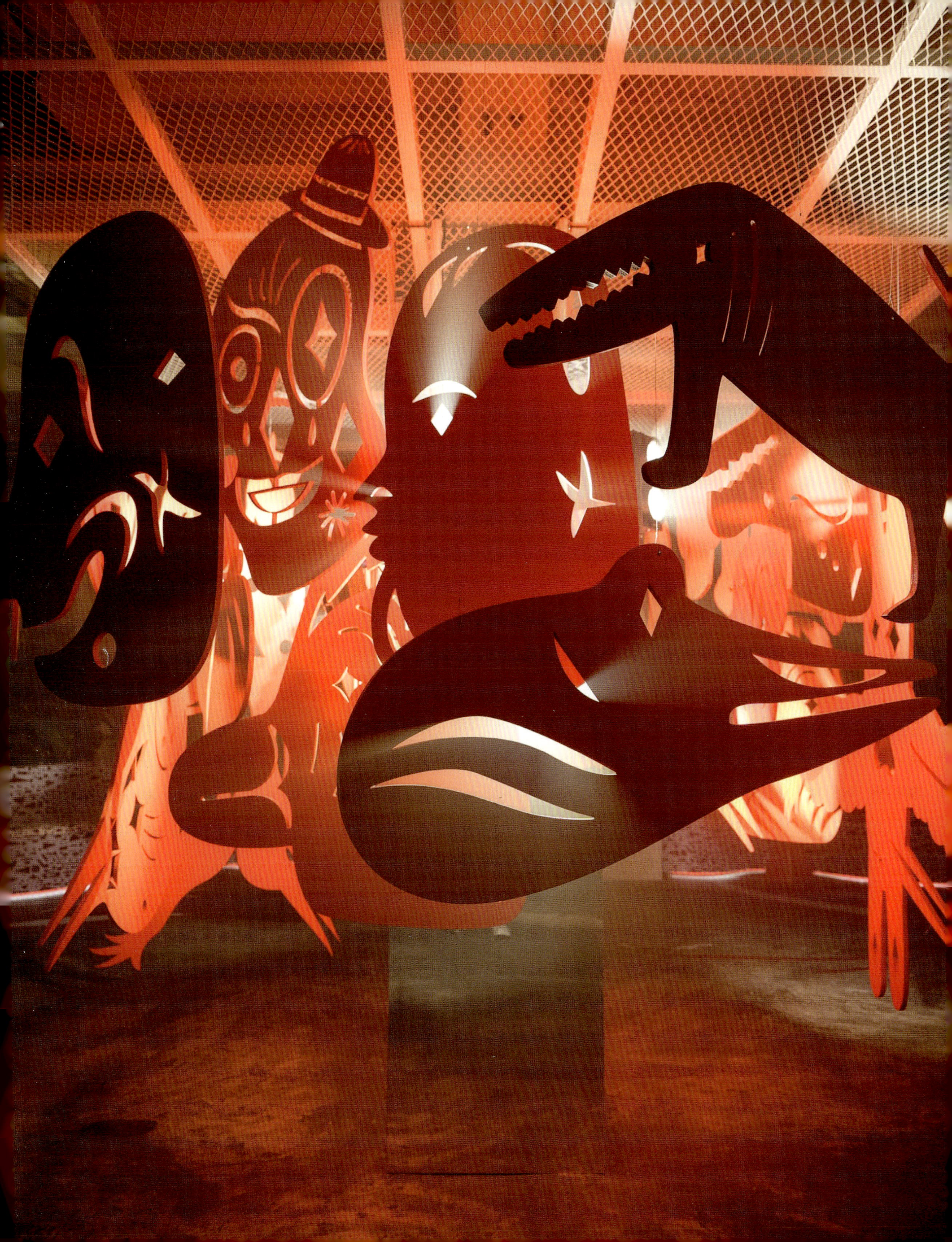

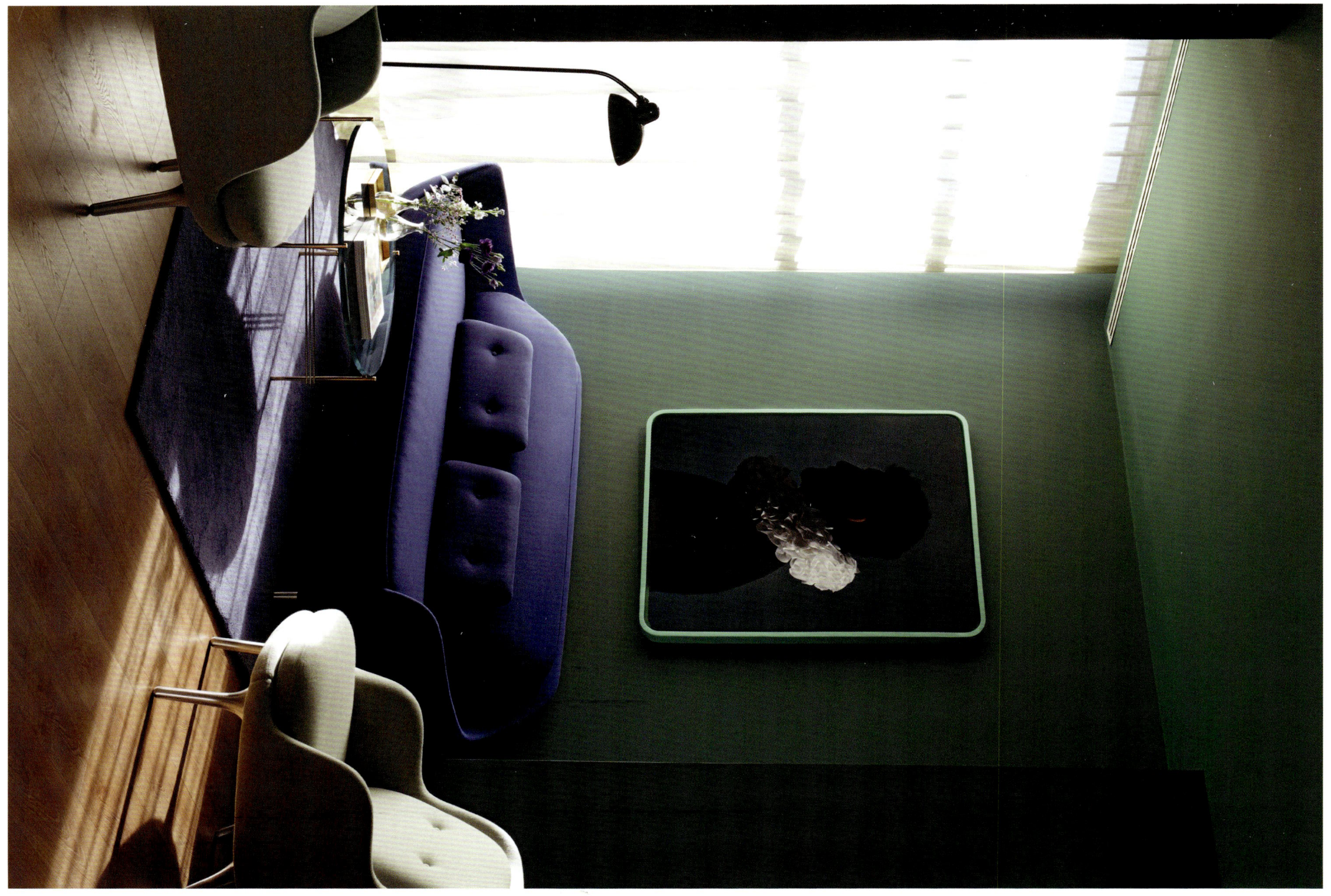

↑ Barceló Torre de Madrid Hotel—Interior design, Madrid, Spain, 2016
↓ Camper Store—Interior design, Tokyo, Japan, 2009

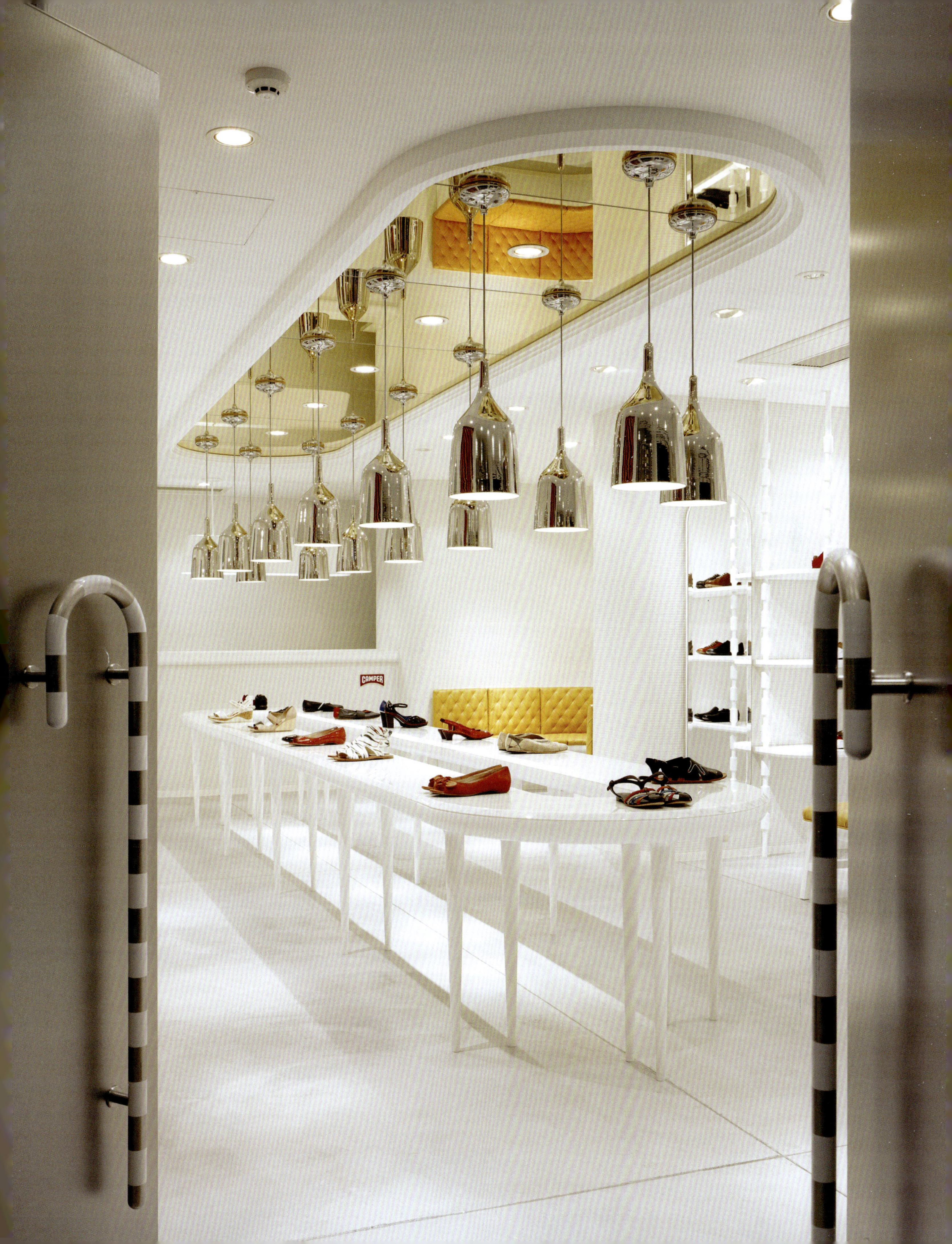

CAMPER

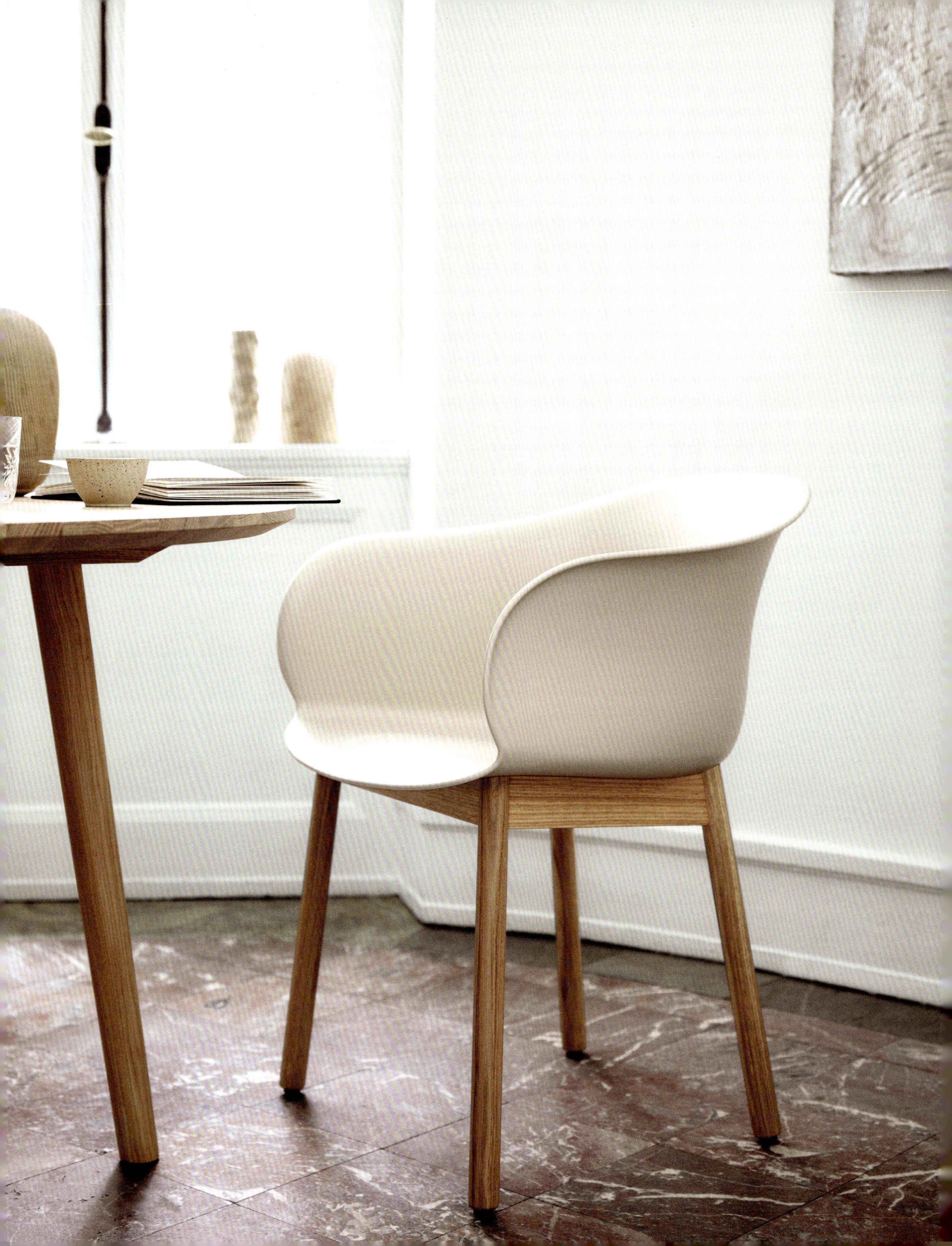

↑ Elefy—Chair for &Tradition, 2019
↓ Happy Susto—Ceramic vases for BD Barcelona Design, 2017

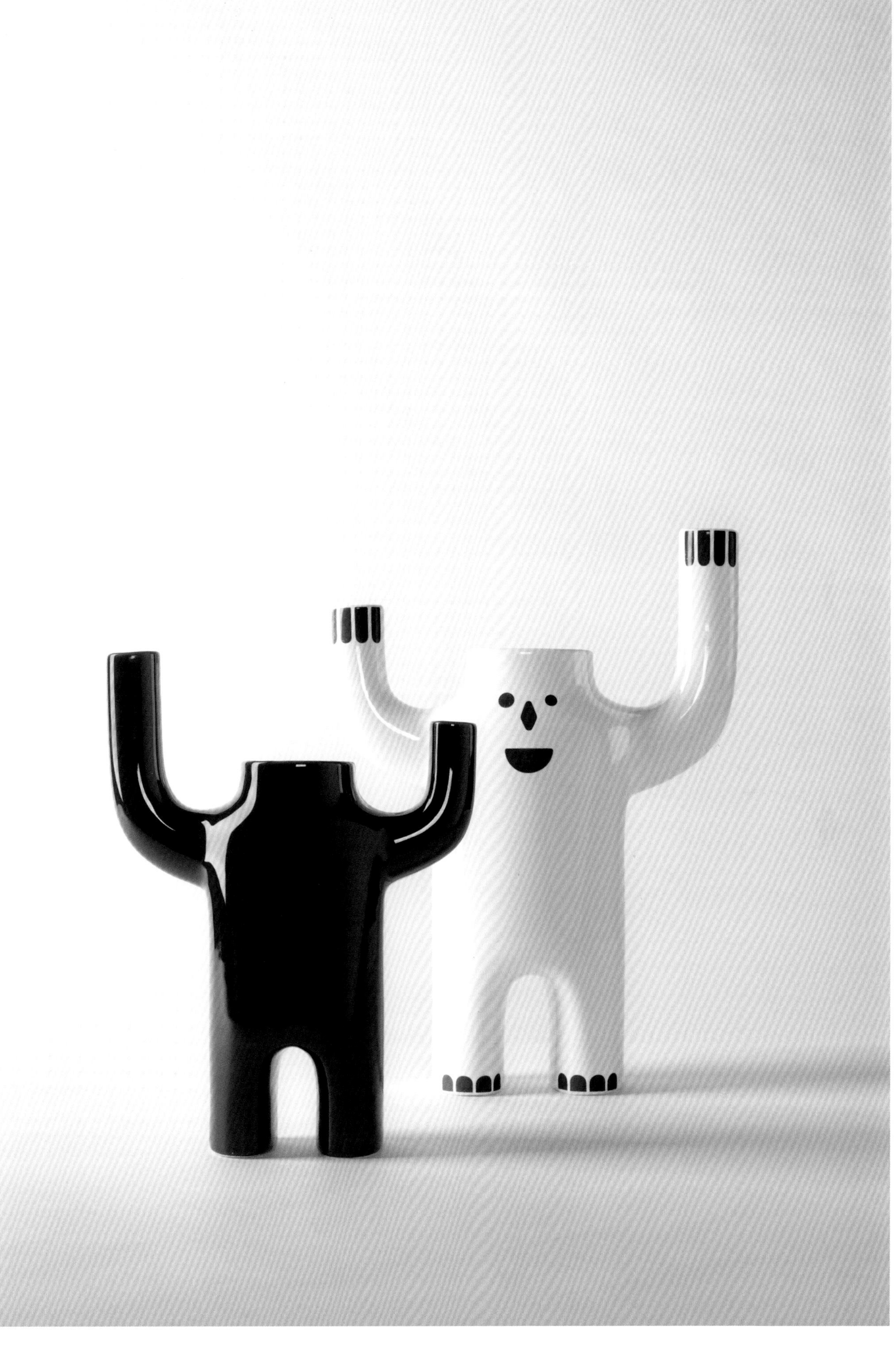

285

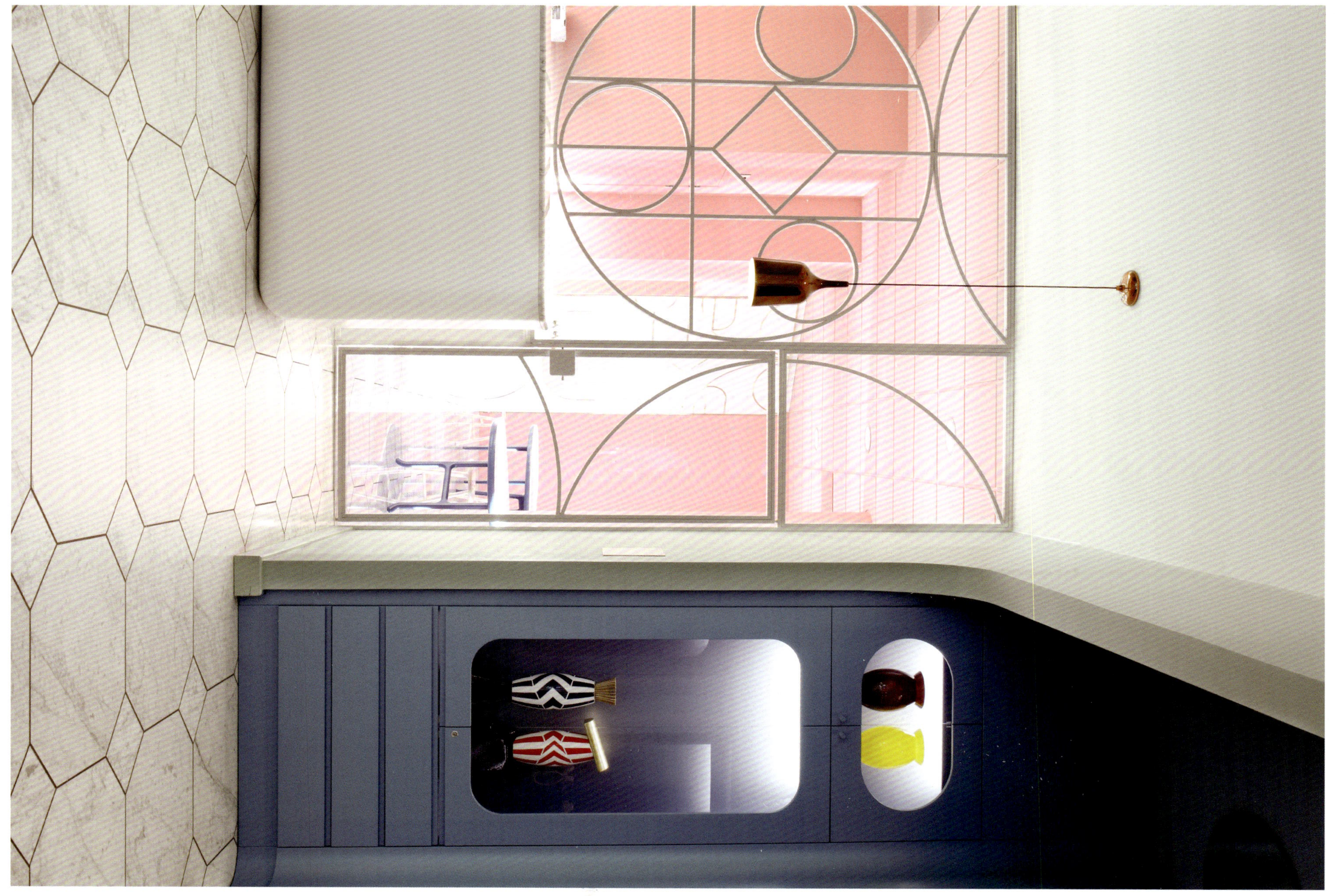

↑ Groninger Museum Family Lab—Interior design, Groningen, Netherlands, 2014
↓ Ro—Lounge chair for Fritz Hansen, 2013

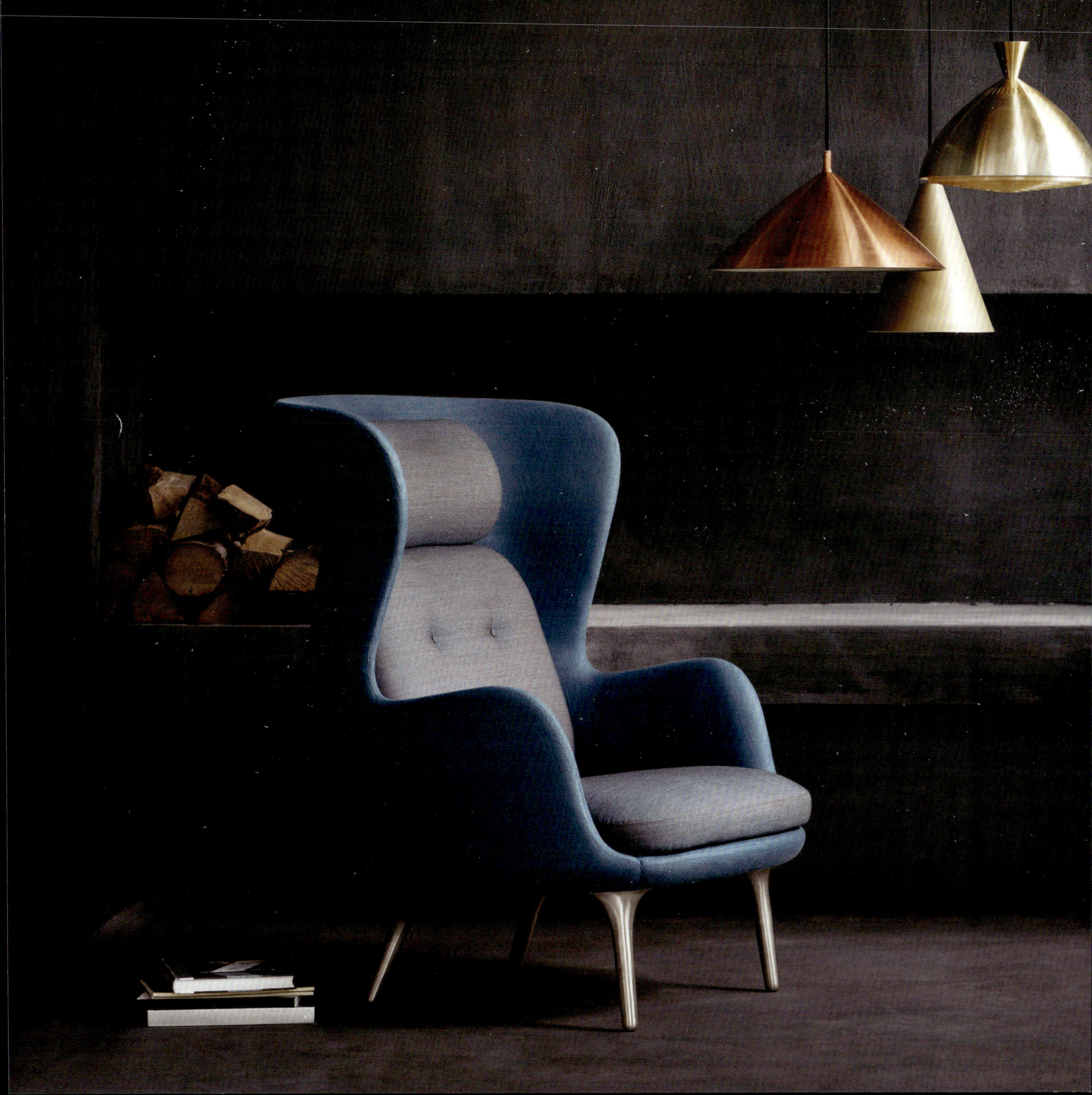

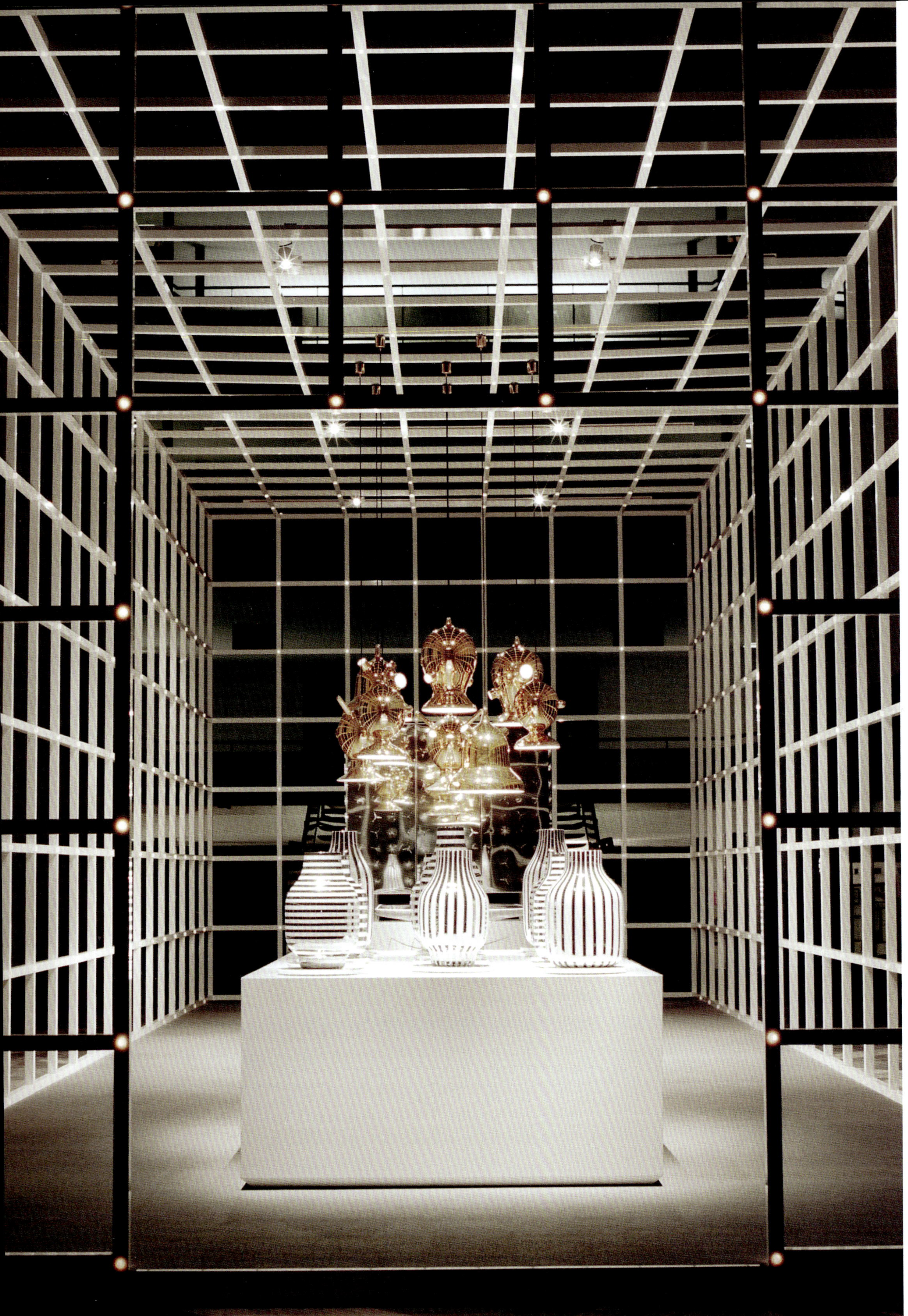

↑ Smart Grid Gallery—Installation: ceramic Grid vases and Scuba lamps, Milan, Italy, 2010
↓ Lune—sofa for Fritz Hansen, 2017

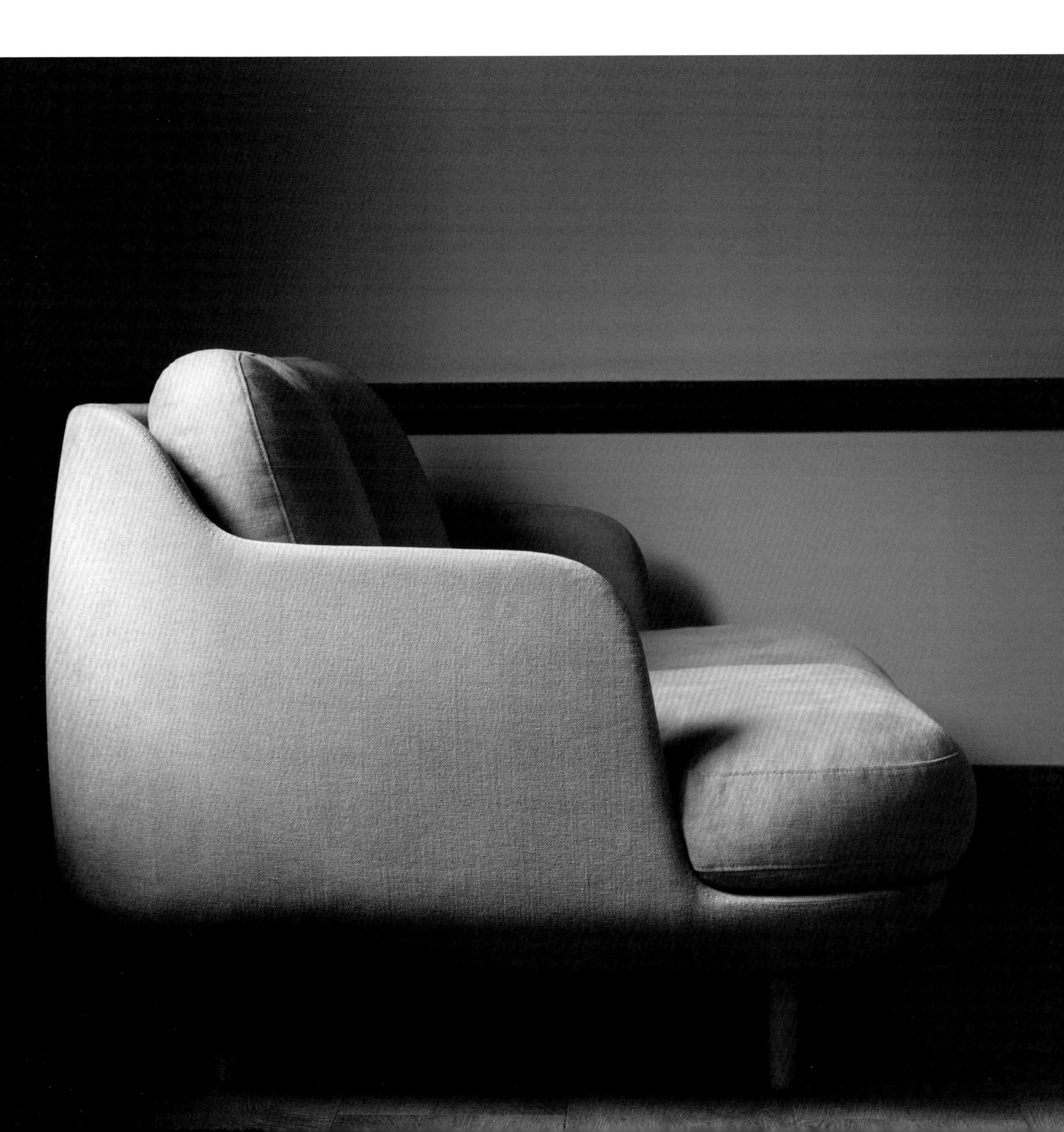

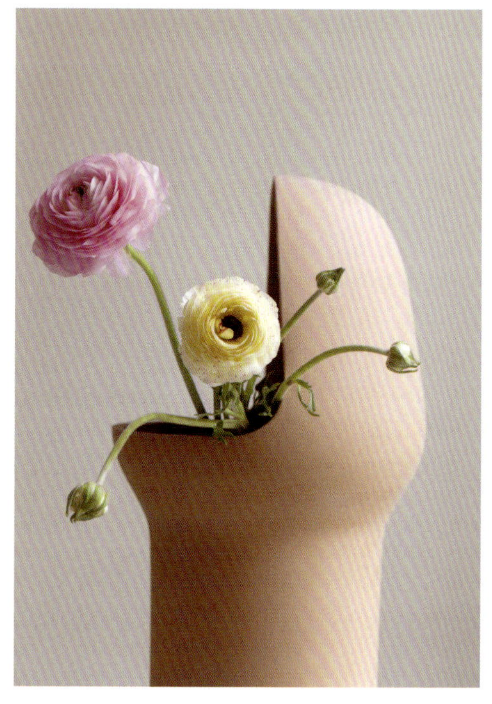

↑ Gardenias—Ceramic vase for BD Barcelona Design, 2013
↓ Flower Garden and the Blue That Saved Them, 3—Acrylic on canvas, 160 ×160 cm, 2021

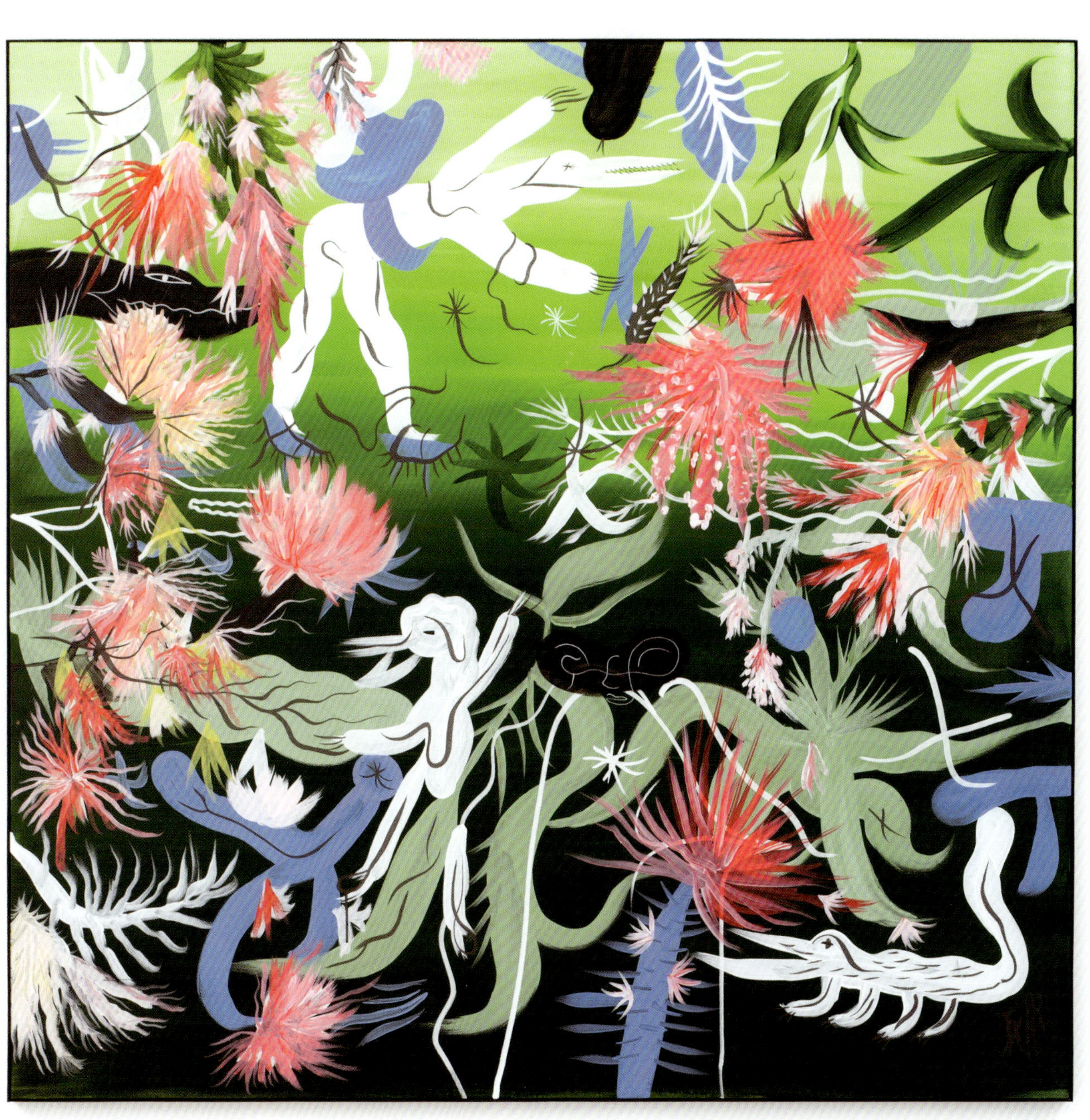

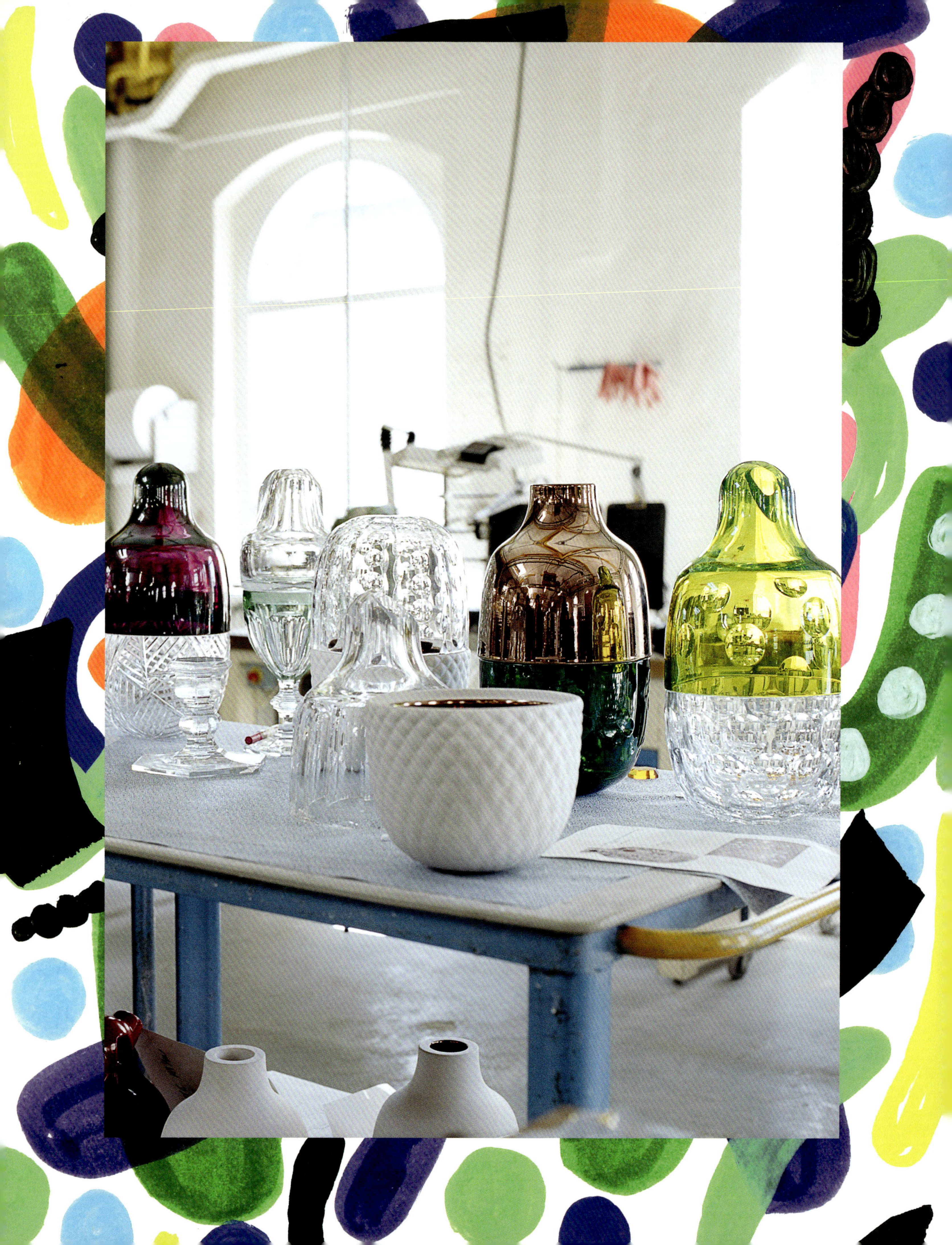

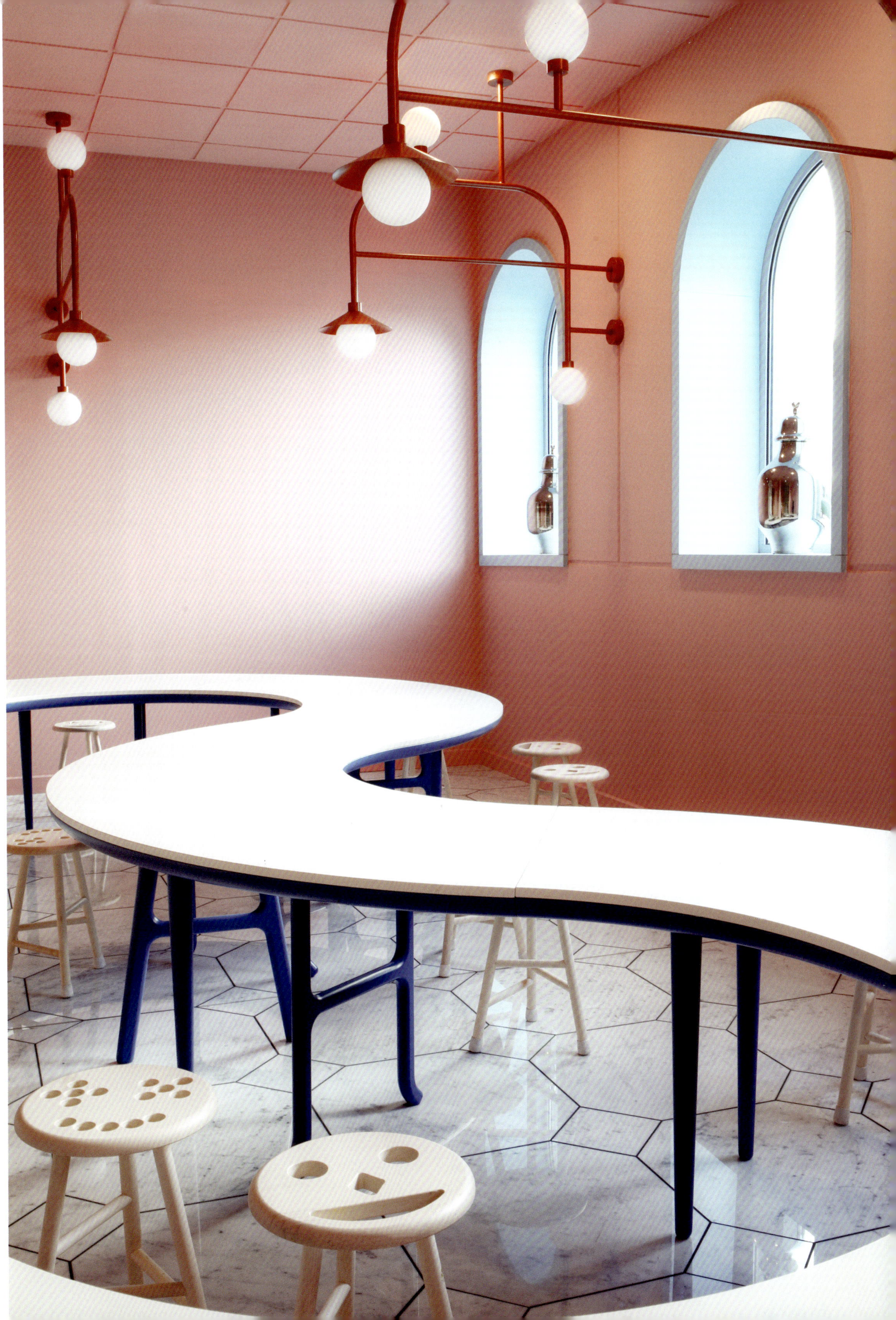

↑ Crystal Candy Set workshop at Baccarat atelier, France, 2009
↓ Groninger Museum Family Lab—Interior design, Groningen, Netherlands, 2015

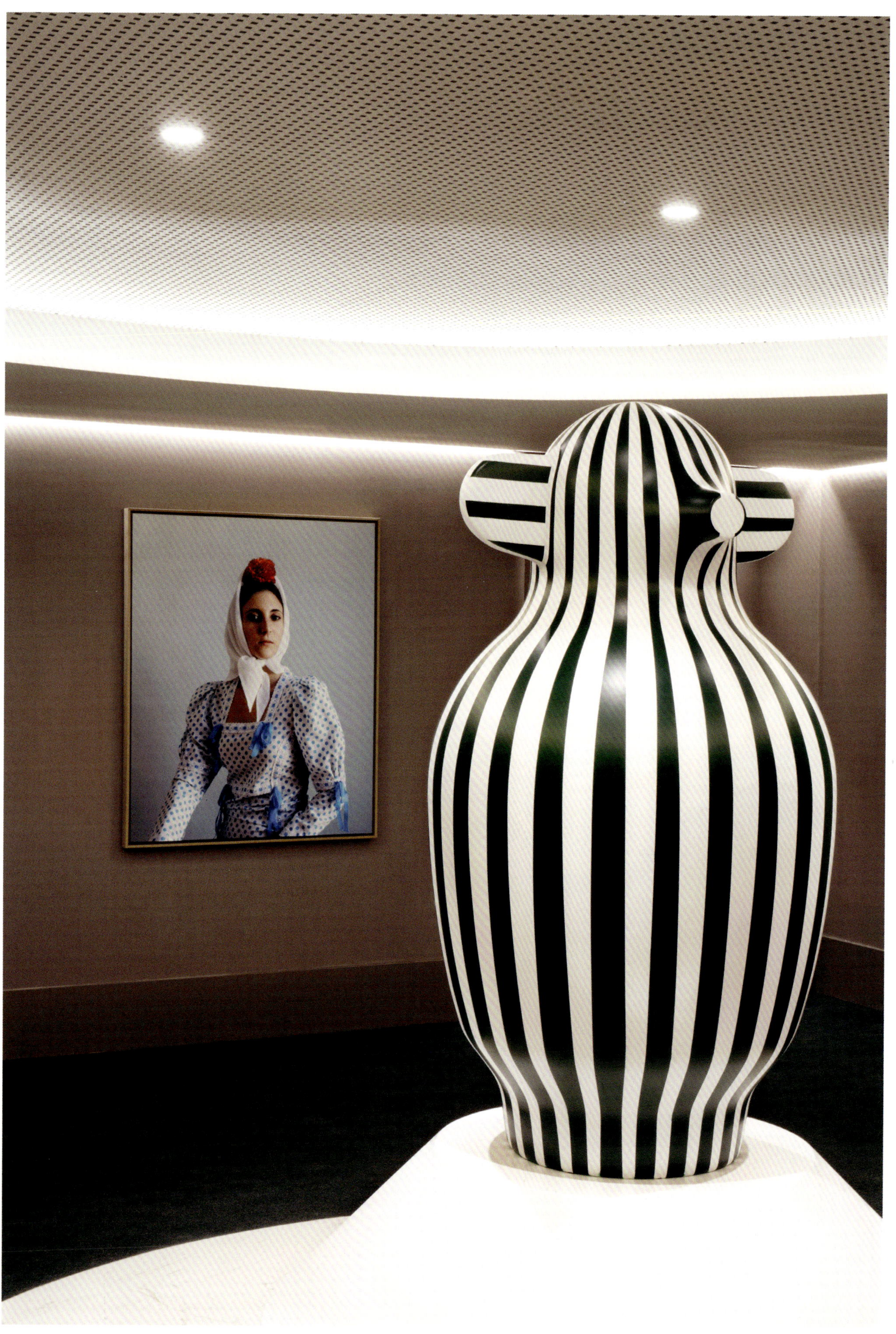

↑ Barceló Torre de Madrid Hotel—Interior design, detail, Madrid, Spain, 2016
↓ Sketches

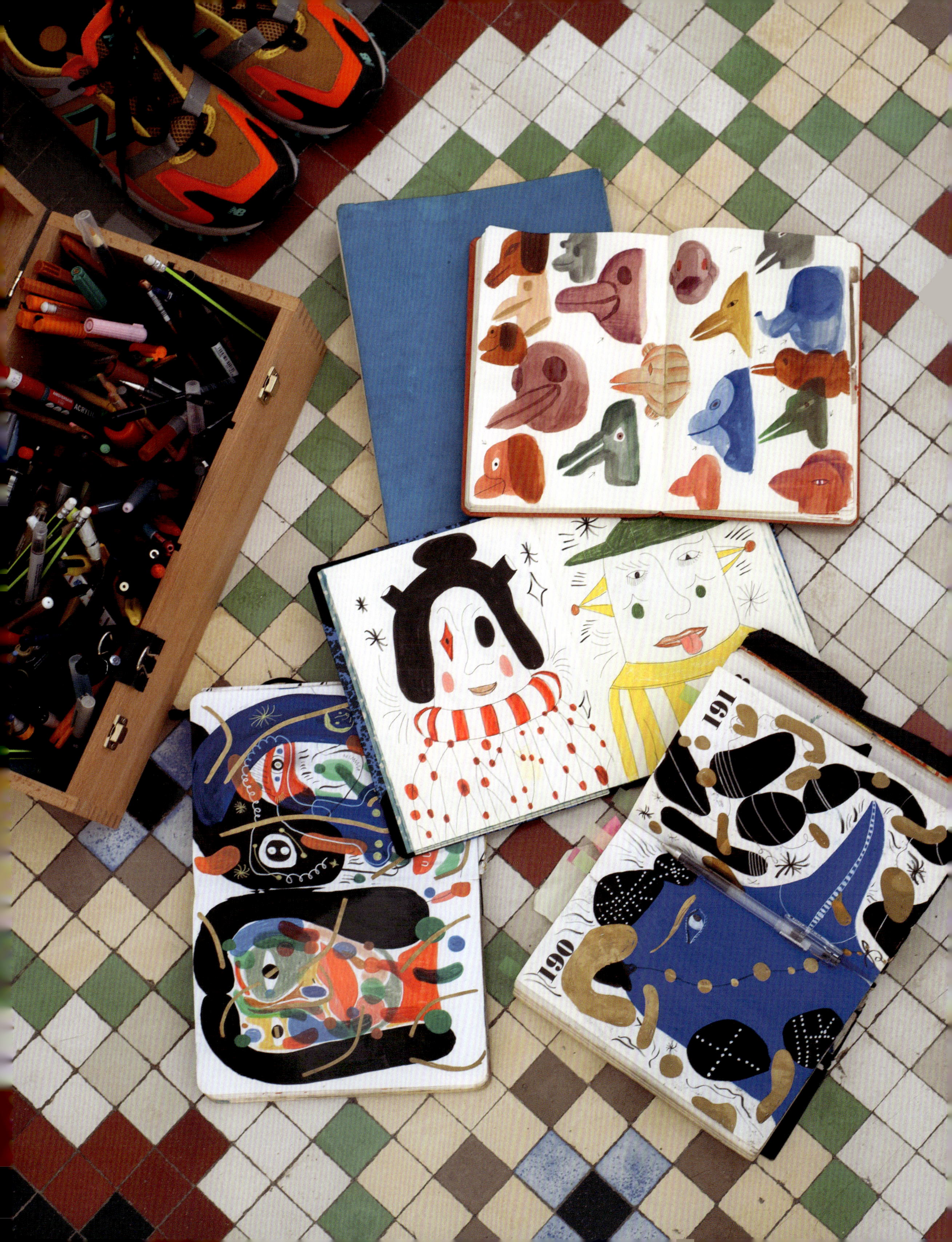

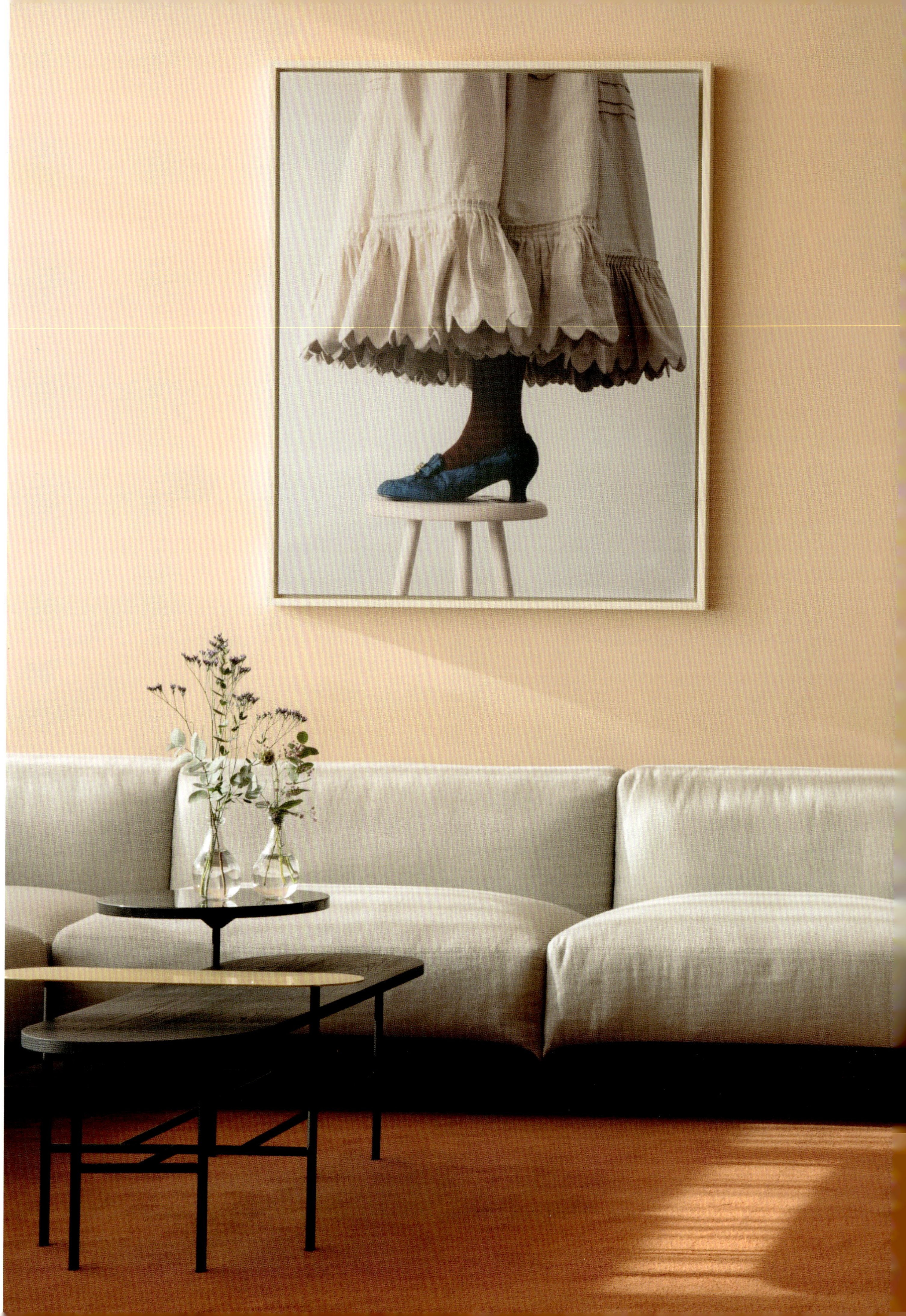

↓ Barceló Torre de Madrid Hotel—Interior design, Madrid, Spain, 2016

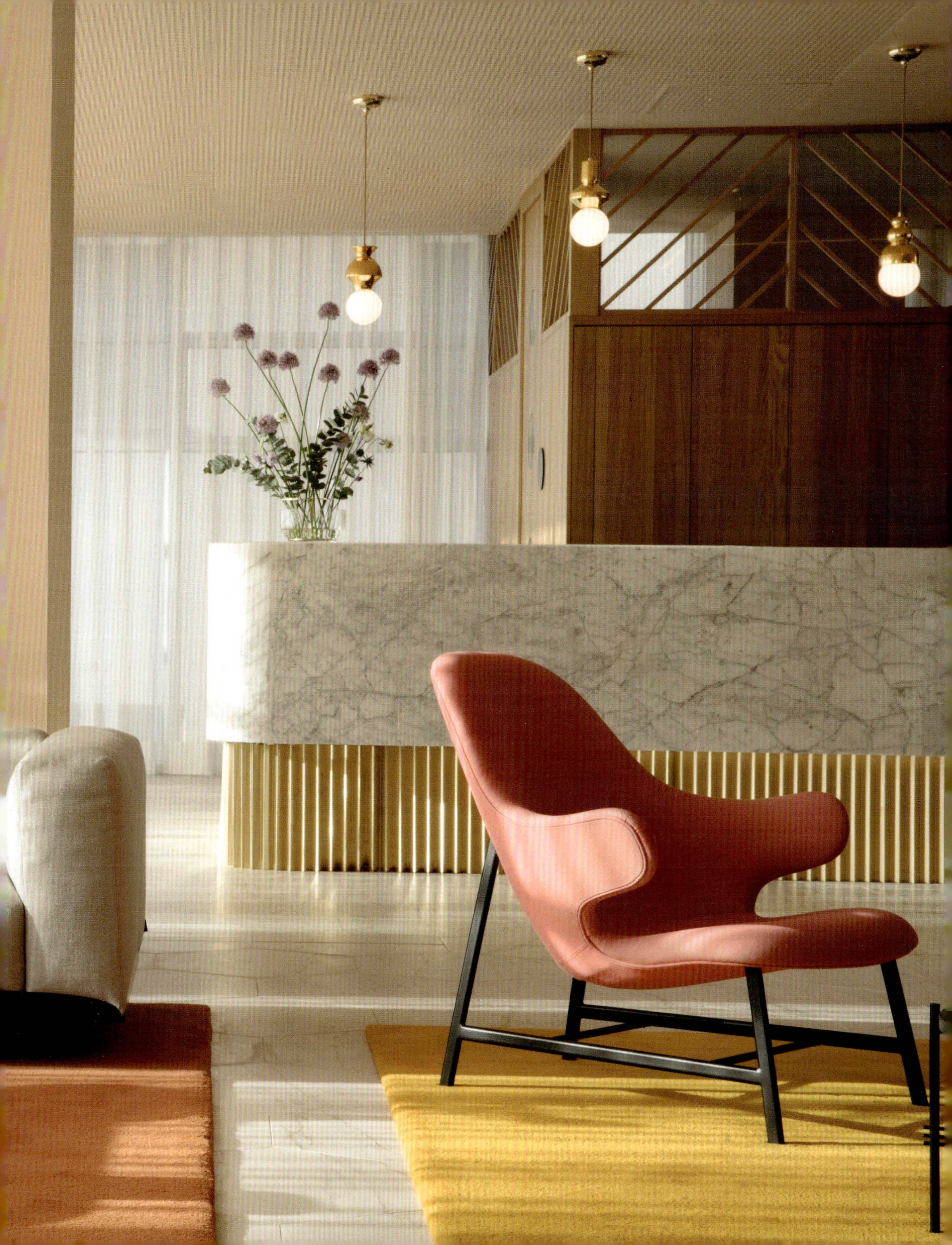

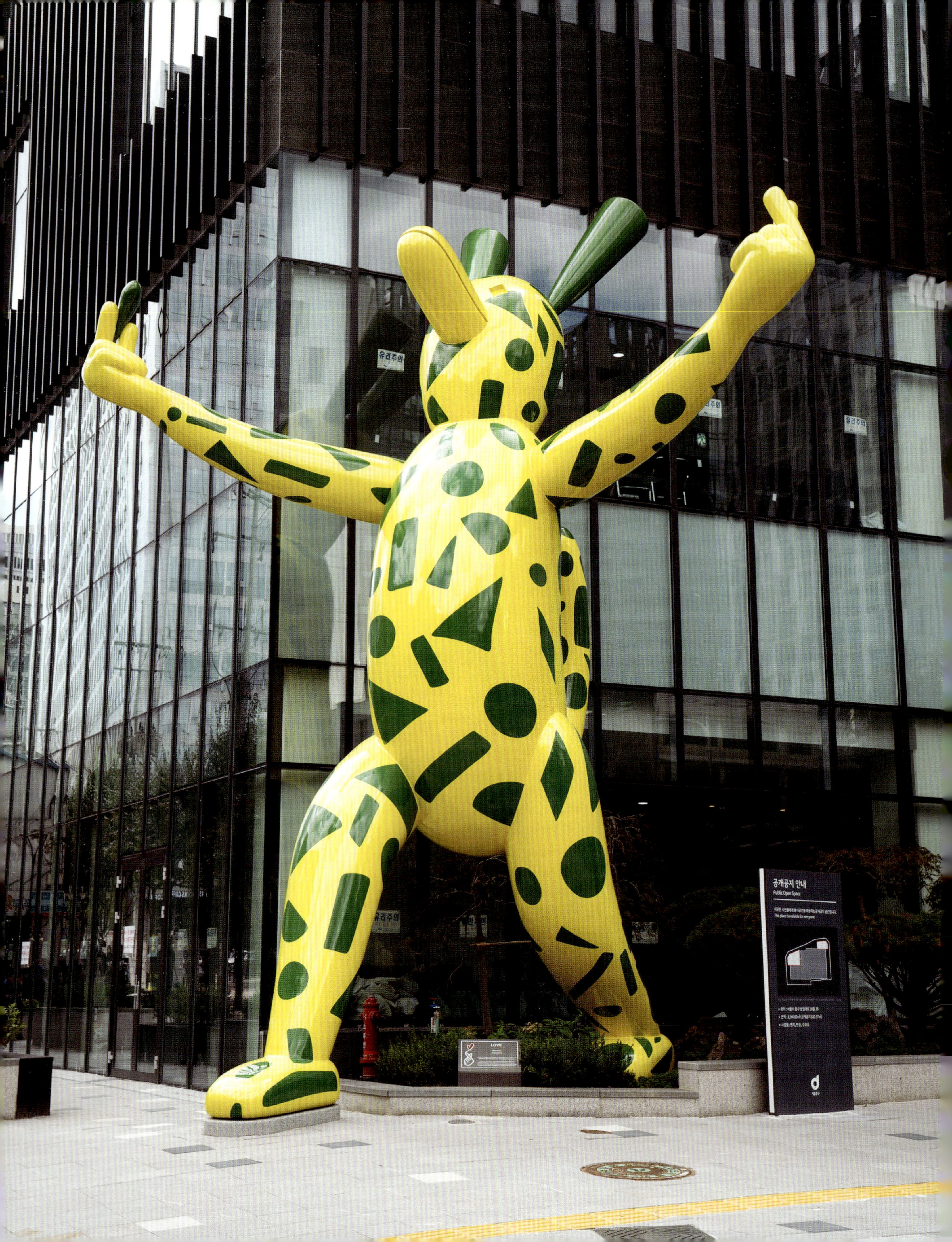
공개공지 안내
Public Open Space
이 공간은 시민 누구에게나 휴식공간을 제공하는 공개공지 공간입니다.
This place is available for everyone.
위치 : 서울시 중구 삼일대로 10길 35
면적 : 1,546.00㎡ (공개공지 182.97㎡)
시설물 : 벤치, 판석, 수목류
서울중구

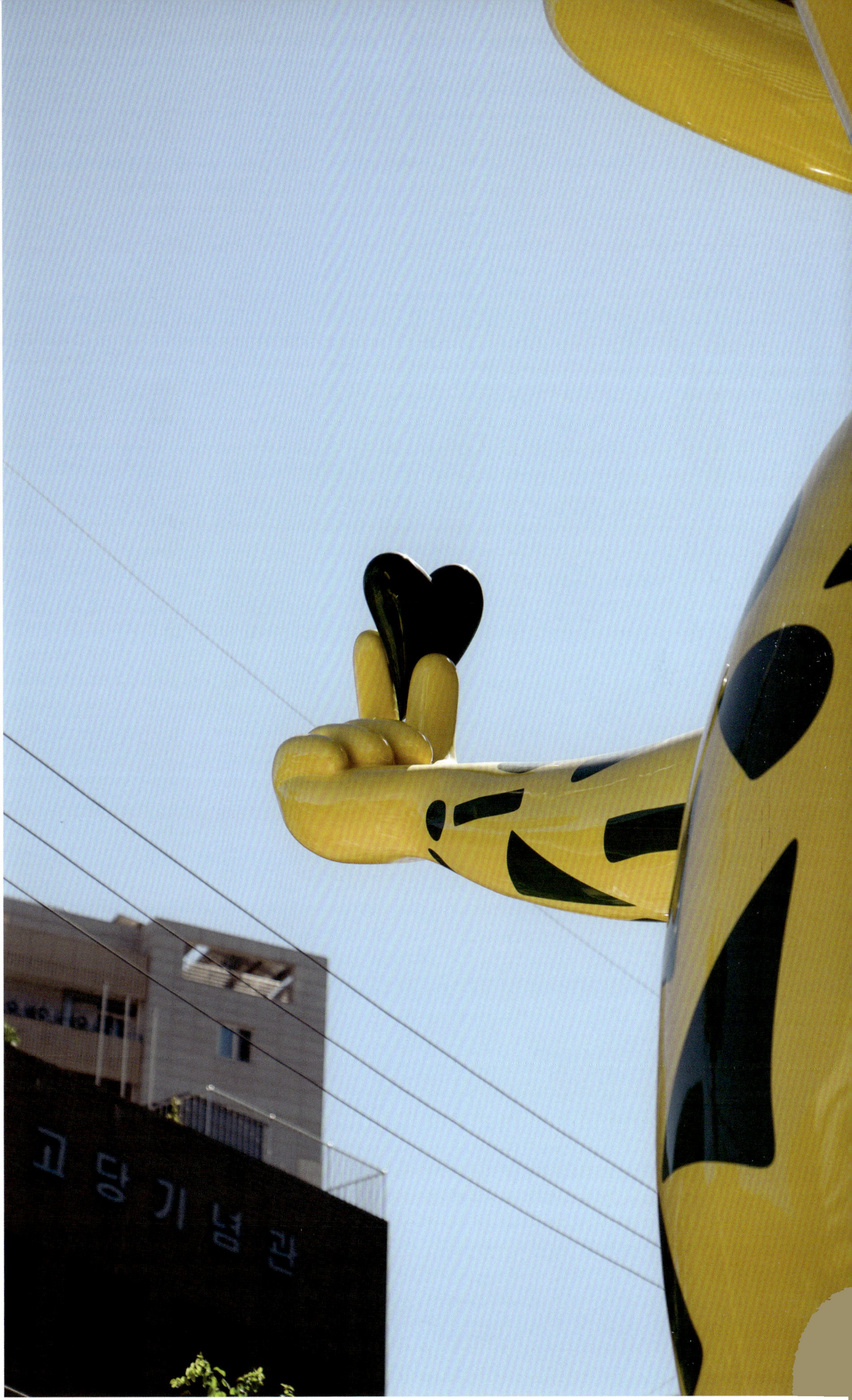

↑↓ Love—Public sculpture, Seoul, South Korea, 2020

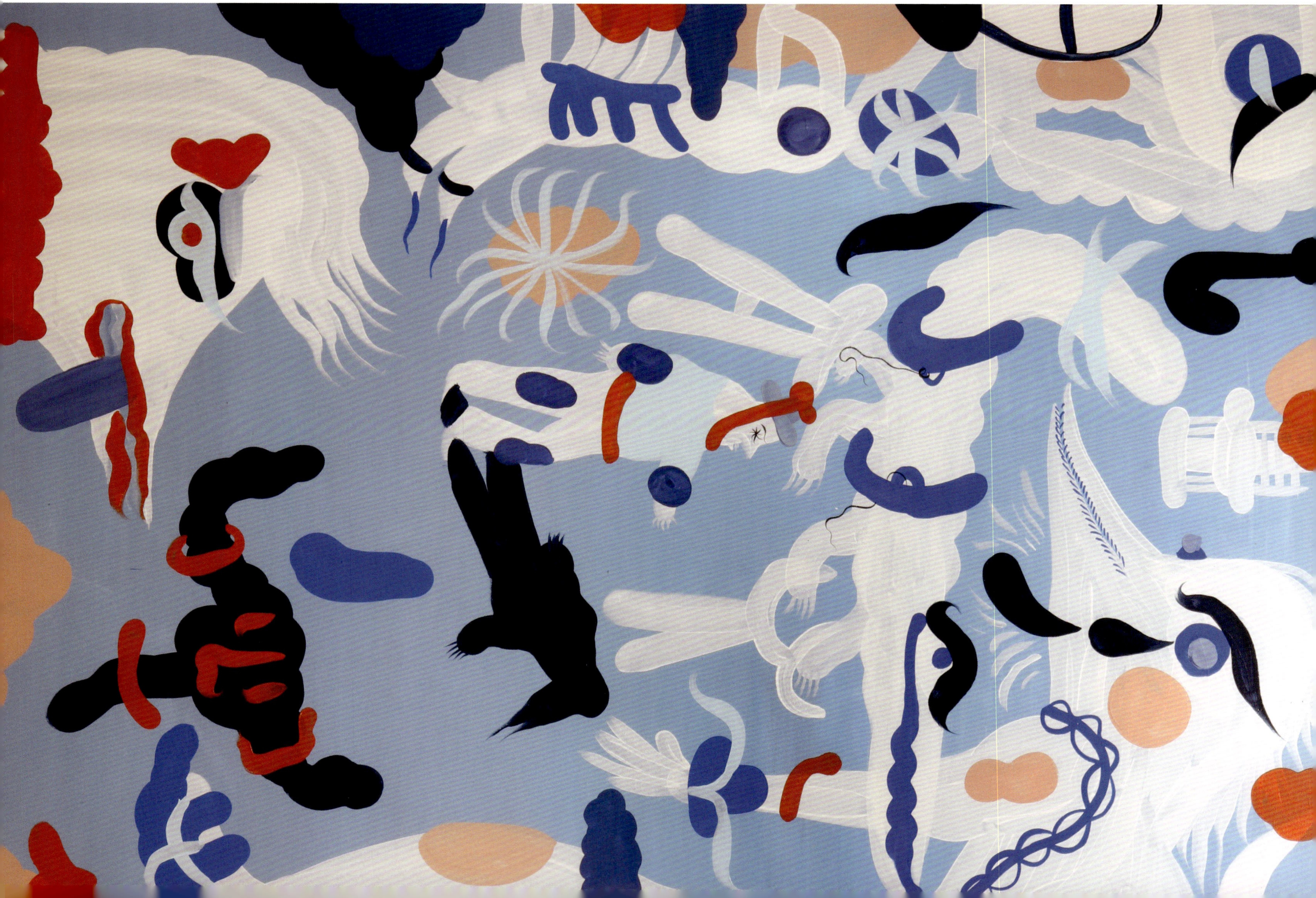

↙ The Castle of Transgression—Acrylic on canvas, 180 × 250 cm, 2022

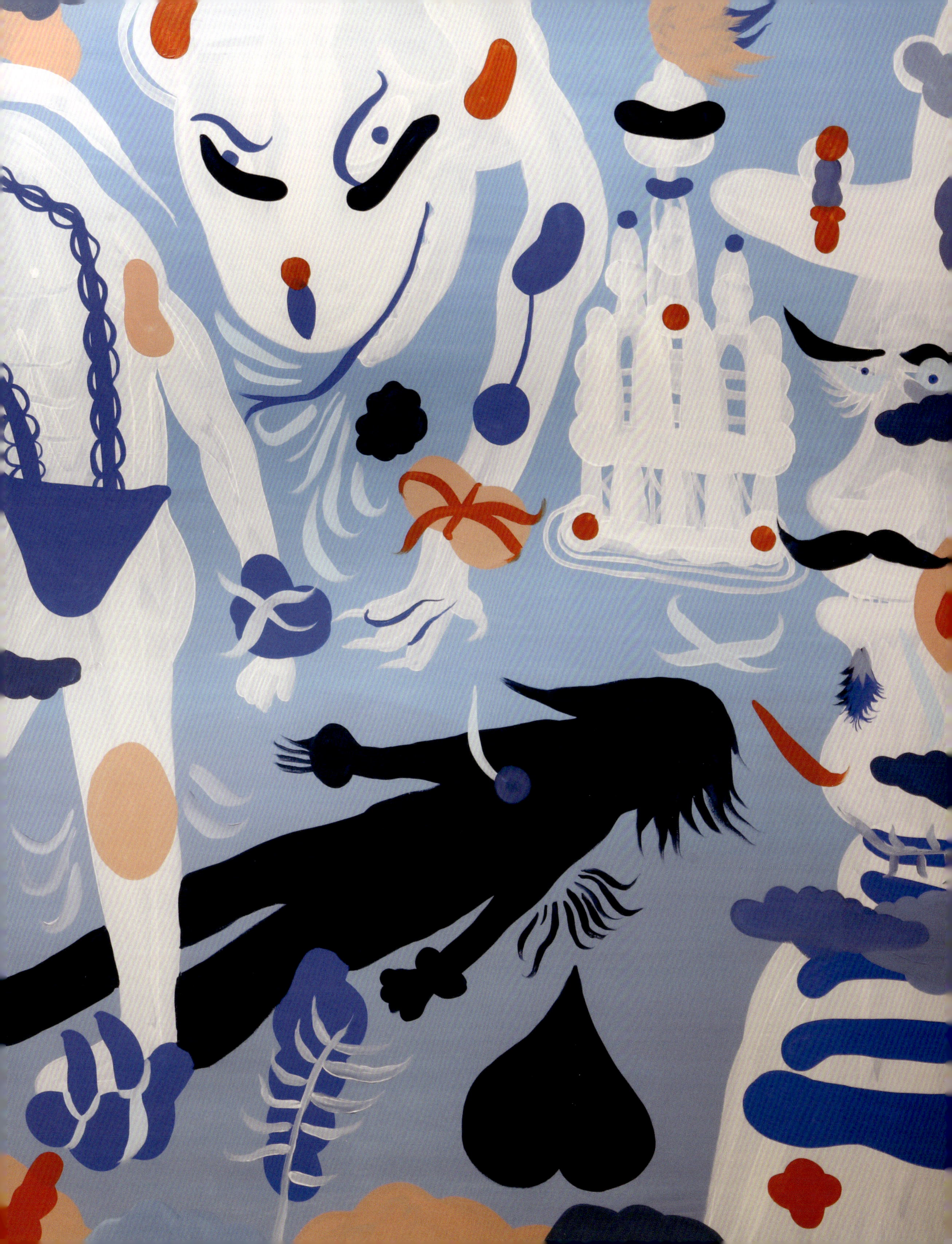

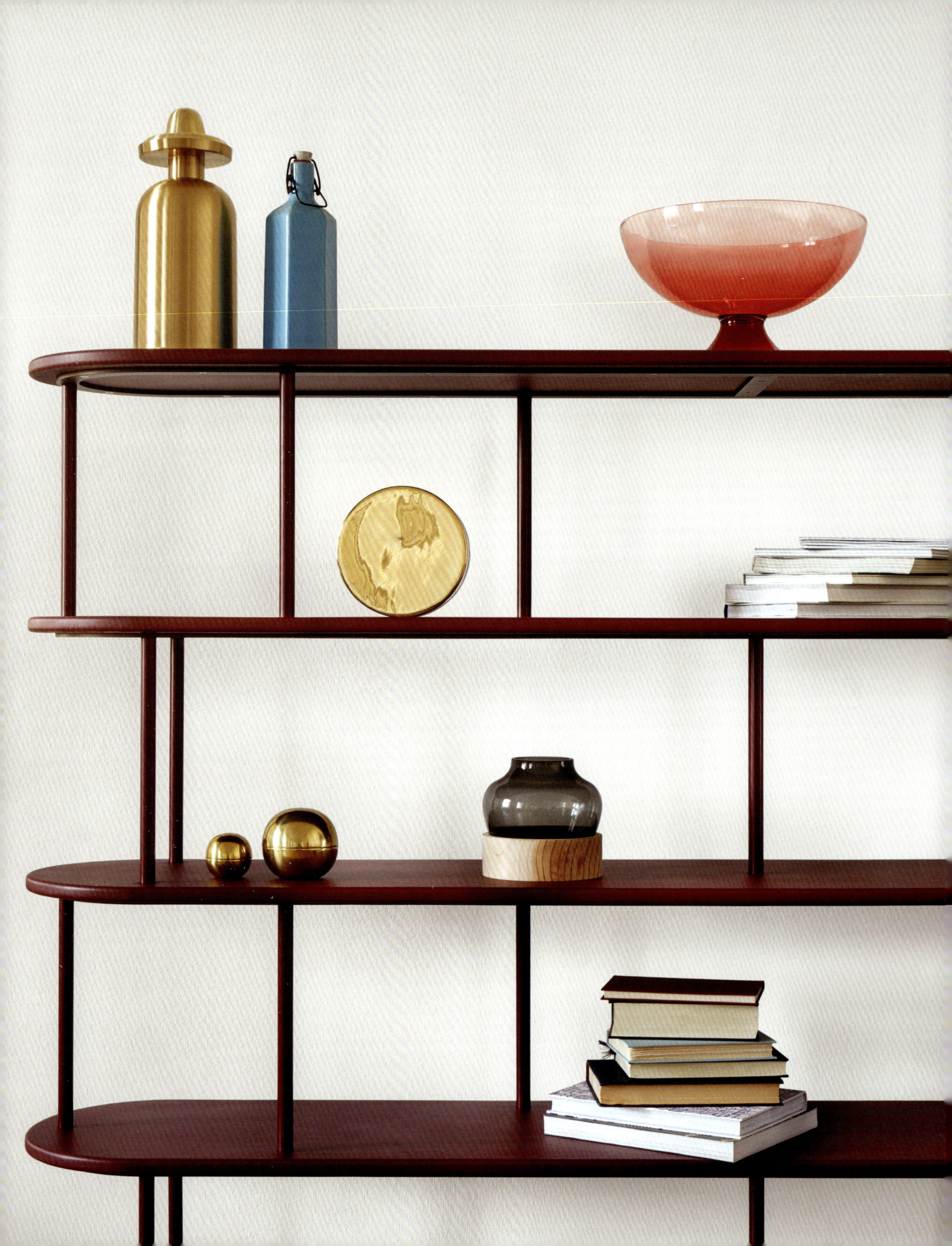

↑ MD shelf—Wittmann, 2016
↓ Fritz Hansen Showroom—Interior design, floor detail, Xi'an, China, 2019

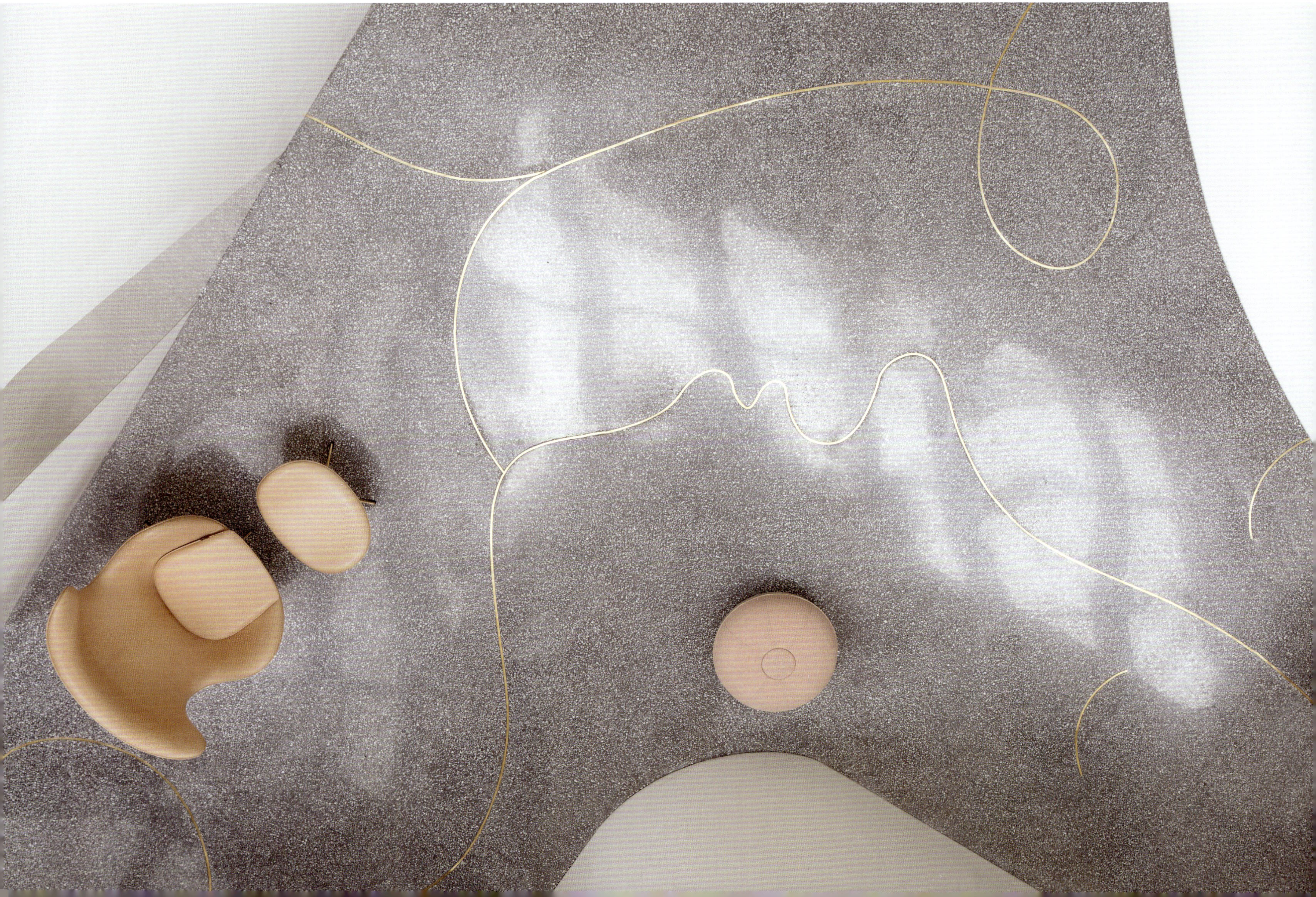

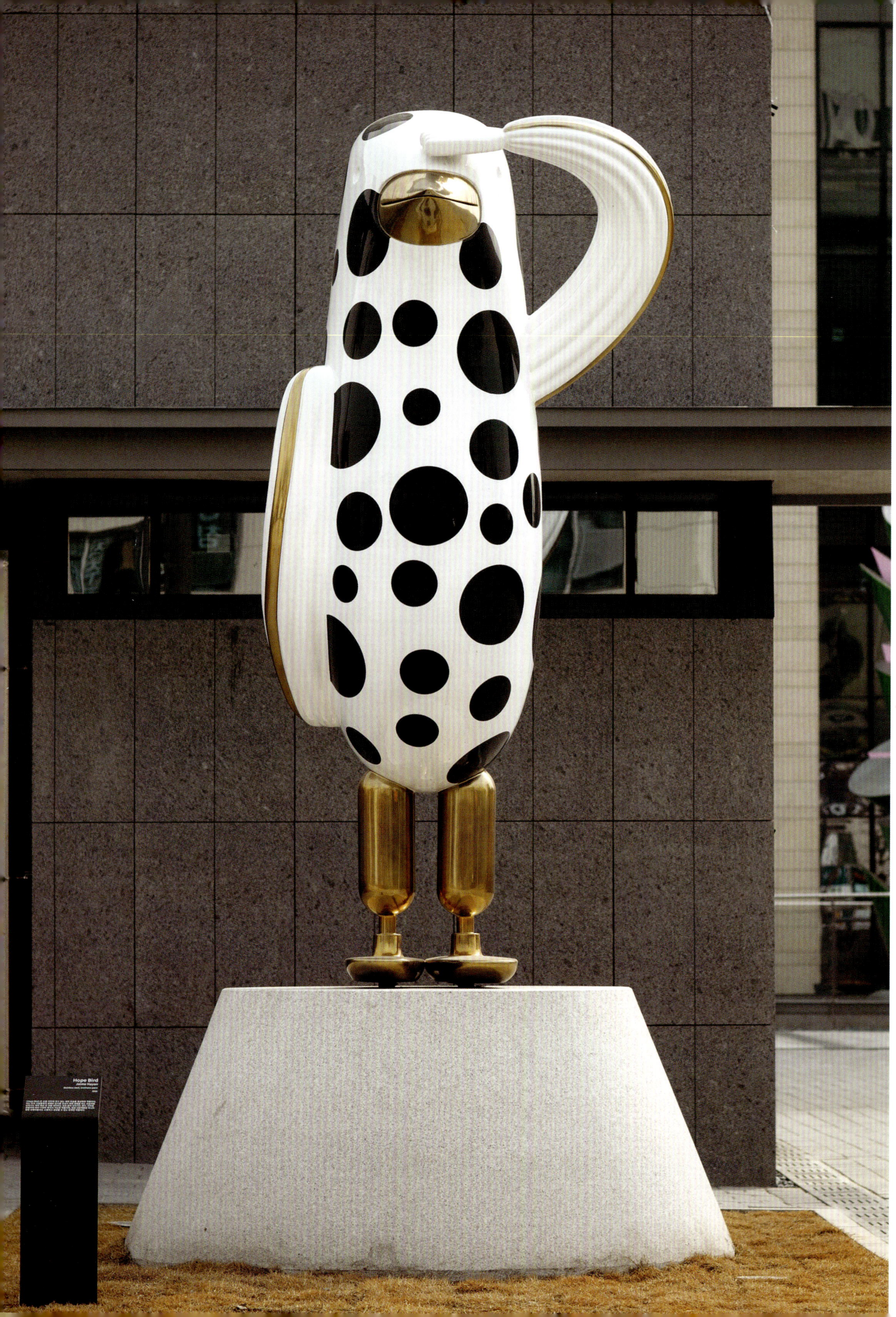

† Hope Bird—Public sculpture at Ehwa Women's Hospital, Seoul, South Korea, 2018